The Palgrave Handbook of Ethnicity

Steven Ratuva
Editor

The Palgrave Handbook of Ethnicity

Volume 1

With 46 Figures and 57 Tables

Editor
Steven Ratuva
Department of Anthropology and Sociology
University of Canterbury
Christchurch, New Zealand

Macmillan Brown Centre for Pacific Studies
University of Canterbury
Christchurch, New Zealand

ISBN 978-981-13-2897-8   ISBN 978-981-13-2898-5 (eBook)
ISBN 978-981-13-2899-2 (print and electronic bundle)
https://doi.org/10.1007/978-981-13-2898-5

© Springer Nature Singapore Pte Ltd. 2019, corrected publication 2020
This work is subject to copyright. All rights are solely and exclusively licensed by the Publisher, whether the whole or part of the material is concerned, specifically the rights of translation, reprinting, reuse of illustrations, recitation, broadcasting, reproduction on microfilms or in any other physical way, and transmission or information storage and retrieval, electronic adaptation, computer software, or by similar or dissimilar methodology now known or hereafter developed.
The use of general descriptive names, registered names, trademarks, service marks, etc. in this publication does not imply, even in the absence of a specific statement, that such names are exempt from the relevant protective laws and regulations and therefore free for general use.
The publisher, the authors, and the editors are safe to assume that the advice and information in this book are believed to be true and accurate at the date of publication. Neither the publisher nor the authors or the editors give a warranty, express or implied, with respect to the material contained herein or for any errors or omissions that may have been made. The publisher remains neutral with regard to jurisdictional claims in published maps and institutional affiliations.

This Palgrave Macmillan imprint is published by the registered company Springer Nature Singapore Pte Ltd.
The registered company address is: 152 Beach Road, #21-01/04 Gateway East, Singapore 189721, Singapore

Preface

Since the end of the cold war, the world has seen an unprecedented multimodal transformation involving the complex interplay of various forces such as globalization and nationalism; the resurgence of extreme right and the unrelenting response from the left; the consolidation of neoliberal hegemony and creation of conditions for its own crisis; the rise of authoritarian leadership and the widespread democratic reactions; the popularization of the social media and the declaration of cyber wars; and the rise of China and how this poses a threat to US hegemony. A salient feature of many of these is the multiple expressions of ethnicity as a factor in shaping geopolitical, socioeconomic, and sociocultural relations. The explosion of ethno-nationalist conflicts and religious tension; the resurgence and electoral mainstreaming of ultra-right political groups with racial supremacist ideals; the widespread expressions of extremist Islamic groups; the anti-immigration policies of President Trump and various European states; the use of the cyberspace as an arena for racial vilification; the rise of extremist and terroristic violence; and the fluid nature of ethnic relations are just some of the manifestations of the new transformation. These have justifiably inspired a surge in interest in research and discourses around ethnicity.

Commissioned by Palgrave Macmillan, this comprehensive work on global ethnicity – which spans diverse national, political, cultural, and ideological boundaries, schools of thought, and methodological approaches – is a result of an exhaustive international search for the right experts, mobilization of a wide range of resources, writing, editing, reviewing, and production over 3 years. With 102 chapters (and more than 90 authors from around the world), this was a mammoth task, which involved the collective synergies of the editor-in-chief, section editors, chapter authors, the Palgrave editorial team, and the production team. It is a great example of transnational cooperation, innovative communication, systematic networking, and durable patience. At a time when academia is obsessed with the fetishization of individual output, as a result of the pervading audit and metric culture wrought by neoliberal reforms, a collaborative interdisciplinary and transnational effort of this scope and magnitude is a rarity. This is why all those involved in this mega project deserve whole-hearted congratulations.

The different parts and individual themes of the chapters are connected in a complex web of historical, intellectual, sociocultural, and political narratives and are meant to converse with each other using different contextual yet familiar discourses. Ostensibly, while they encapsulate different schools of thought and disciplinary traditions, they share a common thread of optimism and hope of expanding the horizons of knowledge of humanity and contributing to debates and discussions about creating a better world.

Ethnicity is not an easy subject to deal with because of its intersectional relationship with a host of factors including identity, inequality, conflict, religion, economic distribution, class, politics, and other aspects of everyday life. History is littered with the residues of ethnicity's connection with wars, mass killings, terrorism, poverty, and discrimination. History is also blessed with moments of interethnic embracement, multicultural engagements, and collective voices of humanity crying for justice and yearning for equality against the forces of discrimination, abuse, and oppression. These three volumes echo the multiple sentiments of history and capture some of the moments of human frailty and strength, human fiasco and fortitude, human retardation and progress, manifested in the different corners of the globe.

Some chapters are theoretical and some are based on empirical case studies and cover more than 70 countries around the world. Due to the massive size of the undertaking and the limited time available for its completion, the volumes are not able to cover all the countries in the world. Nevertheless, the existing chapters provide a wealth of discourses, experiences, reflections, and analysis, which would no doubt enrich our understanding of ethnicity as complex developments in our contemporary world unfold over time. The volumes are meant to inspire further debate and research and not meant to provide the panacea for global ethnic utopia. They are meant for a wide range of interests including scholars and researchers, policy makers, political leaders, corporate personnel, international agencies, peacebuilders, educators, security community, civil society organizations, and the public at large. This diversity reflects the underlying normative sentiments of inclusivity, accessibility, (in)formativeness, and enrichment.

Some chapters provide practical solutions to problems, while some provide abstract analyses of complex dynamics to unpack deeper and latent manifestations of social realities. While some are concerned with the global context, some revolve around geopolitical and geocultural regions, and some are focused on national and even local situation. These multiple layers of narratives are interconnected and provide intellectual enrichment for each other. The volumes do not pretend to provide definitive and conclusive analysis of ethnic issues that enshroud our times, but rather speak to them and raise important issues that need closer and serious scrutiny with the ambitious goal and sincere hope of making the world a better place for humanity.

Department of Anthropology and Sociology   Steven Ratuva
University of Canterbury   Editor
Christchurch, New Zealand

Macmillan Brown Centre for Pacific Studies
University of Canterbury
Christchurch, New Zealand

Contents

Volume 1

1   Exploring Global Ethnicity: A Broad Sociological Synopsis   1
Steven Ratuva

Part I   Nexus Between Ethnicity and Identity   27

2   Ethno-cultural Symbolism and Group Identity   29
Elya Tzaneva

3   Cultural Socialization and Ethnic Consciousness   49
Sara N. Amin

4   Historical Memory and Ethnic Myths   65
Cindy Zeiher

5   Indian Identity in South Africa   77
Kathryn Pillay

6   The State and Minority Nationalities (Ethnic Groups) in
China   93
Roland Boer

7   Ethnic Blindness in Ethnically Divided Society: Implications
for Ethnic Relations in Fiji   109
Romitesh Kant

8   Post-Arab Spring: The Arab World Between the Dilemma of
the Nation-State and the Rise of Identity Conflicts   131
Hassanein Ali

Part II   The State, Society, and Ethnopolitics   147

9   The Significance of Ethno-politics in Modern States
and Society   149
Joseph R. Rudolph

10	**Religion and Political Mobilization** Jóhanna K. Birnir and Henry D. Overos	169
11	**Foreign Military Occupations and Ethnicity** Radomir Compel	187
12	**Ethnic Politics and Global Justice** Geoff Pfeifer	209
13	**Shared Citizenship and Sovereignty: The Case of the Cook Islands' and Niue's Relationship with New Zealand** Zbigniew Dumieński	221
14	**State Hegemony and Ethnicity: Fiji's Problematic Colonial Past** Sanjay Ramesh	247
15	**Ethnicity and Politics in Kenya** Jacob Mwathi Mati	265
16	**Ethno-politics in the People's Republic of China** Matthew Hoddie	283
17	**Ethnicity and Cultural Rights in Tibet** Jianxia Lin	301
18	**Volga Tatars: Continuing Resilience in the Age of Uncertainty** Renat Shaykhutdinov	315
19	**Identity and Conflict in Northern Ireland** Cathal McManus	331
20	**Immigration Policy and Left-Right Politics in Western Europe** Trevor J. Allen and Misty Knight-Finley	347
21	**Lost in Europe: Roma and the Search for Political Legitimacy** Neil Cruickshank	363
Part III	**Stereotypes and Prejudices**	**381**
22	**Race and Racism: Some Salient Issues** Vijay Naidu	383
23	**Media and Stereotypes** Tara Ross	397
24	**Japanese Representation in Philippine Media** Karl Ian Uy Cheng Chua	415

25	Racism in Colonial Zimbabwe Alois S. Mlambo	429
26	Ethnic Riots in United Kingdom in 2001 Paul Bagguley and Yasmin Hussain	447
27	Racialized Identity Under Apartheid in South Africa Suryakanthie Chetty	463
28	Racism and Stereotypes Paul Spoonley	483
29	Discussing Contemporary Racial Justice in Academic Spaces: Minimizing Epistemic Exploitation While Neutralizing White Fragility Adele Norris	499
30	Ethnicity, Race, and Black People in Europe Stephen Small	513

Volume 2

Part IV Ethno-nationalism and Power 535

31	Contemporary Ethnic Politics and Violence Adis Maksic	539
32	Ethnic Conflict and Militias Andrew Thomson	559
33	Evolution of Palestinian Civil Society and the Role of Nationalism, Occupation, and Religion Yaser Alashqar	577
34	Ethno-nationalism and Political Conflict in Bosnia (Europe) Aleksandra Zdeb	595
35	Ethnic Conflicts and Peace-Building Sergio Luiz Cruz Aguilar	613
36	Ethnicity and Violence in Sri Lanka: An Ethnohistorical Narrative Premakumara de Silva, Farzana Haniffa, and Rohan Bastin	633
37	Ethno-communal Conflict in Sudan and South Sudan Johan Brosché	655
38	Patterns and Drivers of Communal Conflict in Kenya Emma Elfversson	675

39	Elites in Between Ethnic Mongolians and the Han in China Chelegeer	695
40	Ethnicity and Cultural Wounding: Ethnic Conflict, Loss of Home, and the Drive to Return Amanda Kearney	715
41	Constitutional Features of Presidential Elections and the Failure of Cross-ethnic Coalitions to Institutionalize M. Bashir Mobasher	735
42	The Making of a Mobile Caliphate State in the African Sahel Hamdy Hassan	755
43	Consequences of Globalization for the Middle East Political Geography Mostafa Entezarulmahdy	773
44	National Imaginary, Ethnic Plurality, and State Formation in Indonesia Paul J. Carnegie	791
45	Ethno-nationalism and Ethnic Dynamics in Trinidad and Tobago: Toward Designing an Inclusivist Form of Governance Ralph Premdas	809
46	Islam in Trinidad Nasser Mustapha	825

Part V Indigeneity, Gender, and Sexuality 847

47	Indigenous Rights and Neoliberalism in Latin America Jeffrey A. Gardner and Patricia Richards	849
48	Settler Colonialism and Biculturalism in Aotearoa/New Zealand Jessica Terruhn	867
49	Nuclear Testing and Racism in the Pacific Islands Nic Maclellan	885
50	Nagas Identity and Nationalism: Indigenous Movement of the Zeliangrong Nagas in the North East India Aphun Kamei	907
51	Reclaiming Hawaiian Sovereignty Keakaokawai Varner Hemi	927

52	**Perpetual Exclusion and Second-Order Minorities in Theaters of Civil Wars** Jovanie Camacho Espesor	967
53	**Indigenous Australian Identity in Colonial and Postcolonial Contexts** Michael Davis	993
54	**China: Modernization, Development, and Ethnic Unrest in Xinjiang** Kate Hannan	1011
55	**Ethnicity and Class Nexus: A Philosophical Approach** Rodrigo Luiz Cunha Gonsalves	1033
56	**Islamic Identity and Sexuality in Indonesia** Sharyn Graham Davies	1063
57	**LGBT and Ethnicity** Arjun Rajkhowa	1077
58	**Migration and Managing Manhood: Congolese Migrant Men in South Africa** Joseph Rudigi Rukema and Beatrice Umubyeyi	1111
59	**Race and Sexuality: Colonial Ghosts and Contemporary Orientalisms** Monique Mulholland	1129

Part VI   Globalization and Diaspora **1147**

60	**Diaspora as Transnational Actors: Globalization and the Role of Ethnic Memory** Masaki Kataoka	1149
61	**Global Chinese Diaspora** Zhifang Song	1167
62	**Greek Identity in Australia** Rebecca Fanany and Maria-Irini Avgoulas	1185
63	**Italian Identity in the United States** Stefano Luconi	1203
64	**Faamatai: A Globalized Pacific Identity** Melani Anae	1223
65	**Migrant Illegalization and Minoritized Populations** Paloma E. Villegas and Francisco J. Villegas	1247

66 Indian Diaspora in New Zealand 1265
    Todd Nachowitz

67 Ethnic Migrants and Casinos in Singapore and Macau 1313
    Juan Zhang

68 Ethnic Minorities and Criminalization of Immigration Policies
    in the United States 1331
    Felicia Arriaga

69 Diaspora and Ethnic Contestation in Guyana 1351
    Ralph Premdas and Bishnu Ragoonath

Volume 3

Part VII   Ethnic Relations and Policy Responses 1363

70 Role of Crown Health Policy in Entrenched Health Inequities
    in Aotearoa, New Zealand 1365
    Sarah Herbert, Heather Came, Tim McCreanor, and Emmanuel Badu

71 Aboriginal and Torres Strait Islander Secondary Students'
    Experiences of Racism 1383
    Gawaian Bodkin-Andrews, Treena Clark, and Shannon Foster

72 Stereotypes of Minorities and Education 1407
    Jean M. Allen and Melinda Webber

73 Rural Farmer Empowerment Through Organic Food Exports:
    Lessons from Uganda and Ghana 1427
    Kristen Lyons

74 Local Peacebuilding After Communal Violence 1445
    Birgit Bräuchler

75 Cultural Identity and Textbooks in Japan: Japanese Ethnic and
    Cultural Nationalism in Middle-School History Textbooks 1465
    Ryota Nishino

76 Asian Americans and the Affirmative Action Debate in the
    United States 1483
    Mitchell James Chang

77 Affirmative Action: Its Nature and Dynamics 1501
    Ralph Premdas

78 Negotiating Ethnic Conflict in Deeply Divided Societies: Political
    Bargaining and Power Sharing as Institutional Strategies 1515
    Madhushree Sekher, Mansi Awasthi, Allen Thomas, Rajesh Kumar,
    and Subhankar Nayak

Part VIII Ethnic Cleansing and Genocide 1537

79 The Threat of Genocide: Understanding and Preventing the "Crime of Crimes" 1539
Eyal Mayroz

80 Separation Versus Reunification: Institutional Stagnation and Conflict Between Iraq and Kurdistan Region 1555
Nyaz N. Noori

81 Ethnic Cleansing of the Rohingya People 1575
Nasir Uddin

82 Displaced Minorities: The Wayuu and Miskito People 1593
Christian Cwik

83 Ethnic Conflict and Genocide in Rwanda 1611
Wendy Lambourne

Part IX Ethnicity, Migration, and Labor 1643

84 Policing Ethnic Minorities: Disentangling a Landscape of Conceptual and Practice Tensions 1647
Isabelle Bartkowiak-Théron and Nicole L. Asquith

85 Romanian Identity and Immigration in Europe 1671
Remus Gabriel Anghel, Stefánia Toma, and László Fosztó

86 Refugee Protection and Settlement Policy in New Zealand 1689
Louise Humpage

87 Indian Indentured Laborers in the Caribbean 1711
Sherry-Ann Singh

88 New Middle-Class Labor Migrants 1729
Sam Scott

89 Slavery, Health, and Epidemics in Mauritius 1721–1860 1749
Sadasivam Jaganada Reddi and Sheetal Sheena Sookrajowa

90 The Legacy of Indentured Labor 1767
Kathleen Harrington-Watt

91 Global Capitalism and Cheap Labor: The Case of Indenture ... 1795
Brinsley Samaroo

92 United Nations Migrant Workers Convention 1813
Sheetal Sheena Sookrajowa and Antoine Pécoud

93 The Rhetoric of Hungarian Premier Victor Orban: Inside X Outside in the Context of Immigration Crisis 1829
Bruno Mendelski

94 Different Legacies, Common Pressures, and Converging Institutions: The Politics of Muslim Integration in Austria and Germany 1853
Ryosuke Amiya-Nakada

95 Intended Illegal Infiltration or Compelled Migration: Debates on Settlements of Rohingya Muslims in India 1877
Sangit Kumar Ragi

96 Indonesia and ASEAN Responses on Rohingya Refugees 1891
Badrus Sholeh

Part X Cultural Celebration and Resistance 1907

97 Rewriting the World: Pacific People, Media, and Cultural Resistance 1909
Sereana Naepi and Sam Manuela

98 Kava and Ethno-cultural Identity in Oceania 1923
S. Apo Aporosa

99 Museums and Identity: Celebrating Diversity in an Ethnically Diverse World 1939
Tarisi Vunidilo

100 Artistic Expressions and Ethno-cultural Identity: A Case Study of Acehnese Body Percussion in Indonesia 1957
Murtala Murtala, Alfira O'Sullivan, and Paul H. Mason

101 Ethnic Film in South Africa: History, Meaning, and Change ... 1977
Gairoonisa Paleker

102 Multiculturalism and Citizenship in the Netherlands 1993
Igor Boog

Correction to: Diaspora and Ethnic Contestation in Guyana C1

Index 2015

About the Editor

Steven Ratuva
Department of Anthropology and Sociology
University of Canterbury
Christchurch, New Zealand

Macmillan Brown Centre for Pacific Studies
University of Canterbury
Christchurch, New Zealand

Steven Ratuva is Director of the Macmillan Brown Center for Pacific Studies and Professor in the Department of Anthropology and Sociology at the University of Canterbury. He was Fulbright Professor at UCLA, Duke University, and Georgetown University and currently Chair of the International Political Science Association Research Committee on Security, Conflict, and Democratization. With a Ph.D. from the Institute of Development Studies at the University of Sussex, Ratuva is an interdisciplinary scholar who has written or edited a number of books and published numerous papers on a range of issues including ethnicity, security, affirmative action, indigenous intellectual property, geopolitical strategies, social protection, militarization, ethno-nationalism, development, peace, and neoliberalism. He has been a consultant and advisor for a number of international organizations such as the UNDP, International Labour Organization, International Institute for Democracy and Electoral Assistance, Commonwealth Secretariat, and the Asian Development Bank, and has worked in a number of universities around the world including in Australia, USA, New Zealand, Fiji, and UK.

About the Section Editors

Steven Ratuva
Department of Anthropology and Sociology
University of Canterbury
Christchurch, New Zealand

Macmillan Brown Centre for Pacific Studies
University of Canterbury
Christchurch, New Zealand

Steven Ratuva is Director of the Macmillan Brown Center for Pacific Studies and Professor in the Department of Anthropology and Sociology at the University of Canterbury. He was Fulbright Professor at UCLA, Duke University, and Georgetown University and currently Chair of the International Political Science Association Research Committee on Security, Conflict, and Democratization. With a Ph.D. from the Institute of Development Studies at the University of Sussex, Ratuva is an interdisciplinary scholar who has written or edited a number of books and published numerous papers on a range of issues including ethnicity, security, affirmative action, indigenous intellectual property, geopolitical strategies, social protection, militarization, ethno-nationalism, development, peace, and neoliberalism. He has been a consultant and advisor for a number of international organizations such as the UNDP, International Labour Organization, International Institute for Democracy and Electoral Assistance, Commonwealth Secretariat, and the Asian Development Bank, and has worked in a number of universities around the world including in Australia, USA, New Zealand, Fiji, and UK.

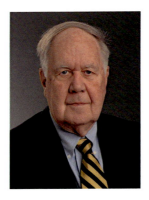

Joseph R. Rudolph
Department of Political Science
Towson University
Baltimore, MA, USA

Joseph R. Rudolph, Jr. received his Ph.D. from the University of Virginia and is currently a Professor in the Department of Political Science at Towson University (Baltimore, Maryland, USA). He has served as a Fulbright appointee to Czechoslovakia (1991–1992) and Kosovo (2011–2012), and has published in the field of ethnic and nationalist politics for more than 30 years. Since 1997, he has also frequently been a part of the democratization operations of the Organization for Security and Cooperation in Europe (OSCE) in areas of the former Yugoslavia and former Soviet Union. His Palgrave publication *Politics and Ethnicity: A Comparative* Study (2006) is now in its second printing. More recent work includes compiling and contributing to *The Encyclopedia of Modern Ethnic Conflicts* (editor, 2nd edition, 2015), and *From Mediation to Nation Building: Third Parties and the Management of Communal Conflict* (coeditor, 2013).

Vijay Naidu
University of the South Pacific
Suva, Fiji

Vijay Naidu completed his undergraduate and M.A. studies at the University of the South Pacific in Fiji, and his doctoral degree at the University of Sussex in the UK. He has been Professor and Director of Development Studies in the School of Government, Development, and International Affairs at the University of the South Pacific (USP), and the School of Geography, Environment, and Earth Sciences at the Victoria University of Wellington. He is a Pacific development scholar and has written on aid, electoral politics, ethnicity, higher education, land tenure, migration, urbanization, social exclusion, the state, poverty and social protection, informal settlements, human security, and MDGs.

Paul J. Carnegie
Institute of Asian Studies
Universiti Brunei Darussalam
Bandar Seri Begawan, Brunei Darussalam

Paul J. Carnegie is Associate Professor of Politics and International Relations at the Institute of Asian Studies, Universiti Brunei Darussalam and the former Director of the Postgraduate Governance Program at the University of the South Pacific. He has research specializations in comparative democratization, human security, and localized responses to militant extremism in Southeast Asia, MENA, and the Asia Pacific with a particular focus on Indonesia. Paul has published widely in his fields including the monograph *The Road from Authoritarianism to Democratization in Indonesia* (Palgrave Macmillan) and the coedited volume *Human Insecurities in Southeast Asia* (Springer). He has been awarded multiple research grants with related output in leading international journals including *Pacific Affairs*, *Australian Journal of Politics and History*, the *Middle East Quarterly*, and the *Australian Journal of International Affairs*. Paul has extensive applied research experience and networks having lived and worked previously in Australia, Brunei Darussalam, Egypt, Fiji, and the United Arab Emirates.

Airini
Faculty of Education and Social Work
Thompson Rivers University
Kamloops, BC, Canada

Professor Airini is Dean of the Faculty of Education and Social Work at Thompson Rivers University, British Columbia, Canada (https://www.tru.ca/), and previously at the University of Auckland, Aoteraoa New Zealand. Airini's research looks at how to build world-class education systems where success for all means all. Her current focus is on closing education achievement gaps experienced by Indigenous school and university students in Canada and internationally. Airini is the recipient of national research and teaching awards in New Zealand (*Success for All: What university teaching practices help/hinder Maori and Pasifika student success*) and Canada (*Knowledge Makers: Indigenous undergraduate and graduate student research mentoring*). To identify how we can influence better outcomes for all, Airini went to Washington DC as a Fulbright Scholar and investigated how to convert tertiary education policy into better results for underserved students (E-mail: airini@tru.ca; Twitter: @truAirini; LinkedIn: https://ca.linkedin.come/in/airini).

Melani Anae
Pacific Studies|School of Māori Studies
and Pacific Studies,
Te Wānanga o Waipapa
University of Auckland
Auckland, New Zealand

Lupematasila, Misatauveve Dr. Melani Anae, is Senior Lecturer in Pacific Studies, Te Wānanga o Waipapa, at the University of Auckland. Anae has been a former Director of the Centre for Pacific Studies (2002–2007), a recipient of the Fulbright New Zealand Senior Scholar Award (2007), and was awarded the Companion to the Queen's Service Order for services to Pacific communities in New Zealand (2008). In 2014, she was awarded the prestigious Marsden Grant from the Royal Society of New Zealand for her project "Samoan transnational matai (chiefs): ancestor god avatars or merely title-holders?" Focusing on her research interests of ethnic identity for first-/second-generation Pacific peoples born in the diaspora, social justice and Pacific activism, and the development of her teu le va paradigm in relational ethics, her transformational work has successfully developed strategies for policy formation, service delivery, and optimal research outcomes for Pacific peoples/families and communities across the sectors of education, health, and well-being for Pacific peoples, families, and communities in New Zealand. She has taught, researched, and published extensively in these specialty areas and is currently focused on transnational identity construction of Pacific peoples and communities in the diaspora. She carries two Samoan chiefly titles from the villages of Siumu and Falelatai in Samoa, is part of a large transnational Samoan aiga, and is a grandmother and mother of three children.

Radomir Compel
School of Global Humanities and Social Sciences
Nagasaki University
Nagasaki, Japan

Radomir Compel is Associate Professor of comparative politics at the Global School of Humanities and Social Sciences of Nagasaki University in Japan. He has edited or coauthored several books, including *Guns and Roses: Comparative Civil-Military Relations in the Changing Security Environment* (2019), *Hito to Kaiyo no Kyosei wo Mezashite VI* (2013), and *Ashida Hitoshi Nikki 1905–1945 V* (2012), and has published articles in Japanese and English on Okinawa, Japan, East Asia, Middle East, and maritime issues. He obtained a Ph.D. from Yokohama National University, and taught at Hosei University, Yokohama National University, Nihon University, University of Oulu, and other educational institutions in Japan and Europe.

Sergio Luiz Cruz Aguilar
Sao Paulo State University (UNESP)
Marilia, São Paulo, Brazil

Sergio Luiz Cruz Aguilar holds a Ph.D. in History (UNESP), and is Associate Professor at the Sao Paulo State University (UNESP), Brazil, where he coordinates the Group of Studies and Research of International Conflicts and the International Conflicts Observatory. He is also Professor of the postgraduation programs San Tiago Dantas Program on International Relations (UNESP/UNICAMP/PUC-SP) and Social Sciences (UNESP – Campus of Marilia/SP). He was visiting researcher at the Department of Politics and International Relations – University of Oxford, UK. He was military observer on the United Nations Peace Force (UNPF) and on United Nations Transitional Administration for Eastern Slavonia (UNTAES), during the civil war in the former Yugoslavia. Sergio was also Director of the Brazilian Defense Studies Association (ABED) and wrote four books, edited five books, and published many journal articles in Portuguese, English, and Spanish languages.

Lyndon Fraser
Department of Sociology and Anthropology
University of Canterbury
Christchurch, New Zealand

Historian **Lyndon Fraser** is currently the Head of Department (Sociology and Anthropology) at the University of Canterbury, Christchurch, New Zealand, and Research Fellow in Human History at the Canterbury Museum. He is coeditor (with Linda Bryder) of the *New Zealand Journal of History*, and his recent publications include *Rushing for Gold: Life and Commerce on the Goldfields of Australia and New Zealand* (Otago University Press, 2016, with Lloyd Carpenter) and *History Making a Difference: New Approaches from Aotearoa* (Cambridge Scholars Publishing, 2017, coedited with Katie Pickles, Marguerite Hill, Sarah Murray, and Greg Ryan).

Contributors

Sergio Luiz Cruz Aguilar Sao Paulo State University (UNESP), Marilia, São Paulo, Brazil

Yaser Alashqar Trinity College Dublin (the University of Dublin), Dublin, Ireland

Hassanein Ali Department of International Studies, College of Humanities and Social Sciences, Zayed University, Dubai, United Arab Emirates

Jean M. Allen Faculty of Education and Social Work, The University of Auckland, Auckland, New Zealand

Trevor J. Allen Department of Political Science, Central Connecticut State University, New Britain, CT, USA

Sara N. Amin School of Social Sciences, Faculty of Arts, Law and Education, The University of the South Pacific, Suva, Fiji Islands

Ryosuke Amiya-Nakada Tsuda University, Kodaira, Japan

Melani Anae Pacific Studies|School of Māori Studies and Pacific Studies, Te Wānanga o Waipapa, University of Auckland, Auckland, New Zealand

Remus Gabriel Anghel The Romanian Institute for Research on National Minorities, Cluj Napoca, Romania

S. Apo Aporosa Te Huataki Waiora: Faculty of Health, Sport and Human Performance, University of Waikato, Hamilton, Waikato, New Zealand

Felicia Arriaga Sociology Department, Appalachian State University, Boone, NC, USA

Nicole L. Asquith Western Sydney University, Kingswood, NSW, Australia

Maria-Irini Avgoulas School of Psychology and Public Health, College of Science, Health and Engineering, La Trobe University, Bundoora, VIC, Australia

Mansi Awasthi Tata Institute of Social Sciences (TISS), Mumbai, India

Emmanuel Badu Faculty of Health and Environmental Studies, Auckland University of Technology, Auckland, New Zealand

Paul Bagguley School of Sociology and Social Policy, University of Leeds, Leeds, UK

Isabelle Bartkowiak-Théron Tasmanian Institute of Law Enforcement Studies, University of Tasmania, Hobart, TAS, Australia

Rohan Bastin School of Humanities and Social Sciences, Deakin University, Geelong, VIC, Australia

Jóhanna K. Birnir Government and Politics, University of Maryland, College Park, MD, USA

Gawaian Bodkin-Andrews Centre for the Advancement of Indigenous Knowledges, University of Technology Sydney, Broadway, NSW, Australia

Roland Boer School of Liberal Arts, Renmin University of China, Beijing, People's Republic of China

Igor Boog Institute of Cultural Anthropology and Development Sociology, Leiden University, Leiden, The Netherlands

Birgit Bräuchler Monash University, Melbourne, VIC, Australia

Johan Brosché Department of Peace- and Conflict Research, Uppsala University, Uppsala, Sweden

Heather Came Faculty of Health and Environmental Studies, Auckland University of Technology, Auckland, New Zealand

Paul J. Carnegie Institute of Asian Studies, Universiti Brunei Darussalam, Bandar Seri Begawan, Brunei Darussalam

Mitchell James Chang University of California, Los Angeles, Los Angeles, CA, USA

Chelegeer University of Leeds, Leeds, UK

Karl Ian Uy Cheng Chua History Department, Ateneo de Manila University, Quezon City, Philippines

Suryakanthie Chetty University of South Africa, Pretoria, South Africa

Treena Clark Centre for the Advancement of Indigenous Knowledges, University of Technology Sydney, Broadway, NSW, Australia

Radomir Compel School of Global Humanities and Social Sciences, Nagasaki University, Nagasaki, Japan

Neil Cruickshank Political Scientist and Dean of the Faculty of Arts, Science, and Technology, North Island College, Courtenay, BC, Canada

Faculty Associate, Centre for European Studies, Carleton University, Ottawa, ON, Canada

Christian Cwik Department of History, The University of the West Indies, St Augustine, Trinidad and Tobago

Sharyn Graham Davies Auckland University of Technology, Aotearoa, New Zealand

Michael Davis Department of Sociology and Social Policy, The University of Sydney, Sydney, NSW, Australia

Premakumara de Silva Department of Sociology, University of Colombo, Colombo, Sri Lanka

Zbigniew Dumieński Auckland University of Technology, Auckland, New Zealand

Emma Elfversson Department of Peace and Conflict Research, Uppsala University, Uppsala, Sweden

Mostafa Entezarulmahdy Political Science Department, Robat Karim Branch, Islamic Azad University, Tehran, Iran

Jovanie Camacho Espesor Department of Political Science and International Relations, University of Canterbury, Christchurch, New Zealand

Department of Political Science, Mindanao State University, General Santos City, Philippines

Center for Middle East and Global Peace Studies, Universitas Islam Negeri Syarif Hidayatullah Jakarta, Tangerang, Indonesia

Rebecca Fanany School of Health, Medical and Applied Sciences, Central Queensland University, Melbourne, VIC, Australia

Shannon Foster Centre for the Advancement of Indigenous Knowledges, University of Technology Sydney, Broadway, NSW, Australia

László Fosztó The Romanian Institute for Research on National Minorities, Cluj Napoca, Romania

Jeffrey A. Gardner Department of Sociology, Sam Houston State University, Huntsville, TX, USA

Rodrigo Luiz Cunha Gonsalves European Graduate School (EGS), Saas fee, Switzerland

University of Sao Paulo (IPUSP), Sao Paulo, Brazil

Farzana Haniffa Department of Sociology, University of Colombo, Colombo, Sri Lanka

Kate Hannan Department of History and Politics, University of Wollongong, Wollongong, NSW, Australia

Kathleen Harrington-Watt Anthropology, Canterbury University, Christchurch, New Zealand

Hamdy Hassan College of Humanities and Social Sciences, Zayed University, Dubai, UAE

Keakaokawai Varner Hemi University of Waikato, Hamilton, New Zealand

Sarah Herbert Faculty of Health and Environmental Studies, Auckland University of Technology, Auckland, New Zealand

Matthew Hoddie Department of Political Science, Towson University, Towson, MD, USA

Louise Humpage Sociology, Faculty of Arts, University of Auckland, Auckland, New Zealand

Yasmin Hussain School of Sociology and Social Policy, University of Leeds, Leeds, UK

Aphun Kamei Department of Sociology, Delhi School of Economics, University of Delhi, Delhi, India

Romitesh Kant Institute for Human Security and Social Change (IHSSC), College of Arts and Social Sciences, La Trobe University, Melbourne, VIC, Australia

Masaki Kataoka University of Canterbury, Christchurch, New Zealand

Institute of Developing Economies, Japan External Trade Organization, Chiba, Japan

Amanda Kearney College of Humanities, Arts and Social Sciences, Flinders University, Bedford Park, SA, Australia

Misty Knight-Finley Department of Political Science and Economics, Rowan University, Glassboro, NJ, USA

Rajesh Kumar Tata Institute of Social Sciences (TISS), Mumbai, India

Wendy Lambourne Department of Peace and Conflict Studies, University of Sydney, Sydney, NSW, Australia

Jianxia Lin University of Leeds, Leeds, UK

Stefano Luconi Department of Education (DISFOR), University of Genoa, Genoa, Italy

Kristen Lyons School of Social Science, University of Queensland, Brisbane, QLD, Australia

Nic Maclellan Melbourne, Australia

Adis Maksic International Burch University, Sarajevo, Bosnia and Herzegovina

Sam Manuela University of Auckland, Auckland, New Zealand

Paul H. Mason School of Social Sciences, Monash University, Clayton, VIC, Australia

Department of Anthropology, Macquarie University, North Ryde, NSW, Australia

Jacob Mwathi Mati School of Social Sciences, Faculty of Arts, Law and Education (FALE), The University of the South Pacific, Suva, Fiji Islands

Society, Work and Politics (SWOP) Institute, The University of the Witwatersrand, Johannesburg, South Africa

Eyal Mayroz University of Sydney, Sydney, NSW, Australia

Tim McCreanor Te Rōpū Whāriki, Massey University, Auckland, New Zealand

Cathal McManus School of Social Sciences, Education and Social Work, Queen's University Belfast, Belfast, Northern Ireland

Bruno Mendelski Institute of International Relations (IREL), University of Brasilia, Brasilia, Brazil

International Relations at Department of Economics, University of Santa Cruz do Sul, Santa Cruz do Sul, Viamão, Brazil

Alois S. Mlambo University of Pretoria, Pretoria, South Africa

M. Bashir Mobasher Department of Political Science, American University of Afghanistan, Kabul, Afghanistan

Monique Mulholland College of Humanities, Arts and Social Sciences, The Flinders University of South Australia, Adelaide, Australia

Murtala Murtala Suara Indonesia Dance Troupe, Sydney, NSW, Australia

Nasser Mustapha Department of Behavioural Sciences, University of the West Indies, St Augustine, Trinidad and Tobago

Todd Nachowitz University of Waikato, Hamilton, New Zealand

Sereana Naepi Thompson Rivers University, Kamloops, Canada

Vijay Naidu University of the South Pacific, Suva, Fiji

Subhankar Nayak Tata Institute of Social Sciences (TISS), Mumbai, India

Ryota Nishino University of the South Pacific, Suva, Fiji

International Research Center for Japanese Studies (Nichibunken), Kyoto, Japan

Nyaz N. Noori Department of Economic History, Uppsala University, Uppsala, Sweden

Lecturer, Department of Economics, University of Sulaymaniyah, Sulaimaniyah, Kurdistan Region, Iraq

Adele Norris School of Social Sciences, Sociology and Sociology Program, The University of Waikato, Hamilton, New Zealand

Alfira O'Sullivan Suara Indonesia Dance Troupe, Sydney, NSW, Australia

Henry D. Overos Government and Politics, University of Maryland, College Park, MD, USA

Gairoonisa Paleker Department of Historical and Heritage Studies, University of Pretoria, Pretoria, South Africa

Antoine Pécoud University of Paris 13, Paris, France

Geoff Pfeifer Worcester Polytechnic Institute, Worcester, MA, USA

Kathryn Pillay University of KwaZulu-Natal, Durban, South Africa

Ralph Premdas University of the West Indies, St. Augustine, Trinidad and Tobago

Sangit Kumar Ragi Department of Political Science, Social Science Building, North Campus, University of Delhi, Delhi, India

Bishnu Ragoonath Department of Political Science, University of the West Indies Trinidad, St. Augustine, Trinidad and Tobago

Arjun Rajkhowa University of Melbourne, Melbourne, Australia

Sanjay Ramesh Department of Peace and Conflict Studies, University of Sydney, Camperdown, NSW, Australia

Steven Ratuva Department of Anthropology and Sociology, University of Canterbury, Christchurch, New Zealand

Macmillan Brown Centre for Pacific Studies, University of Canterbury, Christchurch, New Zealand

Sadasivam Jaganada Reddi Réduit, Mauritius

Patricia Richards Department of Sociology, University of Georgia, Athens, GA, USA

Tara Ross University of Canterbury, Christchurch, New Zealand

Joseph R. Rudolph Department of Political Science, Towson University, Baltimore, MA, USA

Joseph Rudigi Rukema School of Social Sciences, University of KwaZulu-Natal, Durban, South Africa

Brinsley Samaroo History Department, University of the West Indies, St. Augustine, Trinidad and Tobago

Sam Scott University of Gloucestershire, Cheltenham, UK

Madhushree Sekher Centre for Study of Social Exclusion and Inclusive Policies (CSSEIP), Tata Institute of Social Sciences (TISS), Mumbai, India

Renat Shaykhutdinov Florida Atlantic University, Boca Raton, FL, USA

Badrus Sholeh Department of International Relations, Faculty of Social and Political Sciences, Syarif Hidayatullah State Islamic University, Jakarta, Indonesia

Sherry-Ann Singh The University of the West Indies, St. Augustine, Trinidad and Tobago

Stephen Small Department of African American Studies, University of California, Berkeley, Berkeley, CA, USA

Zhifang Song University of Canterbury, Canterbury, New Zealand

Sheetal Sheena Sookrajowa Department of History and Political Science, Faculty of Social Sciences and Humanities, University of Mauritius, Réduit, Mauritius

Paul Spoonley College of Humanities and Social Sciences, Massey University, Auckland, New Zealand

Jessica Terruhn Massey University, Auckland, New Zealand

Allen Thomas Tata Institute of Social Sciences (TISS), Mumbai, India

Andrew Thomson Queens University of Belfast, Belfast, UK

Stefánia Toma The Romanian Institute for Research on National Minorities, Cluj Napoca, Romania

Elya Tzaneva Institute of Ethnology and Folklore Studies with Ethnographic Museum, Bulgarian Academy of sciences, Sofia, Bulgaria

Nasir Uddin Department of Anthropology, University of Chittagong, Chittagong, Bangladesh

Beatrice Umubyeyi School of Built and Environmental Studies, University of KwaZulu-Natal, Durban, South Africa

Francisco J. Villegas Department of Anthropology and Sociology, Kalamazoo College, Kalamazoo, MI, USA

Paloma E. Villegas Sociology, California State University, San Bernardino, CA, USA

Tarisi Vunidilo Department of Anthropology, University of Hawaii-Hilo, Hilo, HI, USA

Melinda Webber Faculty of Education and Social Work, The University of Auckland, Auckland, New Zealand

Aleksandra Zdeb Centre for Southeast European Studies of the University of Graz, University of Graz, Graz, Austria

Cindy Zeiher University of Canterbury, Christchurch, New Zealand

Juan Zhang Department of Anthropology and Archaeology, University of Bristol, Bristol, UK

Exploring Global Ethnicity: A Broad Sociological Synopsis

Steven Ratuva

Contents

Introduction	2
Exploring Some Sociological Debates	4
Ethnicity, Communal Boundaries, and Group Dynamics	6
Ethnicity and Nationalism	7
Ethnicity and Race	9
Shifting Ethnicity, Self, and Others	10
Ethnicity and the State	12
Racism and Subconscious Bias	14
Ethnic Diversity and Assimilation	17
The Process of De-ethnicization	18
Ethnicity and Intersectionality	20
Ethnicity and Affirmative Action	21
Conclusion	23
References	24

Abstract

This ethnicity project brings together a diverse range of international scholars from various disciplinary orientations, theoretical inclinations, and methodological approaches but connected by their shared expertise and interest in ethnicity or ethnicity-related issues. Ethnicity is more than just complex. It is contested, has the capacity to be politically provocative and intellectually mystifying, especially in an age where the parameter of its scholarly use is ever changing in response to unfolding social realities. A result of collective social construction, it influences and in turn influenced by attitudes, perceptions, practices, policies, laws, and norms and is reproduced through multiple societal means of socialization. It is a

S. Ratuva (✉)
Department of Anthropology and Sociology, University of Canterbury, Christchurch, New Zealand

Macmillan Brown Centre for Pacific Studies, University of Canterbury, Christchurch, New Zealand
e-mail: steven.ratuva@canterbury.ac.nz

© The Author(s), under exclusive license to Springer Nature Singapore Pte Ltd. 2019
S. Ratuva (ed.), *The Palgrave Handbook of Ethnicity*,
https://doi.org/10.1007/978-981-13-2898-5_1

means with which we define ourselves and how we categorize individuals and groups. What is ethnicity and how can we understand its manifestations, influences, and social dynamics? the three volumes provides multiple prisms through which ethnicity can be understood and articulated. This chapter is a broad introduction which raises a number of critical issues about ethnicity which are articulated, unpacked, analyzed, and critiqued in about a 102 chapters in this major Palgrave global ethnicity handbook project. This is the most comprehensive coverage of a subject that has been part of human development and consciousness since time immemorial.

Keywords
Ethnicity · Identity · Racism · Nationalism · Globalization · Race

Introduction

Mobilizing the array of international expertise in this project was not a simple undertaking as it involved pulling together scholars with diverse disciplinary, theoretical, and methodological orientations into a harmonious ensemble of multiple voices. In a world where ethnicity is an inescapable part of our humanity and everyday life, a critical understanding of ethnic identity as a complex, contested, provocative, and sometimes mystifying subject is of utmost importance. The surge in interest in the phenomenon of ethnicity in the post-cold war era has been enthused by a number of factors including: the proliferation of ethno-nationalism and ethnic-based conflict; terrorism and associated ethno-cultural ideologies; institutionalized subconscious racial prejudice and bias; expressions of racially motivated tension in many parts of the world; growth in anti-foreigner sentiments; rise in populist right wing political agitations in Europe and the United States; President Donald Trump's anti-Muslim immigration policies; sectarian religious conflicts; ongoing refugee crisis; pervading inequality and the increasing demands for sovereignty by indigenous peoples and marginalized ethnic minorities. Associated with these is the growing desire by many to reconnect with their own sense of identity, humanity, and culture in response to a pervading sense of alienation associated with globalization.

While ethnicity itself is a form of sociocultural identification, its intersection with other factors, such as class, competition for political power, resources distribution, historical grievances, human rights abuse, marginalization, and discrimination, makes it as potent force for political mobilization. Ethnic differences on their own may not "cause" conflict but how these differences intersect with or interplay with other social, economic, and political factors may prove potentially explosive.

Although ethnicity has continued to evolve as a result of social transformation and globalization, it still remains as a primary means of identification and mobilization for many in response to external threats to their groups and the uncertainties of the contemporary world. Sometimes, ethnicity can also be used as a convenient way to advance one's political and economic interests or as a means to scapegoat a group in times of crisis. Over the years, wars have been waged, governments have been overthrown, groups have been oppressed, societies have been torn apart, and millions of lives have been lost in the name of ethnicity. The trend continues unabated in different degrees and manifestations.

Thus understanding how ethnicity is constructed and how it manifests itself in everyday life is critical in illuminating our own self-perception and view of others in our dramatically transforming social world. This is especially so because of the multiple ways in which ethnicity is projected and deployed including justification for political ideas and practices; imposition or opposition to affirmative action policies; support for liberation movements; imposition of repressive rule; carrying out genocide; discrimination against immigrants; organizing revolutions; hiring and firing employees; and the list goes on. To many, it is an almost inescapable part of everyday reality in a globalizing world.

The three volumes provide a diverse and comprehensive exploration of ethnicity in its conceptual and empirical manifestations. They do not claim to provide definitive answers but rather raise important issues associated with ethnicity in our contemporary era. The authors were chosen because of their respective expertise and research proficiency across the broad academic spectrum of anthropology, sociology, political science, psychology, economics, literature, gender studies, development studies, and indigenous studies, to name a few. The different contributors employ a range of conceptual narratives including classical sociological and anthropological prisms, critical social discourses, gender lenses, intersectional framework, postmodern narratives, and postcolonial analysis to illuminate some of the manifest and latent expressions of ethnicity and their meanings in a whole range of case studies in different parts of the world. The case studies are not presented in a comparative way but are articulated as unique social contexts in their own right with their own unique voices and identities which converse with each other through strands of shared themes and conceptual narratives. One of this shared themes is that ethnicity needs to be understood as a form of collective identification constructed by a group or by others outside the group to emphasize exclusive claim to various forms of social symbolisms, historical experience, ancestry, or cultural heritage (Rex 1970). As a form of collective identification, ethnicity is closely associated with cultural norms, religious beliefs, claims to motherland, historical memory, collective mythology, land rights, nation states, and other forms of sociocultural symbolisms that are associated with many conflicts today.

The handbook is meant for researchers, students, teachers, professionals, policy makers, community leaders, and general public. It is organized into ten parts based on subthemes. Part I (Nexus Between Ethnicity and Identity) is edited by Steven Ratuva; Part II (The State, Society, and Ethnopolitics) by Joseph Rudolph; Part III (Stereotypes and Prejudices) by Vijay Naidu; Part IV (Ethno-nationalism and Power) by Paul Carnegie; Part V (Indigeneity, Gender, and Sexuality) by Airini and Steven Ratuva; Part VI (Globalization and Diaspora) by Melani Anae; Part VII (Ethnic Relations and Policy Responses) by Radomir Compel; Part VIII (Ethnic Cleansing and Genocide) by Sergio Aguilar; Part IX (Ethnicity, Migration, and Labor) by Lyndon Fraser; and Part X (Cultural Celebration and Resistance) by Steven Ratuva.

This chapter is largely introductory and provides some basic conceptual approaches to the ever expanding area of ethnicity. It draws from the multiplicity of approaches provided by the individual chapters and provides a broad framework for the handbook.

Exploring Some Sociological Debates

The notion of ethnicity has varying sociological undertones. The term "ethnic," from which it is derived, originates from the Greek term *ethnos* and the meaning in different languages evolved in specific circumstances. Its use in the English language evolved from reference to heathens and pagans around the eighteenth century to association with "race" during the nineteenth century. The interchangeable use with the term race (which is defined in relation to inherited biological features) has created some confusion and this continues today. Debates on the nature and dynamics of ethnicity has continued in different forms until today as a result of changing circumstances and new ways of framing identity in a globalized and conflict-prone world. We have to recognize the fact that the terms race and ethnicity are for historical, political, and other reasons used in different ways in different countries; thus we have to understand them in relation to their contextuality and variability.

Because of its subjectivity, it is important to surmise at the outset that conceptions of ethnicity are often contested. For instance, those who frame it within the primordialist discourse tend to view ethnicity as more or less innate, fixed, and permanent (Erikson 2010), in "a state of intense and comprehensive solidarity" (quoted in McKay 1982: 398) and associated with "tribalism, parochialism, communalism" (Geertz 1963: 261). The critics of this view argue that it lacks human agency in that ethnicity has "innate disposition" (Cohen 1974: xii), and as such tends to purvey "a picture of underives and socially-unconstructed emotions that are unanalysable and overpowering..." and "a more unintelligible and unsociological concept would be hard to imagine" (Eller and Coughlan 1993: 187). Because of this tendency, primordialism fails to explain the changing patterns of social organization, identity, and culture and tends towards a static and almost biologically deterministic view of human society. Associated to some degree with primordialism is the notion of essentialism which tries to frame complex ethnic issues into a single category with given characteristics which are often based on generalizations and assumptions of some given features which are often devoid of time and place (Erikson 2010; Seibers 2017).

Most of the critics of the primordialist and essentialist positions emanate from the other end of the sociological camp. These are principally the social constructionists and instrumentalists who see human intent, experience, belief, and action, not innate determinism, as basis for constructing ethnic identity. The instrumentalist approach conceives of ethnicity in terms of how people subjectively select aspects of cultural norms and institutions to serve their purposes (Barth 1969). So rather than assuming that ethnic identity is inborn and permanent, Bath argues that it is situational and ever-changing depending on people's subjective needs in response to changing circumstances. In some ways, Max Weber, who earlier on used the term ethnicity, generally had a similar view that ethnicity does not constitute a group as such but simply acts as facilitator for group formation in a political environment (Weber 1971). In a similar strand of thought, Everett Hughes talks about ethnicity as a result of the way in which the "ins" and "outs" groups define each other's space on the basis of difference and separation (Hughes 1994). In a way, Weber and Hughes influenced the later social constructionist conception of ethnicity which can be summed up as: "ethnic groups are what people believe or think them to be; cultural differences mark 'group-ness', they do not cause it (or indelibly characterise it); ethnic identification arises out of, and within, interaction between groups" (Jenkins 1997: 11).

Along the same trend, while the instrumentalists see ethnicity as subject to selective and conscious manipulation, the social constructionist view sees it as a constantly "constructed" and reproduced phenomenon. The emphasis is the mechanics of construction, the purpose behind the process, and by whom. There are three main subapproaches to the social constructionist discourse. The first is that individuals through social interaction construct various symbolisms which constitute the collective ethnic identity. The second is that discursive formations are agents of social construction and create meanings which frame and differentiate a group from one another (Fearon and Laitin 2000). The third and most prominent of the social constructionist subcategories is the idea that ethnicity is a result of the complex interplay between social, economic, cultural, and political forces linked to colonialism, globalization, modernity, postmodernity, cultural commodification, cyberspace identity, nationalism, and the formation of the nation-state (Erikson 2002, 2010).

By the 1980s, the growth of the postmodern approach shifted the debate from grand narratives of ethnic identity as a social phenomenon to casting it as a reflection of consciousness. Postmodernists argue that identity is superfluous, fragmented, and transactional and must not be considered as a durable social phenomenon (Jenkins 2008). In addition, ethnicity was also seen through the lenses of intersectionality and how issues such as ethnicity must not be understood on its own but should be framed in terms of their relationship with other interconnecting factors such as gender, class, sexuality, ability, age, country of origin, and education as these factors shape ethnicity and each other in complex ways (Collins and Chepp 2013). Meanwhile, at the other extreme end of the postmodern continuum are those like Carter and Fenton (2009) who argue that ethnicity should be abandoned altogether as a useful conceptual tool.

The idea of ethnicity and race as being superfluous is further developed by postcolonial writers. An icon of postcolonial discourse, Stuart Hall, asserts that the historical conditions are construction grounds for new forms of identification. For instance, the changing nature of ethic representation among the diaspora contributes to "new ethnicities" which are constructed from the old forms of postcolonial representations (Hall 1996). Hall does not see ethnicity as a "thing" but lenses through which social dynamics and structures must be explored (Grossberg 2007). In all social processes, race is to be understood in its internality because it is lived and experienced as well as woven into the fabric of inequality (Alexander 2009).

Along this line of thought, the historical agenda of colonialism was the construction and institutionalization of separate ethnic identities and how this was leveraged as part of the broader ideological, socioeconomic, political, and cultural project of domination that kept colonized ethnic groups marginalized and divided.

Ethnicity, Communal Boundaries, and Group Dynamics

A number of chapters speak to the salience of boundaries and group dynamics. The critical significance of ethnicity, according to Ratcliffe (1994: 6), "lies in its salience for group consciousness and collective action." The idea of collectivity and shared characteristics such as kinship, religion, language, shared territory, nationality, or physical appearance are often used as factors in defining ethnicity. Eriksen (2010) suggests that, far from being an unchangeable characteristic of groups, ethnicity is a dynamic and as such constantly transforms aspects of social relationships which cannot be detached from other social identifiers such as class, gender, and nationhood, as well as major contemporary issues of racism, globalization, and multiculturalism.

In this context, ethnicity cannot be easily divorced from other forms of group identity such as shared language (ethno-linguistic), shared nationality (ethno-national), shared region (ethno-regional), or shared religions (ethno-religious) because of the way that it emphasizes the common characteristics of people within the group. In these cases, ethnicity is not only an identifier; it is also a force for mobilization of common interests as well as a defensive mechanism against threats to the group. These forms of mobilization are often referred to as communal nationalism or ethno-communalism. Communalism is a broad term which is defined by identifiers such as language, religion, nationality, region, and other forms of group identification. For Cohen, community is based on simultaneous symbolic construction of similarities and differences:

> "Community" thus seems to imply simultaneously both similarity and difference. The word thus expressed a *relational* idea: the opposition of one community to others or to other social entities...The use of the word is only occasioned by the desire or need to express such a distinction. It seems appropriate, therefore, to focus our examination of the nature of community on the element which embodies this sense of discrimination, namely, the *boundary*. (Cohen 1985: 12, original emphasis)

Communal boundaries are defined either internally by the group itself based on its historical claims, mythology, and symbolisms, reproduced and passed down over generations or externally by others based on how they see the group from "outside." These internal and external definitions of boundaries could be based either on consensus or differences. The state, as an all-powerful external force, may impose its boundaries according to its own political interests and use laws to legitimize this. In other cases, the state may allow members of the group to self-classify. The variables used to define ethnic boundaries consist of an array of factors such as common cultural descent, common history, genetic and kinship links, sociopolitical symbolisms, and notion of motherland (Erikson 2010). Boundaries become tightly drawn as a defensive mechanism during times of political conflict and socioeconomic crisis as certain groups are targeted, stereotyped, scapegoated, and framed as "undesirables" or even "enemies." In the recent refugee crisis around the world, migrants were branded as such as their ethnic groups were publicly named to profile them. Discursive branding through "naming" is a way of shaming as well as drawing a tight boundary around a group. It is also a way of drawing attention to the plight of these groups either in a tokenistic and patronizing way or in an empowering manner.

Boundaries are often contested and subverted even from within as societies become more transnational and cultures interact. In contemporary multiethnic societies, where intermarriages, global transmigration, and cultural interaction are common, communal boundaries become more porous and volatile as new generations assimilate new cultures, languages, and new forms of identity. The new globalized middle class in many communities find themselves assuming more internationalized identities and interests which are outside their "traditional" communal boundaries.

One of the most significant factors in group identity is "sense of belonging." Identification with a primary group through language, nation, religion, territory, tribe, cultural symbolism, or historical association provides a sense of individual and collective bond in an "imagined community" where people who do not know each other share common bonds (Anderson 2006). The feeling that others share similar sense of belonging, no matter where they might be around the world and no matter how much they understand about their original language, religion, or other aspects of their culture, is often reassuring and gives people a sense of purpose and meaning in a globalizing and fast-changing world.

Ethnicity and Nationalism

A common strand in the handbook is the relationship between ethnicity and nationalism. The surge of nationalism worldwide has transformed the political landscape significantly because of its tendency to inflame differences and tension. It is important to note that nationalism has two rival conceptions which have competed for historical legitimacy up to now. The first is what may be termed civic nationalism, referring to the creation of collective identity in relation to the state, and this may express itself in the form of a secular ideology for a common civil identity across the within a state. Ethnic characteristics are subsumed under a single national identity within the territory of a sovereign state. This, according to Stavenhagen (1996: 3), may be referred to as "territorial or civic nationhood, and is determined by the state itself through law and shared experience."

The second conception, ethno-nationalism, refers to intracommunal mobilization using social markers such as language, religion, tribe, ethnicity, and other forms of historically determined links and loyalties, either to establish claims for a separate state or to consolidate domination of a group within an existing state. Unlike civic nationhood, the fundamental determining factor is cultural identity, not formal citizenship. Sometimes, territory is a necessary aspect of identification, not so much as a space for the application of formal citizenship as for creating an historic homeland to which primordial identification could be made. In this regard, ethnic nationalism attempts to mobilize ethnic groups in relation to actual territories as the ethnic motherland. In these cases, we see a double process of defining a nation around a territorially based state, and of making one particular group the privileged bearer of national identity, defining and controlling the symbols of that identity (Stavenhagen 1996).

The two forms of nationalism have a syncretic relationship which involves the simultaneous interplay between contradiction, accommodation, negotiation, and even selective synthesis. In many case, the need to unify ethnic groups under a common civic nation is often counteracted by the demand for separate ethnic identity, but this is often mediated my moderate elements within the community who attempt to balance the two. Sometimes, the state plays an active role in mediating this relationship and in certain circumstances this may involve the ethnicization of political space for political, military and other forms of mobilization (Enloe 1980). Sometimes, a particular ethnic group may be dominant with a certain degree of control of the state institutions through the deployment of ideological, legal, political, or cultural mechanisms to maintain hegemony. The dominant ethnic group may even attempt to create and impose a "common" national identity as an ethnic cultural arbitrary. Ethnic conflict between two groups within a state boundary does not necessarily result from ethnic differences in themselves as suggested by advocates of pluralism such as Furnivall (1948) but from a complex interplay of identity with ideological, political, and socioeconomic forces.

The creation of an ethno-nationalist ideology is underpinned by four fundamental factors. Firstly, the "nation" may constitute a community with a distinctive culture and group consciousness articulated in cultural symbols such as language, historical memory, genealogical system, mythology and folkways. Secondly, the group has claim to a common history about common ancestry and the need to perpetuate the unbroken link with the past. Thirdly, the concretization of the ancestral narratives through claims to territorial Motherland, Fatherland, or Homeland. Fourthly, it is the demand that communal and cultural distinctiveness is deserving of political and cultural autonomy (Stavenhagen 1996). These four traits are intertwined and reproduced over time as ideological, cultural, and political basis for ethno-nationalism. But it must be noted that there are other factors such as human rights violation, inequality, resources distribution, political repression, and marginalization which may spawn or trigger the expressions of ethno-nationalism as well as determine its magnitude.

Nevertheless, a nation and nationalism are not always neatly defined through collective familiarity as Benedict Anderson suggests. To Anderson, a nation is "an imagined political community-and imagined as both inherently limited and sovereign" (Anderson 2006: 6). It is imagined because members of the nation do not know of other's existence, yet they feel that they are part of the same group. It is limited because it includes some people and excludes some, and sovereign because nationalism can be associated with independence and self- government. While Anderson assumes that nationalism and racism may be dissimilar, Robert Miles counter-argues that the ideological foundation of nationalism and racism are very much the same, because both assume "the existence of a natural division of people of the world's population into discrete groups" and are used as justification for a group's superiority over another (Miles 1989, 1993).

The idea that nationalism is fundamentally an ideological construction pervades. For instance, Eriksen asserts that nationalism and ethnicity are different but argues that a nationalist ideology is fundamentally an ethnic ideology and is a celebration of the setting up of a state on behalf of an ethnic group (Eriksen 1993). Immanuel Wallerstein (1991) stretches the argument further by contending that the reality of the modern world is that people have "ambiguous identity" and our complex sociohistorical conditions make precise definition and labelling of social groups absurd. Ethnic and nationalist concepts, he argues, are purely ideological forms of representation and explanations relating to nationalist and ethnic relations must be sought in relation to the "world system" paradigm. Ethnicity is a social construct and a legitimizing tool of capitalist expansion in the world economy. The positions of ethnic groups or nations in the global economic hierarchy are results of the internationalization of capital and labor, Wallerstein continues. In this context, ethnic consciousness can be seen as both situational and subject to "shifting contexts" Horowitz (1985: 4). This means that collective enmities can be created, manipulated, and reproduced at different historical junctures and these may impact upon the direction and degree of social change.

Thus in a broad way, nationalism can be identified and framed at different levels: at the national level where there is an attempt to unify the country as a single political and ideological construct and the creation of a homogeneous and collective identity, or at the local level where the exertion of conflicting identities within a common political space, based on narrow and localized constructs.

Ethnicity and Race

As some of the chapters show, both race and ethnicity are social constructs which are often used interchangeably. In a rather simplistic way, race is usually associated with the collective identity of people sharing the same physical attributes while ethnicity is often related to shared cultural inheritance. But it does not end here. Underlying the assumptions about race is the idea that primordial physical characteristics are intrinsically associated with people within a geographical boundary and sharing similar cultural traits. For instance, when references to "Chinese race," "Aboriginal race," or "Irish race" are made, there is an implicit assumption of interrelationship between both biological and social characteristics. Sometimes race is used as broad sociobiological construct used as generic constructs such as "black race," "white race," or "Aryan race," which often have political or ideological connotations attached to them to demarcate (horizontally and vertically) groups from one another.

In some countries (such as the USA and South Africa), the generic concept of race is officially employed to demarcate and categorize groups of people with perceived similarities – the notions of "black" and "white" are central to this classification. But these color codes are associated with perceptions and attributes which go beyond just the skin pigmentation into the realm of cultural hierarchy and even level of intelligence (Fredrickson 2015). The racialization of intelligence and superiority of culture has underpinned racism over the years but despite criticisms, it still exists in various institutionalized and subtle forms. The belief in the link between race and sociocultural progress still lurks in subconscious ways in many academic discourses such as psychology, economic development, and political development. In his book, *The Bell curve*, Herrnstein and Murray (1994), tried to make the argument that race and intelligence had some association. The modernization theory which has been a dominant narrative in economics, sociology, political science, and other social science disciplines is based on the assumption that societies can be ranked on a unilineal scale based on their level of cultural, technological, and scientific progress and superiority. Even the use of indexes in analytical templates such as the United Nations Human Development Index, Fragile State Index, Corruption Index, Governance Index and other forms of country classifications, selectively use indicators which favor "Western" countries and associated cultural groups over postcolonial societies which are largely populated by "less superior" racial groups.

Recent advances in the area of genetic studies have helped reshape some of the assumptions about ethnicity and race. DNA mapping of human groups show that there are no genetic basis for racial differences thus nullifying the age-old myths of racial superiority on which scientific racism is based. It is now a scientifically proven reality that human genetic variation occurs more within geographically distinct groups (85%) than between them. Thus racism as a constructed behavioral disposition is based on flimsy myths of differences rather than on any scientifically sound basis (Rutherford 2017).

Shifting Ethnicity, Self, and Others

Several chapters deal with the challenges of ethnicity in a changing and complex social environment and collective definition. In an increasingly complex world, ethnicity has become relational with constantly constructed and shifting boundaries based on responses to the changing contexts. This is a theme elaborated by Barth (1969), who used the social anthropology framework to understand how groups mediate and define themselves in relation to others. This requires the use of symbolism to unify individuals and create a commonly shared sense of belonging. These symbolisms express cultural narratives and values which often change over time. According to Jenkins (1997: 40), ethnicity involves cultural "differentiation" (although identity is always dialectic between similarity and difference) as well as "variable" and "manipulable" as well as both "externalized" and "internalized." Because it is manipulable, ethnicity is potentially explosive and fraught with intellectual and political prejudice and controversy, as Horowitz wrote: "Ethnicity has fought and bled and burned its way into public and scholarly consciousness" (Horowitz 1985: xi). It is sometimes conceived of as being "situational" (Ratcliffe

1994) because ethnic identities are created in relation to certain situations; or "mobilizational" (McKay 1982) because ethnicity is based on mobilizing along certain identities to serve certain purposes. As a way of sustaining their collective identity in a situation of change, groups will continue to "reinvent" identity and tradition (Hobsbawm and Ranger 1983).

Ethnicity is also transactional in two ways. Firstly, the processes of internal definition where members of a group collectively define their own individual and group identity in relation to some recognizable culturally specific practices; and secondly, is external definition where individuals and groups are collectively defined by "others." External definition could either entail validation of other's internal definition of themselves or the imposition and characterization by others which may significantly affect the social experiences of the categorized (Eriksen 2010). The processes of internal and external definition are, in the complex day-to-day social life, interrelated in a dialectical way. External definition takes place within an active social relationship between individuals and groups.

As Jenkins (2008) further suggests, the "us" and "them" or "in group" and "out group" definitions are fundamental to the process of ethnicity formation. It involves the interrelated processes of production, reproduction, and transformation of the "groupness" of culturally differentiated collectivities. Here, the distinction between "groups" and "categories" must be made. A group (as in ethnic group) represents a collectivity as meaningfully conceptualized and defined by its members, and self-awareness of their distinctiveness; while category (as in ethnic category) is a collectivity defined externally in relation to criteria formulated by sociologists or anthropologists.

External definition could be a mirror for internal definition since it has an impact on conceptualization of the self (Harter 2015). It can also pose a threat to a group since external definition could imply stereotyping or worse, undermining of internal definition or worse still, a prelude to political interference and even ethnic cleansing as we saw in Rwanda and Bosnia. Defense of threatened identities could be a basis for political mobilization, around certain culturally specific or historically constructed symbols such as flags, land, mythology, or language. Collective identification is a result of acculturation into an ethnic group identity through complex processes of formal and informal socialization at different stages in life. These may include family nurturing; routine public interaction; sexual relationships; communal relationships; membership of informal groups; marriage and kinship; market relationships; employment; administrative allocation; organized politics; official classification (Jenkins 2008).

Moreover, external categorization may be "internalized" by the categorized group in different ways and these may have implications on intergroup relations. Sometimes, external definitions may complement and validate existing internal definitions, and this has potential to open up group boundaries to allow for greater interaction. Sometimes, external definitions which are incompatible with internal definitions can create hostility and invoke resistance thus tightening intergroup boundaries further. In times of crisis and conflict, intergroup definitions could become intensely political and the ethnic boundaries drawn more rigidly and well-guarded. In some cases, external definitions may be externally imposed by more powerful groups, sometimes with the help of the state, and this has the potential effect of creating a subaltern identity under the hegemonic shadows of a dominant group. External categorization can mean intervening into and changing others' social world and experiences as we have seen in the case of vulnerable minority groups such as the Rohingya in Myanmar, Aborigines in Australia or certain indigenous minorities in China.

Also, in times of conflict, claims to land, rights, identity, religion, history, language, and other aspects are constructed as a way of legitimizing political demands or as protective mechanisms against counter-claims. These claims are often articulated as immemorial and even primordial and involve invoking genealogical continuity and intimate embeddedness in ancestral land. This may involve reproducing myths of common ancestry, origin, migration, and history as a basis for constructing an ethnic ideology. To Stavenhagen (1996), the ideological consciousness arising from identification as a "kinship myth" community could remain embedded in the communal psyche for a long time and deployed in various forms as a justification underscoring demands for various political rights, economic rights and nationalistic causes. Thus ethnic solidarity tends to intensify as the struggle over scarce resources escalates. The ethnic myths reproduced over time can define the moral and political character of the "us" in relation to "them." An important component of these ethnic myths is ethnic stereotypes that collectively embody the identity with strangers in an "imagined community" (Anderson 1983).

Ethnicity and the State

A number of chapters in the project deal with the complex relationship between ethnicity and the state. Ethnicity is often conceptualized partly as an ideology employed by individuals and the state to resolve insecurities arising from the power structure within which they are located (Brown 1994: 1). The relationship between ethnicity and the state is complex, especially when associated with contestation for power and wealth. In its role in the distribution of power, status, wealth, and security arrangements in society, the state may align itself with certain groups over others on grounds of religion, language or cultural identity. In addition, the state may impose a power structure and impose an ideology to define the parameters within which ethnic identity and consciousness of particular groups should exist. The state may even derive its official ideology from the cultural values of a particular ethnic group using cultural markers such as language, religion, and territory. Some examples such as Malaysia, Iran, and Indonesia where Islamic values are associated with state ideology, come to mind. Even in "Western" states such as France, assimilation into the dominant "liberal" French values are enforced by the state through banning of certain cultural symbols such as burka in various places.

States differ greatly in their capacity, legitimacy, autonomy and organizing ideologies in relation to dealing with the challenges of ethnic relations. Perhaps a broad and arbitrary distinction could be made between "autonomous" and "non-autonomous" states, as two ends of a continuum, based on their deployment of ethnic policies. States which tend towards being autonomous would be "ethnically impartial" or ethnically depoliticized, that is, ethnicity arises only as a factor in national integration and development. On the other hand, states which have nonautonomous tendencies have a strong ethnic orientation in relation to state ideology, resource allocation, and political mobilization. This is where the hegemony of the ethnic paradigm as a state ideology is more likely to be a dominant trend. This does not mean that the state creates ethnicity. Rather, the state, because of its control of the power structure, is able to intervene and influence the operationalization of ethnic relations through subtle legal means, direct coercion, or a mixture of both. Reaction to this intervention can be determined by how much state power threatens existing in-group identity (Brown 1994).

The state-ethnicity power dynamics may involve the stratification of political power and resource ownership along ethnic lines. A particular ethnic group may, for historical reasons, be able to control and use the state machinery to make territorial claims and to advance its political and economic interests, ahead of the interests of other subaltern ethnic groups. The state is rarely an innocent bystander as state power could be used by "dominant elites to impose, preserve or extend their hegemony over other ethnies or over territory which they claim as their own"; this becomes destabilizing because "power in the state rests principally with a dominant or majority ethnic group, or when the national society constitutes an ethnically stratified system" (Stavenhagan 1996: 1–2). The relationship between the state and ethnicity is a complex and dynamic one which changes and manifests itself in different ways because ethnicity can be political as well as well as a potential central ingredient in the construction and mobilization of state power (Enloe 1980).

The state presides over a terrain of class and ethnic complexity which it shapes and in turn shapes the character of the state. The capacity of the state to sustain its hegemony depends on how it maps out the ethnic terrain, selectively nurtures ethnic categories, and carries out political and economic mobilization along constructed ethnic divisions. Thus the role of the state is a deliberately active one, either to contain ethnic friction or encourage ethnic conflict and hegemony through direct or indirect alignment to ethnic-based values in a direct or very subtle ways. The state's role in ameliorating ethnic conflict through affirmative action, truth and reconciliation commissions, diversity policies, and other measures have sometimes led to stability, but in some cases, these have encouraged essentializing groups and further ethnicization of the state (Ratuva 2013). The state's control and monopoly over force and the legal process enables it to construct and reproduce ethnicity in ways that are consistent with certain elite interests. This could feed into what Enloe (1980) refers to as "ethnic mapping" or how the state stratifies ethnic groups in terms of trustworthiness and potential threat to the state. After 9/11, people of Middle Eastern origin were regarded as posing the largest threat to the USA and many were publicly attacked and vilified. In Israel, those of Palestinian origin are regarded as least trustworthy while in many European countries, migrants of non-European background are seen suspiciously as potential threats to the state and the European culture.

Weiner (1987) notes that when the state acts as an agency for a dominant ethnic community and acts to accommodate its cultural, economic, and political interest in a highly institutionalized way, it becomes an "ethnocratic state." To Brown, the ethnocratic state has three main aspects; firstly, the state overwhelmingly recruits from members of the dominant ethnic category into the state elite positions (such as military and civil service); secondly, the national ideology is based on the values of the dominant ethnic category and; thirdly, the superstructural arrangements (constitution, law, political structures) serve to maintain monopolization of power by an ethnic group (Brown 1994: 36–37). In this sense, policies pertaining to multiculturalism or national integration often translate to cultural assimilation of subaltern communities into the values of a dominant ethnic group.

Moreover, one of the levers of interethnic engagement in "plural" state is to generate consensus by elites of competing ethnic groups through what Lijphart refers to as "consociationalism." Consociationalism contends that arriving at social homogeneity and political consensus is an essential prerequisite for maintaining a stable democracy (Lijphart 1968). This requires that competing ethnic leaders engage in coalescent rather than adversarial decision-making. However, this could lead to elite bargaining and consensus based on narrow self-interest and because of this, the idea of constitutional and electoral engineering is seen by some as a way of maintaining ethnic balance and stability (Horowitz 1985).

The state's engagement with ethnicity could be multidimensional and contradictory. For instance, the state may be involved in strategies to minimize ethnic tension, while on the other hand, it may contribute to conflict through policies which exacerbate inequality, unemployment, loss of educational opportunities and human rights abuse. Or states my articulate humanistic liberal policies such as multiculturalism at one level but engage in institutionalized and subconscious discrimination and marginalization of some groups at the same time. A significant number of conflicts around the world today revolve around this state-ethnicity dynamics. Responses to state-sponsored injustices, oppression, and malpractices may even take the form of violence and succession and these can lead to interrogation of the legitimacy of the states.

In recent years, the assault of the state from both the "right" (which demands more power to corporations and particular ethnic groups) and the "left" (which demands more ethnic diversity and more power to the people) has raised fundamental questions about the role and capacity of the state in dealing with the complex issues relating to ethnicity. States have been forced to rethink their strategies by either taking a more exclusive strategy or swing down the path of exclusivity. This is happening in the context of the weakening of the state through the neoliberal agenda including the privatization of state functions (including the military), undermining of state autonomy and sovereignty through global trade agreements, growth of the social media, as a means of mass mobilization, increase in arms deal outside the ambit of states and growth of people's movements. We are bound to see these trends increasing in the near future.

Racism and Subconscious Bias

A number of chapters cover how racism and subconscious bias play out in various situations and countries. At the outset, it is important to note that a vital ingredient of ethnic relations is people's interpretation of other's experiences, perceptions, attitudes, and behavior, as well as norms, belief systems, and institutional policies and laws. Negative attitudes towards others are often referred to as "racism," the belief that one's own race is superior than others. The notion of superiority is perceived to permeate many aspects of human ability and capacity such as intelligence, culture, technology, political systems, economic systems, and belief systems (Kivel 2017).

There are various types and degrees of discrimination and prejudices, ranging from genocide to more subtle forms such as subconscious bias in everyday life (Levison 2012). History is littered with killing of people on grounds of ethnicity and this continues today (Wolff 2006). Many indigenous groups suffered massacres and oppression in the hands of colonial invaders because they were seen to be subhuman and thus dispensable. Even in postcolonial societies, some of the ethnic stereotypes constructed during the colonial days became the basis for ethnopolitical tension and even violence in new states. Prejudice can be publicly invoked by competition for control of economic resources, employment, land, political power, and other aspects of life where any form of competition can easily digress into scapegoating and racialization. Racism and colonialism were symbiotic in many ways because while racism provided justification for colonialism, colonialism and its civilizing mission was also used to justify racism (Ross 1982). Slavery, like colonialism, was justified on the grounds that there were certain people who were destined to be subservient because of their inferiority in the natural order of humanity. This was the ideological narrative used to justify exploitation of cheap labor to generate profit for the globally expanding colonial capitalism and also a way of softening the moral burden of the largely Christian European society which was involved in slavery, colonialism, and other forms of human subjugation (Williams 1994).

Racial prejudice can be institutionalized in a deliberate or subconscious way through the use of policies or practices which favor a dominant group while subconscious racism is far more subtle and not easy to "detect" although it can be "felt" in a profoundly subjective way by victims. Because of this, it is easy to deny it. People's prejudices are developed through religion, home upbringing, education, media, and other means of socialization. Often these are "normalized" and deeply embedded in our psyche, and they are articulated through thoughts, language, behavior, and actions. Subconscious racism pervades a whole range of our daily activities including marking student essays, selection of a football team, recruitment in a firm, service in a restaurant, or catching a taxi. Some forms of subconscious bias are more subtle than others. For victims of racism who have been subjected to "normalized" prejudices, their interpretation of language and action can be colored by preconceptions of prejudice. Thus victims can also manifest subconscious bias but in a different way from the perpetrators. Policies and laws often have deeply entrenched implicit biases against subaltern groups – this by and large reflects the racialized and unequal nature of the legal system and society generally (Levinson and Smith 2012).

The electoral victory of the far right and neo-Nazi political parties in some countries in Europe and Trump's ethnic policies in the USA has helped "normalized" racial prejudice and deepened ethnic divide. To be clear, the divide is not so much between the "racial" categories of "whites" and "non-whites" but between the supporters and opponents of white supremacy, an ideology which believes in the natural superiority of whites. Many opponents of white supremacy are moderate and progressive whites themselves. However, as Robin DiAngelo observes in her book, *White fragility*, even liberals contribute to racism through self-serving attitudes and by pretending to be vanguards of multiculturalism (DiAngelo 2018). One of the misleading assumptions is that racial supremacy is only manifested by neo-Nazi groups making public political demands. The reality is that the belief in racial and cultural superiority is also subtly embedded in a range of dominant discourses in development (Western form of economics is superior), politics (Western form of politics is more advanced), psychology (Westerners are more motivated), and the list goes on. Subtle variations of supremacy are wired into educational curriculum, medical practice, sports, Hollywood films, mainstream media, and other daily activities, but the fact that these have been mainstreamed makes their prejudice "invisible." Through Christianity and modern education, dominant ethnocentric views also become mainstreamed and act as yardstick for defining progress, civilization, and modernity.

Constant reproduction of prejudice as part of the normal moral discourse can be overwhelming and even victims themselves often end up internalizing the imageries, stereotypes, and prejudices against them, and they may even consider them as natural. Accepting one's own cultural and intellectual inferiority is reinforced by the education system, Hollywood movies, literature, media, and other forms of communication. This can be traumatizing for some groups who are caught between the rock and a hard place – on one hand, the desire to protect their identity and, on the other hand, the pressure and expectation by society to assimilate into the bigger social and political environment.

Racism is not only between a dominant group and a minority; it also exists amongst minority and marginalized groups. For instance, as Matori (2015) found out, in a situation where several minorities are victims of racism, the competition to be accepted by the dominant group can create tense contestation. Often the idea is to determine the most recognized and privileged within in a pecking order determined by the dominant whites or who best emulates the dominant white racial ideal. Matori found that competing minorities have created racial hierarchies and boundaries which they passionately guard from each other. The irony of utilizing the standard of "whiteness" as basis for intra-minority racism – where those with the darker skin and fuzzy hair are considered inferior to those with fairer skin and straighter hair – adds a new dimension to intergroup racism.

Racism can also be time and context bond and people's subconscious bias may change in relation to changing circumstances. For instance, Johnson and Jone (2015) note that the perception in the 1800s in the USA that Asians, especially Chinese and Japanese, were culturally and intellectually inferior and good only for manual labor, changed over time as a result of the Asians' achievements in education, commerce, and various professional undertakings. While there is still contextual racial bias, the Chinese and Japanese are now often regarded as equals or even better than whites in educational areas such as mathematics, science, and technology. But then these successes are often seen as results of narrow mechanical role learning, an Asian educational trait, as opposed to enlightened critical thinking, a feature of "Western" scholarship. Despite these contextual shifts (contextual because it can be seen as just temporary or exception of the norms), there is still a belief that success of minorities can be just due to the assimilation into the superior dominant ways rather than a manifestation of equality of intelligence or skills between the dominant and minority groups.

Beyond perception, racism and the imposition of dominant values is more durable and permanent when embedded and reproduced in powerful institutions and systems such as education, economy, health, religion, and sports. While these institutions provide means of empowerment social mobility, they can also breed inequality and deprivation and those without the means to climb up the ladder may find themselves caught up in a vicious cycle of inequality over generations. As discussed by Thomas and Clarke (2013), the global neoliberal economic agenda has further marginalized many ethnic minorities whose land has been appropriated for corporate business or who remain disempowered unskilled workers. The growth in global labor migration from various poor communities (mostly from the Global South) around the world has added a very visible ethnic dimension to capitalism's global division of labor. Global neoliberalism has created a dynamic nexus between international labor and ethnicity through the creation of a globally mobile working class who continue to be subjected to racial profiling in countries where they work whether they be Latinos in the USA, Asians in the Middle East, Eastern Europeans in Western Europe, Africans in Europe, or Pacific Islanders in New Zealand.

The increase in migration and refugees has also heightened the incidents of racist attacks in various parts of the world such as in Europe. Migrants and refugees are seen not only as economic liabilities but also as threats to local culture and security (Fekete 2018). The fact that most migrants and refugees into Europe are non-whites draws a clear racial line of demarcation between "them" and "us" and the public visibility of the "them" makes them very vulnerable to attacks by right-wing groups and anti-migrant ordinary citizens.

Ethnic Diversity and Assimilation

A number of articles directly speak to the notion of ethnic diversity. A concept often associated with diversity is assimilation. Assimilation refers to smaller groups being absorbed into a large one through voluntary association, use of force, or through tactical co-option. This can lead to different scenarios such as subjugation to the dominant culture, negotiation over one's place in the new order, marginalization due to failure by the dominant group to acknowledge minorities or outright resistance and conflict. Integrating into the new order is challenging because of the existing structures of social, political, and economic inequality which automatically slot people into class and racial silos. Without education, language proficiency (especially English), and professional skills, it would be very difficult for new immigrants to be absorbed mutually into mainstream society. For migrant minorities, assimilation often means, firstly, facing up to the complex paradoxes of acquiring the host country's culture while threatening to lose one's own and secondly, being part of a structure of socioeconomic inequality and political subalternation and racism which keep them marginalized. Reaction and resistance to this can build up over time and could be expressed in violent forms such as terrorism (Chrichlow et al. 2018).

Examples of this abound. In France, whose colonial rule equated to "Frenchnization" of colonized people, assimilation meant "de-ethnicizing" and transforming one's identity to become "French" and may include banning of cultural symbols such as dress and artifacts from public places in the name of secularism (Thomas 2013). The haunting paradox is that French secularism not only forces migrants to integrate into the French culture, the French society itself does not accept them as equals, thus creating a class and ethnic schism which has contributed to instability and violence. In Britain, while ethnic minorities can continue to celebrate their unique cultures, in latent ways, they are also expected to assimilate to certain values, behavior, and thinking consistent with being "British." The notion of Britishness is contested between those who believe in maintaining the old imperial symbolisms and those who want it redefined and rearticulated to reflect the country's globalized and diverse character (Erel 2016). Although assimilation has its own problems, in many European countries, it has now come under assault by the emerging populist right-wing parties and political groups campaigning against migration. In the USA, the intersection between class and racial inequality has made a mockery of the mythical ideals of accommodation to the "American dream," "land of the free," and "god's own country" which define the virtue of "Americaness" as millions of people sink into poverty while corporate America continues to prosper (Chomsky 2017).

One of the criticisms of assimilation is that the economic, cultural, and political structures which are meant to facilitate the process of acceptance and integration actually create the conditions which promote class inequality and racial separation. It is difficult to assimilate horizontally when the structures of inequality still create vertical separation and marginalization of migrant minorities. This often breeds grievances and sometimes violent reaction. Cultural assimilation often involves redefining identities, readapting to a new cultural sphere, and sometimes reinventing one's own ethnicity. This requires constant negotiation between the original identity and the new one and people deploy one over the other to suit their interests in different contexts.

The Process of De-ethnicization

A number of articles elude to the issue of de-ethnicization in indirect ways, although the term itself (de-ethnicization) may not be used. The term refers to the process of erasing ethnic aspects of identity of a person, group, or object voluntarily, through legal mandate or forcefully through political coercion. Sometimes this can be subtle and institutionalized such as the removal of ethnic labels and symbols and reducing people into quantifiable statistical information as consumers, citizens, or population, a common form of categorization by economists.

Deliberate de-ethnicization by neoliberal forces has impacted significantly on indigenous groups around the world. For instance, indigenous people who sit on profitable land are seen not as cultural groups with a history but as impediments to the march of modernity (Thomas and Clarke 2013). The desire for greater privatization, profit-making, and free trade has led to the reframing of indigenous culture, knowledge, identity, and even people (through their labor) as mere marketable commodities devoid of human qualities. This is quite pronounced in the area of indigenous intellectual property where through the process of biopiracy, pharmaceutical companies have transformed traditional mediational knowledge into profitable market commodities. The loss of indigenous knowledge for the purpose of making corporate profit has stripped away the connection between ethnicity and knowledge, an ethical issue which has resonated in recent decades (Ratuva 2009).

In professional sports, de-ethnicization of individuals is part of the commodification of their physical prowess and their identity is associated with sports brands and sponsoring companies (Poli 2007). The same goes for high achievers in various fields, where the media often portrays people in terms of their nationality and place of residence rather than ethnicity. A particular form of commodification is the way in which identity has been "digitized" in the cyberspace world. Often that cyber identity has to be paid for. Engagement with the cyber world requires people to reconstruct new virtual and digital identities to connect with other digital identities globally. In this realm, ethnicity as a social category is overshadowed by a virtual personality. However, the dynamics may change when the virtual space is used for ethnic and cultural networking either to promote or subvert ethnic identity as Sullivan and Chen (2016) have shown in the case of Chinese speaking or "Sinophone" virtual discussants.

De-ethnicization can also take place through assimilation as we have seen earlier. Diversity and equal citizenship policies can be used as Trojan horse for assimilation and de-ethnicization of minority groups. In some cases, attempts by states to de-ethnicize and impose a new identity has been met with creative and innovative means of "resistance." For instance, research in China has shown that people have used common religious beliefs as new cultural unifying forces that transcend people's ethnic identity imposed by the state (Lim 2015). In other cases, the process of granting citizenship for migrants can lead to de-ethnicization through provision of a new identity (re-ethnicization) based on the values of the new nation and residency. Loyalty to the new state, or civic nationalism becomes an overriding consideration over loyalty to one's ethnicity. Creating a new civic identity and de-ethnicization may become complementary forces in the new experience and this may enhance symbolic assimilation where people will show outward loyalty but latent resistance (Joppke 2003).

Another strategy which is linked to de-ethnicization is the use of "color blindness" as a means of responding to the challenges of relationships in a multi-ethnic society. This entails removing ethnicity from daily discourse and treating people on the basis of "equality." While this may seem like a just and morally virtuous approach, the reality is much more complex since removal of ethnic labels only helps to conceal the structural and historical inequalities and injustices suffered by the de-ethnicized minorities. These inequalities are linked to income, education, and opportunities and to gloss over through "color blind" policies may hide the situations of the minorities and marginalized further thus in effects legitimizing them (Fryberg 2010).

Although on the surface, de-ethnicization could be regarded as a progressive approach to creating a harmonious and diverse society, the subjective reality is far more complex. For dominant groups, this means disregarding race, a rather difficult subject to deal with, as an important factor in interpreting and understanding inequality. For minorities who are victims of discrimination, this may hide the very factors which keep them in a disadvantaged position. The argument that needs to be made here is that ethnicity has to be illuminated and consciously dealt with to reveal how it disadvantages some groups and privileges some. One of the ways to address this is endorsement of ethnic and cultural diversity and acceptance of differences as social capital for interracial harmony (McCabe 2011)

Ethnicity and Intersectionality

Ethnicity intersects in complex ways with other social factors such as class, gender, and political ideology. In situations of "ethnic" conflict, the major causes could be structurally associated with economic inequality, competition over resources, or contestation over political power. Often ethnicity becomes a conduit through which conflict is expressed. The situation is much sharper in societies where there is a clear relationship between class and ethnicity, especially where an entire ethnic group constitutes the economically subaltern class (Healey 2011).

In many postcolonial societies, the deep rifts resulting from the intersection between ethnicity and socioeconomic class is a result of historical processes such as colonialism that involved the transmigration of ethnic labor to provide cheap labor for colonial capitalism. Slavery, indentured labor, and other forms of cheap labor recruitment created a new class of international migrant workers from Africa, Asia, Pacific, and other parts of the world. Although colonialism and slavery have long gone, the impacts are still felt today in terms of how many descends of slavery and other forms of transnational laborers still face poverty and marginalization.

The disjuncture between high economic expectations and lack of opportunities has potential to nurture grievances amongst the young and this can easily translate into mobilization of ethnic identity and expressions of resistance. This could be worsened by the racialized policies of some states which neglect the ethnic poor. In the long run this can breed violent forms of ethno-nationalism. The assimilationist policies of the state aimed at domesticating poor ethnic minorities has not been totally successful as many young people seek alternative support systems and modes of expression such as "terrorism" (Zizek 2016). In the USA and Brazil, the descendants of former slaves, still remain at the bottom of the social rug and their opportunities are worsened by the neoliberal policies which impact negatively on housing, health, and employment.

The issue of gender is closely tied to ethnicity in various forms. Women in minority groups are subordinated in multiple ways because of their gender, ethnic background, as well as socioeconomic status. In some societies, minority women often suffer not only masculine violence, also racism in everyday life and sexism at work (Healey 2011). The rise of black feminism as a discourse of resistance is a response to the ethnicity-gender intersectionality and the oppression and marginalization of poor colored women. Similarly, discrimination against members of the LBGT (lesbian, bi-sexual, gay and trans-gender) community is even more discernible if one is colored or belongs to an ethnic minority. Dominant masculine notions of morality often institutionalized in religious, legal, cultural, and political institutions are usually based on dominant European sensibilities.

Globalization has transformed the politics and spaces of intersectionality which links together ethnicity with class and gender within states and between states. Although globalization may appear to be integrating peoples and cultures into a unifying embrace, the reality is that it has created significant power inequality, a class of vulnerable subalterns, and a deeply racialized global society (Chrichlow et al. 2018).

Ethnicity and Affirmative Action

As some chapters indicate, attempts to address ethnic tension abound and affirmative action is just one of them. Affirmative action refers to policies and programs aimed at redressing the disadvantaged position of groups who have historically been denied opportunities, power, and resources. Many countries have used it as policy response to issues of racism, inequality, and lack of opportunities resulting from a history of racial discrimination, denied opportunities, and oppression (Arthur 2007; Kahlenberg 1997). The types and intensity of racial discrimination and separation differs from country to country, although the justifications may be similar (Ratuva 2013).

The philosophical justifications for affirmative action include reparation for past wrongs and injustices, creation of a more equal playing field and allowing equal opportunity, or as a form of conflict resolution (Ratuva 2013; Arthur 2007). In the USA, some states still allow race-based affirmative action for blacks and other minorities, while some like California have banned it altogether in favor of diversity-based approaches. In Malaysia, affirmative action started in 1970 under the New Economic Policy to equalize wealth distribution between the Chinese and Malays and both South Africa and Fiji copied the Malaysian model (Ratuva 2013). In India, there is ongoing affirmative action for the scheduled caste, who are also often regarded as belonging to an ethnic group. A number of countries like Brazil, Canada, and New Zealand, among others, also practice affirmative action as a way of redressing the disadvantaged socioeconomic situation of their indigenous people. Ethnic-based affirmative action is justified on the principles of justice and equity and the recognition of the faults of history that need to be rectified or at least acknowledged. In this case, it is a matter of moral consideration and a matter for the conscience of the nation (West 2001).

Critics of affirmative action have provided different counter narratives and some have referred to affirmative action as a form of "reverse discrimination" basing their arguments on the fact that through preferential resources distribution, whites and other nondesignated groups are denied their rights of access and natural justice. Along this reasoning, there have been some challenges in US courts over the years on university entry either by white or Asian students (Kennedy 2015), one of the latest being on Harvard's diversity-based admission policies which allegedly disqualified entry by some Asian students. There is a claim that characteristics such as sex, religion, or race, used as basis for arbitrary discrimination, should not be used as basis for compensation (Faundez 1994). For instance, the use of ethnicity as ground for affirmative action to counter previous acts of discrimination that were based on ethnicity, tantamount to another form of discrimination. Some like Gross (1978) and Goldman (1979) argue that affirmative action, if it is compensatory, is unjustified.

One of the counter arguments against the reverse discrimination theory is that it does not consider the historical and structural aspects of discrimination and the effects on the subalternation of an entire group. Along this line of logic, affirmative action should be seen as contributing to equity creation in the broader context of society rather than an attempt to deprive the more privileged groups. Demands for more equitable distribution through affirmative action is often met with resistance by more privileged groups in society because of fear that it would undermine their dominant position, take away their rights they are entitled to, and that the designated groups need to work harder rather than rely on handouts.

Nickle (1977) argues that affirmative action does not really involve reverse discrimination because it involves reparations for past wrongs and as such is not based on morally irrelevant factors. Affirmative action is also a way of making up for the losses incurred under discriminatory systems such as slavery and Jim Crow laws in the USA or apartheid in South Africa (Katznelson 2006). These forms of inequality were hegemonic, predatory, and exploitative and meant to maintain racial supremacy, while affirmative action attempts to create a level playing field. It is important also to note that the playing field is never level in the USA, despite myths of the "American dream," because of the complex ways in which the interplay between ethnic and economic inequality are institutionalized in the corporate US society. Even the black middle class is not fully accepted into the white corporate America, and race still matters in defining class membership and privileges (West 2001).

Perhaps one of the most successful forms of affirmative action has been education while other programs in the area of business have been problematic. For instance, in cases such as Malaysia, South Africa and Fiji, affirmative action in education has created a vibrant and large middle class while preferential policies in the area of commerce has led to institutionalized corruption by ethnic elites working in collusion with state bureaucrats and business (Ratuva 2013). Some of the biggest beneficiaries of affirmative action are state aligned elites, their cronies, and families.

One of the controversial issues refers to the question of whether affirmative action should take place within the context of group or individual rights. Critics of group rights such as Cowan (1977) argue that affirmative action is only justified as a remedy for individuals who have suffered discrimination. On the other hand, Nickle (1977) admits that individuals need compensation but mainly because they were part of a group that suffered discrimination; hence the only solution is for the entire group to be compensated. It is important to note that in most cases of ethnic inequality, group and not individual identity was the basis for discrimination and marginalization, thus affirmative action needs to have a group focus.

A central tenet of affirmative action is the issue of justice and whether it has the potential to heal some of the wounds of the past. As a mode of distributive justice and a means of peace-building in societies where ethnic strife is part of the political and social life, affirmative action can either be built into law or maintain a voluntary status. The issue of whether affirmative action should remain strictly ethnic or become more class-based is a critical one, particularly with the increase in the number of well-off individuals from the designated group and the need to address the socioeconomic issues of the poorest people among the subaltern groups. Creating opportunities for the most disadvantaged is a moral imperative which transcends race and class – it is fundamentally a humanity-driven concern.

Conclusion

Ethnicity is one of the most basic forms of identification but over the years, the way it is defined by groups and by those outside the groups has been subjected to revaluation and reconceptualization as a result of changing contexts. Globalization has worked in diverse ways in terms of creating new forms of identification including the de-ethnicization of identities and at the same time it has created conditions which have spawned the growth of re-ethnicization as individuals and groups try to reconstruct their identities as protective, reactive, proactive, or mobilizational tools in response to perceived threats.

Ethnicity is complex and contentious, and there are diverse approaches used to understand the underlying forces which frame it as well as some of its manifestations. This chapter has briefly examined a number of issues focusing on some sociological debates; ethnic boundaries and group dynamics; nationalism; ethnicity and race; ethnicity and the state; racism and subconscious bias; ethnic diversity, assimilation, and integration; de-ethnicization; intersectionality; and affirmative action. There are a number of lessons that we can learn from this chapter – perhaps the most important is that ethnicity is a social construct which is framed and articulated at the whims of groups and individuals. Because it defines our humanity and sense of being, ethnicity is shrouded with emotion and often with imprecise boundaries. Historically, people have killed and destroyed in the name of ethnicity and a lot of today's conflicts and wars are associated, either directly or indirectly with ethnicity. The rise of Trump and his racially loaded policies and political narratives; the war on terror; the conflict in the Middle East, Africa, Europe, and Asia; and the rise of right-wing parties and groups in response to immigration show that old forms of ethnic identity can be reimagined and reinvented and used as justifications for new interests.

Ethnicity is closely aligned with other social forms of identity such as class and gender and when laced with political and religious ideologies, the outcome can be dramatically transformative. Ethnicity is transformative, and at the same time, it is being transformed and will continue to be a defining force for human identity and destiny.

References

Alexander C (2009) Stuart Hall and "race". Cult Stud 23(4):45–482
Anderson B (1983) Imagined communities. Verso, London
Anderson B (2006) Imagined communities: reflections on the origin and spread of nationalism. Verso, London
Arthur J (2007) Race, equality and the burdens of history. Cambridge University Press, Cambridge, UK
Barth F (1969) Introduction. In: Ethnic groups and boundaries: the social organization of culture difference. George Allen & Unwin, London
Brown D (1994) The state and ethnic politics in South East Asia. Routledge, London
Carter B, Fenton S (2009) Not thinking ethnicity: a critique of ethnicity paradigm in an over-ethnicized sociology. J Theory Soc Behav 40(1):1–18
Chomsky N (2017) Requiem for the American dream. Seven Stories Press, New York
Chrichlow M, Northover P, Guisti-Cordero J (2018) Race and rurality: in the global economy. State University of New York Press, New York
Cohen A (1974) Introduction: the lesson of ethnicity. In: Cohen A (ed) Urban ethnicity. Tavistock, London, pp ix–xxiv
Cohen A (1985) The symbolic construction of community. Ellis Hardwood, London
Collins P, Chepp V (2013) Intersectionality. In: Celis K, Kantola J, Waylen G, Weklon J (eds) The Oxford handbook of gender and politics. Oxford University Press, Oxford
Cowan LJ (1977) Inverse discrimination. In Gross BR (ed) Discrimination in reverse. New York State University, New York
DiAngelo R (2018) White fragility: why it's so hard for white people to talk about racism. Beacon Press, New York
Eller JD, Coughlan RM (1993) The poverty of primordialism: the demystification of ethnic attachments. Ethn Racial Stud 16(2):185–202
Enloe C (1980) Ethnic soldiers: state security in a divided society. Penguin, London
Erel U (2016) Migrant women transforming citizenship: life stories from Britain and Germany. Routledge, London
Eriksen TH (1993) Ethnicity and nationalism: an anthropological perspective. Pluto, London
Erikson T (2002) Ethnicity and nationalism: anthropological perspectives, 2nd edn. Pluto Press, London
Erikson T (2010) Ethnicity and nationalism: anthropological perspectives, 3rd edn. Pluto Press, London
Faundez J (1994) Affirmative action: international perspective. International labour Organization, Geneva
Fearon DJ, Laitin DD (2000) Violence and social construction of identity. Int Organ 54(4):845–877
Fekete L (2018) Europe's fault line: racism and the rise of the right. Verso Books, London
Fredrickson G (2015) Racism: a short history. Princeton University Press, Princeton

Fryberg SM (2010) When the world is colorblind, American Indians are invisible: a diversity science approach. Psychol Inq 21(2):115–119
Furnivall JS (1948) Colonial policy and practice. Cambridge University Press, Cambridge, UK
Geertz C (1963) The integrative revolution: primordial sentiments and civil politics in the new states. In: Geertz C (ed) Old societies and new states: the quest for modernity in Asia and Africa. The Free Press of Glencoe, Collier-MacMillan, London, pp 105–157
Goldman A (1979) Justice and reverse discrimination. New York State University Press, New York
Gross BR (1978) Discrimination in reverse. New York State University Press, New York
Grossberg L (2007) Stuart Hall on race and racism: cultural studies and the practice of contextualism. In: Meeks B (ed) Culture, politics, race and diaspora: the thought of Stuart Hall. Lawrence & Wishart, London
Hall S (1996) New ethnicities. In: Morley D, Chen K (eds) Stuart Hall: critical dialogue in cultural studies. Routledge, New York, pp 441–449
Harter S (2015) The construction of the self: developmental and sociocultural foundations. Guilford Press, New York
Healey J (2011) Race, ethnicity, gender and class: the sociology of group conflict and change. Sage, London
Herrnstein R, Murray C (1994) The bell curve. Free Press, New York
Hobsbawm E, Ranger T (1983) The invention of tradition. Cambridge University Press, Cambridge, UK
Horowitz D (1985) Ethnic groups in conflict. University of California Press, Berkeley
Hughes E (1994) On work, race and the sociological imagination. Chicago University Press, Chicago
Jenkins R (1997) Rethinking ethnicity: arguments and explorations. Sage, London
Jenkins R (2008) Rethinking ethnicity: arguments and explorations, 2nd edn. Sage, London
Johnson E, Jones C (2015) Chinese and Japanese in America: the immigration controversies. Westphalia Press, New York
Joppke C (2003) Citizenship between de-and re-ethnicization. Eur J Sociol 44(3):429–458
Kahlenberg R (1997) The remedy: class, race, and affirmative action. Basic Books, New York
Katznelson I (2006) When affirmative action was white: an untold story of racial inequality in twentieth century America. W.W. Norton, New York
Kennedy R (2015) For discrimination: race, affirmative action and the law. Knopf Doubleday, New York
Kivel P (2017) Uprooting racism: how white people can work for racial justice. New Society Publishers, Gabriola
Levison A (2012) The white working class today: who they are, how they think and how progressives can regain their support. Democratic Strategic Press, New York
Levison J, Smith R (eds) (2012) Implicit racial bias across the law. Cambridge University Press, Cambridge, UK
Lijphart A (1968) The politics of accommodation. University of California Press, Berkeley
Lim F (2015) Religious revival and de-ethnicization in the ethnic minority regions of China. Working paper no. 231. Asia Research Institute, Singapore
Matori JL (2015) Stigma and culture: last-place anxiety in black America. University of Chicago Press, Chicago
McCabe J (2011) Doing multiculturalism: an interactionist analysis of the practices of a multicultural sorority. J Contemp Ethnogr 40(5):521–549
McKay J (1982) An exploratory synthesis of primordialist and mobilizationist approaches to ethnic phenomena. Ethn Racial Stud 5:395–420
Miles R (1989) Racism. Routledge, London
Mile R (1993) Racism after race relations. Routledge, London
Nickle JW (1977) Should reparation be to individuals or groups? In: Gross BR (ed) Discrimination in reverse. New York State University Press, New York

Poli R (2007) The denationalization of sport: de-ethnicization of the nation and identity deterritorialization. Sport Soc 10(4):646–661

Ratcliffe P (1994) Race, ethnicity and nation: international perspectives on social conflict. UCL Press, London

Ratuva S (2009) Commodifying cultural knowledge: corporatized western science and Pacific indigenous knowledge. Int Soc Sci J 195(1):153–163

Ratuva S (2013) Coerced preferences: horizontal inequality and affirmative action in Fiji. In: Premdas R, Gometz T (eds) Affirmative action, ethnicity and conflict. Routledge, Oxford

Rex J (1970) Race relations in sociological theory. Weidenfeld & Nicolson, London

Ross R (ed) (1982) Racism and colonialism. Springer, London

Rutherford A (2017) A brief history of everyone who ever lived: the human story retold through our genes. Weidenfeld & Nicolson, London

Siebers H (2017) "Race" versus "ethnicity"? Critical race essentialism and the exclusion and oppression of migrants in the Netherlands. Ethn Racial Stud Rev 40(3):369–387

Stavenhagen R (1996) Ethnic conflicts and the nation state. Macmillan Press, London

Sullivan J, Chen Y-W (2016) Ethnicity in Sinophone cyberspace. Asian Ethn 16:269–273

Thomas D (2013) Africa and France: post-colonial cultures, migration and racism. Indiana University Press, Bloomington

Thomas D, Clarke K (2013) Globalization and race: structures of inequality, new sovereignties, and citizenship in a neoliberal era. Annu Rev Anthropol 42:305–325

Wallerstein I (1991) The construction of peoplehood: racism, nationalism and ethnicity. In: Wallerstein I, Balibar E (eds) Race, nation and class: ambiguous identities. Verso, New York, pp 71–85

Weber M (1971) Max Weber on race and society (trans.). Soc Res 38:30–41. (Original work published 1910)

Weiner M (1987) Political change: Asia, Africa and Middle East. In: Weiner M, Huntington S (eds) Understanding political development. Little Brown, Boston

West C (2001) Race matters. Random House, New York

Williams E (1994) Capitalism and slavery. The University of North Carolina Press, Chapel Hill

Wolff S (2006) Ethnic conflict: a global perspective. Oxford University Press, Oxford

Zizek S (2016) Refugees, terror and other troubles with the neighbours: against the double blackmail. Melville House Publishing, London

Part I
Nexus Between Ethnicity and Identity

Part Introduction

Ethnicity is an expression of identity, yet how the two interplay and shape each other is complex and takes multiple forms. Ethnic identity is framed and articulated in diverse ways, including symbolisms, sense of belonging, shared consciousness, collective imageries, historical memories, genealogical ties, and even institutionalized definitions and policies.

Symbolisms help in defining ethnocultural group identity as Elya Tzaneva discusses. To sustain this sense of group identification, a common sense of belonging and consciousness, inculcated through cultural socialization, is needed, a theme expounded by Sara Amin. Group identity evolves and constructs its sociocultural trajectory through cosmological, mythological, or ideological reference points, which are often inspired by a group's historical memory. This is a theme explored by Cindy Zeiher who connects historical memory to ethnic myths. As a binding force for collective identity, historical memory is strongly tied to a group's sense of kinship, genealogy, and affinity. Furthermore, in everyday life, these identity relationships are projected outwards and negotiated through various lenses. Perceptions and imageries often inform the way social groups are framed and classified in a multiethnic society. An important factor, which interplays in a prominent way with ethnicity is class. There are different angles from which this is approached and Rodrigo Gonsalves takes a more philosophical and psychoanalytical approach in analyzing the nexus between ethnicity and class.

The above articles are more conceptual in their use of different sociological and philosophical framing of the nexus between identity and ethnicity, while the rest of the articles are more empirical-based in terms of how this nexus plays out in various social contexts. The dynamics in different societies are specific to the historical, political, and sociocultural conditions. One of the challenges for minority ethnic groups is how they are able to maintain their identities within a hegemonic state system which imposes an external definition as well as determines the limits of their political rights. Roland Boer provides a comprehensive analysis of how minority ethnic groups are redefined and provided official identities by the Chinese state. Such construction of official ethnic boundaries and formal identities also characterize the situation in South Africa, where state-based categorizations have raised serious dilemmas in the post-apartheid era, as Kathryn Pillay observes.

The interplay between the state and ethnic identity is multifaceted and can be syncretic – that is, it can be contradictory while at the same time accommodating. The state, as we have seen in the case of China and South Africa, may impose formally constituted identities as a form of control, and at the same time, the state itself maybe transformed and threatened by identity conflicts. Hassanein Ali shines light on the latter by discussing the dilemma of the nation-state and the rise of identity conflicts in the post-Arab spring. Interestingly, sometimes, the state may even supress formal articulation of ethnic identity through policies of "ethnic blindness" with the hope of exercising greater state hegemonic control. This is explored by Romitesh Kant who focuses on ethnic blindness in ethnically divided societies, drawing on the Fiji example.

While the theme of ethnicity and identity runs through the entire handbook, the focus of this part is to explore some initial conceptual narratives, which other parts will expand on using different approaches and a diversity of comparative case studies from around the world.

Steven Ratuva

Ethno-cultural Symbolism and Group Identity

2

Elya Tzaneva

Contents

Introduction	30
Conclusion	45
Cross-References	46
References	46

Abstract

This chapter is aimed at helping researchers study the ways in which communities and individuals perceive their own ethnic identity under the conditions of cosmopolitanism, transnationalism and mobility. Such analysis, the chapter argues, can be successfully conducted within three main contexts: in the era of constant movement around the globe, the *ethnic* mobilizes and expresses its *multiidentical*, *situational*, and *contextual* nature. Thoughts are shared on the necessity of finding a precise scholarly lexicon and suitable combined approach to ethnic phenomena today. The term *ethnic* as a scholarly construct is suggested to combine the contents of both *ethnos* and *ethnicity* and to denominate the past and present specifics and processes of ethnic identity phenomenon. Also suggested is the use of *ethno-symbolism* to order and sort out, trace the dynamics, and reveal the malleable position of different identity components. Discussed are some specifics of the ethnic symbols, along with their classification and role at the ethnic/national level. Finally, some ideas are provided about the scale and order of the cultural symbols and their development in the recent global situation.

E. Tzaneva (✉)
Institute of Ethnology and Folklore Studies with Ethnographic Museum, Bulgarian Academy of sciences, Sofia, Bulgaria
e-mail: etzaneva@gmail.com

Keywords

Ethnic · Identity · Cultural symbols · Ethno-symbolism · Globalization · Multiculturalism

Introduction

Approaching the end of the new millennium's second decade, social scientists and researchers should admit that the predicted and mostly expected tendency towards ethnic and cultural relational rearrangement, leading to unification/regimentation as a result of globalization (Bauman 1996; Rosencrane 2001; Cohen 2004), did not occur in social reality, and as a result minority cultures have not been assimilated into the leading industrialized nation states.

On the contrary, amidst the recent process of democratization in many different zones of older or newly promoted ethno-cultural contacts, a globalization-related dynamics and social reconfigurations happened, such as a rather unexpected flowering of ethnic movements, the activation of voluntary and forced migration and other forms of mobility, and changes in attitudes to ethnic values. With people easily moving around the globe, many areas – not only throughout their entire history but especially today – represent an explosive ethnic mixture of conflicting social, economic, and political as well as cultural views and respective interests. Many regions today offer rich diversity in issues of rivalries and conflicts, as well as border and memory issues associated with traditional and new ethnicities and their cultures. The reason for this is that, in most developing countries, **ethnic cultures** are expressions of long-established tactics of survival and the protection of groups' livelihood, embodying life experiences and adapting useful influences, that today, even more than before, the group chooses to cherish and transmit. The ethnically diverse population, maintaining its contacts and keeping its different social and cultural characteristics, continues to create ideas, theories, programs, and respective tactics and strategies in the current social practice, which, whether officially promoted or neglected, feed into the various ethnic conflicts. If neglected or treated incompetently, the present forms of ethnic solidarity, confrontation, and movements within multiethnic states arising from past ethnic sentiments and current interests can create national and national-territorial problems in a global world and complicate the contemporary transition of many states to a political, economic, and ideological pluralism and democratic structure.

Mobility, **migration,** and **refugees** are today the key instruments of population change in Europe. As a result of mobility, migration, and integration, many communities and group members develop multiple affiliations and more complex **group identities** (Castles and Miller 1993; Vertovec and Cohen 1999), while keeping their ethnic loyalties strong. In many cases, the acculturation processes from the past are significantly substituted by the strengthening of ethnic identification and self-identification on a large scale. This has an impact on the current population size in Europe with migration flows of two million non-EU immigrants, with foreign citizens making up to 7.5% of persons living in the EU Member States in 2017, and almost 22 million non-EU citizens living in the EU (Eurostat 2017). According to a demographic projection (Lanzieri 2011), by 2060, persons of all nationalities with at least one foreign-born parent are expected to account for about 33% of the EU-27 population. The national countries and their societies will inevitably become increasingly diverse in an ethno-cultural sense. Remaining an important aspect of group consciousness, the ethnic identity shows its malleable nature in adapting to the new circumstances.

The discourse of ethnic culture in its dynamics as a mediator for a "rearrangement of national space due to 'globalizing' forces" (Berking 2003) is therefore a logical and analytical way to discuss the relationship between current **ethnization** and **globalization**. With such an approach, a twofold problem comes to the fore: on one hand, what is happening with **the *national*** in the context of increasing contemporary ethno-cultural diversity?; and on the other, what is the destiny of **the *ethnic*** in the contemporary nation state, which is usually multiethnic and multinational? Actually, this is the question of how *ethnic* the *national culture* is today, and, in a more general context, how can the *ethnic* be defined today on a canvas of mobility, escalating a population's diversification and cultural variety, since it is beyond doubt that cultural diversity is the main characteristic of today's "global village." The following text offers a view on those problems by focusing on the methodological and historiographical points of the subject and projecting them onto the contemporary social background.

Contexts of investigation. Research on how group identity is constructed through symbols is especially meaningful for communities demanding self-determination and rights; respective claims for them are usually underwritten by the ethno-symbolic cultural definitions of identity. Actually, the interplay between this diversity and contemporary national societies is analyzed within the interpretative framework provided since the rise of modernization theory and, later, by the theoretical study of nationalism. As a result, a distinctive characteristic in the study of ethnic phenomena in the last few decades became the growing convergence of its subject with the theme of nation and nationalism. This convergence of research fields directed scholars' interest either to the mechanisms that create social cohesion among an ethnically distinctive group of people – a cohesion which under different circumstances can reach a certain degree of intensity and make that group significant in some sense, usually political – or towards the examination of emerging loyalties to the state and their transformation from attachments to the previously existing ethnic formation. This rapprochement between the notions of *national* and *ethnic* occurred at the end of the nineteenth century, and even today in the sociological literature there is a tendency to consider these two viewpoints of ethnicity, nations and nationalism together (Koptseva et al. 2011; Smith 2009; Eriksen 1993; Hutchinson 1994; Hutchinson and Smith 1996; Guibernau and Rex 1997). No matter how old and criticized these approaches are, both aspects are important today, for example, in the adaptation of migrants, refugees, seasonal workers, to a receiving country's culture and life through the processes of the *melting pot, assimilation, acculturation, homogenization, pluralism, multi-, inter-, and transculturalism.*

Despite the variety of approaches, the research on *ethnos/ethnicity* and the other ethnic issues (all of them interweaved in the notion of *ethnic identity*) remains one of those themes in social sciences that seem to not only generate recurrent and intensive debates, but also feed doubts about how correctly the subject has been investigated, especially on the theoretical level. The confusion derives from the different substances advanced by scholars in these categories in the past and today as both social and research phenomena. Recently, based on the analysis of case studies, it is not difficult to conceptualize their dynamics (Cohen 2004; Leoussi and Grosby 2006; Tzaneva 2015): Today's countries, with their national societies in a globalized environment, are modern constructs often fashioned from selectively chosen and reworked premodern materials, receiving additional activation and change, new components, and contents under the motive of new interests and goals.

Their dual character, as modern and global inventions constructed largely from reworked premodern materials, has made the interplay among nations and their old and new ethnic essence difficult to fathom for scholars working in both the "Western" and "Eastern" liberal social-science traditions. Both "schools," however, agree that to express and frame theoretically their existence today is to ascribe to the groups within a nation, certain identity. Identity itself is an immutable, subjective, and evolving concept, defined by the process of identification. Among the various identifications, the only ethnic identity that matters is the one that the individuals as members of the group ascribe to. It is socially constructed as self-identified, and is perceived as such. It is constructed under the direct influence and guidance of societal interests and culture in interplay. The process of its establishment draws much of its content and energy from preexisting and newly added forms of solidarity and multifaceted images of collective belonging. It respectively explores the formation and expression of national identity by examining the role of cultural and "culturalized" political and economic factors and the way these have been shaped, adapted, reordered, and changed over time by the mobilizing power of those factors. The scholarly approach should therefore seek the development of contemporary globalized ethnic identities as changes in consciousness brought about by cultural shifts (motivated and driven by societal powers and interests). Recently, many attempts have been made to conceptualize the methodological bases of ethno-cultural studies under the conditions of globalization (Tomlinson 1999; James and Mandaville 2010; Lechner and Boli 2012). Intended to give some historiographical and methodological insights for a possible interpretation of the state of the ethnic in the contemporary global world, the text below begins with some basic notions from the ethnic lexicon in use, judged according to their potentials to adequately analyze the present-day social processes.

Being one of the major forms of group (collective) identity, ethnic identity often surprises today's researcher with its malleable character. Both components of the phenomenon's nomination – the classification of *ethnic* and *identity* – are problematic regarding their content and form. The outset and early development of the globalized world set standards and tried to argue perspectives about the academic future of both these components. However, the social and political reality produced its own picture and caused significant turns in the line of scholarly investigation. The variations of ethnic terms such as *ethnic, ethnos, ethnie, ethnicity, core/kernel of ethnos*, *identity*, and *nation* are steadily being used in the public language. In scholarly discourse, however, they are often omitted or substituted due to *ethnic nihilism*, which was fashionable at the start of the millennium, and especially strong (at terminological level) in the Russian social science. "I don't use the term 'ethnos'," wrote V. Tishkov (the most prominent representative of the school which actually invented *ethnos*), "because I don't know what it is" (Tishkov 2003). Up to the present day, in trying to adequately reflect the processes, the term *ethnos* acquired gradually different nuances: from denotation of a social-cultural historical group with certain specifics, through bio-cultural and natural-geographic formation with mainly behavioral uniting characteristics, to an ethnic substance present in a member of a group (Bromley 2008; Rybakov 1998), the last coming closer to an attributive understanding of *ethnic* as present in the non-Russian schools of thought. Recently, in the global era, some scholars, especially ethnologists, have tended to interpret *ethnic* only as a tool for scholarly analyses, devised and used by academicians (Tishkov 2001; Banks 1996). In neo-Marxist "ethnos theory," the idea was shared that the only way to make sense of the variety of branched and subordinated ethnic terms is to view the main one among them – *ethnos* (adopted from the meaning of the original Ancient Greek) – as such a category of classification and an academic construct that serves analytical purposes (Tzaneva 2015).

The potential definitional problems were outlined early in the etymological history of the term (beginning in the 1950s) in Western social science as well. At that time, *ethnicity* was first used to characterize the "quality of ethnic groups." The conceptual framework elaborated in the United States later saw the alignment of national-cultural particularities within the formation of a homogeneous and culturally standardized society – a society quite different from our contemporary one. Hence, the earliest conceptions of a *melting pot* and *ethnic pluralism*, which sought to explain such diverse phenomena as social and political changes, nation building, identity formation, and cultural and political assimilation (and in some attempts even race relations), are now often empty vessels in most cases, and more or less of historiographical interest only, although they can still prove adequate and vivid in some real situations in our ethnically dynamic world.

It is in the field of socio-anthropological literature and the conceptual apparatus of contemporary ethnology where *ethnicity* is generally defined in terms of a cultural ethos, such as shared customs, institutions, rituals, values, intentions, relations, and behavior. Yet the members of an ethnic group who possess a common "cultural ethos" were always seen as sharing "a genetic and/or a linguistic, religious, national and social connection." Meanwhile, more than 20 years after M. Weber's successful attempt to combine the cultural and political aspects of *ethnic*, many scholars still think that a distinction must be made between cultural and political ethnicity (the former referring to a belief in shared cultural values, the latter to a political awareness or mobilization). Actually, this highlights the complex incorporation of several forms of identity in today's world also known as **multiple identities**. Suggested and elaborated in the past, this context is workable today in the situation of constant mobility and settlements in unfamiliar environments, when the multitude of identities receives its concrete and detailed expressions.

The further determination of *ethnicity* through cultural identification, but with respect to some characteristics of sociological type, was an advanced way of looking at the phenomenon. In this context, each present study should adopt the idea that ethnic formations cannot exist in isolation but only in contrast to other such groups. That is, the boundaries distinguish between two or more "somethings" which carry their own initial distinctiveness. Also entailed is the idea of a choice in the expression of ethnic identity or what is called "**situational ethnicity**" – that components of identity emerge and change situationally and do not express permanent absolutes. Respectively, when included in a territorial state, "the conflict potential of ethnicity is highlighted" because of the contrasts in the differences of religion, language, descent, and history that reflect on groups' social psychological modes. Living as a minority in a multiethnic society builds existing relationships to one's own ethnicity (both in the foreign country and at home) and the host society simultaneously. This is expressed through identity components chosen for preferable identification in different situations of the new, often hostile, social milieu. Ethnic identity therefore also becomes contextual when forced to communicate these components within the milieu. So, *ethnic* in the era of mobility and migration mobilizes and expresses its *multiidentical, situational*, and *contextual* nature, and these are the three possible contexts within which it could be studied successfully today.

According to the latest research, other basic notions related to *ethnos* and *ethnicity*, such as *kernel of ethnos, ethnic/nonethnic groups, symbolic ethnicity, multiethnicity, dual ethnicity, and quasi-ethnicity*, are presented in both the contemporary Western and today's Russian science with regards to the globalization processes (Wiener 2005; Koptseva et al. 2011). Still in use are the previous terms of *ethnic groups, ethnic identity, ethnic community, ethnic unit*, and *ethnic relations* as synonyms to *ethnic*, but they are being stepped back as they are subject to much misinterpretation today. To reveal the characteristics of *ethnic* today, both *ethnos* and *ethnicity* have a place for the following distinction in their meaning that seems reasonable and consensual: the first designates the grouping of culturally related people, associated with territory, economy, history, lifestyle, etc., while the latter – their psychological unity based on rationalization of the features mentioned and expressed in some standards of their behavior. Some scholars are in search of a combined term. A. D. Smith uses the concept of *ethnie*, perceived as the prerequisite of a nation, tied to both premodern and modern phenomena (Smith 1986). Also suggested (and used in this text) is the attributive *ethnic*, designating the social category and its symbolic content, also acknowledging the importance of the circumstances for their appearance. In the substantial body of literature on the subject in both schools, the notion and dominant meaning of *ethnic* is considered in continuously developing aspects, although some of its important characteristics still appear to be untranslatable into a language of theory. Even today, after a century-long study, many researchers of *ethnic* recognize that not all its meanings can be grasped through objective scientific methodology, especially those linked to psychological elements such as thinking, will, memory, and the main focus of *ethnic* – the *ethnic identity*. Conceptualizing ethnic identity is the general context for the investigation of *ethnic* today, and it demands the approbation and application of multiple and manifold viewpoints, even if this might sometimes seem eclectic.

A suggested convergence of research schools. It is the ethno-cultural approach that from the outset recognizes nations as modern constructs often devised from available and selected premodern, but also newly incorporated, materials. This is also true for the contemporary multiethnic civil nations which are willingly or forcibly accommodating ethnic newcomers who are trying to balance their cultural identifications between "foreignness and indigeneity," and so are the host-countries. Because of this complexity, it is difficult to fit contemporary ethnic and national phenomena into accepted conceptualizations and established theories (e.g., the nation as a mode of production, or the nation defined in class and economic terms, as a product of industrialization, modernization/postmodernism and progress, or of institutional and political conflicts). The problem becomes more complicated when trying to clarify the mechanisms involved in the changes of ethnic, nation, and its identity under the influence of contemporary population motilities. Discussion on the relationship between *ethnic* and *nation* includes first the question how the scholar approaches the nation with its ethnic content, choosing between or combining the above-defined specifics of *ethnos* and *ethnicity*: as an intellectually constructed concept, an "instrumental" creation serving particular rationalized interests, or as a specific historically established ethnic and social formation. As stated, this was the main dilemma between the "theory of ethnos" and the "theory of ethnicity," and the answer gives radically different directions for today's presence of *ethnic* in the national picture of the global world. Therefore, for such research, the possibilities for bringing both concepts closer together in one integrated vision to study the phenomenon of *ethnic* must be considered. Before suggesting this, an analysis is needed to relate the developments traced to certain similar, even parallel, antinomies in the orthodox Eastern European and mainstream Western European/American theories of ethnicity, ethnos, nation, and identity. There are recent studies that seek to demonstrate, rather than a simple convergence between the two general approaches, a similarity in the impasse, which scholars in the two traditions experienced in the face of nations' dual characters and the re-appropriation of ethnically different materials in modern forms for novel purposes. How modern nations draw upon simple continuations of premodern (before) or foreign (recently) ethnic memories and cultural legacies but are growing to be different and even contradict them, is a complex process, focused on the social circumstances and procedural tools that allow nations to use and shape various characteristics in their need to construct innovative thinking and social sensibility.

To extract and analyze the cultural essence of *ethnic* today, its attachment to the two abovementioned contrasting concepts (approaches) of investigation should be conceptualized. According to a **"primordialist" ("essentialist")** position, which has grown unfashionable in recent years, the social markers (manifested as loyalties, attachments, endowments, etc.) were primary, or taken as given. This approach emphasized the naturalness and stability of culture, religion, history, and emotional links within communities that derived from place of birth, kinship relationships, religion, language, and social practices through members' lives that are "natural" for them and that provide a basis for an easy affinity with other people from the same background. These attachments constitute the givens of the human condition and might be rooted in the nonrational foundations of personality. They develop in childhood and remain with the person through the whole life; consciously or not, they often provide a basis for the formation of social and political groupings. Even in threatening moments – for example, when the objective cultural markers do not really exist, including under foreign political domination and forced and voluntary migrations, or in situations when people are removed from their origins or have rejected their childhood identifications (refuge cases) – ethnic loyalties are supposed to continue reflecting not real but imagined, memorized, or idealized uniting/ distinguishing factors. Therefore, the resulting identity is often viewed as being "based on national and ethnic factors rather than civilizational ones" with "old heroes and narratives, with ethnicity and religion playing a major role" (Martins 2010). According to C. Geertz, the personal and collective identity of the ethnic groups' members, although an interplay between contemporary dynamics and past loyalties, is mostly driven by ties of blood, mother tongue and language, homeland, religion, historical memories and images, and traditional attachments (Geertz 1996). So, the main advantage of a primordial perspective, applied to present-day situations, is focusing the attention on the active emotional power of ethnic ties. But in using this view, the researcher cannot explain the dynamics of past and contemporary *ethnics* or the political consequences sometimes marked by quick changes in political partners, loyalties and preferences, and group political behavior. The contrary idea that cultural symbols and cultural affinities are used by a certain group of interests, or an elite, seeking instrumental advantage for themselves or the group they claim to represent, is central for the modern perspective on ethnicity in all its branches: "instrumental/situational/mobilizationist." Ethnicity is seen as strategically "constructed" and susceptible to redefinition in concrete situations, needing to be assessed in each context separately. The mobilization of loyalties obviously affects the self-definition of the group and its boundaries, which can be shifted and extended, so ethnicity appears to be an artifact imagined by political and cultural leaders in accordance with their particular interests. This approach tends towards an idea that ethnicity has no content of its own, no independent status; it is "nothing but a tool for pursuing nonethnic goals" for different interest/status-groups. Within constructivist readings of ethnicity dynamics, "material terms" are elaborated, such as competition for resources, distribution of resources, elite strategies, status and wealth, and power and rational choice (Banton 2008). They do not deny the existence of bonding through symbols and loyalties but view symbols and culture as resources for achieving positions desired by different groups' elites.

Although this perspective pervades in the modern debates on the subject, ethnic phenomena are much more than just manipulative instruments. No doubt, ethnic boundaries are fluid; they move and change, but some immanent characteristics of the group keep the balance within those boundaries and maintain them. So, despite the "natural" temptation for the researchers to give preference to one or another of the existing approaches, and to apply it critically to their concrete study, and also because of the comprehensive and changing character of the ethnic phenomena themselves, a theoretical and methodological strategy combining these approaches should be employed in the study of *ethnic*. Today, there is no doubt that fruitful ideas and concepts from different approaches and perspectives may be combined to reveal the nature of the phenomenon more adequately. Even in the early 1980s, within the dominant modernist perspective, there were some reasonable suggestions to create "an exploratory synthesis of primordial and mobilizationist approaches" to developing ethnicity for the purpose of an adequate study (McKay 1982). Later, a huge breakthrough happened by recognizing that "approaches to ethnicity are not necessarily mutually exclusive" (Tishkov 2001).

A fruitful suggestion was offered in the field of anthropology, in which ethnicity was assessed as referring to people's classification in a context of **"self-other" distinctions** on the cultural level (Eriksen 1993). Accordingly, the ethnic identity is viewed as referring to: "the individual level of identification with a culturally defined collectivity ..." (Hutchinson and Smith 1996). The separate existence of a given ethnic formation is defined by the unique balance between **universal cultural features** (characteristic for the whole of human civilization), the **general** (characteristic for a large group of neighboring or somehow related peoples), and the **particular** (characteristic only for a given local group). In combination, these features create a cultural configuration that makes the "cultural level" of the group objectively different and unique and determines it as such in a specific social context; within a spatial frame, corresponding characteristics will be global, regional, and local (Genchev 1984). Because of the distinctive combination of those features, the ethnically determined grouping looks to be distinct from all similar establishments; it looks different to its "own" people, as well as to "strangers" or "outsiders." If brought together, the "own" people and the "outsiders" should share the unique notions of the mentioned cultural "foreignness and indigeneity" in an effort to create their mutual belonging to a political and cultural community of the whole state (Castles 2000).

To study how these notions develop towards successful co-existence, an approach and investigative mechanism should be suggested that brings together the expertise of the above dichotomized views. It will help to use the contrasting views and scholarly debates for providing useful explanatory and normative insights for understanding the phenomenon. This approach should combine the earlier established (and often considered "essential") attachments and loyalties within their historical trajectory and transformation, with their recent ("modernist," "postmodernist," and "globalized") applications. This approach, labeled as ***ethno-symbolism***, was developed from the 1980s mostly by Anthony D. Smith and his followers within the tradition of historical sociology, stressing cultural continuity and the role of historically preserved and transferred affiliations. As an academic current, the *ethno-symbolic approach* reflects the interest in the creation and representation of complex identities, as well as their adoption and modeling by the ethnic group over time, and therefore contains potentials for application within the constructivist perspective. In recent decades, serious and successful attempts have been made to apply the ethno-symbolic approach as a working synthesis in this perspective (Hutchinson and Smith 1994; Guibernau and Hutchinson 2004; Leoussi and Grosby 2006; Smith 2009; Kaplan et al. 2011; Tzaneva 2015). Now, "the question is rather how far such synthesis can be empirically helpful" (Hutchinson and Smith 1996).

To avoid the controversial debate about its predominantly "essentialist nature," I would suggest using ethno-symbolism as an instrumental research body (a set of contexts, symbols, and analytical methods) for studying how a national community, both in the past and global, could be considered and sustained. Such a view should be based on a consensual idea of *ethnic* that also combines the potentials of the existing concepts and opens up fields for the study of its symbols. A possible new anthropological direction understands *ethnic* as a complex cultural integrity of a group, existing in all individual members as an ethnic substance, with united external and internal components which are ordered and symbolically expressed (Rybakov 1998; Koptseva et al. 2011). Ethnic substance is an attribute of the personality – it is always in the individual, and visible in symbolic signs, even if, outside the main group, the person still carries a certain model of ethnic values and expresses them in sticking to norms, models and certain behaviors. Personal ethnic features are very stable, existing regardless of such conditions as change of territory, language, and even religion. Emotions and all their manifestations in loyalties, attachments, endowments, etc., are deeply associated with *ethnic*, and this also characterizes today's ethnic groups living in multiethnic states. Such a view is obviously a combination of classical **theories of ethnos and ethnicity** through distinguishing objective and subjective ethnic properties. It also comes closer to the representatives of Western ethno-symbolism by indicating the presence of some stable ethnic structures in a person that are susceptible to mobilization and change.

Ethno-symbolism in this perspective handles the question of how cultural markers, or complex symbolic practices as expressions of these structures, appear and function as characteristics of a group. It can be used as an investigative textual and contextual tool for the dynamics of national identity in conditions of ethnic mobility – not as a theoretical approach (as stated by its founders), but as an instrumental construct for sorting out, tracing the changes, and revealing the malleable position of different identity components. Even serving as "actors" on a "cultural scene," ethnic symbols have a serious political role when used to enhance ethnic/national awareness, and legitimize self-determination demands (Guibernau and Hutchinson 2004). By accepting the changeable nature of **ethno-cultural symbols**, ethno-symbolism also provides a terrain for studying their manipulation and the pressure on them from different social forces and interests, and also the mechanisms of their forced or voluntary adjustment to new social, political, and economic environments.

Investigating ethnic as an indexed and dynamic cultural hybridity. Culture, history, religion, language, and other markers not only shape but objectively distinguish ethnic groupings. They are also subjectively distinguishing and uniting indicators as far as group members interpret all these markers according to their different values and standards, and the historical and social contexts of their lives. The sum of these changeable interpretations creates the sense of community, or the sense of identity. For the existence and maintenance of that identity, the balance of the group's markers needs to be rationalized. This necessity makes the dichotomy sameness/distinctiveness an element of a consciousness or identity and a subjective category. It is precisely this rationalization which provides the content of *ethnic* as a specific sense of identity. Hence, the conclusion that *ethnic* is that characteristic of the group which keeps its cultural content and inner integrity sufficiently balanced so that it can exist as a whole, without changing its boundaries as a group. In this light, the main analytical concept concerns the simultaneous historical/chronological alongside the situational/contextual character of the phenomenon, whose constitutive elements undergo change as actors seek to keep *ethnic* alive, or changes in the cultural content within the ethnic boundaries should be studied as a main research problem. Therefore, a suggested synthesis between the essentialist/primordial and situational/instrumental approaches to the *ethnic* in ethno-symbolic instrumental analysis, applied to and organized around the theory of symbolic boundary maintenance and development, seems reasonable.

Two other related research perspectives could be also of use: the "transactionalist" and "socio-psychological." But the most detailed interpretation of the much-needed concept which emphasizes the persistence, transformation, and resurgence of ethnos/ethnicity through the device of cultural symbolism pervades the works of J. Armstrong (in the early 1980s) and especially A. Smith and his school (late 1980s to early 1990s and to the present), followed by a number of talented scholars, although their ideas are still not unanimously accepted in the literature as a general theoretical framework of the *ethni*c (Barth 1994; Horowitz 1996, 2004; Smith 2009). The validation of these ideas can be proven or rejected only by a multitude of case-study investigations. In this light, ethno-symbolism analyzes the nature of ethnic and interprets it as an embodiment of a hybrid cultural amalgamation of malleable markers.

Cultural hybridization is a result of cultural encounters that happen during the increasingly intense mobility of our time. In their fulfillment, ethnic contacts and contradictions, interaction, and exchange occur. Both "hosts" and "outsiders" participate in these processes with their look, dress style, manners and foods, music and dances, followed by more communicational means as feasts and celebrations, religion (faith, beliefs), stereotypes, education, and morals and values. Moving around globally, individuals and groups, families and kins, households, companies and neighbors, carrying this set of endowments, try to (1) keep their home identities and (2) construct their new ones. The former process is loyalty to an inherited and approbated cultural survival mechanism brought from home, the latter an adaptation to the new environments and experiences with the purpose of survival. This is obviously the interplay between long-established (primordial) and newly learned (constructed) norms, which again is in favor of the ethno-symbolic research mechanism combining the two linked but separate investigations. In this interplay, old and new values can mix and change their roles, places, and significance as identity factors and can also disappear or minimize their presence among the markers.

This approach is closely associated with elaborated and approbated indexes of **identity markers**. The present reading of those markers understands them as susceptible to disappearance and evolution, to change and variation, over time and according to the particular interests of the people, the members of the group, involved. To study *ethnic* through its symbols, the concept of identity construction and dynamics through different socio-political periods should first be "loaded" with concrete and precise content, and then the dynamics should be traced. The investigation of identity's structure as composed of a number of identifiers is the necessary beginning. The distinguishing features of *ethnic* as a sense of identity, and of a multiethnically composed contemporary nation, are usually organized in lists of criteria associated with both phenomena.

As a whole, those lists show an impressive stability and steady contents through time. One of the first attempts to formulate the attributes or "prerequisites" of identity on the national level was made by the Royal Institute of International Affairs in 1939. It formulated six criteria, which were rather formal in their expression (Nationalism 1966). About two decades later, B. Shafer, taking up this report, and using on the latest factual material, listed the following historical-political ingredients normally essential to the existence of nationhood. This list, which Shafer himself regarded as incomplete, consisted of ten statements: (1) an undivided territory actually or virtually held; (2) features in common, such as language, literature, and customs; (3) a minimum of common social (including religious) and economic institutions; (4) a common independent or sovereign government either actually or virtually in existence (type does not matter), or, with rare exceptions, the desire for one; (5) a shared belief in a common history and often in a common ethnic origin sometimes thought to be religious or racial; (6) some common values held by all nationals, or preference and esteem for fellow nationals; that is for those who share the common culture, institutions, interests, and heritage, or at least greater preference and esteem for them than for members of other similar groups (the "foreigners") who do not share these; (7) pride in the successes and chagrin at the failures of national policy; (8) contempt for or hostility to foreign nationalities; (9) a devotion to the entity (even if little comprehended) called the nation (or patria, or fatherland) that embodies or symbolizes the territory, people, culture, institutions, interests, heritage and whatever else the people have or think they have in common; and (10) hope for the future national power. They do not all have to be present at the same time and in the same way or to the same degree. The varieties of combinations and emphases are manifold. The components of identity do not define the process of its creation in a global aspect, but taken together they describe its basic attributes, both real and mythical. J. Hutchinson and A. D. Smith, in their introduction to a volume of readings on ethnicity (Smith introduced ethno-symbolism in 1986 and 1991), list six main features of this type of community. They compose and create a specific set of endowments, loyalties, and identifications that every individual shares with other group members, and that are symbolically expressed: (1) a collective proper name; (2) a myth of common ancestry; (3) shared memories of a common past (4) one or more differentiating elements of common culture, normally including religion, custom, or language; (5) an association with a specific "homeland"; and (6) a sense of solidarity among major sectors of the population. This is one expanded list of the mostly concentrated index by Smith's famous teacher H. S. Watson, who listed four factors in the process of the formation of national consciousness in the following order: "State, Geography, Religion and Language." As pointed out by M. Nash, these: "index features ... must be easily seen, grasped, understood, and reacted to in social situations" (Nash 1989). That is why the suggested lists or enumerations are similar in many respects; as already listed, they usually include such markers as proper name, common ancestral origin and kinship, common history, same culture, territorial boundedness, language and religion (sometimes also race or physical characteristics), sense of peoplehood and endogamy. The effectiveness of symbols in keeping ethnic group identity as distinct derives from the fact that these symbols represent features of the group which are usually considered objective by the members. During mobility and migration, the **group boundaries** are threatened and the process of the transformation of some subjectively perceived and fluid traits into more concrete objective ethnic features is more dynamic and strong (Smith 1981). Accordingly, the attachment to them can also get stronger, as if they are real, rather than imagined or invented symbols.

Having in mind the present picture of population structure as a result of mass mobilities, the differentiation between the so-called *status* and *auxiliary* symbols of *ethnic*, also called ascriptive (fixed by birth) and achieved (e.g., through culture, language, or religion), takes on a greater role. The first group of symbols consists of visible marks such as skin pigmentation, face and hair type, standardized body gestures, and other physical features and provides an important basis for making the "first-glance" distinction. When displayed, these symbols can differentiate and unite members of the group with both majority and minority status and in this way play an important part in systems of social composition. The psychological ground for this lies in the fundamental of ethnic groupings – since they are believed to consist of people who are alike by virtue of common ancestry, these conventionalized hereditary markers naturally become symbols of identification. But they cannot be the only or even the most important defining ethnic markers. To be recognized as valid by the members of a group, they must always be combined with other symbols of belonging, such as clothing, decals, adornments, flags, manner of behavior, language, dietary habits, and this is equally valid for areas where ethnic groups from the same race or population stock have long been in contact, so physical differentiation therefore becomes progressively more difficult. Their role is clearly rationalized today by "hosts" and "newcomers": The debate in Europe about, for example, the *burqa*, *hijab*, *niqab*, etc., which might serve as a public affirmation of a group's ethnic claim, becomes significant. In such cases, what Smith calls the "auxiliary symbols" of belonging and identity achieve a greater significance. Ethnic identity is viewed by some scholars along two other axes: a cognitive/affective axis and a specific/universal axis (Cohen 2004), where the ethnic symbols are organized with various presences at ethnic and national levels. The symbols are created in a cultural sense (Smith 1986), and their acceptance by the whole cultural environment is an aim of the civilized efforts of the states. Investigation through narratives, personal behavioral actions, and groups' social and political activities, as sources for changeable order and meaning of the mentioned marker-indicators of identity, is a precise research path valid for each study in the handling of the problem.

Current Dynamics of Indexed Symbols. The scholarly thought behind the research in identity dynamics is that the listed components of identity are far from fixed and stable categories. They are in fact very malleable notions, which can be mobilized, activated, and ordered differently in different discursive contexts. According to the ethno-symbolic concept, each case study explores the dynamics of identity in the selectively chosen mobilization forms of collective attachments. For a better structuring of identity research, the investigated ethnic loyalties can be grouped according to their ethno-political and ethno-cultural parameters. The former are associated with all nuances of group members' lives in political, economic, and social meaning, and their attitude to all state-related elements – territorial bound, market unity, government, institutions of power and authority, army, etc. – also including the emotional expression and feelings they provoke in members, such as pride, glory, dignity, sense of collective possession, and readiness to defend. This scale of ethnic symbols begins with ethnic labeling. The latter includes the rationalization of features with cultural meaning focusing on linguistic and religious and ending with **ethnic imageology**. In a situation of settlement in a host-country, the use of these symbols may reinforce the group's assertiveness of self-determination claims and respective demands, as many case studies show (Kaya and Keranen 2015). Together, they create the group's ethnic identity, which is transferable and variable in its content. As stated by A. D. Smith: "collective cultural identity refers not to a uniformity of elements over generations but to a sense of continuity on the part of successive generations of a given cultural unit . . ." (Smith 1991).

The systematic research on today's choices of ethnic labeling is still an emerging field (Phinney 2003). Subsuming the different loyalties and the stock of endowments and identifications is the group's ethnic name, the so-called ***ethnonym***, considered the most significant among the ethnic symbols. The "proper ethnic name" is usually mentioned as the first marker of the *ethnic* by most existing classifications of identity's attributes or features. The ethnonym is claimed by or ascribed to the group. A study of certain ethnic labeling and naming practices is an expression of the extent of the communication process in a contemporary global situation. Also proposed is research in the process of encoding an "identification idea" into a word or group of words and the decoding of that idea among the members of a group. Encoding refers to the selection of the term that the person (a member of the migrating group) feels best conveys the meaning intended; decoding refers to the fact that the hearer (a member of the host-group) must interpret it according to their own understanding. The accuracy of the interpretation depends on a mutual understanding between both groups. The content and meaning of ethnic names in the case of migration indicate the level of identity of both bearers of the ethnonym (newcomers) and users of it from outside (hosts); the adequacy of the mutual understanding shows the level of the spread of identity among the population and is a sign of the level of settlement and the acculturation process.

The researcher of ethnic names today should be aware of the fact that ethno-naming is always a "placing of labels for identification purposes" (Lampe 1982). "At home," these are labels or signs of identification a person shares from the first moment of socialization into the family and kin group. The ethnic name is a group convention and has been identified as one of the first dimensions of language. Like all other kinds of naming, the ethnonym entails the establishment of certain verbal symbols to refer to specific things or categories, in this case ethnically determined values. This allows members of a group to make verbal distinctions whenever ethnic things and categories are concerned; these distinctions are regarded as *correct* and *important* within the group. When the members of an ethnic group learn appropriate words, they also learn the corresponding attitudes and behaviors that accompany them. The ethnonym (together with its variants and respective adjectives) generalizes all ethnic values and loyalties, especially when used as a differentiator. Its diffusion, frequency, and usage provide clear signs of the level of ethnic development and the degree of old and inherited/newly established identity purposes. Despite the limits of case studies, and although dependent on a combination of contextual factors, the authors agree that, in our global world, "ethnic labels have been increasingly used as prominent and meaningful markers of identity" (Phinney 2003). In a situation of mobility, their use has an extended ethno-uniting and ethno-distinguishing role. An important aspect of research will focus on the changing of personal ethnic names for employment, status, or other purposes, which has recently gained scholars' attention (Giampapa and Canagarajah 2017).

The formation of a new identity consists of the creation of new ethnic categories, possibly through an extension of existing ethnic symbols and investing them with new content. The study of the ethno-cultural dimensions of *ethnic* investigates the development of those ethnic markers that have a distinct cultural denotation. This involves the further evolution and change of existing symbols, as well as the selection of new symbols and their infusion with national content, resulting in enhanced internal cultural cohesion. The first requirement in this process is the creation (based on the prior revitalization) of a shared **belief in a common descent**, fate and history, and the reinterpretation of the past. This process can be observed today in some Western European countries where migrants and refugees consciously identify their common historical symbols from the homeland with the attempt to share and pass them along to the younger members of the group. Research on this process involves a textual and contextual investigation into the question of whether, as a group, the members remember and commemorate the past, in what form and image, and who made the selection and how. Also, did this remembrance change and, if so, what was its reflection on the group's consciousness, and is the purpose of the process identifiable?

Besides the ethnic labeling, the ethno-linguistic and ethno-religious sensibilities of nationhood form the next vital aspects or macro-strategies of what is called a "discursive construction of narratives" of national identity (Wodak and DeCillia 2007). At home, in the Heimatland, certain myths about language and religion were certainly major elements of the national project for the people who later chose to move. **Language** has often provided the initial criterion in delineating imagined social formations. The function of language in creating new loyalties is fundamental, as is evidenced by the interest which each nation has in the broadest possible acceptance of the worth and survival of its culture. The ethnic language is usually that aspect of *ethnic* that receives an immediate and most thorough rationalization in the ethnic identity of the group; consistently, no matter the culture, all people who speak an unknown language are considered "foreigners." The relationship between the present-day migration (both skilled and not) and language is complex and nuanced, even if there is no doubt that the employment chances for the migrants are mediated through the main language. Some migration studies have proven the connection between the language in host communities with levels of the overall success of migrants (Adsera and Pytlikova 2010; Dustmann and Fabbri 2003). The native language has a greater importance in the everyday lives of all social types of migration and definitely preserves positions during at least two to three generations at their homes. The language dominant in the host country is a strong but controversial tool for redefining the identity dynamic of the newcomers (Giampapa and Canagarajah 2017).

Religion is a distinct dimension of human organization and one that often lies close to the sources of self-awareness and grounds of personal identification. Historical, literary, and folklore documents displaying ethnic identity show that its manifestations in many of today's sending and host countries for migrants were connected with religion and interrelated with the religious dimension of identity. In most of them, religious consciousness does not possess a separate quality different in content from social consciousness in general. Belief involves other forms of social awareness and affects ideas of ethnic characteristics, both prenational and national. The relationship between ethnic characteristics and religious identities in the construction process of nationality and nation-building is especially evident where those formations had a stable premodern ethnic origin but lacked statehood and their own forms of religious and cultural organization. Together with cultures and identities, religions are also brought together in direct communication by the process of globalization and migration (Beyer and Beaman 2007). Specific for the religious encounters is that, today, religions enter through migration into a circle of controversies and conflicts, and as a result migrants' religious identities are often reinforced.

The phenomenon of *national imagining* is complex and multidimensional and is designed in the context of the longue durée civilizational development of the society. Each contemporary study of newly appeared or changed ethnic images follows the cultural discourse as a prominent feature of the ethno-symbolic approach and claims engagement with the idea that the effort to trace the appearance of national images and self-images is actually a study of how the past (brought from the home cultures) cultural and spiritual achievements are "soaked" into the modern nation as a civilizational overlay. This is a contribution to understanding "the *inner world* of ethnicity and nationalism through the analysis of symbolic elements and subjective dimensions" (Smith 2009). It aims to study ethno-images as a constructive canvas for the national stereotypes, and ethnic imaginary as an aggregate of the technique of image-making, social practice of perception, and expression of the "otherness." The role of ethno-symbolism as a tool for image and stereotype formation is viewed in the attendance of "myth, memory, symbol and tradition that modern national identities are reconstituted in each generation, as the nation becomes more inclusive and as its members cope with new challenges" (Ibid). These ethno-political and ethno-cultural dimensions – language, religion, traditions, historical memories, and images – are established in the early stages of ethnogenesis and developed later in accordance with the accelerating integration of the people involved. Here, it seems, the researcher comes to the crucial word of analysis – *communication*. The ancient and medieval world lacked the necessary level of communications among the people from same ethnic group for them to begin identifying themselves in national categories. One specific example of this idea was provided by Lerner in the 1960s, when he revealed the role of literacy, empathy, and the mass media in the process of the "achievement of mobility" by the ethnic group. This mobility, consisting of different kinds of communication, is necessary for the group to enter the political arena and announce its political demands. Later, K. Deutsch, pointing again to the role of communication, suggested that modernization does not refer primarily to the entrance of a large number of people into the political scene but to the creation, through the communication of a new knowledge of the world, a new set of aspirations, visions, and statuses, together with an intensive network of shared memories and messages among the members of the group. These communications intensified the integration of the society; eventually, they are the link between its economic status and the processes of group formation. The character of the internal ties in a given society marks the level of its social, political, economic, and cultural development; it also signifies the stage of ethnic development in this society, evidencing the readiness of the ethnic group to enter into those relationships that characterize nationhood. What must be studied in this process is the growth of "loyalties transcending those of primary [ethnic] groups." The general view of K. Deutsch is that *ethnic* – as a network of communication that seeks to ascertain how culture, religion, language, and other "symbolic codes" bind the members of communities together and how this connection lasts for generations – is also a basic thesis for the time of globalization when the internal dynamics of this network come to the fore. The contemporary situation in the era of postmodernism and globalization is viewed by some authors as a process of "accelerating connectivity" (Tomlinson 1999), which again places communication at the center of social change. The engagement with the historical, political, and social dynamics through which culture comes to matter is, however, at the center of identity's substance. What was once said of national identity as a "multidimensional concept [that includes E.T.] a specific language, sentiments and symbolism" (Smith 1991) is also true for the global situation and processes about the identity of composed civil state-organized nations. Single case studies should be directed towards revealing which among those indexed features are the major elements or "symbolic codes" of the "conscience collective" in the situation of a global population's mobility and that provide the driving force for changing group identification. When a minority group lives and tries to survive in a multiethnic state (no matter if this is a recent migration in a global world or a historic settlement), the use by the individuals of "our" or "their" cultural symbols creates certain behavioral forms that signify the existence of an often confusing "**dual identity**," as has been reported (Vertovec and Cohen 1999).

Conclusion

Today, many scholars assume that the leading characteristic of the societies in the world is their multiculturalism – precisely the people in them, and the groups and their identities shaped by more than one single culture, usually associated with territory, home and fatherland, mother tongue, memories, etc. (Sotshangane 2002). The effect of globalization is greater if, using these sets of existing identifications, new group and personal consciousness is built above the old one, which unites people within newly established parties. In this sense globalization appears to be a concept of uniformization. But if approaching cultural processes via the understanding of the effects of globalization "as they are felt within particular localities" (Tomlinson 1999), the much-needed creation of the united (not uniform), multiple, situational, and contextual identities of the ethnic groups living together will be visible.

Cross-References

► Cultural Socialization and Ethnic Consciousness
► Diaspora as Transnational Actors: Globalization and the Role of Ethnic Memory
► Ethnicity and Cultural Wounding: Ethnic Conflict, Loss of Home, and the Drive to Return
► Historical Memory and Ethnic Myths
► Religion and Political Mobilization
► The Significance of Ethno-politics in Modern States and Society

References

Adsera A, Pytlikova M (2010) The role of language in shaping international migration: evidence from OECD countries 1985–2006. Econ J 125(586):F49–F81
Banks M (1996) Ethnicity: anthropological constructions. Routledge, London
Banton M (2008) The sociology of ethnic relations. ERS 31:1267–1285
Barth F (1994) Enduring and emerging issues in the analysis of ethnicity. In: Vermeulen H, Govers C (eds) The anthropology of ethnicity. Beyond "ethnic groups and boundaries". Het Spinhuis, Amsterdam
Bauman Z (1996) Glokalisierung oder Was für die einen Globalisierung, ist für die anderen Lokalisierung. Argumentation 217:653–664
Berking H (2003) 'Ethnicity is everywhere': on globalization and the transformation of cultural identity. Curr Sociol 51:248–264
Beyer P, Beaman L (2007) Religion, globalization, and culture. Koninklijke Brill NV, Leiden
Bromley Y (2008) Essays on the theory of ethnos, 2nd edn. Nauka, Moscow
Castles S (2000) Ethnicity and globalization. Sage, London
Castles S, Miller M (1993) The age of migration: international population movements in the modern world. Macmillan, London
Cohen E (2004) Components and symbols of ethnic identity: a case study in informal education and identity formation in diaspora. Appl Psychol Int Rev 53:87–112
Dustmann C, Fabbri F (2003) Language proficiency and labour market performance of immigrants in the U.K. Econ J 113:695–717
Eriksen T (1993) Ethnicity and nationalism. Anthropological perspectives. Pluto Press, London
Eurostat (2017) Eurostat regional yearbook 2017. http://ec.europa.eu/eurostat/documents/3217494/8222062/KS-HA-17-001-EN-N.pdf

Geertz C (1996) Primordial Ties. In: Hutchinson J, Smith A (eds) Ethnicity. Oxford University Press, Oxford, pp 40–45
Genchev S (1984) Folk culture and ethnography. Nauka i Iskustvo, Sofia
Giampapa F, Canagarajah S (2017) Skilled migration and global English. Glob Soc Educ 15:1–4
Guibernau M, Hutchinson J (eds) (2004) History and national destiny: ethnosymbolism and its critics. Blackwell, Oxford
Guibernau M, Rex J (1997) The ethnicity reader. Nationalism, multiculturalism and migration. Blackwell, Malden
Horowitz D (1996) Symbolic politics and ethnic status. In: Hutchinson J, Smith A (eds) Ethnicity. Oxford University Press, Oxford, pp 285–291
Horowitz D (2004) The primordialists. In: Conversi D (ed) Ethno-nationalism in the contemporary world: Walker connor and the study of nationalism. Routledge, London, pp 72–82
Hutchinson J, Smith A (eds) (1994) Nationalism. Oxford University Press, Oxford
Hutchinson J (1994) Modern Nationalism. Fontana Press, London
Hutchinson J, Smith AD (eds) (1996) Ethnicity. Oxford University Press, Oxford
James P, Mandaville P (2010) Globalization and culture 2: globalizing religions. Sage, London
Kaplan D, Catterall P, Rembold E (2011) Introduction to special issue: national identities in retrospect. National Identities 13:325–327
Kaya Z, Keranen O (2015) Constructing identity through symbols by groups demanding self-determination: Bosnian Serbs and Iraqi Kurds. Ethnopolitics 14:505–512
Koptseva N, Bakhova N, Medyantseva N (2011) Classical and contemporary approaches to ethno-cultural studies. Kernel Ethnos SibFU J Humanit Soc Sci 5:615–632
Lampe P (1982) Ethnic labels: naming or name calling? Ethn Racial Stud 5:542–548
Lanzieri G (2011) Fewer, older and multicultural? Projections of the EU populations by foreign/national background Eurostatt, European Commission
Lechner F, Boli J (eds) (2012) The globalization reader. 4th edn. Wiley-Blackwell, West Sussex.
Leoussi A, Grosby S (eds) (2006) Nationalism and ethnosymbolism: history, culture and ethnicity in the formation of nations. Edinburgh University Press, Edinburgh
Martins J (2010) Berger S, Lorenz C (eds) The contested nation: ethnicity, class and gender in national identities. Palgrave Macmillan, Houndmills.. Book review. Nations Natl 16:189–200
McKay J (1982) An exploratory synthesis of primordial and mobilisationist approaches to ethnic phenomena. Ethn Racial Stud 5:395–420
Nash M (1989) The cauldron of ethnicity in the modern world. University of Chicago Press, Chicago/London
Nationalism (1966) Nationalism: a report by a study group of members of the Royal Institute of International Affairs, 2nd edn. Augusta M/Kelley, New York
Phinney J (2003) Ethnic identity and acculturation. In: Chun K, Organista P, Marin G (eds) Acculturation: advances in theory, measurement, and applied research. APA, Washington, DC, pp 63–81
Rosencrane R (2001) Das globale Dorf, New Economy und das Ende des Nationalstaates. Patmos, Düsseldorf
Rybakov S (1998) On the concept of "ethos": the philosophical and anthropological aspect. Ethnographic Rev 6:3–15
Smith A (1981) The ethnic revival in the modern world. Cambridge University Press, Cambridge
Smith AD (1986) The ethnic origins of nations. Basil Blackwell, New York
Smith A (1991) National identity. Penguin Books, London
Smith A (2009) Ethno-symbolism and nationalism: a cultural approach. Routhledge, London
Sotshangane N (2002) What impact globalization has on cultural diversity? Altern-Turkish J Intl Rel 1:4. Retrieved from http://dergipark.gov.tr/alternatives/issue/1722/20963
Tishkov V (2001) Ethnology and politics. Political journalism. Nauka, Moscow
Tishkov V (2003) Requiem for ethnos: studies in social-cultural anthropology. Nauka, Moscow
Tomlinson J (1999) Globalization and culture. Chicago University Press, Chicago

Tzaneva E (2015) Ethnosymbolism and the dynamics of identity. Cambridge Scholars Publishing, Newcastle

Vertovec S, Cohen R (eds) (1999) Migration, diasporas, and transnationalism. Edward Elgar, Cheltenham

Wiener B (2005) Forms of ethnicity, whether the ethnicity has the essence and what the supporters of the academic Bromley can obtain from the new theories. JSSA 8:142–164

Wodak R, DeCillia R (2007) Commemorating the past: the discursive construction of official narratives about the 'Rebirth of the Second Austrian Republic'. Discourse Commun 1:315–341. Sage Publications: www.sagepublications.com

Cultural Socialization and Ethnic Consciousness

3

Sara N. Amin

Contents

Introduction	50
Neoliberal Globalization and the Commodification of Culture	51
Tourism	54
Development	57
Social Media	59
Conclusion	61
Cross-References	62
References	62

Abstract

In this chapter, I argue that cultural socialization processes of ethnic consciousness need to be understood in the context of the contemporary global political-economic order. To do so, I first discuss the commodification of culture under neoliberal globalization and its role in heightening ethnic consciousness. This discussion points to three spaces in which cultural encounters, cultural knowledge, and identity have been intensified in the Global South: tourism, development, and social media. The chapter explores what are some key characteristics of cultural socialization of ethnic consciousness in these three sites and their implications for heightening or diminishing ethnic consciousness. I suggest that with the commodification and globalization of "ethnicity" and "culture," researchers looking into cultural socialization practices and what is heightening or diluting ethnic consciousness need to look beyond the social relations in the family, peers, education, and "traditional" media and examine the economy –

S. N. Amin (✉)
School of Social Sciences, Faculty of Arts, Law and Education, The University of the South Pacific, Suva, Fiji Islands
e-mail: sara.amin@usp.ac.fj; saranuzhat.amin@gmail.com

© The Author(s), under exclusive license to Springer Nature Singapore Pte Ltd. 2019
S. Ratuva (ed.), *The Palgrave Handbook of Ethnicity*,
https://doi.org/10.1007/978-981-13-2898-5_3

especially in the areas of tourism, the development industry, and the performance of identity in social media.

Keywords
Ethnic consciousness · Cultural socialization · Neoliberal globalization · Commodification of culture · Tourism · Development · Social media

Introduction

Ethnic consciousness has been conceptualized in different ways, including an awareness of membership in an ethnic group (Gold and Miller 2015), the extent to which one understands human social relations through notions of ethnicity (Banton 2014) and the degree to which awareness and understanding of ethnic identity shapes social and political action (Gibson and Gouws 2000). There have been at least two major concerns in relation to the study of ethnic consciousness: what produces (or diminishes) ethnic consciousness and what are the consequences of heightened/diminished ethnic consciousness (Vermeulen and Govers 1997). In an important way, answers to these questions vary by disciplinary focus.

Psychological theorization of how ethnic consciousness is fostered in the individual has focused on the role of the family (see review by Hughes et al. 2006) or peers (Wang et al. 2015) and has identified four key sets of practices, which taken together can be understood as constituting ethnic socialization: cultural socialization, preparation for bias, promotion of mistrust, and promotion of egalitarianism and/or silence. Cultural socialization has usually been understood as a set of practices of social actors in fostering awareness of (and pride in) one's ancestry, origin, and cultural heritage (Hughes et al. 2006). While preparation of bias includes teaching one how to cope with racialized/ethnic discrimination in society, promotion of mistrust involves practices that warn one to be cautious or suspicious of interracial/interethnic interactions (Hughes and Johnson 2001). The promotion of egalitarianism or silence about ethnic issues involves encouraging one to focus on individual/nonethnic characteristics of one self and others or "simply" not discussing ethnicity (Hughes et al. 2006). Researchers have explored the role of these four types of processes in impacting on aspects of self-esteem, as well as education, employment, and health outcomes. In their review of the research on ethnic socialization in the family, Hughes et al. (2006) state that unlike the evidence for preparation of bias, promotion of mistrust and egalitarianism, which is mixed and limited, there is clear evidence that cultural socialization practices of parents that nurture awareness and pride of cultural heritage and contribute to heightened ethnic consciousness have positive effects on youth's social and well-being outcomes. Most of this line of work, like much of psychological research, has focused on ethnic and racialized minorities in the American context and has been characterized by a focus on the positive role cultural socialization practices by the family can have on integration processes and intergroup relations.

In contrast, sociological and anthropological theorizations of the processes by which ethnic consciousness is fostered in groups in a given society have tended to examine the sociopolitical and economic processes that impact on people's consciousness of ethnic membership, the meanings attached to that membership, and the type of social and political actions that result from that consciousness. Central to sociological discussions of the formation of ethnic consciousness is the argument that ethnic consciousness is shaped in important ways by the extent to which distribution of resources, opportunities, belonging, and power are (primarily) organized along ethnic lines (Rex 2013; Banton 2014). One important implication of this is that there is a political economy of ancestry, origin, and cultural heritage, shaping the kinds of stories, symbols, and meanings that are mobilized to construct ethnic consciousness (Castells 2010; Tilly 2015). As such, cultural socialization practices and the impact of these practices on ethnic consciousness are contested, multiple, and context-specific. This body of work has been more global and comparative, but there has been a tendency to focus on the conflict-generating consequences of ethnic consciousness in relation to intergroup relations, examining the role of educational, media, social movement, and nation-building institutions of the state.

Keeping in mind the insights in psychological, sociological, and anthropological research noted above, I suggest in this chapter that cultural socialization processes of ethnic consciousness need to be understood in the context of the contemporary global political-economic order. To do so, I first discuss the commodification of culture under neoliberal globalization and its role in heightening ethnic consciousness. This discussion points to three spaces in which cultural encounters, cultural knowledge, and identity have been intensified in the Global South: tourism, development, and social media. I then explore what are some key characteristics of cultural socialization of ethnic consciousness in these three sites and their implications for heightening or diminishing ethnic consciousness.

Neoliberal Globalization and the Commodification of Culture

While both neoliberalism and globalization remain contested concepts (Brenner et al. 2010; Bowles 2005; Castells 2010), it is possible to distinguish key features of the process of neoliberal globalization. Neoliberal globalization can be understood as the politically guided process of producing increased interconnection, time-space compression, deterritorialization of social action and processes, and intensified interdependence through the dominant logics of marketization, privatization, and deregulation. Neoliberal globalization involves the reconfiguration of the purpose and structure of state and government to facilitate greater free trade, expand the flow of goods and capital, and allow for the penetration of market logic and privatization processes across societal transactions (Brenner et al. 2010; Castells 2010).

Neoliberal globalization also involves the creation of new forms of political subjects, where attachment to cultural identity has become important in surviving, resisting, succeeding, or transforming the sociopolitical and economic changes brought about by neoliberal globalization (Castells 2010). A major feature of contemporary neoliberal globalization in the late twentieth century and early twenty-first century is the significant expansion of global trade regimes into areas of knowledge, diversity, and information. This includes extending the enforcement of intellectual property (IP) rights into areas of genetic resources and the recognition of traditional knowledge. It has also included new protections for biological diversity and efforts to understand cultural knowledge as proprietary assets. Coombe (2016) argues that as a result of this expansion of neoliberal globalization into the realm of diversity and culture:

> Culture is reified and animated as an asset base that can be competitively leveraged by communities to market distinctive places, goods, and experiences. Appearing to possess cultural distinction also provides collateral for attracting developmental investment and attention, receipt of which provides further demands for making cultural goods legible to new publics and interlocutors ... Efforts to expand market relations into culturally defined zones of life tend to incite new forms of struggle, knowledge mobilization and identity formation. I are witnessing a proliferation of reterritorialization that are legitimated on grounds of cultural difference and animated by global policy principles in which collective subjects become legible as communities" holding distinguishing assets. (pp. 251–252)

The commodification of culture produces contested cultural socialization practices, especially between state projects of mobilizing ethnic markers for profit (through tourism, service and performance industries, and export markets) and community-level or group projects of resisting state control/regulation/co-option of cultural identity or asserting autonomy. While contestations may revolve around what markers of identity should be suppressed, celebrated, or represented, the resulting consequence of such contestations is that ethnic consciousness is heightened and intensified overall in society. Moreover, the technologies of neoliberal globalization enable ethnically defined groups to reach out to non-state actors within and beyond state borders to either resist the commodification of cultural goods for profit, to claim ownership of such goods to demand the accrual of such profit to the group, or to leverage their market value for greater political power (Escobar 2010). However, the need for predictable and stable societies to allow for the dominance of market processes (as well as the continuation of state power) often requires the reigning in of such practices by the state of cultural groups while simultaneously profiting or marketing certain aspects of these groups' ethnic identity.

Writing about the impact of neoliberal economic policies on the Caribbean and cultural identity, Scher (2011, pp. 8–9) argues that:

> The structuring force of neoliberalism produces an emphasis on culture (a non-competitive market niche), yet also provides the hegemonic model of what counts as culture; that which is remembered and recalled by consumers as appropriate and legitimate to a region, is shaped by both global factors and local history or tradition. Cultural products then need to be recognizable to the target consumer...The result is a greater investment in managing cultural products and practices in order to preserve their economic potential and serve the expectations of consumers.

This "culturalist market" (Scher 2011, p. 8) includes "ethnically marked" agricultural produce, spices, foods, drinks, fabrics, clothes, designs, and artisanal crafts, as well as various "religious"/"traditional" rituals, practices, and artistic (oral, visual) performances. Bodies also become marked in this market, exoticized and ethnically marked for purposes of consumption in the entertainment, sports, fashion, or sex industries, locally and globally. DeHart (2010) illustrates how cultural knowledge and membership in an ethnic group have become new forms of "human" capital, producing ethnic entrepreneurs as key agents of economic development in Latin America.

Debates about authenticity, appropriation, exploitation, and ownership ensue as contests between state, corporations, and the "marked" group, between groups and within groups, leading to persistent questions about who are we, who are they, and how do we (should we) relate to "others." Consequently, there is a lot of "ethnicity" these days – "a lot of ethnic awareness, ethnic assertion, ethnic sentiment, ethno talk…it is increasingly the stuff of existential passion, of the self-conscious fashioning of meaningful, morally anchored selfhood. It is also more corporate, more commodified, more implicated than ever before in the economics of everyday life (Comaroff and Comaroff 2009, p. 1)."

While these processes are not limited to any particular ethnically defined group, it is worth noting that a distinct feature of ethnic consciousness in the contemporary era is that indigenous communities and indigeneity as a type of ethnic marker have come under the spotlight (Comaroff and Comaroff 2009). Cansessa (2014) noted this dynamic in relation to the identity category of indigeneity and indigenous in claims-making in Bolivia, pointing to the conflict between a self-acclaimed indigenous state, its self-identified indigenous supporters, and its self-identified indigenous opposition. The resulting consequences of such contested claims-making around a given ethnic marker include an intensified rhetoric (and practice) around the indigeneity. Canessa (2014) suggests that we can distinguish between two types of claims around indigeneity in the Global South, one that aims to co-opt the state and one that seeks protection from the state. What is worth noting is that claims of indigeneity are increasing globally (Canessa 2014). Some have linked this to the expansion of international treaties and law which has given a means for some groups to make claims against the state (Holder and Corntassel 2002). Others have also noted that the commodification of culture, and especially of essentialist conceptualizations of indigeneity including ideas about relationship to land and environment have place a premium on indigenous knowledge and identity in development discourse (Chandler 2008). This is in contrast to a history of marginalization of indigenous identity in relation to development: for a long time, indigeneity was seen as equivalent to marginal, backward, left behind, and not productive; yet very recently, they are lauded for their relevance, potential, and importance in terms of economies and solving development issues (Smits 2014; Chandler 2008).

In their important text *Ethnicity, Inc.,* Comaroff and Comaroff (2009) provide a diverse range of examples on how indigenous culture is commodified and mobilized. They use these examples to make the argument that neoliberal globalization has produced *Ethnicity, Inc.* (the incorporation of identity and commodification of culture) and is linked to the current history of capital. In this, they point to the role of the "entrepreneurial (singular) and ethno-preneural (collective) subject

(p. 141)"; the role of the intellectual property regime (as seen above) in reducing the "cultural being to inalienable rights, immaterial assets, private effects (p. 141)"; and to a global economy of difference and desire. Importantly, they highlight the consequences of this and the complicated nature of these consequences: On the one hand, these identity economies seem to have created important opportunities and possibilities for indigenous and cultural communities that have been historically marginalized and excluded. On the other hand, it is unclear to what extent these have the potential to improve the well-being of these communities and reduce power inequalities between these groups and long-standing relationships of power. With regard to the latter, they caution that culture as commodity usually means that the "big players from both inside and out" dominate and lead, creating new divisions and inequalities; and that it subjects cultural voice, meaning and belonging to "vagaries of commerce, which demands that the alienation of heritage ride a delicate balance between exoticism and banalization (p. 141)." They also point to the violent potential of all of this, through the processes that heighten politics, political organization, and political mobilization on the basis of ethnic identity and ethnic consciousness. At the same time, they underscore that these processes are not deterministic and singular – they have multiple potential trajectories and outcomes and that sometimes the "dissolution" of identity politics into commercial spaces can "turn carnage into commerce, perdition into patrimony" (p. 145). What is possible and what happens, they argue is dependent on historical contingency, including resources, geographic location, economic and political conditions that allow for greater or lesser capacity for transforming "ethnicity"/cultural material into capital (Comaroff and Comaroff 2009).

In short, cultural socialization of ethnic consciousness is currently occurring in a context where cultural markers of ethnic identity are potentially available for commodification and are subject to political contests, economic appropriation, and globalizing processes. The historical contingency in which this is happening for a given ethnic/cultural group and its contemporary socio-political-economic context are crucial in understanding what kind of cultural material is available for producing ethnic consciousness, how it is being utilized and its potential consequences (Tsing 2011; Comaroff and Comaroff 2009; Castells 2010).

Nevertheless, the commodification of culture, neoliberalism, and accelerated globalization have led to three sites in which cultural socialization processes of ethnic consciousness have heightened: tourism, development, and social media. I look next at the specific dynamics of cultural socialization and ethnic consciousness in these three sites. I conclude that the roles of the economy and social media have become major factors in how ethnic consciousness is being produced.

Tourism

Cultural socialization, as noted earlier, refers to a set of practices of social actors in fostering awareness of (and pride in) one's ancestry, origin, and cultural heritage. While tourism can and often is linked to "natural" delights of land- and seascapes, it is also an industry in which ancestry, origin, and cultural heritage are selectively (re) presented and consumed. Researchers have often focused on the political economy of tourism and its role in essentializing culture, ethnicity, and identity, as well as the objectifying gaze of tourism in which those providing the touristic experience are located in a subordinate position of power, relative to the tourist (Hannam 2002; Urry 1990). Postcolonial critiques also point to how performers, service providers, and even governments providing the touristic experience work to destabilize this apparent hierarchical power and assert their cultural identity on their own terms (Kanemasu 2013; Amoamo 2007; Hollinshead 1999).

The impact of neoliberal globalization on tourism is multifold. Urry (1990) pointed out that new technologies of communication and mobility have facilitated the increase and diversification of tourists, which in turn has increased the revenue making potential in tourism. This potential along with the commodification of culture has expanded the market of tourism providers while increasing and intensifying competition. As a result, tourist providers and workers compete to provide a unique experience while at the same time making their culture accessible to larger numbers of diverse tourists.

What are the consequences of all of this for cultural socialization and ethnic consciousness? On the one hand, there is greater flexibility in what ancestry, origin, and cultural heritage are mobilized, reproduced, and claimed. The search for providing a different experience often requires ethnic-preneurship, in which one is able to take cultural identity material and represent it as unique. This may mean that more narratives about what "makes us us (and them them)" (Comaroff and Comaroff 2009; Urry 1990). As such, the processes that normally produce dominant narratives about identity are in some ways destabilized and decentralized as a result, and the material for cultural socialization is thus shifted.

An example of this is in the context of the indigenous peoples of Bangladesh, who self-identify as jumma, where we can identify the ways that even state-based tourism can unintentionally create empowering spaces for nationally marginalized groups. While any form of political resistance by jumma peoples is violently suppressed in Bangladesh (Chakma 2010), jumma culture (or certain aspects of its culture) have been amplified and mobilized by the state and the military (Ahmed 2017; Alamgir 2017). In particular, the national agenda of expanding the tourism industry, embodied in part in the "Beautiful Bangladesh" campaign launched in the context of the 2011 World Cup of the International Cricket Council, hosted in Bangladesh, centers and privileges the jumma people in billboards, advertisements, and the type of experiences one can have (Ahmed 2017). (The largest group of non-Bangla communities in Bangladesh live in the Chittagong Hill Tracts (CHT), one of the eight administrative divisions of Bangladesh and made up of three divisions: Khagrachhari, Bandarban, and Rangamati. These groups in the CHT self-identify as jumma and are constituted by the 11 different who have lived there for generations: Chakma, Marma, Tripura, Tanchangya, Chak, Pankhoya, Mro, Bawm, Lushai, Khyang, and Khumi.) Similarly, while the lack of assimilation of jumma people into mainstream Bengali culture is seen as cause of suspicion, threat, and even deserving violent regulation by ordinary Bengalis (Chowdhury 2016), aspects of jumma culture have also become the object of entertainment, pleasure, and desire. Jumma women in "traditional" clothing, jumma people in their "natural settings," Buddhist temples in hills, "untouched hills and natural beauty" of the customary lands of the jumma peoples, jumma cultural artefacts, and jumma festivals are part of the experience package being sold by the state and the military for profit and consumed by the Bengali and foreign tourist to CHT (Ahmed 2017). Jumma cultural practices around dance, handicraft, fashion, and food are not only commodified for tourism and development in these processes; they become legitimate sites around which jumma pride can be constructed and where jumma identities can be celebrated. As such, cultural socialization processes of the jumma peoples find these practices as sites of building empowerment and confidence in their own community, especially since these can be shared with the dominant majority without threat of violence. Additionally, while unintended, the consumption of these cultural products by the Bengali majority and their use in nation branding tourism campaigns challenge the dominant Bengali-Muslim national narrative (Schendel 2001). It is important to underscore that we cannot minimize the powerful effect the lived everyday violence experienced by jumma peoples in CHT (and more broadly in Bangladesh) has on producing heighted ethnic consciousness around their cultural identities. This is particularly so when we recall the conceptualization of ethnic consciousness as constituting awareness of membership in an ethnic group (Gold and Miller 2015) and the degree to which awareness and understanding of ethnic identity shapes social and political action, including inter-ethnic relations (Gibson and Gouws 2000). However, the neoliberal globalization pressures that lead the state and military controlled tourism to make use of jumma culture creates unintended encounters, spaces, and opportunities to challenge both the narrowly defined Bengali-Muslim national identity and empower jumma identity.

Another related consequence of the search for providing a competitive and unique tourist experience is that more and more aspects of people's daily lives become identified through the lens of culture and ethnicity, heightening ethnic consciousness in the communities that become part of the touristic experience. As such, local coffee rituals (Lyon 2013), weddings (Toyota 2006), and village life become sites of tourism. Sometimes, these have taken more dramatic forms as noted in the works of Lennon and Foley (2000) on "dark tourism" and O'Rourke (1988) in "holidays from hell," where jails, abandoned coal mines, and massacre trails become part of the tourist trail. All of these are potentially important in selecting what is "our" culture for the society and communities that enter the global tourism path, either as reactions against or in privileging these narratives, spaces, and practices further (Haldrup and Larsen 2010).

On the other hand, the need to make culture accessible to the tourist has also meant that what is "ethnic" or "cultural" often starts to look similar across distinct spaces. Ancestry, origin, and heritage are remolded to ensure that the tourist can enjoy and digest identity quickly and easily. While this is done with the intention to place the tourist at ease, it has an important impact on the performing community as well: Over time with repeated performances, the performance becomes what is familiar and known to the community itself as its own, changing the material of cultural socialization in the community itself and in some ways making its own identity more similar to other "ethnic" sites elsewhere. Thus, tourism in the context of neoliberal globalization produces both heightened ethnic consciousness but also makes "ethnicity" and how it is performed, socialized, and understood similar across different spaces (Urry 1990). As such, artisans in the Chittagong Hill Tracts of Bangladesh, in Chiang Mai in Thailand, and in Bali in Indonesia are often in the process of producing weaves that are not specific to their own practices but that match some idea of ethnic handicrafts being circulated in the global tourist market. While some can critique this phenomenon in terms of how "authentic" practices are being lost, others have noted that the search for authentic itself is an elusive one and subject to who is evaluating what is authentic (Shepherd 2002). In addition, irrespective of the "origins" of a particular practice, it is possible that the "new" practice itself becomes thought of as one's own and that is the knowledge that is passed on as "our culture." Whether this is a loss to be grieved and resisted or not, what is important in the context of understanding how neoliberal globalization is impacting on cultural socialization is that a global tourism is leading to "culture" being commodified and performed in similar ways.

Development

While modernization theory tended to view Global South culture and ethnic identity as problems to be changed for development to occur, in the context of commodification of culture under neoliberal globalization, culture and ethnic identity have come to be seen as ways to support development (see examples in Chandler 2008), provide new solutions to developmental challenges (e.g., Boillat and Berkes 2013), or provide legitimacy to neoliberal strategies of development (e.g., Smits 2014). As such, ethnic identity and associated cultural material to foster that identity gain a premium, not only to create belonging, pride, and community but as a means to see how social problems can be addressed. Cultural knowledge as such has become an important competence in the development industry, and consequently, cultural socialization of such knowledge takes place in trainings, workplaces, and educational centers. In particular, the relevance of traditional and indigenous knowledge has increasingly gained ground in relation to issues of environmental justice, sustainability, and dealing with climate change (Nyong et al. 2007; Schlosberg and Carruthers 2010).

This is not to suggest that such cultural socialization is thus necessarily appropriately contextualized, nuanced, or embedded in the communities in which the knowledge will be applied; power dynamics mediate what is defined, appropriated, and utilized as cultural knowledge (Briggs 2005). However, it does implicate cultural socialization of ethnic identity has become an important element of development work, and like in tourism, ethnicity, culture, and identity matter more, thus heightening ethnic consciousness.

Another way that neoliberal globalization impacts on development with implications for cultural socialization and ethnic consciousness relates to the phenomena of nation branding as a means for economic development. Nation branding, an engine of neoliberal globalization, directly utilizes a reductive and essentialist logic, in which national identity is articulated through the logic of market relations (Jansen 2008). It is seen as a means to increase a country's economic competitiveness and enhance solidarity in the country and the self-esteem of the nation and its citizens. Development, in a neoliberal globalized world, becomes a problem of "recognition, visibility and self-esteem," ignoring all other socio-economic and political mechanisms that sustain poverty and (under)development (Browning 2016, p. 52). Scholarly literature on nation branding has examined the processes of branding that can increase a country's competitive advantage (Moilanen and Rajnisto 2009), how branding impacts on a country's soft power (van Ham 2008), and the relationship of nation branding to identity politics, citizenship, and social control of communities (Aronczyk 2008). Browning (2016) has also pointed out that nation branding has taken on a special role in development of countries in the Global South, where the reputation and image of developing countries as "problematic" leads to a lack of needed investment and, therefore, rebranding the nation would help to correct the issue. Browning (2016) criticizes this argument, highlighting that while national image may be some part of a developmental challenge, nation (re-)branding as a solution is disingenuous, playing to the needs of international branding consultants, as well as ignoring the fact that both the diagnosis and the prescription reinforce a neoliberal understanding of development. He further notes:

> ...nation branding also contributes to the subordination of states to market logics, while simultaneously shifting responsibility for development onto the poor states themselves by emphasising their need to take ownership of their national brands. Beyond this, however, nation-branding practices can also be viewed as a neo-colonial governmental technology, which empowers (largely Western) experts in establishing what constitutes relevant knowledge in a globalising world, which subordinates questions of national identity to market preferences, and which extends governance responsibilities beyond the state through the expectation that civil society will become actively engaged in branding processes. (Browning 2016, p. 52)

Despite these important critiques, nation branding is a growing phenomenon, with countries in the world creating branding commissions and hiring consultants. "Amazing Thailand," "Incredible India," and "Malaysia – Truly Asia" are all highly visible examples of this, with other less well-known ones including "Nigeria – Irrepressible Giant" and "Beautiful Bangladesh." Nation branding is more than about just creating a name for (foreign investors). A type of commercial nationalism, nation-branding implicates its populace to live and perform the brand, with citizens being asked to live the brand responsibly (Volcic and Andrejevic 2011). Consider the online ad contest Get Wildly Creative About South Africa that the International Marketing Council of South Africa launched in 2010, as a part of a major nation branding research project. In the creative brief for the contest, they note that the nation brand's should be able to:

> imprint on the minds of decision-makers, opinion leaders and trendsetters everywhere – the target audience – an image of South Africa as a desirable and distinctive place to visit,

conduct business, invest, source products, services and ideas, host gatherings and experience a unique, unrestrained blending of cultures and hospitable, friendly people. (Zooppa.com contest center)

The discourse of nation-branding for development implicates both that the nation is constituted of a particular type of individual and that its citizens need to act like that, today and for the future. For the nation-brand to work, it needs to resonate, and it needs to be (re)produced. As such, nation branding becomes a major element of cultural socialization – the campaigns of nation-branding are not only for international relations and public management of the nation's image but also to instill in its own citizenry a prescriptive identity and behavior. However, as Jansen (2008) has noted, it is both undemocratic and a "risky business," since the process of nation branding is based on the "cultural knowledge" of select individuals and their "creative" understanding and articulation of that knowledge. What is important in our discussion of cultural socialization and ethnic consciousness is that this phenomenon of nation-branding to promote development in the Global South has become an important element of cultural socialization processes that need to be examined further. Nation branding seems to also be part and parcel of the dynamic of privileging cultural frames to understand problems and opportunities, thus playing to heightening ethnic consciousness. Relatedly, it is important to ask, in the context of ethnically diverse societies, how do marginalized or minority ethnic groups relate to national brands, especially in how cultural, ethnic, and national pride are fostered. Jansen (2008) points to Umberto's concept of "semiotic guerrilla warfare" as a strategy of how branding can be both disrupted and made more democratic. Examining these kinds of discursive warfare of nation-branding at macro and micro levels would be an important site to understand how cultural socialization practices are being impacted in the context of neoliberal globalization and their consequences for ethnic consciousness in the contemporary era.

Social Media

The emergence of social media spaces including Facebook and Instagram are important sites in which cultural socialization processes play out that are both similar to "older" socialization processes by families, peers, schools, religious and community institutions, media, and the state. To the extent that these spaces replicate "real"-life networks and ties, these spaces will be sites in which offline messages about "who one is" and "who we are" will be reinforced. However, social media spaces are also distinct in several ways. Firstly, their reach in terms of the networks and agents at play go beyond the territorially bounded nature of "traditional" social actors involved in cultural socialization processes. It becomes more possible for territorially dispersed communities to create a shared sense of ethnic identity and to maintain such identity. As such diaspora, (im)migrant, and minority identities are able to maintain, reproduce, and even expand themselves (Georgiou 2006). Examining the utilization of social media among Filipino and Polish migrants to Ireland, Komito (2011) argues that:

> If the first wave of Internet applications helped extend personal networks and building bridging capital, this second wave of social media applications is, in addition, enhancing and supporting communities by contributing to bonding capital. Migrants are able to maintain contact with those who live remotely...Migrants have the opportunity [through these spaces] have the opportunity to not be so much 'connected migrants' as 'virtual migrants': their physical locality can be irrelevant for their identity. (pp. 28–29)

In a study on adolescent Russian immigrants to Israel, Elias and Lemish (2009) found that social media spaces were utilized simultaneously to learn about the new society but also to reinforce their ethnic identity and to actively claim their Russian identity, often in response to negative reactions in the host society. Social media spaces become a way to present one's ethnic identity to others, learn more about it, and create emotional connections to the ethnic community.

Secondly, the degree of control one experiences in the socialization process is expanded both in terms of externalized and internalized control. In particular, externalized control of what constitutes the narrative one is socialized in to is produced through algorithms that repeat and reinforce "more of the same," while our ability to select what we see and don't see allows us to exercise greater internalized control of the narrative as well. Relatedly, social media ICTs are unique in their ability to amplify or dilute socialization outcomes more intensively than "traditional" socializing agents because in these spaces one can actively choose to belong more tightly to one community or make it a space to escape one's ethnic community. Castells (2010) noted how social media has become a major medium of "selective social interaction and symbolic belonging (p. 37)."

Finally, recent discussions on how social media spaces are politicized and how they are potentially being utilized to amplify hate speech and impacting on election and collective violence indicate the degree to which social media spaces are playing a major role in the construction of ethnic consciousness. The most visible form of this has been in discussions on how Facebook was utilized in the most recent violence against the Rohingya population in Myanmar (Mozur 2018). In particular, to what extent do these materials in social media spaces that have been designed and crafted ("fake news," photoshopped images, edited videos) become cultural material for the socialization of ethnicity in the future? Cultural socialization material and ethnic identity have always relied on myths, where "truth" is of less importance. Social media spaces seem to have intensified how much "truth" can be brushed aside and how new realities can be created with very real consequences. The more tightly bound people's social networks in social media spaces are, these tendencies can be manipulated with dangerous consequences for how ethnic consciousness works. At the same time, researchers have noted that indigenous and other marginalized cultural groups have found social media as empowering spaces, in which "lost" traditions, stories, and communities can be reclaimed, performed, and built (Carlson 2013; Srinivasan 2006).

To what extent does the neoliberal globalization context impact on these aspects of social media's role in cultural socialization of ethnic consciousness? One way to consider this is in the rise of "influencers": The commodification of culture combined with individualization dynamics implicated by both neoliberal globalization and the functioning of social media spaces means have meant that "producing" and "performing" culture is an important way one can make a lifestyle and opinion profitable. Becoming an "influencer" on Instagram or Facebook can become a career, but it requires creative selection of "cultural materials" that are simultaneously personalized yet accessible. Consider Nas Daily (Nuseir Yassin), an Arab-Israeli vlogger who travels across the world not only "educating" his audience about "cultures" in 1-min clips but has also become an icon of what kind of positive relationships may be possible between Arabs and Israelis. His narratives and his own perspectives are followed by over six million people on Facebook and are potentially becoming part of the cultural material utilized to create a sense of pride and tell heritage stories among both Arab and Jewish Israelis. Cultural socialization material has always included heroes, leaders, other important people and their lives, actions, and ideas as part of what makes a community who they are. What is happening in the contemporary era in social media spaces is that "ordinary" (albeit often still from privileged backgrounds) individuals can become part of that cultural material now through how they can amplify their voices through social media spaces. As such, future research needs to investigate to what extent these influencers in social media spaces are becoming part of both the content of cultural socialization and shaping how "pride," "heritage," and identity conversations are occurring in communities.

Conclusion

In the above discussion, I have pointed to how cultural socialization and ethnic consciousness are being impacted in tourism, development, and social media spaces in the context of neoliberal globalization. Several processes seem to be occurring simultaneously, where culture and ethnic identity have greater value to be leveraged for economic and political gains, more and more of social and economic life are viewed through a cultural or ethnic lens, and where the disruptive power of culture/ethnicity seem to be heightened in some contexts and diluted in others. Neoliberal globalization seems to thus produce both reductive, essentialist, and violent tendencies in cultural material and ethnic consciousness and expansive, diversified, and empowering potentials of ethnic belonging. Related to Gidden's argument about how in the post-traditional context, self-identity is reflexive (Giddens 1991), neoliberal globalization seems to have created a context in which one is apparently free to choose, not only one's own self-identity but what cultural material one can utilize and how one interprets it to be who they want to be and who they choose to identify with; in fact, it seems to become almost necessary to be entrepreneurial with one's cultural heritage. How do these entrepreneurial choices of culture impact on both the content and the process of how cultural socialization of ethnicity occurs among our contemporaries and future generations? I would suggest that with the commodification and globalization of "ethnicity" and "culture," researchers looking into cultural socialization practices and what is heightening or diluting ethnic consciousness need to look beyond the social relations in the family, peers, education, and "traditional" media and examine the economy – especially in the areas of tourism, the development industry, and the performance of identity in social media.

Cross-References

▶ Ethno-cultural Symbolism and Group Identity
▶ Indigenous Rights and Neoliberalism in Latin America
▶ Media and Stereotypes
▶ The Significance of Ethno-politics in Modern States and Society

References

Ahmed HS (2017) Tourism and state violence in the Chittagong Hill Tracts of Bangladesh. Unpublished MA thesis, Electronic thesis and Dissertation Repository, University of Western Ontario, Ontario. https://ir.lib.uwo.ca/etd/4840

Alamgir F (2017) Land politics in Chittagong Hill Tracts of Bangladesh: dynamics of property, identity and authority. Doctoral thesis, University of East Anglia. https://ueaeprints.uea.ac.uk/66964/1/Alamgir_Land_Politics_in_CHT_of_Bangladesh_September_17.pdf

Amoamo M (2007) Māori tourism: image and identity – a postcolonial perspective. Ann Leis Res 10(3–4):454–474

Aronczyk M (2008) 'Living the brand': nationality, globality, and the identity strategies of nation branding consultants. Int J Commun 2:25

Banton M (2014) Ethnic and racial consciousness. Routledge, New York

Boillat S, Berkes F (2013) Perception and interpretation of climate change among Quechua farmers of Bolivia: indigenous knowledge as a resource for adaptive capacity. Ecol Soc 18(4):21. https://doi.org/10.5751/ES-05894-180421

Bowles P (2005) Globalization and neoliberalism: a taxonomy and some implications for anti-globalization. Can J Dev Stud/Revue canadienne d'études du développement 26(1):67–87

Brenner N, Peck J, Theodore N (2010) Variegated neoliberalization: geographies, modalities, pathways. Global Netw 10(2):182–222

Briggs J (2005) The use of indigenous knowledge in development: problems and challenges. Prog Dev Stud 5(2):99–114

Browning CS (2016) Nation branding and development: poverty panacea or business as usual? J Int Relat Dev 19(1):50–75

Canessa A (2014) Conflict, claim and contradiction in the new 'indigenous' state of Bolivia. Crit Anthropol 34(2):153–173

Carlson B (2013) The 'new frontier': emergent indigenous identities and social media. In M. Harris, M. Nakata & B. Carlson (Eds.), *The Politics of Identity: Emerging Indigeneity* (pp. 147–168). Sydney: University of Technology Sydney E-Press

Castells M (2010) The power of identity: the information age: economy, society and culture, vol II. Blackwell Publishing, Sussex

Chakma B (2010) Structural roots of violence in the Chittagong Hill Tracts. Econ Polit Wkly 45(12):19–21

Chandler RM (2008) Artisans and the marketing of ethnicity: globalization, indigenous identity and nobility principle in micro-enterprise development. Ethn Stud Rev 31(1):10–18

Chowdhury TM (2016) Indigenous identity in South Asia: making claims in the colonial Chittagong Hill Tracts. Routledge advances in South Asian studies. Taylor and Francis, London

Comaroff JL, Comaroff J (2009) *Ethnicity, Inc*. The University of Chicago Press, Chicago

Coombe RJ (2016) The knowledge economy and its cultures: neoliberal technologies and Latin American reterritorializations. HAU: J Ethnogr Theory 6(3):247–275

DeHart M (2010) Ethnic entrepreneurs: identity and development politics in Latin America. Stanford University Press, Stanford

Elias N, Lemish D (2009) Spinning the web of identity: the roles of the internet in the lives of immigrant adolescents. New Media Soc 11(4):533–551

Escobar A (2010) Latin America at a crossroads: alternative modernizations, post-liberalism or post-development? Cult Stud 24(1):1–65

Georgiou M (2006) Diaspora, identity and the media: diasporic transnationalism and mediated spatialities. Hampton Press, Cresskill

Gibson JL, Gouws A (2000) Social identities and political intolerance: linkages within the South African mass public. Am J Polit Sci 44:278–292

Giddens A (1991) Modernity and self-identity. Self and society in the Late Modern Age. Polity Press, Cambridge

Gold SJ, Miller P (2015) Race and ethnic consciousness. In: The Blackwell encyclopedia of sociology. https://doi.org/10.1002/9781405165518.wbeosr004.pub2

Haldrup M, Larsen J (2010) Tourism, performance and the everyday. Routledge, London

Hannam K (2002) Tourism and development I: globalization and power. Prog Dev Stud 2:227–234

Holder CL, Corntassel JJ (2002) Indigenous peoples and multicultural citizenship: bridging collective and individual rights. Hum Rights Q 24(1):126–151

Hollinshead K (1999) Surveillance of the worlds of tourism: Foucault and the eye-of-power. Tour Manag 20(1):7–23

Hughes D, Johnson DJ (2001) Correlates in children's experiences of parents' racial socialization behaviors. J Marriage Fam 63:981–995

Hughes D, Rodriguez J, Smith EP, Johnson DJ, Stevenson HC, Spicer P (2006) Parents' ethnic-racial socialization practices: a review of research and directions for future study. Dev Psychol 42(5):747

Jansen SC (2008) Designer nations: neo-liberal nation branding-Brand Estonia. Soc Ident 14(1):121–142

Kanemasu Y (2013) A national pride or a colonial construct? Touristic representation and the politics of Fijian identity construction. Soc Ident 19(1):71–89

Komito L (2011) Social media and migration: virtual community 2.0. J Am Soc Inf Sci Technol 62(6):1075–1086

Lennon J, Foley M (2000) Dark tourism. Continuum, London

Lyon S (2013) Coffee tourism and community development in Guatemala. Hum Organ 72(3):188–198

Moilanen T, Rainisto S (2009) How to brand nations, cities and destinations. A planning book for place branding. Palgrave MacMillan, pp 65–75

Mozur P (2018) A genocide incited on Facebook, with posts from Myanmar's military. The New York Times, 15 Oct. https://www.nytimes.com/2018/10/15/technology/myanmar-facebook-genocide.html

Nyong A, Adesina F, Elasha BO (2007) The value of indigenous knowledge in climate change mitigation and adaptation strategies in the African Sahel. Mitig Adapt Strateg Glob Chang 12(5):787–797

O'Rourke PJ (1988) Holidays in hell. Atlantic Monthly Review, New York

Rex J (2013) Race, colonialism and the city. Routledge, London

Schendel WV (2001) Who speaks for the nation? Nationalist rhetoric and the challenge of cultural pluralism in Bangladesh. In: van Schendel W, Zurcher EJ (eds) Identity politics in Central

Asia and the Muslim world: nationalism, ethnicity and labour in the twentieth century. I.B. Tauris Publishers, London, pp 107–147

Scher PW (2011) Heritage tourism in the Caribbean: the politics of culture after neoliberalism. Bull Lat Am Res 30(1):7–20

Schlosberg D, Carruthers D (2010) Indigenous struggles, environmental justice, and community capabilities. Glob Environ Polit 10(4):12–35

Shepherd R (2002) Commodification, culture and tourism. Tour Stud 2(2):183–201

Smits K (2014) The neoliberal state and the uses of indigenous culture. Nationalism Ethn Polit 20(1):43–62

Srinivasan R (2006) Indigenous, ethnic and cultural articulations of new media. Int J Cult Stud 9(4):497–518

Tilly C (2015) Identities, boundaries and social ties. Routledge, New York

Toyota M (2006) Consuming images: young female Japanese tourists in Bali. In: Meethan K, Anderson A, Miles S (eds) Tourism, consumption and representation. CABI, Wallingford, pp 158–177

Tsing AL (2011) Friction: an ethnography of global connection. Princeton University Press, Princeton

Urry J (1990) The 'consumption' of tourism. *Sociology* 24(1):23–35

Van Ham P (2008) Place branding: the state of the art. Ann Am Acad Pol Soc Sci 616(1):126–149

Vermeulen H, Govers C (1997) From political mobilization to the politics of consciousness. In: The politics of ethnic consciousness. Palgrave Macmillan, London, pp 1–30

Volcic Z, Andrejevic M (2011) Nation branding in the era of commercial nationalism. Int J Commun 5:21

Wang Y, Benner AD, Kim SY (2015) The cultural socialization scale: assessing family and peer socialization toward heritage and mainstream cultures. Psychol Assess 27(4):1452

Historical Memory and Ethnic Myths

Cindy Zeiher

Abstract
The tracking of historical events and memory serve as affective pivots for myth to be cultivated and to thrive throughout generations. From a Freudian perspective, this chapter tracks selected traumatic events such as the Holocaust, and discusses how the historicizing process operates in order for us to have a coherent memory of the past, even of our recent past, through invoking repetitious patterns. Also discussed is the notion of recognized authority, who in speaking to the past, is able to pinpoint particular historical agitations and witnesses in order to write a logical history from which myths emanate.

Keywords
History · Authority · Memory · Myth · Ethnicity · Trauma · Freud

The mythology of a nation doesn't emerge by the history of a nation; by means of a mythology of a nation, the history of a nation is composed. (Berk 2016, p. 70)

We cannot fall out of this world. It is a feeling, then, of being indissolubly bound up with and belonging to the whole of the world outside of oneself. (Freud 1899, p. 2)

In the ancient Greek myth, Pygmalion falls in love with a statue he has made. At the festival of Aphrodite, he reveals his desire that the statue becomes a real woman and much to his delight it does. Although this myth seems innocuously romantic,

---

C. Zeiher (✉)
University of Canterbury, Christchurch, New Zealand
e-mail: cindy.zeiher@canterbury.ac.nz

© The Author(s), under exclusive license to Springer Nature Singapore Pte Ltd. 2019
S. Ratuva (ed.), *The Palgrave Handbook of Ethnicity*,
https://doi.org/10.1007/978-981-13-2898-5_7

nevertheless the reason for Pygmalion's desire is revealing in the context of this being a reaction against his boredom with the company of women surrounding him. His fantasy that this sculpture representing his ideal version of beauty be a real woman overshadows his disgust for the many women including the prostitutes he consorts with. His fantasized ideal of a silent and beautiful woman reflecting the female virtues most important to him is the embodiment of his myth.

Myths play an important even critical role in the constitution of social identities and cultural heritage. This is because we are all, both individually and collectively meaning-seekers. However, the function of myth is much more than this: myth plays a key role not only in the making of history but also in the continuation of legacy through the geography and politics of memory. Myths and mythmaking manifest variously in human culture which itself, according to Girard, emanates from religion (2010, p. 123). Roland Barthes contends that myth is not a concept but rather a system of speech; thus mythology derives from schematic movement between Saussurean signs and signifiers (1957). That we can believe in the possible allows us to reject or at least reconcile with the often-traumatic actualities of life which are ironically, what led to myth being imagined in the first place. For Pygmalion, the statue embodying his fantasy, thanks to the intervention of Aphrodite, triumphs his real life. Although on one level just a myth, this portrayal of desire in terms of fantasy made real resonates even today. In his *Interpretation of Dreams*, Freud considers how we might relate the occurrences of the past to the present and the future, particularly when these events are horrific or traumatic; how might we arrange them so that they become liveable in the present? In order to situate ourselves in history, we cannot privilege its claimed facts over cultivation of the imaginary through myth. Such a historicizing process must take place in order for us to have a coherent memory of the past, even of our recent past, and may span several generations through invoking repetitious patterns. Alongside this there must be in place a recognized authority who in speaking to the past is able to pinpoint particular historical agitations and witnesses in order to write a logical history.

Between each historical event lies a lapsus manifesting as dimly perceived continuity which is necessarily presupposed by the event. We cannot fully know history and everything which constitutes it either as event or continuity, and organizing these as history involves both subjective and collective interpretation. This process renders a history which may also be absorbed into historical memory as particularly societal groups identify with certain events, both actual and imaginary, as a way of transmitting narrative. This identification includes oral histories, storytelling, artifacts, collective memories, and superstitions. These combine in maintaining social, cultural, and political bonds as well as providing laws and prohibitions on the nuances of everyday life. Thus, history provides the basis to an ongoing historical praxis of collective destiny. As history continues to be written by different authorities, it inevitably presents a range of interpretations and perspectives. The problem with this positivist approach to history is that not only events but *everything speaks*, often all at once and changing all the time insofar as history can never be laid to rest. Freud in part addresses this problem by insisting that it is

4 Historical Memory and Ethnic Myths

precisely because *everything speaks* that no single history or historian can have precedence and that all of them are potentially significant.

In his reading of Freud's elements of mythology, Rancière highlights that *everything speaks* in terms of the interdependence of science and myth which structures ethnic identity (2009, p. 35):

> [Freud] gives the insignificant details of the prose of the world their power of poetic signification. In the topography of the plaza, the physiognomy of a façade, the pattern or wear of a piece of clothing, the chaos of a pile of merchandise or trash, he recognises the elements of a mythology. He makes the true history of a society, an age, or a people visible in the figures of this mythology, foreshadowing individual or collective destiny. *Everything speaks* is the abolition of the hierarchies of the representative order [emphasis in original].

Certainly, ethnic identities are often associated with myths both past and present in being constructed by us through an imaginative process which allows us to capture moments of belief in matters beyond the purely empirical. There is something atemporal about this process of and investment in mythmaking, as is also the case with cultural and ethnic identities: each gives us clues as to the form and substance of the other. In this way we can situate myth as an often extraordinary or supernatural story which explains a social, cultural, or natural occurrence. Defining a myth requires attention to its various constituents: its linear narrative reveals a protagonist who for the most part has the role of serving the actions or values of the narrative, for example, Narcissus's preoccupation with his reflection is a warning against loneliness, vanity, and self-absorption. Freud's 1914 essay, *On Narcissism*, considers the myth of Narcissus as one which belongs to us all in that ultimately, we are all strangers (or, rather, strange objects) to ourselves; therefore we should be aware of falling in love with ourselves. Both secular and sacred myths have a function additional to that of transmitting folklore or explaining human foibles. Myths created by recent history as a result of particularly traumatic events which confound us allow the interrogation of pervasive and troubling ways of thinking whose outcomes we don't want repeated. Thus, myth has the function of giving free reign to our imagination but within limits so that the rational element of the imaginary can be harnessed. Myth conveys a cultural worldview, both metaphorical and actual, and facilitates the establishment of identities secured in history. The medium of all myth is language which helps order the world and thereby create history.

E.H. Carr's *What is History?* (1961) helps us in establishing what constitutes a historical fact. For Carr the historical fact is also a cult, and although not referencing Freud, he considers the historical fact to be something of a fetish in that it becomes an object infused with the enjoyment of meaning-making. Here he is problematizing traditional empirical historical method through insisting that in studying the facts of the past, we need to study the historian (p. 23):

> Study the historian before you begin to study the facts. This is, after all, not very abstruse. It is what is already done by the intelligent undergraduate who, when recommended to read a work by that great scholar Jones of St. Jude's, goes round to a friend at St. Jude's to ask what

sort of chap Jones is, and what bees he has in his bonnet. When you read a work of history, always listen out for the buzzing. If you can detect none, either you are tone deaf or your historian is a dull dog. The facts are really not at all like fish on the fishmonger's slab. They are like fish swimming about in a vast and sometimes inaccessible ocean; and what the historian catches will depend, partly on chance, but mainly on what part of the ocean he chooses to fish in and what tackle he chooses to use – these two factors being, of course, determined by the kind of fish he wants to catch. By and large, the historian will get the kind of facts he wants. History means interpretation.

Thus for Carr there is no such thing as an objective history, let alone an objective fact. Rather, ideas are compiled and collated and, in this way, provide the answer to Carr's question which serves as the title of his book: "a continuous process of interaction between the historian and his facts, an unending dialogue between the past and the present" (p. 30). Although he acknowledges the importance of the social sphere from which the individual is shaped and asserts that we are, as individuals, by-products of history, in this theorization of history, only certain people or groups shine or are privileged as embodying historical facts. For example, he cites Lenin as one who because he shaped social forces exemplifies an historical fact. Žižek agrees, observing however that Lenin's actions on his own authority did not take into account factors which we today would consider essential (2017, p. xiv):

> Not only was Lenin understandably blind to many of the problems that are now central to contemporary life (ecology, struggles for emancipated sexualities, etc) but also his brutal political practice is totally out of sync with current democratic sensitivities, his vision of the new society as a centralised industrial system run by the state is simply irreverent, etc. Instead of desperately attempting to salvage the authentic Leninist core from the Stalinist alluvium, would it not be more advisable to forget Lenin and return to Marx?

In attempting to reconcile with the failed Leninist project, Žižek asks of us to do something provocative regarding the telos of history: notwithstanding that history repeats itself, reinterpret the facts at hand in order to gain insight into the present. Here unlike Carr, Žižek is not troubled by bias; indeed he embraces it as a productive method which he claims we unconsciously employ anyway. Contradiction, bias, and cherry-picking are parts of the historical method and always have been. For Žižek the true challenge lies in what we choose to highlight and how we interpret it, a challenge emanating from Aristotle's position that history is no more than something that might have happened and whose cultivation constrains the mind's faculties. For Aristotle, images projected by imagination and memory, even if opaque, hold more resonance.

Here we come to the importance of historical memory. As Bonnet puts it (unpaginated):

> The process [of cultivating memory] went something like this: it began with a real or imagined incident or event that was worth repeating, something so intriguing that we were compelled to repeat it. It was passed along by word of mouth, from person to person and from generation to generation until it had been told and retold millions of times and existed in a hundred different versions around the world.

With this framing of historical memory, feminist scholars in particular will be familiar. They point out that history has been written largely by men as social reproduction serving the masculine enterprise of retaining privilege and power in the political, social, intellectual, and public domains. In such history women may be left out, which is certainly in contradiction to historical-sociological perspectives. Even if women do appear, they may be cast as compensatory, for example, the necessity for women's labor during wartime, on top of their ongoing unpaid and sometime unacknowledged domestic labor. The limited consideration to women's history has compromised their placement as historical fact and facilitated subsequent myths about women, their labor and care, to thrive in men's histories. However, this is not necessarily as intentional as Calvi states in her essay on Jewish women factory workers in early twentieth-century New York (1990). Rather, documents from the time were poorly kept and untrustworthy and even include stories from women who, under pressure and still dependent on male family members, recount positive experiences of working in overcrowded factories with poor conditions and pay. The myth that working women at this time and later were emancipated ignores its origin in the necessity of self-preservation. Paid work does not necessarily lead to emancipation, argues Calvi, citing as a testament of history the discordance women of the time suffered, which is overshadowed by the accumulation of other historical events (p. 202):

> The condition of the great majority of working women, indeed, as regards skills and efficiency, is probably worse now than that of their grandmothers who were not wage-earners. Before the introduction of machinery women were, probably on the whole, as compared with men workers, more skilful and efficient than they are to-day... Gradually however, as girls have been forced on the one hand by machinery... and on the other hand by divisions of labour... to undertake tasks which have no direct interests to them as prospective wives and mothers, there has grown up a class of women workers in whose lives there is contradiction and internal discord. Their work has become merely a means of furnishing food, shelter and clothing during a waiting period which has, meanwhile, gradually lengthened out as the average age of marriage increased. Their work no longer fits in with their ideals and has lost its charm.

Both paid and unpaid domestic work were far from being privileged, and female paid labor was seen as merely supplementary to a possibly failing domestic circumstance which required women to work because more money was needed. Factory work did not accord with the prevailing essentialized view of women, yet it coexisted with the profile of Calvi's "mythical woman/mother" (p. 206) which retains motherhood as the woman's profession *par excellence*. Thus, factory work, arguably the bedrock of political consciousness and trade unionism, held ambivalent emancipatory power, in that it had the potential both to strip women of their traditional roles and also men of their historical masculine heroic status. The upholding of myth can be said to reside in the politics of labor.

The intersection of ethnicity and myth is explicitly stated in the case of matriarchal societies. In their field studies of the Chinese *Na* tribe, Hua (1997) and Godelier (2004) describe how this provincial minority functions without marriage, husbands, fathers, or even father figures. Lineage is passed on via the mother whose authority determines each household. Sexual relationships between men and women are based simply on the premise that society needs to reproduce itself; women and men freely engage in various simultaneous sexual relationships. What is most interesting about this tribe is that its operative pragmatics stem from the mythical component of procreation which sustains the community. Sperm is not recognized as essential to conception, its function being merely to water in a pre-existing fetus deposited by the goddess, *Abaogdu*. Thus, the child does not belong solely to the mother. Similarly, a tribe on the Trobriand Islands, off the east coast of New Guinea, practices matrilineal and matriarchal customs which involve symbolically limiting the man's role in child-rearing. Subjective existence for these two tribes lies in the singularity of specific events, bodily located within women's experiences and which in turn structure the ongoing social bond of the community. There is no practical link between sex and pregnancy (Weiner 1988). This is how the human reality of the tribes is symbolized and where their cultural law is legitimized.

Belonging to a particular ethnicity requires that one identifies, even if ambivalently, with one's cultural history, including its mythologies, superstitions, and shared nuances of behavior. To claim a particular ethnic signifier for oneself serves as public recognition of a personal identification. Being in these ways either too constricting or too broad, ethnicity is problematic for the social sciences, notwithstanding that the kernel of ethnic identity is always an agreement between ourselves as individuals and the history we feel compelled to possess. What is most important regarding these two studies is that historical memory is made by women who have the authority to signify ethnicity via the transmission of myth.

Implicit in Carr's theorization of history is the important question, who writes history to which we feel able to belong? Here we are faced with an interesting conundrum. The authority figure in history may or may not inspire us, for example, Žižek's account of Lenin's incapacity and blindness is a cautionary tale for all who aspire to make history. The problem posed by history lies not only in method as Carr and Žižek rightly assert but also in the will to keep particular past memories symbolically alive in the present. If we can't remember, then how do we piece together fragments of history which don't always align? Here psychoanalysis provides the solution that we act out in contradictory ways. We contend with conflicting narratives which together form the foundation for multiple social identities. In his history of the *bourgeoisie*, Moretti (2013) notes that like workers in the factories, the French *bourgeoisie* of the mid-1700s, unsettled by turbulence and social change, bolstered their social identities by championing the fight against inequality while nevertheless retaining their enjoyment of continuing regular privilege. Moretti contends that the *bourgeoisie* held on to this regularity, that is, the myth of sameness, in order to create a narrative of solidarity in the face of the uncertainties posed by capitalist innovation.

How to cultivate an authority of individual and collective identities is an ongoing question for the human sciences. Kojève maintains that authority reveals itself in a typology consisting of consciousness and behavior; we must for the common good remain critical regarding how authority is legitimized and not accept the facts or structures of history without inquiring who the authority is and why its version of history has been cast in such a way. Kojève describes the nature of authority thus (2014, p. 7):

> There is Authority only where there is (real, or at least possible) movement, change, and action. Authority is held only over that which can 'react', that is to say, that which can change according to what or who represents ('embodies', realises or exercises) Authority. And quite obviously, Authority belongs to the person who can effect change and not to the one subjected to change: Authority is essentially active and not *passive* [emphasis in original] (Kojève insists on writing Authority with a capital – this can be interpreted as a pun on the word, *capital* as being reliant on Authority as an essence necessary to circulate within its own logic).

Here authority is a social relation relying on an agent which acts on behalf of people. This relation manifests in our use of objects, especially technologies, and via our shared, often-traumatic experiences which are inescapably intertwined and mediated through language. Nevertheless Kojève argues, we don't necessarily need to *do* anything in order to exert authority, but there must be at least an intention to act authoritatively.

How does Kojève's account of authority relate to myth and history? If we follow Kojève's main influence, Hegel, then we must conclude that myth too is a theory, a sort of discursive revelation of method. Myth presents a narrative which those of other myths might negate. Myths may speak to each other as adversaries or may engage in dialogue and discussion. Here, in the collision of opinions we can witness how every truth reveals its own error, and is this not the very conundrum of history, that it contends with itself as an inadequacy?

Jankélévitch addresses this inadequacy by refusing to propagate ethnic myths which may accompany history. For Jankélévitch, not only the Nazi's but the entire German people were culpable for the Holocaust (1996). Influenced by Freud and Bergson and rejecting German philosophy, Jankélévitch contributed influential texts on forgiveness, the apology, politics, and social nuances such as charm and grace. For Jankélévitch an essential part of forgiveness is that memory must be maintained and not erased by it. Through Jankélévitch's stand on German culpability, we can link memory, myth, and ethnicity as a triad constructing history via subjective trauma, in which it is essential that memory must be maintained over forgiveness: "Nothing could be more evident: in order to forgive, it is necessary to remember" (1967, p. 56). When history is a narrative of hysteria, which in its psychoanalytical sense constantly questions that nature of existence, there is always an "other" with which to contend. For Jankélévitch this other is not only the Nazi's; all Germans occupy his radical alterity, thereby providing the discursive thread from which he can approach the present via the past. Jankélévitch attempts to make a cut in history and in so doing identifies with the myth that all Germans are culpable. Of course, this is certainly untrue – not *all* German people supported the Nazi's, and some indeed paid the price for being outspoken against them. However, that *all* Germans are culpable is a myth which has arguably been taken up by the German people and colonized as a national myth in order to exclude the possibility of a future Holocaust.

In this way myth has a rhetorical function which serves to simplify and obfuscate the inconsistencies of actuality. For its part the German government has taken responsibility by enacting the law against genocide.

In *Totem and Taboo* (1913), Freud addresses symbolic laws protecting people which must be universally enforced as the regulation of culture. Levi-Strauss's 1949 studies of cultural regulation in South America and Australia focus on social practices in which women, property, and objects are valued and exchanged; he observes how in the overlap of nature with culture (p. 56), "[a] man or a woman separated from his/her biological family in order to be united with a member of another clan assures perpetuation of the species."

He further observes these people are unconsciously operating within the law, and although they know the regulations of, for example, marriage, exchanging animals, and so on, they may necessarily understand that their role is to maintain social bonds. For all of us, the laws of cultural regulation make unconscious knowledge conscious and enable us to handle trauma and perhaps also guilt. Psychoanalytically speaking guilt is a symptom through which we address lack and thereby come to terms with life which would otherwise be unliveable. The symptom offers a sort of enjoyment but within limits; it must be confronted in warding off the unbearable. This is arguably the reality of the unconscious: it serves to protect memory.

In the not too distant future, all remaining Holocaust survivors will have died. Nevertheless, we still have these people among us to testify what happened. We have their collective stories, the fragments of their experiences, at least those they are able to articulate. Alongside these stories are preserved artifacts: the concentrations camps, published Nazi propaganda, film footage, historian's commentary, and so on. In all this we are determined to preserve memory of these horrific events so that they never happen again, but insofar as genocide still occurs, particularly in countries that are experiencing civil unrest, we have failed in our efforts to learn from the past. The embarrassingly honest saying about German guilt – that there is no guilt quite like that of Germany – is perhaps explained by its combination of morality, guilt by association, bystander guilt, and, as Jaspers calls it (1965), metaphysical guilt. Arguably within this unique guilt permeating post war, Germany lurks the function of the confessional including the fantasies of forgiveness and even of self-justification. Such guilt preserves historical memory of traumatic events in a specific way, namely, in terms of political as much as social affect. It would be dangerous to relinquish the Holocaust in favor of a history made more palatable by the inclusion of forgiveness because it is precisely the hysteria of history which we rely upon to not only record the historical event but also to instill a discipline of history enabling recognition of one's self in it. This in turn provides evidence that it is particular historical facts, including myths and affect, which allow a constitution of the subject.

Here historical and social memories are inextricably bound within the collective construction and privileging of narratives concerning particular historical events. For example, although the infamous Nazi book burnings were undertaken for reasons of social purification and in order to reconstruct historical memory by eliminating texts ranging from Marx to Jack London, nevertheless the effect of this attempted historical erasure was the complete opposite of its intention. Ironically, in casting

4 Historical Memory and Ethnic Myths

these texts as subversive, political authority helped to preserve their legacy. Here the politics of historical memory, in attempting to construct identities in a particular way, merely serve to reconstruct them in way which is self-defeating.

There is a difference between memory, the capacity to store experiences, and recollection, the process of recalling them (Nikulin 2015). Historical memory, being the uptake of what is already known, accepted and enforced functions as a symbolic law wherein the events of history are transmitted as lived history, as something we can identify with. Such a history manifests an ethnic dimension in that it can be passed from generation to generation among people belonging to a social group having a specific location, language, and culture. Thus through ethnicity the past is adopted involuntarily. Identification with a particular ethnicity is to declare recognition of its unique transmission of history, including myth. History and memory enabling connection to one's past, together with certain rules and expectations, are what constitute ethnicity.

In *Civilisation and its Discontents* (1930), Freud describes the feeling of connection with the past as an "oceanic" feeling akin to "oneness with the universe" (p. 7), where the past, the present, and the future synchronize to produce a sense of belonging, both for oneself and others. His account of Rome as the "Eternal City" eloquently illustrates this (pp. 5–6):

> This brings us to the more general problem of preservation in the sphere of the mind. The subject has hardly been studied as yet; but it is so attractive and important that we may be allowed to turn our attention to it for a little, even though our excuse is insufficient. Since we overcame the error of supposing that the forgetting we are familiar with signified a destruction of the memory-trace — that is, its annihilation — we have been inclined to take the opposite view, that in mental life nothing which has once been formed can perish — that everything is somehow preserved and that in suitable circumstances (when, for instance, regression goes back far enough) it can once more be brought to light. Let us try to grasp what this assumption involves by taking an analogy from another field. We will choose as an example the history of the Eternal City. Historians tell us that the oldest Rome was the Roma Quadrata, a fenced settlement on the Palatine. Then followed the phase of the Septimontium) a federation of the settlements on the different hills; after that came the city bounded by the Servian wall; and later still, after all the transformations during the periods of the republic and the early Caesars, the city which the Emperor Aurelian surrounded with his walls. We will not follow the changes which the city went through any further, but we will ask ourselves how much a visitor, whom we will supposed to be equipped with the most complete historical and topographical knowledge, may still find left of these early stages in the Rome of to-day. Except for a few gaps, he will see the wall of Aurelian almost unchanged. In some places he will be able to find sections of the Servian wall where they have been excavated and brought to light. If he knows enough — more than present-day archaeology does — he may perhaps be able to trace out in the plan of the city the whole course of that wall and the outline of the Roma Quadrata. Of the buildings which once occupied this ancient area he will find nothing, or only scanty remains, for they exist no longer. The best information about Rome in the republican era would only enable him at the most to point out the sites where the temples and public buildings of that period stood. Their place is now taken by ruins, but not by ruins of themselves but of later restorations made after fires or destruction. It is hardly necessary to remark that all these remains of ancient Rome are found dovetailed into the jumble of a great metropolis which has grown up in the last few centuries since the Renaissance. There is certainly not a little that is ancient still

buried in the soil of the city or beneath its modern buildings. This is the manner in which the past is preserved in historical sites like Rome.

In connecting the artifacts and the physicality of the great Eternal City with the hustle and bustle of the present, Freud is claiming that history is more than just ruins insofar as wistful contemplation of them invokes an altogether wider dimension, namely, oceanic worldview of life. Such a worldview is sustained through our obligation to language in conveying that what was past is still ever present. What happens during this transmission constitutes and sustains the oceanic feeling as symbolic recognition of what lingers in memory. Yet we cannot be separated from symbolic recognition because our relation to the other is maintained as the promise of a meaning to come.

We are constantly yet unconsciously entwined in the production of myth. Regarding guilt it is usually myth which surfaces to confront trauma and thereby perhaps enable a liveable alternative which does not forget. In this way myth and trauma provide us with a past which is at least usable if not entirely liveable. Arguably this is what Žižek and Jankélévitch are claiming; that we need to constantly stir up the past in order to figure out the present.

Enabling the social bond is a greater continuity and interdependence between historical memory, myth, and ethnicity than might appear. Sociability relies on the recognition, cultivation, and transmission of language, and memory is more than just a cognitive faculty; it is what grounds the structure of subjectivity. Historical memory cultivates the historicity of myth within contemporary manifestations of subjective ethnicity.

Cross-References

▶ Cultural Socialization and Ethnic Consciousness
▶ Ethnic Politics and Global Justice
▶ Ethnicity and Class Nexus: A Philosophical Approach

References

Barthes R (1957) Mythologies. Les Lettres Nouvelles, Paris
Berk F (2016) The role of mythology as a cultural identity and a cultural heritage: the case of phrygian mythology. Procedia – Soc Behav Sci 225(14):67–73
Bonnett J (unpaginated) How the great myths and legends were created. From Writers Store. https://www.writersstore.com/how-the-great-myths-and-legends-were-created/
Calvi G (1990) Women in the factory: women's networks and social life in America (1900–1915). In: Muir E, Ruggiero G (eds) Sex and gender in historical perspective. The John Hopkins University Press, Baltimore, pp 200–234
Carr EH (1961) What is history? University of Cambridge Press, Cambridge, UK
Freud S (1899) Interpretation of dreams. Macmillan, Austria
Freud S (1913) Totem and taboo. Beacon Press, Boston

Freud S (1914) On narcissism. The standard edition of the complete psychological works of Sigmund Freud, volume XIV (1914–1916): on the history of the psycho-analytic movement, papers on metapsychology and other works. Hogarth Press, London
Freud S (1930) Civilisation and its discontents. Penguin, London
Girard R (2010) Kültürün Kökenleri (trans: Ayten Er). Dost Publishers, Ankara
Godelier M (2004) Metamorphoses of kinship. Verso, London
Hua C (1997) A society without fathers: the Na of China. MIT Press
Jankélévitch V (1967) Forgiveness. University of Chicago Press, Chicago
Jankélévitch V (1996) Should we pardon them? Crit Inq 22(3):552–572
Jaspers K (1965) The question of German guilt. Piper Verlag, München
Kojève A (2014) The notion of authority. Verso, London
Levi-Strauss C (1949) The elementary structures of kinship. Beacon Press, Boston
Moretti F (2013) The bourgeois. Verso, London
Nikulin D (2015) Memory in ancient philosophy. In: Nikulin D (ed) Memory: A history. Oxford University Press, Oxford
Rancière J (2009) The aesthetic unconscious. Polity, Cambridge, MA
Weiner A (1988) The Trobrianders of Papua New Guinea. Harcourt Brace Jovanovich, Orlando
Žižek S (2017) Lenin. Verso, London

Indian Identity in South Africa

5

Kathryn Pillay

Contents

Introduction	78
Community and Belonging	80
Isolation and Exclusiveness	82
Fixed Identity	86
Conclusion	87
Cross-References	90
References	90

Abstract

After the first democratic election took place in 1994, a commitment was made, by the ANC led government, to "nonracialism" based on a Constitution, adopted in 1996, which was inclusive of all who lived in the country. This chapter argues that even though the democratic state acknowledges South Africans of Indian descent as part of the national discourse, it nevertheless still perpetuates the notion of essential "differences" between "peoples" which originated in colonialism was entrenched further after the formation of the Union and legitimized through various policies during apartheid. This continuation of such "race" classification in legislated and bureaucratic form, conflates race and ethnicity, and ensures racialization and "race thinking," which is evident in self-perceptions and the perceptions of "others." The argument is demonstrated by examining the role of the South African state historically in the maintenance of racial categories which in turn allow "Indians" to be stereotyped, homogenized, and labeled as a separate and distinct group. This formal process ultimately results in the confirmed perception of them as "a people" or "community" with fixed and essentialized identities and ultimately "belonging" to another country, to which they

K. Pillay (✉)
University of KwaZulu-Natal, Durban, South Africa
e-mail: pillaykat@ukzn.zc.za

© The Author(s), under exclusive license to Springer Nature Singapore Pte Ltd. 2019
S. Ratuva (ed.), *The Palgrave Handbook of Ethnicity*,
https://doi.org/10.1007/978-981-13-2898-5_9

could *easily* "return," as evidenced by calls to "go home" echoed at various points in time during the post-1994 democratic era. Processes of othering and anti-"Indian" sentiment, reminiscent of the political eras prior to democracy, persist therefore in public and popular discourse in contemporary South African society and are exposed at various junctures.

Keywords
Indian · Race · South Africa · Classification · Xenophobia · Identity

Introduction

Indians were initially brought to southern Africa to work as indentured laborers in the colony of Natal in 1860. However a "second stream of migrants" followed after under the colony's ordinary immigration laws (Mesthrie 1997, 100). Although they were mainly Muslim and Hindu traders predominantly from the Gujarat area, there were some Christian Indians, including teachers, interpreters, catechists, and traders who also migrated to southern Africa (Mesthrie 1997, 100). This second wave of migrants were referred to as "passenger Indians" as they paid for their own journey to South Africa.

Just over half of the Indian laborers that travelled aboard the Truro (the first ship to transport indentured laborers from India to Natal in 1860) stayed on in South Africa after they had served out their indenture, while the rest boarded the Red Riding Hood, which was the first ship to carry repatriated Indians back to India in 1871 (Motwani et al. 1993). The Indian repatriates aboard this ship carried with them stories of misery, as they complained of beatings and unfair treatment by their "colonial masters." This resulted in the tightening of immigration control laws by the British Government of India (Ebr.-Vally 2001). The colonial authorities in Natal, and thereafter the South African government (after 1910), frequently used the threat of repatriation as a form of intimidation, and to create insecurity among the indentured laborers, as they were reminded of their constant impermanence in the country. This system of indentured labor, however, continued until 1911 when a resolution was passed in India, preventing the further recruitment of indentured labor for Natal, and the last sailing vessel, the Umlazi, arrived in Natal in July 1911 carrying the final group of indentured laborers.

With the arrival of these indentured laborers, a new era of racialization began in southern Africa, as until the beginning of the twentieth century all people who were not considered to be "European" or "black" were regarded as "colored" (Christopher 2002, 2009; Erasmus 2007; Maré 2011). By as late as 1950, the National Party (NP) was still hopeful that the descendants of these Indian immigrants who had been born in South Africa would "return" to India, and so they were still classified as "coloreds" for the purposes of population enumeration. According to Christopher (2002, 405), the classification "colored" was a broad umbrella category which included "Indian, Chinese, Cape Malay and Griqua subgroups in addition to the basic Cape Coloured group." At that stage the NP together with its supporters attempted actively to demonstrate why "Indians" could not be integrated into South Africa or become South African citizens (Ebr.-Vally 2001).

According to Klotz (1997), the debates on inclusion in the country focused on "Indians" as consensus on the exclusion of "black" people was already reached, as one of the policies of apartheid, developed in the 1930s and 1940s and implemented in 1948 by the National Party government of South Africa, was to create "homelands" for "black" people and thereby exclude them politically, economically and socially from mainstream South African society. Unlike the Australian government which in 1918 granted full citizenship rights to Indians who had arrived in the country in the nineteenth century (Yarwood 1964), the South African government continued with anti-"Indian" legislation, dating back from 1885. For example, the Union Nationality and Flags Act, No. 40 of 1927 denied "Indians" the right to become citizens by naturalization (Maasdorp and Pillay 1977; Davenport 1991). Other restrictions included the prohibition of "Indians" in the Orange Free State from engaging in agriculture, trading, or ownership of property. They were also not allowed to travel freely between provinces until 1975. In addition the Asiatic Land Tenure and Indian Representation Act No. 28 of 1946, also referred to as the "Ghetto Act," was devised to restrict "Indian" property ownership in "white" areas in Natal (Maasdorp and Pillay 1977; Davenport 1991).

There were plans designed to persuade "Indians" to willfully return to India and taxes were levied against indentured laborers, and their descendants thereafter, who refused to do so. In addition expensive repatriation strategies were implemented by the Department of the Interior to tempt "Indians" to go back to India. The NP together with those who opposed immigration also argued that "Indians" would not be able to integrate culturally; an example of this was the deliberations around whether or not non-Christian marriages could be considered legal.

"Indians" only became a permanent population, in the eyes of the governing authorities, in 1961 when these many plans to "repatriate" them had failed. This was not due to any kindness on the part of the South African government but was done so that the Indian government would no longer interfere in South African affairs, especially regarding the treatment of "Indians." India, it should be noted, was the first country to impose sanctions on South Africa. This was initially done to publicly express their disapproval with the discriminatory laws against "Indians" in South Africa. It was later extended to show support for all those suffering under the oppressive regime. In addition to this, in 1946, Indian officials made representation to the United Nations about the racist practices in South Africa generally and the treatment of "Indians" in particular. The political context of South Africa at that point in time seemed to mirror what was happening in India where freedom from oppressive rule was being fought for. Indeed, for a period of almost 100 years after the arrival of the first indentured laborers, the impermanent status of Indians and people of Indian descent continued.

It is against this political backdrop that this chapter aims to trace the construction of an "Indian" identity in South Africa. The word "Indian" is placed within inverted commas to denote the category assigned to people of Indian descent in South Africa, which was legitimized by the former apartheid government. This classification was based on physical external appearance and the initial unproblematic combination of group arrival and hence bureaucratic labelling (Erasmus 2007). However, this category is still employed in contemporary South Africa as it is regarded as an "official" racial category by the state. The inverted commas signify in the first instance that the category "Indian" is not accepted as a biologically meaningful category but nevertheless as a very real social construct. Secondly it is used in this chapter, without quotation marks, to create a distinction between South Africans of Indian descent and Indian nationals from India.

Community and Belonging

An analysis of South African "Indian" identity, by its very nature, demands an engagement with notions of "community" in relation to South Africans of Indian descent. Most of the literature points to discriminatory legislation during and after colonialism, as well as, most notably, apartheid later on as contributing factors to the construction of an "Indian" community. The construction of a separate "Indian" identity was seen to be an essential component of the apartheid state's strategy of divide and rule and the idea therefore of "Indians" as a homogenous ethnic group was fostered.

Zegeye and Ahluwalia (2002, 394) and MacDonald (2006, 3) point out that an "Indian" identity, as with all other "races," emerged then in response to "white" racism and ultimately political experiences. The apartheid government, by giving rights of citizenship to one group and denying it to others, created communities of the various "race" groups. "White" people and specifically Afrikaners, through governing the country were able to assert their status as South Africans, whereas "Indians" were largely categorized as "'others' or 'out-groups'" and were thus never viewed as South Africans (Zegeye and Ahluwalia 2002, 395).

So although "Indians" were divided in terms of class, caste, language, and religion, they were nevertheless all "legislatively defined or described themselves as part of the 'Indian Community'" and as a discrete racial category (Padaychee 1999, 393; see also Vahed 2002, 79). Bhana (1997a, 5) posits that as a result of being consistently indiscriminately grouped together, "Indians" progressively viewed themselves as a uniform unit who were compelled to respond accordingly. Vahed (2001, 125) writes that even though a multitude of identities that were founded on language, class, religion, and customs existed together within the category "Indian," these fundamentally different individuals were drawn together and as a result a common "Indian" identity surfaced in response to various political and economic exclusions.

Singh and Vawda (1988, 2) too argue that not only was the category "Indian community" a creation of the state but was also a tool used by "Indian" politicians for challenging the status quo. For example, the political strategies of the Natal Indian Congress (NIC), which was established in 1894, included considering the oppressed as fragmented according to "race" and thus appealed to the sentiments of "Indians" as one of the oppressed ethnic groups (Singh and Vawda 1988; Rastogi

2008; Bhana 1997a). The NIC then were responsible for creating an awareness of, preserving, and upholding the notion of "Indianness" (Bhana 1997b). According to Bhana (1997b, 100),

> The Natal Indian Congress (NIC) sought to weld together the diverse cultural and religious immigrants from the Indian subcontinent into a single, coherent, and secular organization. In the process of the NIC's creation, 'Indianness' came into being and subsequently became firmly embedded in South Africa's politics. In the early years of the NIC's existence, 'Indianness', in its restricted sense, was central to the organization's efforts to win rights for the immigrants. Examples of these include documents, pamphlets, advertorials and the like which appealed to this politically manufactured category.

For instance a document of the NIC indicated that "it had welded all classes of Indians into a coherent whole" (Singh and Vawda 1988, 5). This sentiment portrayed the "community" then as homogenous with a common political agenda. So in spite of the NIC's arguments that its political goals emanated out of the given historical and socio-political context, it nevertheless appeared to lend credence to apartheid notions of ethnic enculturation (Singh and Vawda 1988).

For instance, the following statement appeared in *Flash*, the newsletter of the NIC, in 1946 (cited in Naidoo 1998), which displays one of the many ways that "Indianness" was aroused during the resistance campaign:

> It is for us as true sons and daughters of Mother India to follow in their footsteps and vindicate the honour of our community and our motherland. As a true Indian, you must become a passive resistance volunteer in order to protect the honour and dignity of our people.

It should be noted that by 1946 over 80% of the "Indians" residing in the country at that point in time had been born there and knew no other home (Gell 1951, 432). The discourse of the NIC then perpetuated ethnic categories and divisions by dealing with national agendas through the narrow lens of "community politics and ethnic mobilization" (Singh and Vawda 1988, 12).

The language used in the various publications and advertorials of the NIC also perpetuated the notion that "Indian" struggles could be easily separated from that of the other oppressed groups in society and this then strengthened the belief that "... Indians as a 'community' have something specific or different to be fearful about, that they are threatened in ways that other people are not" (Singh and Vawda 1988, 13).

In analyzing the political tactics and activities of the NIC Bhana (1997a, 22) refers to this instance of political conduct as "sojourner politics" in that the leaders of the NIC did not regard South Africa as their home, as most had been born in India, and still regarded their birthplace as their "motherland." Bhana (1997a) suggests that this then may provide a rationale for their inability to identify, at that point in time, with the other oppressed groups in South Africa. Some years earlier, Singh and Vawda (1988, 14) made a similar point that the view of the NIC was that "Indians" were a complete and independent unit in and of itself, and that other such insulated communities existed was evident in their communiqués to the public. They argue that in addition broad statements made by NIC politicians and activists, such as the ones below, indicated their conception of "Indians" as a homogenous, culturally unified group rather than a politically and socially constructed category:

> That there are Indians, Coloureds, Africans and Whites [national groups] in our country is a self evident and undeniable reality. It is a reality precisely because each of those national groups has its own heritage, culture, language, customs and traditions. (Zac Yacoob cited in Singh and Vawda 1988, 14)

> We have the potential to become the only authentic political body representing the Indian community... We have gauged from our fieldwork that generally the community looks to us as the guardians of the people. We have been around for a long time – 90 years – and intend remaining in the forefront of Indian politics. (Pravin Gordhan cited in Singh and Vawda 1988, 14)

Vahed (2001, 112) maintains that by encouraging "race" and culture to be a part of the sensibilities of people, the chasms between the different racial groupings were further widened. He argues that these instances together with the states measures of separation cemented the idea of "racial" communities and counteracted any attempts for people to organize at the level of class. As Ginwala (1977, 5) notes, during the height of apartheid, the demands for exclusion and isolation were from forces external to the "Indian" group and penalties were issued for noncompliance to the restrictive, discriminatory laws.

Isolation and Exclusiveness

The arguments provided by the various writers discussed above explain the formation of the "Indian" community as emanating from external pressures, thus forcing isolation and exclusivity, and resulting ultimately in acceptance of the "community" from "within." Vahed (2001, 111) states that the purpose of such divisive pieces of legislation, such as the Group Areas Act of 1950, at its very core was an attempt completely to sever or at the very least diminish interaction between "Indians," "Africans," and "whites" and "... reinforced in children the idea that they belonged to a specific race, by virtue of the absence of others." The Group Areas Act (GAA) separated people therefore on the basis of "race," i.e., where a person resided or was allowed to reside was determined by "race." This therefore introduced the dynamics of proximity, which is crucial as identity construction would have been different if "Indians" resided in smaller locales or culturally mixed locales.

The Group Areas Act resulted ultimately in the forced removals of "Indians," who were already settled in specific areas, to inferior housing in areas distinctly set aside for "Indians." Freund (1995) argues that approximately 80% of the "Indian" population in Durban was affected by the systematic execution of the program of forced removals. In commenting on the Group Areas legislation the then Prime Minister of South Africa D.F. Malan stated in a parliamentary debate that, "I do not think there is any other Bill, affecting the relations between different races, the non-

Europeans and the Europeans of this country, which determines the future of South Africa and of all population groups as much as this Bill does." (Hansard 1950: col.7722 cited in Christopher 2001, 4). Many argued that the purpose of the Group Areas Act was to "ruin" the "Indians" in South Africa and force them to "repatriate." W.A. Maree, who eventually became the Minister of Indian Affairs, was reported in 1956 to have said, "After the effects of the Group Areas Act had been felt, Indians would be only too pleased to get out of S.A." ("NT," *Natal Witness*, June 23, 1956).

What facilitated the implementation of this Act however was the passing of the Population Registration Act (PRA) of 1950. The purpose of this act was to provide a register of everyone in the country according to "race." The "race group" that each person was assigned then became their "official classification" in the eyes of the state and thus all other resources pertaining to that "race" applied (Christopher 2002, 405). This act then was tied to the GAA as both worked together to govern where individuals could live, as the Group Areas Act allowed for the creation of residential spaces for each "race"/population group. According to Christopher (2002, 405), the classification system reflected the divisions used by the state since 1911 which initially included only three racial classifications, namely, European or "white," "bantu" or "native," and "colored" (Christopher 2009, 104). West (1988) argues that the term "population group" was created by the Apartheid government for its use in its programs of governance and was unique to South Africa. What made this racial classification system even more pronounced was the fixing of cultural attributes to each "race" to provide cultural descriptions of each "race," and along with that, ethnic stereotypes (Posel 2001, 53).

Hockey et al. (2005, 12) maintain that,

> Birds can be classified in many ways – by size, shape, colour or even palatability – but biologists strive to classify organisms in a hierarchy that reflects their evolutionary relationships. Such a natural classification has to be inferred from the pattern of shared derived characters ...

In much of a similar way, these imagined shared characteristics of "Indians" was perpetuated via discourse and entrenched through legislation. As Posel argues (2001, 53) "Race, in their view, was a judgment about 'social standing', made on the strength of prevailing social conventions about difference." "Race" during apartheid, and because of apartheid's programs, according to Posel (2001, 53) was distinguishable by both biology and culture, which were interchangeable to the apartheid government. "Indians" then were viewed as "Indians" biologically and culturally and thus inferior in a hierarchy of racial superiority. And as Balibar and Wallerstein (1991, 228) point out, although "race" is continually being constructed, it can become solidified and "meaningful" for the people who appropriate the classification. The stereotypes then became essential characteristics in the minds of people. The categories created by the government required people to abide by it and identify as such in order to receive services and resources. Government policies, or the official discourse, then filtered down to the formal and informal settings and became part of the discourse in every sphere of society, from employment and education to family life. These discourses then offered to people, meanings, and identifications in the construction of their identity (Siebers 2004, 90).

The state, in addition to creating geographic racial silos, also failed to make provision for basic amenities and facilities in the residential areas it created for "Indian" occupation. Jagarnath (2009) argues that a single building would serve a multitude of functions such as serving as a classroom by day and then be converted into a community hall for meetings, or a temple where religious practices were conducted, and thereafter into a movie theatre where films could be shown.

In terms of sporting facilities, these were nonexistent in areas set aside for "Indian" occupation as the following Table 1 (prepared by the City Estates Manager in 1936) reveals:

So even though "Indians" paid the obligatory rates and taxes, there we no sporting amenities in the residential areas in which "Indians" resided (Govender 2010). This lack of provision of facilities meant that "Indians" of all classes had to join together to finance these projects. In addition, the construction of schools to educate "Indian" children was done not only by wealthy traders but also by individuals who worked for very little wages who would assign a portion of their earnings toward educating the children (Vahed 2001, 110). Gwala (2010, 7) adds that one particular individual, Hajee Malukmohammed Lappa Sultan, had a "... deep desire to see that all Indian people were educated," and as a result he formed the ML Sultan Charitable and Educational Fund. Contributions from this fund assisted in building the ML Sultan College in 1949, which was regarded as the first higher education institution for "Indians." Vahed (2001) argues that this co-operation then across class lines in building much needed facilities and amenities, strengthened notions of a racial community.

Another factor that contributed to racial exclusivity was that of segregated sport. In his foreword to Desai et al's *Blacks in Whites: A Century of Cricket Struggles in KwaZulu-Natal* (Desai et al. 2002, ix), Naidoo states that, "Cricket, like much of South African society, has a history of racial compartmentalization ... This division between Black and White cricket reflected the broader divisions in South African society." Cricket then, as with all other sport, was not a means to advance interaction between race groups, but instead was used as a tool to divide people on "ethnic grounds," and the playing of nonracial sport therefore was considered a legal offence (Khoapa 2007, 25).

Table 1 Sporting facilities in "Indian" areas – 1936 (Desai et al. 2002, 98)

Area	Indian population	Facilities
Greenwood Park	8054	None
Sydenham	14,123	None
Mayville	14,821	Reserved 15 acres – not developed
Umhlatuzana	3212	Reserved 7 acres – not developed
South Coast Junction	17,324	None

"Indians," in order to provide for their own recreation, had to work within the confines of their racial category to achieve their sporting goals. For instance, Govender (2010, 33) points to the fact that,

> ...for [Indian] footballers to prove themselves, there had to be soccer grounds and organised leagues ... KwaZulu-Natal had people like the articulate, handlebar-moustached SL Singh, Sooboo Rajah, Charles Pillay, Bobby Naidoo and in the Transvaal the Rev. BLE Sigamoney and Bob Pavadai set up district football associations. They laid the ground for the introduction of provincial associations and eventually the South African Indian Football Association.

The idea of "Indianness" then was furthered through common participation of "Indians" in various sporting activities. In addition as a result of the Group Areas Act "black" spectators were forbidden by law from attending sporting matches with people of other races (Khoapa 2007, 25). Desai et al. (2002, 6) note that a newspaper of the day, the *Sporting Star*, proposed in May 1912 that a specific "enclosure should be set aside for respectable and decent Asians" at the Wanderers Stadium in Johannesburg. Segregated sport then made it inevitable that "races" would not cross or mix even during sporting activities, and the fact that sporting associations as well as civic ones were formed along racial lines made it difficult to promote the growth of nonracial affiliations (Vahed 2001). Sport then played into the creation and maintenance of group identities and allowed only for a particular version of society to develop.

In addition to exclusionary sports, "Indian" people also had to provide their own social and cultural activities such as performing their own plays, singing songs, re-enacting religious stories, and the like, which further created a sense of a racial community (Vahed 2001, 109). A significant factor that contributed to the development of a so-called "Indian identity" was that of Indian film (Jagarnath 2009, 200). Initially silent films were imported and would be screened on building walls and "... the entire community of people would gather and pay their money to see the moving pictures" (Jagarnath 2009, 201).

In addition, the religious festival of Muhurram was also significant in shaping, what Vahed (2002, 77) refers to as, a "pan-Indian 'Indianness' within a white and African colonial society." He argues that even though the origins of this festival lay in mourning the death of a Muslim martyr both Hindus and Muslims participated, blending both Muslim and Hindu customs thus making it a "pan-Indian festival" and he argues that this then contributed to an important aspect of forging an "Indian community," beyond the otherwise religious separation. By participating as a collective Vahed (2002, 92) argues that this festival contributed to a "fraternal feeling and 'Indianness'" stating further,

> Muharram provided an opportunity for developing and expressing a self-conscious local community identity, in the first instance, but also signalled the participation of Indians in a broader collective. Muharram strengthened links between the individual and 'community', and was important in constituting a diverse collection of people into a collectivity, while also excluding others, whites and Africans ...

Common experiences under the discriminatory regimes during and after colonialism and of apartheid then fostered a sense of "Indianness" as is reflected in these writings around notions of "Indian" community. There was no external pressure to conform to a single South African identity and so, creating residential pockets of "Indian" groups encouraged "Indians" to construct an insular identity through shared participation in sports, religious activities, and other social and cultural processes.

Fixed Identity

This shared oppression reinforced the impression of a fixed "Indian" identity, not only from the "outside" but also by those who define themselves as belonging to this group. As Posel (2001, 51) makes clear "... decades of racial reasoning, the idea that South African society comprises four distinct races – Whites, Coloureds, Indian and Africans – has become a habit of thought and experience, a facet of popular common sense still widely in evidence." There is a propensity therefore to consider racial classifications as essential, as something that cannot be changed and that is stable over time.

Further to this, in South Africa the category "Indian" was both racialized and ethnicized. In other words it was used as a racial category but also denoted people from a different geographic location with different traditions, customs, and religions. The state perpetuated the idea of ethnic groups and used it to further divide people and justify policies such as the Group Areas Act of 1950 and the Bantustan strategy. For example, in South Africa, people were born into a context of racial categorization and separation. In addition to this the state actively encouraged people to regard themselves in even more minuscule ways such as, as Xhosa, Zulu, or Venda for example. The idea was to create and perpetuate difference between "race" groups and the further subdivided ethnic/language groups. According to Edwards (1992, 6), "Central to these models was the belief in the intrinsic relationship between the physical, biological nature of man and his cultural, moral and intellectual nature. Thus culture was seen as being biologically determined." Although the idea of "race" as determined by biology has been undermined, it has been replaced by an equally debatable idea of "culture," where "race" is considered to be cultural formations (MacDonald 2006, 1). The claims of culture and "race" and the conflation of the two, as in the case of "Indians" are problematic in that it essentializes and fixes identity, suggesting then that cultural attributes are determined by physical ones, and that racial groups are culturally distinct (Erasmus 2008, 172; Bass et al. 2012).

Hinkle and Brown (1990, 48) contend that, "our sense of who we are stems in large part from our membership of affiliation to various social groups, which are said to form our social identity. This identity is thought to be maintained through evaluative comparisons between in-groups and relevant out-groups." The political system of apartheid in South Africa fostered group sensibilities which forced people to fight for rights and resources and in turn against the restrictive, discriminatory regime as distinct groups, i.e., to identify as "Indians" or as "black" or in more minute terms as "Zulu" or "Xhosa." The official apartheid discourse of an "Indian" "race group" appeared to solidify the notion of "Indianness" both in social discourse and in the minds of the so-called "Indian" people themselves. Through segregated education, housing, amenities, and the like, "Indians" were told in no uncertain terms who they were. This placed limits not only on their identity choices but also on how they were perceived by others. In other words they could not be identified as anything other than "Indian," and the classification itself carried all the stereotypes of the foreign other perpetuated in the media and political discourse since the arrival of the very first immigrants from India in 1860 (Pillay 2017). Racial difference was so infused into society that "race" thinking was a norm and was evident in almost every sphere. As Omi and Winant (1986) argue, racial categories are made real by processes in society such as the political systems of the day and via the media, and as Jacobs and Manzi (2000, 37) point out, "... discourses and rhetoric are effective tools to exert dominance."

Dominance in South Africa was constructed through a process legitimized by state laws and reified through the media and popular discourse. Lerner (1997, 195) articulates further that this enforces a "group identity" where "Negative characteristics are arbitrarily selected and affixed to the group. Then these negative characteristics are ascribed to each member of the group ..." an example of which was that all "Indians" were exploitative and inherently dishonest (Pillay 2017, 83). By pitting one group against another, the apartheid government attempted to ensure that the oppressed made up of "black," "colored," and "Indian" people would not unite to effectively challenge the regime. It further added to this by creating subdivisions within the "black" "race group" by classifying "black" people according to language and creating homelands based on "ethnicity." Bantustans, or Homelands, as they were also commonly referred to, were the specific areas that were demarcated by the apartheid state as part of their grand plan to house ethnic groups. It was anticipated that attempts for political participation within these homelands would occur thus creating even further ethnic fractures in the South African landscape and lending credence to the National Party's false propaganda of South Africa being made up of diverse "ethnic nations" (Maré and Hamilton 1987). "White" people however who also originated from different countries, including most countries in Europe, were lumped under one category of "white" with no distinction created between the various "language" groups. The institutionalized discrimination which included a wide range of laws to enforce the discriminatory ethos of the state including specific acts targeted at "Indians" reinforced the belief of the "group" as foreign prior to 1961 and as different and "other," after.

Conclusion

Even though they were officially given permanent status in 1961, South Africans of Indian descent were still regarded very much in popular discourse as foreign and were viewed in general as a threat, as exploitative, as wealthy (this myth, derived from a legacy of stereotypes against "Indians" as exploitative merchants and traders, was erroneously perpetuated throughout the years and even into democracy), and ultimately as belonging elsewhere (Pillay 2019). The notions of "Indians" as foreigners and as not belonging that had been perpetuated through the media and more especially political discourse over time became part of the perceptions people had regarding "Indians." As Mamdani (2001, 7) argues, "...identities both become reified and get turned into a basis of legal discrimination – between those who are said to belong and those who are said not to belong, between insiders entitled to rights and outsiders deprived of these rights ... Prevented from changing, [racial] identities become frozen."

Third, fourth and fifth generation South Africans of Indian descent, the majority of whom could only speak English and knew no other Indian language, were perpetual foreigners. The xenophobic discourse around "Indians" was so pervasive and extreme that "Indians" could not be viewed in a way other than as belonging elsewhere. The colonial government, the Union, and subsequently the apartheid government prior to 1961 had made every attempt to politicize their status in South Africa as immigrants, laws were created around "Indians" as immigrants, they were recorded in an immigrants register, and there were still plans to repatriate them. Accepting "Indians" as South Africans on paper could not remove the "stigma" of being foreign that had been perpetuated for over a century.

Indeed, 24 years into democracy, notions of "Indians" as other and not belonging, still exist. For example, statements from the public and political sphere have forced crude notions of identity and community to dominate (Pillay 2017). The category "Indian" in South Africa as mentioned earlier was always a racial as well as an ethnic one, and according to Park (2008, 3), "Ethnic identity involves setting boundaries – determining who is a member and who is not – and deciding what ethnic features are to be used to identify those members at a particular time and place." These classifications, although imposed upon individuals, in terms of the Population Registration Act under apartheid, and with the categories being unquestioningly employed in different ways in postapartheid South Africa, individuals also, as Cornell and Hartmann (1998, 79) argue "accept, resist, choose, specify, invent, redefine, reject, actively defend" identities. In describing the extent and effect of the Population Registration Act, Ebr.-Vally (2001, 52) states that this law, "... gave each South African an objective racial/ethnic identity ... an imposed identity, like the identity given to an object through a name, or through a label stuck onto it depending on its shape and origin. The law determined the membership of a group through the apparent phenotype, and through a wide array of religious, linguistic and cultural criteria, which went as far as including clothing and social habits."

These divisive acts however have left a lasting legacy on the social fabric of South Africa. For example, even though the Group Areas Act was rescinded in 1991, the damage to communities and families had already been done, and the spatial and racial landscape of South Africa has been irrevocably changed. The different residential locations for each of the "races," in contemporary South African society, have been the virulent legacy of apartheid. Most suburbs have retained its "old" racial composition especially formerly "Indian" and "black" townships.

A *South African* community then does not exist, except in rhetoric, but what is apparent however is a country comprising a number of "communities." The "Indian community" is one such branch whose basis as a community was established and promoted by the state, chiefly through various administrative and census undertakings to count and quantify this "community," but also accepted by politicians who used it as a vehicle to gain rights and privileges, and thereafter accepted uncritically by those so labelled. In addition to this, inhabiting a shared geographic space, and having common ancestry, the community thus appears logical to "insiders" and "outsiders," as this spatial legacy of apartheid contributes to notions of the self and others as racial subjects.

In addition, as mentioned earlier, racial categories in South Africa persist in everyday discourse and practices because it has been implemented in state law. Categories, no matter what their intent or purpose, cannot exist without hierarchies and ultimately discrimination. As Maré (2011, 617) explains, "'Race', when applied to human beings, can never be a neutral descriptive term but carries the historical baggage of exploitation, domination and dehumanization." Research has revealed that South Africans of Indian descent from the various generations assert a strong South African identity, but nevertheless uncritically accept the label "Indian" as a "race" classification with some pointing to its ties to "culture" (Pillay 2015). The fact that South Africans are products of "an experiment in human engineering" (Gorra 1997, 67) is largely ignored and this is chiefly because "race thinking," exacerbated by state emphasis on "race" classification, has become so embedded in the national psyche and continues to be passed down to each generation (Pillay 2015).

South Africans then are deeply ingrained to view society, i.e., people, places, events, and the like, in terms of "race," as "white," "black," "colored," and "Indian." "Indians" in South Africa are thus constructed and perceived as a homogenous group with a single, unified identity. This perception of "Indians" as a separate community is entrenched in social and political discourse and raises questions on citizenship and belonging, and what it means to be or "become" a South African. In 1996, the then Deputy President of South Africa Thabo Mbeki delivered a speech titled "I am an African" on behalf of the ANC on the passing of the new Constitution of South Africa. The speech drew on the history of the origin of the inhabitants of the country, with Mbeki claiming his identity as African being "born" out of all the experiences of the ancestors of the land, the speech stated: "I come of those who were transported from India and China, whose being resided in the fact, solely, that they were able to provide physical labour, who taught me that we could both *be at home and be foreign*" (Mbeki 1996). This however is exactly the dilemma faced by South Africans of Indian descent today. In a land that they call home, they are stigmatized as belonging to a place that is not South Africa. It is telling that just over 150 years after the first indentured laborers arrived in South Africa, it is nevertheless *still* necessary for "Indians" to stress their belonging to South Africa as a homeland.

Cross-References

▶ Ethno-cultural Symbolism and Group Identity
▶ Racialized Identity Under Apartheid in South Africa
▶ The Legacy of Indentured Labor

References

Balibar E, Wallerstein I (1991) Race, nation and class: ambiguous identities. Verso, London
Bass O, Erwin K, Kinners A, Maré G (2012) The possibilities of researching non-racialism: reflections on racialism in South Africa. Politikon 39:29–40
Bhana S (1997a) Gandhi's legacy: the Natal Indian Congress 1894–1994. University of Natal Press, Pietermaritzburg
Bhana S (1997b) Indianness reconfigured 1944–1960: the Natal Indian Congress in South Africa. Comp Stud South Asia Afr Middle East 17:100–107
Christopher AJ (2001) The atlas of a changing South Africa. Routledge, London
Christopher AJ (2002) 'To define the indefinable': population classification and the census in South Africa. Area 34(4):401–408
Christopher AJ (2009) Delineating the nation: South African censuses 1865–2007. Polit Geogr 28:101–109
Cornell S, Hartmann D (1998) Ethnicity and race: making identities in a changing world. Pine Forge, Thousand Oaks
Davenport TRH (1991) South Africa: a modern history. Macmillan Press, London
Desai A, Padayachee V, Reddy K, Vahed G (2002) Blacks in whites: a century of cricket struggles in KwaZulu-Natal. University of Natal Press, Pietermaritzburg
Ebr.-Vally R (2001) Kala pani: caste and colour in South Africa. Kwela Books, Cape Town
Edwards E (1992) Introduction. In: Edwards E (ed) Anthropology and photography: 1860–1920. Yale University Press, New Haven, pp 3–17
Erasmus Y (2007) Racial (re)classification during apartheid South Africa: regulations, experiences and the meaning(s) of race. Unpublished Doctoral Dissertation. St George's, University of London
Erasmus Z (2008) Race. In: Shepherd N, Robins S (eds) New South African keywords. Ohio University Press, Ohio, pp 169–182
Freund B (1995) Insiders and outsiders: the Indian working class of Durban, 1910–1990. University of Natal Press, Pietermaritzburg
Gell CWM (1951) The Indians in South Africa. Fortnightly 176:429–438
Ginwala F (1977) Indian South Africans. Minority Rights Group 34:5–20
Gorra M (1997) After empire: Scott, naipaul, rushdie. University of Chicago Press, Chicago
Govender R (2010, 6 June) The glory days: football was once the most popular sport among Indians. Sunday Tribune, p 33
Gwala V (2010, 5 June) Self-made businessman with a passion for education. The Independent on Saturday, p 7
Hinkle S, Brown R (1990) Intergroup comparisons and social identity: some links and lacunae. In: Abrams D, Hogg MA (eds) Social identity theory: constructive and critical advances. Springer, New York, pp 48–70
Hockey PAR, Dean WRJ, Ryan P (2005) Roberts birds of southern Africa. The Trustees of the John Voelcker Bird Book Fund, Cape Town
Jacobs K, Manzi T (2000) Evaluating the social constructionist paradigm in housing research. Hous Theory Soc 17:35–42

Jagarnath V (2009) "Filmi very filmi". The influence of popular Indian film in shaping the cultural and social identity of the diasporic community of South African Indians. In: Klemencic M, Harris MN (eds) European migrants, diasporas and indigenous ethnic minorities. Pisa University Press, Pisa, pp 197–209

Khoapa B (2007) A heritage and arena for struggle and development. In: Rosenberg L (ed) Wellspring of hope: the legacy of a sports field. Durban University of Technology, Durban, p 25

Klotz A (1997) International relations and migration in Southern Africa. African Security Review 6:38–45

Lerner G (1997) Why history matters: life and thought. Oxford University Press, Oxford

Maasdorp G, Pillay N (1977) Urban relocation and racial segregation: the case of Indian South Africans. University of Natal Press, Durban

MacDonald M (2006) Why race matters in South Africa. University of KwaZulu-Natal Press, Pietermaritzburg

Mamdani M (2001, 8 August) Making sense of non-revolutionary violence: some lessons from the Rwandan genocide. Paper presented at the Frantz Fanon Lecture, University of Durban-Westville, Durban

Maré G (2011) 'Fear of numbers': reflections on the South African case. Curr Sociol 59:616–634

Maré G, Hamilton G (1987) An appetite for power: Buthelezi's Inkatha and South Africa. Ravan Press, Johannesburg

Mbeki T (1996, 8 May) Statement of Deputy President TM Mbeki, on behalf of the ANC, on the occasion of the adoption by the Constitutional Assembly of The Republic of South Africa Constitution Bill 1996. https://www.mbeki.org/2016/06/01/i-am-an-african-speech-by-president-thabo-mbeki-8-may-1996/. Accessed 5 Sept 2018

Mesthrie US (1997) From advocacy to mobilization Indian Opinion, 1903–1914. In: Switzer L (ed) South Africa's alternative press: voices of protest and resistance, 1880s–1960s. Cambridge University Press, Cambridge, pp 99–126

Motwani JK, Gosine M, Barot-Motwani J, Global Organization of People of Indian Origin (1993) Global Indian diaspora: yesterday, today and tomorrow. Global Organization of People of Indian Origin (GOPIO), New York

Naidoo K (1998) Class, consciousness and organisation: Indian political resistance in Durban, South Africa 1979–1996. https://www.sahistory.org.za/archive/class-consciousness-and-organisation-political-development-indian-south-africans-1860-1979. Accessed 1 June 2018

Omi M, Winant H (1986) Racial formation in the United States. Routledge, New York

Padayachee V (1999) Struggle, collaboration and democracy: the 'Indian community' in South Africa, 1860–1999. Econ Polit Wkly 34:393–395

Park YJ (2008) A matter of honour: being Chinese in South Africa. Jacana Media, Auckland Park

Pillay K (2015) South African families of Indian descent: transmission of racial identity. J Comp Fam Stud XLVI:121–135

Pillay K (2017) AmaNdiya, they're not South Africans! In: Ballantine C, Chapman M, Erwin K, Maré G (eds) Living together, living apart? Social cohesion in a future South Africa. UKZN Press, Pietermaritzburg, pp 80–87

Pillay K (2019) The 'Indian' question: examining autochthony, citizenship, and belonging in South Africa. In: Essed P, Farquharson K, Pillay K, White EJ (eds) Relating worlds of racism: dehumanisation, belonging, and the normativity of European whiteness. Palgrave Macmillan, London, pp 63–87

Posel D (2001) What's in a name?: racial categorisation under apartheid and their afterlife. Transformation 47:50–74

Rastogi P (2008) Afrindian fictions: diaspora, race, and national desire in South Africa. The Ohio State University Press, Columbus

Siebers H (2004) Identity formation: issues, challenges and tools. In: Kalb D, Pansters W, Siebers H (eds) Globalization and development. Kluwer Academic Publishers, Dordrecht, pp 75–102

Singh R, Vawda S (1988) What's in a name?: some reflections on the Natal Indian Congress. Transformation 6:1–21

Vahed G (2001) Race or class? Community and conflict amongst Indian municipal employees in Durban, 1914–1949. J South Afr Stud 27:105–125

Vahed G (2002) Constructions of community and identity among Indians in colonial Natal, 1860–1910: the role of the muharram festival. J Afr Hist 43:77–93

West M (1988) Confusing categories: population groups, national states and citizenship. In: Boonzaier E, Sharp J (eds) South African keywords: the uses and abuses of political concepts. David Philip, Johannesburg, pp 100–110

Yarwood AT (1964) Asian migration to Australia: the background to exclusion, 1896–1923. Melbourne University Press, Victoria

Zegeye A, Ahluwalia P (2002) Transforming culture: street life in an apartheid city. Soc Identities 8:393–430

The State and Minority Nationalities (Ethnic Groups) in China

6

Roland Boer

Contents

Introduction	94
Defining Nationality	94
Chinese Nationalities Policy	96
Problems	99
Terrorism or Separatism?	100
An Alternative Approach to Human Rights	102
Conclusion: Between Autonomy and Unity	105
Cross-References	106
References	106

Abstract

In the context of racial tensions in the USA, questions over the EU project from those who have not benefitted, the treatment of asylum seekers with increasing harshness in places like Australia, and the response to refugees in Europe, a rather different example of ethnic and cultural diversity is worth attention – that of China. As the country with the largest population in the world and due to a complex history, China now has 56 officially recognized nationalities, including the Han, who number 1.2 billion. Even so, the next nine nationalities number 6–19 million each – larger than the total population of many countries in the world.

How does China deal with this situation? To begin with, the term *minzu* is badly translated as "ethnic group." It is better translated as "nationality." With its multiple nationalities, China has developed a "preferential policy" that initially followed the model of the Soviet Union and was revised substantially in the 1990s. The policy entails support for economic development, cultural traditions, language, education, literature, and local political leadership. However, the policy

---

R. Boer (✉)
School of Liberal Arts, Renmin University of China, Beijing, People's Republic of China
e-mail: 20147014@ruc.edu.cn

has also created some problems: the inherent difficulties of government classification and their unintended effects; the tensions over "separatism, extremism, and terrorism," which has included foreign interference; and differences over the understanding and application of human rights in light of distinct traditions. Ultimately, the policy turns on the contradiction between autonomy for nationalities and the unity of the Chinese state. The question is how one deals with such a contradiction.

Keywords
China · Nationality · Preferential policies · Terrorism · Human rights

Introduction

The Chinese approach to ethnic minorities offers a distinct alternative to approaches elsewhere, so it is important to understand this approach properly. To begin with, the terminology prefers "nationality [*minzu*]" rather than "ethnic group." This preference is the result of a long Marxist tradition and the reality that ethnicity is not necessarily a defining feature of such groups. Further, the Chinese government has since the 1950s developed and revised a "preferential policy [*youhui zhengce*]," in which socio-economic wellbeing is paramount, although it also includes culture, governance, language, and education. This is not to say that the policy and its practice is without problems: government definitions; pressures concerning what some international observers call "separatism" and the Chinese and other international observers call "terrorism"; and different emphases in fostering human rights (with the primary right to economic wellbeing). However, the core feature of the preferential policy is a dialectical connection between two poles of a contradiction. On the one hand, the policies have increasingly (since the 1990s) emphasized greater autonomy; on the other hand, the inviolability of China's borders is without question. Throughout the following analysis, the concern is to understand the logic behind the Chinese approach and how this is manifested in actions. How one assesses such an approach is another question.

Defining Nationality

The Chinese term for "ethnic group" is *minzu*. But there is a catch: "ethnic group" is a bad translation for this term. Instead, "nationality" is more accurate. The better Chinese word for "ethnic group" is *zuqun*, a term that is used in some recent scholarship (Bulag 2010) but is not used commonly and in relation to government policies. For this reason, this study uses "nationality," although some further explanation is needed.

Let us begin with an example: the Hui nationality. If one visits Xi'an and the famous "snack street," one will see many men and some of the women wearing small white caps. Indeed, some – but not all – of the women wear head-scarves. Why? They are Hui people, identified in terms of adherence to Islam. How did they get to Xi'an? Some 1400–1100 years ago the Tang Dynasty ruled China. At that time, Xi'an (then known as Chang'an) in the more western parts of China was the most populous city in the world. Tang power swayed across significant parts of China, culture and learning flourished, Buddhism was fostered, trade boomed, and international connections were made far and wide. In order to encourage further trade, the Tang Emperors invited Muslim peoples from further west to Xi'an, since they had a reputation for hard work and the fostering of trade. Their descendants have been in Xi'an, and now many others parts of China, for more than a millennium.

But were they an identifiable ethnic group at the time? Not at all. As with all such groups, their history is mixed (Dillon 1999; Gladney 1991). The Tang, as well as the later Song and Yuan dynasties, encouraged immigration to China of peoples from more western parts of the world, as far west as Persia. A long history of intermarriage with Han people led to the development of what is now known as the Hui. But the Hui now includes converts to Islam among the Han, as well as other Muslim groups on Hainan island, among the Bai people and Tibetan Muslims. The key to their identification is religion, even if such identification pertains only to certain customs, dietary patterns, and dress, rather than religious practice per se. The vast majority of the Hui speak Mandarin and most of their customs are common to the Han. Obviously, ethnic identity is not a defining feature of the Hui. But there is a twist: the Hui have become strongly conscious of being a distinct nationality. This means that the complex and overlaid history of the Hui, with migration, intermarriage, state decisions, and policies, has led to, if not produced, a strong sense of a distinct identity (Gladney 1991, 323).

The implications of this example for defining *minzu*, or nationality, are as follows. First, since the Hui, as with any such group, is the result of a long history of movement, inter-mingling, and development, it may be suggested that no "ethnic group" is what might be called pure, for what counts as such a group is really a history of intermingling with many other groups, which are themselves the result of further mingling. Second, the Hui are one of 56 officially recognized groups in China. Out of these groups, the Hui are among the largest of the non-Han, with a population of 10 million. They are outnumbered by others, such as the Zhuang with 19 million (larger than the populations of many countries), but the Hui are far more numerous than the smallest groups, which number only a few thousand.

Let us return to question of terminology. Although "ethnic minority" or "ethnic group" is commonly used in English, it assumes ethnicity as the primary defining feature of the group. As the brief account of the Hui indicates, this is hardly the case (if indeed for any group). Further, the Chinese term is *minzu*, made up of two characters: 民族. The first, *min*, has the basic sense of "people." The second character, *zu*, means a class or group of things with common features. So *minzu* means a group of people with similar or common features. The situation becomes even more complex: *minzu* is a word borrowed from Japanese in order to translate the Russian word, *natsional'nost'*, which designates a particular group within a state that has overlaid common characteristics. The Russian terminology was itself the result of long debates and deliberations – from the turn to the twentieth century – concerning what was called the "national question" in countries with significant diversity, such as Austria and Russia (Suny 1993; Suny and Martin 2001; Egry 2005; Boer 2017, 142–156). In these debates, a nationality designated a distinct group within a state, a group defined by language, location, cultural history, economic shape, and at times religion. Most importantly, such nationalities lived within a larger state (which was not called a "nation"), and they included majority and minority groups as "nationalities." This is the tradition to which Chinese terminology and understanding is deeply indebted. So the best translation of *minzu* is "nationality." The problem with becoming used to this usage rather than "ethnic group" is that – in English at least – it has become overlaid with another sense. This is the relatively recent category of "imagined communities" (Anderson 1991), in which "nation" came to designate the modern European state, which is often called the "nation-state." While relatively common, this usage can be misleading, for it obscures the older and richer tradition.

Chinese Nationalities Policy

With this in mind, we may now deal with the Chinese situation from 1949 (for Qing dynasty approaches, see Crossley et al. 2006). As mentioned, the Chinese government identifies 56 official *minzu*, or nationalities. This includes the majority Han (themselves the result of a long history of intermarriage with other groups) and 55 other groups, ranging in number from almost 20 million to a few thousand (Mackerras 2003, 182–193; Hill and Zhou 2009, 3–8).

The policy dealing with minority nationalities is known as *youhui zhengce* (优惠政策), which may be translated as "preferential policies" or "positive (action) policies" (Zhou 2009, 47). The term appeared in its earliest form in 1949 in what is called the Common Program (from 29 September) and has been consistent in Chinese constitutions to the present. It was initially modeled on the Soviet Union, the world's first "affirmative action" state (Martin 2001), although China clearly developed its own approach in light of distinct circumstances and history. Debate ranges over whether Moscow pulled the strings, whether China continued imperial and republican practices, or whether it developed its own approach after Liberation in 1949 (Dreyer 1976, 43–60; Connor 1984, 87–88; Sautman 1998b; Zhou 2009). The best answer is that multiple factors influenced the development of the policy, although Marxist approaches provided the overall framework.

Theoretically, the definition first offered by none other than Stalin (1913 [1953], 307) formed the basis of determining different nationalities: "A nation is a historically constituted, stable community of people, formed on the basis of a common language, territory, economic life, and psychological storehouse manifested in a common culture" (translation modified). In the context of the Soviet Union, the key to fostering nationalities was not so much a tension between assimilation and recognition of differences, but a dialectical approach that went through the international category of class to generate a specifically local and national policy focused on difference (a crucial point entirely missed by Connor 2009; Zhou 2009, 58–59). In other words, this approach entailed a counter-intuitive move: one begins not with diversity in order to find some unity, but with the unifying category of class that in turn produced a whole new level of diversity that recognized and fostered distinct identities. It was nothing less than the application of the Marxist dialectic to a concrete situation (Boer 2017, 151–156).

In China in the 1950s, this definition and its larger text were the subject of much study by Chinese scholars (Mackerras 2003, 2; but see also the criticisms by Tapp 1995), with the resulting identification of 40 nationalities (including the Han) in the census of 1954. Ten years later the number was increased to 54, with two more added later, the last being the Juno, from Yunnan, in 1979 (Mackerras 2003, 19–55; Zhou 2009, 58–63).

However, with signs of problems in the Soviet Union already in the 1980s and especially after the union's breakup in 1991, Chinese scholars and policy makers carefully studied the situation and concluded that a major factor concerned tensions and mistakes in the nationalities policy (Hill and Zhou 2009, 8–10). These mistakes resulted in complex power imbalances and economic inequality. On the one hand, the policy of autonomy and self-determination of nationalities had led to a desire in some parts for secession from the union; on the other hand, the need to develop a common culture and language based around the Russian majority had entrenched the economic and power inequalities in favor of the majority Russian nationality, a situation that exacerbated the desire to break away (Suny 1993, 127–160). As a result of these findings, the Chinese approach was thoroughly revised and enhanced, leading to what some have called a shift from a Soviet model to a Chinese model, based on *duo yuan yi ti*, "one state with diversity" (Hill and Zhou 2009, 10–13).

But what does all this actually entail? It is best to begin with article 4 of the Chinese constitution of 1982, an article that has remained the same even with subsequent amendments elsewhere in the constitution (see http://www.npc.gov.cn/englishnpc/Constitution/node_2825.htm):

> All nationalities in the People's Republic of China are equal. The State protects the lawful rights and interests of the minority nationalities and upholds and develops a relationship of equality, unity and mutual assistance among all of China's nationalities. Discrimination against and oppression of any nationality are prohibited; any act which undermines the unity of the nationalities or instigates division is prohibited. The State assists areas inhabited by minority nationalities in accelerating their economic and cultural development according to the characteristics and needs of the various minority nationalities. Regional autonomy is practised in areas where people of minority nationalities live in concentrated communities; in these areas organs of self-government are established to exercise the power of autonomy. All national autonomous areas are integral parts of the People's Republic of China. All nationalities have the freedom to use and develop their own spoken and written languages and to preserve or reform their own folkways and customs.

Four features of this article are worth more attention: cultural autonomy, with a focus on language, folkways, and education; political autonomy; economic development; and the inviolability of China's borders. Let us take each in turn.

Culturally, local languages continue to be fostered (National People's Congress 2001, article 37), which entails media, education, and literature. For larger groups, this is easier to achieve, but for the small groups of only a few thousand the task is much more difficult and the threat remains that such languages may die out. Local customs, rituals, festivals, and especially religions are not merely permitted but actively fostered, with temples, churches, and mosques constructed and maintained with state funds – so much so that minority peoples are far more religious than the Han nationality. In terms of education, school children receive classes in their local language, alongside the obligatory classes in Mandarin. At university level, a quota system applies, as well as extra points given to students from minority nationalities for the all-important entrance examinations, the *gaokao* (Wang 2009). To be added here is the practice of having *minzu* universities in all regions. Although all students may apply, these universities focus on students from minority nationalities (Sautman 1998a). The result: between 1964 and 1982, the percentage of minority nationalities in universities rose marginally from 5.76 to 6.7 percent. However, from 1982 to 1990, the percentage rose to 8.04 percent (Mackerras 2003, 27).

Politically, it means both regional autonomy (such regions now number almost 160 in China) and representation in the Chinese People's Political Consultative Conference. Minority governance in autonomous regions is ensured through proportional representation, while at a national level elections – both direct at a local level and indirect at higher levels – are held annually in order to elect delegates to the CPPCC. The CPPCC is known as a "democratic front" that includes representatives from all political parties and all nationalities. It meets annually and provides informed advice and guidance to the legislative activities of the National People's Congress, the supreme decision-making body in China. Indeed, participation in the NPC by nationalities is also substantial. Further, there has also been a consistent long-term rise in the percentage of national minorities in the CPC. In 1980, only three percent of the total number of members were from minority nationalities. By 2001, the percentage had grown to 6.2 percent, albeit still behind the percentage of minority nationalities among the population as a whole, which is 8.14 percent (Mackerras 2003, 42).

Already with political matters we begin to see a tension, between autonomy and unity. This tension appears even more strongly with the core economic dimension of the nationalities policy. One the one hand, autonomous regional development is crucial, with a perpetual search for entrepreneurial activities that will boost local economies. On the other hand, these local initiatives could not happen without central government involvement. For example, the central government provides significant additional resources for economic development (Hill and Zhou 2009, 13), which appears in terms of subsidies for infrastructure and higher levels of public works funding. Here we find that the expansion of the Chinese rail and road system – which now leads the world in terms of extent and technical prowess – focuses on providing transport infrastructure for areas of concentrated minority nationality presence, especially since they tend to live in remote and relatively inaccessible areas. In businesses, both publicly owned companies (the major economic drivers) and private companies are provided with incentives for preferential treatment in employing people from smaller nationalities. And businesses run by minority nationalities receive interest-free loans from the government. The clear purpose is to encourage economic development in regions where minority nationalities live, for they tend to reside in parts of China that are only now beginning to experience the full benefit of the economic progress in the east.

This tension – between autonomy and unity – is a constitutive feature of Chinese preferential policies. Indeed, this tension is a major feature of the substantial revisions to this policy in the 1990s (after in-depth study of the causes of the collapse of the Soviet Union). Thus, in the amended *Law on Regional National Autonomy*, which was first promulgated in 1984 and substantially revised in 2001, autonomy at all levels has been enhanced – culturally, linguistically, politically, and economically. On the other hand, the law makes it quite clear that the borders of the country remain unchanged and inviolable. We may see this approach as a balancing act, as Mackerras observes (2003, 39): "the two demands in some ways balance each other, because some people do in fact see advantages in remaining part of a comparatively successful state where their lives have indeed greatly improved." Or we may see it terms of a Chinese approach to contradictions, concerning which there will be more comment in the conclusion.

Problems

At the same time, the nationalities preferential action policy is not without its problems. Some problems may be dealt with briefly, while two – terrorism and human rights – require some more detail. One problem, germane to any government policy, concerns how one defines a distinct nationality. What is the key determining factor? Is it language, culture, history, territory, or religion? In policy terms, it seems to be determined mostly by religion, culture, and territory. For instance, the Hui (see above) have no definable territory, since they are to be found all over China (albeit with a concentration in the north-west). The determining factor in this case is clearly observance, at however a nominal level, of Islam (Mackerras 2003, 114–126). By contrast, the determination of the Zhuang is based on territory. When empirical research was first undertaken for the sake of identifying distinct nationalities, the social scientists in question found that almost every tribal group in the south-western mountains of China saw themselves as distinct even from the group in the next valley. If the policy makers allowed full scope for such sensibilities, it would lead to thousands of distinct nationalities. So self-perception was relegated to a minor level. Instead, territory became crucial. People with largely similar ways of life, customs, and language living in similar territory were grouped together and identified as a nationality (Kaup 2002). Yet, even with these inherent problems in government definitions, Mackerras (2003, 3) points out that the vast majority of people agree with and accept the classifications, not merely because nationality is a rubbery term at best, but because in most cases the designations are reasonably valid.

Further problems with government administration include: a certain paternalism, in which the minority peoples need to be brought up to the cultural and indeed political level of the majority, and the trap of focusing on exotic items of national identity, in terms of clothing, rituals, customs, and food, a trap found especially with increasing tourism to such areas (Hillman 2003); the sense at times is that the economic development is largely in the hands of Han Chinese, who move into the minority areas as jobs and economic prospects increase. Let us elaborate on the last point, where a paradox emerges: fluency in *putonghua* (Mandarin) enables young people from minority backgrounds to gain employment. In Xinjiang, for example, it appears that Uyghur students who attend regular school with Han students have greater fluency than those who attend minority schools with Uyghur teachers, where Mandarin is taught as a second language. The outcome is that the former students do much better, even than Han young people, in attaining good jobs (Ma 2009).

Terrorism or Separatism?

One problem that requires further comment is that of terrorism, or as some international observers call it, "separatism." This topic relates specifically to the areas of Tibet and Xinjiang (and Taiwan and Hong Kong), each of which is autonomous in many respects but also part of the Chinese state. These areas tend to receive a significant portion of attention by some international media and human rights agencies, which attempt to paint a picture of systematic and unreasonable "repression" of the minorities in these areas (Human Rights Watch 2018, 143–145). Such a focus also distorts the overall situation concerning minority nationalities in China, so we need to be wary of falling into the same trap. Further, given the close alignment of bodies such as "Human Rights Watch" with the US State Department, and given the tendency of some Western media to selective sensationalism, it is better to rely on careful and balanced scholarly research (Sautman 1998b, 2010; Norbu 2001; Mackerras 2003; Davis 2013, 74–112). We also need to be wary of skewing the picture by relying only on treatments of such regions, for there are many other minority nationalities in China who contribute willingly and peacefully to society.

With this in mind, let us address a number of issues. To begin with, there is the simple historical question. Although accounts differ in relation to Tibet, the reality is that this region has been subject to China in various ways since the eighteenth century under the Qing dynasty. Claims to some form of independence hark back to an image of the Tibetan empire from the seventh to the eleventh centuries. As for Xinjiang, it was incorporated into the Chinese state in the 1750s and eventually became a full province in 1884, marking the western border of the Chinese state under the Qing. Obviously, the history of both areas in relation to Chinese control goes back centuries.

Second, the terminology of "separatism" and "terrorism" is selective, depending on who uses it. From one perspective, the attack on the World Trade Centre in New York in 2001 is "terrorist," while the efforts by some in Tibet and Xinjiang are peaceful and "separatist," seeking independence. From another perspective, the deadly 2008 riots in Llasa, Tibet, in which some Tibetans burned, looted, and killed Han Chinese and Muslims are "terrorist." Or the attempted suicide attack on a China

6 The State and Minority Nationalities (Ethnic Groups) in China 101

Southern flight in 2008, threats to attack the Beijing Olympics in 2008, a car ramming in Tiananmen Square in 2013 and the knife attack in Kunming railway station, perpetrated by Uyghur radical Muslims and in which many were killed and even more injured, are "terrorist" acts. To add a twist, the Chinese government typically uses a three-character phrase, "separatism, extremism and terrorism," which is not restricted to religion (Davis 2013, 98). Whether we agree or not, the connection between separatism and terrorism informs government policy.

Third, a crucial feature of Chinese sovereignty is the resistance to all forms of foreign interference. This approach to sovereignty arises from the anticolonial struggles of the nineteenth and twentieth centuries, in which Chinese independence from semi-colonialism developed a strong sense of the need to prevent foreign intervention. (It also influences China's dealings with other countries, in which it avoids any effort to change political, economic and social patterns.) Thus, there had been a profoundly negative effect from the CIA's intervention in Tibet in the 1950s, funding the Dalai Llama and inciting the ill-fated uprising in 1959, in which tens of thousands of Tibetans died and the Dalai Llama and his entourage fled to India. CIA operations wound up in the 1970s, only to be replaced with western propaganda, funding, and organization – especially by the United States' National Endowment for Democracy that carries on the work of the CIA – of protests in Tibet, all of which are based on a particular interpretation of "democracy" and "human rights" (Norbu 2001, 263–282; Mackerras 2003, 32–35, 157–165; Davis 2013, 89–92). These activities have also focused on Xinjiang, with the added dimension of a distinct increase in influence from Islamic radicalism from further west in the 1990s. The discovery of Uyghurs training with al-Qaeda in Afghanistan, or links with militant groups in restive parts of Pakistan, as well as various radical fronts focused on Xinjiang and passing weapons, explosives, and militants along drug routes (Davis 2013, 102–103, 108), made it clear that another form of foreign interference had arisen. All of these efforts are seen as profound challenges to Chinese sovereignty.

A fourth issue concerns the tensions between autonomy and unity (a recurring theme). One might argue that it is precisely the preferential nationalities policy and its fostering of local identities and cultures that has generated such movements (as had happened in the Soviet Union). By giving minority nationalities the economic resources and encouragement for cultural, linguistic, educational, and political self-management, the potential is to create a desire for distinct identity separate from the state that fostered such identity. At the same time, we must balance this with the resolute emphasis in the Chinese constitution and nationalities policy that China's borders will remain unchanged. There is no right to secession for any part of China (unlike the Soviet Union) and any such move is strongly prevented, so much that those entertaining these possibilities are in a relatively weak position.

Finally, there is a distinct variation of emphasis. Some foreign critics of China in relation to Tibet and more recently Xinjiang – especially the United States, Canada, Germany, Great Britain, and India – focus on cultural issues, with religion playing a major role (Tibetan Buddhism and Islam among the Uyghur). A crucial feature here again is that any sign of outside meddling – as with any religious group in China – is seen as a challenge to Chinese sovereignty. However, on the matter of culture it is worth noting the most thorough treatment of the issue by Mackarras, who observes, "what strikes me most forcefully about the period since 1980 or so is not how much the Chinese have harmed Tibetan culture, but how much they have allowed, even encouraged it to revive; not how weak it is, but how strong" (Mackerras 2003, 46; see also Sautman 2003, 2006). The same could be said of Xinjiang, especially if one keeps in mind that Mackerras's focus is on citizens living in these regions, rather than those who have not lived there for more than a generation or two.

The Chinese emphasis is consistently on economic issues as the core reason for unrest. This is a distinctly Marxist approach, with massive investment and preferential economic treatment for Tibet and Xinjiang (Davis 2013, 85–87, 96–98). For example, when unrest in Xinjiang rose to a new level in the 1990s, much analysis and policy revision followed. The result was two-pronged: an immediate focus on comprehensive security (which is a core feature of Chinese society at many levels) and a long-term effort to improve economic conditions in a region that still lagged behind the much of eastern China (Mackerras 2003, 53). Not all such incentives have been as successful as might have been hoped, with the various nationalities in Xinjiang – not merely Uyghur, but also including Han, Hui, Kazak, Mongol, and Kirgiz – benefitting at different levels. The most significant project to date is the massive "Belt and Road Initiative," launched in 2014. Although its geographical scope is much vaster than the western parts of China, the economic effect is already being felt in these parts. Thus, it is reasonable to say that there has been a marked improvement in the economic wellbeing of all those who live in these and other regions, such as Yunnan and Guizhou. The basic position is that if people see that their living conditions have improved, they will more willingly see themselves as part of the greater whole – as we find, for example, with another major Muslim group, the Hui (Davis 2013, 100). However, this variation of emphasis between culture and economy brings us to the next issue: human rights.

An Alternative Approach to Human Rights

For some foreign interventionists, the separatism-terrorism description is a smokescreen for systemic abuses of human rights; for others – not merely the Chinese – the threat is real and the solution focuses on economic wellbeing. How are we to understand these differences?

Rather than resorting to tit-for-tat exchanges (Human Rights Watch 2018; Amnesty International 2018; State Council 2018), we need to ask a deeper question. The key is to identify distinct traditions of human rights and resist the effort to universalize one of those traditions so that it is imposed on others. Context, history, and culture determine the nature of the traditions. Thus, the European tradition focuses on civil and political rights, such as freedom of speech, freedom of assembly, the right to life, equality before the law, the right to a fair trial, freedom of religion, and so on. Such is the hegemonic power of this tradition that many assume it designates "human rights" as such. Yet, the history of this tradition is telling: the modern meaning of "right," Latin *ius*, began to arise in the European twelfth century. It meant a natural innate force or power that leads human beings to act rightly. In other words, it was a "natural" force that arose from the innate power of reason. It was closely connected with another word, *dominium*, which designated the mastery exercised by a rational and free-willing individual. The outcome: a right can work only if one has power or mastery to enact it (Tierney 1997). These senses did not arise in a vacuum, for they were the result of the rediscovery and application of ancient Roman law by the "lawyer popes" of the eleventh century (Gianaris 1996, 20; Miéville 2004, 95–97). Central to this rediscovery was the idea of private property, which the Romans called *dominium*. Why this word? It entailed in the first instance mastery – by a master or *dominus* – over a slave, who was seen as a thing and therefore property, but then came to apply to all private property (Wolff 1951, 67; Patterson 1982, 32; Graeber 2011, 201). The upshot is that the European development of the idea of a right and therefore a human right was seen as private property, over which one had mastery. This would later develop into the idea that one would have mastery over one's individual speech, political expression, religion, ability to assemble, and so on. The history of the term and its exercise is clearly important for understanding its later emphases, a history that was intimately connected with the development of private property and thereby slavery, so much so that the Dutch lawyer Hugo Grotius (1625 [2005], I.1.5) – who was responsible for a major step developing the European tradition of human rights – argued that a human right is the power over ourselves or power over others, such as slaves. This he called liberty.

A Chinese (and Marxist) approach to human rights comes from a different tradition. The following points are drawn from the comprehensive study by Sun Pinghua, *Human Rights Protection System in China* (2014). To begin with, it recognizes not absolute or singular universals, but rooted universals, or contextualized commonalities. This means that there are universals that may apply to all peoples, but they can and do arise in different contexts and cultures. Crucially, we must always remember the specific context, for it reveals the history, promises, and limitations of the tradition in question. In this way, the idea of "rooted universals" moves past the facile distinction between relative and absolute (Sun 2014, 132–135). On the question of human rights, this means that the European tradition may contribute some features to international human rights, but it neglects other features.

Let us consider the Chinese tradition's approach to human rights. To begin with, in contrast to the Euro-American tradition's emphasis on individual mastery, a Chinese approach emphasizes not merely the collective but recognizes both individual and collective. A good example is the first statement of the United Nations' *Universal Declaration of Human Rights* (1948): "All human beings are born free and equal in dignity and rights. They are endowed with reason and conscience and should act towards one another in a spirit of brotherhood." Why is this a good example of a Chinese approach to human rights? It comes through P.C. Chang (Zhang Pengchun), who was vice-chair of the Commission on Human Rights. It is well documented that Chang proposed the term "conscience," which is drawn from the Confucian term *ren*. Indeed, Chang explained that a better translation of *ren* is "two-person mindedness." Obviously, this is a collective emphasis that balances the individual dimensions of the first half of the statement.

A further point is that while the Euro-American tradition emphasizes the inalienable right of individuals and downplays the role of sovereign governments, a Chinese approach to human rights stresses the foundational role of sovereignty. This point relates not merely to the fact that individual states need to ratify and enact the international treaties, especially from the United Nations, but to the more important fact that a colonized country cannot exercise any rights whatsoever. In a Chinese situation, the struggle against colonialism – the time of "humiliation" – is usually put in terms of the three mountains: imperialism, feudal relics, and bureaucratic capitalism. Only when these three were overcome, from 1949, could sovereignty begin to be exercised and rights enacted. There are two implications: first, is sovereignty determinative of human rights? The answer is no: sovereignty is an inescapable basis,"but human rights are the most essential and at the highest level" (Sun 2014, 121). In robust Chinese debates, one finds that sovereignty is simply an assumed basis (see, for example, Luo and Song 2012). Second, this approach to sovereignty arises from the anticolonial struggle (see above). In light of this history, one may understand the resolute emphasis on avoiding and resisting foreign interference at all levels.

Third and most importantly, while the Euro-American tradition focuses on civil and political rights, it neglects a whole other dimension. This is the right to economic wellbeing for all, which includes the right to work and to development. These are foundational in a Chinese context. They are not seen as a "second generation" of human rights, with civil and political rights as the "first generation" (Vasak 1977), for the idea of these generations indicates the Euro-American tradition. Instead, the Chinese emphasis goes back in more immediate history to the Jiangxi-Fujian Soviet of the early 1930s, with its capital in Ruijin. Here developed what may be called the "Ruijin ethos": focus first on the people's need for food, shelter, clothing, and security; only when these are secured will they become communists. In the longer tradition, the Confucian ethos is strong, particularly with the Confucian influence in terms of the desire for at least a *xiaokang* society, meaning that one is moderately well-off, healthy, and peaceful. Thus, the basic human right in China remains the right to economic wellbeing. We can see this in the consistent focus of minority nationalities policy, on the long-term poverty alleviation program, the Belt and Road Initiative, and also with the long-term emphasis on economic improvement in the trouble spots of Tibet and Xinjiang. This particular emphasis has indeed become a rooted universal, acknowledged, and ratified by others – although not the United States – in terms of the United Nations' *International Covenant on Economic, Social, and Cultural Rights* (1976). Article 11(1) is relevant here, which mentions that state parties "recognize the rights of everyone to an adequate standard of living for himself and his family, including adequate food, clothing, and housing, and to the continuous improvement of living conditions" (see also ASEAN 2012).

The implications of this distinct tradition of human rights in relation to minority nationalities are as follows: human rights apply as much to the collective or group as the individual – in this case the group in question is the nationality; foreign interference in such matters is an affront to Chinese sovereignty, which is not to say that the Chinese policy studies do not learn much from other practices (notably the collapse of the Soviet Union); and the right to economic wellbeing and development remains foundational to the preferential policy in relation to minority nationalities. This emphasis appears not merely with long-term programs in relation to trouble spots, but more generally because minority nationalities tend to live in remote areas where the benefits of China's development have been relatively slow to materialize.

Conclusion: Between Autonomy and Unity

How we assess the Chinese approach minority nationalities, trouble spots, and the different traditions of human rights is another matter and beyond the remit of this study, but it is important to understand how this approach has been developed and how it works.

In closing, three matters are important. First and as mentioned earlier, the minority nationalities "preferential policy" operates in terms of a tension, particularly after the revisions of the 1990s. This is a tension between autonomy and unity – greater autonomy for the nationalities and the absolute unity of the Chinese state. Obviously, this is a contradiction. But rather than the European tradition's tendency to see contradictions in terms of an opposition between either-or, it is useful to consider a distinctly Chinese approach to contradictions. In other words, what are opposites – such as unity and diversity in this case – can operate as a non-antagonistic contradiction. Or, as the old saying puts it, "*xiangfan xiangcheng,*" "Things that oppose each other also complement each other" (Mao 1937 [1965], 343). This point is not pure philosophical speculation, for significant evidence exists that cultural activism among the many nationalities (such as the Dai, Bai, and Muslim Hui in Yunnan province), especially in terms of economics, but also with regard to language, education, and religion, actually enhances and strengthens the sense of belonging to China as a whole (McCarthy 2000; Postiglione et al. 2009). The key, of course, is economic, for the Chinese tradition stresses that economic wellbeing enhances one's desire to remain part of the larger whole.

This economic focus raises a further question: is it enough? The preferential policy may stress economic wellbeing, but it also includes culture, language, literature, education, and governance. These features have at times been secondary to the economic focus, which has provided ground for some international critics. In this context, it is worth noting that at the nineteenth congress of the Communist Party of China (November 2017), Xi Jinping (2017, 14) announced a new primary contradiction: the contradiction between unbalanced and inadequate development and the people's ever-growing needs for a better life. Not only does this need to identify a primary contradiction come from Mao Zedong, and not only is it the first change in 36 years, but it also raises a question: is this yet another recognition that life – including that for minority nationalities – requires more than economic wellbeing?

Cross-References

▶ Cultural Socialization and Ethnic Consciousness
▶ Ethno-politics in the People's Republic of China

References

Amnesty International (2018) Amnesty International report 2017/18: the state of the World's human rights. Amnesty International, London
Anderson B (1991) Imagined Communities, Revised edn. Verso, London
ASEAN (2012) ASEAN human rights declaration. Asea-Pacific Human Rights Center, Osaka
Boer R (2017) Stalin: from theology to the philosophy of socialism in power. Springer, Beijing
Bulag U (2010) Alter/native mongolian identity: from nationality to ethnic group. In: Perry E, Selden M (eds) Chinese society: change, conflict and resistance. Routledge, London, pp 262–287
Connor W (1984) The National question in marxist-leninist theory and strategy. Princeton University Press, Princeton
Connor W (2009) Mandarins, marxists, and minorities. In: Zhou M, Hill AM (eds) Affirmative action in China and the U.S.: a dialogue on inequality and minority education. Palgrave Macmillan, New York, pp 27–46
Crossley P, Siu H, Sutton D (2006) Empire at the margins: culture, ethnicity, and frontier in early modern China. Stanford University Press, Berkeley
Davis EVW (2013) Ruling, resources and religion in China: managing the multiethnic state in the 21st century. Palgrave Macmillan, Houndmills
Dillon M (1999) China's Muslim Hui community: migration, settlement and sects. Routledge, London
Dreyer JT (1976) China's forty millions. Harvard Univerity Press, Cambridge
Egry G (2005) Social democracy and the nationalities question. In: Feitl I, Sipos B (eds) Regimes and transformations: hungary in the twentieth century. Napvilág Kiadó, Budapest, pp 95–118
Gianaris N (1996) Modern capitalism: privatization, employee ownership, and industrial democracy. Greenwood Publishing, Westport
Gladney D (1991) Muslim Chinese: ethnic nationalism in the People's Republic. Council on East Asian Studies, Harvard University, Cambridge
Graeber D (2011) Debt: the first 5,000 years. Melville House, New York
Grotius H (1625 [2005]) The rights of war and peace. Translated by John Clarke. Edited by Richard Tuck. 3 vols. Liberty Fund, Indianapolis
Hill AM, Zhou M (2009) Introduction. In: Zhou M, Hill AM (eds) Affirmative action in China and the U.S.: a dialogue on inequality and minority education. Palgrave Macmillan, New York, pp 1–24
Hillman B (2003) Paradise under construction: minorities, myths and modernity in northwest Yunnan. Asian Ethn 4(2):177–190
Human Rights Watch (2018) World report 2018: events of 2017. Human Rights Watch, New York
Kaup K (2002) Regionalism versus ethnic nationalism. China Q 172:863–884
Luo H, Song G (2012) Balance and imbalance in human rights law. Soc Sci China 33(1):55–70
Ma R (2009) Issues of minority education in Xinjiang, China. In: Zhou M, Hill AM (eds) Affirmative action in China and the U.S.: a dialogue on inequality and minority education. Palgrave Macmillan, New York, pp 179–198
Mackerras C (2003) China's ethnic minorities and globalisation. RoutledgeCurzon, London
Mao Z (1937 [1965]) On contradiction. In: Selected works of Mao Tse-Tung, vol 1. Foreign Languages Press, Beijing, pp 311–347

Martin T (2001) The affirmative action empire: nations and nationalism in the Soviet Union, 1923–1939. Cornell University Press, Ithaca

McCarthy S (2000) Ethno-religious mobilisation and citizenship discourse in the People's Republic of China. Asian Ethn 1(2):107–116

Miéville C (2004) Between equal rights: a Marxist theory of international law, Original edn. Brill/Pluto, Leiden/London, p 2005

National People's Congress (2001) Zhonghua renmin gongheguo Minzu quyu zizhi fa (Law of the People's Republic of China on regional national autonomy). Ethnic Publishing House, Beijing

Norbu D (2001) China's Tibet policy. Curzon, Richmond

Patterson O (1982) Slavery and social death: a comparative study. Harvard University Press, Cambridge

Postiglione G, Jiao B, Tsering N (2009) Tibetan student perspectives on neidi schools. In: Zhou M, Hill AM (eds) Affirmative action in China and the U.S.: a dialogue on inequality and minority education. Palgrave Macmillan, New York, pp 127–142

Sautman B (1998a) Affirmative action, ethnic minorities and China's universities. Pac Rim Law Policy J 7(1):77–116

Sautman B (1998b) Preferential policies for ethnic minorities in China: the case of Xinjiang. Nationalism Ethnic Politics 4(1–2):86–118

Sautman B (2003) 'Cultural genocide' and Tibet. Texas Int Law J 38(2):173–246

Sautman B (2006) Colonialism genocide, and Tibet. Asian Ethn 7(3):243–265

Sautman B (2010) 'Vegetarian between meals': the Dalai Llama, war, and violence. Positions 18 (1):89–143

Stalin IV (1913 [1953]) Marxism and the National Question. In: Works, vol 2. Foreign Languages Publishing House, Moscow, pp 300–381

State Council Information Office of the People's Republic of China (2018) Human rights record of the United States in 2017. State Council, Beijing

Sun P (2014) Human rights protection system in China. Springer, Heidelberg

Suny RG (1993) The revenge of the past: nationalism, revolution, and the collapse of the Soviet Union. Stanford University Press, Stanford

Suny RG, Martin T (2001) A state of nations: empire and nation-making in the age of Lenin and Stalin. Oxford University Press, Oxford

Tapp N (1995) Minority nationality in China: policy and practice. In: Barnes RH, Gray A, Kingsbury B (eds) Indigenous peoples of Asia. Association for Asian Studies, Ann Arbor, pp 195–220

Tierney B (1997) The idea of natural rights: studies on natural rights, natural law and church law 1150–1625. Scholar's Press, Atlanta

UN General Assembly (1976) International covenant on economic, social, and cultural rights, United Nations treaty series, vol 993. United Nations, New York

Vasak K (1977) Human rights: a thirty-year struggle: the sustained efforts to give force of law to the universal declaration of human rights. UNESCO Cour 30(11):29–32

Wang T (2009) Preferential policies for minority college admission in China: recent developments, necessity, and impact. In: Zhou M, Hill AM (eds) Affirmative action in China and the U.S.: a dialogue on inequality and minority education. Palgrave Macmillan, New York, pp 71–82

Wolff HJ (1951) Roman law: an historical introduction. University of Oklahoma Press, Norman

Xi J (2017) Secure a decisive victory in building a moderately prosperous society in all respects and strive for the great success of socialism with Chinese characteristics for a new era: report to the 19th National Congress of the Communist Party of China, October 18, 2017. Foreign Languages Press, Beijing

Zhou M (2009) Tracking the historical development of China's positive and preferential policies for minority education: continuities and discontinuities. In: Zhou M, Hill AM (eds) Affirmative action in China and the U.S.: a dialogue on inequality and minority education. Palgrave Macmillan, New York, pp 47–70

Ethnic Blindness in Ethnically Divided Society: Implications for Ethnic Relations in Fiji

Romitesh Kant

Contents

Introduction	110
Ethnic Blindness	111
The Integration (Ethnic Blindness): Accommodation Debates	112
Accommodation	113
Integration	113
Colonial Rule and the Politicization of Ethnicity in Fiji	114
Constitutionalizing Ethnicity in Post-independent Fiji	115
Reorientation to Authoritarian Civic Nationalism	119
The Indigenous Fijian Challenges to "Ethnic Blindness"	121
Conclusion	124
References	126

Abstract

This chapter critically examines Fiji's approach to ethnicity by adopting an "ethnically blind" approach to constitutional and political reform since the 2006 military coup. As a multiethnic and culturally diverse society, Fiji has witnessed political conflicts arising from this ethnic and cultural diversity. Since gaining independence from the United Kingdom in 1970, Fiji politics have been marked by an alternating pattern of coups and constitutional reform. The country has instituted various constitutional arrangements with a view to meeting group claims to difference and equality. While the 1970 and 1997 Constitutions sought a form of multicultural compromise with the realities of Fiji's demographic makeup, demands for continued ethno-political paramountcy by sections of the indigenous Fijian (*iTaukei*) population led to the overthrow of the democratically elected governments in 1987 and 2000. The 1990 Constitution institutionalized

---

R. Kant (✉)
Institute for Human Security and Social Change (IHSSC), College of Arts and Social Sciences, La Trobe University, Melbourne, VIC, Australia
e-mail: r.kant@latrobe.edu.au; romit.fj@gmail.com

the privileged ethno-political status of indigenous Fijians. Following the 2006 military coup, Fiji embarked on a nation-building program designed, inter alia, to create unity by eliminating official categorization based on ethnicity. It is argued that national integration in the Fijian context has been an attempt to forge "unity in diversity," seeking to wish away sociocultural differences and imposing uniformity in spite of complex cultural, ethnic, and religious diversity. This "ethnically blind" approach has the potential to create more conflict and pose obstacles to unity, peaceful coexistence, progress, and stable development. It recommends that national integration and its benefits can be realized only with the development and entrenchment of a supportive public culture, understanding, respecting, and tolerating differences occasioned by sociocultural diversity.

Keywords

Ethnic diversity · Ethnic conflict · Divided societies · Ethnic blindness Constitutional reform · Fiji politics

Introduction

Constitutional deliberations in pre- and post-independent Fiji have mostly revolved around the issue of ethnic distribution of power. Constitutional frameworks in Fiji prior to the 2006 coup were organized on the basis of treating ethnic communities as corporate entities with group rights. The first three post-independent constitutions in Fiji (the 1970 Independence Constitution, the 1990 Constitution, and the 1997 Constitution) were based on the assumptions that there are distinct communities divided by their race; that these communities are homogeneous, sharing common interests; and that their group interests are opposed. Despite the tumultuous history of constitutional democracy, Fiji embarked on yet another, constitution-making process in 2012, fifth in its 48 years since independence, the result of which is the 2013 Constitution, touted as an "ethnically blind" constitution. Claims have been made that this constitution would usher in an era of democratic consolidation and provide much needed political stability.

In the four decades since independence in 1970, Fiji has had six coups (four successful, two unsuccessful) and a mutiny (2000). Up till 2017, no fewer than four constitutional approaches have been adopted in Fiji highlighting the obstacles faced by many divided societies in designing appropriate constitutions. Fiji's post-independence history of constitutional reform has been defined by competition between three very different conceptions of the Fijian nation and (hence) of Fijian nationalism. Constitutional discourse in Fiji has presented ideological security to citizens in the form of three visions, represented as "ethno-cultural," "civic," and "multiculturalist."

The first approach, in the lead up to independence in 1970, was evident in a series of discussions and debates held in Fiji and Britain. It involved a contestation between civic and ethnic nationalism resulting in constitutional recognition of the three most prominent ethnic groups through the electoral provisions in the constitution and entrenchment of indigenous Fijian interests with veto power granted to the Great

Council of Chiefs nominees to the Senate. A second approach, prompted by the coups of 1987, paid even more attention to differences, constitutionalizing indigenous Fijian hegemony and transforming Fiji into a hegemonic ethnic democracy. The instability created by the hegemonic ethnic democracy prompted a new set of constitutional debates producing yet another approach. This third approach, beginning in the-mid 1900s, involved a transition from the hegemonic ethnic state to a more multicultural democracy. The strategy involved the adoption of a constitution that recognized ethnic groups as corporate consociations while aiming to transcend ethnic differences in the long run through the centripetal electoral system and provisions for a multi-party executive. This transformation did not provide the desired democratic stability as Fiji suffered more attempted removals of democratically elected governments in 2000 and 2006.

2012 marked the beginning of yet another set of debates and negotiations that have continued to the present. It produced a fourth approach that was version of the civic nationalist strategy proposed, but rejected, in the lead-up to independence. The motive behind this approach is to move Fiji away from accommodating ethnic group interests to an "ethnically blind constitution," aimed at de-ethnicization of the political sphere and the creation of a unified civic state. However, this latest approach has been compromised by the militarized transition to democracy intended to preserve the pre-2014 status quo, an expanded role of the military in domestic politics, and the persistence of popular belief in the paramountcy of indigenous Fijian interests.

Ethnic Blindness

The concept of "ethnic blindness" is closely associated with the "color-blind" ideal. While explicit racism validates beliefs about racial superiority and social inequity, color-blind racial approaches embody a repudiation of racism even in extending to contest the concept of race itself (Bonilla-Silva 1997).

The theory of color-blindness proposes that racial categories do not matter and should not be considered when making decisions. The primary tenet of this approach is that social categories should be dismantled and disregarded and everyone should be treated as equal individuals (Walton et al. 2014: 112; Schofield 1997: 252; Ullucci and Battey 2011: 1196; Vorauer et al. 2009: 838–839; Ryan et al. 2007). Ethnic blindness as an approach to issues of ethnic-racial difference centers on the premise "that racial group membership and race-based differences should not be taken into account when decisions are made, impressions are formed and behaviors are enacted" (Apfelbaum et al. 2012: 205). In other words, everybody should be "judged as individual human beings without regard to race or ethnicity" (Ryan et al. 2006, 2007: 618; Neville et al. 2000). Ethnic blindness is related to the notion of a post-racial society where ethnicity/race does not matter and racism is a thing of the past (Appiah and Gutmann 1996; Cho 2009; Ono 2009). Calls for ethnic blindness are not just normative but prescriptive as well, which is briefly expounded on the following section. Acknowledging the existence of ethnic groups emphasizes differences, which then brings about discrimination and is seen as a system of perpetuating stereotyping (Markus et al. 2000; Tajfel and Turner 1979; Peery 2011: 473). Ethnic blindness can prevent prejudice and discrimination: "If people or institutions do not even notice race [or ethnicity], then they cannot act in a racially biased manner" (Apfelbaum et al. 2012: 205). Therefore, proponents of ethnic blindness choose to avoid or ignore race in interpersonal interactions under the belief that it would decrease racism.

The concept of ethnic blindness for the purposes of this chapter is closely linked to the idea of color blindness in that an ethnically blind constitution is one which does not recognize ethnic differences but treats all citizens equally giving them equal recognition. This is reflected in the theories of "politics of universalism" integration and civic nationalism.

The Integration (Ethnic Blindness): Accommodation Debates

The question of how constitutions should respond to the challenges of ethnic nationalism has prompted two main approaches to constitutional design: (i) states which tend to disregard ethnic differences and to treat all persons as citizens with equal rights and obligations (sometimes described as "the liberal" or ethnically blind state) and (ii) states which are based on the political recognition of ethnic groups as rights-bearing entities ("ethnic-based states"). The latter can be subdivided into two groups: one in which a majority dominates other communities ("hegemonic state") and the other which is more consensual and aims at power sharing and proportionality ("consociational state").

Academics overwhelmingly assert that ethnically divided societies require accommodative constitutional designs to avert political instability and violent conflict. This stance has variously been characterized as "widely held," "dominant," and "a panacea" (Reilly 2001: 20; Binningsbø 2013: 89). By contrast, "the scholarly orthodoxy has long rejected majoritarian approaches" (Reilly 2001: 20). Arend Lijphart declared in 1994 that consociationalism is "the only workable type of democracy in deeply divided societies" (as cited by Reilly 2001: 169). Timothy Sisk and Andrew Reynolds assert "the alternative [to accommodation] is nearly always a catastrophic breakdown of the state and society" (Reynolds and Sisk 1998: 30). Reynolds later elaborated "parliamentarism, proportional representation, and power- sharing structures provide the foundational level of inclusion needed by precariously divided societies to pull themselves out of the maelstrom of ethnic conflict and democratic instability" (Reynolds 1999: 268). By contrast, he insisted, integrationist constitutional frameworks lead to "increased ethnic hostility" and "political instability" (Reynolds 1999: 269).

However, a smaller but slowly growing group of academics is skeptical that accommodative institutions are the only, or even the best, constitutional design to promote political stability in deeply divided societies. These scholars argue that accommodating groups on the basis of their differences serves to manifest and sharpen these divisions, perpetuating and intensifying intergroup conflict. They further contend that guaranteeing government posts or other benefits to particular groups is anti-democratic and undermines the political competition necessary to promote good governance via accountability. Fixed quotas also can prove particularly divisive over time if there is a significant change in the underlying dynamics on which they were based (Roeder and Rothchild 2005: 37).

The ongoing debate whether states should accommodate or attempt to integrate the ethnic differences of citizens demonstrates a fundamental normative disagreement over the mechanisms of inter-ethnic cooperation. Each approach proceeds from different assumptions and epistemological positions regarding the durability and malleability of politically mobilized ethnic identities. Integrationists focus primarily on the long-term normative vision of the state, while accommodationists are (allegedly) more concerned with the immediate, short-term pressures states face (Pildes 2008: 175). Both approaches translate into a much broader set of policy options with regard to constitutional design in divided societies than the familiar Lijphart–Horowitz debate has generated (Choudhry 2008, p. 27). In the following section, I will briefly summarize the principle differences between the accommodationist and integrationist approaches to managing ethnic difference.

Accommodation

In general terms, accommodationists promote dual or multiple public identities and advocate equality with institutional respect for difference (Choudhry 2008: 27). They assume ethnic identities in segmented societies are resilient and not susceptible to short-term transformation. However, they do not necessarily believe identities are primordial and fixed (Bertrand 2008: 209; McGarry et al. 2008: 52).

Accommodationists seek to ensure each ethnic group has the public space necessary to express its identity, make its own decisions in areas of critical importance, and protect itself against the majority (McGarry et al. 2008: 42). The result is the design of public policy, which permits the institutional expression of differences in the public sphere, such as minority language rights. Consociational techniques advocated by Arend Lijphart (1975, 1977, 2008) and others (McGarry and O'Leary 2005; McGarry et al. 2008; etc.) are examples of approaches to accommodating cultural pluralism (power-sharing executives; proportionality; segmental autonomy, territorial or corporate, along ethnic lines; mutual veto rights among groups; and arbitration mechanisms). Centripetalism, advocated principally by Donald Horowitz (1991, 2000, 2002, 2007), is another example of how states can accommodate ethnic difference, albeit at the integrationist end of the spectrum. The political incentives this approach advocates to encourage intergroup cooperation assume that the existence of ethnic political parties is inevitable (Choudhry 2008: 27).

Integration

Integrationists, by contrast, believe political instability and even further conflict are a consequence of group-based partisanship in political institutions, since they empower elites that have a vested interest in maintaining these social divisions.

They reject the idea that ethnic difference should necessarily translate into political differences and instead argue for the possibility of a common (civic) public identity (Choudhry 2008: 27). As McGarry, O'Leary, and Simeon note (2008: 73), integrationists advocate such an approach even when ethnicity is served as the basis of political mobilization, since they believe ethnic identities are seldom as long-standing or as deep as supporters of accommodation suggest. Accordingly, integrationists support constitutional strategies that promote a common public identity, which transcends, crosscuts, and minimizes ethnic cleavages, without (importantly) demanding ethno-cultural uniformity in the private sphere. Examples of such strategies include common state institutions, "ethnically blind" public policies, the promotion of individual rather than communal rights, the design of mixed or nonethnic territorial entities, and electoral systems which encourage the formation of pre-election coalitions across ethnic divides (Sisk 1996: xi).

Integration/ethnically blind constitutional design is concerned with de-ethnicization of politics emphasizing the importance of state neutrality among different sub-national identities. The difference between integration and accommodation models is that the accommodation models acknowledge the importance of recognizing public and private ethnic groups, identities, needs, and aspirations, although to varying degrees. The accommodationist models of constitutional design can be anywhere on a spectrum from mild ethnicization to appropriation of the state by a dominant ethnic group. Centripetalists are closer in their commitment to the long-term de-ethnicization of politics by focusing on the need to design institutions that reward moderates from different groups as opposed to the radicals. Consociationalism is more open to greater recognition of ethnic groups than centripetalists by being inclusive of radicals. On the extreme end of accommodation is hegemonic control, whereby the state and the dominant ethnic group appropriates its institutions for the purposes of promoting the dominant group's demand for political control of the state.

To contextualize the integrationist-accommodationist debate in Fiji's political landscape, throughout the history of nation building in Fiji especially after 1970, there emerged two competing visions of the emerging nation-state: a struggle between claims for indigenous Fijian ethno-nationalism and civic nationalism. Debates around constitutional design have exposed a persistent tension between civic nationalism and ethno-nationalism, that is, between political equality, on the one hand, and the need to maintain distinct identities, on the other.

Colonial Rule and the Politicization of Ethnicity in Fiji

Political instabilities in post-independent Fiji are a result of colonial policies that were instituted since British colonization in 1874. Policies of indirect rule aimed at placating indigenous Fijians and the divide and rule policies that separated ethnic groups since the introduction of indentured Indian laborers has had a lasting impact on solidifying ethnic identities in Fiji. These policies later created problems for the British government in the lead-up to independence, contributing to political instabilities after independence.

In order to thwart European settler exploitation of indigenous Fijian labor and land, and protect indigenous Fijian culture and tradition, Fiji's first Governor General, Sir Arthur Gordon, reorganized the social modes of control to keep order and stability in Fiji (Robertson and Tamanisau 1988: 7; Srebrnik 2002; 189). This meant that preserving the doctrine of the "paramountcy of [indigenous] Fijian interests," implied in the Deed of Cession, was of the utmost importance. Gordon instituted a policy of "divide and rule," of which indirect rule was a major part of this policy.

Through the divide and rule policies, constitutional policy in colonial Fiji was developed with regard to ethnic differences. Initially, the Legislative Council was composed exclusively of nominees by the Governor. Although indigenous Fijian chiefly hierarchy was integrated into the running of district administrations, the Council of Chiefs played an advisory role at the national level (MacNaught 1982). Subsequent changes, from 1904, to representation in the Legislative Council incorporated nominees of the Council of Chiefs, elected nonofficial Europeans, and, from 1929, Indo-Fijian representatives elected from a communal roll. Despite granting franchise to Europeans and Indo-Fijians, effective power was retained by the Governor and his Executive Council. As moves toward independence gained momentum in the 1960s, adult franchise was extended to indigenous Fijians (much to the opposition of indigenous Fijian chiefs), women, and other groups. Since the end of indenture in 1918, Indo-Fijians had consistently demanded common roll and political equality (Gillion 1977; 130). However, the colonial administration and especially European members of the Legislative Council resisted these demands fearing that open franchise combined with a majoritarian system would end up with Indo-Fijian political dominance. They therefore supported communally based electoral rolls. Nevertheless in 1929, the colonial government agreed to the principle of parity in representation in the Legislative Council between elected representatives from the three major communities despite discrepancies in population between Europeans on the one hand and Indo-Fijians and indigenous Fijians on the other. The main outcome of this was that this policy created and fostered many misperceptions between the two major ethnic groups.

Constitutionalizing Ethnicity in Post-independent Fiji

Since decolonization began in Fiji in the 1960s, debates around constitutional design have witnessed contentious debates around integrated, nonracial state, based on individual rights and those who favor of a political order based on ethnic communities: civic and ethnic nationalisms. Until the coup of 2006 and the resulting 2013 Constitution, the issue of nation building and citizenship in Fiji has been secondary to ethnicity and ethnic accommodation.

In the lead-up to independence, while Indo-Fijian leaders through the Federation Party advocated common roll electoral design and political integration, indigenous Fijian leaders through the Fijian Association, together with European political leaders, opposed common roll and political integration (Norton 2002; 134). They were suspicious of the Federation Party proposals, as the demographic changes during that period would mean Indo-Fijian political domination.

Indigenous Fijians viewed the Deed of Cession as a "protective" document that would preserve and protect their "rights and interests with regards to ownership of land and chiefly titles," arguing that their interests should be paramount. As independence became imminent, this protective understanding turned into a more "assertive" one fueled by uncertainty of how their "interests would receive special recognition in the new constitutional order" (Norton 2013; 426). Indigenous Fijian demands were seen as providing for rules and structures that would ensure and provide for political paramountcy – that "only if Fijians were in control of Fiji's political leadership, their interests could be protected" (Norton 2002; 134).

The solution, after intense series of closed-door negotiations in 1969 and 1970 between the leaders of the two major ethnic groups, was a consociational arrangement, encapsulated in the 1970 Constitution, whereby the indigenous Fijians and Indo-Fijians were allocated the same number of parliamentary seats (for an in-depth analysis of the provisions of the 1970 Constitution, see Ghai and Cottrell 2008). To appease indigenous Fijian concerns, which feared political domination by Indo-Fijians and loss of land and political rights, there was agreement that the Senate would provide greater indigenous Fijian representation with veto powers over legislation affecting indigenous Fijian interests (Vasil 1972; 28).

The 1970 Constitution provided hopes that democracy could be made to work in Fiji. In the peaceful transition to independence, leaders from both parties worked well together, establishing a good personal rapport proving to people in Fiji and abroad that genuine multicultural cooperation was possible. Despite this, ethnic polarization was still evident during elections, with voters choosing the comfort of the ethnically based parties, a result of the racially based electoral system (Alley 1970, 184–186; Ghai and Cottrell 2008; 291–292).

In the April 1987 elections, the NFP/Fiji Labor Party coalition defeated the incumbent Alliance Party. Three weeks after the elections, Sitiveni Rabuka led a military coup, with the support of the iTaukei movement and the chiefs, to oust the NFP/FLP government. Initially, Rabuka claimed national security, alluding to the threat posed by the Taukei Movement's agitation and demonstrations, as the reason for carrying out the coup (Ghai 1990: 13; Lawson 1991: 257–259). However, the language that materialized after the coup revealed the reason to be threats of an Indo-Fijian-dominated government to indigenous Fijian political supremacy (Ghai 1990: 13; Lawson 1991: 260–261).

In a subsequent coup in September 1987, Rabuka declared Fiji a Republic, severing all ties with the British monarchy (Lal 1993: 276, 2002). This led to the abrogation of the 1970 Constitution and the promulgation of a new constitution constructed to secure "paramountcy of [indigenous] Fijian interests" (Lal 1993: 274). The 1990 Constitution provided for indigenous Fijian domination in the legislature and executive – 37 out of the 71 seats in the lower house were reserved for them and 24 out of 34 Senate members were to be nominated by the Great Council of Chiefs (GCC). In addition, the President appointed by the GCC would always be a Fijian chief, and the posts of the Prime Minister and other ministries were reserved for indigenous Fijians seats (for an in-depth analysis of the provisions of the 1990 Constitution, see Ghai and Cottrell 2008).

The constitution also "enhanced the entrenchment of legislation protecting Fijian land and other interests" (Ghai and Cottrell 2007: 297–300). The protection provided to specific acts of parliament now encompassed any bill "affecting land, customs or customary rights." (These acts included the Fijian Affairs Act, the Native Lands Trust Act, the Natives Land Act, the Fiji Development Fund Act, the Rotuma Act, the Rotuma Lands Act, the Banaban Lands Act, and the Banaban Settlement Act. Relevant sections?) The GCC Senate appointees were accorded the power of veto with rules specifying that no less than 18 of the 24 Senate members appointed by the GCC had to support it for the bill to pass (Section 78, *Constitution of the Sovereign Republic of Fiji 1990)*. The parliament and the executive were also given unlimited powers to establish affirmative action programs and policies for "promoting and safeguarding the economic, social, educational, cultural, traditional and other interests of the [indigenous] Fijian and Rotuman people" (Chap. 3, "Fijian and Rotuman Interests," *Constitution of the Sovereign Republic of Fiji 1990*).

Despite its ethnically biased orientation, there was one bright spot in the Constitution; it provided for a review of the Constitution before the end of 7 years after its promulgation (Section 161, *Constitution of the Sovereign Republic of Fiji 1990*). In 1995 the government set up a three-member Constitutional Review Committee (CRC), tasked with recommending changes to the 1990 Constitution. In doing so, the Commission had to balance the principle of indigenous Fijian interests while also guaranteeing having full regard to the rights, interests, and concerns of all ethnic groups. While the Commission's recommendations indicated their intention to radically transform Fiji politics through arrangements aimed at de-ethnicization of politics (see Reeves et al. 1996), the Joint Parliamentary Sector Committee's (JPSC's) deviation from these recommendations signaled their intention for cosmetic transformation thereby retaining the fundamentally ethnic character of the state while making some efforts toward dismantling the hegemonic ethnic state.

The 1997 Constitutional arrangements included a mixture of consociational and centripetal features. The communal allocation of almost two-thirds of seats in the House of Representatives is a feature of corporate consociationalism, treating major ethnic groups as corporate entities. It also attempted to move away from race-based politics through the introduction of 25 common roll seats. An appointed 32-member Senate was retained; however, there was a reduction in the number of GCC nominees from 24 to 14 who retained their power of veto over all legislation affecting indigenous Fijians thereby retaining the principle of paramountcy of [indigenous] Fijian interests' but only in a protective sense. The GCC was granted constitutional recognition in the 1990 Constitution; however the 1997 Constitution went further and provided for its roles and functions (Section 116, *Fiji Islands Constitutional Amendment Act 1997*). Chapter 13 of the Constitution (Group Rights) also provided for entrenchment of laws relating to indigenous Fijians, Rotumans, and Banabans and their land and provided for procedures on how to alter the laws. It also provided for the parliament to enact legislation regarding customary laws and for dispute resolution in accordance with traditional processes, for distribution of royalties to landowners and registered customary fishing rights for mineral and resource extraction (Sections 185–6, *Fiji Islands Constitutional Amendment Act 1997)*. Another feature of consociationalism in the Constitution was the mandatory power sharing in the executive whereby the Prime Minister was constitutionally mandated to invite all parties that attain 10% or more seats in parliament to be part of their cabinet in proportion to their composition in Parliament (Section 99, *Fiji Islands Constitutional Amendment Act 1997*).

The electoral provisions of the 1997 Constitution reflect the preferences of the political scientist Donald Horowitz, who preferred a power-sharing model comprising "centripetal, integrative or incentive-based techniques" which he suggests is most likely to foster moderation and conciliation on the part of all concerned. Horowitz recommends the AV system as the best option for divided societies as he believes that political elites must be afforded political and electoral incentives with the aim of "making moderation pay" (Horowitz 1990: 451–475). The notion behind this system is to provide politicians with incentives to seek electoral support from groups beyond their own ethnic community.

While the alternative vote, preferential voting, seemed like an appealing idea, it did not have the desired impact that the CRC foresaw: it did not encourage cooperation between ethnic groups but led to shady deals across ethnic lines, geared mainly to weaken those parties within ethnic groups committed to racial integration (for more see Fraenkel 2001, 2006). The power-sharing executive provisions also it did not work at all well because of the lack of commitment of the leading parties to sharing power. After the 1999 elections, when the Fiji Labour Party (FLP) won and invited Rabuka's Soqosoqo ni Vakavulewa ni Taukei (SVT) to participate, the latter responded with a number of conditions, which Prime Minister Chaudhry interpreted as a rejection. In 2001, after another coup and return to civilian rule, the Soqosoqo Duavata ni Lewenivanua (SDL) party leader invited the FLP to participate while suggesting that there was "insufficient basis for a workable partnership" and went on to recommend a Cabinet with no FLP members (Supreme Court of Fiji: Qarase v. Chaudhry 2003). Resolution of these disputes has involved repeated resort to the courts. In the first case, the Supreme Court held that Chaudhry was not bound to accept the conditions imposed by the SVT for joining government (Supreme Court of Fiji: President of Fiji Islands v. Kubuabola 1999). In the second case, the Supreme Court held the prime minister in breach of the constitution (Supreme Court of Fiji: Qarase v. Chaudhry 2003). The matter went back to court in 2004 over the precise interpretation of the constitution on allocation of seats (Supreme Court of Fiji: President's Reference, Qarase v. Chaudhry – Decision of the Court 2004).

After the 2006 elections, a power-sharing Cabinet did come into being; before the "conventions" that the Supreme Court had advised could develop, another coup ensued the country a few months later, led by the head of the military, Commodore Bainimarama. Initially Bainimarama insisted that the coup was carried out to protect the 1997 Constitution claiming Qarase was violating the spirit of the Constitution by pursuing a controversial legislation that would grant amnesties to those convicted in the 2000 coup. He argued that this legislation would "divide the nation and will have very serious consequences to our future generations." He proclaimed that the military "not only adheres to the rule of law and the Constitution but more importantly believes in the adherence to the spirit of law and the Constitution" (Ghai and Cottrell 2007: 311).

Reorientation to Authoritarian Civic Nationalism

In April 2007, the Bainimarama regime announced its intentions to review the 1997 Constitution with the goal of "ridding the Constitution of provisions that facilitate and exacerbate the politics of race in such areas as the registration of voters and the election of representatives to the House of Representatives through separate electoral rolls" preferring an electoral system that was based on one person-one vote (Fiji Ministry of Information 2007). Speaking at the UN General Assembly in 2007, Bainimarama argued that Fiji's independence was built on shaky foundations (i.e., race-based constitutions) that separated Fijians. Democratic politics that had been practiced in Fiji was therefore divisive and constrained efforts at nation building. He announced that Fiji had to do away with race-based politics, committing to reforms that would entail greater democratization that would ultimately end coup culture (Bainimarama 2007). The coup and its ideology therefore sought to supplant the politics through a nation-building project.

This was initiated under the guise of a state of emergency. The military government acquired extraordinary powers that permitted the armed and police forces to quell dissent, with force if necessary. In the aftermath of the coup and the eventual abrogation of the 1997 Constitution in April 2009, decrees were put in place that severely restricted freedom of movement, assembly, and expression (including media freedom) (Bhim 2011: 2).

In his quest to de-ethnicize Fijian politics, Bainimarama challenged the Methodist Church and the Great Council of Chiefs, institutions that indigenous Fijians hold dear and with reverence causing much concern among indigenous Fijians (Lal 2009: 31–32, 2009: 77; Norton 2009: 112, 2015: 113–125; Ratuva 2011: 112). Bainimarama stated that the military did not have to please the chiefs nor the Methodist Church and was in the best position to institute political and constitutional reforms that would benefit everyone, regardless of their ethnicity (Norton 2009: 112, 2015). He further argued that indigenous Fijians needed to change their mindset that the nation and democracy belonged or should belong to the chiefs (Bainimarama 2007).

Fiji's transition to democracy that began with the Bainimarama regime's constitution-making process was carried out in a restrictive political environment (Kant and Rakuita 2014; Kant 2014a, b). For 6 years, the regime was successful in controlling and silencing most dissenters and the media. In 2012, the regime released two decrees to pave the way for the drafting of a new constitution: the Fiji Constitutional (Constitution Commission) Process Decree 2012 or Decree 57 and the Fiji Constitutional Process (Constituent Assembly and Adoption of Constitution) Decree 2012 or Decree 58. Decree 57 stipulated 11 nonnegotiable principles which had to be reflected in the constitution which aimed at de-ethnicization of Fijian politics: common and equal citizenry; a secular state; removal of systematic corruption; an independent judiciary; elimination of discrimination; good and transparent governance; social justice; one person, one vote, one value; elimination of ethnic voting; proportional representation; and voting age of 18. A five-member Commission was appointed by the regime, headed by Professor Yash Ghai. The Commissioners started their work in July 2012 and wound up operation in December 2012 with the presentation of a draft Constitution to the President (Kant and Rakuita 2014).

The 2012 Commission's draft constitution marked a departure from previous constitutions, a significant move away from the consociational character that defined previous constitutions to one that was intent on civic nation building and integration. It had a difficult balancing act to manage. While the regime wanted ethnically blind/integrationist provisions in the constitution, the Commission after listening to people's views decided to maintain certain aspects of iTaukei institutions and provide for protection of language, culture, traditions, and practices, although making a distinction between the public and private spheres. In the 1990 and 1997 Constitutions, the GCC had been recognized as a public institution with important powers conferred to it, but in the 2012 draft, the GCC was classified as a civil society organization with only advisory powers. Section 47 provided for rights to join and maintain cultural, linguistic, and religious association and practices. The GCC was given constitutional recognition as a nonpartisan organ of civil society, namely, as a custodian of iTaukei culture and traditions (Section 56, Fiji Constitution Commission Draft Constitution 2012).

In January 2013, the regime dumped the Commission's Draft Constitution. The President informed the people that, the commission's draft while it included some good provisions, "many of the provisions of the Ghai draft position us in the past" (Fiji Times Online 2013). He directed the regime to put together a new draft. The regime released its draft in March and held its own "consultations" on it.

In August 2013, the regime released the final version of the Constitution that would take Fiji to elections, which was promulgated by the President in September. The 2013 Constitution in the Preamble makes references to the indigenous Fijians and Rotumans as the first inhabitants of Fiji, recognizing their lands, unique culture, customs and traditions, and language. It also recognizes the same for all the other later immigrants. For the first time, it makes mention of a common national identity, which remains to this day a thorny issue within the indigenous Fijian community.

The recognition of indigenous Fijian customary land ownership in the Constitution is intended to appease suspicions stirred up by ethno-nationalists over most of Fiji's independent history. It is strengthened by Article 28, which confirms that indigenous Fijian, Rotuman, and Banaban land rights are inalienable, while Section 30 provides for fair distribution of royalties from minerals extracted from traditional lands and/or customary fishing grounds.

In terms of institutions, the Senate and the Great Council of Chiefs, both already defunct in practice, are no longer constitutionally recognized. A single-chamber Parliament is introduced, to be elected via a system of proportional representation of party lists (Section 53, Constitution of the Republic of Fiji 2013). With some symbolic importance, Article 53 provides very explicitly: "each voter has one vote, with each vote being of equal value, in a single national electoral roll comprising all the registered voters." Ethnic electoral rolls, and ethnic representation in Parliament, are thus abolished. With indigenous people now constituting a majority of the population, this measure was not as controversial as it would once have been. In all other regards, Fiji's institutions under the terms of this Constitution are Westminster-inspired. The relationship between Parliament and the Cabinet is a reaffirmed codification of British custom; the President, appointed by Parliament, is a purely ceremonial head of state, bound to act solely on his ministers' advice (Section 82, Constitution of the Republic of Fiji 2013).

The Indigenous Fijian Challenges to "Ethnic Blindness"

With minimal recognition to ethnic and cultural identities, the 2013 Constitution aims to develop a culture of civic nationhood. However, the transition to the "ethnically blind" ideology is fraught with challenges (Kant 2017). Indigenous Fijian political and traditional elites have opposed the provisions of the 2013 Constitution condemning the "interim military government" for "failure to protect the group rights of indigenous Fijians" and for appropriating control over "native Fijians semiautonomous government (Matanitu Taukei)" (Lalabalavu and Kepa 2013). Local NGOs (including the newly formed Fiji Native Tribal Congress (FNTC)) protested to the United Nations Committee on Elimination of Racial Discrimination (UN CERD) about the regime abolishing the GCC without consulting the indigenous Fijians. Similarly, the NGO Coalition on Human Rights (NGOCHR) objected to the regime's actions registering concern around the "dismantling and restructuring of what have hitherto been identified as indigenous institutions without appropriate consultation with stakeholders," calling on the regime to "conduct an open dialogue process with the iTaukei people on the change to their name, the removal of the Great Council of Chiefs (GCC) and revision of land laws in recognition of the 2007 United Nations Declaration on the Rights of Indigenous Peoples" (NGO Coalition for Human Rights 2012: 10–11). The NCOHR further called on the regime to publicly declare its position on "the status of the iTaukei people so as to provide certainty to them of their position in the future society of Fiji" (NGO Coalition for Human Rights 2012: 10–11).

The FNTC, in its submission to the UN CERD Committee, objected to the regime's move via decree that all citizens would be known as "Fijians," a term that previously was used to refer only to the indigenous Fijians. "The Decree changed all references of "Fijian "indigenous" or "native" that appeared in the law, government publications and communications, replacing it with the term "iTaukei"" (Fiji Government 2010).

The FNTC submission claimed that the regime violated rights of indigenous Fijians and that the actions and rhetoric of the regime were to "wipe out entirely the group rights of indigenous Fijians and to thereby make Fiji a plural society of individuals where individual rights only is paramount" (Fiji Native Tribal Congress (FNTC) 2012: 42).

The UN CERD Committee, while noting the regime's moves to provide development on the basis of need rather than ethnicity, was concerned about the lack of consultation with indigenous Fijians on reforms relating to indigenous Fijian institutions. The Committee recommended that the government initiate appropriate processes for consultation with indigenous Fijians on policies which affect "their identity, ways of living and resources, in line with the Convention, the United Nations Declaration on the Rights of Indigenous Peoples and the ILO Convention on 169 on Indigenous and Tribal Peoples" (UN Committee on the Elimination of Racial Discrimination (CERD) 2012: 4).

The calls by indigenous Fijian political and traditional elites, the CSOs, and the UN CERD Committee have gone unheeded by the regime. The promulgation of the 2013 Constitution paved the way for parliamentary elections in September 2014. The constitution had brought an end to communal voting, a feature of previous constitutional arrangements. Seven political parties contested the election; however, the main competition was between FijiFirst and SODELPA.

FijiFirst promised a new, modern, secular Fiji free of the crippling legacies of a racially divided past and was more toward the reformist, secularist, modernist, and multiethnic end of the political spectrum, while the SODELPA promised the restoration recognition and power for the iTaukei greater protection for indigenous Fijian land ownership, the restoration of the Great Council of Chiefs, reservation of "Fijian" as the identity for indigenous Fijians, and the establishment of a Christian state placing it at the "protectionist, ethno-nationalistic and conservative end of the continuum" (Ratuva 2015: 143–145). The NFP, FLP, and PDP advocated multiculturalism while also promising to review the Constitution and provide recognition and a role for the GCC.

Describing the 2013 Constitution as "Godless," SODELPA manifesto spoke of how the Constitution "ignored the role of Christianity in the development of Fiji." Secularism became cast as an attempt "to encourage worship of an unknown deity." SODELPA insisted that when it formed government, a new constitution would "ensure God's rightful place in our supreme law" and "uphold Christian values and principles" (Social Democratic Liberal Party (SODELPA) 2014). SODELPA's leadership constantly attacked the Bainimarama Government and the 2013 Constitution for undermining indigenous rights, claiming that by abrogating the 1997 Constitution, the entrenched protection of native land rights had been removed. One specific objection was that without a Senate, and the representation afforded to the GCC through this body, all that was required to change Taukei land ownership in the new unicameral legislature was a simple majority vote in parliament (Fiji Times, 11 September 2014: 29).

Beginning with the usual reference to the 1874 Deed of Cession as the basis for iTaukei monopoly of land ownership, SODELPA's manifesto proceeded to list all the actions of the Bainimarama Government that had purportedly undermined these. The list included appointing government sympathizers to staff the Native Land Trust Board (NTLB, now iTaukei Land Trust Board) and opposition to the Qarase government's Qoliqoli Bill dealing with the ownership of coastal areas, including those used for surfing. The manifesto also made clear that its principal objection was to the transfer of control over native lands away from the chiefs, manifested in the GCC, to the Minister responsible for indigenous Fijian affairs.

The main opposition party SODELPA, managed to secure almost 28% of total votes cast (more than 98% from indigenous Fijians) during the 2014 elections. SODELPA increased its popularity in the 2018 elections as they received almost 40% of total votes. These votes were overwhelmingly from indigenous Fijians due to SODELPAs appeal to the Christian religion, and indigenous Fijian tradition and culture. It thus seems that there remains strong support for constitutional recognition of indigenous Fijian culture and tradition and indigenous Fijian hegemony. The image of indigenous Fijians as iTaukei (owners of the land) remains a potent symbol. What distinguishes Fiji from most divided societies is the presence of an ethnic group with claims of indigeneity, which has created a higher and more abstract level of belonging than just citizenship. The idea of prior occupation has afforded indigenous Fijians grounds for insisting on being given priority in the political and cultural spheres.

Since elections in 2014, SODELPA in parliament has consistently raised issues with regard to Bainimarama's regime and FijiFirst's blatant disregard for issues important to indigenous Fijians and the suppression of indigenous rights since the 2006 coup. MP Niko Nawaikula claimed that Bainimarama – and later his 2013 Constitution – contravened UN-mandated indigenous rights by abolishing the GCC and the exclusive Fijian name and by denying indigenous Fijian self-determination (FBC News 2017).

In response to SODELPA, Bainimarama claimed that "SODELPA keeps summoning up the past and preying on the fears of the iTaukei people about the security of their land and their way of life," ... "it is divisive. It is offensive. And it simply isn't true … There is no threat to iTaukei – to our land, culture, institutions or religion" (Fiji Sun 2015).

Other signs of indigenous Fijian disquiet emerged. Fear of losing privileged constitutional status, small groups of indigenous Fijians in Nadroga/Navosa and Ra provinces, under the influence of an indigenous Fijian expatriate, residing in Australia, who urged them to rise up against the Bainimarama government, declared their provinces sovereign Christian states. Those involved in this blamed the secular, ethnically blind 2013 Constitution. A statement from the group echoed familiar ethno-nationalist themes about alleged British failure at independence in 1970 to return Fiji to descendants of the original signatories of the 1874 Deed of Cession. The Ra group denounced the "oppressive, dictatorial and tyrannical nature of the Bainimarama/Khaiyum regime," with its "nirvana concept of a polity of equality," and "dream" of a "modern progressive Fiji." The Uluda Declaration purported to express the aspirations of "ethnic peoples, first nation peoples of Fiji and therefore sovereign people of this land." It criticized the government's "perverse form of social engineering which employs constitutionally enshrined laws of 'mainstreaming' with which it enforces intensive assimilation that selects only the native Fijian race as its target group" (Field 2015).

As a consequence, by September 2015, 63 persons had been arrested and charged with sedition (Armbruster 2015). Fifteen people charged with sedition in Ra were all found guilty in September 2017, while court proceedings are underway for those changed in Nadroga/Navosa case (Deo 2015).

While for the time being Bainimarama has been successful in restraining and suppressing indigenous Fijian nationalism, SODELPA has demonstrated that appeals to ethno-nationalism remain a potent force with a large enough section of the indigenous Fijian population. Demographic changes in Fiji's population especially the continuing decline in the Indo-Fijian population since the 1980s do not guarantee that demands for indigenous Fijian political dominance are likely to disappear in the near future.

Conclusion

In recent decades, liberal constitutionalism, integration, and ethnic-blindness have come under criticism for enforcing homogeneity thereby ignoring diversity that exists within many nation-states by political theorists (Tully 1995: 58; Taylor 1992: 38; Kymlicka 1996; Parekh 2000). Charles Taylor (1992: 38) locates his reflections on the politics of recognition in multicultural countries against the historical setting of the development of the modern idea of identity, since in his view this idea also explains the growth of the politics of difference. Recognition, Taylor states, indicates mutual relations between individuals, who regard each other as both equal yet separate (Taylor 1992: 25). James Tully (1995) states that different groups (based on immigrant status, gender, indigeneity, linguistic and religious differences) seek constitutional recognition of their cultural diversity. In criticizing liberal constitutionalism, he argues that constitutions are based on the assumption that societies are of a homogenous culture; however in practice it is structured in a way whereby diversity is either excluded or attempts are made to assimilate people (Tully 1995: 58). He further points out that a constitutional order that attempts to provide a structure for the resolution of issues that deal with the interests of the state and its diverse communities cannot be seen to be just if it prevents different cultural objectives for self-determination and government (Tully 1995: 6). His recommendation is that a constitution should be a "form of accommodation" of cultural diversity, of inter-ethnic conversation in which people from culturally diverse backgrounds negotiate settlements on their forms of association over time.

Numerous attempts at constitutional design in Fiji have endeavored to reconcile demands for democracy with demands by some indigenous Fijians that the state should promote their indigenous Fijian nationalist aspirations. Colonial rule shaped a state structure symbolized not only by the political divisions of indigenous Fijians from other groups but in a system that kept them tied to an increasingly "traditional way of life" under the authority of chiefs. The entrenchment of a doctrine of paramountcy of indigenous interests, while well-meaning in its initial design, has been a catalyst for a highly narrow-minded form of ethno-nationalism. Political instabilities in Fiji while detrimental to social and economic relations have also presented an opportunity for dialogue. Coup-makers and their supporters have relied on designing and implementing constitutions to support their objectives, whether they be in the form of indigenous Fijian nationalism in the case of 1987 and 2000 or of promoting civic nationalism and ridding Fiji of communal and ethnic divisions (in the case of 2006 coup). However, the problem with the opportunities offered has been political manipulation by the victors of coups to design constitutions to ensure their short-term political survival rather than attempting to truly find solutions to Fiji's problems.

In a divided society, people will be reluctant to work together unless ethnic groups to which they belong are afforded recognition. However, civic integration (ethnic-blindness) is also important because it urges people to work together politically thus making it easier to allocate goods and services within the state; for democracy to take root, recognition of ethnic groups might be warranted, while for democracy to consolidate, people must be willing to transcend their ethnic group interests and take a broader view (common good).

This constant negotiation and redefinition of inter-ethnic relations is a price divided societies has to pay if consolidation of democracy is to be achieved. Constitutional (re)design is not a final solution as norms, processes, and institutions have to be modified in an ever-changing process and should be viewed as chains of recurring intercultural dialogues and negotiations. As Hanna Lerner and James Tully suggest, constitution-making and reforms in divided societies should not be seen as revolutionary moments but as an evolutionary process (Tully 1995: 183–184; Lerner 2011: 39;194). While a constitution can address the institutional aspects of democracy relatively straightforwardly, addressing the foundational features is more complex as in a divided society there are contending perspectives on the character of the state. Similarly, Adeno Addis (2009: 75) contends that constitutional design in divided societies should not be seen as an attempt to be a final solution to the persistent problems the society faces. Tully, Lerner and Addis argue that controversial issues such as national identity, nation-building, and official language, and state religion should be deferred for future deliberation, arguing in favor of constitutional ambiguity on these issues as an initially. Conflict is highly probable if the constitution attempts resolve the foundational problems of a divided society.

In Fiji, as in many divided societies coming out of conflict, it is clear that the short-term pressure to democratize has not been sufficient to foster democratic stability. What is required is ensuring sustainable long-term systems and processes of reconciliation that aims to bring about profound change in attitude, in conduct, and in the quality of governance systems, socioeconomic environment, structures, and institutions. Transitions to democracy usually involved political elites without much regard to necessary societal changes to ensure future stability. These elite negotiated agreements most times assume that these political resolutions will allow conflicting groups to reconcile and live in harmony. This view overlooks the deep cleavages that still exist. Post-conflict reconciliation in divided societies requires a process that goes beyond inclusion of elites; therefore it should be designed in such a way that is long-term and involves civil society organizations and the community at large. Overlooking a process of deeper reconciliation at the grassroots has the potential to create more problems for the transition and compromises long-term stability.

References

Addis A (2009) Deliberative democracy in severely fractured societies. Ind J Glob Legal Stud 16(1):59–83
Alley R (1970) Independence for Fiji: recent constitutional and political developments. Aust Outlook 24(2):184–186
Apfelbaum EP, Norton MI, Sommers SR (2012) Racial color-blindness: emergence, practice and implications. Curr Dir Psychol Sci 21:205–209
Appiah KA, Gutmann A (1996) Color conscious: the political morality of race. Princeton University Press, Princeton
Armbruster S (2015) Fiji PM 'Distracts' with Overseas Plotter Threat. SBS News, 31. http://www.sbs.com.au/news/article/2015/08/31/fiji-pm-distracts-overseas-plotter-threat. Accessed 30 Apr 2017
Bainimarama VJ (2007) Statement by H.E. Commodore Josaia Voreqe Bainimarama, Prime Minister of the Republic of Fiji Islands. 62nd session of the UN General Assembly, New York
Bhim M (2011) Stifling opposition: an analysis of the approach of the Fiji Government after the 2006 Coup, Canberra: SSGM Discussion Paper Series
Binningsbø H (2013) Power sharing, peace and democracy: any obvious relationships? Int Area Stud Rev 16(1):89–112
Bonilla-Silva E (1997) Rethinking racism: toward a structural interpretation. Am Sociol Rev 62(3):456–480
Cho S (2009) Post-racialism. Law Rev 84:1589–1649
Choudhry S (2008) Bridging comparative politics and comparative constitutional law: constitutional design in divided societies. In: Choudhry S (ed) Constitutional design for divided societies: integration or accommodation? Oxford University Press, New York, pp 3–40
Deo D (2015) 15 people charged with sedition found guilty by the high court. Fiji Village (Suva, Fiji, 23 September 2015), http://fijivillage.com/news-feature/15-people-charged-with-sedition-found-guilty-by-High-Court-Judge-r52ks9/. Accessed 30 Sept 2017
FBC News (2017) Nawaikula brings up constitution and rights. (Suva, Fiji, 13 September), http://www.fbc.com.fj/fiji/54456/nawaikula-brings-up-constitution-and-rights. Accessed 19 Sept 2017
Fiji Government (2010) Fijian Affairs (Amendment) Decree 2010. Decree 31 of 2010. Government Printer, Suva
Field M (2015) On snake gods and edition in Fiji. Micheal J. Field. http://michaeljfield.tumblr.com/post/128137108353/on-snake-gods-and-sedition-in-fiji-these-are-the. Accessed 25 Mar 2016
Fiji Ministry of Information (2007) Moving in the right direction. Retrieved March 14, 2017, from Fiji Ministry of Information: http://www.fiji.gov.fj/uploads/Roadmap_2007.pdf
Fiji Native Tribal Congress (FNTC) (2012) Supplementary report to the committee on the elimination of racial discrimination for the Republic of Fiji. Fiji Native Tribal Congress (FNTC), Suva
Fiji Sun (2015) Full speech: new Kadavu Provincial Council Opening. http://fijisun.com.fj/2015/02/19/full-speech-new-kadavu-provincial-council-opening/. Accessed 25 Mar 2016
Fiji Times Online (2013) The President Ratu Epeli Nailatikau's Address on Fiji's Constitution and Constituent Assembly. January 10. Retrieved September 29, 2015, from Fiji Times Online: http://www.fijitimes.com.fj/story.aspx?id=222129
Fraenkel J (2001) The alternative vote system in Fiji: electoral engineering or ballot-rigging? Commonw Comp Polit 39(2):1–31
Fraenkel J (2008) Political consequences of Pacific Island electoral laws. In: Rich R, Hambly L (eds) Political parties in the Pacific Islands. ANU Press, Canberra, pp 43–68
Ghai Y (1990) A coup by another name? Politics of legality. Contemp Pac 2(1):11–35
Ghai Y, Cottrell J (2007) A tale of three constitutions: ethnicity and politics in Fiji. Int J Const Law 5(4):639–669

Ghai Y, Cottrell J (2008) A tale of three constitutions: ethnicity and politics in Fiji. In: Choudhry S (ed) Constitutional design for divided societies: integration or accommodation? Oxford University Press, Oxford, pp 287–315

Gillion K (1977) The Fiji Indians: challenge to European dominance, 1920–1946. ANU Press, Canberra

Horowitz D (1990) Making moderation pay: the comparative politics of ethnic conflict management. In: Montville JV (ed) Conflict and peacemaking in multiethnic societies. Lexington Books, Lexington, pp 451–475

Horowitz D (1991) A democratic south Africa: constitutional engineering in a divided society. University of California Press, Berkley

Horowitz D (2000) Ethnic groups in conflict. University of California Press, London

Horowitz D (2002) Explaining the Northern Ireland agreement: the sources of an unlikely constitutional consensus. Br J Polit Sci 32(2):193–220

Horowitz DL (2007) The many uses of federalism. Drake Law Rev 55:953–966

Kant R (2014a) Constitution monitoring report: September 2013–September 2014. In: Citizen's Constitutional Forum Limited (ed) Fiji in transition: towards a sustainable constitutional democracy. Citizen's Constitutional Forum Limited, Suva, pp 105–146

Kant R (2014b) The roadmap to democracy and Fiji's 2012 constitution-making process, SSGM In-Brief Series. The Australian National University, Canberra

Kant R (2017) Casting a blind-eye: is Fiji's 2013 'Ethnically-blind' constitution a path to democratic stability. J South Pac Law: Spec Issue, 3–36. https://www.usp.ac.fj/index.php?id=22271

Kant R, Rakuita E (2014) Public participation and constitution-making in Fiji: a critique of the 2012 constitution-making process, SSGM Discussion Paper Series. The Australian National University, Canberra

Kymlicka W (1996) Multicultural citizenship: a liberal theory of minority rights. Oxford University Press, Oxford

Lal B (1993) Chiefs and Indians: elections and politics in contemporary pacific. Contemp Pac 5(2):275–301

Lal, Brij V. 2009. 'Anxiety, uncertainty and fear in our land': Fiji's road to military coup. The 2006 military takeover in Fiji: a coup to end all coups?. Jon Fraenkel, Stewart Firth Brij V. Lal, 21–42. Canberra: ANU E Press

Lalabalavu N, Kepa T (2013) Paramount Chief of Rewa, and Head of Burebasaga Tribal Confederacy Ratu Naiqama Lalabalavu, Tui Cakau, Paramount Chief of Cakaudrove and Head of Tovata Tribal Confederacy. Retrieved February 15, 2017, from Coup 4.5: www.coupfourandahalf.com/2013/10/the-statement-from-rewa-and cakaudrove.html

Lawson S (1991) The failure of democratic politics in Fiji. Oxford University Press, Oxford

Lerner H (2011) Making constitutions in deeply divided societies. Cambridge University Press, Cambridge

Lijphart A (1975) The comparable-cases strategy in comparative research. Comp Pol Stud 8(2):158–177

Lijphart A (1977) Democracy in plural societies: a comparative exploration. Yale University Press, New York

Lijphart A (2008) Thinking about democracy. Power Sharing and majority rule in theory and practice. Routledge, London

MacNaught T (1982) The Fijian colonial experience: a study of the Neotraditional Order under British colonial rule prior to World War II. ANU eView, Canberra

Markus HR, Steele CM, Steele DM (2000) Colorblindness as a barrier to inclusion: assimilation and nonimmigrant minorities. Daedalus 129(4):233–259

McGarry J, O'Leary B (2007) Iraq's constitution of 2005: liberal consociation as political prescription. Int J Constit Law 5(4):670–698

McGarry J, O'Leary B, Simeon R (2008) Integration or accommodation? The enduring debate in conflict regulation. In: Choudhry S (ed) Constitutional design for divided societies: integration or accommodation? Oxford University Press, Oxford, pp 41–88

Neville H, Lilly R, Duran G, Lee R, Browne LV (2000) Construction and initial validation of the color-blind racial attitudes scale. J Couns Psychol 47:59–70

NGO Coalition for Human Rights (2012) NGO alternate report to the committee on the elimination of racial discrimination for the republic of Fiji. Retrieved March 18, 2017, from Office of the High Commissioner for Human Rights: http://tbinternet.ohchr.org/Treaties/CERD/Shared%20Documents/FJI/INT_CERD_NGO_FJI_13663_E.pdf

Norton R (2002) Accommodating indigenous privilege: Britain's dilemma in decolonizing Fiji. J Pac Hist 37(2):133–156

Norton R (2009) The Changing role of the Great Council of Chiefs. In: Fraenkel J, Firth S (ed) The 2006 military coup in Fiji: a coup to end all coups? ANU E Press, Canberra, pp 97–116

Norton R (2015) The troubled quest for national political leadership in Fiji. Round Table 104 (2):113–125

Norton R (2013) Averting 'irresponsible nationalism': political origins of Ratu Sukuna's Fijian administration. J Pac Hist 48(4):409–428

Ono K (2009) Postracism: a theory of the "post-" as political strategy. J Commun Inq 34:227–233

Parekh BC (2000) Rethinking multiculturalism: cultural diversity and political theory. Macmillan, London

Peery D (2011) The colorblind ideal in a race-conscious reality: the case for a new legal ideal for race relations. Northwest J Law Soc Policy 6(2):473–495

Pildes H (2008) Ethnic identity and democratic institutions: a dynamic perspective. In: Choudhry S (ed) Constitutional design for divided societies: integration or accommodation? Oxford University Press, Oxford, pp 173–204

Ratuva S (2011) The military coups in Fiji: reactive and transformative tendencies. Asian J Polit Sci 19(1):96–120

Ratuva S (2015) Protectionism versus reformism: the battle for Taukei ascendancy in Fiji's 2014 general election. Round Table: Commonw J Int Aff 104(2):137–149

Reeves P, Vakatora TR, Lal BV (1996) The Fiji Islands: towards a united future, parliamentary, Paper no. 34 of 1996. Government Printer, Suva

Reilly B (2001) Democracy in divided societies. Electoral engineering for conflict management. Cambridge University Press, Cambridge

Reynolds A (1999) Electoral systems and democratization in Southern Africa. Oxford University Press, New York

Reynolds A, Sisk TD (1998) Elections and electoral systems: implications for conflict management. In: Reynolds A, Sisk TD (eds) Elections and conflict management in Africa. United States Institute of Peace Press, Washington, DC, pp 19–28

Robertson R, Tamanisau A (1988) Fiji: shattered coups. Pluto Press, Leichhardt

Roeder PG, Rothchild D (2005) Power sharing as an impediment to peace and democracy. In: Roeder PG, Rothchild D (eds) Sustainable peace: power and democracy after civil war. Cornell University Press, Ithaca, pp 29–50

Ryan AM, Gee GC, Laflamme DF (2006) The association between self- reported discrimination, physical health and blood pressure: findings from African Americans, black immigrants, and Latino immigrants in New Hampshire. J Health Care Poor Underserved 17:116–132

Ryan CS, Hunt JS, Weible JA, Peterson CR, Casas JF (2007) Multicultural and colorblind ideology, stereotypes, and ethnocentrism among Black and White Americans. Group Process Intergroup Relat 10(4):617–637

Schofield JW (1997) Causes and consequences of the colorblind perspective. In: Banks J, Banks CM (eds) Multicultural education: issues and perspectives. Allyn & Bacon, Needham Heights, pp 251–271

Social Democratic Liberal Party (SODELPA) (2014) Land-the truth and nothing but the truth: a statement and a challenge by the social democratic liberal party (SODELPA). *Fiji Times*, 11 September, 29

Sisk TD (1996) Power sharing and international mediation in ethnic conflicts. United States Institute of Peace Press, Washington, DC

Srebrnik H (2002) Ethnicity, religion, and the issue of aboriginality in a small Island State: why does Fiji Flounder? Round Table 364:187–210
Tajfel H, Turner J (1979) An integrative theory of intergroup conflict. In: Austin WG, Worchel S (eds) The social psychology of intergroup relations. Brooks/Cole, Monterey, pp 33–47
Taylor C (1992) Multiculturalism and "The politics of recognition": an essay. Princeton University Press, Princeton
Tully J (1995) Strange multiplicity: constitutionalism in the age of diversity. Cambridge University Press, Cambridge
Ullucci K, Battey D (2011) Exposing color blindness/grounding color consciousness: challenges for teacher education. Urban Educ 46(6):1195–1225
UN Committee on the Elimination of Racial Discrimination (CERD) (2012) UN Committee on the elimination of racial discrimination: concluding observations, Fiji 31 August. CERD/C/FJI/CO/18-20, New York
Vasil RK (1972) Communalism and constitution-making in Fiji. Pac Aff 45(1):21–41
Vorauer JD, Gagnon A, Sasaki SJ (2009) Salient intergroup ideology and intergroup interaction. Psychol Sci 20(7):838–845
Walton J, Priest NC, Kowal E, Brickwood K, White F, Paradies Y (2014) Talking culture? Egalitarianism, color-blindness and racism in Australian elementary schools. Teach Teach Educ 39:112–122

Legislations

Fiji Constitution Commission (2012) Draft constitution 2012. Fiji Constitution Commission, Suva
Fiji Government (1970) Fiji Independence Order 1970 and Constitution of Fiji
Fiji Government (1990) Constitution of the Sovereign Republic of Fiji 1990
Fiji Government (1997) Fiji Islands Constitutional Amendment Act 1997
Fiji Government (2013) Constitution of the Republic of Fiji 2013

Court Cases

President of Fiji Islands v. Kubuabola (1999) FJSC 8, Misc. Case No. 1 of 1999 (3 September 1999)
Qarase v. Chaudhry (2003) F.J.S.C. 1, CBV0004.2002S (18 July 2003)
The President's Reference, Qarase v. Chaudhry—Decision of the Court (2004) FJSC 1; MISC 001.2003 (9 July 2004)

Post-Arab Spring: The Arab World Between the Dilemma of the Nation-State and the Rise of Identity Conflicts

Hassanein Ali

Contents

Introduction	132
Origins and Causes of the Structural Crisis of the Nation-State Building in the Arab World	133
Identity Conflicts in the Arab World Before and After the Arab Spring	135
Political and Socioeconomic Dimensions of Identity Conflicts in the Arab World	140
External Dimensions of the Identity Conflicts in the Arab World	140
The Islamic State Organization (DAESH) and the Decline Nation- State System in the Arab World	141
The High Cost of Identity Conflicts in the Arab World	142
Conclusion: The Future of the Arab World Between the Protracted Identity Conflicts and the Nation-State Failure	143
References	144

Abstract

The Arab world is one of the most volatile regions in the world suffering from identity conflicts. These conflicts, which revolve around religious, sectarian, ethnic, and tribal issues, represent the other side of the crisis of nation-state building in the Arab world in the postindependence era. Although identity conflicts are not new to the region, they have intensified after the US invasion of Iraq in 2003 and the revolutions of the so-called Arab Spring. These two events revealed the deep crisis of the nation-state, thereby highlighting the failure of the postindependence ruling elites to establish nation states that can maintain a position of legitimacy and effectiveness. Being both legitimate and effective enables a state to include religious, sectarian, ethnic, and tribal pluralism within

H. Ali (✉)
Department of International Studies, College of Humanities and Social Sciences, Zayed University, Dubai, United Arab Emirates
e-mail: Hassanin79@hotmail.com

the framework of its national identity, based on the foundations and principles of citizenship, rule of law, respect for human rights, minority rights, and social justice.

Additionally, identity conflicts are linked to two other factors that escalated after the US invasion of Iraq and the events of the "Arab spring." First, was the increased politicization of religious, sectarian, and tribal affiliations, which was used to serve political ends, either by ruling regimes, political parties, or non-state actors. Second, is the current expansion of the political polarization between the forces of political Islam which rose rapidly after the "Arab spring" on one hand and the liberal, leftist, and national civil forces on the other hand. This polarization reflects the deep gap between the advocates of the "religious state" and the advocates of the "civil state." The purpose of this chapter is to analyze and interpret the dimensions of the relationship between the deep crisis of the nation–state and identity conflicts in the post-Arab spring era

Keywords
Nation-State · Identity conflicts · Arab Spring · Sectarianism · Failed states · Civil Wars

Introduction

The concept of identity conflicts refers to intrastate divisions and conflicts that are related to one or more religious, sectarian, ethnic, or tribal dimensions. Identity conflicts also have its political, economic, and social dimensions, and are often influenced by external interference. The Arab world experienced many identity conflicts in the pre-Arab Spring period, and they increased after the Arab Spring. Due to the collapse of the state institutions, internal conflicts and civil wars broke out in Libya, Syria and Yemen, threatening their existence as political entities. They face the risk of failure and disintegration like Somalia. Many other Arab countries like Lebanon, Iraq, Sudan, etc. suffer from state weakness and internal conflicts related to the issue of identity in varying degrees and different forms (Lynch 2016; Kamrava 2016; Hashemi and Postel 2017; Guzansky and Berti 2013; Eshel 2012).

This chapter argues that the identity conflicts in the Arab world are the other side of the crisis of the nation-state building which has its roots in the western colonial stage and has been continued in the postindependence period. The ruling elites failed in many cases to build a legitimate and effective state that can include the societal pluralism (religious, ethnic, sectarian, and tribal) within the framework of a national identity. Therefore, these subidentities have become a big challenge to the state from below (religious, sectarian, ethnic, and tribal communities) and above (Islamic movements that reject the nation-state and rise the slogans of the Islamic state).

When the state collapses or weakens, it becomes unable to monopolize the use of force (which is one of the most important characteristics of the modern state) and loses the ability to impose its control over its territory and to provide security, protection, and basic needs to its citizens. In this case, citizens will revive their subidentities as an alternative to the national identity embodied by the nation-state. Tribal, religious, ethnic, and sectarian groups provide them with what the state failed to provide in terms of security, protection, and basic needs. Thus, loyalty to these sub entities becomes more important than loyalty to a weak or failed state.

This chapter aims to analyze the dimensions of the relationship between the crisis of nation-state building in the Arab world on one hand, and the escalation of identity conflicts, especially in the post-Arab spring period, on the other hand. In this context, it will highlight the features and causes of the structural crisis of the nation-state in the Arab world. It will also analyze the patterns of identity conflicts that represent the other side of the state crisis and discuss the negative impacts of these conflicts on both the state and society. In addition, the chapter seeks to explore the future of the Arab state in the light of post Arab Spring transformations and to develop some of the conditions and requirements necessary to overcome the worst scenario, the collapse of some Arab states. This worst scenario will create serious negative impacts on the security, stability, and development in the region.

Origins and Causes of the Structural Crisis of the Nation-State Building in the Arab World

The Arab states are currently experiencing a real structural crisis. There are states that are threatened in their presence as political entities such as Libya, Syria, Yemen, and Iraq. There are other states such as Lebanon, Sudan, Egypt, Jordan, Morocco, Tunisia, Algeria, Mauritania, and others that do not face the risk of failure and disintegration but suffer from a state of weakness that makes them unable to carry out their main functions effectively and efficiently. This deepens the internal political, economic, social, security crises, and negatively affects the relationship of the state with its society as well as with the abroad. In addition, some Arab states, especially in the Gulf region, suffer from a gap between their political frameworks on one hand and their demographic, economic, social, and technological changes on the other hand. While they have achieved big achievements in economic, technological, and social fields, their political structures still reflect traditional features. In the light of all these and other considerations, the legitimacy of the nation-state in the Arab world has become a major challenge (Corm 2016; Benhabib 2014; Ahram and Lust 2016; Salamey 2017).

It is well-known that the origins of the modern nation-state crisis in the Arab world relates to the period of Western colonialism and settlements of the First World War. Many Arab states are artificial entities because the policies of the colonial powers are based on the division of some regions and the unification of multiple areas into a larger entity. The colonial powers also drew boundaries between many countries according to their own goals and interests, not according to the realities of geography, history, and social entities. The colonial powers also used the minority card and "divide and rule" strategies to achieve their goals. The Sykes-Picot agreements are the best evidence of the role of the colonial powers in creating the roots of the modern nation-state crisis in the Arab world (Mansfield 2013).

While the roots of the structural crisis of the nation-state in the Arab world were associated with circumstances of its establishment, it continued and even worsened after the independence. The fundamental reason for this phenomenon is the failure of ruling elites to establish legitimate and effective states that include religious, sectarian, ethnic, and tribal subidentities within a national identity that is based on the principles of citizenship, the rule of law, and tolerance. Because of the desire to monopolize power and wealth, the main interest of most postcolonial political regimes was to build repression institutions and establish an authoritarian rule rather than building a strong and legitimate nation-state.

In many cases, postindependence ruling elites have practiced various types of discrimination against some groups of society based on ethnic, sectarian, and tribal lines and used this as a mechanism to ensure survival of their regimes. The Assad regime (father and son) in Syria is based on the Alawite community and marginalized the Sunni majority. In Iraq, Saddam Hussein's regime relied on its tribal Sunni base and marginalized most of the Kurds and Shia population. In Libya, Qaddafi's regime used tribal card as one of the main mechanisms to continue in power, by favoring certain tribes and excluding others. All these policies have created a suitable enviroment for the emergence of identity conflicts in the mentioned states (Jazayeri 2016; Al-Sayid 2009; Selvik and Stensile 2011).

In this context, some of the key features of the Arab state crisis include the absence of state independence from the ruler authority and employing its institutions to serve the interests of certain communities which are known for their loyalty to the regime. The Arab state also suffered from the inflation of its administrative structures, the institutionalization of corruption, and the increasing dependence on the outside world (Ayubi 1995). In addition, there is a gap between the state and society, in terms that the state does not have real legitimacy. In this case, subidentities have become a big challenge to the state both from below and above.

The comparative experiences at a global level emphasize that societal pluralism (religious, sectarian, ethnic, linguistic, tribal, etc.) is neither good nor bad. In some societies, societal pluralism has become a source of strength and enrichment to both the state and society. In other societies, it represented a source of division, civil wars, protracted social conflicts, and disintegration of the state itself. The main factor that distinguishes the two cases is the nature of the political system that manages the affairs of the state and society.

The democratic regime with its values, institutions, and procedures allows the management of societal pluralism in peaceful and institutionalized ways, thus consolidating the values of civil peace, stability, a culture of tolerance, and adherence to peaceful methods of conflict resolution. By contrast, the authoritarian regime – which is based on monopolization of power, political exclusion, repression, and violation of human rights – produces a type of authoritarian stability, which soon declines once the security grip of the regime weakens. This explains the rapid disintegration of state institutions and the frequent emergence of civil wars once the regime is overthrown, as happened in Somalia, Iraq, Libya, Yemen, and others.

Identity Conflicts in the Arab World Before and After the Arab Spring

The Arab world experienced many intrastate conflicts in the pre-Arab Spring period because of the failure to build a legitimate and strong state capable of including societal pluralism within the framework of a national identity. In addition, the ruling regimes in many countries were largely involved in distributing the wealth and power according to tribal, ethnic, and sectarian lines. We can refer to the civil war in Sudan, which lasted for decades and ended with the separation of the south; the civil war in Lebanon from 1975 to 1990; and the civil war in Somalia, which began since the early nineties of the last century and ended with the failure and collapse of the Somali state. Iraq also experienced internal wars before and after the American invasion and occupation in 2003 (O'Ballance 1998; Ali and Matthews 1999).

In the Light of the Arab Spring transformations, identity conflicts have escalated in many Arab countries. In **Libya**, following the overthrow of the Qaddafi regime in 2011, the central authority disappeared, and the state apparatus and institutions disintegrated. Large areas of the country were falling under the control of armed militias, tribes, and religious organizations. This led to many internal wars influenced by various tribal, religious, political, military, and economic factors. In this context, moderate and radical Islamist parties and organizations emerged, some of which introduced the Islamic identity of the state in exchange for national identity. Also, tribal and ethnic conflicts broke out in some areas for various reasons. For example, the frequent armed confrontations among Arab, Tabu, and Tuareg tribes across the southern regions of Libya (Wehrey 2017).

In the light of the above, the political and security situation in Libya became more complicated and fragmented. There are three governments at the same time, the interim government headed by Abdullah al-Thani, the National Salvation government headed by Khalifa al-Ghawil, and the Presidency Council of the Government of National Accord headed by Fayez Alsarraj. Also, there are two armies, the first is under the leadership of Khalifa Haftar in eastern Libya, and the second is affiliated to the Presidency Council of the Government of National Accord. It controls parts of the city of Tripoli, not to mention the presence of dozens of armed battalions, militias, and tribes, which controls many of the Libyan cities and villages as mentioned above. In addition, there are divisions among the regional and international actors concerned with the Libyan crisis (Sadiki 2012; Vandewalle 2014; Wehrey 2018; Aghayev 2013).

Despite the many attempts to reach a settlement in Libya, the last one is the action plan proposed by the UN envoy to Libya, Dr. Ghassan Salama, in last September 2017 – which centered on the achievement of national reconciliation, issuing a new constitution for Libya, and holding legislative and presidential elections in 2018. Despite the importance of this plan, there are many obstacles which make its implementation difficult, including the continued division at the military and political levels, where there are three governments and two armies. In addition, there are many internal conflicts and confrontations between the tribes, armed groups, and terrorist jihadist organizations.

In **Yemen**, the state suffered from weakness and fragility in the pre-Arab Spring. The state lost control over its territory consequent to the increased tribal influence and interference, the expansion of al-Qaeda in the Yemen, the repetition of Huthi's rebellion, and the persistent tendency toward separatism in the south. In the context of this complex reality, the former Yemeni President Ali Abdullah Saleh used the tribal card as means for the survival of his regime (Boucek and Ottaway 2010; Alley 2010; Juneau 2010). After his departure from power, the Shia Huthi group supported by Iran took control of Yemen in 2014. On 26 March 2015, the Arab coalition led by Saudi Arabia launched a military campaign against the Huthis that continues till now. The protracted conflict in Yemen has its own tribal, sectarian, political, and strategic factors (International Crisis Group 2012, 2013; Schmitz 2012).

Although majority of the parties involved and concerned with Yemeni conflict – including the Arab Alliance, led by Saudi Arabia's call for political solution of the conflict – there are no immediate signs of a settlement. This means that the war in Yemen will continue for at least the foreseeable future, especially in light of the failure of all previous attempts to settle it. There are several factors which have led to the continuation of the conflict, including the intransigence of the Houthis and their rejection of all solution references (International Crisis Group 2017). In addition to this is the weakness of the Yemeni government and its inability to impose control and security in the areas liberated from Houthi's control. Also, some political forces in south Yemen began to call again for the separation of the south. In this context, non-Houthi armed actors have been able to strengthen their influence in Yemen, including Islamic State organization (DAESH) and al-Qaeda. DAESH has strengthened its presence, especially in the governorates of Hadramawt, Aden, Lahj, and Abyan. Al-Qaeda had a prominent presence in Yemen in the pre- Arab Spring and strengthened in the light of the conflict in Yemen. Therefore, some of the military operations of the Arab alliance target al-Qaeda strongholds in Yemen.

In **Syria**, the revolution was initially peaceful, but the regime's sharp repression response against it led to the rise of armed actions. This paved the way for many local, regional, and international actors to intervene in the conflict with their own goals and agendas. This dramatic change has made Syria the arena for several wars at the same time, which overlap the ethnic, sectarian, religious, political, and strategic dimensions, especially since the al-Assad regime used the sectarian card as one of its mechanisms of survival. It created a state of fear for Shia Alawites and other minorities in case the regime is overthrown (Diehl 2012; Tasopoulos 2014).

Also, some regional actors got involved in the conflict along political and sectarian considerations. Al-Assad regime is still receiving significant military support from both Iran and its ally Hezbollah. At the same time, Saudi Arabia, Turkey, and some other Arab countries have been supporting armed groups opposing the regime (Kassab and Al-Shami 2018).

On the political front, Syrian political opposition forces have been fragmented to the point that they are unable to form a unified front against the regime. In light of this complex reality, the tracks of the Syrian crisis and its conflicts of identity have become dominated primarily by balances and interactions between the external powers (regional and international) that have their presence on the Syrian arena.

Due to the divergence of agendas and conflict of interests, attempts to resolve the crisis peacefully through the Geneva and Astana tracks were stalled until now (Rath 2017).

During the years 2017 and 2018, significant developments took place in the Syrian arena. The most prominent of these were the military defeat of Islamic State organization (DAESH) and its expulsion from most of the territories it controlled. In this context, the Syrian regime began to impose its control over more territories supported by the large military role played by Russia on the Syrian arena. This supported Assad regime's position in any arrangements related to the future of Syria; especially there is a clear shift in the positions of many regional and international parties toward the Syrian regime. The countries that were making Assad's departure a condition for any real political settlement in Syria such as Turkey, France, Saudi Arabia, the United States of America, and others have changed their positions on this issue.

Despite the importance of the military and political developments that have taken place in Syria in recent times, there is no sign that a political settlement of the crisis and the related identity conflicts are imminent. There are still many complex issues that impede the settlement, including the constitution and arrangements for the transitional period, the nature of the political system, the reconstruction challenge, and the tragedy of refugees and displaced persons. In addition to this, there are other challenges that are the demands of the Kurds of Syria to apply federalism in the country to ensure the establishment of a federal entity, which is rejected by both the regime and the Syrian opposition and strongly rejected by Turkey (Radpey 2016). Under these complex conditions, Syria is likely to remain a model case for state disintegration and identity conflicts, at least in the short and medium term.

Iraq under Saddam Hussein witnessed many ethnic and sectarian conflicts. The regime has used excessive force in dealing with Shiites, Kurds, and Sunni Arab opponents. But identity conflicts have risen sharply in Iraq following the USA invasion and occupation in 2003, especially after Washington dismantled the Iraqi state and its institutions and favored Shiites and Kurds on the one hand and excluded Sunnis on the other hand. In this context, some have spoken of "the awakening of the Shiites," "the Shiite crescent," and "the empowerment of the Shiites," especially after Iraq became "the first state in the Arab world ruled by a Shiite majority." Accordingly, many religious Shiite and Sunni parties have emerged, thus deepening the process of politicizing sectarianism (International Crisis Group 2014; Walker 2006; Nasr 2006).

As the sectarianism has become strong at the level of politics, it has presented the same force in the fields of media, economy, and finance, where the media has become governed by sectarian tendencies and agendas. The corruption has been institutionalized in the wake of successive governments – especially the Maliki government, which is based on sectarian lines in the distribution of economic and social benefits. All this has contributed to the weakening of the national identity and deepening of the tribal, sectarian, and religious identities. In this context the identity conflicts escalated sharply through ethnic and sectarian violence, forced displacement, and even to the extent of mutual targeting of mosques by Shiite and Sunni elements. All these and others contributed to the creation of suitable environment for the expansion of terrorist jihadist organizations and armed militias such as al-Qaeda, DAESH, and the Shia's Popular Mobilization Forces ("Al-Hashad al-Shaabi") (Haddad 2014; Nasr 2006; Fei 2016; Selim 2012; Cole 2003).

The overthrow of Saddam Hussein in 2003 marked the beginning of a new phase in the history of the Kurdish problem. Post-Saddam policies and developments contributed to the strengthening of the influence of both Kurds and Shiites at the expense of the Sunnis, especially after the adoption of federalism as a new formula for the Iraqi state. However, the political clashes between the Kurds and the central government in Baghdad continued due to many issues, particularly the disputed areas between the two parties. But the biggest challenge in terms of relationship between the two was the referendum which was organized on September 2017 by Kurdistan Regional Authorities to determine the independence of the territory from Iraq.

Kurdistan Regional Authorities ignored the rejection of the referendum by the central government in Baghdad, the Iraqi parliament (the House of Representatives), and the Federal Supreme Court in Iraq. Also, it ignored the regional and international opposition to the referendum results by Turkey, Iran, the Security Council, and others. More than 90% of the total voters who participated in referendum supported the separation of the territory from the Iraqi state. Against this backdrop, the central governments in Baghdad, Turkey, and Iran have taken aggressive punitive steps against the Kurdistan region. After a series of political skirmishes and some military clashes between the government and Kurdish forces, the government of the Kurdistan region was subjected to rule by Baghdad, and the referendum was nullified, especially as it created more tensions between the political forces within the region (Sowell 2017; Toorn 2017).

The recent Parliamentary elections held on May 12, 2018 in Iraq confirmed that the sectarian dimension continues to have a strong impact on the political process. The two electoral alliances that have won the largest number of seats are the Saeroon Alliance led by the Shia Muslim cleric Muqtada al-Sadr's, which came first with 54 out of 329 seats, and the Fatah alliance, which mainly represents Iranian-backed militias named Popular Mobilization Forces, came second with 47 seats. Both are polarized political forces at the Iraqi Political arena.

Although the identity tensions and conflicts have eased a bit as the government of Haider Al-Abadi combats and attains victory in the fight against the Islamic State organization "DAESH," there is nothing to prevent the renewal of sectarian conflicts at any time. To avoid further escalation of sectarianism, a few conditions are necessary. These include a historic reconciliation between the major components of the Iraqi people (Shia, Sunnis, and Kurds), establishment of a national Iraqi state that breaks with the system and policies of sectarian quotas, ensuring a political system based on the principles of citizenship, providing for the rule of law and respect for human rights, including rights of minorities, as well as reducing external interference in the internal affairs of the Iraqi state.

Since 2003, **Sudan** has been suffering from internal wars between the governmental forces and many armed movements in Darfur, South Kordofan, and Blue

Nile. All these wars are having tribal, economic, and political dimensions. Many serious attempts have been made to resolve these conflicts, but different internal and external forces are sabotaging these efforts (Bassil 2013). Therefore, these conflicts represent a real challenge to the unity of the Sudanese state, especially after the independence of South Sudan in July 2011.These conflicts also deplete state resources, disrupt development plans, and deepen the economic and social crises in Sudan.

Because of the weakness of the **Lebanese** state and the complexity of its sectarian structure, it remained subject to sectarian tensions, especially under Hezbollah's involvement in the Syrian conflict, contrary to the state's official policy (Salloukh et al. 2015). It's known that there are 18 religious communities officially recognized by the state in Lebanon. The largest of these communities are Shia, Sunni, Druze, Catholic, Orthodox, and Maronite (Al Ariss and Sidani 2016).

Sectarian tensions and political divisions have often disrupted political life in Lebanon. No consensus was reached on the election of Michel Aoun as president of the country until 888 days after Lebanon remained without a president. The processes of forming new governments often face many difficulties because of internal politicization of sectarianism and external interventions.

Since the 1970s, **Egypt** has been experiencing sectarian tensions between Muslims and Copts. These tensions were related to the rise of Islamic movements (Muslim Brotherhood, Salafists, and jihadists) before and after the Arab Spring. During these tensions, many Coptic churches and properties were targeted. In general, the tensions and sectarian events that happened in Egypt since the 1970s have been in the context of intellectual and political debate about the nature of the relationship between the Egyptian state and the church. In this context, several scholars discussed and evaluated the response of successive regimes to Copts' demands (Stephanous 2010; Guirguis 2017; Naiem 2018; Ibrahim 2011).

Over the past two decades, tensions and sectarian confrontations have been a prominent feature of the political and security developments in **Bahrain**. Shiite groups have engaged in demonstrations and riots, and there have been terrorist attacks and confrontations between security forces and Shiite organizations. The Bahraini government has often accused Iran of interfering in its internal affairs by providing military and financial support to groups that practice violence and terrorism against state and society (Byman 2014; Al-Sayyid 2009; Gengler 2015).

After the Arab spring, many Arab countries such as Egypt, Tunisia, and others have witnessed a sharp polarization between the forces of political Islam on one hand, and civil forces of nationalists, liberals, and leftists on the other hand. This polarization reflects the big gap between the advocates of the "religious state" and the advocates of the "civic state." This polarization is also related to "politicization of religion," which means using it to achieve political goals. The tensions between islamists and secularists revolved around many issues such as the application of Sharia, the rights of women and minorities, and the exercise of some public freedoms (Cross and Sorens 2016; Lust et al. 2012; Ciftci 2013).

Political and Socioeconomic Dimensions of Identity Conflicts in the Arab World

While identity conflicts in the Arab region are related primarily to religious, sectarian, ethnic, and tribal dimensions, they also have political, economic, and social dimensions. This is linked to the polices adopted before and after Arab spring by ruling regimes in countries like Syria, Libya, Iraq, Yemen, Lebanon, and others, where political powers and social and economic benefits are distributed according to ethnic, sectarian, and tribal lines (Selvik and Stensile 2011). In addition, in many Arab states, subidentities have been politicized and employed to achieve political objectives for regimes, opposition forces, and armed non-state actors.

As for the economic dimensions of identity conflicts, some examples can be mentioned. In Iraq, ethnic and sectarian tensions and conflicts are partly linked to the issue of oil wealth which is concentrated in the north (Kurds) and the south (Shia), while middle areas (Sunni) are poor. Also, post Saddam era, the Sunni community has been excluded and marginalized politically and economically (International Crisis Group 2013; Haddad 2014).

In Sudan, the long civil war that led to the separatism of the south was linked to economic dimensions, where the south remained the most underdeveloped area despite most of oil wealth within its land. Also, the conflict in Darfur has its own political and economic dimensions, as well as its tribal and ethnic dimensions.

In general, in countries such as Iraq and Lebanon, the system of power-sharing based on sectarian quotas has:

> ...led to a divvying up the national pie along sectarian or ethnic lines, nepotism, cronyism, and corruption proliferated. Electoral laws in both countries were designed to guarantee the continued election of the sectarian elite, enabling politicians to hijack representation in their individual communities. This also allow them to maintain control over state institutions. (Yahya 2017: 7)

External Dimensions of the Identity Conflicts in the Arab World

The identity conflicts in the Arab world also have their external (regional and international) geo-strategic dimensions. Both before and after Arab Spring era, the competition between some regional and international powers for gaining influence and control over the region has posed direct and indirect effects on the intensity and frequency of the intrastate conflicts. In this context, some regional and international powers were involved in many Arab crises and conflicts by creating and supporting local allies and using this as means to achieve their strategic objectives. Also, the local parties involved in these conflicts are associated with regional and international actors that provide them with financial and military support.

Based on the previous analysis, it is possible to refer to what Gause called "The New Middle East Cold War" in which Iran and Saudi Arabia are the main actors. The Cold War between the two states has its influence on many crises and conflicts in the region such as in Yemen, Iraq, Syria, Lebanon, Bahrain, and elsewhere (Gause III 2014; Alsultan and Saeid 2017).

Alongside, the United States and Russia have been involved in a cold war over the Syrian arena. In Iraq, following the overthrow of Saddam Hussein's regime in 2003, the United States played a prominent role in reviving and feeding identity conflicts in Iraq. It dismantled the Iraqi's state apparatus and institutions, especially the army, security services, and some other vital institutions. It has also adopted a "sectarian quota" approach to the formation of political institutions as well as post-Saddam governments. Moreover, the US-backed sectarian orientation extended to the electoral law and the new Iraqi constitution. The United States has also favored Shiites and Kurds in exchange for the exclusion and marginalization of the Sunnis (Ismael and Fuller 2009). In addition to all these examples, the Turkish role in both Syria and Iraq cannot be ignored as it is linked to the protracted Kurdish question (Abdel Hameed and Mostafa 2018).

The Islamic State Organization (DAESH) and the Decline Nation-State System in the Arab World

Between 2013 and 2017, "DAESH" expanded its presence in both Syria and Iraq. According to some estimates, it occupied about half of Syria and one third of Iraq. It also removed the internationally recognized borders between the two countries and announced the establishment of the "Islamic Caliphate State" in June 2014. This dramatic change, especially after the defeat of the Iraqi army by DAESH fighters in Mosul, represented the top threat to the nation-state system in the Arab world. It confirmed the weakness and fragility of the nation-state. DAESH's aggressive practices against Shia and religious minorities contributed to deepen identity conflicts in Iraq. The Islamic state has used the sectarian card and presented:

> ...itself as a tool of vindication for Sunnis. In its media and face-to-face outreach, the group uses the narratives of Sunni humiliation and discrimination, as well as the goal of bringing the world back to the "correct" path of Islam by fighting apostates (those who pledged allegiance to the Islamic State and later defected), infidels (including Christians and other minorities), traitors (Sunnis who do not support the group), and rafidha (a discriminatory Sunni reference to Shia. (Khatib 2015: 8)

In addition, DAESH tried to create internal sectarian strife in both Saudi Arabia and Kuwait by targeting Shia mosques in both countries in 2015. The liberation of the Iraqi and Syrian territories from DAESH control was carried out through a big war in the two fronts. Many local, regional, and international actors participated in this war including the US-led international coalition to fight DAESH in both Iraq and Syria. The military defeat of DAESH does not mean the end of the organization and its Takfiri ideology. Also, it does not mean the end of the structural crisis of the nation-state and identity conflicts in both Syria and Iraq.

The High Cost of Identity Conflicts in the Arab World

The expansion of internal conflicts and civil wars related to the identity question in many Arab countries such as Libya, Syria, Iraq, Yemen, and others has had major consequences. Most importantly, millions of people were killed and wounded by wars and armed confrontations, many infrastructure, facilities, and services have been destroyed in the concerned countries. This means that large sectors of the population are denied access to the minimum of basic goods and services such as food, clean water, electricity, education, health care, transportation, and housing. This represented a major paradox in countries rich in oil resources such as Libya and Iraq.

In this disastrous situation, post-conflict reconstruction (in the case of ending the conflicts and building peace) has become a major issue in the concerned states, requiring enormous financial resources, new laws and rules, as well as efficient institutions to achieve this goal. All these requirements are not easy to provide. Perhaps the experience of reconstruction in Iraq in the post-Saddam Hussein era is an ideal case of failure to achieve this goal despite all the resources that Iraq has, compared to countries such as Syria, Lebanon, Sudan, and Yemen.

Accordingly, the human and social capital of many Arab countries that are experiencing internal conflicts and civil wars was destroyed. The standard of living of large sectors of the population deteriorated, they relied mainly on foreign aid. The problems of education, health care, transportation, housing, and security have worsened. The result is that the current generation in those countries is headed toward an unknown future in the dark shadows of chaos, insecurity, destroyed infrastructure, and widespread use of weaponry.

Identity conflicts also produced millions of refugees and internally displaced people. For example, according to some estimates, about half the population of Syria is currently refugees abroad or displaced within Syria. The problem of the Syrian refugees has become burdensome for neighboring Arab countries, which suffer mainly from the weakness of their resources and capabilities, such as Lebanon and Jordan. The return of the refugees and displaced people to their homes has become one of the major challenges of post-conflict era in countries such as Syria, Iraq, Yemen, and Libya (Garriaud-Maylam 2017). All these consequences of identity conflicts will complicate the post-conflict rehabilitation and reconstruction process. Large amounts of funding, new rules, regulations, and an effective and efficient institutional system will be required to accomplish this task.

The phenomenon of identity conflicts has contributed to the fragmentation of societies, especially considering the spread of violent non-state actors. In addition, these conflicts deepened psychological barriers; revenge desires among the people of one nation; and the spread of a culture of violence, extremism, and terrorism instead of the values and culture of tolerance and moderation. Such profound moral, social, and psychological effects need time to be satisfactorily addressed to reestablish and consolidate the values of civil peace; coexistence; and religious, intellectual, and political tolerance among different groups of society.

In addition, Identity conflicts may lead to state failure and disintegration. Countries such as Syria, Iraq, Libya, and Yemen are threatened by their existence as political entities. As this scenario occurs, these countries will become safe havens for armed non-state actors, whether they are terrorist jihadist organizations such as DAESH & al-Qaeda or organized crime gangs.

Conclusion: The Future of the Arab World Between the Protracted Identity Conflicts and the Nation-State Failure

Currently, the Arab world is standing at the crossroads, facing serious challenges and problems at once. After the evaporation of the Arab spring promises in terms of freedom, democracy, human dignity, and social justice, internal conflicts and civil wars have swept through many countries in the region, threatening their existence as political entities. There are also many other Arab states that are vulnerable and fragile, unable to carry out their main functions efficiently and effectively. As a result, the economic and social problems increased, political authoritarianism has been consolidated, opportunities for development and democratic transformation were reduced, and non-state armed actors expanded.

The major issues of the Arab world are being influenced by external powers such as the United States of America, Russia, Israel, Iran, and Turkey. Therefore, we can't explore the future of the Arab world without taking into consideration their political, military, and economic roles.

There are two main possible scenarios for the future of the Arab world:

First, the continuation of internal conflicts, civil wars, and the state of disintegration suffered by some big Arab countries such as Syria, Libya, Iraq, and Yemen. In this case, these states will become safe havens for armed non-state actors such as terrorist organizations and organized criminal gangs as mentioned above. This scenario will have catastrophic effects on security and stability not only at the regional level but also at the international level.

Second, achieving historic settlements of the wars in Syria, Libya, Yemen, and Iraq. However, the reality suggests that the conditions and terms of the settlement in any of these wars do not appear to have matured in the near future. In light of this, the biggest challenge facing the Arab league and the regional and international actors involved in the affairs of the region and its conflicts is how to mature the requirements and conditions of achieving historic settlements of these conflicts, taking into account that some external actors such as Iran, Israel, and others are working to fuel these conflicts not solve them as this serves its objectives and interests.

In this complex situation, a major part of the responsibility lies on the key local actors involved in the conflicts, some of whom view the conflict as a zero-sum game, with a predominant and ambiguous logic, complicating the chances of a political settlement. For example, some Libyan actors are blocking the chances of a political solution in Libya. The Huthis' persistence has contributed to prolonging the conflict in Yemen, and the divisions within Syria's political opposition have made it ineffective in the equation of the conflict. In addition, there are deep and persistent divisions between internal political actors in Iraq, Lebanon, and Sudan.

The divisions among the regional and international actors involved in the internal strife and wars in many Arab countries are no less dangerous than the divisions and disagreements among the actors at home. The internal divisions are often an extension of the external divisions. Considering the continuing internal and external divisions, it is unlikely that there will be historic settlements to the internal conflicts and civil wars that are afflicting Libya, Syria, Yemen, and to a certain extent Iraq and Sudan, in the foreseeable future.

In the light of the current protracted crises, the Arab world will still suffer at least during the short and medium terms from authoritarianism or semiauthoritarianism, the absence of governance, poor human development record, continuation of identity conflicts, and the expansion of violent non-state actors. Also, it is expected that many Arab states will witness collective protests for economic and social reasons as happened in Tunisia and Jordan during 2018.

References

Abdel Hameed MA, Mostafa MM (2018) Turkish foreign policy towards Syria since 2002. Asian Soc Sci 14:57–68
Aghayev E (2013) Analysis and background of the "Arab spring" in Libya. Eur Res 39:139–198
Ahram AI, Lust E (2016) The decline and fall of the Arab state. Survival 58:7–34
Al Ariss A, Sidani YM (2016) Understanding religious diversity: implications from Lebanon and France. Cross Cult Strateg Manag 23:467–480
Ali TM, Matthews RO (eds) (1999) Civil wars in Africa: roots and resolution. McGill-Queen's University Press, Montreal
Alley AL (2010) Yemen's multiple crises. J Democr 21:72–86
Al-Sayyid MK (2009) Identity and security in Arab countries. IDS Bull 40:62–69
Alsultan FM, Saeid P (2017) The development of Saudi-Iranian relations since the 1990s: between conflict and accommodation. Routledge, London
Ayubi NN (1995) Over-stating the Arab state: politics and society in the Middle East. I.B. Tauris, London
Bassil NR (2013) The post-colonial state and civil war in Sudan: the origins of conflict in Darfur. I.B. Tauris, London
Benhabib S (2014) The new legitimation crises of Arab states and Turkey. Philos Soc Criticism 40:349–358
Boucek C, Ottaway M (eds) (2010) Yemen on the brink. Carnegie Endowment for International Peace, Washington, DC
Byman D (2014) Sectarianism afflicts the new Middle East. Survival 56:79–100
Ciftci S (2013) Secular-Islamist cleavage, values, and support for democracy and shari'a in the Arab world. Polit Res Q 66:781–793
Cole J (2003) The United State and Shi'ite religious factions in post – Ba'thist Iraq. Middle East J 57:543–566
Corm G (2016) The crisis of Arab states, ethics, and citizenship. Philos Soc Criticism 42:357–362
Cross E, Sorens J (2016) Arab spring constitution-making: polarization, exclusion, and constraints. Democratization 23:1292–1312
Diehl J (2012) Lines in the sand: assad plays the sectarian card. World Aff 175:7–15
Eshel D (2012) The "Arab spring": turning into a long ethnic/religion war. Mil Technol 1:239–242

Fei E (2016) Towards a Shi'a bloc? The new gulf after 2003: Shi'a empowerment and sectarianism. Hemisphers 31:5–12

Garriaud-Maylam J (2017) The war in Syria and Iraq: humanitarian aspects, Committee on the Civil Dimension of Security, NATO Parliamentary Assembly. https://www.natopa.int/downloadfile?filename=sites/default/files/2017. Accessed 11 Sept 2018

Gause FG III (2014) Beyond sectarianism: the new Middle East cold war. Brookings Doha Cent Anal Pap 11:1–33

Gengler J (2015) Group conflict and political mobilization in Bahrain and the Arab gulf: rethinking the rentier state. Indiana University Press, Bloomington

Guirguis L (2017) Copts and the security state: violence, coercion, and sectarianism in contemporary Egypt. Stanford University Press, Stanford

Guzansky Y, Berti B (2013) Is the new Middle East stuck in its sectarian past? The unspoken dimension of the "Arab spring". Orbis 57:135–151

Haddad F (2014) A Sectarian awakening: reinventing Sunni identity in Iraq after 2003. Curr Trends Islamist Ideology 17:70–101

Hashemi N, Postel D (eds) (2017) Sectarianization: mapping the new politics of the Middle East. Oxford University Press, Oxford

Ibrahim V (2011) The Copts of Egypt: the challenges of modernisation and identity. I.B. Tauris, London

International Crisis Group (2012) Yemen: enduring conflicts, threatened transition. Middle East Rep 125:1–44

International Crisis Group (2013) Yemen's southern question: avoiding a breakdown. Middle East Rep 145:1–32

International Crisis Group (2014) Make or break: Iraq's Sunnis and the state. Middle East Rep 144:1–46

International Crisis Group (2017) A Huthi missile, a Saudi purge and a Lebanese resignation shake the Middle East. https://www.crisisgroup.org/middle-east-north-africa/huthi-missile-saudi-purge-and-lebanese-resignation-shake-middle-east. Accessed 20 May 2018

Ismael TY, Fuller M (2009) The disintegration of Iraq: the manufacturing and politicization of sectarianism. Int J Contemp Iraqi Stud 2:434–473

Jazayeri KB (2016) Identity – based political inequality and protest: the dynamic relationship between political power and protest in the Middle East and North Africa. Confl Manag Peace Sci 33:400–422

Juneau T (2010) Yemen: prospects for state failure implications and remedies. Middle East Policy XVII:134–152

Kamrava M (ed) (2016) Fragile politics: weak states in the greater Middle East. C. Hurst & Co. Publishers, London

Kassab RY, Al-Shami L (2018) Burning country: Syrians in revolution and war. Pluto Press, London

Khatib L (2015) The Islamic State's strategy: lasting and expanding. Carnegie Endowment for International Peace, Carnegie Middle East Center, Washington, DC

Lynch M (2016) The new Arab wars: uprisings and anarchy in the Middle East. PublicAffairs, New York

Lust E, Soltan G, Wichmann J (2012) After the Arab spring: Islamism, secularism, and democracy. Curr Hist 111:362–364

Mansfield P (2013) A history of the Middle East, 4th edn. Penguin Books, New York

Naiem G (2018) Egypt's identities in conflict: the political and religious landscape of Copts and Muslims. Mcfarland & Company, Inc., Publishers, North Carolina

Nasr V (2006) The Shi'a revival: how conflict within Islam will shape the future. W.W. Norton and Company, New York

O'Ballance E (1998) Civil war in Lebanon, 1975–92. Palgrave Macmillan, New York

Radpey L (2016) Kurdish self-rule administration in Syria: a new model of statehood and its status in international law compared to Kurdistan Regional Government (KRG) in Iraq. Jpn J Polit Sci 17:468–488

Rath SK (2017) Searching a political solution for Syria. India Q: J Int Aff 73:180–195
Sadiki L (2012) Libya's Arab spring: the long road from revolution to democracy. Int Stud 49:285–314
Salamey I (2017) The decline of nation states after the Arab spring: the rise of communitocracy. Routledge, London
Salloukh B et al (2015) The politics of sectarianism in postwar Lebanon. Pluto Press, London
Schmitz C (2012) Building a better Yemen. The Carnegie papers, Middle East: 1–20
Selim JM (2012) The impact of post – Saddam Iraq on the cause of democratization in the Arab world. Int J Contemp Iraqi Stud 6:53–87
Selvik K, Stensile S (2011) Stability and change in the modern Middle East. I.B. Tauris, London
Sowell KH (2017) Ethnic dimensions of the Kurdistan referendum. Sada, Carnegie Endowment for International Peace. http://carnegieendowment.org/sada/73187. Accessed 15 May 2018
Stephanous AZ (2010) Political Islam, citizenship, and minorities: the future of Arab Christians in the Islamic Middle East. University Press of America, Lanham
Tasopoulos I (2014) Religious minorities in turbulent periods: the recurring dilemmas for Christians in Syria. Hemisph Stud Cult Soc 29:71–83
Toorn CMVD (2017) Internal divides behind the Kurdistan referendum. Sada, Carnegie Endowment for International Peace. http://carnegieendowment.org/sada/73359. Accessed 13 May 2018
Vandewalle D (2014) Beyond the civil war in Libya: toward a new ruling bargain. In: Kamrava M (ed) Beyond the Arab Spring: the evolving ruling bargain in the Middle East. Hurst & Company, London, pp 437–458
Walker M (2006) The revenge of the Shia. Wilson Q 30:16–20
Wehrey F (2017) Insecurity and governance challenges in Southern Libya. Carnegie Endowment for International Peace, Washington, DC
Wehrey F (2018) The burning shores: inside the battle of the new Libya. Farrar, Straus and Giroux, New York
Yahya M (2017) The summer of discontent: states and citizens in Lebanon and Iraq. Carnegie Endowment for International Peace, Carnegie Middle East Center, Washington, DC

Part II

The State, Society, and Ethnopolitics

Part Introduction

The study of ethnicity is necessarily a multi- and interdisciplinary one, and it does not lose that character when its focus is ethnonationalism and other forms of ethnopolitics. It is also of global concern, as the dozen essays assembled in this part suggest, drawing as they do on the contributions of scholars in various institutions stretched across six different countries and addressing instances of ethnic and/or ethnonational politics on five different continents.

Following the editor's introductory essay on the goals and difficulties of accommodating ethnoterritorial and ethnoclass conflict, Johanna Birnir and Henry Overos remind us that, in addition to often being a characteristic differentiating ethnic groups, religion can be an important agent for political mobilization in its own right. Radomir Compel's following essay on military occupation and ethnicity moves the conversation across the dial to a consideration of coercive relationships and ethnic rights, including the right to self-determination. Finally, concluding this introductory segment, Geoff Pfeifer places the world of ethnopolitics into the broader search for justice of oppressed groups around the world.

The group of chapters which follows takes us into the specific world of ethnoterritorial politics and case studies of the search for control over their own affairs of territorially concentrated peoples. In some instances, as Zbigniew Dumienski's essay on the Cook Islands and Nine notes, these can involve peoples who have already achieved self-determination, but in the form of small polities that still need the assistance of a larger state to remain economically and politically viable. Sanjay Ramesh's study of Fiji offers another study of a mini state, but with an attention to legacy politics and the effect that a former colonial system can still have on politics in a multination state half a century after independence – a theme that is central as well in Jacob Mwathi Mati's study of politics in Kenya.

There follow a trio of essays devoted to the tribulations of groups struggling for meaningful autonomy in states disinclined to grant it, beginning with Matthew Hoddie's general chapter on ethnopolitics in China itself, followed by Jiaxia's Lin's study of the search for cultural rights of Tibetans in particular living under China's control. Renat Shaykhutdinov rounds out this segment with a chapter on the oft-overlooked efforts of the Volga Tatars to maintain their identity in a Russia now engaging in intense Russianization efforts and having effectively ended Tatar autonomy in 2017.

Drawing this thematic focus to a close, Cathal McManus' study of politics in Northern Ireland underscores how complex ethnoterritorial politics can be when ethnic differences are reinforced by class considerations, and each community is seeking a territorial settlement in which it will be or remain the numerical majority.

The final segment shifts the focus yet again; this time to a study of ethnoclass politics involving territorially intermingled majority and minority populations separated by both ethnic identity and socioeconomic status. The continent is Europe, where politics often involves a supranational (European Union) as well as national and sometimes subnational (regional and state) authorities. And the time is now, with Trevor Allen and Misty Knight-Finley focusing on the politics of immigration in Western Europe and Neil Cruickshank exploring outsider politics in his essay on the Roma's search for political legitimacy.

Joseph Rudolph

The Significance of Ethno-politics in Modern States and Society

9

Joseph R. Rudolph

Contents

Introduction	150
The Ethnie, Nations, and the Faces of Ethno-politics in the Contemporary World	150
Means, Goals, Dreams, and Ethno-politics	156
Negotiating Ethno-political Demands	164
Conclusion	166
Cross-References	166
References	166

Abstract

Ethnic identity, the oldest basis for social association and the building block of most national identities, remains a potent force in societies as well as in domestic and international politics throughout the world. Significant as a uniting and dividing line in its own right, ethnic identity has often proven to be most salient when reinforced by social class differences and/or territorial identity in the minds of those consciously distinguishing themselves from others. Although even authoritarian governments often find that accommodating ethno-political demands is less costly than efforts to repress them, the greatest bargaining between governments and ethno-political groups – and especially those motivated by ethno-class considerations (e.g., anti-immigrant parties) and those pursuing ethno-regional and ethnonational agendas (including separatist movements) – occurs in the democratic and democratizing worlds.

Keywords

Nation · Ethnonationalism · Ethno-class conflict · Exclusionary nationalism · Constitutional engineering

---

J. R. Rudolph (✉)
Department of Political Science, Towson University, Baltimore, MA, USA
e-mail: jrudolph@towson.edu

Introduction

In explaining a complicated topic, the grave advice of the King (okay, the King in *Alice in Wonderland*) is usually reliable. "Begin at the beginning...and go on until you come to the end: then stop." Here, however, there seems little end to the influence of ethno-politics in the daily events and shaping histories of modern states and societies. Ethnic identify formed the basis for the nineteenth-century development of national identities and demands for self-determination throughout much of Europe. Contrary to the respective predictions of Marxists, who put their faith in social class, and of the postindustrialists who foresaw modern politics revolving around quality of life issues, it endured as a most potent factor in the destabilization of the multinational states given their independence by their colonial powers after World War II. More recently, ethnonationalism lay at the heart of the implosion of the Soviet Union and explosion of Yugoslavia into, combined, more than a score of states, and the durability of "old," ethnicity based national identity has blocked the pathway of those who would build new democracies on a civic identity rather than an ethnic one in numerous post-civil war states. Likewise, today exclusionary nationalism and ethnic identity are shaping the politics of the world's oldest democracies as they react negatively to the growing presence of "others" in their increasingly multicultural societies.

No, the end of this centuries' long run of ethno-political considerations and movements shaping politics around the globe is not in sight, but it is possible to begin, as the King would suggest, at a beginning with some basic definitions and by identifying many of the characteristics of contemporary ethno-politics.

The Ethnie, Nations, and the Faces of Ethno-politics in the Contemporary World

Ethnic and National Identity. A well-respected dictionary on the terminology of ethnicity and nationalism defines the ethnie, or ethnic group broadly – as opposed to narrowly in terms of genetic traits – as a people "who identify themselves or are identified by others in cultural terms, such as language, religion, tribe, nationality, and possibly race" (Spiro 1999: 207). Members of the group are thus able to identify one another by the more outwardly visible manifestations of their groupness, such as language and perhaps attire. The same characteristics, however, also allow outsiders to identify the group's "otherness."

In contrast, a nation largely exists only in the realm of an individual's sense of identity. To use Rupert Emerson's still serviceable definition, a nation is "the largest community which, when the chips are down, effectively commands men's loyalty, overriding the claims both of the lesser communities within it and those which cut across it or potentially enfold it within a still greater society" (Emerson 1960: 95–96). Nonetheless, as in the past, in much of the contemporary world there remains an extremely close link between national identity and ethnic identity. There *are* multiethnic/multicultural nation-states, in which the people identify with one another as a nation despite their ethnic diversity, and with the government as *their* legitimate government. The United States still is often cited as a successful example of one; that is, a civic nation-state based on the shared political culture and civic identity of its various ethnic communities. Such states are, however, extremely rare, especially compared to multinational states incorporating two or more different national communities, which account for the vast and still growing majority of states in the contemporary world.

The more common thread is for nations to be rooted in an ethnically distinct community. It is almost axiomatic that people are most prone to develop a common sense of identity with others with whom they already share much in common in terms of such outwardly apparent variables as language, religious, and other cultural practices, and perhaps appearance. Collective histories and daily contact also play a role in fostering the development of a common sense of national identity. Hence, with relatively rare exceptions nations emerge only within ethnic groups concentrated in a common territorial homeland, whereas ethnic groups often retain their identity even when geographically dispersed among a wider population. In both instances, however, significant political conflict is most likely to result when ethnic or ethnonational identity is reinforced by other factors.

From Identify to Conflict. As Aristide Zolberg noted, culture, class, and territory tend to define the principal arenas in which political activity currently occurs (Zolberg 1976). Samuel Huntington's description of the last days of the twentieth century as a *Clash of Civilizations* involving differing cultures and religions rather than state interests offers an example of the first (Huntington 1996). The historic bloodletting resulting from the schisms within Christianity and within Islam provides other examples here. So does the persecution of Jewish and Catholic immigrants from Europe by the Ku Klux Klan and other white Christian (i.e., Protestant) supremacists in the post-Civil War United States' south, which by the 1880s had become so notorious that the Italian government threatened to halt the further immigration of its citizens if Washington did not intervene.

Rivaling the influence of religion on politics within the states of the Western World, in the nineteenth century social class differences intensified by the Industrial Revolution began to shape societies and begat political upheavals before evolving into the basis of party systems inside most developed industrial democracies in the twentieth century. The divisions between the rich and the poor, the middle class and the working class, the ultra-wealthy and the average citizen still shape and shake their politics, from the annual decisions involving the movement of monies in national and subnational budgets to law and order issues involving crime and controlling the violence in protests against economically "unjust" systems.

Thirdly, there is the territorial segmentation of societies across state boundaries and within state systems. Former United States House of Representatives Speaker Thomas Phillip "Tip" O'Neill, and one of the principal facilitators of the Anglo-Irish (Good Friday) Agreement of 1985 that began the process of bringing peace to the troubled region of Northern Ireland, remains best known in many circles for his aphorism that "all politics is local." His actual meaning was more appropriate to democracies insofar as he was primarily referencing the skills needed to win local elections, especially those involving representation in municipal and state governments. In a much wider sense, though, all politics *is* territorial in the sense that it plays out on a territorial game board. There, for democratic and nondemocratic forms of government alike, struggles for influence pit locales against locales, regions against regions, regions against central authorities, and states against states in the world of international politics.

Ethno-Class Conflict. Zolbert's principal point for the comparative study of ethno-politics was, nevertheless, not the existence of these three distinguishable arenas for political action, but rather that they often intersect with a profound impact on the nature and tractability of ethnic and national politics. The overlay of reinforcing ethnic and social class lines of segmentation, for example, can result in ethno-class conflict more intense than would be the product of rivalry between two members of the same ethnic group or social class. Civil rights laws produced extremely tense politics where the only advantage of, say, unskilled French workers or white southerners over immigrant laborers or unskilled African-Americans lay in the fact that they were, respectively, native French rather than of foreign origin, and white rather than black, and hence occupied a higher step near the bottom of the socio-economic ladder. Indeed, such ethno-class politics have not only been divisive on both sides of the Atlantic Ocean, but have spawned a series of anti-immigrant parties throughout Europe and have long sustained racist sentiments in the United States. The 1978 slogan of Jean-Marie Le Pen's National Front party in France – "Two Million Unemployed is Two Million Immigrants Too Many!" – has not lost its evocative nature with the passage of time. Indeed, ethno-class segmentation and politics have seemingly intensified with the arrival in Europe and elsewhere of the hundreds of thousands of twenty-first-century refugees displaced by the violent, often ethnic civil wars in the Middle East and Africa.

Immigrants, war refugees, and transitory migrants like the Romany customarily take more lowly jobs and possess lower social status than their host populations, and to the extent that they come from culturally as well as geographically remote areas, they are apt to stand out in the populations of economically advanced democracies. As such, they constitute ripe targets for local partisan profiteering, especially because they rarely have the right to vote. The same, ironically, can also be true where the immigrants are more educated, skilled, and/or affluent than host populations as a whole. Such tends to be true even in economically developing areas, where Ibos may face discrimination as the "Jews of Africa" outside Nigeria. It remains an epithet also attached to the Chinese throughout Asia and those of Indian origin in Africa. And sometimes conflict between two tribes within the same country can feed on overlapping ethno-class divisions and end in tragic consequences, as occurred in Rwanda in early April of 1994, when tens of thousands of the historically privileged Tutsis were massacred by members of the majority Hutu tribe.

Finally, lest we overlook the more distant past in this short and hardly exhaustive inventory of instances of ethno-class differentiation and conflict, ethno-class divisions also shaped history in the settler societies of the New World in North and South America, Australia, and New Zealand. Almost immediately upon their arrival, Europeans quickly appropriated the best land and established commerce-based societies that they deemed innately superior to what they perceived to be the primitive ways of the native tribes and aborigines (Headrick 1981).

Ethno-Territorial Conflict. At least equally significant in its impact on domestic and international politics has been the intersection of territorial identity and ethnic identity, which has often led to map-redrawing ethnonational demands for and accomplishment of national self-determination (Connor 1972). Yet even where territorialized majorities do not develop a nationalistic desire for independence in states where, overall, they constitute minorities, their ethno-regional demands involving regional languages, regional economic conditions, and ethno-political representation in a country's capital can redefine the constitutional order. Belgium, for example, during the last three decades of the twentieth century went from being Western Europe's most centralized unitary system to becoming almost a confederate association of its Flemish, Brussels and Walloon regions in its efforts to accommodate the escalating demands of the ethno-regional and ethnonational parties springing up in those areas.

Nor are such ethno-regional and ethnonational demands limited to regions where the territorial majority is a system-wide minority. In a truly terrible pun referring to the politics of ethno-nationalism, Walker Connor once quipped that "nothing *secedes* like success." Rich minority regions can tire of subsidizing what they see as ungrateful majority areas and think in terms of going their separate ways, as events involving Catalonia's recent efforts to secede from Spain underscore. Likewise, nationalists speaking for ethnically distinct communities both occupying the richest region and constituting the numerical majority in a multinational state may push separatist agendas, as Flemish nationalists in Belgium have been doing for nearly two generations.

That noted, by far the most common form of ethno-territorial conflict shaping domestic and international politics over the last several decades has been the demand for self-determination by territorialized minorities constituting a majority in their region and striving, violently if necessary, for independence. The Soviet Union imploded during the winter of 1991–1992 into 15 sovereign (but still mostly multinational) states when its non-Russian union republics seceded peacefully. The same period, however, marked the beginning of a decade of violent warfare that split the former Yugoslavia into seven states when Kosovo, recognized by approximately half of the countries in the world, is included.

The Soviet and Yugoslavia examples of state multiplication by secession fit into the long post-World War II period in which warfare has shifted from battles fought across international frontiers to domestic civil wars. A Heidelberg's Institution for International Conflict Research report filed more than a decade after the 1995 Dayton Accord officially ended the war involving, Serbia, Bosnia-Herzegovina, and Croatia is telling. Of the 254 conflicts tabulated that year, only 91 were interstate, all 30 of the instances of violence characterized as "severe crises" occurred within a single state, and eight of the nine conflicts identified as constituting warfare were intrastate. (Heidelberg Institute 2008) Not surprisingly given the stakes involved by regional minorities seeking to secede on the one hand and state leaders trying to avoid the dismemberment of their state on the one hand – the most violent civil wars continue to trend towards ethnic civil wars.

Moreover, although the most violent of these wars gain at least initial news coverage, minority struggles for regional autonomy and/or independence are far more widespread, both geographically and in number, than a reliance on headlines would suggest. Including such groups as the Chiapas in Mexico, China's Xinjiang separatists, English language separatists in Cameroon, and the Karens and Rohingyas in Myanmar (*nee* Burma, and often described as the scene of the world's longest running civil war), at any given moment there are at least 40 ethnic civil wars occurring around the globe. In some instances, the central government prevails – as when the government of Sri Lanka, after more than a quarter century of warfare, finally defeated the efforts of its Tamil minority to carve an independent Tamil state out of the north of that island. Sometimes the separatists prevail, as in the case of Slovenia, Croatia, and Bosnia achieving their independence from Serbia's leaders in Belgrade, albeit with outside support.

Outside support can also result in a state of diplomatic limbo and "frozen" conflict when a third party intervenes on behalf a breakaway minority, resulting in a de facto state with only one country in the world diplomatically recognizing it. Perhaps the best known of these entities is the Northern Cyprus Turkish Republic, which emerged in 1974 following Turkey's invasion of Cyprus to prevent its Greek Cypriot leaders from collaborating in a Greece takeover of the island. It is still independent of Nicosia's rule, although Nicosia has remained the pretend ruler of the entire island, a status last sanctioned by the European Union when it admitted Cyprus in 2004.

Other frozen conflicts exist, many dating from the breakup of the Soviet Union in the early 1990s. It was then that Moldova's Russian population in the east successfully seceded after a brief skirmish with Moldovan authorities to found – with Russian support in the form of both financial aid and troops on the ground – the unrecognized state of Transnistria (officially the Pridnestrovian Moldavian Republic). Neither subsequent warfare not diplomatic recognition has ensued, unlike in Georgia, where the government's 2008 efforts to retake the two northern regions – South Ossetia and Abkhazia – that broke free nearly two decades previously led to Russian military intervention on their behalf. For the greater part, though, these ethnonational conflicts just continue as low-grade warfare because the separatists are not strong enough to break free and the central government is not strong enough to end their rebellion.

Ethno-Territorial-Class Conflict. Finally, Zoberg's model entailed a small sector where all three arenas overlap and territorial, cultural, and class differences reinforce one another in separating communities even in complex industrial and postindustrial democracies where the lines of segmentation – region, age, gender, religion, profession, social class, etc. – normally cross-cut one another, thereby reducing the salience of any single source of cleavage. Such instances of ethnic-class-territorial politics often produce the most complex scenarios and protracted conflicts. Consider the case of politics in Northern Ireland, where the terms "Protestant" and "Catholic" remain short hand for referencing multiple, reinforcing sources of division separating the one from the other.

The Protestants are the descendants of the settler communities who were imported from Great Britain to colonize Ireland and who brought with them a different ethnic heritage, language, and religion from that of the indigenous Gaelic-speaking, religiously Catholic population. Territorially, the Protestants concentrated in Ulster, the northeast quarter of the Island, where most debarked. There, they came to number two-thirds to three-fourths of the population, though rarely exceeding 3% of the population in the rest of Ireland. Throughout the island, however, they became the dominant economic as well as ruling class. The same was true in Ulster, although there they also came to constitute the majority in all socio-economic tiers. All of which produced a dichotomy of territorialized political associations. A minority in Ulster but solid majority in Ireland as a whole, the Catholics became the Nationalists, initially pressing for a full independence from British rule, and continuing to pursue a reunification agenda following the 1921 partition of Ireland and subsequent Irish civil war. The latter set three-fourths of the island on the path to full independence but London retained the northern six counties of Ulster as parts of the rechristened United Kingdom of Great Britain and Northern Ireland. Meanwhile, a small minority in Ireland as a whole but part of an overwhelming ethno-religious majority in the United Kingdom, Ulster's Protestants adopted a staunch Unionist position with respect to their province's continued integration with Great Britain.

The Protestant-Catholic division in Ireland flared again in the 1960s when a civil rights movement by Ulster Catholics inspired by the success of the Civil Rights movement in the United States resulted in a violent counter-reaction in the Protestant community. By 1972, the conflict had reached such a level that the Government in London found it necessary to dismiss Ulster's self-governing assembly in Belfast, place Northern Ireland under direct London rule, and deploy a sizeable peacekeeping force throughout Ulster. Although meant to last for only 12 months, the resistance of the province's Protestant majority to the power-sharing features of London's plan for restoring direct rule turned a temporary, exceptional measure into a political necessity that lasted more than 30 years. Only then, following 20 years of diplomatic negotiations involving United States Senators as well as government and party leaders from the Republic of Ireland, London, and Ulster was a sustained system of provincial self-government restored in Northern Ireland (Mitchell 2001).

Meanwhile, the other most commonly cited example of ethno-class-territorial conflict continues to simmer and the body count on all sides continues to creep up in spite of more than 40 years of international efforts to settle the Palestinian-Israeli conflict. The parallels with the Protestant-Catholic conflict in Ireland are not perfect, but neither are they hard to find. Poorer as a whole than the Israelis, the Palestinians living in the areas occupied by Israel since 1967 are Arab in their ethnic roots and Muslim in religion. Many of the leaders of Israel can trace their roots to the Zionist European immigrants that settled Israel when it was a League of Nations Mandate between World War I and World War II, or who came to Israel from Europe (including Russia) following World War II. In the Fertile Crescent area in which they live, the population is overwhelmingly Arab and Muslim, but their desire for statehood remains opposed by the Israel government with authority over them, and much of their territory on the West Bank continues to be the subject of Israeli settlements reducing it in size.

All of which leads us to a consideration of the means employed by and goals of ethno-political groups, and of the oft difficulty of accommodating them, all of which are significantly affected by whether the group is a territorialized majority or a minority broadly distributed within the country in which it resides.

Means, Goals, Dreams, and Ethno-politics

Means. As the examples above indicate, those pursuing ethno-political agendas exist in open and closed systems alike; however, the same options for pressing their demands do not. Where the political process permits it, they may form interest groups to protest government actions or lobby for policies as varied as those championed by White Supremacists in the United States and the Welsh Language Society in Britain. They may also form parties and openly contest for political power to advance their agendas from within; for example, the National Front party in France and its anti-immigrant, antirefugees kin campaigning on essentially ethno-class issues throughout Europe, Australia (the Australia First Party), Japan (the Japan First Party), Latin America (the Free Brazil Movement), and elsewhere around the world. Almost equally ubiquitous in our world of multinational states are the various Nationalist parties with a capital "N" focused on achieving federal status if not independence for their ethno-territorial communities. Of course, articulating demands does not guarantee that they will be addressed. Especially when the demands emanate from a regionalized community seeking greater autonomy, they are apt to be initially ignored. Alternately, the state may challenge the legitimacy of those raising the issues, as Belgium's ruling parties once chose to do with the slogan: "Federalism = Separatism."

Contrastingly, in less open systems, where dissent is repressed regardless of the grievances or nature of the demands, the vehicles of ethno-political assertiveness are more likely to be clandestine and engage in various levels of political violence. There were, for example, the essentially nuisance attacks on French television transmitting stations by *Breton* nationalists in France during the de Gaulle era when the official policy was to deny that France contained ethno-linguist minorities. At the other end of the spectrum lie the dark days of cross-burning and lynching by the Ku Klux Klan during the late nineteenth- and early twentieth-century United States. To this can be added the fighting in Ulster between the Irish Republic Army and the Order of the Orange's defenders of Protestant rule, and the civil warfare in Franco;s Spain between the Government in Madrid and the Basque ETA (*Euskadi Ta Askatasuna*, Basque Homeland and Liberty). Such para-military expressions of ethno-political objectives and communities are even more likely to be the carrier movements in repressive regimes where opposition opinions are unwanted and potentially fatal.

The focus here, then, is much more on ethno-politics in more open societies inclined towards accommodative policies, noting that even here both government receptivity towards the demands of ethno-political communities and the demands themselves can be affected by a wide set of variables, two of which stand out. First, there is the hitherto noted issue of pluralism. In complex social and economic systems, individuals tend to be members of a variety of different associations and carry multiple identities. Ethnic origin is one. Territorial concerns can be another and separate. Age and gender can affect outlooks, as can the importance of specific issues to different groups depending on their class, employment, social status, religion, and philosophies of life. The more these identities and associations crosscut one another, the more they can dilute – at least on a day-to-day basis – the salience of any single identity, including ethnicity.

The other element involves the community's ability to engage in cost-benefit analysis in pursuing courses of action rooted in ethnic or national identity. In part, this may be a function of outlook. Hypothetically, the more cosmopolitan and less provincial, the more likely options will be viewed dispassionately. Likewise, outlook may reflect different levels of education – the more educated the individual or group, the more likely a greater set of consequences will be taken into account in evaluating courses of action. Popular referendums on independence provide some support for these conjectures. At a time of a global economic recession, the French-speaking majority in Quebec voted against pursing independence from Canada. Their province's economy depended on the continued presence of English-owned businesses in Quebec, and its budget relied extensively on economic transfers from Canada's government in Ottawa.

The calculus changes, of course, depending on the subjective weight assigned to the benefits of self-determination – almost always a powerful Siren's call to a minority national community feeling itself under the shadow of a more famous and majoritarian one. No referendum was held to test its weight, but no one in Slovakia at the time doubts that those steering it towards independence knew well that their poorer region would be economically worse off disconnected from the Czech lands yet still went forward with their demands to separate in the early 1990s.

At least as frequently, however, unfavorable conditions can significantly limit ethno-political options. The resurfacing of ethnonational movements in the regions of many European states only in the last third of the twentieth century is largely explicable in terms of the circumstances of twentieth-century Europe until that time. Surviving and recovering from a World War, an interwar depression, another World War, an even more challenging round of postwar reconstruction, and warding off an expansionistic Soviet Union were all challenges that called for larger, rather than smaller scale political undertakings. They offered little political space in which ethno-regionalists and nationalists could operate in lobbying for greater autonomy, much less independence. Only after a generation or more of peace and economic growth, during which the system-wide governments lost a bit of their luster by having to relinquish their empires, did the luxury of pushing the nationalist agenda emerge.

The same applies to a degree, but only to a degree, to the ethno-class based agendas of the anti-immigrant parties of Europe. The need for foreign laborers to rebuild the countries of Western Europe following World War II was beyond dispute and it was therefore not until the recession of the 1970s, with domestic unemployment rising, that parties like the French National Front could find the political space to argue against their presence as a threat to French workers.

Goals. As for their goals, nearly four decades ago John Wildgen helpfully noted that the demands of ethnic and nationalist organizations and movements can be grouped under one or more of four headings. Some are output-oriented demands, some are authority-focused in nature, still others challenge the nature of the constitutional regime and – the most difficult to accommodate – there are those that challenge the definition of the political community (Rudolph 2006: 230). In the intervening period, ethno-political, and especially ethnonational, conflicts have grown in number, spawned greater divisiveness in even established democracies, and produced horrific body counts, but the distinction remains a useful one.

Output Goals. At a minimum, those articulating the interests of ethnic groups and national aspirations are interested, like interest groups in general, in government outputs; that is, *what* government does in terms of the policies adopted and the actions to which governments commit themselves. Racial minorities and immigrant groups, for example, might be particularly interested in the passage of anti-discrimination, housing and employment laws – interests they might share with other memories of their societies with whom they might collectively try to influence government. Likewise regional minorities with national self-determination on their minds might join the ethno-regionalists of similarly poorer regions in lobbying for regional development funds and better regional infrastructure – demands, again, in which the support of less ethnically mobilized others might be coopted. Alternately, linguistic minorities like the Welsh Language Society in Britain may by themselves successfully push objectives of a more narrow interest – for example, having their languages taught in local schools, public documents translated into their tongue, and public television programming in their language – given a government interested in accommodation.

Accommodating this set of demands is easier than dealing with authority-, regime-, or community-focused ones insofar as they do not require those in authority to relinquish any of their decision-making authority; however, in practice they have not usually found readily receptive audiences. Quite apart from the fact that the system may not have the resources to fund the desired courses of action, the demands themselves have often lacked legitimacy in the eyes of decision-makers in the capitals. Regionalists in France long failed to gain the right to teach their languages in the public schools in Alsace and Corsica because the French government classified their tongues as bastardized mixtures, respectively, of French and German and of Italian and French. Likewise, those seeking to advance the rights of foreign workers in Germany found little support until forced by the European Union to adopt naturalization procedures because the official policy of the Federal Republic of Germany was that it was not an immigrant country but a *returnee* states. Translated, that policy meant that those of German blood who were cut off from Germany by Cold War borders could return to Germany as citizens, but that the Turkish workers and their descendants born in Germany remained foreigners under the country's *jus sanguinis* citizenship laws, subject to a termination of their residency should they lose their jobs.

Authority-Focused Objectives. Even less likely to fall immediately on receptive ears among the decision-makers or to draw support from others in society have been the authority-focused demands of ethnic organizations centering on *who* makes the decisions. Unlike output-oriented demands, these are of a zero-sum nature in the sense that they necessarily dilute the authority of the decision-making Establishment, even if they do not displace it. The most common of these demands involves some variant on proportionality if not parity for minority groups in decision-making processes (in the Cabinets in parliamentary systems, for example), and perhaps as well within the higher ranks of the military and policy level bureaucrats. The preference is normally for a policy codified in the constitutional order; however, informal adherence has frequently become the rule. Even judiciaries may succumb to the practice, as has been true in both the United States and Canada for more than half a century. The US Supreme Court has had a "black seat" ever since Thurgood Marshall joined its other eight Justices in 1967 – a time when African-Americans constituted approximately one-ninth of the country's population. In a like manner, with approximately a third of Canada's population, Quebec continues to be the home province of a third of the Canadian Supreme Court justices despite the fact that the effort to write that figure into the Canadian Constitution (the Lake Meech Accord) failed more than 30 years ago.

Closely related to the desires of ethno-class and ethno-territorial groups to have a presence in executive and/or judicial decision-making arenas have been their efforts to secure a presence in the legislative assemblies. Such has been constitutionally achieved in a few states. Kosovo's constitution thus not only mandates that 30% of the seats be held by women, but also mandates that seats be allocated to the country's smallest minorities, which individually constitute less than 1% of the population. More commonly, however, the debate has focused on electoral arrangements. Because single-member-district/winner-by-plurality systems favor the stronger parties overall, majorities are loathe to consider other arrangements. Minorities, and not just ethnic minorities, on the other hand, often press for the adoption of Proportional Representation (PR) systems in general and especially regional PR systems with low threshold requirements.

At first blush, such systems seem tailor made to enhance the influence of both ethno-territorial parties and those with an (ethno-class) anti-immigrant focus. The differences in outcomes resulting from the two systems are obvious in the parliaments of Europe. The Freedom Party in Austria has long profited from the country's PR system to the point where it has frequently been part of the country's coalition governments. With a similar share of the popular vote, France's National Front party has seldom been able to advance beyond the first round of voting in France's single-member district system to win even a single seat in the country's Chamber of Deputies.

Less anecdotally, broader studies generally confirm the correlation between the use of PR voting systems and an enhanced representation of small cadre parties, single issue parties, and especially starter-up political competitors in democratic systems (Richie et al. 2000). At the same time, scholarly examinations of the value of PR systems in empowering ethno-political associations in particular have been less decisive in concluding that, on a long term basis, they benefit the electoral fortunes of such parties. To the contrary, John Huber, a political scientist at Columbia

University in New York, has noted that PR systems may actually lead to less politicization and promotion of ethno-political causes in pluralist systems than single member district systems because PR arrangements encourage multiple other interests to organized and carry their appeals directly to the voters, thus further fragmenting the vote over a wider number of parties (Huber 2010).

Finally, in terms of authority-focused demands and possible concessions, there are the power sharing arrangements that have become increasingly popular international recommendations for areas restoring democratic governments in the aftermath of ethnic civil wars and/or multinational countries transitioning from nondemocratic to democratic regimes. As noted with respect to Northern Ireland, solid ethnic and national majorities tend to resist such schemes, so to date they have most often been imposed on communities by "outsiders" as the price of achieving self-government; for example, London vis a vis Ulster, and the negotiators at Dayton and UN administrators vis a vis Bosnia-Herzegovina's ethnonational communities. Yet even where successfully imposed, power-sharing arrangements do not necessary result in collective decision-making. Rather, as in the case of Bosnia, constitutions whose future evolution depends on decisions collectively agreed upon by all ethnic communities may remain locked in the time of their origin. On the other hand, policy paralysis does not necessarily mark these peace-making schemes as failures. Political limbo is preferable to the resumptions of civil war.

Regime Change Demands and Constitutional Engineering. Constitutional engineering – the practice of designing institutional arrangements in order to address problems previously besetting a political process and/or to minimize anticipated future problems – has a long history, to some scholars reaching as far back as Socrates' search for the perfect polity in Plato's *Republic*. Its modern birth is usually accredited to James Madison, and the intended horizontal (federalism) and vertical (separation of powers) fragmentation of authority in the United States' Constitution he designed in order to assure the fearful that the resultant government would not be too powerful. The twentieth century saw Charles de Gaulle adopt the opposite approach – a powerful, directly elected president to offset the fragmentary tendencies in French society often resulting in a multiparty system and paralysis in the French assembly. A similar system was adopted in Russia in the early 1990s when endowing the Russian legislature with most political authority led to policy paralysis and sometimes fisticuffs. Most recently, it has been in the international efforts to reconstruct states in a democratic fashion in postcommunist and post-civil war countries that the practice has most enjoyed a renaissance, with the Juan Linz school (Linz 1996, 1996) stressing the value of federal formulae and others embracing Arendt Lijphart's power-sharing approach in postconflict institution-building (Lijphart 1977, 2008). But its use has not been limited to those situations.

Whereas both spatially dispersed ethno-class groups and territorialized ethno-regional and ethnonational interests can profit from output and authority concessions as well as make demands in these areas, demands for some variant of regime change – including power-sharing designs – are most likely to emanate from ethno-territorialized communities seeking greater control over their own affairs. Moreover, even authoritarian systems have found it useful to respond to such demands at least in part. It can be far less expensive to accommodate and try to co-opt the support of ethno-regional groups than to garrison an unruly area, and bitterly divisive politics sometimes may be lessened by decentralizing decision-making responsibility to localized communities not necessarily sharing the system's dominant political culture. Thus, within the fold of the unitary and controlling Communist Party of the Soviet Union (CPSU) and in accordance with the process that the Soviet Union labeled national delimitation, the Soviet state was federally divided into 15 national republics (the Soviet Socialist republics, or SSRs). Then, within many of these, decision-making authority was further distributed downwardly to semi-autonomous provinces, districts, and locales in order to accommodate the Soviet Union's numerous ethnic subregions.

For democratic states lacking an integrative machine like the CPSU, the costs of regime change involving territorial concessions to regionalized minorities can be higher in terms their control of the overall political process. The existing options are nonetheless much the same. A unitary state can decentralize administratively by allowing more local governments adjust centrally made laws to local conditions or – more far reaching – by giving local councils the ability to make law in specific areas (for example, educational curriculum). In each instance, the primacy of the central government remains clear. Constitutional engineering schemes that devolve legislative and administrative authority to *regionally* elected governments, however, stretch the nature of unitary governance in a decidedly federal direction. It is one thing politically to recall a prior grant of authority to a local government; it is quite another to tell an elected regional assembly that it no longer has the authority previously devolved to it because the center that giveth can constitutionally taketh it away.

Making concessions beyond regionalization requires formally crossing the gap separating a unitary system in which the center legally retains the totality of political authority, to a federal system in which multiple levels of government exist, each with the ability to make, adjudicate, and execute laws in the areas assigned to it. Furthermore, crossing that line may itself trigger a new set of demands, with the federal entity's leaders demanding the transfer of an expanding list of decision-making powers from the center to the state.

One other note here. Although the debate involving regime change most commonly focuses on the territorial management of power, it need not exclusively do so in democracies and democratizing states. Beyond power-sharing arrangements involving geographically dispersed ethnic communities, the drafting and revising of constitutions can also entail the adoption of a Bill of Rights backed by a system of judicial review to protect the interests of spatial and nonspatial minorities alike.

Finally, with respect to the organization of government at the center, although the United States' separation of branches/checks and balances model has generally been shunned, the issue of whether to adopt a conventional parliamentary system or a hybrid system in which a directly elected President is vested with wide domestic as well as foreign policy decision-making authority has received considerable attention. The latter offers the promise of more decisive government in states with a highly fragmented political culture, resultant extreme multiparty systems, reliance on weak coalition cabinets, and potentially legislative paralysis. Ukraine's recent experience with a presidential system, however, suggests it can aggravate ethno-political tensions in a bi-national state if the presidency is perceived to be clearly favoring the interest of one nation over the strongly held preferences of the other, thus propelling the "losing" side towards decidedly undemocratic courses of action, including violently challenging the terms of the union itself.

Differing Definitions of the Political Community. To summarize briefly before venturing into the world of extra-constitutional politics, to a high degree ethno-politics and conflicts reflect both where they take place (weak multinational states, racially divided societies, societies feeling besieged by the unwanted but clearly rising tide of multiculturalism within) and what they are about. In the older, established democracies, most political quarrels – including those involving spatial and nonspatially distributed ethnic communities – occur over *what* government does; that is, the conventional, who gets what, when, and in what form dimension of politics. Where groups feel left out, the debate may escalate to focus on *who* makes the decision. Demands for affirmative action programs to push into leadership positions groups previously left out, for parity or proportionality as a basis for staffing government positions, and power-sharing are frequently chosen examples of internal conflict management devices here. And, as just noted, sometimes the debate will escalate to *where* the decision is to be made, as in federal system where sensitive issues can be down-loaded for treatment in provinces corresponding to the boundaries of minority nationalities.

Nevertheless, sometimes the issue that cannot be side-stepped boils down to the definition of the political community itself and the legitimacy of the state's existing borders in countries with territorialized ethnic communities. Or, simply stated, what is the nation's homeland? Is it Scotland or Great Britain, Alsace or France, Catalonia or Spain? These are the most difficult conflicts to manage. Where they are particularly ugly – and as noted, ethnic civil wars are often the ugliest of all forms of warfare because each side believes that it is in the right – they can become the subject of international intervention because of a flagrant disregard for human rights and/or because they result in a regionally destabilizing, massive flow of refugees into neighboring areas. It is at this point that the politics of accommodation and compromise are most likely to break down.

To be sure, dichotomous definitions of the political community need not end in violence. In a variation of Arend Lijphart's conceptualization of consociational democracy, leaders of the national communities may choose to work together to hold the state together lest its pieces individually suffer. The menace posed by Soviet expansionism inclined the leaders of Yugoslavia's Macedonia, Croatian, and Slovene union republics to accept Belgrade's rule even after the death of Tito until the Soviet Union imploded. There is also a precedent for the separation of ethnonational communities by a peacefully negotiated division of territory and shared property in the "velvet divorce" dissolution of Czechoslovakia into two sovereign states. In the same manner, at this writing, to enhance their chances of admission to the European Union, Serbia and Kosovo are trying to work out a land swap: the northern, heavily Serbian part of Kosovo to go to Serbia in exchange for Serbia transferring a strip of predominantly Albania-Muslim populated areas in eastern Serbia abutting Kosovo.

And Quebec remains in Canada, the beneficiary of a greater transfer of decision-making power from Ottawa than enjoyed by the English-speaking states in the Canadian federation.

Today's "management" devices for resolving community-based conflicts nonetheless do often involve those of an extra-constitutional nature; that is, means that lie outside the normal processes for conflict resolution inside a political system. Secession, whether successful or otherwise, can provide a definitive answer to the question of what constitutes the state's official political community. The prevalence of the North over the South in the United States Civil War determined the future development of national identity there. There would be no separate country carved out of the rebellious states around which one could continue to develop a sense of national identity. The Ibos may continue to hold a separate national identity in multinational Nigeria, but the failure of Biafra's effort to secede ended the question of whether they would enjoy national self-determination. The same applies to the Tamils' failed effort in multinational Sri Lanka to win a state of their own. Alternately, Croatia, Slovenia, Macedonia, and Bosnia-Herzegovina prevailed in their series of wars with Serbia, as did Bangla Dash (nee East Pakistan) a quarter century earlier in its efforts to liberate itself from the rule of (West) Pakistan. Civil Wars are a costly way of deciding issues of self-determination, and those mentioned above took a horrific toll in lives lost and an even greater number in lives disrupted, often irrevocably. Nevertheless, in their outcome civil wars effectively function as extra-constitutional means of determining the nature of the state's political community, even if it is to remain a multinational one.

Other, for the most part less drastic approaches to ethno-political conflict also fall under the extra-constitutional/extra-systemic umbrella. To the extent that ethnonational conflict is resulting in unrestrained separatist violence and/or border conflicts threatening regional stability, especially in strategically important areas, there is the possibility of third parties – states, international organizations, even mediation-offering non-government actors – offering pathways to conflict resolution in the form of good office diplomacy and third-party peacekeeping operations. In the event of a total breakdown of the system, the third party may become a direct part of the conflict resolution process, assuming a form of international tutelage over the area in question and overseeing democracy-building activities, as the UN did in both Bosnia-Herzegovina and Kosovo in intervening in the wars in Yugoslavia affecting those regions.

Third party involvement in ethno-class conflict *inside* a country must usually be indirect. Absent the aforementioned violent breakdown of the legal and political systems, what happens inside a state is still sheltered from the outside world by the principle of state sovereignty. But it is not immune from influence. Outside states have an interest in the treatment of their ethnic kin settled in other countries and on occasion may be able to affect their treatment short of direct intervention. Hungary thus held up Slovakia's application for membership in the Council of Europe until the government in Bratislava retreated from the more discriminating practices it aimed at its Hungarian minority shortly after Slovakia gained independence. Likewise, the Baltic Republics with substantial Russian populations operate with a full awareness that Moscow is monitoring their treatment in Latvia and Estonia, where ethnic Russians constitute approximately a quarter of the population.

The watchfulness of outside countries over the treatment of their immigrants abroad is paralleled by the role that international organizations like the United Nations and nongovernmental actors like Amnesty International play in reporting on the treatment of minorities more generally. Beyond publicizing the mistreatment, however, their options are few and they normally lack any means of forcing changes in policy, but not always. The European Union's efforts to end much of the more egregious anti-Romany policies in its member states under threat of economic sanctions, for example, have produced some positive results. Still, for the most part outside advice is unwanted and normally ineffective in terms of improving the conditions of ethno-class minorities in states throughout the world. Likewise, most ethno-territorial conflicts either continue or reach some form of resolution without the direct involvement of outside parties if for no other reason than if it is at all possible to do so, states prefer to treat their social and political conflicts themselves.

Negotiating Ethno-political Demands

Negotiating ethno-political issues is not always possible. Apart from the fact that a demand for independence by an ethno-territorial community may be nonnegotiable, those raising them may be doing so for private reason, and more interested in the personal benefits of exploiting them than resolving them. The championing of Greater Serbian Nationalism by Milosevic, for example, had more to do with his desire to hold power in postcommunist Yugoslavia than the treatment of Serbs in those union republics where they were in a minority, and no country holds a monopoly on demagoguery.

Meanwhile, the prospects for both more ethno-politically sensitive politics (the relatively recent re-examination of the rights of native groups in the settler states of the North America, Australia, and New Zealand, for example) *and* ethnic and national conflict continue to grow. Migration from the poorer south to the richer states of the developed democratic world, as noted previously, continues to turn formerly homogeneous, or nearly homogeneous societies with little experience with diversity into multicultural, multiracial, and to a large extent de facto multilingual countries. One result of this migration has been the revival of a negative species of nationalism, most conspicuously in the EU zone and Trump's America. Nor has this sharpening of differences between majorities and minorities within the developed democratic world been limited to conflict between the host and immigrant populations. The growth in anti-Semitism, racially motivated violence, anti-Muslim sentiment, and overt discrimination against Roma minorities in North America and Europe all reflect a rise in ethno-class conflict and decline of tolerance in established democracies of the Northern Hemisphere. Meanwhile, to the south conflicts seem to just continue to grow in the multinational and multiethnic states of the developing world, with the most recent entrant literally during the creation of this Handbook – the secession movement by Anglophones in Cameroon sparked the government's crackdown on the English-speaking minority territorialized in its southwest (Searcey 2018; O'Grady 2019).

Still elsewhere in the world of ethno-territorial conflict, with each newly created state carved out of separatist, civil war torn states as an approach to ending the conflict – Kosovo, East Timor, South Sudan – there is an additional incentive for others to plow the same field in the hope that if the conflict is awful enough third parties may step in and grant their wishes. The same state-creating process likewise encourages areas with far greater prospects of being economically viable independent states to press their own cases in Spain (Catalonia), Belgium (Flanders), the United Kingdom (Scotland), and elsewhere. Nearly 40 years before the European Communities morphed into the European Union, a French politician, Guy Heraud, predicted that by the time Europe grew to be as politically united a federation as the United States of American, it would contain nearly as many member states (Heraud 1973).

Even where there is a sincere interest in peacefully managing divisive issues, the complexity of the negotiating process can itself become a problem. Different voices weigh in with different intensity in different settings. An ethno-territorial or anti-immigrant party that commands a third of the regional vote speaks more forcefully than one with – perhaps only initially – a smaller following. Spatial minorities with close ties to a major party – for example, African Americans and the United States Democratic Party – may have considerable influence compared to other spatially distributed minorities, but only when that party is in power. And sometimes an important participant in an ethno-political conflict may scarcely have a voice in the domestic political process, as in the case of foreign workers and/or refugees who more often than otherwise are the target of political debate rather than effective advocates for their interests.

For those actively involved in a negotiating process, other obstacles loom. Because it *is* or is likely to become a negotiating process, merging the minimum gains that ethno-political groups will accept with the maximum points on which governments will compromise can be a long, tense process constantly on the edge of breaking down. Those making demands are apt to ask for more than they candidly want in order to give themselves room for compromise. Similarly, governments are hesitant to offer too much, lest they encourage an escalation in the demands confronting them. On the other hand, governments need to be mindful of the dangers of stonewalling moderate bargainers who are pressing ethno-political agendas. Ultimately the ability to accommodate spatial and non-spatially distributed groups depends on them accepting that the offers they receive are being made in good faith by majorities whose previous adherence to the rule of law, equality of rights, and civil liberties may not always have been above suspicion. Finding a middle ground with ethno-regionalists and nationalists has proven to be even more difficult. As Walker Connor posited more than 40 years ago,

> ethnonationalism appears to feed on adversity and denial (the Jewish and Kurdish movement). It also appears to feed on concession: permissive perpetuation of the cultural manifestation or of political structures that reflect the nation's distribution become constant reminders of separate identity and rallying points for further demands (Franco-Canadians, Ibos, and the nations of the Soviet Union). (Connor 1973: 21)

Conclusion

Finally, and with specific reference to the matter of accommodating ethno-political demands, a distinction must be drawn between the demands of ethno-political movements and their leadership on the one hand and the durability of ethno-political *sentiment* on the other. Inevitably the accommodation process addresses the former, and studies for decades have shown that it has often been successful, at least in the short term, in abating if not deflating the momentum of ethno-political movements. Affirmative action programs and wars on poverty for minorities, symbolic concessions, the right to teach regional languages in regional schools, parity arrangements, and the cooptation of ethnonational parties into governing coalitions have all paid dividends in reducing the salience of ethno-politics at various juncture of time and place.

Muting ethnic identity and sentiment is another matter. This most primal basis for social association and political organization has continued to exert its influence in multicultural and multinational states in spite of the efforts of the nation-builders who would create new, post-civil war societies based on a civic identity superseding the ethnic and national identities of their diverse peoples. Seventy years of Moscow's intense efforts to displace national identities in its non-Russian Soviet Socialist republics in favor of the "New Soviet Man" did not even slow the unraveling of the Soviet Union in the winter of 1991–1992, the legacy of slavery continues to haunt racial relations in the United States, Muslim and African refugees remain unwanted in large parts of the European Union, and tribal warfare continues to infect the countries of Africa six decades since independence. Sometimes managed and sometimes accommodated, ethnic identities, sentiment, and goals continue to shape state and society alike around our early twenty-first-century globe.

Cross-References

► Ethnic Conflicts and Peace-Building
► Negotiating Ethnic Conflict in Deeply Divided Societies: Political Bargaining and Power Sharing as Institutional Strategies

References

Connor W (1972) National-building or nation destroying? World Polit 24(3):319–355
Connor W (1973) The politics of ethnonationalism. J Int Aff 22(1):1–21
Emerson R (1960) From empire to nation: the rise of self assertion of Asian and African peoples. Cambridge, MA: Harvard University Press
Headrick D (1981) The tools of empire: technology and European imperialism in the nineteenth century. New York: Oxford University Press
Heidelberg Institute for International Conflict Research (2008) Conflict barometer 2008: crises, wars, coups d'Etats, negotiations, mediations, peace settlements, 19th annual conflict analysis. Accessed last 6 Dec 2011 at http://hiik.de/en/konfliktbarometer/

Heraud G (1973) Contre les Etats: les regions d'Europe. Paris: Presses d'Europe

Huber J (2010) Measuring ethnic voting: does proportional representation politicize ethnicity? http://www.columbia.edu/~jdh39/Site/Research_files/ethnic_voting.pdf. Last accessed 21 Nov 2018

Lijphart A (1977) Democracy in plural societies. Yale University Press

Lijphart A (2008) Thinking about democracy: power sharing and majority rule in theory and practice. Routledge

Linz J (1994) The failure of presidential democracy: comparative perspectives, vol 1. Johns Hopkins University Press

Linz J (1996) Problems of democratic transition and consolidation: southern Europe, South America, and post-communist Europe. Johns Hopkins University Press

Mitchell G (2001) Making peace. Oakland, CA: University of California Press

New Huntington S (1996) The clash of civilizations and the remaking of world order. New York: Simon and Schuster

O'Grady S (2019) Cameroon's lethal linguistic fault line: a crackdown on English speakers by francophone authorities fuels a separatist movement. The Washington Post, 6 February 2019

Richie R, Amy D, McBride F (2000) How proportional representation can empower minorities and the poor. https://www.fairvote.org/how_proportional_representation_can_empower_minorities_and_the_poor. Last accessed 21 Nov 2018

Rudolph J (2006) Politics and ethnicity: a comparative study. Palgrave Macmillan

Searcey D (2018) Cameroon on brink of civil war as english speakers recount 'Unbearable' horrors. The Washington Post, 6 October 2018

Spiro T (1999) Nationalism and ethnicity terminologies: an encyclopedic dictionary and research guide. Gulf Breeze, FL: Academic International Press

Zolberg A (1976) Culture, territory, class: ethnicity demystified. A paper presented at the international political science association congress, Edinburgh

Religion and Political Mobilization

10

Jóhanna K. Birnir and Henry D. Overos

Contents

Introduction	170
Implications of Secularization Theory	171
Surging Interest in Violent Religious Mobilization	174
Theology as a Mechanism for Mobilization	175
An Endogenous View of Religious Mobilization	176
Future Directions	178
Peacemaking	178
Formal and Informal Institutions	179
Direction of the Causal Arrow?	179
Gender, Religion, and Issues of Private Versus Public Life	180
The Empirical Analysis of Religion and Mobilization	180
Conclusion	181
Cross-References	181
References	181

Abstract

What is the role of religion in political mobilization? In this chapter, we examine developments in the literature as it considers the role of religion in political mobilization. Broadly speaking we outline two predominant lines of thinking about religion as a driver of political mobilization, the marketplace and theology. The former strand of thinking, we show, traces its roots as far back as the behavioral revolution and even further still. The second strand, popularized by global conflict events framed in religious terms, focuses on theology and differences between religions as motivating factors in mobilization. This line of thinking has largely been supplanted, while at the same time, it has forced the acknowledgment that while religion is an intervening instrument in mobilization

---

J. K. Birnir (✉) · H. D. Overos
Government and Politics, University of Maryland, College Park, MD, USA
e-mail: jkbirnir@umd.edu; hoveros@terpmail.umd.edu

© The Author(s), under exclusive license to Springer Nature Singapore Pte Ltd. 2019
S. Ratuva (ed.), *The Palgrave Handbook of Ethnicity*,
https://doi.org/10.1007/978-981-13-2898-5_22

across theology, religious experience likely plays a role in motivating elites and lay believers alike to mobilize. Finally, we outline some emerging areas for further research, including inquiry into the causes of religious preferences, mapping of the mechanisms of mobilization of the devout, clarification of the nexus of democracy and religion, and the increasing availability of data for continued exploration of the role of religion in mobilization.

Keywords

Religion · Political mobilization · Ethnic conflict · Marketplace of religion · Secularization · Religious institutions · Theology

Introduction

What is the role of religion in political mobilization? Mobilization has received a great deal of attention in Comparative Politics (Gurr 2015; Habyarimana et al. 2009; Lipset 1960; Mecham 2017; Norris 2002). However, the role of religion in the mobilization process is not fully understood – in part – because in international politics, the topic of religion in politics remained understudied for decades (Gill 2001; Gryzmala-Busse 2016; Wald and Wilcox 2006). This lack of attention is in stark contrast to foundational works across the social sciences, many of which considered religion a cornerstone of preferences and political activity (see Smith 2007; Weber 1958).

One likely reason for the more recent dearth of interest in religion in politics is secularization theory or the long-standing prediction that modernizing societies would grow more secular over time. In the long run, secularization theory essentially renders religion irrelevant as either an explanatory variable or an outcome (Berger 1967; Bruce 2002; Dobbelaere 1981; Durkheim 2001; Marx and Engels 2012). However, contrary to this prediction, accumulation of empirical evidence shows that religiosity and/or practice are not only present within industrialized democracies (Dalton 2013) but are, in some societies, expanding (Broughton and ten Napel 2000; Finke and Iannacone 1993; Finke and Stark 1992; Iannaccone 1991). The continued importance of religion worldwide (see Gill 2001; Inglehart et al. 1998), along with global events involving political actors using religious symbolism and framing, in the twenty-first century, has brought religion again to the forefront in the study of international politics.

In this chapter we trace developments in the thinking about the role of religion in literature discussing political mobilization. Broadly speaking, we outline two predominant arguments, developing somewhat sequentially, in journals and books published primarily in the United States and Britain. We conclude that the current line of thinking portrays religion as an instrument for mobilization of and by a population, while the root causes for the mobilization generally are not thought to be theological. This strand of thinking, we show, traces its roots as far back as the behavioral revolution in political science and even further still. The second strand, set in motion by global conflict events framed in religious terms, focused on theology and differences between religions as motivating factors in mobilization. This line of thinking has largely been supplanted. Even so, it did force the acknowledgment that while religion is an intervening instrument in mobilization, belief may at the same time sincerely motivate the leader of mobilization and the individual followers mobilizing. However, this does not mean theology is considered a driving factor of religious movements in a static and differential sense. In contrast, the literature considers theologies as fluid doctrinal teachings, endogenous to historical and social contexts, all of which may at different times motivate individuals to mobilize.

We define political mobilization as a process of activating a social movement for political ends (Tilly 1978). In turn, a social movement can be defined as "a network of informal interactions between a plurality of individuals, groups and/or organizations, engaged in a political or cultural conflict, on the basis of a shared collective identity" (Diani 1992, p. 13). Notably this outcome-centered definition, focusing on activation, encompasses both peaceful and violent political conflict that may remain informal or become formally organized and for a wide range of political outcomes. In explaining activation, we touch upon a variety of theories that highlight, among other things, incentives, structure, grievance, opportunity, framing, and theology. We do not specifically separate works by the great variety of terms that are used to describe mobilization of religion and range in content from mobilization of religious parties for explicitly secular goals as opposed to more informal organization of actors, sometimes seeking more explicitly religious goals, as long as those goals have political ramifications.

The subsequent discussion is roughly organized temporally to illustrate some major developments of the two main themes, the instrumental use of religion and theological drivers of mobilization. Within these two themes, we recognize at least two parallel and often overlapping sets of inquiries – one pertaining to electoral politics and the other to the politics of violence. Next we discuss the current state of our understanding of the role of religion in mobilization. Finally, we suggest some considerations for future research on the role of religion in political mobilization.

Implications of Secularization Theory

Early writings about the role of religion in mobilization tended to focus principally on the peaceful albeit contentious variety that over time was channeled through formal political structures. Foundational theories of the role of religion in political mobilization include Adam Smith's *An Inquiry into the Wealth of Nations* that devotes a chapter to a theory of the relationship between church, state, and members of congregations. Starting with the assumption that the clergy are rational, self-interested, political actors, Smith argues that the relationship between elite leaders of religious groups and their followers, and the state, depends on the marketplace of religion. To summarize, the driver in Smith's argument is the source of the clergy's income (Anderson 1988). Specifically, focusing on Catholic and Protestant churches in Europe, Smith suggests that if church income draws on state resources (taxes or mandatory tithes), the clergy will seek to align with the government to protect the clergy's monopoly in the marketplace of religions, against competing churches. In contrast, if the clergy's income is supplied directly by congregations, leaders of religious groups will be more zealous in courting the congregation. Thus, the economic relationship between the state and leaders of religions alters the incentives of the clergy to mobilize congregations. In turn, governments and political groups may align themselves with religious organizations to win more support, especially in times of conflict. In this way, Smith suggests that elite representatives of religious groups can become key political operatives within a state.

Behavioralist perspectives, in the middle of the twentieth century, shifted the view of religion in mobilization to an expression of a cleavage conflict that emerged in the course of consolidating nation states. However, similarly to Smith, the driver of mobilization was also located in the relationship between the church and state, which conditioned the relationship between the church and the constituency. Arguing that the role of the church and religions in society was one of the three main political issues confronting Western Nations, Lipset observed a general pattern across Western nations. Catholic churches, which had a closer alignment with the aristocracy, tended to mobilize through the parties on the right that were associated with the establishment. In contrast, Protestants and Jewish constituencies tended to align with the left against the landed aristocracy (Lipset 1960). Lipset and Rokkan (1967) further elaborated the process by which they argued national revolutions in Europe pitted against each other members of various prominent cleavages, among these secular against religious cleavages, leading to the political mobilization and static (frozen) alignment of citizens into the West European party systems of the time.

In the 1970s, religion in mobilization featured in the debate about the role of grievance versus resources in mobilization. In Gurr's view, the key to mobilization was relative deprivation or the current or predicted future inequality in a desired but unattained good (either political, territorial, or economic). Specifically, with respect to religion and mobilization, he argued that new religious movements often mobilized as a result of such grievances, against the establishment associated with the religious status quo (Gurr 1994). Some of Gurr's examples included proletariat protests in nineteenth-century Britain that took on religious frames and nationalist movements in Africa that capitalized on religious membership in mobilization against colonial powers (Regan and Norton 2005).

Objecting that grievances exist for many groups that have not mobilized politically, Tilly, in contrast, thought of religion as an organizational resource solution to Olson's (1965) collective action problem. According to Tilly, common identity and strong social networks result in better group organization, which in turn gives the group higher mobilization potential. While attempting to explain workers' mobilization rather than mobilization of the religious, Tilly used the religion of the Catholic Church as one example of an identity that by way of organizational network structure contributes to greater mobilizing capacity of a group engaged in political contestation over state power (Tilly 1978).

In turn, Tarrow explained mobilization in contentious politics arising out of changes in political opportunities for groups. While individuals may desire political change for a variety of reasons (from the material to the imaginative), mobilization requires individuals in a social network have opportunities to express discontent without excessive repression from the government (Tarrow 2011). However, sustained political mobilization requires more than opportunity and grievance, according to Tarrow. Sustained mobilization also requires "solidarity," or the recognition by participants that common interests exist in their groups. Among several strategies, solidarity can be created when leaders of religious movements tap into individual devotion and convince believers that their group-level grievances are connected to their religious identity (Tarrow 2011, p. 6).

Simultaneously, culturalists worked to better understand the individual-level mechanisms driving the "high political mobilization potential of religious identities" (Young 1976, p. 52). Young suggested that religious rituals provide the individual with continuous reaffirmation of membership while at the same time demarcating the group. He also argued that religious symbols provide the bases for shared emotional reactions to real and imagined external threats and for calls for defense of the faith as sanctioned by the divine. Similarly, Geertz' 1966 thick anthropological description pinpoints religious symbols as synthesizing an "ethos" and people's "ideas of order" (p. 3), thus helping to justify a particular social order (Geertz 1973).

At the same time, in an attempt to explain the perceived decrease in religiosity, in part conceptualized as falling church memberships in higher-income countries, secularization theory gained steam. The theory proposed that the increasing complexity of society due to modernization (primarily the separation of public and private life as well as the increasing rise of income and introduction of national or global market economies) would cause secular activities to become more important over time, while at the same time people had less resources to devote to religion (Bellah 1986; Berger and Luckmann 1967; Bruce 2002; Dobbelaere 1981).

Pushing back against secularization theory, one of the more prominent contributions to the thinking about religion and mobilization was the fundamentalist project (Marty and Appleby 1994). In contrast to secularization, the authors argued modernization magnifies the role of religious mobilization rather than suppressing it. Following up on the fundamentalist project, Almond et al. (2003) defined "fundamentalism" as a "discernible pattern of religious militancy by which self-styled 'true believers' attempt to arrest the erosion of religious identity, fortify the borders of the religious community, and create viable alternatives to secular institutions and behaviors" (p. 17).

Others highlighted the fact that the evidence showed increasing religiosity in less developed nations and in largely secular nations a high number of people that professed a belief in some form of a higher power (Gill 2001). Consequent refinements of the theory included Norris and Inglehart (2004) who proposed that with modernization, individual existential insecurity diminished and thus decreased individual need in more developed countries for faith in religious salvation.

The substantial empirical variance in religious activities in the group of higher-income nations, for instance, highlighting large religious populations in United States ignited further inquiry. Building on Smith's ideas about the marketplace of religion to explain this variance, scholars suggested state-funded church leaders – for example, in several countries in Europe – lacked an incentive to recruit and/or keep rank and file involved and excited about the church, since that would increase the funded church leaders' work load. Consequently, they proposed that, where religion is funded by the state, religious state institutions survive without the necessity to maintain and/or recruit adherents and adherents turn away from organized religion. In contrast, under conditions of pluralist religious competition where church leaders rely on their constituency for income, as in the United States, religious leaders must work to keep adherents involved and mobilized. Larger or more robust religious organizations continually adapt their teachings or practices to meet demands and gain new members (see Anderson 1988; Iannaccone 1998; Stark and Finke 2000, 2002; Stark and Iannaccone 1994; Stark et al. 1996 for examples). Furthermore, if religious leaders think that addressing political topics helps mobilizing the devout, religious rhetoric takes on increasingly overt political overtones (Jelen and Wilcox 2002).

Others developed arguments to emphasize individual incentives for joining and participating in religious organizations. These suggest, for example, that in addition to spiritual payoffs, there are significant individual benefits to engagement with religion including networks and shared symbols that develop human capital, resources, and organization. Furthermore, religious mobilization is influenced by associated opportunity costs. If wages or employment decreases, opportunity costs associated with religious activities diminish, and religious involvement of the rank and file increases (Carr and Landa 1983; Durkin and Greeley 1991; Iannaccone 1991).

Auxiliary, theorized mechanisms of the role of religion in mobilization highlighted the importance of religious framing by leaders of social movements in pursuit of a political goal (McAdam et al. 1996). Scholars also showed elites using their public status to shape the political discourse relating to mobilization (Djupe and Gilbert 2002) and relying on common religious group language to frame what correct political behavior looks like for their followers (Wald et al. 2005). Others illustrated the role of historical legacies in influencing party formation in new democracies, including suppression of political mobilization of religion (Grzymala-Busse 2013). The research also illustrated how organizational capacity of the religious institution matters for political mobilization (Kalyvas 1996, 2000). For example, organizations that are hierarchical, like the Catholic Church, can more easily mobilize loose religious networks than can horizontally oriented institutions of various Islamic sects and schools (Pfaff and Gill 2006). Even so, Muslims have successfully mobilized at local and regional levels, although the evidence shows this is not uniform across Muslim communities (Fox 2006; Koopmans 2004; Koopmans and Statham 1999; Pfaff and Gill 2006), suggesting that hierarchical organizational structures facilitate mobilization but vertical structures likely do not prevent it.

Surging Interest in Violent Religious Mobilization

Huntington's (1996) clash of civilizations thesis was another prominent contribution at this time. His argument contended that the end of the Cold War marked a new era in which liberal democracy would have to contend with Islamic and Asian civilizations defined by differing cultural systems and world views. The theory itself is noted for being somewhat vague, contradictory, and anecdotal, especially with respect to the mechanisms by which members of these clashing cultures supposedly mobilize for conflict (Gurr 1994; Hassner and Huntington 1997; Hassner 2011). Still, the general cultural distinctions discussed in Huntington's thesis correspond with prominent religious differences, and Huntington himself argued religion was a central motivator of mobilization (Fox 2001; Huntington 1996, p. 66). Subsequent empirical research examining the role of religion in conflict mobilization as intimated by Huntingtonian ideas, for the most part, did not find a direct empirical relationship (Chiozza 2002; Fox 2004; Henderson and Tucker 2001), especially not for conflict between Islam and other religions (Gartzke and Gleditsch 2006; Gleditsch and Rudolfsen 2016).

Nonetheless, global events – especially 9/11 and the war on terror – coupled with Huntington's theory eclipsed other types of inquiries into the role of religion in violent mobilization for the next decade. To date the google scholar citation count for Huntington's 1993 Foreign Affairs article is well over 13 thousand, and the citation count for his book (Huntington 1996) with a similar title exceeds 22 thousand, revealing the enormous influence of this work for both scholars seeking to support and/or refute it. This line of research produced a large body of literature that delved into theology – especially Islamic doctrine – in search of mechanisms to explain the contribution of religion to violent mobilization.

Theology as a Mechanism for Mobilization

Borum summarizes the fruits of the first decade of the literature on radical mobilization – especially radical Islamic mobilization – as conceptual, rather than empicial, and mostly offering a "descriptive narrative of a typical transformative process" (Borum 2011, p. 38). Even so taken together, this body of work makes clear that while Islam is often used as a tool for radical mobilization, there is little evidence that there is anything inherent to Islam that distinguishes this theology in that it necessarily drives adherents to violence. Rather similarly to mobilization in other religious traditions, Islamic theological concepts are often developed and used to appeal to susceptible individuals.

The cross-national literature supports this view showing that while Muslims are overrepresented in conflict, this is for reasons that a Huntingtonian theory of civilizations cannot fully explain. For example, the predominant type of conflict Muslims are involved in is intra-religious (Fox 2004; Gartzke and Gleditsch 2006; Gleditsch and Rudolfsen 2016; Toft 2007). Fox (2001) suggests that waves of Islamist violence after the 1970s and again in the 1990s likely reflect an important change in geopolitics. De Soysa and Nordås (2007) find that regional effects unique to the Middle East have a great impact on receptiveness to democracy, repression of civil and human rights, and the probability of acts of violence. Some of these regional effects include having largely oil-based export economies, low income per capita, and historical repression of civil liberties or civil wars. As Gunning and Jackson (2011) point out, even if it were true that Islamist groups committed more deadly acts of terrorism, that alone does not imply causality between theology and violence.

Individual-level evidence similarly suggests that Islamic doctrine is not the cause of terrorist mobilization. Toft (2013) suggests terrorist organizations adopt religious ideology for material and strategic benefits. Toft and Zhukov (2015) provide evidence that with the exception of how they respond to counter-terrorism measures, Islamists mostly behave similarly to secular nationalists. Furthermore, they posit that Islamist's unusual resilience in the face of indiscriminate violence against their population by a national government is related to the transnational funding and support that Islamist organizations receive from coreligionists abroad rather than any sort of theological uniqueness.

Indeed, radical Islamist militants do not necessarily appear to have a particularly good understanding of theology. For example, although Hegghammer (2017) and Juergensmeyer (2018) argue that Daesh's mobilization draws on a global diaspora of supporters that share the organization's values, their research shows that many members of the group demonstrated little knowledge of their group's theology.

In addition to explaining why the origin of conflict mobilization is not to be found in Islamic theology, the increasing attention to religion in conflict mobilization delivered several important insights. One example is the evidence that religious conflicts are more difficult to end than are other types of conflicts (Fox 2004; Svensson 2007). A possible explanation is that religious claims made during conflict are more intractable because religious belief systems do not easily allow compromise or bargaining over the state (Fox 2004; Toft 2007; Wentz 1987).

Other scholars elucidate why and how entrepreneurs use religious symbols and doctrines for purposes of religious mobilization across religious traditions (Haynes 2006; Jelen and Wilcox 2002). For example, even though their goals are ostensibly secular, religion is the front and center in religious nationalist movements of the twentieth century, according to Juergensmeyer, because these are often driven by a fundamentalist reactions to modernization and earlier secular nationalist movements (Juergensmeyer 2010).

With respect to the international dimension of religious mobilization, Toft (2007) explains that the transnational nature of religion allows for increased elite outreach and augmentation of network ties. Indeed, as globalization progresses, the importance of transnational religious movements is intensified (Haynes 2016b). In a globalizing environment, religious leaders with large mobilized constituencies have the ability to challenge international norms via global networks that can attract compliance. At two ends of the spectrum, these networks include terrorist groups with fundamentalist ideology, such as Al Qaeda, and humanitarian and democratic organizations connected to institutions like the Vatican (Haynes 2016b, p. 5).

An Endogenous View of Religious Mobilization

Current research shows that while not the root cause of political conflict, religion is one identity type that individuals may choose to activate in their "identity repertoire" (Chandra 2012, p. 22) and one dimension of identity that political entrepreneurs seek to mobilize among their constituency (Birnir and Satana forthcoming; McCauley 2014; Posner 2017). Religion provides the structures and tools, including organization but also the symbolic rituals and language, for salient group coordination, fund-raising, and resource allocation (Haynes 2016a; Jelen and Wilcox 2002; Juergensmeyer 2000, 2013; Toft 2007). Thus, religion can be used as an instrument for mobilization, sometimes with objectives that possibly differ from other types of political mobilization.

For instance, Brubaker (2015) suggests that mobilization of religiously based, substantive regulation of public life is distinct. Similarly, McCauley suggests that political entrepreneurs evoke religion for support of policy issues that differ from issues for which they seek ethnic support (McCauley 2012, 2014). Furthermore, it is understood that religious experience can have a strong psychological influence on the individual beyond political identification (Mitchell 2007).

However, religious experience may serve as the foundation for individual mobilization in ways that are simultaneously devout and instrumental. For example, religion and religious experience provide a framework that helps people understand the world around them (Seul 1999). When challenged, the devout may then mobilize to defend this framework (Fox 2002) for reasons that are simultaneously sincere and instrumental.

Conceptualizing religion as an instrument in mobilization underscores that the structural tools for mobilization are common, albeit varied, across religions. Furthermore, it highlights that the root causes for mobilization are exogenous to doctrine. At the same time, this understanding of the role of religion in mobilization accommodates religious experience and sincere belief as a driver of individual preferences and behavior. Therefore, the current framework for researching the role of religion in mobilizations is consistent with theories of the marketplace of religion while at the same time encouraging inquiry into the features of religious experience that across doctrine distinguish, from other types, mobilization centering on religion.

This endogenous point of view makes room for inquiries into a plethora of processes, peaceful and violent, where religion plays a role in mobilization. In the domain of electoral politics, for instance, studies explore the instrumental mobilizing role of Islamic parties across seemingly devout constituencies in the Middle East and South Asia (Contreras-Vejar 2015; Euchner and Preidel 2018) and religious parties more generally across a global sample (Fox 2006). The evidence suggests, for example, that countering secularist politics is in some cases articulated by religious leaders as the mobilizing raison d'être of religious parties (Euchner and Preidel 2018; Gill 2017), sometimes for instrumental reasons.

Others focus on transition where religion features prominently including the democratic transitions during the Arab Spring (Ferrero 2018), suggesting that democracy is harder to achieve when a hegemonic religion is tied to the state (Cesari and Fox 2016). In this vein, Mecham (2017) examines Islamist political mobilization across peaceful and violent settings. Briefly, Mecham argues that internal state crisis or rapid political liberalization serves as a catalyst for Islamist mobilization. This mobilization is led by political entrepreneurs that are poorly incorporated into the state and/or not under the hierarchical or social control of the religious leadership, for example, by way of state patronage. At the individual level, religion plays a role in the mobilization process in that common religious institutions shape preferences for religious policies, create common knowledge about these preferences among worshippers, and lower the cost of collective action by taking advantage of extant religious structures.

Others investigate the role of religion in violent mobilization. Here, the explanations for the high mobilization and conflict potential between divergent ethnoreligious groups are especially well developed. Chiefly, threatened political elites attempt to enhance their religious credentials with their key domestic audiences to take over and/or cement their hold on power. To this end, majority/plurality elite factions instrumentally outbid each other, targeting ethnoreligious minorities (Toft 2013), making ethnoreligious segmentation especially conflict prone (Basedau et al. 2011b, 2016; Stewart 2012). Elaborating the mechanisms of mobilization, overlaying segmented ethnicity and religion increases group loyalties and strengthens social networks, which decreases the cost of recruiting rebels (Ellingsen 2005; Selway 2011; Seul 1999). This allows for the use of religion as a mobilizing vehicle for conflict (Basedau et al. 2011a, 2016; Juan and Hasenclever 2015). Other recent complimentary explanations of how religion becomes mobilized in conflict between religious groups point to minority religious grievances (Akbaba and Taydas 2011), including grievances that are exogenous to religion (Satana et al. 2013), governments' regulatory involvement in religion (Fox 2008, 2015, 2016b), religious repression (Nordås 2015), and salience of religion (Isaacs 2017).

Taken together this literature acknowledges that individuals have religious preferences that create opportunities for mobilization by religious leaders. At the same time, it is understood that mobilization by of the religious further shapes individual preferences with respect to religion.

Future Directions

The wealth of scholarship on religious mobilization has clarified scholarly thinking about identity formation and collective action. Recently revised conceptions of religion, secularism, and modernization have opened new paths for social inquiry. Moving forward we highlight four areas of the literature where we think substantial contributions can be made with respect to the topic of religious mobilization. These are religion and peacemaking, the role of formal and informal religious institutions (within and across religions), the direction and content of the causal arrow between religious identity and mobilization, and the intersectionality of religion and gender. Each of these areas relate not only to questions of mobilization in general but to pertinent global issues such as growing transnational nature of religious organizations, the increasingly prominent role of religion in civil conflicts across diverse states, as well as issues of human rights and political polarization along religious lines.

Peacemaking

Some scholars of conflict have suggested that clergy and other types of religious leaders have a unique position for promoting peace. For example, Sandal (2017) argues that religious leaders can interpret religious texts in a way that bears on conflict. Illustrating this idea, Sandal suggests that religious leaders in Ireland between 1960 and 2000 used their standing in communities to formulate a theology of reconciliation between conflict parties in the Irish conflict. Others suggest that religious institutions may be particularly helpful for peacemaking. For instance, religious institutions can be designed to facilitate reconciliation between enemies, forgiveness, cross-class solidarity, and social justice (Abu-Nimer 2001; Appleby 1999; Gopin 2000, 2002; Sandal and Fox 2013). This literature suggests that the micro-foundations for national peace could be related to how local leaders diffuse theological framing throughout the community, as well as offering social benefits and welfare. Questions building on the literature include whether religious actors are more helpful in certain types of conflicts or at certain times in a conflict.

Formal and Informal Institutions

On a similar, comparative note, we suggest that more research could be done to understand the role that formal and informal religious institutions play in shaping outcomes. Extant research suggests study of institutional organization within and across religions might yield interesting observations. For instance, Mecham (2017) argues that a chief cause of variation in Islamic political mobilization results from differences in informal religious institutions across Islamic contexts. Specifically, he suggests mobilization by Islamic entrepreneurs is easier when they cannot be easily controlled by religious leadership. Thus, Islamic sects that maintain tighter control over social structures and doctrine will, on average, see less Islamic politicization. Livney (forthcoming) adds that informally shared Islamic identity enhances interpersonal trust that helps overcome coordination failures.

In turn, examining political mobilization among Christian Church constituencies, Kalyvas (2000) suggests religious mobilization may partially be a product of the formal organizational structures of the institution. Comparing across religions, hierarchical religions such as Catholicism seemingly are more centralized than is Islam. However, given the variation identified by Mecham (2017) looking across the cases within doctrine, it would be interesting to better understand, for example, the variation in hierarchical control within and across each religion. Furthermore, it would be fascinating to examine whether Livney's argument about religiously based interpersonal trust generalizes across doctrine.

Direction of the Causal Arrow?

Another fascinating line of research explores empirically the endogeneity of religious mobilization. Recent work suggests that under certain circumstances, religious preferences are not just activated but created by political operatives defining a constituency. For instance, Margolis (2018a) argues that in the United States, individual choice in religion is driven by a marketplace of religious entrepreneurs who signal their political identity in religious practice and to which the politically like-minded respond. In other words, individual religious preferences follow political preferences (Campbell et al. 2018; Margolis 2017, 2018a, b). Others suggest more of an endogenous sorting mechanism at work in US politics. Political parties pick up religious platforms, which, in turn, induce constituency sorting into blocks that are increasingly polarized on multiple identity dimensions including religion (Mason 2018). Further exploration of the origin of politically mobilized religious preferences across contexts is sure to elucidate and uncover additional nuances in the direction and content of the causal arrow between religion and mobilization.

Gender, Religion, and Issues of Private Versus Public Life

Another area where additional rigorous work can be done by political scientists is on the intersection of gender studies and religious mobilization. As scholars of the sociology of religion note, faith provides gendered languages and customs that define roles for women in society (Stark and Finke 2000). Furthermore, some argue that there are gender differences in religiosity, with women on average being more religious with possible consequences for political preferences (Miller and Stark 2002; Pew Research Center 2016; Stark 2002). Teele (2018), for example, notes that women's enfranchisement in France was hindered, partially, by the perception of leftist politicians that women's votes were conservative and religious. The role of women in conflict has also been understudied, particularly in religious or ethnically divided conflict (Sales 1997, p. 4).

A growing policy concern about women's rights and public forms of religious expression (Reilly and Scrivner 2014) highlights the importance of research on the intersection of religion and gender. Recent examples include public display of religious symbols such as the hijab (Rosenberger and Sauer 2012) but extend to a broader debate about issues such as individual autonomy, abortion, use of contraceptives, education, and political participation.

The Empirical Analysis of Religion and Mobilization

A final trend, more than direction, that we see as particularly fruitful is the increase in available data for analysis of the various aspects of religion and mobilization. For example, nearly a decade ago, Fox (2012, 2016a) began to compile information on religious freedoms and restrictions across the world. Basedau et al. (2016, 2011b) code ethnic groups for religion in Africa to analyze the effect of ethnoreligious segmentation on conflict outcomes. Other scholars have constructed and examined national-level indicators of shared cultural characteristics including religion (Selway 2011) code, the religion of conflict participants (Lindberg 2008), and their motivation (Svensson 2007; Svensson and Nilsson 2018). A forthcoming dataset A-Religion codes the religion of all socially relevant ethnic groups in the AMAR data

(Birnir et al. forthcoming). Furthermore, a brief survey of datasets held by the Association of the Religion Data Archives, at (http://www.thearda.com/), shows that multiple datasets depict religious populations and their attributes such as population size (Brown and James 2018; Hackett and Stonawski 2017) and religious practices within countries across the globe. In sum, in recent years, we have experienced an explosion in the availability of public data touching on the various aspects of religion, and we hope this trend continues.

Conclusion

In this chapter we sought to synthesize theories of religion as they pertain to mobilization. We traced two divergent paths of literature: the first suggesting that religious identity is used strategically as an instrument for mobilization and, the second, arguing that theology is a mobilizing mechanism. We suggest that the literature currently converges on the idea that while religious belief can be sincere and theology can drive individual preferences, true belief does not exclude the use of religion as a tool for mobilization.

Work on religious belief in politics has pertinent implications for current issues in politics across the globe, including renewed nationalism in countries with higher than average incomes, augmented democratization in countries with lower than average incomes, and the rise of conflicts fought in the name of defending one's faith. In addition to the wealth of knowledge that has been accumulated already, we highlighted four areas where researchers can dive deeper into questions of faith and mobilization with a final note about the promising accumulation of data for the analysis of religion in politics. Further inquiry into this topic will continue to be of great importance.

Cross-References

▶ Ethnic Conflicts and Peace-Building
▶ Evolution of Palestinian Civil Society and the Role of Nationalism, Occupation, and Religion
▶ Identity and Conflict in Northern Ireland

References

Abu-Nimer M (2001) Conflict resolution, culture, and religion: toward a training model of interreligious peacebuilding. J Peace Res 38(6):685–704
Akbaba Y, Taydas Z (2011) Does religious discrimination promote dissent? A quantitative analysis. Ethnopolitics 10(3–4):271–295
Almond GA, Appleby RS, Sivan E (2003) Strong religion: the rise of fundamentalisms around the world. University of Chicago Press, Chicago

Anderson GM (1988) Mr. Smith and the Preachers: the economics of religion in the wealth of nations. J Polit Econ 96(5):1066–1088

Appleby SR (1999) The ambivalence of the sacred: religion, violence, and reconciliation. Rowman & Littlefield Publishers, Lanham, 445 pp

Basedau M, Strüver G et al (2011a) Do religious factors impact armed conflict? empirical evidence from Sub-Saharan Africa. Terror Polit Violence 23(5):752–779

Basedau M, Vüllers J, Strüver G (2011b) Cutting bread or cutting throats? findings from a new database on religion, violence and peace in Sub-Saharan Africa, 1990 to 2008. GIGA, Hamburg

Basedau M, Pfeiffer B, Vüllers J (2016) Bad religion? religion, collective action, and the onset of armed conflict in developing countries. J Confl Resolut 60(2):226–255

Bellah RN (1986) Habits of the heart: individualism and commitment in American life. 1st Perennial Library edn. Harper & Row, New York

Berger PL (1967) The sacred canopy; elements of a sociological theory of religion, 1st edn. Doubleday, Garden City

Berger PL, Luckmann T (1967) The social construction of reality: a treatise in the sociology of knowledge. Anchor books, A589. Anchor Books edn. Doubleday, Garden City

Birnir JK, Satana N (forthcoming) Alternatives in mobilization: religion, ethnicity and conflict. Cambridge University Press, Cambridge

Borum R (2011) Radicalization into violent extremism: A review of social science theories. J Strateg Secur 4(4):2

Broughton D, ten Napel H-M (2000) Religion and mass electoral behaviour in Europe. Routledge, London

Brown D, James P (2018) The religious characteristics of states: classic themes and new evidence for international relations and comparative politics. J Confl Resolut 62(6):1340–1376

Brubaker R (2015) Religious dimensions of political conflict and violence. Sociol Theory 33(1):1–19

Bruce S (2002) God is dead: explaining secularization. Blackwell, Oxford

Campbell DE et al (2018) Putting politics first: the impact of politics on American religious and secular orientations. Am J Polit Sci 62:551–565

Carr JL, Landa JT (1983) The economics of symbols, clan names, and religion. J Leg Stud 12(1):135–156

Cesari J, Fox J (2016) Institutional relations rather than clashes of civilizations: when and how is religion compatible with democracy? Int Political Sociol 10(3):241–257

Chandra K (2012) Constructivist theories of ethnic politics. Oxford University Press, New York

Chiozza G (2002) Is there a clash of civilizations? Evidence from patterns of international conflict involvement, 1946–97. J Peace Res 39(6):711–734

Contreras-Vejar Y (2015) Unorthodox fate. J Relig Polit Pract 1(1):58–72

Dalton RJ (2013) Citizen politics: public opinion and political parties in advanced industrial democracies. CQ Press, Thousand Oaks

De Soysa I, Nordås R (2007) Islam's bloody innards? Religion and political terror, 1980–2000. Int Stud Q 51(4):927–943

Diani M (1992) The concept of social movement. Sociol Rev 40(1):1–25

Djupe P, Gilbert CP (2002) The political voice of clergy. J Polit 64(2):596–609

Dobbelaere K (1981) Secularization – a multidimensional concept. Curr Sociol 29(2):1–216

Durkheim É (2001) The elementary forms of religious life. Oxford world's classics. Oxford University Press, Oxford

Durkin Jr JT, Greeley AM (1991) A model of religious choice under uncertainty: on responding rationally to the non-rational. Ration Soc 3(2):178–196

Ellingsen T (2005) Toward a revival of religion and religious clashes? Terror Polit Violence 17(3):305–332

Euchner E-M, Preidel C (2018) Dropping the curtain: the religious secular party cleavage in german morality politics. Polit Relig 11(2):221–248

Ferrero M (2018) Why the Arab spring turned Islamic: the political economy of Islam. Constit Polit Econ 29(2):230–251
Finke R, Iannacone LR (1993) Supply-side explanations for religious change. Ann Am Acad Pol Soc Sci 527(1):27–39
Finke R, Stark R (1992) The churching of America, 1776–1990: winners and losers in our religious economy. Rutgers University Press, New Brunswick
Fox J (2001) Clash of civilizations or clash of religions. Ethnicities 1(3):295–320
Fox J (2002) Ethnoreligious conflict in the late 20th century: a general theory. Lexington Books, Lanham
Fox J (2004) Religion and state failure: an examination of the extent and magnitude of religious conflict from 1950 to 1996. Int Polit Sci Rev 25(1):55–76
Fox J (2006) World separation of religion and state into the 21st century. Comp Pol Stud 39(5):537–569
Fox J (2008) A world survey of religion and the state. Cambridge University Press, Cambridge. English
Fox J (2012) An introduction to religion and politics: theory and practice. Routledge, London
Fox J (2015) Political secularism, religion, and the state: a time series analysis of worldwide data. Cambridge University Press, New York. English
Fox J (2016a) Secular–religious competition in Western democracies: 1990 to 2014. J Relig Polit Pract 2(2):155–174
Fox J (2016b) The unfree exercise of religion: a world survey of discrimination against religious minorities. Cambridge University Press, New York. English
Gartzke E, Gleditsch KS (2006) Identity and conflict: ties that bind and differences that divide. Eur J Int Rel 12(1):53–87
Geertz C (1966) Religion as a cultural system. In: Banton M (ed) Anthropological approaches to the study of religion. Routeledge Psychology Press, New York
Geertz C (1973) The interpretation of cultures. Basic Books, New York, 484 pp
Gill A (2001) Religion and comparative politics. Annu Rev Polit Sci 4(1):117–138
Gill A (2017) Christian Democracy without romance: the perils of religious politics from a public choice perspective. Perspect Polit Sci 46(1):35–42
Gleditsch NP, Rudolfsen I (2016) Are Muslim countries more prone to violence? Res Polit 3(2):1–9
Gopin M (2000) Between Eden and Armageddon: the future of world religions, violence, and peacemaking. Oxford University Press, Oxford
Gopin M (2002) Holy war, holy peace: how religion can bring peace to the Middle East. Oxford University Press, New York, 280 pp. Google-Books-ID: n0QStb088YUC
Grzymala-Busse A (2013) Why there is (almost) no Christian Democracy in post-communist Europe. Party Polit 19(2):319–342
Grzymala-Busse A (2016) Religion and European politics – Oxford handbooks. In: Fioretos O, Falleti TG, Sheingate A (eds) The Oxford handbook of historical institutionalism. Oxford University Press, Oxford
Gunning J, Jackson R (2011) What's so 'religious' about 'religious terrorism' ? Crit Stud Terror 4(3):369–388
Gurr TR (1994) Peoples against states: ethnopolitical conflict and the changing world system: 1994 Presidential address. Int Stud Q 38(3):347
Gurr TR (2015) Why men rebel. Routledge, London, 579 pp
Habyarimana J et al (2009) Coethnicity: diversity and the dilemmas of collective action. Russell Sage Foundation, New York
Hackett C, Stonawski M (2017) The changing global religious landscape. Washington, DC, Pew Research Center
Hassner RE (2011) Blasphemy and violence 1: blasphemy and violence. Int Stud Q 55(1):23–45
Hassner P, Huntington S (1997) Clashing On: Hassner and Huntington. The National Interest 48:105–111

Haynes J (2006) Religion and international relations in the 21st century: conflict or cooperation? Third World Q 27(3):535–541
Haynes J (2016a) Religion and democratisation: what do we now know? J Relig Polit Prac 2(2):267–272
Haynes J (2016b) Religion, globalization and political culture in the Third World. Springer, New York
Hegghammer T (2017) Jihadi culture. Cambridge University Press, Cambridge
Henderson EA, Tucker R (2001) Clear and present strangers: the clash of civilizations and international conflict. Int Stud Q 45(2):317–338
Huntington SP (1993) The clash of civilizations? Foreign Aff 72:22–49
Huntington S (1996) The clash of civilizations and the remaking of world order. Simon & Schuster, New York
Iannaccone LR (1991) The consequences of religious market structure. Ration Soc 3(2):156–177
Iannaccone LR (1998) Introduction to the economics of religion. J Econ Lit 36(3):1465–1495
Inglehart R, Basáñez M, Moreno A (1998) Human values and beliefs: a cross-cultural sourcebook. University of Michigan Press, Ann Arbor, 557 pp
Isaacs M (2017) Faith in contention: explaining the salience of religion in ethnic conflict. Comp Pol Stud 50(2):200–231
Jelen TG, Wilcox C (2002) Religion and politics in comparative perspective: the one, the few, and the many. Cambridge University Press, Cambridge
Juan AD, Hasenclever A (2015) Framing political violence: success and failure of religious mobilization in the Philippines and Thailand. Civil Wars 17(2):201–221
Juergensmeyer M (2000) Terror in the mind of God: the global rise of religious violence, 2nd edn. University of California Press, Berkeley
Juergensmeyer M (2010) The global rise of religious nationalism. Aust J Int Aff 64(3):262–273
Juergensmeyer M (2013) The sociotheological turn. J Am Acad Relig 81(4):939–948
Juergensmeyer M (2018) Thinking sociologically about religion and violence: the case of ISIS. Sociol Relig 79(1):20–34
Kalyvas SN (1996) The rise of Christian Democracy in Europe. Cornell University Press, Ithaca
Kalyvas SN (2000) Commitment problems in emerging democracies: the case of religious parties. Comp Polit 32(4):379
Koopmans R (2004) Migrant mobilisation and political opportunities: variation among German cities and a comparison with the United Kingdom and the Netherlands. J Ethn Migr Stud 30(3):449–470
Koopmans R, Statham P (1999) Challenging the liberal nation-state? Postnationalism, multiculturalism, and the collective claims making of migrants and ethnic minorities in Britain and Germany. Am J Sociol 105(3):652–696
Lindberg J-E (2008) Running on faith? A quantitative analysis of the effect of religious cleavages on the intensity and duration of internal conflicts. Masters thesis, University of Oslo, Oslo, 133 pp
Lipset SM (1960) Political man: the social basis of modern politics. Doubleday, New York
Lipset SM, Rokkan S (1967) Party systems and voter alignments: cross-national perspectives, vol 7. Free press, New York
Livney A (forthcoming) Trust and the Islamic advantage in Turkey and the Muslim World. Cambridge University Press, Cambridge
Margolis MF (2017) How politics affects religion: partisanship, socialization, and religiosity in America. J Polit 80(1):30–43
Margolis MF (2018a) From politics to the pews: how partisanship and the political environment shape religious identity. University of Chicago Press, Chicago
Margolis MF (2018b) How far does social group influence reach? Identities, elites, and immigration attitudes. J Polit 80(3):772–785
Marty ME, Appleby RS (1994) Fundamentalisms observed, vol 1. University of Chicago Press, Chicago

Marx K, Engels F (2012) On Religion. Courier Corporation, North Chelmsford MA
Mason L (2018) Uncivil agreement: how politics became our identity. University of Chicago Press, Chicago
McAdam D et al (1996) The framing function of movement tactics: strategic dramaturgy in the American civil rights movement. In: Comparative perspectives on social movements: political opportunities, mobilizing structures, and cultural framings. Cambridge University Press, Cambridge, pp 338–355
McCauley JF (2012) Africa's new big man rule? Pentecostalism and patronage in Ghana. Afr Aff 112(446):1–21
McCauley JF (2014) The political mobilization of ethnic and religious identities in Africa. Am Polit Sci Rev 108(4):801–816
Mecham Q (2017) Institutional origins of islamist political mobilization. Cambridge University Press, New York
Miller AS, Stark R (2002) Gender and religiousness: can socialization explanations be saved? Am J Sociol 107(6):1399–1423
Mitchell J (2007) Religion is not a preference. J Polit 69(2):351–362
Nordås R (2015) Beyond religious diversity: religious state repression and intrastate armed conflict. PRIO (Peace Research Institute Oslo) working paper, PRIO, Oslo
Norris P (2002) Democratic phoenix: reinventing political activism. Cambridge University Press, Cambridge
Norris P, Inglehart R (2004) Sacred and secular: religion and politics worldwide. Cambridge studies in social theory, religion, and politics. Cambridge University Press, Cambridge, UK
Olson M (1965) The logic of collective action. Harvard University Press, Cambridge, MA
Pew Research Center (2016) The gender gap in religion around the world Pew Research Center. http://www.pewforum.org/2016/03/22/the-gender-gap-in-religion-around-the-world/. (Visited on 01/09/2019)
Pfaff S, Gill A (2006) Will a million Muslims march?: Muslim interest organizations and political integration in Europe. Comp Pol Stud 39(7):803–828
Posner DN (2017) When and why do some social cleavages become politically salient rather than others? Ethn Racial Stud 40(12):2001–2019
Regan PM, Norton D (2005) Greed, grievance, and mobilization in civil wars. J Confl Resolut 49(3):319–336
Reilly N, Scrivner S (eds) (2014) Religion, gender and the public sphere. Routledge studies in religion. Routledge, New York
Rosenberger S, Sauer B (eds) (2012) Politics religion and gender: framing and regulating the veil. Routledge studies in religion and politics. Routledge, New York
Sales R (1997) Women divided: gender, religion and politics in northern ireland. Routledge, New York
Sandal NA (2017) Religious Leaders and Conflict Transformation: Northern Ireland and Beyond. Cambridge: Cambridge University Press
Sandal NA, Fox J (2013) Religion in international relations theory: interactions and possibilities. Routledge, New York
Satana NS, Inman M, Birnir JK (2013) Religion, government coalitions, and terrorism. Terror Polit Violence 25(1):29–52
Selway JS (2011) Cross-cuttingness, cleavage structures and civil war onset. Br J Polit Sci 41(1):111–138
Seul JR (1999) 'Ours is the way of God': religion, identity, and intergroup conflict. J Peace Res 36(5):553–569
Smith A (2007) In: Soares SM (ed) An inquiry into the nature and causes of the wealth of nations. MetaLibri Digital Library, Lausanne
Stark R (2002) Physiology and faith: addressing the "universal" gender difference in religious commitment. J Sci Study Relig 41(3):495–507
Stark R, Finke R (2000) Acts of faith: explaining the human side of religion. University of California Press, Berkeley

Stark R, Finke R (2002) Beyond church and sect: dynamics and stability in religious economies. In: Sacred markets, sacred canopies: essays on religious markets and religious pluralism. Rowman & Littlefield, Co, Lanham, pp 31–62

Stark R, Iannaccone LR (1994) A supply-side reinterpretation of the "secularization" of Europe. J Sci Study Relig 33:230–252

Stark R, Iannaccone LR, Finke R (1996) Religion, science, and rationality. Am Econ Rev 86(2):433–437

Stewart F (2012) Religion versus ethnicity as a source of mobilization: are there differences? In: Understanding collective political violence. Springer, New York, pp 196–221

Svensson I (2007) Fighting with faith: religion and conflict resolution in civil wars. J Confl Resolut 51(6):930–949

Svensson I, Nilsson D (2018) Disputes over the divine: introducing the religion and armed conflict (RELAC) data, 1975 to 2015. J Confl Resolut 62(5):1127–1148

Tarrow SG (2011) Power in movement: social movements and contentious politics. Cambridge University Press, Cambridge, 353 pp

Teele DL (2018) How the west was won: competition, mobilization, and women's enfranchisement in the United States. J Polit 80(2):442–461

Tilly C (1978) From mobilization to revolution. Addison- Wesley Publishing Co, Reading

Toft MD (2007) Getting religion? The puzzling case of Islam and Civil War. Int Secur 31(4):97–131

Toft MD (2013) The politics of religious outbidding. Rev Faith Int Aff 11(3):10–19

Toft MD, Zhukov YM (2015) Islamists and nationalists: rebel motivation and counterinsurgency in Russia's North Caucasus. Am Polit Sci Rev 109(2):222–238

Wald KD, Wilcox C (2006) Getting religion: has political science rediscovered the faith factor? Am Polit Sci Rev 100(4):523–529

Wald KD, Silverman AL, Fridy KS (2005) Making sense of religion in political life. Annu Rev Polit Sci 8:121–143

Weber M (1958) The protestant ethic and the spirit of capitalism, Student's edn. Scribner Publishing, New York

Wentz RE (1987) Why do people do bad things in the name of religion? Mercer University Press, Macon

Young C (1976) The politics of cultural pluralism. University of Wisconsin Press, Madison

Foreign Military Occupations and Ethnicity

11

Radomir Compel

Contents

Introduction	188
Foreign Military Occupations in Review	188
Dynamics of Ethnicity and Nationalism	193
Ethnicity and Conflict	195
Military Occupation, Colonialism, and Ethnicity	197
Postcolonial Insights into Occupations	198
Strategies for Termination of Occupation	201
Conclusion	205
Cross-References	205
References	206

Abstract

Military occupations are one form of dispute settlement. International security studies and military sciences investigate why military occupations occur and why they have been considered necessary. International law reviews the grounds for their justification and provides normative guidelines for military conduct in the field. What the two disciplines lack is an introspection into what tends to happen in occupations and why most military occupations tend to end in failure, dislocation, and social turmoil. By reviewing a number of exemplary cases of occupation, including Japan and Palestine, this chapter focuses on the need to search for the underlying causes, which destabilize occupations and contribute to their deterioration. It argues that we need to draw upon research in ethnic relations, nationalism, and postcolonial studies, which focus on identity construction, reveal the nature of the knowledge/power nexus, and offer strategies for getting over the occupational and postoccupational setting.

R. Compel (✉)
School of Global Humanities and Social Sciences, Nagasaki University, Nagasaki, Japan
e-mail: cmplrad@nagasaki-u.ac.jp; cmplrad@gmail.com

Keywords
Military occupation · International security · Conflict · Postcolonialism · Identity

Introduction

Military occupations have rarely been treated systematically in social sciences, but they provide opportunities for refinement of empirical and theoretical knowledge across various disciplines. First, they serve as real-world evidence about how entrenched the principle of Westphalian territorial sovereignty has been and how complicated management of conflict can become. Second, they reveal strategies of war termination, which include social transformation on one hand, and the daily conditions such transformation tends to deliver, often ending in despair, humiliation, and resistance. Third, they raise epistemological questions about West-centric biases embodied in occupational policies of democracy and freedom promotion. This chapter argues that while international security studies can explain the reasons for existence of military occupations, comparative political science drawing on identity- and ethnicity-based theories can tell us more about the results of such occupations.

Foreign Military Occupations in Review

Military occupations are a firm part of public international law. As wars are often fought on foreign soil, military occupations of foreign lands have become an integral part of any such wars, and thus, of the customs and laws of war, especially throughout the nineteenth century. Eyal Benvenisti conceives of the "concept of occupation as the mirror-image of the concept of sovereignty," having emerged and evolved together through time (Benvenisti 2012, 21). Hugo Grotius, one of the founders of international law, traces the laws on the treatment of noncombatant civilians in war and occupation to the ancient customs of Greeks, Hebrews, Assyrians, and indeed, he points to the divine origins of the rule (Grotius 1625, 1441).

The rules on belligerent occupation received their first wide-ranging treatment in the Hague Conventions of 1899 and 1907. The convenors of the first Hague conference codified the rules of military occupations into the Convention with respect to the Laws and Customs of War on Land with annexed Regulations respecting the Laws and Customs of War on Land (Section III). Relevant provisions define the status of occupation, duties of the occupant, and rights of the population under occupation. These rules, especially humanitarian provisions emphasizing the rights of the population under occupation, were further promoted by Geneva Convention (IV) on the Protection of Civilian Persons in Time of War in 1949 (Benvenisti 1993; Dinstein 2009; Roberts 1985).

Of particular significance is article 43 of the Hague Convention of 1907, which stipulates that: "The authority of the legitimate power having actually passed into the hands of the occupant, the latter shall take all steps in his power to re-establish and insure, as far as possible, public order and safety, while respecting, unless absolutely prevented, the laws in force in the country" (Oppenheim 1921, 238). The Convention implies valuable rights for the occupant, such as extraction of resources and obedience of the occupied population, but at the same time, through the duty to safeguard and govern, it implies that occupant has to protect the population and is prohibited from altering the sovereignty of the territory in question.

There are two issues associated with the provisions of the Hague and Geneva Conventions, which have substantially influenced thinking and practice of military occupations. The first one is how to strike the balance between extraction of compliance and resources (benefiting the occupant) and protection of the population (benefitting the occupied), which, together with the changing rules of war, has shifted towards the latter (Nabulsi 1999, 240). The second issue is about whether the role of the occupant should be conservationist (conserving the prewar order) or transformative (reforming the society in question), which also has tended to move away from the original conservationist interpretations of the Hague Conventions (Fox 2008, 295; Roberts 2006, 580; Benvenisti 1993, 30). Both of these shifts have strengthened the original purpose of the Conventions, which was safeguarding of the principle of state sovereignty and de-legitimization of territorial conquest, but they extended those objectives further, especially concerning protection of civilians and in humanitarian issues.

How were the two dimensions of occupation (governance of the population and conservation of laws and order) put into practice? Let us briefly examine two classical cases that have received substantial scholarly attention, post-WWII Japan, and Israeli occupation of Palestine.

Occupation of Japan started after Japan's surrender on 14 August 1945 by virtue of accepting the Allied terms put forward in the Potsdam declaration. Paragraph 7 of the declaration set out that the Allies will occupy several points in Japan, paragraph 8 specified the territorial extent of defeated Japan, which would exclude its prewar advances, and paragraph 10 implied that the Allies might retain Japanese governmental authority instead of a direct occupational rule. At the same time, paragraphs 6, 9, 10, and 11 specified that the Allies would eliminate the militaristic regime, instigate war crime trials, and seek disarmament, economic demilitarization, and "strengthening of democratic tendencies among the Japanese people." Paragraph 10 of the declaration states that "(F)reedom of speech, of religion, and of thought as well as respect for the fundamental human rights shall be established," and paragraph 12 requires that the occupation will end when a peacefully inclined and responsible government will be established "in accordance with the freely expressed will of the Japanese people" (MOFA 1966).

The wartime discussions between the Allies laid down some principles of the organizational structure of the occupation. As the United Nations were not in place yet, the top controlling (and later decision-making) body was Far East Advisory Commission (later Far East Commission) with General Douglas MacArthur as the Supreme Commander for Allied Powers and executive agent of the occupation. However, the terms of the Potsdam Declaration, additionally interpreted by US State Secretary Byrnes' reply to the Japanese Government, and also initial policy directives to General MacArthur, military occupation of Japan would not be direct (as in the case of Germany), but indirect, mediated through the Japanese Government (Takemae 2002, 62). MacArthur's powers were not unlimited, but so far as the Far East Commission was pervaded with conflicts and rarely came forward with authoritative decisions, MacArthur achieved to manage the occupation with little intervention from outside, and with cooperation from the Japanese government. Existence of indirect rule and continuity of Japanese government put the first dimension of article 43 of Hague Regulations in some doubt, but it was not the condition of full governmental authority, which raised concerns.

Based on the Allied interpretation of the Potsdam Declaration, MacArthur introduced vigorous reforms of the Japanese social and legal system. First, militarists were purged out of public office, second, political prisoners were released, and fundamental rights of expression, thought, worship, assembly, including labor movement, were promulgated, third, political freedoms were expanded, parties allowed, women enfranchised, and fourth, land reforms were instituted, land was redistributed to impoverished farmers, and industrial conglomerates were dissolved. These sweeping reforms reached the climax with MacArthur's imposition of the new constitution upon the Japanese (Ward and Sakamoto 1987, 125; Dower 1999, 360). Some of the liberal reforms were later softened or "reversed" through amelioration of the democratizing drive and support of economic reconstruction of the former enemy, due to the rise of Cold War tensions (Schaller 1985, 132; Edelstein 2008, 126). Even if the new "reverse course" is combined with MacArthur's overriding concern about symbolically retaining Japanese Emperor on the throne, this does not change the fact that USA-led occupation went far beyond what could possibly be anticipated as acceptable by the article 43 of Hague Regulations.

Many accounts treat MacArthur's Japan as a "success story" of military occupation. From the legal viewpoint, it extended far beyond what had originally been conceived by international law, but as Benvenisti argues, the law of occupation has been changing in correspondence with the expanding role of the state in economic and social life of the society, and what Roberts described as the increasing influence of the Human Rights Law (Benvenisti 1993, 29; Roberts 2006, 591; Arai-Takahashi 2009, 112). However, these legal and technical accounts of military occupation generally leave out the fact that Japanese society has been deeply divided along the lines of constitutional revision for more than 70 years, ever since its introduction in 1946 (Green 2001, 46). Secondly, many historical accounts fail to mention that occupational authority relied on a rather fragile footing and with substantiated fears that their reforms might instigate an insurgency against the foreign occupant (Compel 2017, 39). Such issues do not necessarily deny the gravity of the trend towards transformative occupations, but rather, they call for caution, and for contemplation, especially about the dynamics of nationalism or ethnicity in an occupational context.

The second case is that of Israeli occupation of West Bank and Gaza. In early June of 1967, Israel fought a short 6-day war against Egypt, Jordan, and Syria, it prevailed, and it occupied the Sinai Peninsula and Gaza Strip (from Egypt), West Bank (from Jordan), and Golan Heights (from Syria) (Bergman 2014). Prior to that,

11 Foreign Military Occupations and Ethnicity

the Sinai Peninsula was under Egyptian control, Golan Heights were the border region belonging to the Syrian Republic, and Gaza Strip and West Bank (of Jordan River) were territories of the British Mandate for Palestine. When Israel declared independence in 1948, war ensued, and by the end of the war, Egypt occupied Gaza Strip, and Jordan West Bank. The 1967 war changed the geopolitical map again. West Bank and Gaza Strip were particularly risky areas, because many countries considered them integral parts of the previous British Mandate of Palestine, and Israel aimed at regaining them after the loss in 1948. Since the 1967 war, Israel has occupied both areas, as well as Golan Heights, while returning the control over the Sinai Peninsula back to Egypt in 1982 as a part of the peace treaty concluded in 1979 (Bunton 2013).

Fearing complications in regard to the sovereignty over some Syrian and Egyptian area, Israel evaded from referring to the Geneva Convention (IV), but it promptly occupied and established military government in the Occupied Territories in accordance with the principles of the Hague Regulations and Geneva Convention (IV) provisions. The Proclamation No. 2, Concerning Law and Administration, issued during the 6-day war at the West Bank on 7 June 1967 declared that the law in existence in the Occupied Territories "shall remain in force, insofar as it does not in any way conflict with the provisions of the Proclamation, or any other proclamation or order ...." Israel refrained from mentioning the Geneva Convention (IV) and it refused to recognize Jordan's claims to the territories of the West Bank and East Jerusalem, but it still accepted the validity of the (Arabic) laws existing in each individual occupied territory. Article 43 of the Hague Convention had been observed throughout all the period of the occupation, with the exception of Golan Heights (Dinstein 2009; Benvenisti 1993, 115). The occupation established a two-tiered system of rule through military proclamations and orders, and secondly, through local laws. The administrative system, also in compliance with the Hague Regulations and Geneva provisions, established a system of military administration based on the orders of the military commander, who delegated some authorities to the civilian administration after 1981, which, however, also remained largely under Israeli control and military supervision. Municipalities were allowed to conduct local elections in 1972 and 1976, but as opposition to the Israeli rule accumulated, the elections were further terminated. Judiciary system also came under the direct military rule, with the military setting up military courts, which adjudicated security related infringements, and offenses against the occupation forces (Dinstein 2009, 138). These examples show that throughout more than half a century old occupation, Israeli military authorities followed customary international law of occupation, including the provisions under article 43 of the Hague Regulations, about establishment of an orderly military government.

Has Israel given proper care to the occupied Palestinian community? Not in cases where military administration invoked security concerns and took harsh security measures, which in itself was not inconsistent with the laws of war. But there has been a major political issue, where Israel has been accused of violating the laws of occupation, the issue of Israeli settlers in Palestinian lands, which was contravening the letter of article 49 of the Geneva Convention (IV) prohibiting colonization of the occupied territory (Gorenberg 2006, Chap. 4). Despite the effort to stick to the customs and laws of occupation, in matters of security and policy, the rights of Palestinians were gravely disfavored.

How did Israel figure in the second dimension of article 43 of the Hague Regulations, the conservationist nature of occupation? Israel's policy of expropriation of Palestinian lands and construction of Israeli settlements contravenes the provisions of the Geneva Convention (IV), and implicitly also of the Hague Regulations. This is because Israeli government has to rely on local infrastructure, legislate new territorial plans, and thus change local laws and administrative measures in the interest of Israelis, harming the interest of the occupied Palestinian population. Furthermore, establishment of the settler communities in their new settlements brought with itself the problem of extraterritorial application of Israeli laws in the occupied territory. Also in economic policy, Israel chose to intervene extensively in the Palestinian matters. As Benvenisti argues, occupant state has an option to contain the occupied areas and assist their local development, but the provision which maintains that occupant should provide "public order and civil life" does not preclude the opposite, economic integration of Occupied Territories into one single market of the occupant. Economic integration is not in the provisions of the two Conventions, but can be implied from them, if it provides for the betterment of the lives of the occupied population. The problem is that economic integration brings with itself reliance on laws and decisions taken outside of the occupied territory. Furthermore, as in the case of introduction of the value added tax or other taxation in Occupied Territories, such decisions are transformative and not conservationist, residents do not have the right to vote on them, and new taxation tends not to protect the interests of residents. Policies of economic union in fact amount to nothing less than economic annexation (Benvenisti 1993, 142).

David Edelstein concludes that the outcome of the Israeli occupation of West Bank and Gaza was a failure, and thus it ended with negative results to Israel. He does not base his criteria for comparison of occupations on international law, but rather, on a cost-benefit analysis of maximization of the value to the occupant. To Edelstein, the occupation of Japan yielded acceptable outcomes for the USA, and it has been too lengthy and too costly in terms of human and material costs to Israel (Edelstein 2008, 188). The problem with such evaluation rests in the fact that it fails to account for deeper roots of antagonisms, which laid behind the problem of insurgencies in the Occupied Territories and which negatively influenced wider security environment in the general Middle Eastern region (Edelstein 2008; Dobbins 2003). Edelstein's suggestions about the best strategy for eliminating internal tensions in occupations are to direct attention of the occupied population away from the realities of the occupation against an external enemy, common to the occupant and the occupied. This is a diversionary strategy which does not address the problems of occupation per se, but may succeed when the environment is favorable, as was the emergence of Cold War in the case of the occupation of Japan. Whatever the suggested strategies might be, for Edelstein as well as for many ordinary Americans, Israel failed in Palestine, and the USA succeeded in Japan.

Both international law (Benvenisti) and international security (Edelstein) perspectives make knowledge claims and evaluations of military occupations on epistemological grounds within their area of inquiry. The first bases its argument on normative grounds and the second on policy grounds. However, none of the two does well in explaining the core problem in military occupations, the causes of insurgency. That is because neither is at ease with grasping the social dynamics of identity, such as nationalism, ethnicity, gender, or religion. Military occupation is a system of arbitrary and domination-subordination framework of social life which influences identity. To understand the dynamics of insurgencies, one needs to step beyond international law and international security framework and incorporate perspectives on identity and epistemology, which may tell us more about the importance of nationalism, ethnicity, and postcolonial mind (de Matos and Gerster 2009; de Matos and Ward 2012; Nabulsi 1999, 240; Azoulay and Ophir 2012; Gordon 2008; Roy 2007).

Dynamics of Ethnicity and Nationalism

Military occupations are pervaded with problems related to ethnicity. Occupations comprise vertical relations between the occupant and the occupied, which are often ethnically and culturally very distinct from each other, with the occupant claiming moral and cultural superiority over the occupied society. However, theories on ethnic relations rarely refer to military occupations per se. Thus, we will first turn into theories of ethnic relations within a wider scope of occupation in colonial and postindependence settings. Such theories can be divided into two groups: those, which explain nationalism as ideology of national self-determination, and those, which deal with ethnic conflict within the state. They are treated separately in the following two sections.

What do the theories of nationalism, as ideologies of national self-determination tell? Major approaches to the study of nationalism can be divided into two: modernism and perennialism. The first stream is that of modernists, who associate the project of nation-building with modernization of society, especially in the nineteenth and twentieth century. For them, the primary reason for the rise of nationalism was that the tendencies of a modernizing society tend to dissolve previous parochial allegiances and converge them into collective imaginations about a nation state. They argue that ethnic and regional diversities would fade away in the process of nation-building, and through the realization of national self-determination, they would be transformed into a uniform nation-wide allegiance to the modern nation state. Many political scientists concerned with studying the dynamics of political modernization, most significantly Karl Deutsch, addressed the phenomenon of formation of nation-wide allegiances through the process of nation building. Deutsch was convinced about the importance of modernization, in the form of urbanization, industrialization, education, communication, and transportation, which promoted the capacity of the state to reach to larger segments of population, and would lead to assimilation of cultural minorities (Deutsch 1953, 188). This perspective of Deutsch was widely shared among others in the modernization literature, but Deutsch himself has been more ambivalent in later writings, recognizing that ethnic groups could mobilize not only in support of majority, but also against the state (Deutsch 1969, 27).

Although with a different agenda, Benedict Anderson also embraced the modernization paradigm and especially Deutsch's focus on social communication as the prime mover towards national consolidation. The arrival of modern communication (such as national newspapers) and transportation paved the way towards consolidation of the nation as an imagined community, extending beyond parochial communities and traditional villages (Anderson 1991, 6). What he emphasized was the stickiness of the regimes of colonial occupation after the gaining of independence. The colonial boundaries often disregarded ethnic or tribal affinities, and the same boundaries were retained by the new political regimes. Also, new societies retained institutions and practices of the old regimes, including pilgrimage of Creole functionaries within the state and concentration of provincial newspaper printing houses at happenings beyond the Creole and relevant to the state. In Anderson's eyes, in Southeast Asia and Latin America, these modern tools of administration and print-capitalism were inherited from the colonial period and they contributed to the construction of a nation (Anderson 1991, 65, 140). Many other writers readily accepted the modernist perspective, including the two other who made up the "holy trinity" of the studies on nationalism, Ernest Gellner and Eric Hobsbawm (Breuilly 2016, 627; Gellner 1983, 36).

The arguments of modernists drew many critics. Anthony Smith accused modernists of spreading a fallacy (Smith 1995, 30; 2000, 28). Walter Connor criticized Deutsch for inadequate consideration of the linkage between mobilization and assimilation and for unquestioned acceptance of the notion that modernization disperses ethnic affiliations (Connor 1994, 54). Connor argues that creation of the national identity necessitated nation destroying, and not nation-building, and that only after secession, the new nation-states achieve a sense of common purpose (Connor 1994, 42). Criticisms are directed to Anderson's "imagined communities" too. For example, his treatment of Latin American nationalisms instigated by the elites of the Creoles does not write about the mobilization of the ordinary populations living there. Andreas Wimmer notes that influence of Mexican elites did not reach to remote native tribes (which rarely read newspapers), but still they actively participated in the Mexican rebellion (Wimmer 2002, 115).

The second stream of students of nationalism is primordialists (or in their weaker form, perennialits). They claim that nations have origins prior to the modern era, stemming from the primordial cultural traits of ethnic groups (Grosby 1995, 2005, 59; Hutchinson 2005, 14). Smith takes a position, which questions the value claims that globalization will override the strength of national and ethnic symbolism, such as mythologies, memorials, and value systems through which nationalism can appeal to autonomy, unity, identity, authenticity, homeland, dignity, continuity, and destiny of the nation or ethnic group (Smith 2009, 63). In his eyes, both globalization and modernization are undeniable trends in the world, but they cannot match the power of ethnic historical bonds. He claims that nations are more than modern civic and rational entities, because they incorporate the bonds to the premodern ethnic groups (Smith 2000).

Among criticisms raised against Smith are those, which argue that he makes a presupposition about the unitary nature of states (Guibernau 1996, Chap. 6). Many Third World states and federations do not fit well into such a scenario. This is also true in the case of occupied societies, which are generally rare and relatively short-lived. Particularistic movements for ethnic self-determination may lead to fragmentation along ethnic or religious lines, and reappearance of violence in such societies.

Both Smith (speaking for perennialists) and Anderson (for modernists) agree that nationalism is based on political imagination of communities and thus construction of national identities. However, they differ in the extent that they allow for identity construction and cultural and historical limitations of such construction. This provides a transmission link between nationalism and ethnicity. Nationalist imaginations produced by elites are rarely enough to penetrate the masses, if they are not based on some common references to ethnicity or race (Balibar and Wallerstein 1991, 49, 99).

Ethnicity and Conflict

Topics of ethnicity and race, closely linked to colonial studies, attracted much attention in the late nineteenth and early twentieth century. After the World War II, they were discredited for their contribution to Nazi and fascist ideologies of mass mobilization. Ethnicity studies gained attraction as a new field of inquiry again in the 1970s and 1990s, in response to the rise of nation-building efforts in the Third World, and decline of the Cold War rhetoric. Some scholars called it a new "ethnic turn" (Brubaker and Laitin 1998, 426). Inability of the newly established modernizing bureaucratic systems to deliver the fruits of modernization alienated themselves from the masses and often ended in political confusion and ethnic conflict. As Brubaker persuasively argues, failures of Westernizing elites in the Third World led into the decline of politics of distribution and ended in identity struggles over religious belief and ethnic recognition. Similar explanations were offered in relation to ethnic wars of the 1990s, such as wars in Yugoslavia or breakup of the Soviet Union (Hall 1998, 286).

Ethnic groups are defined by Max Weber as "those human groups that entertain a subjective belief in their common descent because of similarities of physical type or of customs or of both, or because of memories of colonisation or migration" (Weber 1922, 389). In his view, ethnicity or language give us a basis for communality. These then direct us towards the establishment of a political community, which corresponds to the emergence of the state. Many external forces, such as market or warfare, give us strong impetuses to interpret and reinterpret our beliefs about how the community should look like. Group maintenance based on language, culture, or ethnicity gives us a tool, as Anderson pointed out, to create a sense of a community, which transcends individual face-to-face interactions. Ethnic identities are, therefore, socially constructed, but at the same time, they provide precise standards for human organization, that is, for identifying and excluding others. Some ethnic groups identify themselves based on a commonly recognized territory, others on birth, still others on language or cultural affinities.

Three main groups of ethnicity-based theories can be identified in explanation of ethnic conflicts (Kaufmann 2005; Birdal and Squires 2010). The first is instrumental rationalist approach, which emphasizes individual economic reasoning, teleological behavior, individual utilities, and cost-benefit analysis to explain ethnic conflict in a way as any other forms of political struggle. Authors in this tradition emphasize strategic behavior, transaction costs, accumulated grievances, rent seeking, or greed (Fearon and Laitin 1996, 715; Collier et al. 2003). The focus on the instrumental use of ethnicity, however, is vulnerable to the counter arguments that violent conflicts have deeper roots, such as group identities, which cannot be comprehended by observing only economic interests.

Second approach is essentialist, and it was the first to emerge at the time of post WWII decolonization and independence movements. Essentialist scholars such as Donald Horowitz, Roger Petersen, or Joshua Fishman focus on ethnicity as essential human needs, and they explain that conflicts rise from long-lasting historical hatreds within societies (Horowitz 1985; Petersen 2002). Their claims build on the presumption that all humans have needs for collective self-identification, and ethnic identity is the most elementary and the most powerful to satisfy such needs. Essentialists, while providing powerful explanations for underlying reasons of violence, however, have had difficulties in explaining the timing and actual causes of particular conflicts, and also why some conflicts mattered more than others, and why same societies could rest in peace at one time, and fight violent wars at another time.

Third approach is constructivist, and it is the most recent of the three approaches. Similar to the arguments about nationalism, Crawford Young, Benedict Anderson, Charles Taylor, or Eric Hobsbawm argue that the rise of modernity transformed previously locally based identities and awakened the masses into a new framework of ethnic consciousness and meaning (Young 1994; Taylor et al. 1994). Constructivists propose several mechanisms of identity formation, such as mass communications, transportation, education, bureaucracy, colonial rule, or as Taylor argue, the call for dignity and recognition among previously subordinated masses (Taylor et al. 1994, 64). Constructivism, with its detailed focus on historical and anthropological explanation, has become the dominant approach in the studies of ethnicity. It focuses on nation building and ethnic narratives, but it encounters problems when explaining local variations in such enthusiasm. It has many affinities with instrumentalism, with which it shares the focus on interest, entrepreneurialism, and animosity against essentialism, but at the same time, it shares with essentialism the focus on identity and hostility towards short-term individualistic interest-based explanations.

Finally, other theories, such as structuralism or institutionalism, also have their say in accounts of the complexity of ethnic violence (Posen 1993; Horowitz 1985; Posner 2005). At the same time, as all the theories can provide only partial accounts of the large variety of different cases of ethnic conflict, many call for eclecticism and combination of different explanations (Wimmer 2004; Kaufmann 2005; Brubaker and Laitin 1998; Brubaker 2004).

Military Occupation, Colonialism, and Ethnicity

The above debates highlight possible perspectives, which studies of ethnicity can offer in providing explanations for problems that occur in military occupations. Post-WWII military occupations have tended to reform and democratize the society of the former enemy, and with such reforms, they have implanted new political institutions and new platforms for identity refinement and contestation. They serve as a fertile ground for combining constructivist, instrumental, and institutional approaches, to provide an introspection into identity-based mechanisms of collaboration and contestation during and after the periods of military intervention and occupation.

Military occupations are conducted under special conditions, where the occupied society has been denied sovereignty, and the ultimate decision-making is in the occupying authority. Postoccupational governments, if faced with a power vacuum, may easily slide into chaos and fragmentation (as in the case of post-2004 Iraq), or on the other hand, they may fall into authoritarianism, with the backing of the previous occupational authority (post-1968 Czechoslovakia).

Similar features have been observed in the studies of postcolonial societies. Crawford Young discusses the process of establishment and extension of colonial control in postcolonial states. At the beginning, elites were members of the military, which would dominate to provide for the safety of the state, and later they were followed by imposition of order into regions through the establishment of effective regional administration (Young 1994, 286). Such administrations sought security stabilization and economic modernization, and they rested on the support for the leader or for the military through public rituals of allegiance, such as marches and gatherings, with the objective of creating passive and noncritical citizens. Patrimonial and militaristic leadership often relies on ethnicity-based legitimation strategies.

Many colonial administrations have introduced ethnicity-based mechanisms of control. Horowitz advances some mechanisms of group ethnogenesis, which colonizers skilfully exploited. Focusing on the British colonial policy of indirect rule, he illustrated the way the British constructed and manipulated ethnic groups for their administrative purposes. Utilizing a variety of techniques and environments, colonial control led to consolidation of ethnic groups and ethnic categorizations, which would provide new identifications for local populations. Methods of colonial control varied from region to region, they created dichotomies between advanced and backward groups, which deepened with administrative control, and over time, they led to tensions between such groups, leaving a colonial legacy to postcolonial societies (Horowitz 1985, 147; Young 1994, 283). Liberation from the colonial rule has rarely led to the dissolution of ethnic allegiances, as suggested by modernists, and to the contrary, it has exacerbated cleavages along ethnic lines, deepened distrust between ethnic groups, and provided opportunities for secession (Krishna 1999, 26).

Domination of bureaucratic structures in postcolonial states by one ethnic group can also exacerbate ethnic tensions, as argued by Andreas Wimmer. This is especially the case, where colonial administrations left few institutions of civil society, and no procedures to transform societal conflicts into negotiable disagreements. Once legitimacy on ethnic lines is established and ethnic cleavages are politicized, postcolonial bureaucracies have difficulty in reaching inside such groups and regions, and ethnic tension can escalate into conflict (Wimmer 2004, 107). Absence of mutually accepted procedures for mitigation and resolution of conflict leads to aggravation of animosities, militarization of conflicts, and erosion of democratic institutions.

Both instrumental and constructivist approaches, as well as essentialists with their emphasis on primordial ethnies, have some stake in explaining the vicious circle, which leads to the legitimacy deficit and ethnic violence in postcolonial societies. Not all colonial powers and territories entertained same conditions, and thus, different colonial ruling strategies, and different composition of societies, lead to differing political cleavages, and different long-term consequences.

Insights from studies on ethnicity and nationalism provide valuable tools for explanation of occupational environments. Constructivist and instrumental approaches explain the dynamics of formation, change, and manipulation of ethnic identities in newly independent states. Such features are especially salient at the time of foreign military intervention. Essentialist theories can explain why social identities do not switch easily to correspond to the new ideology of the occupying power, but rather may choose resistance over collaboration. Institutionalist theories give us insight into what governments emerge after the termination of occupation or achievement of independence and also what options for manipulation and choice of identity may be possible, and rationally achievable.

Finally, explanations that combine attributes of identity construction, strategic behavior, and institutional environment can give us better tools, which fit real-world scenarios, including military occupations. They provide an analytical framework for understanding the tense relations between the Israeli settlers and Palestinians in Occupied Territories, or ethno-sectarian clashes in postoccupation Iraq. In this way, they can inform us about the reasons why the Hague or Geneva Conventions, or other human rights laws and humanitarian laws are being circumvented at times, or why occupations tend to fail in the achievement of their goals. In the next section, we look to postcolonial theories, which, through posing epistemological and normative questions about colonialism, may provide us with further analytical tools to explain the societal dynamics during and after military occupations.

Postcolonial Insights into Occupations

A view at ethnic relations within an occupied society can give us a clue about why military occupations have problems in coping with nationalism or ethnic conflict. However, to know about the underlying causes of destabilization under occupation, we need to look beyond ethnicity. Postcolonial theories, questioning the power nexus of Western knowledge, may provide additional clues. The focus of postcolonial theories is in undermining the presumably neutral and scientific accounts or Western knowledge, and in revelation of their true and ideological nature of colonialism. They provide analyses of Western scientific discourses and critiques of Western knowledge systems as legitimating colonial domination over the non-Western worldviews.

Taking the position of women in the Third World, Chandra Mohanty argues that any discourse is repressive and ethnocentric despite its call for objective and universal knowledge, because it sets up an implicit referent, a yardstick, by which to encode and represent the cultural other. Power is exercised through such discourse (Mohanty 1984, 336). What the Western discourse accomplishes is marginalization of the cultural others, denial of justice and equality to them, and dispossession of their historical experiences. Two kinds of postcolonial accounts can be identified in such claims (Paolini 1999, 52; Wilkens 2017; Birdal and Squires 2010). The first one is the expression of struggle and anticolonial nationalism, interested in a progressive constitution of self-identity in direct opposition to the Western imperialist ideology. Such claims are represented by Albert Memmi and Frantz Fanon. The second approach, associated with Partha Chatterjee, Homi Bhabha, Gayatri Spivak, or Arjun Appadurai, is the one of differentiation from the Western modularity of modernization, and of disillusionment with the postindependence authoritarian state of affairs in the postcolonial world. They do not militate against the West, their practices of resistance are subtler and indirect, but also more convincing. Many build on the writings of Jacques Derrida, Michel Foucault, or Jacques Lacan and focus on difference, ambivalence, and hybridity.

From among the first stream of authors, Frantz Fanon set the objectives for the postcolonial project as rejection of the colonialist racial representations of the "Other," and he called for the struggle for liberation from such imperialist designs. He wrote: "The violence which has ruled over the ordering of the colonial world, which as ceaselessly drummed the rhythm for the destruction of native social forms ... will be taken over by the native when ... he surges into the forbidden quarters. To wreck the colonial world is henceforward a mental picture of action which is very clear, very easy to understand and which may be assumed by each one of the individuals which constitute the colonized people" (Fanon 1963, 40). However, with decolonization after the WWII, the emancipation of the colonized had not arrived. Rather, most of the newly independent states fell under new authoritarian and militaristic regimes, which inherited the institutions and practices of their former colonial tyrants. Fanon's dreams went awry, and frustration paved the way for the rise of a new intellectual current.

The point of departure for the authors in the second wave was the disillusion with the postindependence state-of-affairs. Partha Chatterjee studied the problem of Indian postindependence nationalism and arrived at the conclusion that postcolonial nations, as long as they remained within the framework of the East-West divide, represented by Orientalist, Andersonian, Gellnerian, or other, especially Marxist approaches, could not achieve true independence and liberation. It is only in the spiritual domain of the inside of the local social world, where culture, religion, family, education, and language provide major moving factors for liberation, revival, and subjectivity, independent of the rhetoric of the West (Chatterjee 1999, 17).

Homi Bhabha viewed the East-West divide in yet deeper form. He has bitterly refused to accept the core liberal representations of modernity by Richard Rorty, Alasdair MacIntyre, or Jurgen Habermas as authentic enough, accusing them of avoiding addressing the problem of the cultural difference and dissonance at the margins of society. In Bhabha's words, they engage in "synchronous constancy of reconstruction and reinvention of the subject" which is unable of escaping the essential gesture of Western modernity (Bhabha 1994, 334). He stands firmly on the side of the colonial subject, being kept in the state of "sly civility," the state of colonial despotism and subjection without rights, and yet rendered ambiguous by uncertain narrative of progress. Bhabha cries out about a perpetration of the colonial condition within the Western metropolis (the Northern Hemisphere of diaspora and migration), as well as within the colony and postcolony (the Southern Hemisphere of slavery). For Bhabha, however, the means of resistance is not Fanonian revolt, but rather Foucauldian "mimicry," a sign of a double articulation. This is on the one hand "a complex strategy of reform, regulation and discipline" in response to the colonial Other, and on the other hand, "the sign of the inappropriate, ... a difference or recalcitrance, which ... intensifies surveillance and poses an immanent threat to both 'normalized' knowledges and disciplinary powers" (122–123). Bhabha views the power of the subordinated in the cultural contextuality of the postcolonial, in the process of differentiation, in finding the "in-between" of the transnational as the translational, a liminal signifying space, and a location of hybridity, which escapes the binary differentiation established by the Western colonizing discourse (248).

What is at the center of the postcolonial critique of the West is the nexus between power and knowledge as the legacy of Enlightenment thought, which embedded scientific knowledge deeply into the web of European cultural and political practices, and thus normalized such knowledge into a universal modernist rationalism. As Dipesh Chakrabarty asserts, this knowledge has been widely and uncritically appropriated by the Third World into particular localities, which were lacking the same kind of cultural background (Chakrabarty 2000, 4). Such appropriations were either accompanied by authoritarian state-led repressive regimes, often little different from the colonial master beforehand, or to the contrary, they met with violent conservative and religious backlash. One feature of such appropriation of knowledge was the entrapment in the webs of power, where knowledge of Euro-America and the West is of utmost importance, and knowledge of the Third World is atavistic, superfluous, and redundant. This asymmetrical interference is what Arjun Appadurai called "legal drama" in his history and anthropology of colonialism. According to Appadurai, introduction of the British legal system led inadvertently to an increase in litigations, and through the process of such legal struggles, the society would adjust to the new institutions and appropriate new norms, often resulting in fragmentation of authority and loss of the social fabric (Appadurai 1981, 226).

From the perspective of military occupations, Roxanne Doty provides an apt analogy with the US postindependence policies in the Philippines and British policies in Kenya where the knowledge asymmetry and power domination was used to establish social relations of dominance and dependency within the framework of the Cold War and their previous colonial experiences. Drawing upon US and British colonial entanglements, the concept of sovereignty in decolonized societies was constructed in a way that it allowed foreign intervention when it was in the interest of the hegemonic power, through de-legitimization of local struggle as terrorism and insurgency. Expert and political discourses over foreign aid, the spread of democracy and of human rights also built on naturalized categories of knowledge and science which were embedded in the context of humanitarian promotion of Western values alongside with practices of hegemony and domination implicitly going against the realization of such values (Doty 1996, 170).

The problem of epistemology, the entanglement of knowledge and power in the modern security, and development discourse was accompanied by the politics of representation. Representations of the West and the "Other" as powerful and powerless, united and fragmented, integral and corrupt, developed and underdeveloped, skillful and unskilled, all these constructed categories through which people would understand and realize their historical agency, and provided the logic to justify defense of the homeland and of the free world, as well as intervention and annexation. At the same time, however, as argued by Homi Bhabha or Judith Butler, no such representations are based on finite concepts, preexisting essences, or foundational categories. Identities are performative, they are contingent on everyday enunciations and continuous repetition of performances, through which they are constructed into the forms that appear natural and foundational (Bhabha 1994, 187). Because they are a part of everyday processes, they offer a potential for enunciation of cultural difference, exhibition of hybridity, delivery of representational uncertainty, and significatory undecidability, which undermine hegemonic practice of domination and provide space for cultural resistance and liberation.

Strategies for Termination of Occupation

Postcolonial and ethnicity approaches outlined in the discussion above reveal the centrality of politics in any discourse on identity in a colonial or postcolonial setting, thus including also military occupations. They offer critiques of Western justifications of occupations, including demilitarization, democratization, and development of the occupied "Other." They provide tools for deconstruction of prevailing theories, and methods for relativization of established discourses on democratization, peacebuilding, humanitarian intervention, or "brotherly assistance." There are three ways in which studies of foreign occupations can benefit from such approaches: exposition of Western bias, focus on cultural and performative features of identity, and account of the dynamics of resistance.

First, postcolonial and ethnicity approaches reveal the Western bias of military and managerial sciences, and of political theories mobilized for occupational purposes. As Dipesh Chakrabarty argued, the phenomenon of political modernity (symbolized by nation-state, bureaucracy, and capitalism) is firmly associated in the world with political concepts, which originated in the European intellectual and theological traditions. The concepts of democracy, civil society, the individual, distinction between public and private, scientific reality, even morality or social justice, they all bear the imprint of the European Enlightenment and post-Enlightenment scientific and political developments (Chakrabarty 2000, 4). Enlightenment humanism has had profound effects in the developing world. Educated middle classes in Africa, Asia, Latin America, and Oceania embraced ideas of rationalism, science, technology, as well as civil liberties, social justice, liberalism, and human rights. They criticized their domestic institutions, authoritarian regimes, corrupt politics, and they engaged in critiques of Western colonialism and imperialism, appropriating the very same European and American theories and methodologies of such criticism. What the new postcolonial thought gave the rise to was an attention to the relations between Western ideas, the outcomes those ideas failed to deliver, and an insight into the European or American provincial background of those ideas (Chakrabarty 2000, 254). This, however, did not happen only in the realm of theories and ideas. To the contrary, Western values about what is modern and what is primitive established a set of values, which were internalized by elites, and by ordinary people in colonies. Thus, colonial societies were always expected to reach modernity, and any diversion from the Western model was considered backward, premodern, prepolitical, inadequate, incomplete, and lacking authenticity (32).

Second, the new approaches address the problem of identity, which political sciences, jurisprudence, or military sciences are often uneasy about. This trinity of sciences is most relevant to military occupations, and yet, none has dealt sufficiently with the problem of extreme power differential and its societal impact, and dynamics of inter-ethnic exchanges between the new foreign authority and the local "Other." This involves both institutional issues of governance and cultural recognition, including the process of permanent indeterminacy of the "translation" between the occupant and the occupied. Homi Bhabha identifies a way to avoid such Western universalizing bias. He calls it vernacular cosmopolitanism, which is an assertion of rights of "global progress from the minoritarian perspective." He deals with vernacular cosmopolitanism in two dimensions, the rights of migrants for recognition, and the rights of minorities for autonomy. A "right to difference in equality," which Bhabha relates to Etienne Balibar, does not necessarily refer to essentialist forms of group identity. Their claim to equality in citizenship has a symbolic aspect in it, which "raises affective and ethical issues connected with cultural differences and social discrimination." Thus, Bhabha claims that vernacular cosmopolitanism is more about a process of constituting emergent groups and affiliations than about affirmation and authentication of ethnic origins, a process of political reconciliation "that works *towards* the shared goals of democratic rule, rather than simply acknowledging already constituted 'marginal' political entities or identities" (Bhabha 1994 [2004], preface xvii–xviii). Bhabha's statement should be read against the context of liberal America and democratic India, where the question of "belonging" has incorporated the notion of basic human rights, and not authoritarian regimes, where claims for any rights may result in grave existential insecurities.

Foreign occupations reverse the migrant-minority logic of Bhabha's vernacular cosmopolitanism. In occupations, the "foreign Other" is not the subaltern, but to the contrary, it is the new celestial elite. In demographic terms, however, it is a tiny minority encircled by masses of the occupied subalterns, "alien" to the occupants. The disempowered (occupied) is the overwhelming majority of the population. Nevertheless, Bhabha's argument on process and performativity of identity applies in a similar manner. Identities are formed and performed in the new environment of occupation, and thus occupational politics reaches beyond the politics of strife for recognition of already constituted primordial ethnic relationships and exploitation of preexisting lines of polarization. Social attitudes and cultural interactions between the occupant and the occupied help overcoming mutual antagonism and open up a new space of negotiation, a place of hybridity.

Third is the way ethnicity and postcolonial theories reason about resistance. Prior to the rise of Subaltern Studies, theories of conflict built heavily upon the rationalist and Marxian versions of modernization. Marxism, which was profoundly influential in the Third World, emphasizes concepts of commodification of labor, uneven rate of development, and dialectics of class struggle as the causes of conflict. It argues about the difficulty of radically changing relations of production in capitalism, and thus for a revolution of laboring classes, overthrow of capitalism, and establishment of a postcapitalist society. Modernization theories also emphasize the focus on the modern industrial democratic society, but more than Marx, they look upon Max Weber, building on rationalism, bureaucratic state, and individual entrepreneurship. Modernist approaches view conflict in terms of differential modernization, social mobilization, social grievances, political power deprivation, fear of domination, individual entrepreneurism, or security dilemma. The common trait to most modernist theories is their focus on rationality and rational decision-making involved in conflict dynamics.

While modernization and Marxist schools exchange heated criticisms of each other, they share many intellectual commonalities, especially the understanding that the rational Western modernity (capitalist or socialist) serves as the developmental model for others. Indian historian Ranajit Guha raises voice against such appropriation of scientific knowledge and historical reality. Guha focuses on the way the British rule in colonial India mobilized knowledge, and building on such knowledge it controlled regional and local elites, and externalized the peasant, denying him the "recognition as a subject of history in his own right" (Guha 1983a, 4, 334). He distinguishes between three types of historical discourses: primary, secondary and tertiary. These discourses differed from one another in terms of the time sequence in which they occurred, and the degree of their identification with the official British administration. Primary discourses appeared in immediate police and military reports produced by officials to describe peasant insurgencies. Secondary discourses were memoirs and narratives of officials sometime after the event. Tertiary discourses were narratives produced by historians who had neither direct experience nor official affiliation with the events in question.

Guha writes about the colonial "code of counter-insurgency" (or code of pacification), which was omnipresent in writings of that time. Colonial bureaucracy and intellectual circles produced and redistributed the code. He deliberates about the process of such ideological transmission from official reports to historical narratives and about how discourses on peasant insurgences excluded the agency of the peasant by stigmatizing him as a primitive, rebel, insurgent, and criminal (Guha 1983b, 2). Official accounts used scientific terminologies and causal explanations to blame wicked landlords and ill-willed local moneylenders to localize conflict, purify colonial administration, and avoid destabilization of British rule. The "code of pacification" was omnipresent in the official accounts. "Objectivity" and scientific knowledge were mobilized in defense of power.

Guha argues that there was nothing primitive or "prepolitical" in Indian insurgencies, which took an indigenous form of collective action. They were modern political movements for self-government. Yet, they did not follow the logic of secular-rational calculations inherent in the Western conception of the political. The peasant in colonies did not have a "backward" consciousness, he was not an anachronism in the modern world, he was part of the colonial modernity of the time, and insurgency was his way to get himself heard, it was his way of a social and political movement for liberation. However, such movements were not practiced in the way in which Western protests would be organized, in a rational-secular manner. Indian peasants were building on their everyday networks and practices, including kinship, traditions, myths, rumors, gods, and spirits. Guha emphasizes that "(r)eligiosity was, by all accounts, central to the *hool*. The notion of power which inspired it, was made up of such ideas and expressed in such words and acts as were explicitly religious in character" (italics as in the original, Guha 1983b, 34). In British eyes, they were seen as spontaneous bursts of religious fanaticism, infused with nativist rhetoric, traditionalism, and superstition. But for Guha, peasant insurgencies were a political struggle turned against the British and their local epigones who symbolized colonial rule and signified furtherance of oppression. Peasants used strategies, which were closest to their everyday lives, but the goals, mobilization, action, and achievements were no "less modern" or "prepolitical" than those, which took place elsewhere in the colonial world.

Guha's descriptions were more than utterances on anticolonial movement in India. They have a commonly acceptable message, which reverberates in the non-Western world. They also provide one of the most significant reasons for the rise of resistance to foreign occupations. And they deliver a warning to over-optimistic ideas for reform. Western ideas, like democracy or free market economy, do not easily fit into non-Western societies. Not because the recipient society would be in a "different stage of development," but because they are made and delivered with a foreign context, which is not easily translatable and deliverable to that society. Foreign occupations are essentially a cultural and ethnic phenomenon, and whatever they deliver is going to be received with doubt. As with Guha's peasants, there is a high probability that occupation will give an impetus to previously marginalized communities to surpass their local fragmentations, and rise in a common goal, the most significant of which is resistance to the newly rising elite, and opposition to the foreign threat. There are examples of "successful" occupations, like Japan and Germany after the WWII, but a closer examination of even such cases reveals precarious nature of the environment of reforms, and casts doubt at the possibility for generalization of such cases. Those reforms may have been "successful" only because they were able to keep potentially dissatisfied communities fragmented, not because they transformed the minds of the occupied society to the Western image. Western bias, cultural insensitivity, language incompetence, identity blindness, and apprehension of resistance are powerful reasons, which call for caution when it comes to occupation of a foreign soil, however just the cause may be.

Conclusion

As mentioned at the beginning of this chapter, Eyal Benvenisti argues that the concept of military occupation has many things in common with the concept of state sovereignty. In history, the practice of occupation has taken two distinct paths. The first one is occupation of territories outside Europe, which does not distinguish occupation from conquest and colonization, and does not recognize full sovereignty to the "uncivilized" people (Benvenisti 2012, 31). The second, "European" one, has separated permanent sovereign rights from the temporary rights of occupation and has paved the way towards today's technical understanding of the term. To find out more about the dynamics of the concept of occupation, however, we need to go beyond international security, or international legal perspectives. To accomplish that, we have to trace the concept of occupation back to the origins of the European/non-European intellectual bifurcation and ask fundamental questions about the nature of the modern state, society, and knowledge, which are facilitated by the studies of nationalism, ethnicity, and postcolonialism treated in this chapter (Anghie 2004, 14, 317).

Cross-References

- ▶ Cultural Socialization and Ethnic Consciousness
- ▶ Ethnic Riots in United Kingdom in 2001
- ▶ Ethnicity and Politics in Kenya
- ▶ Ethnicity and Violence in Sri Lanka: An Ethnohistorical Narrative
- ▶ Exploring Global Ethnicity: A Broad Sociological Synopsis
- ▶ Migrant Illegalization and Minoritized Populations
- ▶ National Imaginary, Ethnic Plurality, and State Formation in Indonesia
- ▶ Perpetual Exclusion and Second-Order Minorities in Theaters of Civil Wars
- ▶ Rewriting the World: Pacific People, Media, and Cultural Resistance
- ▶ The Threat of Genocide: Understanding and Preventing the "Crime of Crimes"

Acknowledgments This research was partially funded by JSPS research Grant No. 18K01414.

References

Anderson B (1991) Imagined communities. Verso, London
Anghie A (2004) Imperialism, sovereignty, and the making of international law. Cambridge University Press, New York
Appadurai A (1981) Worship and conflict under colonial rule: a South Indian case. Cambridge University Press, Cambridge
Arai-Takahashi Y (2009) The law of occupation: continuity and change of international humanitarian law, and its interaction with international human rights law. Martinus Nijhoff Publishers, Leiden
Azoulay A, Ophir A (2012) The one-state condition: occupation and democracy in Israel/Palestine. Stanford University Press, Stanford
Balibar E, Wallerstein I (1991) Race, nation, class: ambiguous identities. Verso, London
Benvenisti E (1993) International law of occupation. Princeton University Press, Princeton
Benvenisti E (2012) International law of occupation, 2nd edn. Oxford University Press, New York
Bergman A (2014) Cursed victory, Israel and the occupied territories: a history. Pegasus Books, New York
Bhabha HK (1994 [2004]) The location of culture, with new preface by the author, Routledge, New York
Birdal AS, Squires J (2010) Ethnicity, nationalism and colonialism. In: Marlin-Bennett R (ed) Oxford research encyclopedia of international studies. Oxford University Press, New York
Breuilly J (2016) Benedict Anderson's imagined communities: a symposium. Nations and Nationalism 22(4):625–659
Brubaker R (2004) Ethnicity without groups. Harvard University Press, Cambridge, MA
Brubaker R, Laitin DD (1998) Ethnic and nationalist violence. Am Rev Sociol 24:423–452
Bunton M (2013) The Palestinian-Israeli conflict. Oxford University Press, New York
Chakrabarty D (2000) Provincializing Europe: postcolonial thought and historical difference. Princeton University Press, Princeton
Chatterjee P (1999) Nationalist thought and the colonial world. Oxford University Press, New York
Collier P, Elliott VL, Hegre H, Hoeffler A, Reynal-Querol M, Sambanis N (2003) Breaking the conflict trap: civil war and development policy. World Bank and Oxford University Press, Washington, DC
Compel R (2017) The lessons from the post-WW2 occupation of Japan. Pacific Dynamics 1(1):33–45
Connor W (1994) Ethnonationalism: the quest for understanding. Princeton University Press, Princeton
de Matos C, Gerster R (eds) (2009) Occupying the "other": Australia and military occupations from Japan to Iraq. Cambridge Scholars Publishing, Newcastle upon Tyne
de Matos C, Ward R (eds) (2012) Gender, power, and military occupations: Asia Pacific and the Middle East since 1945. Routledge, New York
Deutsch KW (1953) Nationalism and social communication: an inquiry into the foundations of nationality. Willey, New York
Deutsch KW (1969) Nationalism and its alternatives. Alfred A. Knopf, New York
Dinstein Y (2009) The international law of belligerent occupation. Cambridge University Press, Cambridge
Dobbins J (2003) America's role in nation-building: from Germany to Iraq. RAND, Santa Monica
Doty RL (1996) Imperial encounters: the politics of representation in North-South relations. University of Minnesota Press, Minneapolis
Dower J (1999) Embracing defeat: Japan in the wake of World War II. W. W Norton, New York
Edelstein DM (2008) Occupational hazards: success and failure in military occupation. Cornell University Press, London
Fanon F (1963) The wretched of the Earth (trans: Farrington C). Grove Press, New York

Fearon J, Laitin D (1996) Explaining interethnic cooperation. Am Polit Sci Rev 90(4):713–735
Fox GH (2008) Humanitarian occupation. Cambridge University Press, Cambridge
Gellner E (1983) Nations and Nationalism. Cornell University Press, Ithaca
Gordon N (2008) Israel's occupation. University of California Press, Berkeley
Gorenberg G (2006) The accidental empire: Israel and the birth of the settlements, 1967–1977. Times Books, New York
Green M (2001) Japan's reluctant realism foreign policy challenges in an era of uncertain power. Palgrave, New York
Grosby S (1995) Territoriality: the transcendental primordial feature of modern societies. Nations and Nationalism 1(2):143–162
Grosby S (2005) Nationalism: a very short introduction. Oxford University Press, New York
Grotius H (1625 [2005]) The rights of war and peace, book III (from the edition by Jan Barbeyrac, edited and with introduction by Richard Tuck). Liberty Fund, Indianapolis
Guha R (1983a) Elementary aspects of peasant insurgency in colonial India. Oxford University Press, Delhi
Guha R (1983b) The prose of counter-insurgency. In: Guha R (ed) Subaltern studies, vol 2. Oxford University Press, Delhi
Guibernau M (1996) Nationalisms. Polity Press, Cambridge
Hall JA (ed) (1998) The state of the nation: Ernest Gellner and the theory of nationalism. Cambridge University Press, New York
Horowitz DL (1985) Ethnic groups in conflict. University of California Press, Berkeley
Hutchinson J (2005) Nations and zones of conflict. Sage, Thousand Oaks
Kaufmann C (2005) Rational choice and progress in the study of ethnic conflict: a review essay. Secur Stud 14(1):178–207
Krishna S (1999) Postcolonial insecurities: India, Sri Lanka, and the question of nationhood. University of Minnesota Press, Minneapolis
MOFA (The Ministry of Foreign Affairs of Japan) (1966) Nihon Gaiko Nenpyo Narabini Shuyo Bunsho: 1840–1945, vol 2 (Japanese diplomatic chronology and basic documents: 1840–1945, vol 2). Ministry of Foreign Affairs, Tokyo
Mohanty CT (1984) Under Western eyes: feminist scholarship and colonial discourses. Boundary 2 12(3):333–358
Nabulsi K (1999) Traditions of war: occupation, resistance, and the law. Oxford University Press, New York
Oppenheim L (1921) International law, vol 2, 3rd edn. Longmans, Green and Co., New York
Paolini AJ (1999) Navigating modernity: postcolonialism, idenitity, and international relations. Lynne Rienner Publishers, Boulder
Petersen RD (2002) Understanding ethnic violence. Cambridge University Press, New York
Posen BR (1993) The security dilemma and ethnic conflict. Survival 35(1):27–47
Posner DN (2005) Institutions and ethnic politics in Africa. Cambridge University Press, New York
Roberts A (1985) What is a military occupation? British Yearbook of International Law 55:249–305
Roberts A (2006) Transformative military occupation: applying the laws of war and human rights. The American Journal of International Law 55:249–305
Roy S (2007) Failing peace: Gaza and the Palestinian-Israeli conflict. Pluto Press, London
Schaller M (1985) The American occupation of Japan: the origins of the Cold War in Asia. Oxford University Press, New York
Smith AD (1995 [2007]) Nations and nationalism in a global era. Polity Press, Cambridge (2007 reprint)
Smith AD (2000) Nation in history: historiographical debates about ethnicity and nationalism. Polity Press, Cambridge
Smith AD (2009) Ethno-symbolism and nationalism: a cultural approach. Routledge, New York
Takemae E (2002) The allied occupation of Japan. Continuum, New York

Taylor C et al (1994) Multiculturalism and the politics of recognition. Princeton University Press, Princeton
Ward RE, Sakamoto Y (eds) (1987) Democratizing Japan: the allied occupation. University of Hawaii Press, Honolulu
Weber M (1922) Economy and society, vol 1. Bedminster Press, New York (1968 edition)
Wilkens J (2017) Postcolonialism in international relations. In: Marlin-Bennett R (ed) Oxford research encyclopedia of international studies. Oxford University Press, New York
Wimmer A (2002) Nationalist Exclusion and Ethnic Conflict: Shadows of Modernity. Cambridge University Press, Cambridge
Wimmer A (2004) Nationalist exclusion and ethnic conflict: shadows of modernity. Cambridge University Press, New York
Young CM (1994) The African colonial state in comparative perspective. Yale University Press, New Haven

Ethnic Politics and Global Justice

12

Geoff Pfeifer

Contents

Justice and Global Justice	210
Globalization	210
Global Justice Issues: A Snapshot	211
Theories of Global Justice: Rawls and Distributive Justice	213
Theories of Global Justice: Cosmopolitanism	213
Theories of Global Justice: Internationalism	214
Theories of Global Justice: Young and Fraser, More Than Just Distribution	215
References	218

Abstract

This chapter outlines the major theories of global justice from those that emerge early in the history of the concept to more contemporary conceptions. It also discusses the connection between global justice theory and practice and the larger process of globalization. The chapter explains some of the many concrete problems global justice theory and global justice activism seek to address such as global poverty, environmental justice, migration justice, and other forms of social and political oppression and exclusion in both national and international contexts. Finally, this chapter discusses the role global justice theory and activism can and does play in ethnic politics and ethnic political struggles against oppression of the forms just mentioned along with many others.

Keywords

Global justice · Globalization · Distributive justice · Representation · Ethnic politics · Philosophy

---

G. Pfeifer (✉)
Worcester Polytechnic Institute, Worcester, MA, USA
e-mail: gpfeifer@wpi.edu

Justice and Global Justice

While there are many theoretical and practical definitions of justice, for the purposes of this chapter, I will identify the main goal of justice to be the conditions under which individuals and groups are accorded material and moral consideration in such a way that each is, to the extent possible, given the opportunity to lead a life that allows for flourishing and is free from various forms of oppression. Thinking through this conception of justice and its proper application then involves making sense of what kinds of considerations we owe each other, what our obligations are to one another, and what structures (social, legal, economic, environmental, etc.) and forms of rights and responsibilities we might put in place, protect, or get rid of in order to achieve justice both between individuals and groups and at the level of wider social relations.

Broadly, global justice is the study of, and recommendations for justice on a worldwide scale and with regard to international institutional arrangements and relations between individuals and groups within and as a part of those institutions. The emergence of global justice as a named subdiscipline in fields such as philosophy, political science, sociology, and global studies as well as in activist circles is a relatively recent phenomenon. It is in the 1970s that we begin to see this term used in relation to questions of justice and the international sphere (Steger and Wilson 2012). The emergence of this subdiscipline tracks also the emergence of the concepts of the "global" and "globalization" at a time in which the processes that these latter terms name were also beginning to be recognized and discussed in a variety of academic, political, economic, and activist circles (James and Steger 2014). For this reason, we cannot understand the global justice movement apart from theoretical and practical developments in relation to the processes named by the term globalization.

Globalization

Globalization is commonly understood (also broadly) as the recent acceleration and deepening of global interconnectedness of peoples and nations in regard to economic processes, human migration, climate conditions, communication, and culture along with the weakening of the power of the nation-state as sole political actor on the international stage (Sassen 1998; Ohmae 1996; Steger 2017). This latter development, namely, the weakening of the power of the nation-state, is evidenced by the rise of extra and non-state regimes of governance, regulation, human rights, finance and trade, also the emergence of international corporate businesses with no single territorial home, and mass communication technologies that put power in the hands of some individuals in ways that did not exist in the past, but are also not distributed in such a way as to allow equal access to all in the world community (Sassen 2006; Castells 2015).

It is the recognition of this repositioning of the nation-state vis-à-vis such international institutions, issues of climate, economy, and technological connection that gives rise to the question of global justice. How, in a globalizing world, can there be justice for all peoples in relation to the questions raised at the outset? For many who thought about questions of justice in the past, it was assumed that such questions were solely, or mostly, national in character – that the seeking of social justice required things like gaining juridical and other forms of recognition for folks as citizens of particular nations that were not receiving them in various ways and also the thinking through of the right ways of equitably distributing social goods such as education, healthcare, housing, access to wealth, and so forth. Prior to the emerging recognition of the global interconnectedness described above, these questions and discussions took place in the context of what Nancy Fraser calls the "Keynesian-Westphalian framing" of social justice as applying within the confines of the nation-state system and Keynesian redistributive economic programs (Fraser 2009). When discussions of justice across international borders were had, they were usually framed in ways that made it the responsibility of nations as the sole international actors to enforce and regulate justice between national communities mostly via strategies such as international law, economic sanctions, and the like (Sen 1999).

While it is the case that issues of social justice within the confines of given national communities still exist and are still being worked on in a variety of ways, with the rise of globalization, this framing of the question of justice is disrupted, and such theoretical and practical discussions of globalization contribute to this disruption. Scholars and activists, recognizing the changes brought about by the age of globalization, begin asking questions about the linkages between individuals, groups, and communities across geographic and national borders, not only as members of national communities, but apart from and beyond them, and also the effects on those groups of various practices and policies that span these regions in ways that do not necessarily bottom out solely in the confines of the nation-state. I will detail a few of these cross-borders of "global" issues below and then turn to responses to them offered by global justice frameworks. We will see, in the context of this, the ways in which global justice conceptions and activist struggles are relevant to ethnic politics.

Global Justice Issues: A Snapshot

As many have pointed out, it is because of capitalist economic globalization that we see a massive increase in economic inequality on a worldwide scale. Not that there did not exist such inequality prior to the rise of globalization, certainly there did. The colonial and neocolonial world of the fifteenth through the early nineteenth centuries saw their resources and peoples exploited in a variety of ways in order to enrich the colonial powers. In this period, the flow of capital, goods, and services was primarily from the colonized world toward the colonial powers. It is in the age of decolonization beginning in the nineteenth century that the global era emerges as newly decolonized communities began competing with the colonial powers for economic prosperity and social goods. As this process proceeds and the advanced capitalist economies become ever more globalized in the middle to late twentieth century, manufacturing moves from its center in the global north to the global south, and those latter economies become the production zones for not only raw materials and cheap labor but also commodities to be used primarily in the more affluent global north (Sachs 1998; Harvey 2007; Fraser 2016). In this process, the global south also becomes the dumping zone for the waste generated in mass production and consumption on a global scale. This process has led some scholars to talk of globalization as a kind recolonization (Harvey 1995). To be sure, there are still many communities in the global north that also find themselves located in such dumping zones, and I will discuss this more below, but the majority are found in the global south and so demands for various forms of global justice also track environmental justice demands on a worldwide scale (Davis 2003; Schlosberg 2004).

The United Nations reports that as of 2016, 783 million people live below the international poverty line of $1.90 US dollars a day. This amounts to almost 10% of the world's population. This affects more women than men globally, and one in four children worldwide is affected by some form of poverty-related issue. The most affected regions of the world are in the global south: the African continent, Central and South America, and so forth (United Nations). There are also, however, pockets of extreme poverty in countries in the global north as well, and such economic inequality has only grown over the last few decades as a result of the same globalized economic processes (Sassen 2014; Temin 2018).

Fossil fuel production and consumption in the global north has also led to further environmental degradation worldwide and negative effects of the accompanying problems associated with anthropogenic climate change such as increased frequency and severity of storms such as hurricanes and typhoons, drought conditions, and sea-level rise are primarily (though not solely) also visited on those same communities that are the most impoverished under globalization. This is, as with poverty, true not only of communities in the global south but also those impoverished communities in the global north as many of the most poor living in countries like the United States live in zones that are also the most affected by these negative effects (Klein 2014; Ciplet et al. 2015).

These are just some of the many examples of interconnection between communities in the global era across geographies and national borders. Global justice theorists ask questions relating to these issues and institutions including (but certainly not limited too): How and in what ways are certain nations and individuals responsible for global economic inequalities and what can be done to alleviate them? What are the duties of the global north to the global south in terms of the effects of fossil fuel production and consumption and the effects of anthropogenic climate change as a result? What are the rights of migrants – many of whom are forced into migration in the global era as a result of climate change and economic inequality on a global scale – and what are the duties of states in relation to them? Given that as note above, around the world, women and people of color tend to be more affected by unjust conditions caused by the above issues and questions, what does global gender, ethnic, and racial justice look like? And so forth.

Theories of Global Justice: Rawls and Distributive Justice

In many of the mainstream contemporary philosophical debates about global justice, the general concerns are around the proper mode of distributive justice. That is, debates tend to be about what constitutes the most equitable distribution of social goods such as those mentioned above (i.e., education, healthcare, wealth, mobility, and so forth), given the responsibilities of governments and individuals across national and international lines. Various theories come down differently on questions of responsibility in this way. John Rawls' work, in both his development of a distributive model of justice more broadly and his famous "Law of Peoples," tends to be the starting point for these mainstream views in philosophical discussions (Rawls 1971, 2001).

Rawls argues that any notion of distributive justice outside of the confines of the nation-state or across national boundaries is unnecessary. This is because, on his view, as long as a there is justice inside the confines of national communities, and as long as that justice affords people the opportunity to lead good lives, then that is all that is needed (Rawls 2001). In other words, differential economic inequalities between peoples within different communities within different states and different institutions are unproblematic on Rawls' view – even if it can be demonstrated that such inequality is enforced and reinforced by practices in one community that affect another. This is because the pursuit of justice is, for Rawls, always found within the institutional frameworks within communities and as a result of a contractual institutional framework there that offers citizens the opportunity to lead decent lives (Rawls 2001). For Rawls then, just relations between states require respect for state sovereignty, with the caveat that states should also respect the rights of their peoples and allow them access to the goods provided by liberal democratic institutions and structures. There are a number of responses to Rawls' view and theoretical developments that emerge in dialogue with its ideas and arguments. One broad category of response is the cosmopolitan human rights-based approach to global justice, and a second is a more internationalist approach. I will say a few words about each of these two broad types of responses and developments in turn before turning to a third position which I take to be much more robust and which tends to dovetail more with approaches to global justice outside of the theoretical realm and in the practical activist one.

Theories of Global Justice: Cosmopolitanism

The cosmopolitan response to Rawls has its foundations in a Kantian claim to the equality of humanity across social, economic, geographic, and political domains (Kant 1983, 2002). Cosmopolitans argue that individuals are primary bearers of rights (and are so equally) regardless of where they are positioned in social hierarchies and regardless of which part of the world they are found. So, in this view, global justice entails respecting those rights and when thinking about how to properly distribute social goods, services, and possibilities for human flourishing, the cosmopolitan position requires of us that we respect the claims of all individuals equally and act accordingly. This requires then in turn not just working to ensure equal access and distribution of social goods within national boundaries but also across them if we are to achieve global justice. Of particular importance for some cosmopolitans is ensuring that certain human "capabilities" are achievable for all human beings (Sen 1999; Nussbaum 2011). These capabilities include things like being healthy which includes access to healthcare but also adequate housing, clean water and healthy food, not dying prematurely from preventable causes, freedom of movement, reproductive choice, living in a world in which the environment is conducive to this, access to economic well-being, and so forth (Nussbaum 2011). On the cosmopolitan view of global justice, state borders are not a factor in determining whose capabilities are respected and advanced; the argument is that all individuals should have access to these and so global governance structures should promote the advancement of capabilities for all humans in this way.

Further, as Thomas Pogge argues (2001), we need to ensure that the global institutional order that exists does not benefit one group to the detriment of others, and given that the current situation is such that the institutional order as it exists now does in fact do this – it emerged out of the brutal history of colonialism which transferred wealth and resources from the colonies to the colonial powers, and the global financial order is a continuation of this process – we have not only a positive duty to global redistributive justice as a corrective to this but also a negative responsibility in the continuation of an unjust global order. That is, insofar as the history of the current global order positions some as winners and some as losers economically and socially, the winners bear responsibility for both this history and its perpetuation. For this reason, as some cosmopolitans argue, correcting this may require the strengthening of global institutions and the weakening of state sovereignty if it is such sovereignty that perpetuates global inequalities (Pogge 1992).

For example, from the cosmopolitan perspective, that there is anthropogenic climate change and that there are some nations and peoples more affected by this than others, requires a global response that makes all nations responsible for the well-being of everyone in ways that weaken national sovereignty around decisions such as levels of carbon emissions and such (see, for instance, Caney 2005). Though there are differences in the ways that various cosmopolitan theories of global justice make sense of how equality among peoples should be determined, the basic view is that because of the fundamental equality among individuals at the most basic level, and because this equality means all have equal claim to human rights, the goal of achieving equality of capabilities at a practical level is the guiding principle regardless of state or national boundaries.

Theories of Global Justice: Internationalism

A second position taken up in relation to Rawls' view, what we can, to use Nancy Fraser's helpful framing, call the more internationalist one, responds to the Rawlsian privileging of the role of distributive justice inside the bounds of the state by arguing that Rawls is correct to an extent – the demands of justice in the social are specially governed and adjudicated within the realm of national communities, but internationalism argues that there should also be weaker duties of justice between national communities (Fraser 2009). One prime example of this approach is given by David Miller in his 2007 *National Responsibility and Global Justice* (for other similar approaches, see Onora O'Neal 2000 and Kok-Chor Tan 2004). Here, Miller argues that global justice is important, but it cannot be a matter of applying the demands of social justice – like those articulated above in the cosmopolitan capabilities approach – as they exist within national boundaries to communities and individuals across such boundaries. Miller seeks to show, in this way, that there is a difference between social and global justice. This is because as Miller argues, national communities have histories in which they have long-running cultural traditions that ultimately construct particular and localized notions of the good and of justice. Miller's further point here is that these traditions and norms are different from one another precisely because they are culturally and historically bound (Miller 2007). He claims that this is a problem for any conception of global justice that simply seeks to apply the principles of social justice writ large (like the cosmopolitan view) because there is no common, cross-cultural/cross-national notion of social justice that can be used as a foundation for such application (Miller 2007). Nations and cultures construct and rank their notions of what counts as social justice and fairness differently (Miller 2007). Furthermore, as Miller argues, even if we could find such a common conception, national preferences for how to achieve such equality will differ as will the paths different nations choose in working toward those goals and will differ in such a way that they cannot be held to account (because they are preferences) in any universal global egalitarian theory we could construct (Miller 2007).

Ultimately, Miller's view is that, given these problems, we should not see global and social justice as making the same demands or offering the same conditions as they are two separate realms. The former demands a weaker set of conditions than the latter. The demands of global justice are such that we can (and should) claim that individuals and communities should have access to basic sets of resources and also that we should work toward ending global forms of poverty. Such a theory does also include the recognition that some nations can be held responsible for violating these two core values (both in their actions in the present and also in their actions in the past), but any more robust conception of justice and equality remains the provenance of the nation and the state (Miller 2007).

Theories of Global Justice: Young and Fraser, More Than Just Distribution

As we have seen, the three broad philosophical versions of global justice discussed so far – the strictly Rawlsian, the cosmopolitan, and the internationalist – spend their time thinking primarily through the lens of distributive justice and argue in various ways for a just redistribution of wealth, capabilities, and opportunity, as well as redistribution of responsibility for various past and present actions that contribute to the preponderance of various forms of global inequality. In connection with this responsibility redistribution, these theories argue that we also need a redistribution of benefit and burden on a global scale. There is another set of theoretical and practical global justice arguments that claim that simply focusing on redistributive justice is not enough.

Iris Marion Young is an early critic of the distributive model-only style discussions of justice described above and offers one version of a reimagined model that takes seriously not only issues of just distribution but also questions of power and oppression that underlie and produce unjust distribution so as to offer a more robust notion of justice (Young 1990). Young's main concern with the distributive model as the sole foundation of thinking about justice is that when we only think of justice in these terms (as redistribution of material goods such as wealth, resources, access to healthcare, etc.), it obscures larger, and perhaps more important, questioning of the power structures – both historical and presently persistent – that create and perpetuate unequal distribution of the various goods described above. Further, Young argues that even when distributive models do consider this and other nonmaterial social goods such as access to certain nonmaterial capabilities as in the cosmopolitan model, or the protection of cultural goods for minoritized populations, or access to power structures for those historically locked out, these things tend to be conceived of as "static things, instead of a function of social relations and processes" (Young 1990, 16).

In relation to the first charge, that distributive-only models of justice fail to understand power structures, Young argues that solely focusing on redistributive justice leaves oppressive social institutions and structures in place. For instance, if we look to a commonly argued for redistributive model of spreading the burden and responsibility for global inequalities in relation to climate impacts like those argued for in distributive "carbon tax" models, we find a means of spreading the "responsibility" for the effect of carbon use but no way of shifting carbon use in ways that change long-standing institutional and power structures (see, for instance, Miller 2008). That is, as long as carbon users and polluters can continue to pay the tax, they remain in control of the structures, and so, in relation to the second problem identified by Young, in this example those who lack such means and power are left out in ways that they have always been insofar as they are given little ability to make polluters stop and hold them accountable in ways outside of the economic.

For instance, enforcing accountability for the negative and marginalizing effects of climate change on culture and tradition on various indigenous communities around the world is impossible and potentially ignored under such models (Adger et al. 2013; Rush 2018). Native Americans and their descendants in the Southern United States who live in coastal communities are, for instance, especially threatened by rising sea levels and have seen their way of life in these communities slowly eroded and disappeared – ways of life that have been subjected to historical repression by the US government such that they were pushed into coastal living in the first place (Rush 2018). Carbon tax-based, distributive justice style climate mitigation strategies do nothing to address these injustices. In this way, Young argues that an expanded model of justice must take account of not only distributional issues but also issues of oppression, marginalization, powerlessness, and cultural imperialism (Young 1990, 2006). Ultimately, for Young, justice requires social and political (and not just material) equity. This means that we must take account of differences between groups and individuals, and their histories and experiences as well as the ways institutions both in the present and in the past have privileged some at the expense of others.

In a similar vein to Young, Nancy Fraser also argues for a more complete theory of justice and hence of global justice. Building on Young's criticism of distributive models of justice, Fraser argues that what is needed is not only just distribution of social and economic goods but also just political representation for all who are affected by various issues and unjust social relations on a global scale, as well as a form of democratic cultural recognition. For Fraser, this constitutes what she describes as a "three-dimensional" notion of global justice (Fraser 2005, 2009). As Fraser argues in this three-dimensional model, there are a variety of ways that individuals and groups suffer injustice – at the economic distributive level, individuals and groups are marginalized, oppressed, or otherwise excluded by economic structures that disallow them the resources for full participation; at the cultural level, individuals and groups may lack social standing via what Fraser describes as "institutional hierarchies of cultural value" which confers a kind of "status inequality" such that those on the lower end of the cultural hierarchy are excluded and marginalized (Fraser 2005).

We have already seen much about the first set of issues of exclusion/marginalization around the economic. For the second set, we can think here of the various ways around the globe that the status of women suffers under patriarchal social relations or how racial and ethnic hierarchies also enforce exclusion and marginalization across geographic and political contexts. For concrete examples of racial and ethnic hierarchies, we can think about the ways in which the Palestinian community faces repression and marginalization at the hand of the state of Israel and the ways in which communities of color in the United States face similar structures of repression – a fact which both Palestinian activists and Black Lives Matter activists have recognized and so begun to work together to understand each other's struggles (Bailey 2016; Malloy 2014). We can also, in this context, think about the ways in which indigenous activists around the world have come to understand their struggles for justice as bound up together in particular ways and so have begun to act together in seeking justice on a global scale around issues of representation (Choudry 2007).

These latter examples are of the ways in which various local movements – for racial and ethnic rights, for movements for indigenous peoples' rights, and for women's rights – connect with one another in order to form larger movements to combat this exclusion and gain power (Fraser 2005; Choudry 2007). Fighting cultural hierarchies in this way is also a form of gaining just representation – the third of the three dimensions in Fraser's account of a proper global justice for the present. It is not only this though, as justice in representation also includes on her accounting of it, the establishing of criteria for membership in the larger community as well as procedures for resolving conflict and injustice among community members (Fraser 2005). As Fraser points out here, the political dimension is that through which questions of distribution and recognition are articulated and so it cannot be neglected in our construction of theories of justice. To be sure, as just noted Fraser does not privilege the representative and the political over-against the economic as the economic is one of the main ways the other forms of injustice are enforced and extended – minoritized and oppressed populations worldwide are also often economically excluded as well and any global justice program must think all three forms of exclusion and injustice at once if it is to succeed in its goals.

As can be seen by the above, conceptions of justice and injustice are integral to various forms of ethnic politics that are concerned with seeking redress for a variety of forms of injustice at the political, social, and economic levels of social structure. And given that much of these struggles take place not just within a bounded national context but in the context of globalized social, economic, and environmental conditions, conceptions of global justice can and do also play a central role.

References

Adger N, Barnett J, Brown K, Marshall N, O'Brien K (2013) Cultural dimensions of climate change impacts and adaptation. Nat Clim Chang 3:112–117
Bailey KD (2016) Dream defenders, black lives matter & ferguson reps take historic trip to Palestine. January 9, Accessed 22 Nov 2018. http://www.ebony.com/news-views/dream-defenders-black-lives-matter-ferguson-reps-take-historic-trip-to-palestine#axzz4afSIFrVS
Caney S (2005) Cosmopolitan justice, responsibility, and global climate change. Leiden J Int Law 18:747–775
Castells M (2015) Network of outrage and hope: social movements in the internet age, 2nd edn. Polity Press, Malden
Choudry A (2007) Transnational activist coalition politics and the de/colonization of pedagogies of mobilization: learning from anti-neoliberal indigenous movement articulations. Int Educ 37(1):97–112
Ciplet D, Roberts T, Khan MR (2015) Power in a warming world: the new global politics of climate change and the remaking of environmental inequality. MIT Press, Cambridge, MA
Davis M (2003) (Reprint 2017) Planet of slums. Verso, London
Fraser N (2005) Reframing justice in a globalizing world. New Left Rev 36:69–89
Fraser N (2009) Scales of justice: reimagining political space in a globalizing world. Columbia University Press, New York
Fraser N (2016) Contradictions of capital and care. New Left Rev 100:99–117
Harvey D (1995) Globalization in question. Rethink Marx 8(4):1–17
Harvey D (2007) A brief history of neoliberalism. Oxford University Press, Oxford
James P, Steger MB (2014) A genealogy of 'Globalization': the career of a concept. Globalizations 11(4):417–434
Kant I (1983) Perpetual peace and other essays (trans: Humphrey T). Hackett, Indianapolis
Kant I (2002) In: Hill TE, Zweig A (eds) Groundwork for the metaphysics of morals. Oxford University Press, Oxford
Klein N (2014) This changes everything: capitalism vs. the climate. Simon and Schuster, New York
Malloy M (2014) Palestinians tweet tear gas advice to protestors in Ferguson. Telegraph UK. Accessed 1 Dec 2018. http://www.telegraph.co.uk/news/worldnews/northamerica/usa/11036190/Palestinians-tweet-tear-gas-advice-to-protesters-in-Ferguson.html
Miller D (2007) National responsibility and global justice. Oxford University Press, Oxford
Miller D (2008) Global justice and climate change: how should responsibility be distributed. The Tanner Lecture on Human Values. Tsinghua University, Beijing

Nussbaum M (2011) Creating capabilities: the human development approach. Harvard University Press, Cambridge, MA

O'Neil O (2000) Bounds of justice. Cambridge University Press, Cambridge, UK

Ohmae K (1996) The end of the nation state: the rise of regional economies. The Free Press, New York

Pogge T (1992) Cosmopolitanism and sovereignty. Ethics 103(3):48–75

Pogge T (2001) Priorities of global justice. Metaphilosophy 32(1–2):6–24

Rawls J (1971) A theory of justice. Harvard University Press, Cambridge, MA

Rawls J (2001) Law of the peoples. Harvard University Press, Cambridge, MA

Rush E (2018) Rising: dispatches from the new American shore. Milkweed, Minneapolis

Sachs J (1998) International economics: unlocking the mysteries of globalization. Foreign Policy. No. 110 (Spring). 97–110. https://www.jstor.org/stable/1149279?casa_token=peDEKwdWbi0AAAAA:8dUbDBips_Z-FMdG-ed8EwKCZpHqzjNw9wTUGY0Fm5S-Nt8cHk3kEl6ACa9c3pMSMjODZdIHP5sO65b-AYOq8Z4Rjk0GvaP53ZxBkTPB7aGHEHGqxU&seq=1#metadata_info_tab_contents

Sassen S (1998) Globalization and its discontents: essays on the new mobility of people and money. The New Press, New York

Sassen S (2006) Territory, authority, rights: from medieval to global assemblages. Princeton University Press, Princeton

Sassen S (2014) Expulsions: brutality and complexity in the global economy. Belknap Press, Cambridge, MA

Schlosberg D (2004) Reconceiving environmental justice: global movements and political theories. Environ Polit 13(3):517–540

Sen A (1999) Development as freedom. Anchor Books, New York

Steger M (2017) Globalization: a very short introduction. Oxford University Press, Oxford

Steger M, Wilson E (2012) Anti-globalization or alter-globalization? Mapping the political ideology of the global justice movement. Int Stud Q 56:439–454

Tan K-C (2004) Justice without borders: cosmopolitanism, nationalism, and patriotism. Cambridge University Press, Cambridge, UK

Temin P (2018) The vanishing middle class: prejudice and power in the dual economy. MIT Press, Cambridge, MA

United Nations Sustainable Development Goals, Goal 1: End Poverty (n.d.) Accessed 15 Nov 2018. https://www.un.org/sustainabledevelopment/poverty/

Young IM (1990) Justice and the politics of difference. Princeton University Press, Princeton

Young IM (2006) Responsibility and global justice: a social connection model. Soc Philos Policy 23(1):102–130

Shared Citizenship and Sovereignty: The Case of the Cook Islands' and Niue's Relationship with New Zealand

13

Zbigniew Dumieński

Contents

Introduction	222
Microstates as Modern Protected States	224
Cook Islands and Niue: Geography, Population, Politics, and History	228
Geography	228
Population	230
Politics	230
History	231
Protected Statehood and the Question of Shared Citizenship	235
Conclusion	240
Cross-References	241
References	241

Abstract

The world in the twenty-first century contains many distinct small polities of varying degree of self-governance, ranging from fully sovereign states to mere autonomies or special administrative regions. Their existence raises the question of the meaning of sovereignty, statehood, and politico-economic viability in the face of extreme geographic and demographic challenges. This question is of particular relevance in the context of one group of diminutive states that have delegated some of the key attributes of their sovereignty to larger states in order to overcome some of the limitations imposed upon them by geography or demographics. This chapter examines two such political units: the Cook Islands and Niue. While formally independent, they have functioned in free association with New Zealand. In addition to receiving significant amounts of financial assistance, as well as delegating authority in such areas as monetary policy or defense to their former metropolitan power, the Cook Islanders and Niueans have remained New

---

Z. Dumieński (✉)
Auckland University of Technology, Auckland, New Zealand
e-mail: dumienski@gmail.com; zdum510@aucklanduni.ac.nz

© The Author(s), under exclusive license to Springer Nature Singapore Pte Ltd. 2019
S. Ratuva (ed.), *The Palgrave Handbook of Ethnicity*,
https://doi.org/10.1007/978-981-13-2898-5_14

Zealand citizens, and their territories have remained treated as part of New Zealand for the purpose of obtaining its citizenship. The existence of such arrangements has been a source of confusion. In particular, it has raised the question of the compatibility of free association and shared citizenship with sovereign statehood. This chapter addresses this question and argues that despite their miniscule size and close association with New Zealand, both the Cook Islands and Niue can and should be seen as sovereign states.

Keywords
Microstates · Small states · Sovereignty · Shared citizenship · Free association · Modern protected states

Introduction

The world in the twenty-first century contains many distinct small polities of varying degree of self-governance, ranging from fully sovereign states to mere autonomies or special administrative regions. Their continued survival, and indeed, often economic and political success, provokes scholarly debates on both the effects of smallness on domestic institutions and the role of diminutive units in the international system dominated by large powers.

While tiny polities are hardly a novelty in international relations (Dommen 1985, 17; Sundhaussen 2003), their current multitude and position in international relations and global economy have both fascinated and perplexed modern historians, sociologists, political scientists, and economists (e.g., Benedict 1967; Harden 1985; Hintjens and Newitt 1992; Hobsbawm 1992; Parrish 1990; Reid 1975; Plischke 1977; Catudal 1975). As noted by Simpson (2007, 29), "there is an extensive and expanding literature concerning small states." Many scholars have been interested not only in the role that small states play in the world dominated by great powers (e.g., Amstrup 1976; East 1973; Goetschel 1998; Harden 1985; Hey 2003; Keohane 1969; Mohamed 2002; Neumann and Gstöhl 2004) but also in the possible effects of diminutive geographic or demographic size on various states' economic performance (e.g., Armstrong and Read 1995, 1998; Baldacchino 2006; Grydehøj 2011; Katzenstein 1985; Mehmet and Tahiroglu 2002; Milne 2000; Srinivasan 1986; Sutton 2011; Tõnurist 2010) and political institutions (e.g., AJPA 1994; Alesina 2003; Bray and Fergus 1986; Schumacher 1973; Veenendaal 2015). This extensive research fits into "a long tradition in the history of political thinking in Europe" (Amstrup 1976, 163) concerned with the effects of size on states' behavior and institutions.

One group of tiny polities appears as especially intriguing. Due to the constraints imposed by their smallness, these states function in close relationships with at least one larger state acting as a benign protector of their political and economic viability. While sovereign, they delegate some of the key attributes of their sovereignty (such as the conduct of foreign policy, defense, key administrative functions, monetary policy) to larger states in order to overcome some of the limitations imposed upon them by geography or demographics. Perhaps unsurprisingly, the existence of such peculiar arrangements, together with these polities' minuscule size and relative obscurity, has led to some confusion regarding their political status and place within the international system. Furthermore, the establishment of close associations between the tiny polities and larger states has raised the questions of the meaning of sovereignty and statehood in the face of extreme geo-demographic challenges and miniscule size.

This chapter looks at two such polities: the Cook Islands and Niue. Both of them are not just miniscule but also located in the middle of the Pacific Ocean, which amplifies the geo-demographic challenges to political and economic viability presented by their size. The key way in which the two entities overcome their limitations is via free, albeit far-reaching and comprehensive, association arrangements with New Zealand, who used to exercise sovereignty over these island territories. The Cook Islands and Niue do not just receive generous financial aid from their former colonial power but also have delegated certain key attributes of sovereignty to New Zealand. In part, this takes place in the form of New Zealand's direct assistance in such fields as the conduct of foreign affairs, military defense, and public administration. However, arguably more importantly and curiously, it is also manifested in the fact that, despite their respective countries' formal independence from New Zealand, both the Cook Islanders and Niueans have remained New Zealand citizens, and their territories have remained treated as part of New Zealand for the purpose of obtaining New Zealand's citizenship. This means that the people of both polities have an unobstructed access to New Zealand's infrastructure, including healthcare, education, and welfare system. By virtue of New Zealand's agreements with Australia, this also provides them with a right to reside and work in Australia and travel visa-free to most countries in the world.

Perhaps not surprisingly, the existence of such close ties between New Zealand and the two island polities, coupled with their remoteness, tiny size, and lack of any strategic resources, has resulted in their political status being often subject to confusion, misunderstanding, or ignorance, both outside the region and even in New Zealand itself. To many people, superficially, the two entities appear to "to occupy the ill-defined no-mans-land between colony and independent statehood" (Smith 2010, 170). In particular, the issue of the two polities' sovereignty and statehood, in light of their association with New Zealand, has been clouded by a high degree of confusion. Can these entities be described as sovereign states? Are there geo-demographic constraints, coupled with close links to New Zealand and lack of separate citizenships compatible with the concept of sovereign statehood?

The aim of this chapter is to clarify and address these questions. Its central argument is that that despite their miniscule size and peculiar geopolitical arrangements, both the Cook Islands and Niue can and should be seen as sovereign states. While rare and complex, the type of arrangements between the Cook Islands, Niue, and New Zealand is not without precedent. Indeed, it aligns with the experience of several other diminutive states that have managed to mitigate geo-demographic constraints and maintain sovereignty thanks to establishing and managing close relations with larger states acting as benign protectors of their political and economic viability.

The chapter begins by presenting the concept of micro-statehood understood as modern protected statehood. It then discusses the case of the Cook Islands and Niue, with a particular emphasis on the issue of free association, shared citizenship and their implications for the countries' sovereignty and politico-economic viability. The analysis is strongly focused on the Cook Islands, primarily because of the fact throughout the late nineteenth and the twentieth century Niue followed (or was forced to follow) the arrangements worked out for or with the Cook Islands, both when it came to colonial administration and the formation of free association with New Zealand.

Microstates as Modern Protected States

There are a number of diminutive polities that claim to be sovereign and that yet delegate the key attributes of sovereignty to larger states. The existence of such arrangements, together with these polities' minuscule size and relative obscurity, has led to some confusion regarding their political status and place within the international system. Much of the puzzlement surrounding the political status of owes to the fact that such polities have rarely, if ever, been studied together as a separate analytical category within the broader scholarship of small states and territories. One of the key characteristics of this rich scholarship is the problem it has with precisely defining "its own subject, 'the small state'" (Amstrup 1976, 165). As noted by Maass (2009, 66): "despite the existence of a substantial specialised literature on small states and the existence of small states in large numbers, the phenomenon of the small state remains vaguely defined, by scholars as well as practitioners." Notwithstanding the long-standing problem of finding meaningful ways to differentiate between small and large states, scholars have recognized that some polities are so diminutive and institutionally peculiar they need to be studied separately from both large and small states. This realization has led to the creation and popular usage of an assumingly distinct, albeit not very precise (Warrington 1994), category of very small political entities: the microstates.

Presumably, microstates are polities distinctive enough to merit being treated separately from both "normal" and "small" states (Warrington 1994). After all, if they were only quantitatively different from other political units, then looking at them in isolation from larger states would make little sense from the scholarly point of view. For political scientists and economists, it is not merely geographic or demographic smallness in itself that should matter but whether or not smallness produces any significant qualitative consequences. In other words, the microstates "as a category of analysis would only be useful in terms of the characteristics of these states and, the relevance of such characteristics to the role they play in the international system" (Mohamed 2002, 3). As such, any viable definition or concept of microstates must facilitate a clear identification of *qualitatively* distinct political units whose peculiarity derives from certain geographic and demographic constraints.

Unfortunately, such a definition is absent from most of the existing scholarship (Orlow 1995). While scholars appear to agree that a microstate is simply a "very small state," there is little consensus (Warrington 1994), or even reasoned argument, over what constitutes both "very small" and "state." Consequently, most of the current definitions of microstates (and most cases of the usage of the term) are hampered by serious problems of inconsistency, arbitrariness, vagueness, and inability to meaningfully isolate *qualitatively* distinct political units.

As an alternative to this problematic approach to defining and identifying microstates, it has been proposed to regard microstates as modern protected states, i.e., sovereign states that have been able unilaterally to depute certain attributes of sovereignty to larger powers in exchange for benign protection of their political and economic viability against their geographic or demographic constraints (Dumienski 2014).

This definition permits identification and isolation of states on the basis of their qualitative political uniqueness resulting from both their own and external perception of resourcelessness, physical constraints, and geographic insignificance. The real or perceived geographic weakness and resourcelessness make microstates' leaders determined to seek or accept external protection and institutional assistance even at the cost of losing some of their sovereign attributes. At the same time, the real or perceived geographic insignificance of microstates, coupled with certain historical, personal, or strategic considerations, induces larger countries' leaders to provide microstates with nonreciprocal, benign protection. Micro-statehood thus entails not only observable geographic or demographic smallness but also the voluntary and *nonreciprocal* delegation by microstate leaders of some "authority normally exclusively retained by [sovereign] self-governing state, often in the field of defence and foreign affairs" in exchange for protection and/or "favourable economic terms such as market access" (Turner 2007, 19).

Importantly, these unique institutional relationships with larger states are both necessitated and permitted by microstates' real or perceived smallness and geopolitical insignificance. From this perspective, microstates are more than merely very small states, but rather are unique political entities worthy of a focused academic enquiry. This approach to the study of microstates permits not only to address the lack of "terminological clarity and theoretical coherence" (Sieber 1983) that characterizes the current small and microstates scholarships but also to study both the political phenomenon of protected statehood and the peculiar politico-economic situation of some of the world's smallest political communities.

While this way of looking at microstates may be seen as novel, it is nonetheless historically justified. Nearly a century ago the League of Nations was faced with the problem of the then called "Lilliputian States" (Crawford 2007, 183). In 1919 and 1920, the Republic of San Marino, the Principality of Monaco, and the Principality of Liechtenstein submitted their applications for membership in the organization. While the first two soon abandoned the idea, Liechtenstein remained persistent in its efforts and "pursued the matter to the full" (Gunter 1974). In response to its request, the League ordered a detailed examination of the applicant's qualifications. In 1920, following an inquiry into Liechtenstein's situation, the Fifth (Admissions) Committee rejected its application arguing that:

> There can be no doubt that juridically the Principality of Liechtenstein is a sovereign State, but by reason of her limited area, small population, and her geographical position, she has chosen to depute to others some of the attributes of sovereignty. (...) For the above reasons, we are of the opinion that the Principality of Liechtenstein could not discharge all the international obligations, which would be imposed on her by the Covenant. (quoted in: Schwebel 1973, p. 108)

While the League did not accept Liechtenstein's application for membership, it did nonetheless manage to provide a qualitative threshold for microstates. It was recognized that such states were entities so geographically and demographically constrained that they independently chose to depute some of their external sovereignty to their larger neighbors.

The existence of such entities may have been seen as peculiar in the early twentieth century. However, a long time before the times of the League of Nations, the theoreticians and practitioners of diplomacy recognized a category of political units called "protected states" (Berridge and Lloyd 2012; Crawford 2007, 286–294). According to such authors as Hugo Grotius (1583–1645), an "unequal alliance," with one state offering benign or amicable protection or patronage over another, was "quite consistent with the sovereignty of the latter" (Crawford 2007, 286). It was in fact widely accepted that "states which were unable to maintain their sovereignty unaided could have their internal autonomy underwritten if a willing major power came forward to protect them" (Herr 1988). Unlike protectorates (especially in their colonial context), the protected states came into existence through genuine, consensual agreements between two or more sovereign parties (Herr 1988, 289) and assumed respect for independence, protection, and assistance offered either unconditionally or in exchange for a rather benign and limited "accommodation to the wishes of the protector in matters of policy" (Baty 1921, 109).

The protected states delegated some of their authority but retained independent control over their domestic affairs and at least some degree of influence over their foreign affairs (Crawford 2007, 288). What was peculiar was the fact that the relative benefits of such arrangements were far greater for the protected than for the protector. At the price of voluntarily choosing to "restrict the exercise of its sovereign rights in a certain area, allowing another [state] to act on its behalf" (James 1986, 100–101) (with an at least theoretical option for terminating the agreement at will), a protected state gained political support or protection and very "favourable economic terms such as market access" (Turner 2007, 19).

While this form of statehood was somewhat common in medieval and early modern Europe, by the nineteenth century, it seemed that the "conception of a really independent, but protected, State had disappeared" (Baty 1921, 111). According to historians, by the second half of the nineteenth century, the protectors gradually dismantled any real independence of their protected states and either annexed them or turned them into nonindependent façade states (Alexandrowicz 1973; Baty 1921; Johnston 1973). Although the term "protected state" was still in use in the twentieth century (and presented in contrast to the term "protectorate"), it referred to political units such as the Malay and Persian Gulf states that were obviously non-sovereign (Crawford 2007, 287; Parry 1960).

Seen from this perspective, the European microstates were indeed "medieval relics" (Hass 2004), but not due to their size but because of being the only surviving protected states. Somewhat paradoxically their survival as protected sovereignties was arguably large due to their extreme smallness, political insignificance, and lack of any natural resources (Duursma 1996; Eccardt 2005; Sundhaussen 2003). The term microsite can thus refer to both quantitative geographic insignificance and a peculiar political status, the two being inherently linked, the small size making sustainable unequal alliance likely and protection making survival despite the odds possible.

If the European microstates had not entered into unequal alliances with larger neighbors, they would have most probably simply disappeared from the political map of the continent. In fact, their continual presence was widely perceived as a "historical accident" (Bartmann 2012; Hass 2004). This may explain the fact that following the League of Nation's decision regarding Liechtenstein very little, if any, attention was dedicated to the issue of micro/protected statehood. It was perhaps assumed that the model of political arrangement adopted by the European Lilliputian state was simply an outdated anachronism of little relevance to any other present or future cases. It was probably expected that such oddities would in any case soon disappear, as they were seen as doomed to economic failure notwithstanding their protection. Indeed, all of the microstates were characterized by poverty (Hobsbawm 1996, 281). Liechtenstein of the 1920s was among the poorest countries in Europe (Hass 2004; Stringer 2006); Monaco had a revolution in 1910 triggered by high unemployment and poverty (Is Monaco Doomed? Other Nations Want It 1910); and San Marino remained a poor, remote, peasant economy (Sundhaussen 2003). Hence, even though the European microstates were truly quantitatively and qualitatively unique entities, they never attracted any significant attention and gradually became little more than cartographic oddities.

In consequence, by the time new political communities quantitatively similar to the European Lilliputian states emerged as a result of decolonization (Herr 1988), the concept of qualitative microstates, i.e., sovereign states that only small but also protected states, had largely been forgotten. Instead, the term microstate has largely become a vague and vast category defined purely in terms of arbitrary (and rather inconsistent) geographic or demographic cutoff points. In practical terms, the only difference between it and the broader "small states" grouping is the, rather unjustified, inclusion of various sub-national jurisdictions within its scope. This conceptual lack of clarity is arguably one of the reasons behind the considerable amount of misunderstanding that surrounds the question of the Cook Islands' and Niue's political status.

As the next sections of the chapter will demonstrate, a more careful analysis of the Cook Islands and Niue's situation and relations with New Zealand can reveal that both entities fit into the proposed qualitative definition of microstates understood as modern protected states. Instead of being seen as inconsistent with sovereignty of the two diminutive polities, the institution of shared citizenship can be viewed as a convenient and durable mechanism for delegating the provision of public goods to the protecting and securing political and economic viability against severe geographic and demographic constraints.

Cook Islands and Niue: Geography, Population, Politics, and History

A detailed examination of the geography, history, and politico-economic situation in both microstates is beyond the scope of this chapter. However, a brief overview is necessary to understand the dynamics of their statehood and relationship with New Zealand.

Geography

The Cook Islands' territory comprises 15 small islands spread across over 2 million km^2 of the Pacific Ocean. The Cook Islands is located south of Kiribati, west of French Polynesia, and east of Niue, Tonga, and Samoa. The country's capital of Avarua lies about 3,000 km northeast of Auckland and approximately 7,500 km southwest of Los Angeles.

The islands belong to two geographically distinct groups: The northern group consisting of sparsely populated coral atolls and the much larger and more densely populated southern group of eight islands. The distance between the two groups is truly enormous. For instance, Avarua is located over 1,350 km away from the northernmost island of Penrhyn. This is the roughly the same distance as between Italy and Norway. The dispersal of this microstate's tiny islands across the ocean gives it a certain macro dimension. While the total land area of the Cook Islands is approximately 240 km^2, thanks to the principles prescribed by the United Nations Convention on the Law of the Sea according to which states have special rights regarding the use and exploitation of marine resources within 200 nautical miles of their coastline, the country claims a vast maritime exclusive economic zone (EEZ) of approximately 2 million km^2, i.e., comparable in size to Mexico or Greenland (Clark et al. 1995; Hein et al. 2015).

The Cook Islands' massive maritime area is a source of both challenges and opportunities. The ocean can be seen as a potential source of valuable living and nonliving resources. In particular, over the last decades, it has been discovered that the Cook Islands' EEZ possesses significant amounts of mineral deposits "with nodules containing concentrations of cobalt, nickel, manganese, and other valuable non-living marine resources" (Clark et al. 1995). A potential successful exploitation of these resources could earn the country "billions of dollars" (Neate 2013), and as such it might one day lead to a significant politico-economic transformation of the Cook Islands, including changes to its form of statehood and association with New Zealand. However, despite encouraging reports and studies (Cardno 2016; Clark et al. 1995; Hein et al. 2015), as of 2016 the Cook Islands is yet to derive any substantial benefits from seabed mining, and the plans to exploit these resources are thwarted by high costs, potential risks, relatively small interest among potential investors (Cooks to take more direct approach to seabed mining 2016), and various environmental concerns (Samoglou 2014; Smylie 2014).

At the same time, the tremendous distance between the sparsely populated islands and the sheer size of the marine area under the Cook Islands' jurisdictions pose such challenges as significant cost of policing and surveillance of the EEZ, high transportation costs, economic isolation (particularly affecting the northern group islands), and logistical and financial difficulties associated with providing public services across the country (Asian Development Bank 2008; Duval and Winchester 2011; Fairbairn and Pearson 1987; Hoffmann-Dumieński 2016). The large size of the maritime area, especially in the context of small population size, can, perhaps paradoxically, therefore be seen as a geographic constraint and source of geopolitical vulnerabilities. As such it also demonstrates the complex nature "smallness" in international politics and reinforces the arguments regarding the need for a departure from relying solely on arbitrary quantitative thresholds for the purpose of identifying and analyzing polities affected by geographic and demographic limitations.

The Cook Islands' location also makes the country vulnerable to a number of natural hazards, most notably devastating tropical cyclones (Asian Development Bank 2008; Cook Islands Government 2015; Ingram 2004). The scarcely populated northern group islands are more exposed to this threat, but the southern group islands are also at risk. During the particularly bad 2005 cyclone season, the southern group experienced five cyclones that caused considerable damage (Asian Development Bank 2008, 31). Other potential hazards include rising sea levels (most notably in the case of flat and low-lying northern group islands), climate change, and environmental degradation of the key tourist spots (Reti 2008; Syme-Buchanan 2015).

Apart from the seabed mineral deposits, the Cook Islands' key natural resources are limited to marine resources (fish and pearls), small areas with fertile land, as well as attractive beaches and lagoons, which, together with warm climate, create favorable conditions for developing a viable tourism industry, especially on the southern group islands of Rarotonga and Aitutaki (Cook Islands Government 2015).

Unlike the Cook Islands, Niue consists of one single, largely flat island, a large uplifted coral atoll with an area of 260 km^2. While Niue's landmass is larger than that the Cook Islands, the concentration of its landmass means that the country enjoys a much smaller (albeit still quite significant – 390,000 km^2) exclusive economic zone than the Cook Islands. The island consists mainly of limestone and has no river of lakes (as rainwater can easily soak through the porous rock), and the entire coastline is dominated by 30 m cliffs broken by chasms and caves. Marine access is difficult due to the lack of natural harbors or beaches (Connell 2007, 2). The lack of large sandy beaches makes it a challenge to develop the island as a "traditional" Pacific destination (Milne 1992, 566).

Soil, while fertile, is sparse, thinly distributed and "nestled in shallow pockets between coral rocks, a terrain that makes cultivation difficult" (Barker 2000, 195). Thirty to forty percent of the island can be considered as "unsuitable for agriculture" (McNicoll 1989, 15).

Due to its location just on the edge of the so-called hurricane belt, the island has frequently suffered from extreme weather systems capable of devastating the islands' agriculture and key infrastructure and posing a challenge to the island's economic viability (Barker 2000, 196). The island lacks any important mineral resources, and its location is not considered to be of any strategic importance "for either military or commercial purposes" (Barker 2000, 195).

Population

According to the 2011 census, the Cook Islands has a total population of 17,794, of which 2,282 were short-term visitors (mainly tourists) (Ministry of Finance and Economic Management 2013). The total population inside the country peaked at 21,322 in 1971 and has generally been in decline, especially when it comes to the number of residents (Cook Islands Government 2015; Ministry of Finance and Economic Management 2013), largely due to emigration (Bertram and Watters 1984, 131; Crocombe et al. 2008), with a notable acceleration of the rate of emigration since 1996 following the economic reforms leading to reduced public sector employment. Over the same period, the total population of Rarotonga increased by 14%, mainly due to internal immigration from the outer islands, as well as increasing numbers of tourists. The outer islands (except touristy Aitutaki) have experienced a significant decline in population size. The situation might appear to be particularly dramatic in the northern group. According to the 2011 census, the entire northern group of islands had just over 1,100 people (Cook Islands Government 2015).

Niue's population of approximately 1,600 people makes it the smallest sovereign country in the world. The number of ethnic Niueans living on the island used to be much higher (5,000 in the mid-1960s), but due to emigration, the vast majority of ethnic Niueans live today in New Zealand, Australia, and elsewhere.

Politics

Despite the significant cultural and geographic differences between the two countries, as well as over half of century of independence, "the systems of government in the Cook Islands still closely resemble the executive, legislative and judicial systems of New Zealand" (Webb 2016). As per 1965 Constitution, the Cook Islands share a monarch with New Zealand with the Queen of New Zealand being also the Cook Islands' head of state. Similar to New Zealand, the Cook Islands "appoints a queen's representative, by recommendation of the prime minister of the Cook Islands" (Webb 2016).

The country can be best described as a constitutional monarchy with a parliamentary democracy largely modeled after New Zealand but also containing some traditional institutions and elements. In particular, the Cook Islands Constitution establishes the *House of Ariki* "comprising up to 14 Ariki (chiefs) appointed by the Queen's representative (on advice from the prime minister)" (Webb 2016) as an institution tasked with providing occasional advice and consultation to the Parliament (T. Ingram and Uhrle 2004, 22). The 24 members of the Parliament are elected for 4-year terms by the "first-past-the-post" single-vote electoral system (Clarke 1979; Jonassen 2011). The Prime Minister heads the country's government. The electoral system contains certain traditional elements with constituencies' boundaries drafted along the traditional land divisions and in result "made up of people who are related by blood and land resources" (Ingram and Uhrle 2004, 15).

In general, it has been noted that "tribalism, religion, political party affiliation and, more recently, gender have become underlying sources of divergence in Cook Islands politics" (Jonassen 2011). While the country has had a number of political parties since its independence (with the two main parties being the Cook Islands Party founded in 1965 by Albert Henry and the Democratic Party established in 1978 by Sir Thomas Davis), just like in the case of Liechtenstein (Veenendaal 2014), there are no substantial ideological differences between the main parties, and party support appears to be based primarily on family, religious, and personal connections of specific candidates and leaders.

Partially due to the above features but also due to other factors (such as the country's small size, legacy of colonialism, and the impact of foreign aid), patronage and nepotism are seen as some of the biggest problems affecting the Cook Islands' political system (Asian Development Bank 2008; Crocombe 1978, 1979; Ingram 2004). Furthermore, the political system of the Cook Islands is affected by a high degree of voters' apathy toward both the politicians and the political system (Jonassen 2011, 2013). Many voters appear to be disillusioned by frequent scandals and political reshuffles and a general perception of corruption (Jonassen 2011). The "thick crust of apathy" (Strickland 1979) is likely the result of broader, more systemic factors rooted in the colonial history of the country (Crocombe 1979).

The Niueans have traditionally had much more egalitarian social structures than most of the other Polynesian societies, including that of the Cook Islands (Connell 2007, 2; Talagi 2013, 16). Niuean society is also characterized as rather "republican" with "weak nationalism" and strong family loyalties (Talagi 2013, 16). Niue's political system is based on the Westminster system of government. Niue's Assembly consists of 20 members, 6 of whom are elected from the common roll and 14 of whom are elected by the constituents in each of the 14 villages (Government of Niue 2017). With approximately 1 member of Parliament per 80 citizens, Niue has arguably one of the most representative parliaments in the world.

History

The early history of the Cook Islands is not well known, largely due to the absence of written records from the pre-colonial period (Gilson 1980, 1). Nonetheless, it is widely recognized that prior to the colonial period, the 15 islands did not exist as a unified political unit (Jonassen 2011, 35) and that despite the fact that all Cook Islanders "belong to the Polynesian branch of the Oceanic peoples," with the exception of the islands of Manihiki and Rakahanga, "no two islands shared the same cultural origins" (Gilson 1980, 3). The largest island of Rarotonga itself had no centralized political authority and instead was divided into three distinct tribal districts with their own hierarchies of chiefs (with *ariki* being the most senior chiefly title in each district) (Gilson 1955, 268, 1980, 6; Whimp 2008, 30).

The history of the post-European contact period is better documented. While the islands were likely sighted by the European explorers as early as 1595, the Cook Islands' remote location lack of any valuable natural resources, and tiny size meant that unlike other parts of Oceania, the islands "escaped the colonizing attentions" of the major political powers (Scott 1991, 30). Christian missionaries of the London Missionary Society (LMS) were the first group of outsiders to establish with a continuous presence on the islands in the early 1800s. They maintained a significant influence over the Cook Islands' society and politico-economic development for much of the century.

Toward the end of the nineteenth century, the island leaders grew increasingly concerned about potential threats to their power due to an increase in the numbers of foreign traders and influences from the growing French presence around Tahiti. In response to these threats, they approached New Zealand's colonial authorities with a request for British protection. Despite New Zealand's support for the move, London initially rejected their request as the British saw no economic or strategic benefits of becoming more involved in this part of the world, in particular as such involvement would require considerable expenses and would potentially be met with opposition from other colonial powers (Gilson 1980, 57; Scott 1991, 30–36).

However, the situation changed in 1888 due to concerns over the strategic implication of the proposed construction of the Panama Canal. The British realized that they lacked any coaling stations between their colonies in Australasia and Panama and that without having control over Rarotonga, the French would hold the dominant position on this potentially important route (Scott 1991, 42–43). In other words, the Cook Islands suddenly acquired a certain strategic significance to the Crown. In consequence, London changed its stance and moved to establish a protectorate over the islands.

It is important to emphasize that British decision did not establish the Cook Islands as a genuine protected state. Unlike in the case of relations between protected states and their benign protectors, the British protectorate over the Cook Islands (particularly with respect to the outer islands) did not assume full respect for the latter's sovereignty. While Britain ostensibly acted in response to the local appeals for assistance, the process of establishing their political presence on the islands was more akin to annexation than a creation of mutually consensual agreement between two sovereign states (Gilson 1980, 60; Scott 1991, 43). While the British demonstrated a degree of respect for the chiefs' authority and ostensibly came to the islands in response to their appeals, it is clear that the Cook Islands (or even just Rarotonga) was not effectively perceived by the British (not to mention any other powers) as a sovereign state. Likewise, while Britain assured the *ariki* that it would respect their laws, customs, and administration over their respective districts, the fact that it "reserved full liberty of action in respect of the type of government to be formed in the islands" (Gilson 1980, 62) and the fact that it unilaterally determined the political status of specific islands imply that Britain became the sovereign power in control of the Cook Islands.

The British move was welcomed and supported by New Zealand that at the time expressed a keen desire to assert itself as an important political entity not just within the British Empire but also on the world stage. New Zealand's colonial adventures, however small and insignificant from the point of view of global affairs, offered hope to make the world's leading powers perceive New Zealand as a "small power" in the South Pacific even when it was still merely a "self-governing colony" (Ross 1964, 294–295). In this context, it is perhaps unsurprising that New Zealand's politicians were convinced that New Zealand should be "the agent and adviser of the Crown in matters of imperial interest in the Pacific" (Gilson 1980, 58).

It is also understandable that New Zealand expressed an interest in further increasing its formal power of the islands. After a short period of ruling on behalf of Britain, New Zealand managed to persuade London to consent to a formal annexation of the islands into New Zealand in 1901 (Gilson 1980).

In many ways, the Cook Islands occupied a peculiar position within New Zealand. While officially the islands were an integral part of the country, they were "outside the ambit of the New Zealand taxation and social security systems and New Zealand wage rates did not apply" (Quentin-Baxter 2000, 430). Indeed, "no New Zealand Act (...) ever operated in the Cooks unless it included a statement to that effect; and the term 'New Zealand' in any Act did not include the Cooks unless a contrary intention appeared" (Stone 1965, 371). Furthermore, the islands had no representative in the New Zealand Parliament (Stone 1971, 4), and New Zealand citizens "not belonging to [the Cook Islands]" had no automatic right to live on the islands (Quentin-Baxter 2000, 430).

Following the decline of New Zealand's imperial aspirations (likely related to the country's departure from a status of a mere colony in need of asserting its place in global politics), the country's politicians no longer paid much attention to the islands perceived as remote and of no political or economic significance. In consequence, "neglect and vague benevolence have been the hallmarks of [New Zealand's] rule" over the islands (Scott 1991, 7). New Zealand lacked the will or even the opportunities (due to the islands' negligible economic potential) to play the role of an "exploitative colonial power" in the Cook Islands, and instead, it has treated the islands with "benign neglect" (Quentin-Baxter 2000, 430).

In the aftermath of World War II, New Zealand's attitude toward the islands started changing. Wellington began to gradually and unilaterally treat the Cook Islands "as if they were not after all part of New Zealand, but had the status of non-self-governing territories over which New Zealand held a form of trusteeship" (Bertram 1987, 26). This remarkable change in attitude likely resulted to a degree out of the perceived conflict between the islands' seemingly anomalous status and the centralist direction took by New Zealand's government. The strongly centralized New Zealand state saw no room for accommodating politically autonomous communities within the framework of the New Zealand state (Bertram 1987, 21–22). More importantly, by the end of the World War II the global sentiment turned against colonial powers. New Zealand, which itself was a former colony, was naturally inclined to support the right to self-determination and was eager to present itself as the champion for small states (Quentin-Baxter 2000, 429). Like the annexation of the Cook Islands in the late nineteenth century, in the post-world war, "decolonizing" the islands was seen by New Zealand's politicians as a way of gaining international prestige (Bertram and Watters 1984, 5; McKinnon 2013).

Despite the fact that the islands were officially an integral part of New Zealand, and as such were not described as a colony, in 1946, the government decided to present them to the United Nations as a non-self-governing territory and consequently commit itself to facilitating their "self-determination" (Quentin-Baxter 2000, 429). However, the problem was that the Cook Islanders themselves, while perhaps opposed to losing their de facto autonomy, expressed little desire for full independence from New Zealand. Independence without any special arrangement with New Zealand seemed unacceptable primarily because of the concerns of the islanders' about the politico-economic viability of their polities in the absence of support from New Zealand (Bertram and Watters 1984, 48–58).

It is in this context that the option of independence with a form of special arrangement, the institution of "free association," was proposed as a compromise solution. The free association was understood as a voluntary arrangement sought by the weaker party, to which the stronger party merely agreed to while respecting the weaker party's sovereignty. As such it was "designed to provide positive discrimination in favour of the small and the weak, enabling them to benefit if they wished from the benevolence of their former colonial power, without incurring any binding reciprocal obligation" (Bertram and Watters 1984, 35). For many Cook Islanders, it represented an acceptable and safe option. For New Zealand's political elites, it offered an acceptable opportunity "to emerge [out of the decolonisation process] with a good reputation both internationally and at home" (Bertram 1987, 22).

On the one hand, the Cook Islanders were aware of the limitations imposed upon them by their tiny size, lack of substantial natural resources, and geographic isolation. As such they were anxious to retain not just the assistance of a larger state for the purpose of preserving their polity' viability but also the socioeconomic opportunities offered by having access to the larger state's market and institutions (including freedom to migrate) (Bertram and Watters 1984, 56). The free association offered the real possibility of overcoming the limitations of geography and demographics while at the same time entering the exclusive club of sovereign states and not only retaining control over domestic policy or the shape of the country's political system and future but also gaining voice and identity in the international arena. Not surprisingly, with time the free association solution, initially seen mainly as the safe, "conservative" option (Bertram and Watters 1984, 47), eventually became more often perceived as "the best of both worlds" (Jonassen 1996, 55; Quentin-Baxter 2009, 629).

On the other hand, a similar perception of the islands' geo-demographic constraints was present among the New Zealand's (and foreign) policymakers who, in light of these challenges, saw the idea of the Cook Islands' independence without any special arrangement with a larger state as "nonsense" (Wilson 1969, 104). This was particularly true in the context of the apparent problems experienced by Western Samoa, a "nonassociated" state that faced "formidable problems in constructing an independent nation" (Bertram 1987, 25) despite being many times larger, more populous, and richer in natural resources than the Cook Islands. At the same time, the miniscule size of the Cook Islands made it more acceptable for New Zealand to show generosity and benevolence toward them.

Just like the Cook Islands, Niue came under the influence of the missionaries from the London Missionary Society who established a quasi-theocratic society (along the local political structures) on the island around the 1850s and the 1860s (Pointer 2015, 50–72). Following the encouragement from the missionaries, the Niueans sought British protection from the perceived threat posed to the island by the Peruvian slave ships and foreign traders (Pointer 2015, 131–146). After initial reluctance (due to similar considerations as in the case of the Cook Islands), Britain agreed to form a colonial protectorate over the islands in 1900, in part in order to pass them under New Zealand's administration in response to the latter's aspirations described in the above sections. In the following year, the islands were formally annexed to New Zealand as part of its annexation of the Cook Islands. In response to the Niueans' pleas, New Zealand agreed to establish a separate administration and a separate Resident Commissioner for Niue (Tafatu and Tukuitoga 1982, 126).

Soon, it became clear that the islands did not represent any significant strategic or economic benefits to New Zealand. Consequently, once the New Zealand administration became more or less constituted, the islands became "all but forgotten for forty years" (Parsons 1968, 243–244).

Niue proved even more reluctant to pursue independence than the Cook Islands (McNicoll 1989, 44–45). This reluctance was dictated primarily by the widespread perception that the island faces even more serious geographic and demographic constraints than the Cook Islands. In light of these constraints, the Niueans "could not feel that, unaided, they were viable as a country" (Quentin-Baxter 1999, 594). New Zealand government recognized Niue's conditions and agreed to add an additional phrase (not present in the Cook Islands Constitution Act 1965) to the Niue Constitution act: "It shall be a continuing responsibility of the Government of New Zealand to provide necessary economic and administrative assistance to Niue" (New Zealand Parliament 1974).

Protected Statehood and the Question of Shared Citizenship

The Cook Islands' Constitution and arrangements with New Zealand have retained certain legal and symbolic ties between the two countries. First of all, the Cook Islands has chosen to recognize "Her Majesty the Queen in right of New Zealand" as its Head of State. Second, the two countries have frequently emphasized their "commitment to shared values" (Quentin-Baxter 2009, 613–617). Third, the Cook Islands' legal system and administration of justice remain to a degree linked to that of New Zealand's. Furthermore, the New Zealand Government has also expressed official commitment to giving (vaguely specified) continual financial and other supports to the Cook Islands (Quentin-Baxter 2009, 613–617). While the above features of the relationship between the two countries might be contributing to the confusion of the Cook Islands' status, they are not significantly different to those present in many other commonwealth countries and relations between them.

What matters from the point of view of sovereign statehood is the fact that the Cook Islands is free to unilaterally end its relationship with New Zealand (Neemia

1995, 127; Quentin-Baxter 1999, 590; Smith 2010, 204–205) and that New Zealand recognizes the Cook Islands' Parliament's (which replaced the Legislative Assembly) exclusive and full powers to unilaterally make and execute its own laws. Significantly, the Constitution Act of 1965 explicitly states that no laws or decisions made by the New Zealand Parliament are applicable to the Cook Islands, without the latter's consent (Bertram and Watters 1984, 56; Cook Islands Parliament 2004; Quentin-Baxter 2009, 611; Smith 2010, 181).

However, the degree of external ambiguity surrounding the Cook Islands' status is primarily related to two other elements of its association with New Zealand: the exercise of sovereign rights in the area of foreign affairs and defense and the question of shared citizenship. Regarding the first one, much of the controversy was largely generated by the 1964 New Zealand statute containing Section 5 that stated the following:

> External affairs and defence – Nothing in this Act or in the Constitution shall affect the responsibilities of Her Majesty the Queen in Right of New Zealand for the external affairs and defence of the Cook Islands, those responsibilities to be discharged after consultation by the Prime Minister of New Zealand with the Prime Minister of the Cook Islands. (New Zealand Parliament 1964)

This section, which became known as "the Riddiford clause" after the chairman of the Island Territories Committee, for some time added significantly to the confusion surrounding the Cook Islands' status in the international affairs, as it was initially understood to mean that the Government of New Zealand retained exclusive power of the Cook Islands' external affairs and defense (Smith 2010, 184). However, this understanding was at odds with the official statement provided by the New Zealand's government to the United Nations in 1965 according to which:

> [In] the matter of external affairs and defence (...) note also these two more fundamental conditions; first, New Zealand has no unilateral power within the Cook Islands to pass laws or make regulations on external affairs or defence or anything else; therefore nothing New Zealand does on behalf of the Cook Islands in these fields can have practical effect there unless the Cook Islands Government takes whatever legislative, executive or administrative action is required. Secondly, New Zealand can discharge these responsibilities only so long as the Cook Islanders so desire; the Cook Islanders have the power, under Article 41 of their Constitution, to change the free association arrangement and discharge these responsibilities for themselves. (Frame 1987, 144)

Indeed, over time "the dominant interpretation" and understanding of the clause have shifted considerably (Smith 2010, 184), and by the 1980s (especially after the Cook Islands' decision to transform its informal External Affairs Division into a formal Ministry of Foreign Affairs), the constitutional convention recognizing the Cook Islands' ultimate decision-making power in these areas had clearly been established (Frame 1987; Smith 2010, 191). This was further and confirmed by the two countries' governments in their 2001 Joint Centenary Declaration, which stated the following:

> In the conduct of its foreign affairs, the Cook Islands interacts with the international community **as a sovereign and independent state** [emphasis added]. The responsibility of international law rests with the Cook Islands in terms of its actions and the exercise of its

international rights and fulfilment of its international obligations (...) Any action taken by New Zealand in respect of its constitutional responsibilities for the foreign affairs of the Cook Islands will be taken on the delegated authority, and as an agent or facilitator at the specific request of the Cook Islands. Section 5 of the Cook Islands Constitution Act 1964 thus records a responsibility to assist the Cook Islands and not a qualification of Cook Islands' statehood. (Joint Centenary Declaration of the Principles of the Relationship between the Cook Islands and New Zealand 2001)

New Zealand's recognition of the Cook Islands' sovereignty is naturally of great significance to any debate on the country's status. However, what matters even more from the point of view of the Cook Islands' position in the international system is the fact that other states have also recognized it as a state in international law (Quentin-Baxter 2009, 618). Since 1965 the Cook Islands has established diplomatic relations with 40 states (including Australia, People's Republic of China, France, and a number of Pacific island states), has become a signatory of over 100 multilateral conventions (including the UN Convention on the Law of the Sea, the Framework Convention on Climate Change and the Geneva Convention), and has become a member of some of the key international organizations (including the World Health Organization; the Educational, Scientific and Cultural Organization; the International Maritime Organization), many of which are explicitly only open to "states" (Smith 2010, 194–196).

Of particular importance was the signing of the bilateral friendship and maritime border treaty between the USA and the Cook Islands. Initially, the US officials were unsure whether or not the Cook Islands was a sovereign state capable of signing such a treaty. Upon receiving confirmation from the New Zealand government that the Cook Islands were indeed capable of entering into treaty relationships with other states, the treaty between the Cook Islands and the United States was signed (Smith 2010, 193; Treaty between the United States of America and the Cook Islands on friendship and delimitation of the maritime boundary between the United States of America and the Cook Islands 1980). The treaty itself does not mention New Zealand and clearly recognizes both the treaty-making ability of the Cook Islands and its sovereignty over the islands covered by the treaty.

It is possible that much of the confusion surrounding the Cook Islands' status in the international arena has historically been likely linked to the existence of many island-polities the size of the Cook Islands that have remained non-sovereign and indeed quite opposed to the idea of becoming sovereign states. Due to the Cook Islands' isolation and relatively low-profile participation in the international affairs, some countries might have assumed that they were akin to one of the equally small but non-sovereign sub-national jurisdictions. Nonetheless, over the last decades, the Cook Islands has gained a wide recognition across the globe, and it is clear that it has the capacity to enter into relations with other states.

However, the issue of shared citizenship may appear as potentially more controversial. In accordance with the Constitution Act, the Cook Islanders have retained New Zealand citizenship:

Nothing in this Act or in the Constitution shall affect the status of any person as a British subject or New Zealand citizen by virtue of the British Nationality and New Zealand Citizenship Act 1948. (New Zealand Parliament 1964)

Likewise, the New Zealand Citizenship Act of 1977 and the Citizenship Amendment Act of 2005 recognize the Cook Islands as part of New Zealand for the purpose of obtaining New Zealand citizenship by birth. Retaining New Zealand citizenship has always been seen by the Cook Islanders as one of the key benefits of their country's special relationship with New Zealand, and its guarantee in the Constitution Act was one of the main reasons why the option of associated statehood was considered to be attractive (Bertram 1987, 26; Bertram and Watters 1984, 49).

In practical terms, the New Zealand citizenship has been seen as important "mainly because it carries with it the right to live, work and study in New Zealand" (Quentin-Baxter 2009, 614). In other words, the New Zealand citizenship is a guarantee of the access to the New Zealand's market and infrastructure (including education and healthcare services). From this practical point of view, it is arguably akin to the rights enjoyed by the citizens of the European microstates (such as Liechtenstein or Monaco) in their respective protecting states by virtue of their bilateral arrangements. However, in the absence of any flexible and liberal arrangements between New Zealand and other Pacific nations (or any credible proposals to create such arrangements for the Cook Islands should the Cook Islanders lose their New Zealand citizenship), it is not surprising that the New Zealand citizenship appears as the only guarantee of continual access to New Zealand. It can also be seen as the simple "window" through which the Cook Islands can "outsource" the provision of some of the key public goods (e.g., sophisticated medical care, high-level education, some elements of welfare and consular assistance) to New Zealand. Furthermore, the fact that Cook Islanders are New Zealand citizens is seen as a factor that strengthens New Zealand's commitment to maintaining the special relationship with the islands.

Why did New Zealand's government agree to allow the Cook Islanders to retain its citizenship, and why has it never seriously considered removing it in all the years that have passed since the Cook Islands attained independence?. Allowing a tiny population of Cook Islanders to remain New Zealand citizens after independence was never seen as particularly problematic or controversial. At the same time, it was clear that without the offer of citizenship, the transition to independence would have encountered much more resistance among the islanders concerned about their future in the new, potentially economically nonviable state (Bertram and Watters 1984, 49). In theory, the New Zealand Parliament could remove the right to obtaining New Zealand citizenship by birth on the Cook Islands or even deprive the Cook Islanders of their New Zealand citizenship (Stone 1971, 193–194). However, such a move would certainly be legally difficult, and it would require a tremendous amount of political support to pass, particularly in light of the fact that approximately 90% of the ethnic Cook Islanders (many of whom are of mixed ancestry and have lived outside the islands for two or three generations) currently reside in New Zealand or Australia (Crocombe et al. 2008, 156). Should New Zealand want to effectively deprive all "Cook Islanders" of their New Zealand citizenship, it would need to not only come up with a sensible way of determining whom it considers to be a "Cook Islander" but also face the fact that such a move could potentially make tens of thousands of residents of New Zealand stateless, which would be problematic from the point of view of the international law (Blocker and Gulati 2017; Sawyer 2013). It is perhaps more plausible that New Zealand might one day decide to stop treating the Cook Islands as part of New Zealand for the purpose of obtaining citizenship by birth, but this move alone would not make much of a difference, other than to encourage more Cook Islanders to move to New Zealand.

Perhaps most importantly, the Cook Islands' population is so small that the Cook Islanders' right to New Zealand citizenship is largely seen as non-problematic, regardless of the other arrangements under the framework of free association. It could, therefore, be argued that shared citizenship is just one of the most interesting but also durable features of the peculiar relations between the Cook Islands and New Zealand. It is the "most tightly protected dimension of free association," as put by one Cook Islander writer (Marsters 2017).

At the same time, the issue of shared citizenship is sometimes presented as inconsistent with the idea that the Cook Islands' is a sovereign state. In particular, it has been (rather casually) argued that due to the fact that the Cook Islanders lack their own citizenship, their country might be ineligible to become a member of the United Nations or that its membership in the organization would result in a loss of New Zealand citizenship (Andrews 2001; Small and Day 2015). This concern has been the key reason why the Cook Islands' government has been reluctant to apply for membership in the organization. However, it is not clear why the lack of separate citizenship or the fact that the Cook Islanders are entitled to New Zealand citizenship should be at odds with the country's eligibility for the United Nations membership. As argued by the Cook Islands' government officials: "there's nothing about having your own and separate citizenship in the criteria for joining the UN" and that they do not believe that the question of the Cook Islands' shared citizenship, should "form part of the discussion" (Cooks citizenship shouldn't be part of UN membership discussion 2015).

The membership is open to "all other peace-loving States which accept the obligations contained in the present Charter and, in the judgment of the Organization, are able and willing to carry out these obligations" (United Nations 1945). As persuasively argued by Smith (2010), the Cook Islands meets all of the above requirements. While there is no official United Nations definition of "states," the Cook Islands not only meets the criteria described in the 1933 Montevideo Convention on the Rights and Duties of States, but its statehood has also "been implicitly acknowledged by most other UN members through their permitting the Cook Islands to become a member of international organisations that are open only to States" (Smith 2010, 201).

In this context it is unclear why New Zealand politicians seem to consider it necessary to potentially discuss amending the citizenship rules should the Cook Islands choose to become a UN member state. One explanation could perhaps be that New Zealand is willing to offer unique privileges to the Cook Islands only for as long as it perceives it as small and vulnerable, but not necessarily if the Cook Islands were to become a more prominent state in the international arena. As noted by Smith, some Cook Islanders believe that for New Zealand, their country's UN membership could be seen as a sign that Zealand "is no longer needed by its former 'colony', and that New Zealand therefore would use the event as a justification for unilaterally terminating the relationship of free association with the Cook Islands" (Smith 2010, 214).

As noted above, the very beginning of Niue's micro-statehood was marked by the recognition of its precarious geo-demographic circumstances both in Niue and in

New Zealand. This not only paved the way for the successful formation of protected statehood, but also intensified the active character of benign protection offered by New Zealand. The analysis of the case of the Cook Islands demonstrated that New Zealand was generally open to providing direct assistance and funding of the relatively large administrative structured it had designed, in order to assist its protected stated states to overcome the perceived limitations imposed upon them by the smallness and other geo-demographic factors. It is therefore not surprising that when a decade after the Cook Islands' move to independence, the same process took place on an island perceived to be even more geographically constrained and vulnerable, Niue's leaders were anxious to secure and the New Zealand's government is willing to provide an even stronger commitment to active protection of the island's politico-economic viability.

Just like the Cook Islanders, Niueans have remained New Zealand citizens, and their territory is considered as part of New Zealand for the purpose of obtaining New Zealand citizenship by birth. The institution of shared citizenship has been the key mechanism through which Niue has been able to outsource the provision of some of the key public goods to its protecting power. At the same time, just like the Cook Islands, shared citizenship should not be interpreted as non-compatible with sovereign statehood.

Politically, Niue meets all the common criteria for statehood. Just like the Cook Islands, it is free to unilaterally break (via a referendum) its relationship with New Zealand at any time, and since its independence, it has gradually established its presence in the international arena (Gillard 2012, 126). It maintains diplomatic relations with a number of larger states including China, India, France, Italy, Brazil, Japan, Turkey, and Australia. It is also a member of some of the key international organization, such as the World Health Organization, Food and Agriculture Organization, and United Nations Educational, Scientific and Cultural Organization.

Conclusion

There has been a considerable amount of confusion regarding the political status and place in the international system of the Cook Islands and Niue. Much of the puzzlement is due to not just their small size or remoteness, but due to the existence of strong institutional links between the two polities and their former metropolitan power, New Zealand. In particular, a lot of controversy has been generated by the fact that, despite their countries' formal independence, both the Cook Islanders and Niueans have retained New Zealand citizenships, and their states have remained considered as part of New Zealand for the purpose of obtaining New Zealand citizenship. On the surface, the institution of shared citizenship, as well as the fact that New Zealand has been acting as the guarantor of the two entities' political survival and economic well-being, might seem to suggest that the Cook Islands and Niue are not sovereign states but rather dependencies or autonomous sub-national jurisdictions of New Zealand.

However, as this chapter has demonstrated, a more careful analysis of these arrangements reveals that such arrangements are not inconsistent with the concept of sovereign statehood. Both the Cook Islands and Niue can be viewed as valid examples of microstates understood as a modern protected states. A combination of their small size, geostrategic insignificance, and specific historical circumstances has led to their formation as New Zealand's protected states. In order to overcome the constraints imposed on them by their geography and demographics, they have voluntarily delegated the exercise of certain basic authority to New Zealand in exchange for benign protection of their political and economic viability, via both direct assistance and the institution of shared citizenship. While this kind of arrangement might seem unorthodox, it is not unlike the arrangements formed between a number of European microstates and their respective larger neighbors. Just like them, the Cook Islands and Niue demonstrate that small size and lack of geopolitical importance are not necessarily handicaps but can be positive factors permitting, given favorable historical circumstances, certain political units to secure and sustain unusually advantageous arrangements with larger powers.

Cross-References

▶ Faamatai: A Globalized Pacific Identity
▶ The Significance of Ethno-politics in Modern States and Society

References

AJPA (1994) Symposium on the governance of small and Island States. Asian J Public Adm 16(1)
Alesina A (2003) The size of countries: does it matter? J Eur Econ Assoc 1(2–3):301–316. https://doi.org/10.1162/154247603322390946. (January 19, 2013)
Alexandrowicz CH (1973) The European-African confrontation: a study in treaty making. Sijthoff, Leiden. http://www.amazon.com/The-European-African-confrontation-treaty-making/dp/9028603034. (November 22, 2012)
Amstrup N (1976) The perennial problem of small states: a survey of research efforts. Coop Confl 11(2):163–182. https://doi.org/10.1177/001083677601100202. (June 20, 2013)
Andrews J (2001) Cook Islands put NZ citizenship first. New Zealand Herald, Auckland
Armstrong HW, Read R (1995) Western European micro-states and EU autonomous regions: the advantages of size and sovereignty. World Dev 23(I):1229–1245. http://www.sciencedirect.com/science/article/pii/0305750X9500040J. (November 12, 2012)
Armstrong HW, Read R (1998) Trade and growth in small states: the impact of global trade liberalisation. World Econ 21(4):563–585. https://doi.org/10.1111/1467-9701.00148
Asian Development Bank (2008) Cook Islands 2008 social and economic report. Asian Development Bank, Manila
Baldacchino G (2006) Small islands versus big cities: lessons in the political economy of regional development from the world's small islands. J Technol Transf 31:91–100. http://www.springerlink.com/index/y3742p94378p32u3.pdf. (September 4, 2013)
Barker JC (2000) Hurricanes and socio-economic development on Niue Island. Asia Pac Viewp 41(2):191–205. https://doi.org/10.1111/1467-8373.00115

Bartmann B (2012) From the wings to the footlights: the international relations of Europe's smallest states. Commonw Comp Polit (March 2013):37–41. http://www.tandfonline.com/doi/abs/10.1080/14662043.2012.729734. (March 10, 2013)

Baty T (1921) Protectorates and Mandates. Br Yearb Int Law 1. http://heinonlinebackup.com/hol-cgi-bin/get_pdf.cgi?handle=hein.journals/byrint2&section=14. (November 20, 2012)

Benedict B (1967) Problem of smaller territories. University of London, Athlone Press, London. http://books.google.com/books?id=NA7QPgAACAAJ&pgis=1. (May 24, 2012)

Berridge GR, Lloyd L (2012) The Palgrave Macmillan dictionary of diplomacy (Google EBook). Palgrave Macmillan. http://books.google.com/books?id=jvarq4iy5MoC&pgis=1. (November 22, 2012)

Bertram G (1987) The political economy of decolonisation and nationhood in small pacific societies. In: Hooper A et al (eds) Class and culture in the Pacific. Centre for Pacific Studies, University of Auckland and Institute of Pacific Studies, University of the South Pacific

Bertram G, Watters R (1984) New Zealand and its small island neighbours: a review of New Zealand Policy toward the Cook Islands, Niue, Tokelau, Kiribati and Tuvalu. Institute of Policy Studies, Working Paper (October). http://ips.ac.nz/publications/files/3aa5ea29775.pdf. (November 17, 2012)

Blocker J, Gulati M (2017) Forced secessions. Law Contemp Probl 220 pp. 215–247

Bray M, Fergus H (1986) The implications of size for educational development in small countries: Montserrat, a Caribbean case study. Compare: 37–41. http://www.tandfonline.com/doi/abs/10.1080/0305792860160106. (February 17, 2013)

Cardno (2016) An assessment of the costs and benefits of mining deep-sea minerals in the Pacific Island Region: deep-sea mining cost-benefit analysis/Pacific Community. SPC Tech, Suva

Catudal HM (1975) The plight of the Lilliputians: an analysis of five European microstates. Geoforum 6:187–204. http://www.sciencedirect.com/science/article/pii/0016718575900238. (November 22, 2012)

Clark AL et al (1995) Economic and developmental potential of manganese nodules within the Cook Islands Exclusive Economic Zone (EEZ). East-West Center, Hawaii

Clarke T (1979) The rules of the game. In: Crocombe R (ed) Cook islands politics: the inside story. Polynesian Press, Auckland

Connell J (2007) 'The best island on the globe': constantly constructing tourism on Niue. Aust Geogr 38(1):1–13. https://doi.org/10.1080/00049180601175832. (November 17, 2012)

Cook Islands Government (2015) Cook Islands: National infrastructure investment plan. Cook Islands Government, Rarotonga

Cook Islands Parliament (2004) Cook Islands constitution. http://www.parliament.gov.ck/Constitution.pdf

Cooks Citizenship Shouldn't Be Part of UN Membership Discussion (2015) Radio New Zealand

Cooks to Take More Direct Approach to Seabed Mining (2016) Radio New Zealand. http://www.radionz.co.nz/international/pacific-news/297239/cooks-to-take-more-direct-approach-to-seabed-mining. (May 6, 2017)

Crawford JR (2007) The creation of states in international law. Oxford University Press, Oxford. http://www.amazon.com/The-Creation-States-International-Law/dp/0199228426. (November 19, 2012)

Crocombe R (1978) Nepotism in the cook islands. J Sociol 14(2):166–172

Crocombe, Ron. 1979. Forces shaping the arena. Cook Islands politics: the inside story. Ron Crocombe. Auckland: Polynesian Press

Crocombe R, Tongia M, Araitia T (2008) Absentee landowners in the Cook Islands: consequences of change to tradition. Making Land Work 2:153–171. http://www.sprep.org/att/IRC/eCOPIES/Pacific_Region/251.pdf#page=158. (September 23, 2013)

Dommen E (1985) States, microstates and islands. Routledge Kegan & Paul, London. http://www.amazon.com/States-Microstates-Islands-Edward-Dommen/dp/0709908628. (August 9, 2012)

Dumienski Z (2014) Microstates as modern protected states: towards a new definition of micro-statehood. Center for Small States Studies, Reykjavik

Duursma JC (1996) Fragmentation and the international relations of micro-states: self-determination and statehood. Cambridge University Press, Cambridge, UK. http://books.google.com/books?hl=en&lr=&id=CgVDprXjkIYC&pgis=1. (November 22, 2012)

Duval DT, Winchester N (2011) Cost sharing in air-service provision. J Air Law Commer 76:77–96

East MA (1973) Size and foreign policy behavior: a test of two models. World Polit: Q J Int 25(4):556–576. http://www.jstor.org/stable/10.2307/2009952. (March 11, 2013)

Eccardt TM (2005) Secrets of the seven smallest states of Europe: Andorra, Liechtenstein, Luxemborg, Malta, Monaco, San Marino, and Vatican City. Hippocrene Books, New York. http://books.google.com/books?hl=en&lr=&id=gQFzO_v_uwwC&pgis=1. (November 22, 2012)

Fairbairn T'o IJ, Pearson JM (1987) Entrepreneurship in the Cook Islands. East-West Center, Honolulu

Frame A (1987) The external affairs and defence of the Cook Islands – the 'Riddiford Clause' considered. Vic Univ Wellingt Law Rev 17:141–151

Gillard CA (2012) 1994 sovereignty, self-determination and the South-West Pacific: a comparison of the status of Pacific Island Territorial Entities in International Law. University of Waikato. http://researchcommons.waikato.ac.nz/handle/10289/7589. (July 8, 2014)

Gilson RP (1955) The background of New Zealand's early land policy in Rarotonga. J Polynesian Soc 64(3):267–280

Gilson RP (1980) In: Crocombe R (ed) The Cook Islands 1820–1950. Victoria University Press, Wellington. http://books.google.co.ck/books/about/The_Cook_Islands_1820_1950.html?id=CMxwbTquFlgC&pgis=1. (October 7, 2013)

Goetschel L (1998) Small states inside and outside the European Union interests and policies. Springer, New York. http://www.amazon.com/States-Outside-European-Interests-Policies/dp/0792382803. (March 11, 2013)

Government of Niue (2017) Parliament. http://www.gov.nu/wb/pages/parliament.php

Grydehøj A (2011) Making the most of smallness: economic policy in microstates and sub-national island jurisdictions. Space Polity. https://doi.org/10.1080/13562576.2011.692578. (November 12, 2012)

Gunter MM (1974) Liechtenstein and the league of nations: a precedent for the united nation's ministate problem? Am J Int Law 68(3):496–501. http://www.jstor.org/stable/10.2307/2200519. (November 29, 2013)

Harden S (1985) Small is dangerous: micro states in a macro world. Palgrave Macmillan, London. http://www.amazon.com/Small-Is-Dangerous-Micro-States/dp/0312729812. (July 11, 2012)

Hass MA (2004) Geopolitics and nations: why Liechtensteiners exist. SSRN Electron J. 1–35. http://www.ssrn.com/abstract=958866

Hein JR et al (2015) Critical metals in manganese nodules from the Cook Islands EEZ, abundances and distributions. Ore Geol Rev 68:97–116. https://doi.org/10.1016/j.oregeorev.2014.12.011

Herr RA (1988) Microstate sovereignty in the South Pacific: is small practical? Contemp Southeast Asia 10(2):182–196. http://www.jstor.org/stable/10.2307/25798002. (May 7, 2012)

Hey JAK (2003) Small states in world politics: explaining foreign policy behavior. Lynne Rienner Publishers, Boulder. http://books.google.com/books?hl=en&lr=&id=WP1_-k2RGoMC&pgis=1. (March 11, 2013)

Hintjens HM, Newitt MDD (1992) The political economy of small tropical islands: the importance of being small. University of Exeter Press, Exeter. http://books.google.com/books?hl=en&lr=&id=V3rF_DgXtC0C&pgis=1. (April 17, 2012)

Hobsbawm E (1992) Nations and nationalism since 1780: programme, myth, reality. Cambridge University Press, Cambridge, UK. http://books.google.com/books?id=OHz70fY8t2UC&pgis=1. (November 19, 2012)

Hobsbawm E (1996) The age of extremes: a history of the world, 1914–1991. Vintage, New York. http://www.amazon.com/The-Age-Extremes-History-1914-1991/dp/0679730052. (May 23, 2012)

Hoffmann-Dumieński K (2016) Professional development across the islands of the South Pacific a qualitative study of blended learning facilitators in the Cook Islands. J Open Flex Dist Learn 22:66–78

Ingram IP (2004) The need to review land use in the cook islands and the potential for community visioning:1–5

Ingram T, Uhrle M (2004) Transparency international country study report: Cook Islands 2004. Transparency International Australia, Victoria

Is Monaco Doomed? Other Nations Want It (1910) The New York Times

James A (1986) Sovereign statehood: the basis of international society. Allen & Unwin, London

Johnston WR (1973) Sovereignty and protection: a study of British jurisdictional imperialism in the late nineteenth century. Published for the Duke University Commonwealth-Studies Center [by] Duke University Press. http://books.google.com/books?id=ShiOAAAAMAAJ&pgis=1. (November 22, 2012)

Joint Centenary Declaration of the Principles of the Relationship between the Cook Islands and New Zealand (2001)

Jonassen JTM (1996) Disappearing islands?: management of microstate foreign affairs and the potential impact of alternative general futures: the case of the Cook Islands. University of Hawaii. http://scholar.google.com/scholar?hl=en&btnG=Search&q=intitle:Disappearing+islands+?+Management+of+microstate+foreign+affairs+and+the+Potential+Impact+of+Alternative+General+Fututres:+the+Case+of+the+Cook+Islands#0. (November 12, 2012)

Jonassen JTM (2011) Cook islands. In: Levine S (ed) Pacific ways: government and politics in the Pacific Islands. Victoria University Press, Wellington. http://www.ingentaconnect.com/content/paaf/paaf/2011/00000084/00000002/art00056

Jonassen JTM (2013) Cook islands political reform: toward 2055. In: Crowl L, Crocombe MT, Dixon R (eds) Ron Crocombe: E Toa! Pacific writings to celebrate his life and work. University of South Pacific Press, Suva

Katzenstein PJ (1985) Small states in world markets: industrial policy in Europe (Cornell studies in political economy). Cornell University Press, Ithaca. http://www.amazon.com/Small-States-World-Markets-Industrial/dp/0801493269. (February 5, 2013)

Keohane RO (1969) Lilliputians' dilemmas: small states in international politics. Int Organ 23(02):291–310. http://www.journals.cambridge.org/abstract_S002081830003160X. (June 27, 2013)

Maass M (2009) The elusive definition of the small state. Int Polit 46(1):65–83. http://www.palgrave-journals.com/doifinder/10.1057/ip.2008.37. (March 4, 2014)

Marsters E (2017) Rethinking Cook Islands Free Association Agreement with NZ, part 2. Impolitikal. https://impolitikal.com/2017/04/06/rethinking-the-cook-islands-free-association-agreement-with-nz-part-2/

McKinnon M (2013) Interdependence and foreign policy: New Zealand in the world since 1935. Auckland University Press, Auckland. https://books.google.co.nz/books?id=0tZaAwAAQBAJ&printsec=frontcover&dq=inauthor:%22Malcolm+McKinnon%22&hl=en&sa=X&ved=0ahUKEwi2n6WiwKrVAhXCtpQKHSWoDvkQ6AEINTAD#v=onepage&q=cookislands&f=false. (July 28, 2017)

McNicoll IJ (1989) Government policies toward the development of the Chatham Islands: a comparison with the Niue experience

Mehmet O, Tahiroglu M (2002) Growth and equity in microstates: does size matter in development? Int J Soc Econ 29(1/2):152–162. http://www.emeraldinsight.com/10.1108/03068290210413047. (March 4, 2012)

Milne S (1992) Tourism development in Niue. Ann Tour Res 1988(Milne 1988):565–569. http://scholar.google.com/scholar?hl=en&btnG=Search&q=intitle:Tourism+Development+in+Niue#0. (May 27, 2014)

Milne D (2000) Ten lessons for economic development in small jurisdictions: the European perspective. http://www.upei.ca/iis/rep_dm_1. (April 25, 2012)

Ministry of Finance and Economic Management (2013) Cook Islands demographic profile 2006–2011. Cook Islands Government, Rarotonga

Mohamed AN (2002) The diplomacy of micro-states. Int Relat. http://www.nbiz.nl/publications/2002/20020100_cli_paper_dip_issue78.pdf. (May 17, 2012)

13 Shared Citizenship and Sovereignty: The Case of the Cook Islands'... 245

Neate R (2013) Seabed mining could earn Cook Islands 'Tens of Billions of Dollars'. The Guardian. https://www.theguardian.com/business/2013/aug/05/seabed-mining-cook-islands-billions. (May 6, 2017)

Neemia UF (1995) Smallness, Islandness and foreign policy behaviour: aspects of island microstates foreign policy behaviour with special reference to Cook Islands and Kiribati. University of Wollongong. http://ro.uow.edu.au/theses/1439/. (March 8, 2013)

Neumann IB, Gstöhl S (2004) Lilliputians in Gulliver's world? Small states in international relations. University of Iceland, Reykjavik

New Zealand Parliament (1964) Cook islands constitution act. http://www.legislation.govt.nz/act/public/1964/0069/latest/whole.html

New Zealand Parliament (1974) Niue Constitution Act. New Zealand Parliament, Wellington

Orlow D (1995) Of nations small: the small state in international law. Temp Int Comp Law J 1. http://heinonlinebackup.com/hol-cgi-bin/get_pdf.cgi?handle=hein.journals/tclj9&section=10. (November 18, 2012)

Parrish W (1990) The security of very small states. University of Maryland, College Park

Parry C (1960) Nationality and citizenship laws of the commonwealth and the republic of Ireland. Stevens & Sons. http://www.amazon.co.uk/Nationality-Citizenship-Commonwealth-Republic-Ireland/dp/0420372601. (November 22, 2012)

Parsons R (1968) Self-determination and political development in Niue. J Polynesian Soc 77(3):242–262. http://scholar.google.com/scholar?hl=en&btnG=Search&q=intitle:SELF-DETERMINATION+AND+POLITICAL+DEVELOPMENT+IN+NIUE#1. (June 3, 2014)

Plischke E (1977) Microstates in world affairs: policy problems and options (studies in foreign policy). AEI Press. http://www.amazon.com/Microstates-World-Affairs-Problems-Options/dp/0844732419. (July 11, 2012)

Pointer M (2015) Niue 1774–1974: 200 years of contact and change. Otago University Press, Dunedin

Quentin-Baxter A (1999) Niue's relationship of free association with New Zealand. Victoria Univ Wellingt Law Rev 30:589–598

Quentin-Baxter A (2000) The problems of islands. Vic Univ Wellingt Law Rev 31:429

Quentin-Baxter A (2009) The New Zealand model of free association: what does it mean for New Zealand? Victoria Univ Wellingt Law Rev 39:607–634

Reid GL (1975) Impact of very small size on the international behaviour of microstates (international studies). Sage, London. http://www.amazon.com/Impact-International-Behaviour-Microstates-Studies/dp/0803904061. (March 24, 2013)

Reti MJ (2008) An assessment of the impact of climate an assessment of the impact of climate change on agriculture and food security in the Pacific: a case study in the Cook Islands. Food and Agriculture Organization of the United Nations, Rome

Ross A (1964) New Zealand aspirations in the pacific in the nineteenth century. Clarendon Press, Oxford

Samoglou E (2014) Seabed mining: need to protect environment. Cook Islands News. http://www.cookislandsnews.com/item/46770-seabed-mining-need-to-protect-environment/46770-seabed-mining-need-to-protect-environment. (May 6, 2017)

Sawyer C (2013) The loss of birthright citizenship in New Zealand. Vic Univ Wellingt Law Rev 44:653–674

Schumacher EF (1973) 9 nature methods small is beautiful. http://www.ncbi.nlm.nih.gov/pubmed/24687246

Schwebel SM (1973) Mini-states and a more effective United Nations. Am J Int Law 67(1):108–116. http://www.jstor.org/stable/10.2307/2199098. (November 13, 2012)

Scott D (1991) Years of the pooh-bah: a Cook Islands history. CITC, Auckland

Sieber M (1983) Dimensions of small states dependence: the case of Switzerland. In: Small states in Europe and dependence. Austrian Institute for International Affairs, Vienna, pp 107–129

Simpson AW (2007) A theory of disfunctionality: the European micro-states as disfunctional states in the international system. University of Aberdeen. http://gradworks.umi.com/U2/33/U233251.html. (July 28, 2014)

Small V, Day S (2015). Cook Islands push for independence from NZ. Stuff.co.nz. http://www.stuff.co.nz/world/south-pacific/68986939/cook-islands-push-for-independence-from-nz

Smith SE (2010) Uncharted waters: has the Cook Islands become eligible for membership in the United Nations. NZJPIL 1. http://heinonlinebackup.com/hol-cgi-bin/get_pdf.cgi?handle=hein.journals/nzjpubinl8&section=16. (November 20, 2012)

Smylie C (2014) The devil in the deep blue sea. NZ Listener. http://www.noted.co.nz/archive/listener-nz-2014/the-devil-in-the-deep-blue-sea/. (May 6, 2017)

Srinivasan TN (1986) The costs and benefits of being a small, remote, island, landlocked, or Ministate economy. World Bank Res Obs 1(2):205–218. http://wbro.oxfordjournals.org/content/1/2/205.short. (July 19, 2012)

Stone DJ (1965) Self-determination in the Cook Islands: a reply. J Polynesian Soc 74(3). http://www.jstor.org/stable/20704261

Stone DJ (1971) Self-rule in the Cook Islands: the government and politics of a new micro-state. Australian National University, Canberra

Strickland M (1979) Self-government and the new colonialism. In: Crocombe R (ed) Cook Islands politics: the inside story. Polynesian Press, Auckland

Stringer K (2006) An economic diagnosis of Palau through the Liechtenstein lens. East West Centre working papers. http://scholarspace.manoa.hawaii.edu/bitstream/handle/10125/3281/IGSCwp026.pdf?sequence=1. (April 10, 2012)

Sundhaussen U (2003) Peasants and the process of building democratic polities: lessons from San Marino. Aust J Polit Hist 49(2):211–221. https://doi.org/10.1111/1467-8497.00305/abstract. (November 22, 2012)

Sutton P (2011) The concept of small states in the international political economy. Round Table 100(413):141–153. http://www.tandfonline.com/doi/abs/10.1080/00358533.2011.565625. (March 25, 2013)

Syme-Buchanan F (2015) Lagoon national disaster! Cook Islands News. http://www.cookislandsnews.com/national/local/item/55320-lagoon-national-disaster/55320-lagoon-national-disaster. (May 7, 2017)

Tafatu O, Tukuitoga IJ (1982) Developments to annexation. In: Niue: a history of the island. Institute of Pacific Studies of the University of the South Pacific, Suva

Talagi M (2013) Politics, propositions and perspectives: Niue and nationhood. Solomua Press, Niue

Tõnurist P (2010) What is a 'Small State' in a globalizing economy? Halduskultuur Adm Cult 11(1):8–29

Treaty between the United States of America and the Cook Islands on Friendship and Delimitation of the Maritime Boundary between the United States of America and the Cook Islands (1980)

Turner W (2007) History of philosophy (3 vols. set). Global Vision Publishing Ho. http://books.google.com/books?id=vmyN0bMTth8C&pgis=1. (March 20, 2013)

United Nations (1945) Charter of the United Nations

Veenendaal W (2014) A big prince in a tiny realm: smallness, monarchy, and political legitimacy in the principality of Liechtenstein. Swiss Polit Sci Rev: n/a-n/a. http://doi.wiley.com/10.1111/spsr.12138. (November 9, 2014)

Veenendaal W (2015) Politics and democracy in microstates. Routledge, New York

Warrington E (1994) Lilliputs revisited. Asian J Public Adm 16(1):1–13

Webb P (2016) Cook Islands. In: Levine S (ed) Pacific ways: government and politics in the Pacific Islands. Victoria University Press, Wellington

Whimp G (2008) Writing the colony: Walter Edward gudgeon in the Cook Islands, 1898 to 1909. Victoria University of Wellington, Wellington

Wilson SD (1969) Cook islands development 1945–65. In: Ross A (ed) New Zealand's record in the Pacific Islands in the twentieth century. Longman Paul Limited, Auckland

State Hegemony and Ethnicity: Fiji's Problematic Colonial Past

14

Sanjay Ramesh

Contents

Introduction	248
Pre-cession Fiji: Establishing Bipolar Ethnicity	249
The Colony of Fiji: Toward Tri-Ethnic Discourse	253
Conclusion	261
References	262

Abstract

Indigenous Fijian polity before European contact was characterized by political contests and inter-tribal rivalry among indigenous Fijians. However, with the arrival of Europeans and their technology, indigenous warfare changed, enabling the chiefdom of Bau to become a hegemonic power in eastern Fiji via tactical political positioning and strategic maneuvers. The alliance between the chiefs and the Europeans was strengthened by the formation of the Cakobau government in 1871, but internal conflict between indigenous Fijians and Europeans over governance and security forced the Europeans and the chiefs to cede Fiji to Britain, which modeled indigenous administration as humanitarian colonialism. Disparate groups of indigenous Fijians subscribed to a singular cultural identity and the authority on indigenous land lay with the Council of Chiefs. In addition, the British introduced a new ethnic category to the colony of Fiji in the form of Indian indentured laborers, and this new ethnic group led to a three-tier ethnic structure where indigenous Fijians were owners of the land, Europeans controlled commerce and the economy, and Indians and Indo-Fijians provided cheap labor. The ethnic terrain chartered by the colonial administration in Fiji created a problematic historical landscape with constant Indian agitations for political equality and common roll before independence and indigenous Fijian and European resistance to Indian demands.

S. Ramesh (✉)
Department of Peace and Conflict Studies, University of Sydney, Camperdown, NSW, Australia
e-mail: sanjay.ramesh@sydney.edu.au

This chapter explores the ethnic history before cession and the historical and political dynamics of conflicting ethnic social forces.

Keywords

Bau · Chiefs · Europeans · Land · Gordon · Indians · Humanitarian colonialism

Introduction

Indigenous Fijian cultural history before European contact is little known, but the social order that existed provided for rich diverse cultural experience, even though violence and incessant warfare were common. Before the acceptance of the Wesley Mission by the Bauan chief, Ratu Seru Cakobau, indigenous Fijian tribes fought bloody battles and engaged in cannibal feasts as documented by colonial historian R. A. Derrick (1950). However, following contact with Europeans and the introduction of firearms, the chiefdom of Bau, in eastern Fiji, emerged as a hegemonic political power in eastern Fiji.

Europeans exploited indigenous resources for profit and formed alliances with various indigenous chiefs who mobilized commoners to harvest sandalwood and beche-de-mer, which were priced commodities overseas. With increased trade came demands for a stable government. However, divergent interests of chiefs and Europeans led to conflict and the eventual demise of the Cakobau government, established in 1871 by settlers to increase trade and investment in the Fiji islands. Fearing political instability and further conflict between Europeans and indigenous Fijians, the chiefs of Fiji ceded Fiji to Britain, which implemented a paternalistic indigenous policy based on the cultural experience of Bau. Not long after cession to Britain, conflict between the chiefs and the Europeans re-surfaced. Indigenous chiefs expressed concern over alienation of indigenous land, and as a result, the Native Land Ordinance was passed. Under the leadership of Governor Arthur Gordon, indigenous Fijian land rights were strengthened, and a new cultural group in the form of Indian indentured laborers was introduced. While Governor Gordon wanted to shield indigenous Fijians from the devastating effects of plantation labor, he had introduced to Fiji Indians who were politically active and after indenture in 1920 demanded political equality. Indigenous Fijian chiefs were concerned with the introduction of Indian laborers as successive governors, after Gordon, heightened fear among chiefs with calls for changing land legislations and introducing indigenous Fijians to plantation labor and commerce. In the end, the indigenous chiefs prevailed following the affirmation of Gordon's policies by the colonial authorities in the form of humanitarian governance (Lester and Dussart 2014). This chapter aims to trace the history of indigenous Fijians from pre-cession Fiji and in particular addresses the issue of colonial constitution on ethnicity which was established by largely the European conceptualization and understanding of indigenous Fijian culture and tradition. More importantly, there were competing ethnic social forces and political alliances in pre-cession and post-cession Fiji that influenced transition to self-rule.

Pre-cession Fiji: Establishing Bipolar Ethnicity

Indigenous Fijian chiefs are an important component in the indigenous social structure of Fiji. The chiefly system is not well understood by non-indigenous Fijians because the complexity of indigenous custom is based on the inter-relatedness of land (vanua), kalou (god), ratu (chief), and matanitu (body politic). Before and after European contact, the chiefs remained at the top of the indigenous Fijian social hierarchy. In most part of Fiji, chiefly clans were able to establish strategic alliances with their compatriots and form kingdoms and assert political hegemony. Out of these kingdoms emerged a group of powerful indigenous chiefs from eastern Fiji who competed for political power through incessant warfare and political control. According to Aubrey Parke (2014: 85):

> The most complex form of socio-organisational confederation is found in the eastern parts of Fiji, especially in areas which have come into close contact with influences and ideologies originating from outside Fiji, particularly those of monarchical or near-monarchical Tonga and perhaps also the highly stratified and status-differentiating Samoa.

In fact, in eastern Fiji, the war chiefs of Kubuna became paramount authority on matanitu as the eastern chiefs of Fiji became political power brokers in the first half of the nineteenth century and used their customary influences to position themselves strategically with collaborative partnership with Europeans. There were special rules regarding chiefs, and these were enforced with extreme prejudice, and as colonial historian R. A. Derrick (1950: 16) observed: "no person might reach for an object above the chief's head without first asking for and obtaining permission." Failure to adhere to customary laws meant punitive punishment including death, and the chiefs usually imposed their law with the assistance of the priests and warriors. In pre-cession Fiji warfare, rivalry among indigenous tribes was also widespread. Indigenous women from outside the tribe were aggressively sought by indigenous chiefs, and as a result abduction of women was commonplace. Besides competition for women, indigenous chiefs actively extended their tributary through violent invasions and subjugation of conquered territories.

Historian R. A. Derrick critically looked at the indigenous Fijian warfare strategy. According to him:

> A party would steal upon the sleeping village, surround it, and at the faint light of day, fire the houses. Then the stage was set for one of those scenes of horror that made Fijian's name infamous. Men, women, and children were butchered as they ran from the burning houses. (Derrick 1950: 25–26)

While endless feuding was a permanent character of pre-cession Fiji, there nevertheless existed an interdependent relationship among indigenous chiefs, village priests, warriors, and commoners. However, contact with the Polynesian Tonga modified the pre-cession Fijian social order and influenced the rise of the indigenous polity of Bau.

The Tongans had a long relationship with eastern Fijians. There were established movements of people, ideas, and objects between Tonga and Fiji.

By 1700, if not earlier, this traffic had become regularised in the form of Tongan and Samoan bark clothes, mats and whale teeth for Fijians canoes, red feathers, pottery, and sandalwood. Most of the transportation was done by Tongans but in Fijian type canoes (bartered directly from Fijians) or built by Tongans in Fiji. (Oliver 1989: 1151)

As a result of trade and movement of a large number of people, by 1840 a number of Tongans reside in Fiji. Some of them were living as craftsmen or traders or mercenaries in Fijian villages and some in colonies of their own (Oliver 1989: 1151). The long and extensive contact with Tonga produced a hierarchical political organization in the eastern parts of the Fiji Islands, including Bau, Lau, Bua, Macuata, Cakaudrove, Lakeba, and Moala.

In eastern Fiji, a Polynesian form of hierarchical social structure existed long before European contact. Shelley Ann Sayes explains the political hierarchy in Cakaudrove.

> The political organisation of Cakaudrove approximated the Polynesian model- an extensive pyramid of groups capped by the lineage and following a high chief. The head of vanua Cakaudrove, the Tui Cakau who was the member of the i Sokula lineage was the paramount chief of the matanitu. Subordinates of the Tui Cakau thought of them (members of the i Sokula lineage) as sacred, the descendants and representatives of the ancestral gods and as such, gods themselves. (Sayes 1984: 3)

Even though eastern Fiji had hierarchical social structures, the interdependence of the chiefs and his people remained intact, but with the European contact, the indigenous Fijian social system was restructured. Most significant European import was the introduction of firearms. According to J.D. Legge (1958: 11), "the introduction of firearms was perhaps the most momentous effect of the coming of Europeans, for it added a new feature to native wars and radically altered the balance of power between native kingdoms." In addition, European commercial ships started trading with the indigenous chiefs following a shipwreck in Lakeba which led to the discovery of sandalwood. The Europeans brought into Fiji muskets, steel implements, flint, navigational equipment, and foreign goods. According to R. A. Derrick (1950: 38), "from the islands in eastern Fiji, where the first white men landed, evidence of a strange new world emerged beyond the horizons of Fiji and Tonga spread westward throughout the group."

R. A. Derrick notes that every stick of sandalwood had blood upon it. He argued that "chief fought with chief in laying claim to patches of trees that had suddenly become valuable. They drove their people to cut logs, quarrelling over the spoils" (Derrick 1950: 43). However, David Routledge (1985: 44) claimed that the sandalwood trade involved limited contact between indigenous Fijians and Europeans. His position was supported by Peter France, who argued that "the effect of this trade on the lives of indigenous Fijians was limited to the provision of iron tools and glass beads for the common people and to military assistance for the chiefs of a small area on the west coast of Vanua Levu" (France 1969: 25).

The introduction of guns and iron tools radically altered the indigenous Fijian social structure. Traditional weapons such as spears, arrows, and clubs became ineffective in warfare, and after the 1830s, with increased trade, possession of a musket became an essential requisite of a properly equipped indigenous Fijian warrior. Firearms also played a significant role in the emergence of Bau as a hegemonic polity in eastern Fiji since it was first to obtain muskets with the assistance of a European sharpshooter, Charles Savage.

The structural power of Bau soon superseded that of its rivals, and its hegemonic position was established through militarization. Moreover, the leadership of the kingdom was taken up by young chief, Ratu Seru Cakobau, who played an important role in forming strategic alliances with rival chiefs and Europeans. According to R. A. Derrick (1950: 117) "Cakobau lived the best years of his life through a violent period of bloodshed and cannibalism and he took a leading part in all its horrors." After accepting Christianity in 1854, Cakobau formed alliances with European traders, missionaries, rival chiefs, and mercenaries and became the upholder of privilege and the exploiter of ancient indigenous custom. However, there were commercial forces operating in Fiji that were beyond the control of Ratu Cakobau.

European contact made Fiji part of the global political economy of the nineteenth century. In less than 10 years, all sandalwood stands were logged from Fiji. Afterward, European traders found a new marketable commodity called beche-de-mer. Beche-de-mer or dried flesh of the sea cucumbers was highly valued in China. According to R. Gerard Ward (1972), "the rise in beche-de-mer trade in Polynesia and Melanesia was closely linked with that of sandalwood, often providing an alternative income to traders faced with the depletion of the sandalwood resource." The beche-de-mer trade demanded that the islanders learn new tasks and sometimes undertake labor under European direction. The beche-de-mer lasted a little longer than the sandalwood trade (1822–1850), and during this period, traders and beachcombers started to settle on the islands. With growing European interest in Fiji's natural resources, information soon reached imperial centers of the world on potentials for economic investment and Christian missions. The introduction of Christianity transformed old Fiji by outlawing ancient practices such as cannibalism and widow strangulation which were widespread.

On 12 October 1835, the first members of the Wesleyan Methodist Missionary Society arrived in Fiji in the persons of Reverend William Cross and Reverend David Cargill (Clammer 1976: 9). Cross and Cargill realized that the conversion of chiefs to Christianity was a prerequisite for mass conversions of indigenous Fijians. The momentum to covert the indigenous population expanded in 1838 after John Hunt, James Calvert, and Thomas Jagger brought to the island a printing press and published the Bible. The missionaries and their agents utilized existing knowledge of the Tongan language to publish the Bible in the native text, and through the religious teachings of Jesus Christ, indigenous Fijians were encouraged to abandon past heathen and pagan customary practices.

The missionaries were agents of various imperial interests, and their presence on the island of Fiji was aimed at changing the customs of land (France 1969: 29). However, not only customary practices were being overhauled, but ethnic identity of indigenous Fijians was also getting transformed. By attacking the gods of indigenous Fijians, the Christian missionaries restructured the power of the indigenous chiefs. An indigenous Fijian chief derived spiritual power from the ancestral gods, and by discrediting their belief, Christian teachings reduced the old custom and ushered in a more rigid form of ethnic hierarchy (France 1969: 30). However, Christianity was not accepted with open arms by some indigenous Fijians, and for a while, there was fierce warfare between converts and holdouts. The issue of religion, nevertheless, was settled in 1854 when chief Cakobau acceded to a request of the King of Tonga and accepted the Wesleyan Mission (Oliver 1989: 197). By the mid-nineteenth century, the indigenous Fijian traditional social order was successfully transformed by European contact and more importantly by Australian migration (Young 1984). In particular, an influx of Europeans created new inter-ethnic tensions as Europeans established settlements on indigenous land provided for by the chiefs (Tippett 1955: 212–219). However, the new European-inspired social arrangement rested on a fragile socioeconomic arrangement.

There were sporadic attacks on European property, and in one such incident, outrages were committed against an American citizen, who filed a legal suit against the indigenous chiefs of Fiji. European settlers wanted to establish a functioning government to ensure security of European property and investment in the islands. The Europeans manipulated the hegemonic position of Bau and installed Ratu Seru Cakobau as "Tui Viti" or the King of Fiji (Lawson 1991: 48). The move by the Europeans established defacto rule of Bau over all the islands of Fiji, even though there were growing resentment to eastern Fiji from various tribes of western Viti Levu. Moreover, the Europeans were positioning themselves for a more labor-intensive investment in cotton, copra, and potentially sugar.

By the 1860s, the beche-de-mer trade had dropped off significantly, and other export commodities, like coffee and cocoa, were introduced by European settlers. A short-lived cotton boom occurred when world cotton shortage, caused by the American Civil War (1861–1865), prompted many would-be planters to the island, thereby increasing the stake in land and local politics (Oliver 1989: 198). The cotton boom was short, but within this period, there was a surge in migration, and in 1871, Europeans settlers convinced Cakobau to establish a functioning government. Not least among Europeans motivation was the need for political stability, security, and possession of indigenous land. However, factions and divisions emerged between the European community and the chiefs, resulting in the demise of the Cakobau government (France 1969: 92).

The initiative to establish a government enabled European settlers to form political and economic alliances with indigenous chiefs of eastern Fiji. Most significant ally of the Europeans was Cakobau, who was keen on consolidating his authority on all parts of Fiji. In 1873, using the killing of a settler community as an excuse, the Cakobau government launched an invasion against the defiant Hill Tribes of interior Viti Levu (Howard 1991: 23). After defeating the rebels, Cakobau expropriated their land and sold it to the Europeans. The subjugation of the Hill Tribes had a profound impact on the western part of the main island of Viti Levu, where indigenous Fijians carried out attacks against Christian missions and Europeans generally.

Despite the initial subjugation of the rebellious tribes of interior Viti Levu, the Cakobau government failed to provide order and good governance required by the growing European community. As a result, with the assistance of indigenous chiefs, representations were made to a number of imperial powers for the cession of the islands. After initially rejecting the offer, Britain reconsidered its position following reports that British nationals were involved in labor traffic in the Pacific Islands.

The Colony of Fiji: Toward Tri-Ethnic Discourse

Concern about the abuse of Pacific Islanders by commercially minded Europeans was one of the reasons for Fiji's cession. Britain understood Fiji primarily from the interpretations provided by the chiefs of eastern Fiji, where Bauan influence had led to cultural and social synchronization across the tribes in the region. More importantly, the cession of Fiji to Britain strengthened the cultural hegemony of Bau.

On 10 October 1874, the chiefs of eastern Fiji Vunivalu Cakobau, Maafu, Ratu Epeli, Tui Bua, Savenaca, Esekeli, Tui Dreketi, Ritova, Katonivere, Ratu Kini, Matanitobua, and Nacagilevu ceded Fiji to Britain. The cession was inevitable, because the Cakobau government (1871–1874) was virtually bankrupt and the European population wanted a stable political authority to protect their economic interests.

The provisional governor of Fiji, Sir Hercules Robinson, inherited the task of administering Fijians. Borrowing from the political and social organizations of the Bauan chiefdom, he grouped the islands of the colony into provinces, based on boundaries of the old state, and within the province, a number of divisions were created, each compromising a group of villages related by kinship. Each of these administrative units – the village, the district, and the province – was placed in charge of a Fijian, and there was a chain of responsibility from the lowest level to the highest (Roth 1953: 135).

The British colonial government brought to the island the concept of "humanitarian colonialism which was crystallised out of the complex assemblages and networks of the newly expended empire" (Lester and Dussart 2014: 23). The concept of humanitarian colonialism emerged from colonial governance, which continued to consider itself humane. Hence the protectionist project in Fiji initiated a new era in colonial history where ethnicity was established using three forms of categorization: white settlers, indigenous Fijian, and later Indian indentured workers. White settler community and the British colonial administration were the white elite, indigenous Fijians were labeled "exogenous others" who resided within the boundaries of the colonial entity, conveniently excluded from exercising any political authority (Veracini 2011: 26–27) and the "abject others," notably Indian indentured laborers who were permanently excluded via rigid ethnic boundaries and political control.

It is within this humanitarian colonialism and ethnic boundaries the British colonial authorities restructured the indigenous administrative system by giving exclusive jurisdiction on indigenous affairs to the Council of Chiefs, *Boselevu*

Vakaturaga, which was a new institution, based on the collective political experience of the chiefs in the pre-Cession Cakobau Government. Despite dominated by the chiefs from the eastern Fiji, the Council became the official custodian of indigenous land, culture, tradition, customary rights, and social relations. Besides, the Council helped entrench British indirect rule by ensuring acceptance of the imperial rule by indigenous Fijians. The colonial and the indigenous Fijian customary administrations were "networked associations" that "decentered both white and indigenous agency" (Lester and Dussart 2014: 32). The decentered element was the distance between the political hegemony of the colonial administration and the indigenous Fijian administration (Norton 2013: 409–428).

The Council of Chiefs played an important role in steering the colonial policy on indigenous land where the governor consulted indigenous chiefs on the status of indigenous land while reserving the right to make decision on all land alienation. The Deed of Cession of 1874 was interpreted in a way that created the popular myth of a protective or humanitarian colonial policy toward the natives. According to Macnaught, "in the Fijian popular mind the lands had been given by the chiefs to the Queen *Vakaturaga*, that is, by way of a chiefly presentation which entitled them to expect that the Queen in her reciprocal generosity would return the lands to be shared and used by the people" (Macnaught 1982: 30).

The first governor to Fiji, Sir Arthur Hamilton Gordon, cemented a protective and humanitarian colonial policy by establishing and strengthening the Council of Chiefs and the associated Fijian administration, modeled around the customary experience of eastern Fiji and the logic of colonial constitution where the Europeans established political hegemony and indigenous population established their own zones of social transcourse within the colonial socioeconomic system. Gordon was a conservative at heart and campaigned against self-government in the North American Colony of New Brunswick. However, his apparent lack of success in North America left him bitter and disillusioned with London. Nevertheless, he was very well read and had intimate knowledge of the cultural destruction of the indigenous peoples of North America, West Indies, and Australia (Lemarchana 2011). As a convert to preserving indigenous way of life, Gordon was determined to safeguard indigenous Fijian culture. But according to historian Peter France, Gordon's understanding of indigenous Fijian affairs was fundamentally flawed. According to him: "to begin with, Gordon did not speak or write indigenous Fijian and was further estranged by his adoption of the position of a high chief" (France 1969: 104–105). A lack of indigenous languages greatly affected Gordon's ability to comprehend the nuances of indigenous Fijian culture and customary practices. As a result, he relied excessively on interpretations from more nuanced white settlers and their political agents in the colonial administration.

Gordon claimed that the provincial, district, and village indigenous social systems were firmly established in indigenous Fijian tradition. However, this was not the case for all of Fiji. In western Viti Levu, a different form of social organization and hierarchies existed (Brewster 1922). Nevertheless, Gordon saw *Roko Tui* (the Provincial chief), *Buli* (District Chief), and *Turanga-ni-koro* (the village head) working well with the colonial administration, and as a result, a Fijian administration was informally established. Indigenous Fijian labor was regulated through a paternalistic tax policy, where male indigenous Fijian between the ages of 16 and 60 contributed 20 days labor on public works in the province, including road works, improving provincial offices, hospitals, and gardens. Gordon believed that in such a policy, Fijians would have minimum impact in the indigenous way of life and would preserve the communal mode of production of indigenous Fijians.

Besides a paternalistic tax policy, the Deed of Cession allowed the chiefs, together with the colonial government, to oversee the utilization and the alienation of indigenous land. European settlers in Fiji wanted to acquire indigenous land for commercial agriculture and even before cession taken indigenous land through deception. As a result, the Council of Chiefs was reluctant to alienate any indigenous land. However, by the virtue of the Deed, the colonial government had exclusive legal jurisdiction on the economic development of the Colony, and as such, Sir Arthur Gordon decided to develop the sugar industry in the colony by importing Indian indentured laborers from 1879 to 1916 (Lal 1980: 52–70).

It is important to note at this point that Gordon saw coercing indigenous Fijians and bringing them into the colonial plantation economy as an abomination that would ultimately lead to the demise of the native and as Bruce Knaplund observed, Gladstone at the Colonial Secretary Office noted the following: "I think your spirit and feeling towards the natives (in Fiji) is an honour for the empire" (Knaplund 1958: 296), and keeping with the spirit of humanitarian influences in colonial policy, "Gordon sought a stabilising factor between the welfare and prosperity of the Fijians and the commercial success of the white settlers and found it in the introduction of Indian labourers" (Cumpston 1956: 371).

In introducing Indians to the Colony of Fiji, Gordon had introduced a third ethnic group, which had different customary practices to indigenous Fijians and Europeans. The colonial administration controlled the political affairs of the state in collaboration with the white settlers, and indigenous Fijian chiefs provided advice to the governor through the Council of Chiefs and ensured that the Fijian administration in place functioned without much disruption. Indian indentured laborers, however, were permanently excluded from any form of political representation. According to Loretta de Plevitz (2010: 181), Indian laborers "were treated worse than African slaves," but more importantly Gordon was more concerned with "settling tribal disputes" which was a hangover from the problems that emanated from the initial European contact. Nevertheless, the colonial administration had formed an opinion on the pathway for the sugar industry in the Colony of Fiji which required abundant supply of Indian labor. However, this labor was not cheap, and Gordon's insistence on preserving indigenous way of life caused frictions.

> Gordon's plan caused outrage in the humanitarian societies in England. In Fiji the Europeans vociferously rejected it on the grounds that Islanders could be 'got' for £3, half Gordon's proposed annual wage for Indians. Further, Indians would prefer to return home with their wages in hard cash whereas Islanders stimulated the flagging economy by buying, and being paid in, trade goods. The locals proposed an alternative scheme – all Fijian men between the ages of 15 and 50 should be 'apprenticed to the planters for 5 years and in consideration of being taught a valuable industry receive no pay during that time. (de Plevitz 2010: 189)

In the end, Gordon got what he wanted as coolie ships continued to come to Fiji with able bodied men and women, considered ready for sugar plantation. The establishment of the sugar industry led to further alienation and pressure on indigenous land, resulting in intervention from indigenous chiefs and the colonial administration and the enactment of the Native Land Ordinances. While Indian labour proved quite successful in developing and extending a viable sugar economy, indentured labours started agitating for better wages and working conditions. For the colonial government, Indian labor provided indigenous Fijians the time needed to absorb the impact of colonial rule, arrested the steady decline in their numbers, and enabled the indigenous community to enjoy the unusual institutions that had given them a powerful voice in colonial policy (Macnaught 1982: 2). However, after the end of indenture, Indians in Fiji demanded political equality and embarked on a series of anti-colonial campaigns, which caused concern among indigenous Fijian chiefs and the colonial administration.

Realizing that there was a militant ethnic group in the colony, successive governors, after Gordon, attempted without success to introduce indigenous Fijians to commerce and open up indigenous land. The failures it seems emanated from the colonial structure and in particular from the policy of humanitarian colonialism that laid the foundation for protection of indigenous culture and tradition. Demands for air tight protection of native land from the Council of Chiefs in particular led to frictions as new constitution on ethnic governance in the Colony was put into operation. This form of unwritten constitution on ethnicity evolved after the arrival of Indian indentured workers in 1879 and shaped considerably during post-World War II and further matured just before independence.

Following the end of tenure of Governor Gordon in 1880, successive governors largely continued with Gordon's policy. However at the beginning of the twentieth century, governors in Fiji Everard im Thurn and George O' Brien defined indigenous Fijian political autonomy as the governing of the natives through the chiefs and for the chiefs. Governor im Thurn argued that Gordon's interpretation of the Deed of the Cession was a conspiracy to defraud the crown of its legitimate assets: indigenous Fijian land and labor. He reviewed the history of indigenous Fijian land transaction as "one great blunder from the beginning" and emphasized that land boundaries shifted due to tribal conflict in pre-cession Fiji and that determining land boundaries with any degree of accuracy was not possible in the Colony of Fiji (Knapman 1992: 32). Everard im Thurn wanted to release indigenous Fijians from the "iron" customs which, according to the governor, prevented them from participating fully in the colonial economy. However, the ideas of Governors O'Brien and im Thurn were dismissed by the colonial secretary in Great Britain, following intense lobby from members of the Council of Chiefs. The colonial head office reiterated its support for the humanitarian policy toward indigenous Fijians and supported managing competing ethnic interests through greater collaboration between the Council of Chiefs and the colonial administration.

The Chief-Gordon viewpoint found even wider acceptance among indigenous Fijians with the increase in Indian population after the end of indenture in 1920. It was argued by the chiefs that indigenous Fijians not only needed protection from the demands of the colonial economy but from Indians as well. Village leaders, *Turaga ni koros*, were informed by the authorities to keep an eye on any Indians attempting to settle in indigenous villages. Upon discovery of such an activity, Indians were to be promptly arrested and brought back to the labor barracks. William Sutherland notes that the ideology and the practice of racialism perpetrated by the ruling class made a large section of the indigenous Fijian population see themselves primarily as Fijians rather than exploited people (Sutherland 1992: 32). By the mid-twentieth century, the Chief-Gordon viewpoint was firmly in place, and the segregation of the three communities within their respective cultural and ethnic blocs was largely complete.

One of the most avid defender of the colonial government and the Council of Chiefs was Ratu Sukuna, the first indigenous Fijian chief to receive western education. Sukuna was the district commissioner of Lau and a son of a Bauan chief. As the most gifted of the young indigenous chiefs, he was selected to be educated in New Zealand and England. Ratu Sukuna was concerned about the pressure from Europeans and Indians to open up indigenous land for commercial agriculture, and as a result, he played a major role in the establishing the Native Land Trust Board (NLTB) in the 1940s.

The Native Land Trust Ordinance of 1940 was formulated to protect the interests of indigenous Fijian landowners by legalizing indigenous land rights. The objectives of the Ordinance were to protect indigenous interest in their own soil, preserve an area ample for their needs in the future, make provision for suitable and sufficient land for settlement by others, and achieve a continuity of policy and security of leaseholders (Wesley-Coulter 1967: 52). However, as Timothy J. Macnaught (1974: 19) observed: "Ratu Sukuna and the architects of the revitalised Fijian Administration after 1944 felt that the prerequisite of modernisation was to amalgamate the old tikina into more efficient units. The policy failed: the strengths of the old system were undermined; the communities resented their loss of autonomy, and rule by civil servants was considered intolerable." The theme of modernization was also picked up by indigenous Fijian anthropologist Rusiate Nayacakalou (1975) who saw Sukuna's Fijian Administration as an interim solution pending modernization of indigenous Fijian society. However, Nayacakalou emphasized that there was anxiety among the indigenous population due to increasing number of Indian population in the Colony of Fiji.

The tri-modular ethnic structure in Fiji was put in context by the much published Spate Report of 1959. The report is often cited as the baseline for events yet to unfold after independence of the Colony, but many observations in the report highlighted ethnic distance between Indians and Fijians and Europeans. According to Robert Norton (2013: 425), "for the Fijians, the 1950s was a period of rapid change, despite the controlling efforts of the Fijian Affairs Board and especially as migration to towns increased, giving rise to new social problems. Some conflict grew both within the official Fijian leadership and between it and new leaders emerging in trade unions and other urban bodies." By the late 1950s, the polarization of the ethnic communities in Fiji reached full circle. Spate noted in his report:

> The current political situation in Fiji on the face of it, and not only in the tourist literature, appears to be in a state of amiable equilibrium; day-to-day relations between the various races are friendly enough, and although there are symptoms, both amongst Indians and Fijians, of political and social dissatisfaction, it could hardly be said that these are as yet very acute. It seems to me, however, and to informed and thoughtful observers both within and without Fiji, that this equilibrium is highly unstable. The political future is gloomy, and it is indeed difficult to see a solution. (Ward and Spate 1990: 100)

Spate emphasized the whole establishment was at a risk of Indian challenge, and in response Spate recommended education as a reasonable strategy to overcome some if not all of ethnic prejudice in Fiji, but his suggestions were too radical for its time as Indians and indigenous Fijians sought their own separate and untainted cultural representations. A year later in 1960, a report by Alan Burns highlighted deep-seated fears between Fijians and Indians and went further than the Spate report to suggest deportations of some members of the Indian community (Legislative Council Paper No. 1, 1960: 13).

It was in the same year that Indian militancy in the sugarcane areas surfaced and permanently fractured Indian relations with Europeans and indigenous Fijians. At the center of the Indian militancy in the sugarcane areas was India-born A.D. Patel who instigated cane harvest boycott (Pacific Review, 11 August 1960). The position of A.D. Patel was strongly criticized by other Indian leaders for his actions including Fiji-born Ayodhya Prasad (India born) and Fiji-born Vijay R. Singh.

The problem with the Indian leadership in Fiji was that they were making no attempts to negotiate and liaise with either the Europeans or indigenous Fijian chiefs and both these ethnic groups saw Indian leaders moving tactically to usurp power from the Europeans and then having secret plans to alienate indigenous land. Fiji's governor remarked that indigenous Fijian be given additional seats in any new Legislative Council so that they could safeguard indigenous interest against the accesses of Indians in the Colony (Legislative Council Paper No 40, 1960: 3).

Governor Kenneth Maddock (1958–1963) ensured that ethnic representation was effectively codified in the colonial electoral system with four indigenous Fijians for the first time directly elected with further two members appointed by the Council of Chiefs. Indians elected six members and Europeans six. The tri-modular ethnic representation was in train, but Indian members led by A.D. Patel pushed needlessly for common roll. With Indians now a majority in the colony, A.D. Patel called for "independence" which forced other ethnic communities into defensive strategies. Indigenous Fijians and Europeans embraced the Alliance Party led by Lauan Chief Ratu Sir Kamisese Mara, who professed paramountcy of political interest of indigenous Fijians as a baseline for peace and stability. The argument was that it was indigenous Fijian chiefs who ceded the colony to Great Britain and it was Great Britain that was duty bound to return the colony to the chiefs. Indians were seen as agitators and Indian-born leaders influenced by divisive politics of the Indian subcontinent that witnessed bitter partisan of British Indian and communal riots which killed about a million innocent.

Colonial governor, Sir Dereck Jakeway, reiterated that the colonial administration would never allow indigenous population to be placed under the political control of an immigrant community (The Fiji Times, 19 February 1965). In his deliberation, Governor Jakeway reiterated Gordon-Chief viewpoint of protecting indigenous Fijians and continuing with the humanitarian colonial policy toward the natives since the Deed of Cession. Indian leaders were unimpressed and demanded clarity from the colonial administration on decolonization. However, the tri-modular ethnic set up after Cession had deteriorated as members of the European and indigenous communities expressed serious concerns over Indian ambitions and designs.

Ethnic tensions had peaked in the colony by 1965, and the leader of the indigenous Fijian-led Alliance Party, Ratu Sir Kamisese Mara, advised that his community did not want independence from Great Britain and efforts to increase the rights of Indians were "doomed to fail" (Sunday Telegraph, 25 July 1965). Fearing further problems, the colonial government held a constitutional conference in London with representatives from all parties, and it was proposed that indigenous Fijians be given 14 seats, Indians 12 seats, and Europeans 10. These allocations of seats were criticized by the Federation Party as creating further communal and ethnic isolation and argued for common electoral roll of one person, one vote. Indigenous Fijians and their European allies responded by suggesting that common roll was equivalent to Indian control of the government and eventual demise of indigenous land rights.

With the support of the Council of Chiefs, the colonial government in Fiji enacted a new constitution in 1966 based on the recommendations of the constitutional conference of 1965. The colony held general elections under the constitution, but the political atmosphere was incredibly toxic. Federation participated reluctantly in the election and continued with demands on common roll, independence, and equal rights. Indigenous Fijians were deeply concerned about their political position and land rights, and Europeans saw their position of privilege in jeopardy due to increasing Indian activism. The only sign of hope for both indigenous Fijians and Europeans was divisions among Indians and to some extent differences between India-born (Indians) and Fiji-born Indians (Indo-Fijians).

One of the anti-Federation activist was Indo-Fijian Brahma Dass Lachman, who bitterly criticized the Federation Party and called for non-girmitiyas to be placed on work visa. Lachman was particularly incensed by India-born leaders A.D. Patel and Rudranand who were leaders of the Federation Party that advocated equal political rights to all Indians in the colony and immediate independence. However, Lachman argued that indentured laborers who chose to stay in the colony and their descendants were more equal than those Indians who came as free migrants and established small business to compete with Europeans. In a letter to editor to the *Fiji Times*, Rajendra Prasad of Nasinu opined: "I am afraid to say that some of the Fiji born Indo-Fijians openly played into the hands of the Gujaratis (namely A.D. Patel). Previously, the Gujarati dominated us financially, but now, we are politically dominated too" (The Fiji Times, 14 October 1966).

The issue of rights between these two groups, Indo-Fijians and Indians, was never resolved, and on 1 September 1967, a ministerial system of government was introduced by the colonial government. Immediately, the Federation Party took offense and resigned from the Legislative Council. The resignation and the subsequent by-election were seen by indigenous Fijian leaders and Europeans as a political stunt aimed at undermining the 1966 Constitution. To further stir communal emotions, members of the Federation Party increased their votes in the by-elections which were held in 1968. For indigenous Fijians, the Federation Party was unwilling to work with their leaders to understand indigenous concerns and fears. In addition, the resignations of Indian members in 1967 were seen as insulting to the chiefs, especially after the support given by the Council of Chiefs to the constitution. Europeans, while supporting the indigenous Fijian position, were resigned to the fact that Indian tactics had worked and Fiji was heading toward independence.

On 9 May 1968, British representative on the United Nations Decolonization Committee, Creighton Burns, remarked that "Fiji was ready for independence. However, indigenous Fijian leaders are understandably more than content to hasten slowly towards independence. They fear that premature independence could precipitate racial conflict and competition with the Indo-Fijian community" (The Age, 9 May 1968). Furthermore, the Federation Party not only pushed for independence, but its leaders wanted an independent republic (Vasil 1972: 25) modeled along the independent India, and furthermore, they also advocated common roll. However, R.K. Vasil (1972: 26) noted that "the fear of the Fijians with the use of the term Fijian to refer to all the people of Fiji" would lead to the loss of Fijian identity.

The common name remained unresolved before independence, but there was some comfort among Fijian leaders that the colonial government would ensure that indigenous Fijian political interest was preserved in any new constitutional order. Norman Meller (1984: 765) highlighted that there was an understanding between the colonial regime and the Fijian leaders on the continuation of the "Fijian Affairs Ordinance" that allowed for the protection of Fijian land during the colonial rule. Robert Norton (1993: 747) took a different position and argued that there was a degree of accommodation between indigenous Fijian and Indians/Indo-Fijians due to "experience of identity based on intra-group life." No doubt that indigenous Fijian leadership and the Indians and Indo-Fijians were oscillating between extreme conservative views to more accommodating positions with a hope to protect and preserve their communal interests. Brij Lal (2008: 70) analyzed that the "public stand of Fijian leaders was: no independence, at least not yet, no common roll and gratitude to the United Kingdom; nut privately attitudes were changing or at least were being flexible."

During fieldwork in Nadi in 1993, I made the following observations based on extensive discussions with indigenous Fijians: Indian and Indo-Fijian leaders did not understand indigenous Fijian language and culture, and Indian leaders in particular could not comprehend the emotions associated with indigenous land and above all failed to realize that politics was part and parcel of the larger social discourse associated with the vanua. (Extensive fieldwork was undertaken as part of my post-graduate studies on the question of Fiji's independence. Village elders and students from Narewa, Namotomoto, Navoci, and Nakavu were interviewed.) Furthermore, many indigenous Fijians believed that independence had been "forced on to the indigenous Fijian people by Federation leaders and the government of India" and that "independence should have been deferred until indigenous Fijians and their leaders are fully inducted in the democratic processes" and Indian and Indo-Fijian leaders become fully conversant with indigenous language and custom. One interviewee opined that "indigenous Fijians should have had at least twenty years" transition to self-rule. Similar sentiments were expressed by my father who studied at Shri Vivekananda High School in Nadi, where future Indo-Fijian leaders of Fiji were cultivated but none of these leaders understood the nuances of indigenous custom, tradition, and aspirations.

More importantly perhaps as I have noted was the views of India-born non-girmitiyas and those who were India-born and Fiji-born descendants of girmitiyas. As Robert Norton (1993) emphasized, intra-communal dynamics played as much a part in establishing the "accommodation" paradigm as ethnic tensions as the duality within each ethnic group led to political contradictions that continues to be unresolved. Some indigenous Fijians wanted modernity, whereas some Indo-Fijians silently espoused peaceful coexistence. However, at the national level, both communities compromised their extreme communal positions and artificially provided support for independence.

The theme of colonialism playing a central role in ethnic conflict is also discussed by other authors in *The Palgrave Handbook of Ethnicity*. Jacob Mwathi Mati (2019) analyzes ethnicity and politics in Kenya and in particular how anti-colonial struggles were influenced by inter-ethnic, generational, and class alliances which exploited racial antagonisms to rally African unity against the politically dominant white colonial elite. Morsen Moses (2019) looks at colonialism and race in Vanuatu, and both these authors highlight the destructive role of colonialism in ethnic conflict. A more general theoretical contribution on colonialism is from Vijay Naidu (2019) who conceptualizes colonialization as a form of state-sponsored racism where ethnic divisions are institutionalized in support of European hegemony.

Conclusion

The chapter showed that European contact drastically changed indigenous social relations and brought an influence that led to an alliance between the chiefs and the Europeans. In 1871, a government was established but conflict among communities led to the cession of Fiji to Britain, which established an indigenous administration based on experience of the Kingdom of Bau. Moreover, the colonial administration, under the leadership of Sir Arthur Gordon, introduced into the colony a third racial and cultural category in the form of Indian indentured laborers, who started agitations for political equality after end of indenture in 1920. Seeing the rapid growth and progress of Indians, colonial governors, after Gordon, tried without success to introduce indigenous Fijians to commerce. Concerned about the pressures on indigenous Fijians and on indigenous land, Bauan Chief Ratu Sukuna assisted in the formulation and the implementation of the NLTB. In colonial Fiji, indigenous chiefs were increasingly driven by concerns of further indigenous land alienation, introduction of indigenous Fijians to wage labor, and the presence of Indians in the colony. As a result, the chiefs continually reinforced Governor Gordon's viewpoint of protecting indigenous custom and tradition. Conflicting and often oppositional views between Indians and Indo-Fijians and indigenous Fijians and their chiefs came head on in the 1960s as Britain formed the opinion on independence of the colony. The Indian- and Indo-Fijian-led Federation Party argued for common roll electoral system, Fijian as a common name and a republic, whereas indigenous leaders called for protection of indigenous political interest, land, and leadership and emphasized continued relationship with the British crown. The historical ethnic tensions, which were managed by the British colonial administration, surfaced to the forefront in the 1960s to create a problematic inter-ethnic social discourse that remains irreconcilable even to this day.

Other authors in this volume including Jacob Mwathi Mati, Morsen Moses, and Vijay Naidu use similar themes of analyses to demonstrate the role of ethnicity and race in intergroup conflict and tensions during colonial rule in Kenya, Vanuatu, and Fiji.

References

Brewster A (1922) The Hill tribes of Fiji: a record of forty years intimate connection with the tribes of the mountainous interior of Fiji. Service & Company Ltd., Seeley
Clammer J (1976) Literary and social change: a case study of Fiji. E.J. Brill, Leiden
Coulter J (1967) The Drama of Fiji: a contemporary history. Charles E. Tuttle Co., Tokyo
Cumpston I (1956) Sir Arthur Gordon and the introduction of Indians in the Pacific: the West Indian system in Fiji. Pac Hist Rev 25(4):369–388
Derrick RA (1950) A history of Fiji, vol 1. Suva, Government Printer
France P (1969) The charter of the land: custom and colonisation in Fiji. Oxford University Press, Melbourne
Howard M (1991) Race and politics in an Island State. UBC Press, Vancouver
Knaplund P (1958) Sir Arthur Gordon and Fiji: some Gordon-Gladstone letters. Hist Stud 8(31):281–296
Knapman B (1992) Fiji's economic history, 1874–1939, Studies of capitalist colonial development. Pacific research monograph no. 15. ANU Press, Canberra
Lal BV (1980) Approaches to the study of Indian indentured emigration with special reference to Fiji J Pac Hist 15(1):52–70
Lal BV (2008) A time bomb lies buried: 1960–1970. ANU E Press, Canberra
Lawson S (1991) The failure of democratic politics in Fiji. Clarendon Press, Oxford
Legge J (1958) Britain in Fiji 1858–1880. Macmillan, London
Legislative Council Papers (1960) Government Printer, Suva
Lemarchana R (ed) (2011) Forgotten genocides: oblivion, denial and memory. University of Pennsylvania Press, Pennsylvania
Lester A, Dussart F (2014) Colonisation and origins of humanitarian governance: protecting aborigines across the nineteenth-century. Cambridge University Press, Cambridge
Macnaught T (1974) Chiefly civil servants: ambiguity in district administration and the preservation of the Fijian way of life 1896–1940. J Pac Hist 9(1):3–20
Macnaught T (1982) The Fijian colonial experience: a study of neotraditional order under British Colonial Rule Prior to World War II. ANU Press, Canberra
Mati JM (2019) Ethnicity and politics in Kenya. In: The Palgrave handbook of ethnicity. Palgrave, New York
Meller N (1984) Traditional leaders and modern Pacific Island governance. Asian Surv 24(7):759–772

Moses M (2019) Colonialism and race in Vanuatu. In: The Palgrave handbook of ethnicity. Palgrave, New York
Naidu V (2019) Construction and race and racism. In: The Palgrave handbook of ethnicity. Palgrave, New York
Nayacakalou R (1975) Leadership in Fiji. Halstead Press, John Sands
Norton R (1993) Culture and identity in the South Pacific: a comparative analysis. Man 28(4):741–759
Norton R (2013) Averting irresponsible nationalism: Political Origins of Ratu Sukuna's Fijian Administration J Pac Hist 48(4):409–428
Oliver D (1989) Oceania: the native cultures of Australia and the Pacific Islands, vol 2. University of Hawaii Press, Honolulu
Parke A (2014) In: Spriggs M, Scarr D (eds) Descendants: spirits, places and pre-cession Fiji. ANU EPress, Canberra
Plevitz L (2010) Arthur Hamilton Gordon and Adolphe de Plevitz: ambitions for Indian labour in colonial Mauritius and Fiji. Qld Hist J 21(3):181–195
Roth GK (1953) Fijian way of life. Oxford University Press, London
Routledge D (1985) Matanitu: the struggle for power in Early Fiji. The University of the South Pacific Press, Suva
Sayes S (1984) Changing paths of the land: early political hierarchies in Cakaudrove Fiji. J Pac Hist XIX(1):3
Sutherland W (1992) Beyond the politics of race. An alternative history of Fiji to 1992. Political and social change monograph 15. ANU Press, Canberra
Tippett A (1955) Anthropological research and the Fijian people. Int Rev Mission 44(174):212–219
Vasil RK (1972) Communalism and constitution-making in Fiji. Pac Aff 45(1):21–41
Veracini L (2011) Settler colonialism: a theoretical overview. Palgrave, London
Ward R (1972) The Pacific Beche-de-mer trade with special reference to Fiji. In: Ward R (ed) Man in the Pacific. Clarendon Press, Oxford
Ward RG, Spate OHK (1990) Thirty years ago: A view of the Fijian political scene confidential report to the British colonial office, September 1959 J Pac Hist 25(1):103–124
Young J (1984) Adventurous spirits: Australian Migrant Society in pre-cession Fiji. University of Queensland Press, Brisbane

Ethnicity and Politics in Kenya

15

Jacob Mwathi Mati

Contents

Introduction	266
Ethnicity and Politics in Kenya: Theoretical Approaches	267
Atavistic/Residual Cultural Ghost Thesis	268
Ethnicity as an Invention of Colonial State Power	270
Ethnicity as a Form of Social Resistance to Exploitation by Colonial Capitalism	270
Ethnicity as Nationalism or Dissident Sub-nationalism	274
Ethnicity as False Consciousness Ideology that Masks Class Struggle	275
Ethnicity as an Imagined Community	277
Conclusion	279
Cross-References	279
References	279

Abstract

Instrumentalized ethnic identity has been a key variable in the mobilization and molding of Kenyan politics since Britain's colonial divide and rule policies imposed ethnic and racial dualism that emphasized difference. At independence, the post-colonial elite did not dismantle the structural architecture of ethnic-based politics. Ethnic identity therefore remains the basis for mobilization and structuring of politics in contemporary Kenya. This dominance of ethnic-based politics, though explained variously, is a product of the conflation of political economy-induced interests where elites instrumentalize ethnicity in political mobilization to ensure their own survival and reproduction.

J. M. Mati (✉)
School of Social Sciences, Faculty of Arts, Law and Education (FALE), The University of the South Pacific, Suva, Fiji Islands

Society, Work and Politics (SWOP) Institute, The University of the Witwatersrand, Johannesburg, South Africa
e-mail: jacobmati@gmail.com

© The Author(s), under exclusive license to Springer Nature Singapore Pte Ltd. 2019
S. Ratuva (ed.), *The Palgrave Handbook of Ethnicity*,
https://doi.org/10.1007/978-981-13-2898-5_24

Keywords

Ethnicity · Instrumentalized ethnic identity · Politics · Ethnic-based politics · Political mobilization · Political violence · Inter-ethnic violence · Primordialism Kenya

Introduction

Ethnic identity is the most prominent defining feature of political mobilizations across many nations. The all-too-common scenes of anti-immigrant demonstrations across Western nations in the last few years, for example, point to increasing politicization of the way people of different communities use aspects of culture to define belonging and exclusion. In Kenya, instrumentalized ethnicity has been key in the mobilization and molding of political organizations and actions since Britain's formal colonial annexation in 1888 (Maina 1998: 138; Nzomo 2003; Ajulu 2002; Berman 1998, 2010; Omolo 2002; Klopp 2002; Ogude 2002; Mueller 2008; Lonsdale 1994; Bratton and Kimenyi 2008; Lynch 2008). Given this, the relationship between ethnicity and politics or more precisely power has been a fodder for many social scientists with interest in Kenya's sociopolitical developments. This has been especially accentuated since the early 1990s' reintroduction of political party pluralism rekindled what had been assumed to be dying embers of ethnicity in political mobilization, organization, and action.

Ethnic-based political mobilization in competition for power in Kenya as elsewhere in Africa often inflames xenophobic sentiments and, in extreme cases, interethnic violence – a regular ritual every election year since 1992 (Ajulu 2002; Omolo 2002; Klopp 2002; Ogude 2002; Atieno-Odhiambo 2002; Long and Gibson 2015; Long et al. 2013). Some of the violent incidences have been serious enough a threat to have a destabilizing effect. The Shifta War waged by ethnic Somali secessionists in Kenya's Northern frontier from 1963 to 1967 was arguably the most serious of these conflicts. More contemporary examples have manifested as large-scale election-related ethnic violence in parts of the Rift Valley, Coast, Eastern, Nairobi, and Nyanza regions most prominently in 1992, 1997, 2007/2008, 2013, and 2017. There have also been pockets of small-scale inter-ethnic violence in many parts of Kenya especially since the 1990s. These incidences of violence prompted internal as well as foreign interventions aimed at designing institutions to help the country live with or manage its diversity. The 2010 constitution is arguably the best illustrative outcome of such institutional design efforts.

Despite their intensification or rediscovery in the last two and half decades, ethnic identity-based politics and associated violence is not a recent phenomenon in Kenya. Indeed, ethnicity has for long been a very "important political resource" (Lentz 1995). This chapter explains the intransigence of ethnicity in Kenyan politics through a sociohistorical analysis of the emergence and reproduction of ethnic-based politics reinforced by a thematic analysis of the theoretical explanations of the phenomenon. It is argued that ethnicity in the context of Kenyan politics is not a static category. Rather, it is a dynamic product of creative open-ended social and political processes, where "groups appear and disappear, change their names, adapt their cultures, fight over who is or is not a real member of the group, and address a myriad of demands to public institutions and other ethnic groups" (Berman 2010: 3).

Ethnicity and Politics in Kenya: Theoretical Approaches

Scholarly discourses on the ubiquity of ethnicity in Kenyan politics illustrate two dominant tendencies. One is the treatment of ethnicity as an instrumentally socially constituted phenomenon, the other that it is naturally occurring. Within the social construction perspective, ethnicity is viewed as primordial nativism of local orientated and often instrumentally politicized cosmopolite behavior (Mbithi 1974). That is to say that ethnicity results from people trusting their co-ethnics because they self-identify with them while holding others that are different with "suspicion and distrust or dislike" (Glazer et al. 1974: 20). In this regard, ethnicity in Kenya, like in the rest of Africa, is both socially constructed and a lived reality (Atieno-Odhiambo 2002: 230). As an everyday social experience, ethnicity was first constructed and deployed by the colonial state through what Sigmund Freud called "the narcissism of small differences" by "(over)exaggerating difference" (Mamdani 1996: 8).

In this project of conscious exaggeration of difference, language played a significant role. Specifically, the introduction of vernacular reading and writing by Christian missionaries helped in the processes of identification (self or other) – a process involving differentiating and understanding of self as identical to some collective, while separate from others, as well as defining the questions of authority and legitimacy of those that belong or do not belong (Brubaker and Cooper 2000: 4). Specifically, language became a political resource for creating categories of people with shared vernaculars and experiences distinct from others.

As a lived reality, the everyday term for ethnicity is tribalism, a concept Mbithi (1974) defines as cosmopolite behavior that results from "cross-ethnic awareness." Atieno-Odhiambo (2002: 23) argues that tribalism is an "everyday acknowledgment of experiences, contextual practices and political fact, shorthand for the welter of the simultaneously modernising and violent political cultures that have come to typify the post-colony of Kenya." Eminent theorists of ethnicity and politics in Africa, Lonsdale (1994) and Berman (2004), differentiate between what they term moral ethnicity and political tribalism. Moral ethnicity is the "discursive and political arena within which ethnic identities emerge out of renegotiation of the bonds of communal membership and authority, the social rights and obligations of moral economy, and access to land and property" (Berman 2010: 10) (Moral economy for Berman (2010: 4) is "that part of culture that legitimates the inequalities in the distribution of values that mark almost all human communities primarily through principles of redistribution and reciprocity of obligations between rulers and ruled, rich and poor in specific social contexts."). On the other hand, political tribalism is characterized by a struggle of the ethnic elites to gain resources [...through] mobilized communal solidarity and political organization of the community defined by *moral ethnicity*, first against the alien power of the colonial state and then, increasingly, against the competing interests of rival ethnicities for access to the state and its patronage resources, driven by the horizontal inequalities of the colonial political economy. (Berman 2010: 10)

Often, under political tribalism, ethnicity is instrumentalized (at the expense of class identity) as the singular dependable locus for articulation of group interests (Atieno-Odhiambo 2002: 230).

Within the second tendency in the treatment of ethnicity as a naturally occurring phenomenon, ethnic identity is used in collectivizing a group of people on parameters such as sameness of language, other cultural traits, and geographical location. Here, ethnicity is not necessarily a political category or a basis of political action. Simply put, ethnicity in this conception is focused on understanding sameness or difference, rather than amorally instrumentalized to serve political interests. It is however the instrumentalized ethnicity or political tribalism that dominates contemporary Kenyan sociopolitical discourses that is the focus of this chapter. We begin by exploring the explanations of its origins before moving to the analysis of its manifestations. We do this by utilizing a sociohistorical perspective.

The study of ethnicity and politics in Africa has been approached from the standpoint of "analysis of complex causality in which no single set of factors is determinant or can be analysed in isolation from others" (Berman 2010: 3). The predominant preoccupation has been a rather atheoretical empirical explanations of "common factors and the relationships between them to explain not only the similarities of cases, but also their contingent and idiosyncratic differences" (Berman 2010: 3). An influential paper on ethnicity and politics by Lonsdale (1994) indicates that in Kenya as it is for the rest of Africa, existing literature convergences on at least five empirical explanations for the salience of ethnicity in politics. These are (a) ethnicity as a residual category in a modernizing Africa; (b) ethnicity as a form of social resistance to colonial capitalist exploitation; (c) ethnicity as false consciousness that masks class struggle; (d) ethnicity as nationalism or more precisely as per Ogude (2002: 205), "dissident sub-nationalism"; and (e) ethnicity as an imagined community. In what follows, we lay out the key postulations in each of these approaches and their explanations of the production and reproduction ethnicity in Kenya's political sphere as presented in existing literature.

Atavistic/Residual Cultural Ghost Thesis

Early accounts of ethnicity by modernization-inspired Africanist social scientists emphasized primordialism as the "archaic cultural basis of ethnic identities" (Berman 1998: 309). The argument was that as at the time of colonial conquest, there existed different primordial ethno-nations who were forced to belong to a new instrumental Kenya colony. These primordial republics were made up of closely related kinship groups who constituted an ethnic group such as the Giryama, Kikuyu, Luo, Kamba,

Meru, etc. Colonization was justified as necessary in the modernization project (civilizing mission) where different ethno-nations were to be "transformed" into an amalgam Kenyan nation. The underlying assumption was that as African tribesmen are "modernized," ethnicity would die and in its place would emerge a new modern (national) identity (Coleman and Rosberg 1964; Vail 1989).

However ethnicity did not obey the so-called laws of social and political change prescribed by modernization theorists. Even after Kenya gained political independence in 1963, primordial nativism and ethnic consciousness continued to flourish. It however came to be seen by modernization proponents as an "atavistic cultural ghost" (Vail 1989; Berman 1998) that was "strongest amongst those who had least changed" (Lonsdale 1994: 132). By the time of independence and after, the failure of the eight decades of formal colonial modernization project to detribalize the African came to be viewed as a "form of collective irrationality" on the part of the colonized (Vail 1989). The pejorative political term for the native who had "refused to modernise" through the death of the tribe so that the nation would be born and live was a "tribalist" (Mamdani 1996; Lonsdale 1994). Tribalism therefore was and still is for some, routinely denounced as retrogressive, shameful, and an unwelcome aberration in modernity (Berman 1998; Vail 1989; Young 1986; Ekeh 1990). Many continue to blame ethnicity for the copious evils of the postcolonial state in Kenya and elsewhere in Africa.

Modernization's cultural atavism thesis ignored important saliences of ethnicity that ethnic identity is created through everyday practices and experiences. Instead, given the preoccupation with "reproduction of the modernist paradigms of state and society," this paradigm concentrated on explaining "what Africa is not, rather than with explaining what it is" (Berman 1998: 307). Indeed, the contradictory nature of the British colonial administration was that even as it intended to "modernize" native Africa, it also worked hard at maintaining each of its classified tribe(s) as a homogeneous whole. The net effect was that as independence approached, the colonial process of "transforming" the different ethno-nations into Kenya was incomplete. In addition, ethnicity had also been further entrenched through colonial state's activities with the aid of missionaries and anthropologists' "preoccupation with demarcating, classifying and counting subject populations" that propagated false assumptions that African ethnic identity was characterized by "neatly bounded and culturally homogeneous 'tribes'" (Berman 2010: 1). This is to say that a Maasai, for example, was ethnically "pure breed." However evidence from across different Kenya communities indicates that this was not the case. Pre-colonial African social identities were fluid, heterogeneous, and hybrid due to constantly overlapping boundaries, intermingling of individuals and communities, and cultural and linguistic borrowing (Berman 2010; Atieno-Odhiambo 2002). Different ethnic groups, wilfully or through conquest, intermarried with all their neighbors. In this regard, the first president of independent Kenya, Jomo Kenyatta, an ethnic Kikuyu, had a Maasai woman for a grandmother. On account of the fluidity of ethnic identity, it has been argued that a more lucid explanation of ethnicity is that it is instrumentally socially constructed. The dominant narrative is that ethnicity in Kenya is an outgrowth of or an invention of colonial state power.

Ethnicity as an Invention of Colonial State Power

As noted above ethnicity emerged through the practices of classification and categorization by the colonial state. Specifically, the colonial state's divide and rule policies were employed in creating new "neat" categories of ethnic "identities and orders of difference out of eclectic and often contradictory elements of modernity and tradition" (Berman 1998: 306). At the same time, because the idea of racial and ethnic classification was at the heart of the questions of citizenship, rights, and obligations of subject populations, ethnicity became a key political resource because of the way the colonial state treated different groups. For instance, white settlers were citizens, while African tribesmen were subjects of the colonial state and only ethnic citizens in their tribal enclaves (Atieno-Odhiambo 2002; Mamdani 1996). Atieno-Odhiambo (2002) makes a distinction between the two forms of citizenship arguing that ethnic citizenship confers birth right recognition, identity, and patrimony, while state citizenship is a matter of bureaucratic obligation.

Given the colonial politicization of difference and differential treatment of racial and ethnic groups, contrary to modernization's postulations, ethnic identity became "politically more important, not less" (Lonsdale 1994: 132). The reawakening of ethnicity in the early 1960s in the West, especially through the civil rights movement in the United States that busted the cultural melting pot myth, meant that the salience of communal solidarities and ethnicity needed to be understood differently. Across Africa, the result of this retrospection is research that exploded the primordial myth, resulting in a realization that rather than being an "atavistic survival of stagnant primordial 'tribal' identities and communities, African ethnicities are new not old, part of complex responses to colonial modernity" (Berman 2010: 2). It is to these alternative explanations of the salience of ethnicity in politics in Kenya that we turn to.

Ethnicity as a Form of Social Resistance to Exploitation by Colonial Capitalism

This explanation of ethnicity is directly opposed to the modernization paradigm and closely linked to the colonial experience. The principal argument here is that ethnicity emerged as a form of social resistance to colonialism and its attendant capitalist exploitation (Berman 1998, 2004; Lonsdale 1994; Balandier 1955). This view, initially championed by French sociologist Georges Balandier postulates that colonialism was "a crude ordeal that promoted an immoral process of class formation rather than the beneficent 'social mobilisation' of modernisation theory" (Lonsdale 1994: 133). Africans reacted to this process by organizing along primordial ties that largely remained below the surface of colonial state's gaze at it policed Africans' associational life (Fowler and Mati 2019). Ethnicity, therefore, was a "mode of resistance to a predatory state and capitalist exploitation" (Lonsdale 1994; Berman 2004; Bayart 1989; Maina 1998). In this regard, Berman (1998: 305) argues, ethnicity resulted from "internal struggles over moral economy and political legitimacy tied to the definition of ethnic communities – moral ethnicity; and external conflicts over differential access to the resources of modernity and economic accumulation – political tribalism."

In pre-colonial period a moral economy existed in small bands of communities typically under a "big man" who utilized his material resources to reward his network of client subjects who, in return, remained loyal to him (Berman 1998, 2010). These moral economy arrangements were translated to be distinct ethnic groups by the colonial power in the process of demarcating the country into ethnic districts. Further, the colonial state exploited existing distinct moral economies in the contradictory processes of developing a market economy while simultaneously attempting to sustain "traditional" culture and authority through local agents. The strategy was to carefully reconstruct ethnicity as a refuge for local moral order to shield Africans from the "disorders caused by racist state power and externally dominated market" (Lonsdale 1994: 133).

The process of colonial conquest involved divide and rule policies (Lonsdale 1994; Atieno-Odhiambo 2002) that included the "invention of tradition" in the creation of new ethnicities that sometimes bore little, if any, resemblance to pre-colonial identities (Ranger 1983; Berman 2010). These were geared toward facilitating political control and ostensibly preserve social stability. A key strategy was the creation and installation of a clientele of collaborationist chiefs with power resources to either punish or reward their local subjects on the basis of ethnic ascriptive markers (Atieno-Odhiambo 2002; Berman 2010). These developments corrupted local moral orders as chiefs oiled the colonial state's racial dualism machine and the accompanying "regime of ethnic differentiation" or categorization (Mamdani 1996).

One result of this was a powerful colonial state that treated white minority settlers as citizens with political and legal rights, while, on the other, colonized African natives in the insular ethnic district reserves were subjects without the same rights (Maina 1998: 143). In these reserves, Africans were subjected to customary law. The colonial state's appointed indigenous local chiefs and headmen (through patron-client ties with the European field agents of the state) acted directly in aid of colonial power (Mamdani 1996; Berman 1998, 2010). At the same time, the colonial regime attempted to preserve the native to his tribal roots by enforcing and conserving separate native institutions (Mamdani 1996: 6).

The colonial administration was therefore key in providing the "resources and political contexts that Africans, particularly the class of collaborators and educated intelligentsia, could deploy in the internal conflicts that resulted from the unequal and divisive impact of colonial modernity" (Berman 2010: 7). In the post-colonial era, the middle classes and elites continue to reproduce ethnicity because, as Maina (1998: 138) observes, "they are not just members of a class, they are also sons and daughters of the tribe. They are held up as icons of progress and power, its emissaries at negotiations, and their exploits, the stuff of which fireside tales are made."

The colonial system had contradictory strategies and outcomes. To begin with, the colonial system in Kenya was designed to exploit local population through labor and various forms of taxes to make the colony self-financing. As such, even as the colonial state desired to keep African "tribes" segregated in their respective reserves, the colonial political economy's hunger for labor and taxes meant that the native could not be confined to the "reserves" forever, nor would their customs remain preserved and intact once they interacted with others from different ethnic groups. A pan-ethnic Kenyan nationalist identity ultimately emerged. Indeed, as Britons arrived to set up plantation agriculture in the so-called White highlands curved out exclusively for European settlers through violent dislocation of Africans, the demand for African labor increased. In effect, the state imposed taxes to force natives to sell their labor to earn money to pay taxes. At the same time, a system of migrant labor system was set up where African men were recruited to work in the plantations but left their families still rooted in their ethnic district reserves.

Colonial labor recruitment regime was also segregated along ethnic groups aided by the colonial government and capitalist entrepreneurs stereotypical categorization of workers on the basis of their "presumed tribal aptitudes for different sorts of work" (Lonsdale 1994: 134; Atieno-Odhiambo 2002). For example, the martial Maasai were hired as guards, the "hardworking" Kikuyu farm laborers, while Indians were clerks. These laborers were housed in ethnically segregated schemes in the farms and later in urban estates. This system effectively forced Africans into the colonial economic structures (Lonsdale 1994).

Africans reacted to these developments by "reinventing their local societies to regain control over their relations with the external world, if necessary, by shutting it out" (Lonsdale 1994: 133). Atieno-Odhiambo (2002) graphically illustrates these developments among the Luo of Western Kenya. It is noteworthy here that the net effect was that even as Africans started resisting the effects of colonial state's political economy of commodification of daily lives, this resistance was ethnically fractured. It is in this regard that distinctly ethnic-based associations like Young Kikuyu Association, Young Kavirondo Association, North Kavirondo Central Association, and Taita Hills Association (to mention but a few) emerged in the early 1920s. For these groups, tribal ideology was a "source of identity and common purpose" (Atieno-Odhiambo 2002: 234). These associations advocated for distinctly ethnic grievances. Ethnicity in this case was, therefore, a ground or basis for political action.

Even as various struggles against colonialism amalgamated into a nationalist anti-colonial movement after World War II, their distinct ethnic cleavages continued (Mati 2012). This is because the anti-colonial movement was essentially a coalition of "hegemonic ethnic enterprises" (Atieno-Odhiambo 2002), whose leaders were in the business of "essentialist construction of identity" (Haugerand 1995). This was evident in the negotiations for independence when two dominant political forces emerged – the Kenya African National Union (KANU) and the Kenya African Democratic Union (KADU). KANU, said to represent majority ethnic groups, was essentially a Kikuyu-Luo elite alliance which favored a unitary form of government as opposed to KADU's preference for *Majimbo*, a form of consociational federalism (Ogude 2002; Atieno-Odhiambo 2002). KADU on the other hand was a coalition of the leaders of the so-called minority Luhya, Kalenjin, and Miji Kenda communities who had been supported in their opposition to a unitary government by the colonial state. These political formations emerged in a political environment that favored the "cementing of the traditionally, high trust institutions such as the family, clan and tribe' into sites for political activism" (Mati 2012: 83). This was because of the "institutional exclusion of African associational forms and the failure of the colonial state to provide an institutional channel for Africans to express themselves and their grievances" (Nzomo 2003: 186), and up to 1950s, only district level associations were allowed for Africans. In a sense, as Lonsdale (1994: 135) argues, the tribe in this case was transformed into a "modern corporation" rather than an inherited ethnic culture.

The post-colonial elite did not dismantle the structural architecture of ethnicity-based politics. If anything, a political fallout between President Jomo Kenyatta and his deputy, Oginga Odinga, though initially manifesting as an ideological difference in the meaning of *uhuru* (independence), quickly assumed ethnic dimensions. Both invoked instrumentalized ethnicity for political mobilization of support from their co-ethnics (Mati 2012; Atieno-Odhiambo 2002). While revisionist scholarship underplays ethnicity as an issue behind their fallout, Atieno-Odhiambo clearly captures the similarities between Odinga and Kenyatta and their approaches when he writes:

> Both men were deeply cultural and espoused values that were locally rooted, Kenyatta in Gikuyu individual enterprise and personal virtue, Odinga in clan-based communocratic and egalitarian values plus a tradition of resistance to authoritarianism of any sort. Both of them understood the link between the individual and the community, the potency of the emphasis on hard work and unity, and the force and power behind the developmental roots of ethnicity. (2002: 242)

Kenyatta had come to power a captured man after his rehabilitation by the same colonial power that had imprisoned him for 7 years on charges of leading the Mau Mau rebellion. He was released from prison after a spirited campaign by African leaders led by Odinga. Once out of jail and on assuming the leadership of KANU, he assured White settlers that he would respect their right to land and property with his "*hakuna cha bure*" (nothing for free) clarion call. This was a position he shared with others in KANU including Odinga, all who believed in the tyranny of property which had to be protected by state power (Atieno-Odhiambo 2002). Kenyatta's first mission after assuming power was to eliminate the remnants of Mau Mau and any other radicals in the independence movement. Field Marshall Baimuing Marete was among his first victims in the assassination frenzy that the Kenyatta state presided over (Namu 2013). Others, including freedom fighters Pio Gama Pinto, Tom Mboya, and J.M Kariuki, soon followed. Thereafter, believing that his ethnic base was the best way to preserve power, Kenyatta and his men patched together a solidarity of the Gikuyu, Embu, and Meru into what came to be known as GEMA tribe through oathing with the sole purpose of excluding other ethnicities from power (Atieno-Odhiambo 2002). On the other hand, Odinga mobilized his co-ethnics against the Kenyatta regime especially after the assassination of Tom Mboya, a fellow Luo. The net effect of the configurations in the use of cultural structure agency "was to alienate the Luo from the inner sanctums of power for the following three decades"

(Atieno-Odhiambo 2002: 240). In vanquishing Odinga and Luos, the Kenyatta-led state engineered the rise of an ethnocratic state (Ogude 2002) shepherded through runaway GEMA elite corruption.

Nigerian political sociologist Peter Ekeh (1975, 108) provides useful analytical tools for comprehending what was happening and continues to happen in most of post-colonial Africa. Specifically, for the post-independent elite, it was moral to steal from the civic public and distribute to the primordial public. In Ekeh's theorizing, ethnicity continues to spell doom and corrupts African politics and public life because of institutional configurations "where allegiance to kin and lineage provides the moral grounding for people's relations on the one hand, while allowing for amoral or immoral extraction of public resources" to expend in the primordial realm (Fowler and Mati 2019).

In addition, the post-colonial state continued with the same colonial power structures they had inherited complete with a provincial administration system that continued the reproduction of decentralized despotism (Mamdani 1996) and patron-client relationships between national-level political elites and local politicians and chiefs. For an increasing numbers of Kenyans, political independence did not translate to economic prosperity. Issues such as land dispossession that had been part of grievances that had underwritten the anti-colonial struggle remained largely unresolved. Under the circumstance, ethnic mobilization was seen as a "local triumph over national failure" (Lonsdale 1994: 134). The recent realization of an embedded structural decentralization of power along local ethnic groups (county governments) in Kenya as encapsulated in the 2010 constitution needs to be understood in this regard. It is essentially a continuation of primordial understandings of ethnicity as a means to establishing difference or exclusivity for political expediency, which gained greater currency after the reintroduction of multiparty politics in 1991 (Ogude 2002).

Ethnicity as Nationalism or Dissident Sub-nationalism

A closely related narrative to the one above is that ethnicity was a nationalistic response to colonial rule and later to the misrule of the post-colonial elite. Specifically, Africans reacted to colonial penetration by reverting to moral ethnicity with affection networks offering the vernacular for resistance to colonial rule through embedded social institutions (Berman 1998; Maina 1998; Aina 2013). Ogude (2002) refers to this as dissident sub-nationalism which has over the years provided an effective counterweight to the state's hegemonic project of official histories that "have reworked the past to buttress predatory government, ethnic awareness and historiography" (Maina 1998: 138). Ethnic identity in this instance, as Atieno-Odhiambo (2002: 232) observes, is "a strategy for survival in emergent urban social formations" especially those of colonial era which, as already indicated, agitated on behalf of specific ethnic groups.

Here, language is key in the social construction of ethnicity in the sense that it supplies the grammar and metaphor of African politics, as it frames the political and social demands that groups make on the state and other groups (Maina 1998). Atieno-Odhiambo (2002: 244 citing Brubaker) invokes language and cultural idioms in interest articulation:

> Cultural idioms constitute interests as much as they express them. These culturally mediated and thereby culturally constituted interests are not prior to, or independent of, the cultural idioms in which they are expressed. Thus it becomes necessary to study the social production of political languages themselves.

Similarly, Maina (1998: 138) argues that the political language that a tribe or ethnic identity provides "unites people over what to argue about ... the images on which they can base their ideologies (and) ideologies mobilize political support around social divisions." Such political language is encoded in people's histories and customs, as are "their philosophies of power, justice and entitlements" (Maina 1998: 138). In contemporary multiparty era, ethnicity has been used in ethnic mobilizations and even violence as indicated at the beginning of this chapter.

Ethnicity as False Consciousness Ideology that Masks Class Struggle

Another perspective on ethnicity in African politics is Marxist-inspired. Here, scholars using political economy analysis see the basic character of ethnicity as defined by the "tyranny of property" (Atieno-Odhiambo 2002), where the big man politics and patronage networks use ethnicity as a smokescreen to camouflage class differences and interests in their ideological manipulation of subaltern co-ethnics (Berman 2010; Lonsdale 1994; Mueller 2008). Such elites have argued using pseudo-philosophies that pre-colonial Africa was a classless society. However, as Berman (2010: 9–10) argues, this is a myth:

> Africans did not and do not have either class or ethnic identities, but both; and this was reflected in the cultural politics of their communities ... It focused on increasing conflict between rich and poor over their reciprocal obligations, particularly of the former to redistribute their wealth so their dependents and clients could flourish ...

Arguing along the same lines, Atieno-Odhiambo (2002: 234) posits that in colonial Kenya, the Mau Mau was both "an anti-settler and anti-colonial revolt and movement on the one hand, and an intra-Gikuyu civil war on the other." It is such distinctions that the colonial state exploited by accentuating class differences to break the assumed ethnic-class heterogeneity through the 1954 Swynnerton Plan which "entrenched the landed Gikuyu gentry by expanding their landholdings at the expense of the Mau Mau detainees" (Atieno-Odhiambo 2002: 238).

Ethnicity became an important part of the hegemonic apparatus of the new African bourgeoisie for masking class differences and interests in post-colonial Kenya. Specifically, elites become what Atieno-Odhiambo (2002: 232) describes as "ethnic entrepreneurs" who politicized old or newly invented primordial sentiments with a view to accruing personal benefits. It is in this regard that Bates (1974) describes ethnicity as an efficient resource in the competition for the "goods of modernity" (cited in Atieno-Odhiambo 2002: 232). Such ethnic entrepreneurs have also used ethnicity as a tool for protection against "loss of acquired privilege, or as a scapegoat when dissatisfaction with the government is transformed into complaints about the ethnic group or groups presumably in power" (Wallerstein 1960, 1979 cited in Atieno-Odhiambo 2002: 232). In Kenya, the war cry whenever such privileges of a "big man" patron are threatened has been "our tribe is targeted." The key point that Atieno-Odhiambo (2002) makes is that there is a role played by political economy in production of ethnic-based nationalism where elites instrumentalize ethnicity for their own survival and reproduction (Young 1986). It is this form of instrumentalized ethnicity in political competition with other groups that Lonsdale (1994) and Berman (2004, 2010) label political tribalism.

Subalterns fall for this trick through a "false consciousness" of their situated ethnic subjectivities. This is because ideology of kinship makes elites appear as patrons of their tribal constituencies rather than the exploiters of workers and peasants that they are (Arrighi and Saul 1973). This is evident in Kenya where since colonial times, elites have whipped their respective co-ethnics for support in their competition for state power, which is critically important for securing a place at the table for opportunities for rent seeking and sharing of the same. In his analysis of the making of the Kikuyu and Luo ethnicity in post-colonial Kenya, Atieno-Odhiambo (2002: 233) argues that there was deliberate agency in Oginga Odinga and Jomo Kenyatta. In the post-Kenyatta years, Daniel Arap Moi, Mwai Kibaki, and Uhuru Kenyatta regimes have continued the deliberate class interest oriented reproduction of ethnicity in Kenyan politics. The net effect is that subaltern struggles can never unify as their basis for organizing is ethnicity which is wide and fluid, instead of class, which is more precise.

Another version explains the dominance of elite and ethnic-based political mobilization to the fact that arguably, elites are a better organized social group in Kenya to capitalize on "local fears and opportunities" (Mueller 2008; Jenkins 2012; Lynch 2008). The clientelist ethnically driven political parties in Kenya, coupled by the first-past-the-post winner-takes-all electoral system, raises the stakes of winning and even gives rise to ethnic-based political violence, especially since the reintroduction of multi-partyism in 1992 (Mueller 2008). Since then, certain political parties have come to be associated with specific individuals and their ethnic groups, and voting "defensively and fundamentally an ethnic census [attributable to] high degree of mistrust of members of other ethnic groups" (Bratton and Kimenyi 2008: 287). This generated contestations as excluded elites with support from subaltern groups demanded reforms. Similarly, Lynch (2008: 541) shows how "intra-elite cleavages are widened with the support of subordinate groups" sometimes resulting in widespread election related violence. This happens because many Kenyans vote for one of their own co-ethnic political elite based on their own fears of what will happen if the "other" wins power and hopes of what they might gain if one of their "own" wins power (Lonsdale 1994). In this regard, "bottom-up performance of narratives of ethnic territorial exclusion" operate alongside more direct elite involvement, organization, and incitement (Jenkins 2012: 576) in the production of ethnic-based intra-elite competition for power.

Ethnicity as an Imagined Community

A more contemporary explanation of ethnicity in politics is that like nationalism, ethnicity is a product of social imagination that is constructed, invented, or created (Anderson 1983) and must be constantly worked (Atieno-Odhiambo 2002: 231). Within this school of thought, ethnicity is seen as a form of creative "nationalism, an intellectually imaginative political project of liberation that makes claims on behalf of civil rights, directly comparable with European nationalisms, if also sharing their Janus-faced potential for exclusive, jealous evil" (Lonsdale 1994: 136). This approach in not necessarily novel; it borrows from the four afore discussed explanations to argue that ethnicity has been constantly changing since the pre-colonial period. Specifically, Kenyan ethnic communities, it is argued, have evolved geographic specializations. Examples include fisherfolk along the coastal and the western regions due to the presence of large water bodies, highland farmers due to presence of fertile arable land, and plain pastoralists due to existence of large amount of pasture land. Each of these geo-ethnic communities have their own moral economy or means of judging civic virtue (Lonsdale 1994: 137) and a specialized exchange and rulership. The social imagination and self-awareness of ethnic groups, the argument goes, comes through time due to interactions with the external world. This is historically explained, through colonial political economy, which accelerated labor market process as "people begun to compete for the same resources of employment, urban shelter, and security" (Lonsdale 1994: 137).

Other aspects responsible for imagination are the decentralized despotism resulting from the European conquest and attendant domination which gave some people power "to help friends and hurt their enemies" and therein sharpened consciousness of difference (Lonsdale 1994: 138). This resulted in the substitution of moral economy with moral ethnicity. Here, ethnicity acquired a primordial patriotic label and transformation from moral to amoral one. These developments were/are not countered by class fractures due to ethnicity creating and reproducing a false consciousness where wealthier co-ethnics are imagined to have obligation to the poorer co-ethnics. Missionary education accelerated this through creation of vernaculars instead of promotion of the lingua franca for the country.

In the last few decades, politically instigated violence have been incubated in the disorder of ethnicized intra-elite competition and especially buttressed by a stalemate in the constitution review contentions since mid-1990s. This disorder manifests as competing visions for curing existing socioeconomic and political crisis represented on one hand, by a dominant conservative political elite faction obstinately opposed to state reforms. Using state and personal resources, this elite faction occasionally employs violence, patronage, co-optations, as well as piecemeal concessions to stem the reform wave without fundamentally curing existing contradictions. On the other hand, a faction of opposition political elites and middle-class civil society activists united more by their opposition to the dominant elite faction than by the nature of change desired continue to challenge this order (Mati 2013). It is the impasse between these groups and their version of instrumentalized ethnicity, coupled by state institution's inability to mediate intra-elite competition in an environment of widespread dispersal of violence capacity among competing elite groups that has in the last two and half decades resulted in electoral violence, for which 2007/2008 was most poignant.

The resolution of the ethnic-based political violence has involved elite bargains. In 1997, for example, such elite bargains came in the form of the Inter Parties Parliamentary Group (IPPG) agreements that offered the institutional parameters for changing the constitution. However, subsequent ethnic-based elite impasses stalled the process. This impasse ignited the Ufungamano Initiative-led efforts at constitutional reforms (Mati 2012). This effort at reforms was again thwarted even after the merger of the state-led processes with the Ufungamano Initiative, resulting in the rejection of the government supported constitution draft in a 2005 referendum, and subsequently to electoral related inter-ethnic conflict in 2007/2008. The resolution of the 2007/2008 violence jumpstarted the stalled constitution reform project, delivering a new constitution in August 2010. The 2010 constitution introduced institutional arrangements aimed at altering relations between elites and making state institutions to be viable mediators of competing elite groups.

More fundamentally, the 2010 constitution effectively dispersed rent-seeking and patronage opportunities to broader elite factions by creating a two-tier government (county and national) and a bicameral parliament. Importantly, the post-2010 constitutional institutions attempted to constrain elite political behavior, resulting in relative calm in the 2013 elections because state institutions enjoyed relative trust among powerful political elite formations. The recent Kenyan constitutional reforms process and outcomes are illustrative of contemporary theorizations on the political economy of violence in emergent democracies (see, e.g., Arias and Goldstein 2010; North et al. 2013; Von Holdt 2014). In South Africa, for instance, political violence is shaped by "political inclusion and high levels socio-economic exclusion" (Von Holdt 2014: 147). On the other hand, North et al. (2013: 1) argue that in most developing countries, the capacity of violence is widely dispersed among diverse elite groups who, in many instances, refrain from violence but "occasionally find violence a useful tool for pursuing their ends." Such "societies limit violence through the manipulation of economic interests by the political system in order to create rents so that powerful groups and individuals find it in their interest to refrain from using violence" (North et al. 2013: 3). These social arrangements, labelled "limited access orders" by North et al. (2013: 3), specifically limit violence by creating and institutionalizing incentives for leaders of competing groups to coordinate and ensure an agreed or "fair" exclusive sharing of rents among themselves. Such elite bargains can result into elite coalitions or even constitutions that incentivize elite cooperation, deter violence, and even further entrench democratization. For Kenya, the jury is still out on whether the 2010 constitution will be able to finally arrest the beast of ethnic-based politics and attendant violence.

Conclusion

Scholarly discourses on ethnicity in politics in Kenya are centered on two dominant approaches: one is the treatment of ethnicity as an instrumentally constituted social phenomenon and the other is that it is naturally occurring. These are further explained utilizing five arguments presented in this chapter. These are that ethnicity is a modern day residual category of a fast disappearing phenomenon (tribe) as Africa modernizes. The second is that ethnicity is a form of social resistance or an outgrowth – almost an invention – of colonial state power. The third argument is that ethnicity is a product of false conscious ideology used to mask class interests by elites. Fourth is the view that ethnicity is a form of nationalism – primordial or national. Finally the contemporary view is that ethnic identity is socially imagined. As such, following Berman (1998: 305) ethnicity in Kenyan politics is "always simultaneously old and new, grounded in the past and perpetually in creation." Such imagination and creation has resulted to ethnic-based Kenyan politics, which often breeds inter-ethnic conflict and violence. The role played by ethnicity in Kenyan politics provides powerful illustrations of how a convoluted nexus of state institutions and political economy of power and ethnicity results into political tribalism and even political violence. This has called for institutional arrangements to help mediate between competing interests and differences through accommodation. The 2010 constitution's consociational power dispersal model offers a ray of hope in this regard. However the ongoing intra-elite power struggle suggests that the country is yet not out of the woods as far as destructive forces of ethnicity in politics go.

Cross-References

▶ Ethnicity and Violence in Sri Lanka: An Ethnohistorical Narrative
▶ Patterns and Drivers of Communal Conflict in Kenya
▶ Racism in Colonial Zimbabwe
▶ The Significance of Ethno-politics in Modern States and Society

References

Aina T (2013) The state, politics and philanthropy in Africa: framing the context. In: Aina T, Moyo B (eds) Giving to help, helping to give: the context and politics of African philanthropy. Amalion Press, Dakar, pp 1–36

Ajulu R (2002) Politicised ethnicity, competitive politics and conflict in Kenya: A Historical Perspective, African Studies, 61(2):251–268, https://doi.org/10.1080/0002018022000032947

Anderson B (1983) Imagined communities. Verso, London

Arias ED, Goldstein DM (eds) (2010) Violent democracies in Latin America. Duke University Press, Durham

Arrighi G, Saul JS (1973) Essays on the political economy of Africa. Monthly Review Press, New York

Atieno-Odhiambo ES (2002) Hegemonic enterprises and instrumentalities of survival: ethnicity and democracy in Kenya. Afr Stud 61(2):223–249. https://doi.org/10.1080/0002018022000032938a

Balandier G (1955) Sociologie actuelle de 'Afrique noire: Dynamique des changements sociaux en Afrique centrale. Presses Universitaires de France, Paris

Bayart JF (1989) The state in Africa: politics of the belly. Fayard, Paris

Berman BJ (1998) Ethnicity, patronage and the African State: The politics of uncivil nationalism. African Affairs 97:305–341

Berman BJ (2004) Ethnicity, bureaucracy & democracy: The politics of trust. In B. Berman, W. Kymlicka, & D. Eyoh (Eds.), Ethnicity and Democracy in Africa James Currey, Oxford, pp.38–53

Berman B (2010) Ethnicity and democracy in Africa. JICA Research Institute working paper No. 22, November 2010

Bratton M, Kimenyi MS (2008) Voting in Kenya: putting ethnicity in perspective. J East Afr Stud 2(2):272–289

Brubaker R, Cooper F (2000) Beyond identity. Theory Soc 29:1

Coleman J, Rosberg CG (eds) (1964) Political parties and national integration in tropical Africa. University of California Press, Berkley/Los Angeles

Ekeh P (1975) Colonialism and the two publics in Africa: a theoretical statement. Comp Stud Soc Hist 17(1):91–112

Ekeh P (1990) Social anthropology and two contrasting uses of tribalism in Africa. Comp Stud Soc Hist 32:688–689

Fowler A, Mati JM (2019) African gifting: pluralising the concept of philanthropy. Voluntas. https://doi.org/10.1007/s11266-018-00079-z

Glazer, N., Greeley, A.M., Patterson, O. and Moynihan, D.P. (1974). What is ethnicity? Bull Am Acad Arts Sci 27 (8): 16–35

Haugeraud A (1995) The culture of politics. Cambridge University Press, New York

Jenkins S (2012) Ethnicity, violence, and the immigrant-guest metaphor in Kenya. Afr Aff 111(445):576–596

Klopp JM (2002) Can moral ethnicity trump political tribalism? The struggle for land and nation in Kenya. Afr Stud 61(2):269–294

Lentz C (1995) "Tribalism" and ethnicity in Africa. Cah Sci Hum 31(2):303–328

Long JD, Gibson CC (2015) Evaluating the roles of ethnicity and performance in African elections: evidence from an exit poll in Kenya. Polit Res Q 68(4):830–842

Long JD, Kanyinga K, Ferree KE, Gibson C (2013) Choosing peace over democracy. J Democr 24(3):140–155

Lonsdale J (1994) Moral ethnicity and political tribalism. In: Kaarsholm P, Hultin J (eds) Inventions and boundaries: historical and anthropological approaches to the study of ethnicity and nationalism. Roskilde University, Roskilde, pp 131–150

Lynch G (2008) Courting the Kalenjin: the failure of dynasticism and the strength of the ODM wave in Kenya's Rift Valley Province. Afr Aff 107(429):541–568

Maina W (1998) Kenya: the state, donors and the politics of democratization. In: Van Rooy A (ed) Civil society and the aid industry. Earthscan, London, pp 134–167

Mamdani M (1996) Citizen and subject: contemporary Africa and the legacy of late colonialism. Fountain Publishers, Kampala

Mati JM (2012) The power and limits of social movements in promoting political and constitutional change: the case of the ufungamano initiative in Kenya (1999–2005). Doctoral dissertation, University of the Witwatersrand

Mati JM (2013) Antinomies in the struggle for the transformation of the Kenyan constitution (1990–2010). J Contemp Afr Stud 31(2):235–254

Mbithi P (1974) Rural sociology and rural development; its application in Kenya. East African Literature Bureau, Nairobi

Mueller SD (2008) The political economy of Kenya's crisis. J East Afr Stud 2(2):185–210

Namu JA (2013) The first betrayal. https://www.youtube.com/watch?v=B_N5vgg8eD4
North D, Wallis JJ, Webb SB, Weingast BR (eds) (2013) In the shadow of violence: politics, economics and the problems of development. Cambridge University Press, Cambridge, MA
Nzomo M (2003) Civil society in the Kenyan political transition: 1992–2002. In: Oyugi WO, Wanyande P, Odhiambo-Mbai C (eds) The politics of transition in Kenya: from KANU to NARC. Heinrich Böll Foundation, Nairobi, pp 180–211
Ogude J (2002) Ethnicity, nationalism and the making of democracy in Kenya: an introduction. Afr Stud 61(2):205–207
Omolo K (2002) Political ethnicity in the democratisation process in Kenya. Afr Stud 61(2):209–221. https://doi.org/10.1080/0002018022000032938
Ranger T (1983) The invention of tradition in colonial Africa. In: Hobsbawm E, Ranger T (eds) The invention of tradition. Cambridge University Press, Cambridge, MA
Vail L (ed) (1989) The creation of tribalism in southern Africa. James Currey, London
Von Holdt K (2014) On violent democracy. Sociol Rev 62(S2):129–151
Young C (1986) Nationalism, ethnicity and class in Africa: a retrospective. Cah Etud Afr 26(103):421–495

Ethno-politics in the People's Republic of China

16

Matthew Hoddie

Contents

Introduction	284
Diversity in the PRC	284
Changes in the PRC's Minority Policies Over Time	286
The Maoist Era	286
The Reform Era	288
Interethnic Relations in the Reform Era: New and Old Tensions	291
Limits to Autonomy	294
Alternative Approaches to Ethnic Relations in the PRC	296
Conclusion	297
Cross-References	298
References	298

Abstract

This study describes the ethnic diversity that exists within the People's Republic of China (PRC) and how the country's government has approached the issue of interethnic relations. Focusing on the examples of the Tibetan and Uyghur ethnic groups, the essay identifies significant changes that are apparent in the government's posture toward minority communities during the periods of Maoist extremism and the reform era. Recent episodes of protest and violence by minority communities are attributed to continuing social discrimination and significant limitations associated with the government's efforts to address minority grievances. The essay concludes with a consideration of different proposals to reform the government's approach to ethnic relations within the PRC.

Keywords

People's Republic of China (PRC) · Han · Tibetans · Uyghurs · Autonomy

M. Hoddie (✉)
Department of Political Science, Towson University, Towson, MD, USA
e-mail: mhoddie@towson.edu

© The Author(s), under exclusive license to Springer Nature Singapore Pte Ltd. 2019
S. Ratuva (ed.), *The Palgrave Handbook of Ethnicity*,
https://doi.org/10.1007/978-981-13-2898-5_147

Introduction

While the People's Republic of China (PRC) is not typically understood to be a multiethnic state, the country does contain substantial diversity within its borders. The majority of Chinese citizens identify as members of the Han ethnic group, yet the 2010 census reports that 8.49% of people classify themselves as belonging to a minority community. Given a country with the world's largest population, this 8.49% amounts to almost 112 million people – a number that dwarfs the total population of states such as Britain and France.

The discussion that I present in this chapter considers changes over time in the relationship between the government of the PRC and its minority communities. I divide the presentation into five sections. I begin with a description of some of the more notable differences that exist among the groups that comprise China's minority population. A second section identifies distinct historical periods in government policy toward minority communities, highlighting the differences apparent between the periods of Maoist extremism and reform. The third section considers the forms of interethnic tension that have persisted in China despite the government's adoption of limited reforms intended to accommodate minority interests. The section that follows identifies limitations associated with the current government's system of regional autonomy for minority groups and suggests that these limitations may account for the continuing suspicions and hostilities that exist between the majority and minority groups. The essay concludes with a consideration of different means by which the government might reform its approach to interethnic relations.

Diversity in the PRC

The PRC's government recognizes a total of 55 different minority communities, with the most recent census reporting that 9 of these groups are comprised of populations greater than 5 million. In order of population size, the largest groups are the Zhuang (16.9 million), Hui (10.6 million), Manchu (10.4 million), Uyghurs (10.1 million), Miao (9.4 million), Yi (8.7 million), Tujia (8.4 million), Tibetans (6.3 million), and Mongols (6 million).

The Han majority has tended to perceive and characterize the country's minority communities in negative terms. Studies of Chinese media portrayals of minorities highlight that these groups are typically depicted as primitives beset by pathologies such as poverty, illiteracy, and superstition. Characterized in these terms, minorities have come to serve as objects of fascination that are understood to represent China's distant past. This curiosity about the lives of members of these groups is apparent in the presence of minority-themed restaurants and amusement parks in the country, promising to provide the Han with a glimpse of the exotic "other" and their own ancient history. By characterizing minority communities as backward, the Han also tacitly invoke an understanding of their own community as civilized and superior (Blum 2001; Hoddie and Lou 2009).

As one might anticipate, the use of harmful and inaccurate stereotypes to characterize these ethnic groups has had a negative influence of the relationship between majority and minority groups. As a symptom of this tension between communities, minority citizens often highlight the problem of "big Han chauvinism" within the country. At its most benign, this chauvinism is apparent when government representatives promote policies, such as those associated with education or economic development, that do not sufficiently take into account the cultural sensitivities of minorities. At its worst, this chauvinism has been seen in acts of overt discrimination and hostility toward those defined as outside the boundaries of the majority group.

Despite this tendency among members of the majority to characterize minorities through the use of stereotypes, these groups are distinct from one another across a number of significant dimensions. One means by which these groups may be contrasted is in terms of their degree of social differentiation from the Han. A number of these ethnic groups are now largely assimilated with the majority in terms of appearance, language, and culture. Groups such as the Zhuang, Tujia, and Manchu have thus been described as constituting an "ethnic category," with only their identity label signaling their minority status. These assimilated groups stand in contrast to those collectivities described as "ethnic communities" that maintain identity markers that indicate and reinforce their differences with the majority. Included among the groups that might be accurately described as "ethnic communities" are the Tibetans, Uyghurs, and Mongols (Liu 1996, 193–195).

If there is an awareness of China's minority communities in the West, it is of these largely unassimilated "ethnic communities" and the efforts by some members of these groups to press their claims for either greater autonomy or independence from the central government in Beijing. Most prominent among these resistance movements are those associated with the Tibetan and Uyghur ethnic communities.

The Tibetan population of China are adherents to the Buddhist religion and are concentrated on the Tibetan plateau in the country's southwest region. Members of this group have made their demands for greater accommodation by the PRC known in recent years through acts of self-immolation. The first public suicide of this type occurred in 2009. At the time of this writing, there have been a total of 153 instances in which an individual has chosen to set themselves on fire in protest against the Chinese state; 122 of those acts of protest have resulted in death (Self-immolations by Tibetans 2018). Most of those that have attempted to commit suicide in this manner have either been young Buddhist monks or former monks.

China's Uyghur population also has an uncomfortable relationship with the Han majority and an atheist state. Adherents to Islam, and primarily residing in Xinjiang province, some members of this community have sought to make their demands for greater accommodation apparent through acts of terrorist violence. Most prominently, there have been instances in which members of the Uyghur community have engaged in the assassination of government officials and violent attacks targeting public transportation systems. Concerns about terrorist violence often serve as a justification for government surveillance and mass arrests of Uyghurs. This was the case in 2008, as the government engaged in a crackdown against members of this community that they justified based on concerns about possible terrorist attacks during the Beijing Summer Olympics (Jacobs 2008).

Further heightening the stakes of the disputes between these two ethnic groups and the state is the fact that the territories in which these groups reside are rich in natural resources and occupy lands that are considered strategically significant to the Chinese state. The Tibetan Autonomous Region (TAR) occupies a border region between the countries of China and India – two countries that fought a war against one another in 1962 and still have unresolved disagreements over competing territorial claims. The region has a wealth of mineral resources that the Chinese government has been eager to exploit, including copper, lead, zinc, and iron (Johnson 2011, 73–74). Similarly, Xinjiang proves strategically important as it is adjacent to a number of states, including some that were once part of the Soviet Union, such as Kazakhstan and Tajikistan. Xinjiang contains significant oil and natural gas reserves that are important to China's future economic development (Van Wie Davis 2008, 24–25).

Changes in the PRC's Minority Policies Over Time

How has the PRC's government addressed the challenges associated with the diversity that exists within the state? The government has adopted distinctive strategies over time. During most of the era associated with Mao Zedong's leadership, the state proved hostile toward minority communities and sought to promote rapid assimilation with the Han majority. Following Mao's death and the initiation of the reform era, policies shifted substantially toward greater tolerance and efforts to accommodate the distinct interests of minority communities. Here I document the substance of these changes in government policy and describe their influence on the relationship between minority communities and the government.

The Maoist Era

In the early years following the Communist revolution of 1949, both the party and state exercised restraint in their interactions with minorities. Focusing its energies on other tasks associated with the process of the communist transition, the government engaged in what might best be described as "benign neglect" of minority areas. Many minority-concentrated regions were designated as autonomous, with guarantees that the residents of these autonomous regions would have the opportunity to use their own languages and adhere to their own distinct cultural practices (Dreyer 2004, 292–296).

In the case of Tibet, the People's Liberation Army (PLA) initiated attacks on the territory in 1950 with the intention of asserting control over the territory. But even in this instance, the government offered accommodations to minorities. The PRC and the Dalai Lama (the theocratic leader of Tibet) negotiated the Seventeen Point Agreement (SPA) that kept a degree of authority in the hands of the Tibetan people.

In return for recognizing Chinese sovereignty over the region, the SPA provided that Tibet would be allowed to maintain its political system under the Dalai Lama and that the government would not prohibit the practice of Tibetan Buddhism (Goldstein 1997, 47–52; Shakya 1999, 89–90).

This tolerance toward minority communities, both in Tibet and throughout the rest of China, came to an abrupt end with the initiation of the mobilization campaigns that some consider the primary legacies of the Maoist era and that earned Mao his status as one of the greatest mass murderers in history. The most notable of these mobilization campaigns are the Great Leap Forward and the Great Proletarian Cultural Revolution.

The Great Leap Forward (GLF), associated with the years between 1958 and 1961, was Mao's mobilization campaign to initiate rapid economic development in the country through a reliance on the ingenuity and revolutionary zeal of the peasantry. As the title of the campaign suggests, the ambition of the government was for China to take a giant leap into its economic future and provide the country with the means to rival the development of wealthier states.

The era of the Great Leap Forward had disastrous consequences for China's minority communities. Earlier guarantees of autonomy were disavowed by the CPP and state with the initiation of the GLF. Consistent with the characterization of minority cultures as "primitive," distinctive minority practices were now condemned as detrimental to the goal of promoting economic development. As a result, minorities were discouraged from speaking their own languages, wearing distinctive clothing associated with their community, or taking time away from work to engage in prayer (Dreyer 2004, 297–298).

An important element of the GLF was the development of agricultural communes. These communes typically brought together approximately 5000 families who were required to work the land in common. Functions that were once carried out by individual families, such as child care and the preparation of meals, were now the responsibility of the collective. Members of minority communities found these communal arrangements to be particularly difficult to accept as it often required that they compromise their culture values. To note one prominent example, members of Muslim groups, such as the Uyghurs and Kazaks, objected to being served meals that were not prepared in observance of the dietary requirements of their religion (Dreyer 2004, 297–298).

It is clear that many citizens resented and resisted the loss of independence associated with work in the communes, and the often-harsh working conditions imposed on them in the context of the GLF. Events in Tibet serve to represent the exacerbated tensions that emerged between minorities and the Han during this period. Concerned about the growing assertiveness of party officials in Tibet, as well as threats to his own safety, the Dalai Lama fled Tibet in 1959 and established a government-in-exile in neighboring India.

Most of the experiments with management and technology initiated during the GLF proved a failure. In the aftermath of the mobilization campaign, the country experienced widespread famine that resulted in the deaths of tens of millions of people. These famines did not spare minority communities; estimates suggest that thousands of Tibetans died during this period (Sautman 2006, 243).

The Great Proletarian Cultural Revolution (GPCR) serves as the second mobilization campaign that defines the Maoist era. Initiated in 1966, the GPCR was Mao's effort to remove his political rivals from the CCP and give the emerging generation of Chinese a revolutionary experience that would promote a sense of patriotism and fervor for communist ideals. Toward this end, Mao encouraged students from high school and college to abandon their studies and join what were known as the "Red Guards." Red Guards were assigned the task of identifying the enemies of communism who promoted ideas and values contrary to the spirit of the 1949 revolution.

Among the slogans that Mao articulated during this time was the need for society to smash the "four olds" of ideas, culture, customs, and habit. Given the common perception of minority communities as representative of "primitive" cultures, Red Guards understood themselves to have license to participate in acts of intolerance and brutality against these groups. Scholars have documented episodes of violence targeting minority groups such as the Tibetan, Uyghur, Mongolian, and Korean communities. Beyond attacks on citizens, there was also damage and insults to the culture of these societies through the destruction of places of worship (such as Buddhist temples) and cultural symbols (Hoddie 2006, 65–66).

Reviewing the state of ethnic relations following the GPCR, Thomas Heberer (1989, 29) offers the following characterization:

> Humiliation, insults, oppression, and an attempt at forced assimilation; destruction of the ecological equilibrium and ruinous exploitation; economic plundering of the minority regions; these were the consequences of the Cultural Revolution for the national minorities and their regions. It is no wonder that relations between the Han and minorities remain embittered; it will take much time to heal these wounds.

Taken as a whole, it is clear that the extremism associated with the Maoist era served to poison the relationship between the Han majority and minority communities. The distrust that still exists between these communities can trace its roots to the acts of intolerance and violence that took place on Mao's watch. Given what transpired during this period, it is easy to understand why members of many minority communities have sought either greater autonomy or independence from the Chinese state.

The Reform Era

With Mao's passing, China's government embarked on a series of reforms that scaled back government hostility toward minority populations. Why these changes were initiated at this time is not immediately apparent. It may have been the case that the government and party were genuinely interested in providing some level of reparations to minority communities that had suffered a great deal as a result of Maoist extremism. Another possibility is that the government was increasingly concerned about the sense of disaffection for the Chinese state apparent in the border regions of the country in which minorities are concentrated, and in particular how this hostility might serve as a source of vulnerability for the country in its interactions with foreign powers (Hoddie 2006, 67).

Perhaps the most significant benefit that was provided to members of minority communities during the reform period were exemptions from the one-child-per-family policy. Starting in 1979, the PRC's government had imposed a policy that limited couples in the country to a single child. This limit on fertility was deeply resented by couples in China given a cultural preference for large families and ensuring the birth of at least one male heir. This limit on fertility was eased or lifted for many minority communities. In most cases, provided that at least one parent could claim a minority identity, couples residing in urban areas were allowed to have two children. Couples claiming minority heritage from rural areas encountered no limitations and were allowed to have as many children as they wished (Dreyer 2004, 377).

This concession by the state was not costly, as most minorities reside in rural areas with low population density. But the symbolic significance of this policy for minorities proved immense, as it signaled a willingness by the government to allow minority groups to rebuild after years of state-fostered hostility and population losses. The government abandoned the one-child-per-family policy in 2015, and the right to have more than one child was extended to the country's population as a whole.

Even in terms of religion, a controversial issue for an officially atheist state that includes a number of religious minorities, the government sought to offer greater, if incomplete, accommodation. Some have characterized the state's approach to religion during this era as associated with both "soft" and "hard" policies. "Soft" policies are defined by efforts to allow for religious expression, provided that it takes place in the context of state-approved organizations. In the context of both Tibet and Xinjiang, the government has funded the rebuilding or new construction of places of worship. There has also been a willingness to allow for religious activities through state-controlled entities such as the Chinese Islamic Association. At the opposite extreme, "hard" policies are the often-harsh punishments that are meted out to those who engage in religious activities outside of the purview of state authority. Prohibited activities include proselytizing by religious activists and the provision of religious instruction outside of state-approved organizations (Clarke 2008, 279).

Other changes in government policy intended to accommodate minorities that took place during the reform period may be categorized as either political or economic in form. Political changes included the passage of new laws that mandated increasing representation and accommodation for minority communities. In terms of representation in the central state, the 1982 constitution required that a minimum of 12% of seats in the country's legislature – the National People's Congress (NPC) – be reserved for members of minority groups. At the local level, the 1984 Law on Regional Autonomy extended the rights associated with political autonomy to 20% more counties than had previously held this status. The 1984 law reiterates the understanding that autonomous areas maintain the right to determine their own laws governing issues such as economic policy and cultural protections (Dreyer 2004, 375–376; Mackerras 1994, 155–156).

Considering the laws passed by the NPC, Barry Sautman (1999, 288–289) notes a similar trend in prioritizing the interests of minority citizens during the reform era. In his words:

> Of some two hundred NPC laws and State Council regulations created from 1979 to 1995, at least forty contain 'ethnic issues' provisions (Xinhua 3 March 1996). Statistics of this kind are deceptive, however. Some provisions do more than reiterate the power already given under the 1984 Law on Regional Autonomy (LRA) (*minzu quyu zizhi fa*): autonomy areas are empowered to adapt, modify, or supplement national laws according to local conditions (China 1987: 87–10). Other provisions are mere exhortations to take minority interests into account.

Economic reforms initiated during this period were intended to expand the financial resources directed toward minority communities and also enhance the educational and work opportunities for the members of these groups. In recognition of the fact that many autonomous regions are located in areas of the country that are relatively impoverished, the government maintained relatively low tax burdens for these regions while simultaneously investing substantial government funds in local public works projects (Sugimoto 1993, 9–19). These projects often had the potential to hire members of minority communities as workers and thus provided a financial benefit through employment (Sautman 1999, 294).

The government also instituted reforms that enhanced the educational opportunities available to minorities, seeking to address the fact that academic achievement in minority regions has often lagged behind those associated with the Han. Along with the establishment of new schools with the explicit mission of educating minorities, the Chinese state also sought to enhance minority access to existing educational institutions. A policy of affirmative action was established that enhanced the access of minority citizens to university-level education (Kaup 2000, 136). Based on a favorable weighting of their standardized tests scores, thousands of students from minority groups gained admission to universities that would have otherwise proven out of reach (Sautman 1998, 82–83).

Taken together, these policies signaled a dramatic change in the government's attitudes and actions toward minorities in comparison to the Maoist era. Rather than a posture of hostility toward minority communities and pressures to assimilate, programs adopted during the reform era provided these same minority communities with preferential access to government benefits and programs.

One potential indication that this change in the government's minority policy has served to improve interethnic relations appears in China's census data. A comparison of the 1982 and 1990 census enumerations shows a 14 million person increase in the number of individuals claiming a minority identity. Demographers note that this population increase cannot be accounted for by birth rates alone. It is instead a function of a conscious choice by individuals to disavow an earlier affiliation with the majority Han and instead claim membership in a minority group (Hoddie 2006, 69–70).

One interpretation, favored by critics of these reforms, is that this shift in the size of China's minority population reflects a self-interested strategy by some within the

PRC. According to this perspective, the choice to newly assert a minority identity is not based on a rediscovery of an individual's minority heritage. It is instead a cynical ploy to lay claim to benefits that would otherwise remain out of reach. While the possibility of some acts of strategic dissimulation cannot be fully discounted, I am unconvinced that this is the dominant trend. My own interpretation of these changes in identity claims is that it is reflective of the fact that many people within China felt a need to disavow a minority identity during the Maoist era given unremitting government and societal hostility to members of these groups. Once the political winds shifted toward reform, however, these same individuals felt encouraged to reassert what they understood to be their genuine identity (Hoddie 2006, 70).

Interethnic Relations in the Reform Era: New and Old Tensions

While it is clear that the implementation of these changes in policy during the reform era signaled a new approach to addressing the challenges associated with governing a diverse society, they have not proven to be a panacea to the problem of interethnic tensions in China. There is instead evidence of new forms of intergroup hostility emerging in the PRC, while simultaneously some of the old rivalries based on ethnic difference have remained resistant to amelioration.

The relatively new form of intergroup tension within the PRC has taken the form of resentment voiced by members of the Han majority concerning the government-based benefits provided to the members of minority communities. Parallel to the arguments against affirmative action-style policies in the United States and other countries, members of the Han majority have articulated grievances based on claims that they have unequal access to educational and economic opportunities as a result of the preferences reserved for minorities.

Given the paucity of survey research in China on issues related to ethnic issues, it is difficult to gauge exactly how widespread or deeply felt these views critical of preferential policies are in the PRC. At least one observer of ethnic politics in China suggests that while these resentments exist, particularly as they relate to the exemption from family planning laws and preferential access to education, they have never formed the basis for the mobilization of protests or acts of violence (Sautman 1998, 105). While it seems unlikely that these resentments will ever coalesce into the basis of a popular movement, it seems clear that at least some segments of China's majority population would like to see these policies revised or ended.

Beyond the claim that these minority-centered policies are detrimental to the interests of the majority, some critics of these programs further suggest that these programs are counterproductive and actually encourage continued activism and resistance by the members of ethnic minority groups. This perspective is articulated in the work of Ma Rong, a retired sociologist from Beijing University whose work on minority issues has proven increasingly influential in both academic and policymaking circles within China. Central to Ma's perspective is the view that providing political autonomy and economic benefits to individuals on the basis of ethnicity has had the unintended effect of reinforcing divisions between groups and inhibiting the potential for social integration. He articulates this view in the following terms:

> These policies link each minority to a certain geographic area, provide these groups with a political status, administrative power in their "autonomous territory", and guarantee ethnic minorities the potential to develop at a high speed. The process of establishing and implementing these policies and institutions, with their emphasis on "equality among citizens", will inevitably politicize and institutionalize these groups and strengthen their group consciousness. This will have the effect of pushing them away from being "cultural groups" and towards the direction of becoming 'political groups' in the "ethnicity-nation" continuum. (Ma 2007, 14)

Ma suggests that if China fails to alter its ethnic policies, the potential exists that the country will eventually experience the same fate as the Soviet Union and disintegrate along ethnic lines. Tibet and Xinjiang are obvious candidates for forming newly sovereign states should such a scenario be realized.

As an alternative to the current set of policies, Ma Rong advocates an approach that would transition the government away from employing ethnicity as a means of determining access to state resources and benefits. He suggests that the government should instead pursue ethnically blind public policies that prioritize assisting the poor without reference to their ethnic identity label. In a similar vein, he recommends that the current system of autonomous governance for minority areas be phased out with an eye toward discouraging ethnic groups from perceiving themselves as holding ownership over a particular territory (Sautman 2012, 19).

These policy prescriptions seem unlikely to be embraced given the dismay and resistance it would almost certainly invite from China's minority communities. Rather than considering these recommendations as meaningful options for governance, they might instead be best interpreted as an indicator that there now exists within the PRC a certain level of discontent with the current set of minority policies favored by the government and that this has led to a degree of interethnic tension. This Han backlash against the preferences provided to minorities appears to be a new form of interethnic dispute that was not in evidence prior to the initiation of the reform era.

The other form of interethnic tensions that has proven apparent in the context of the reform era is a continuation of the hostility and violence between the Chinese state and those minority groups that were previously characterized as "ethnic communities" in this study – including the Tibetans and Uyghurs. This might appear surprising given the shifts in government policy and the attendant growth in the number of individuals willing to embrace a minority identity. In fact, a close examination of the census data related to shifting identity claims suggests that it is those groups that were among the most assimilated with the majority, which were previously described here as "ethnic categories," that experienced the greatest shifts in population claims. These groups include the Manchu and Tujia. For groups that are more clearly distinctive and alienated from the Han majority, polarization and resistance to the Chinese state remains the norm (Hoddie 2006, 74).

In the case of the Tibetan community, there have been repeated protests and riots that reflect the strong and continuing opposition of members of this group to the Chinese government. Such episodes proved particularly apparent between the years 1987 and 1989. Two examples serve to illustrate the forms of violence that took place during this period. During October 1987, a demonstration held in the provincial capital of Lhasa progressed from a peaceful protest to a large-scale riot. As a result of the violence, both a police station and a number of stores within the city were burned, with estimates suggesting that up to 20 Tibetans were shot by police (Smith 1996, 603; Goldstein 1997, 79; Shakya 1999, 416). Riots in Lhasa also took place in both March 1988 and 1989. In the case of the 1989 disturbance, it is reported that 45 shops were destroyed and up to 150 Tibetans died in confrontations with security forces. As a result of this unrest, martial law was imposed on Tibet and not lifted until the following year (Smith 1996, 617–618).

A second spasm of violence associated with Tibetan resistance to Chinese rule took place during 2008. In this instance, the riots in Lhasa proved much more intense, and the violence spread to much of the rest of the TAR, as well as neighboring provinces with large Tibetan populations. This included protest events in the provinces of Sichuan, Gansu, and Qinghai (Johnson 2011, 92–93). In response to this unrest, the government detained over 1000 people in the TAR alone (Wong 2008).

In the case of Xinjiang, there have also been parallel moments of mass unrest followed by repression by government authorities. Protests and riots against Chinese rule took place during 1990 in Baren township, with similar events inspired by the violence in Baren taking place for a number of years in other cities throughout the province (Holdstock 2014, 4). In 1997, significant protests and unrest again took place. In this case, the city of Yining became the site of resistance activity that lasted for a number of days before government control was reasserted (Holdstock 2014, 4–5). In each of these cases, reports suggest that protestors made their antipathy to Chinese rule apparent by shouting slogans and carrying banners hostile to the Communist state. More recently, Xinjiang's provincial capital city of Urumqi became the center of unrest in the summer of 2009 when a peaceful protest demanding investigation into the deaths of two Uyghurs in an incident outside of Xinjiang evolved into riots in which approximately 200 Han citizens died in the violence (Wong 2009).

There have also been claims made by the Chinese state that Uyghurs have engaged in terrorist activities outside of Xinjiang in an effort to press their demands for a separate state. In most of these cases, it is impossible to verify whether the incidents are genuine examples of terrorist attacks as the only reports available are provided by China's state-controlled media. One instance of this form of violence was the crash and explosion of a jeep in Tiananmen Square – a landmark in the center of Beijing and the site of both the Forbidden City and the Great Hall of the People. Five people were killed in the attack, including 3 passengers in the jeep, and at least 40 people were injured. In this case, the police reported that all occupants of the vehicle were Uyghurs (Holdstock 2014, 6). A second attack that gained a great deal of attention took place during March 2014 at a train station in the city of

Kunming, the capital of the province of Yunnan. A group of 8 individuals stabbed to death 31 people and wounded more than 140. While no organization claimed responsibility for this attack, the Chinese media pointed to evidence that they suggested connected the carnage to Uyghur separatists (Holdstock 2014, 7; Jacobs 2014).

The government's responses to these moments of unrest in Xinjiang and beyond have taken the form of "strike hard" campaigns. Within the PRC, these campaigns typically take the form of focused anti-crime efforts to quickly arrest and imprison those accused of having engaged in a range of different criminal activities. In the case of Xinjiang, however, the focus has almost exclusively been on arresting those believed to be engaged in prohibited religious activities or individuals accused of promoting separatism (Clarke 2008, 280). In recent years, those arrested in these sweeps by security forces have been sent to internment camps. Within these camps, it is claimed that Uyghurs, "...spend their days in a high-pressure indoctrination program, where they are forced to listen to lectures, sing hymns praising the Chinese Communist Party, and write 'self-criticism' essays... (Buckley 2010). Estimates suggest that between a few hundred thousand and approximately one million individuals are imprisoned in these camps at any given time (Buckley 2018).

Limits to Autonomy

Given the government's adoption of policies that are intended to offer a degree of accommodation to these ethnic communities, what accounts for continued evidence of interethnic tensions between the state and some of these groups? One potential means of explaining this phenomenon is to point to the past tensions between majority and minorities within the PRC. Given the long history of Han chauvinism, and periods in which members of minority communities have endured state-supported acts of discrimination and violence, it would not be surprising if the benefits that have been made available in the reform era might be understood to be "too little, too late" to change attitudes and generate support for the Chinese government. Members of minority communities also have reasons to question the durability of these reforms, recognizing that earlier promises to respect the autonomy and self-governance of minority communities have been broken.

Beyond a distrust linked to past relations between groups, it may also be the case that many members of ethnic communities have come to see the policies of accommodation initiated during the reform era as insufficient. This is particularly true as it relates to promises of autonomy – the guarantee that members of territorially concentrated minority groups will have opportunities for self-governance in the context of their regional homelands. A close examination of the practices of autonomy in both Tibet and Xinjiang reveals that there are significant limits to opportunities for self-governance. These harsh and continuing limits on existing autonomy arrangements perhaps best explain the continuing alienation of Tibetans and Uyghurs from the Chinese state.

An obvious means of evaluating the degree to which an ethnic community enjoys true self-governance is in terms of whether members of the community hold positions of power associated with administering the territory. In the case of the TAR, Tibetans hold a majority of cadre positions and occupy a number of high-ranking titles within the state government. The significance of this Tibetan presence within the state is called into doubt, however, by the fact that members of this group hold relatively few positions of influence within the Chinese Communist Party (CCP) itself. Perhaps most notably, the top CCP position within the TAR of party secretary has never been held by a member of the Tibetan ethnicity (Karmel 1995–1996, 500; He 2006, 76; Dodin 2008, 195–196). With the CCP understood to be the true center of power in China, it seems clear that Tibetans do not have opportunities for genuine self-governance.

This pattern of a lack of representation within the CCP is also apparent in Xinjiang. A report from 2008 notes that only 37% of CCP members in Xinjiang hold a minority identity. This same study reports that not 1 of the 124 of the Party secretaries in the province at the "prefectural, municipal, and county level" is a member of a minority community (Clarke 2008, 280–281). Taken together, the relative lack of Tibetans and Uyghurs in their respective provincial governments suggests that the Chinese are unwilling to hand meaningful authority over to the members of these ethnic communities.

It is also clear that the Chinese state still maintains a capacity to monitor religious practice in autonomous regions and interferes with religious activities as it sees fit. In the context of Tibet, government limits in the form of quotas have been set on the number of monks that may be attached to each Buddhist monastery. Those who seek to join a monastery must have a background check completed by the local Party committee to ensure that any applicant has a sufficiently patriotic background. Contrary to earlier practice, the government has also mandated that those seeking to join a monastery must now wait until they reach the age of 18 (Smith 1996, 583; Goldstein et al. 2006).

A further indication of the government's involvement in religious issues is its interference with the selection of new Tibetan Buddhist leaders. By tradition, Tibetan religious authorities have been responsible for identifying the individual who is the reincarnation of a deceased leader. However, when the 10th Panchen Lama (the highest-ranking lama following the Dalai Lama) died in 1989, the Chinese government asserted the right to participate in identifying his reincarnation. After the Dalai Lama announced that he had identified a child within the PRC as the Panchen Lama's reincarnation, the boy and his parents were taken into government custody and have not been seen again (Shakya 1999, 440–447; van Schaik 2011, 262–263). The Chinese state then installed into the role of Panchen Lama a different child, one who proved to be the son of two CCP officials. Tibetans have not embraced the newly installed Panchen Lama as the true reincarnation (Johnson 2011, 164).

Given the Dalai Lama's advanced age, he has become increasingly concerned that the Chinese state will also insert itself into the process of selecting his reincarnated successor. As a result, he has suggested that the means of choosing his successor may differ from past practices. On different occasions he has suggested that he may be the last Dalai Lama; he has also offered the possibility that his reincarnation may be found outside of China. Reports in March 2018 suggest that the government-in-exile is now in discussions about exactly what practices they will adopt to determine the next individual to occupy this leadership role (Narabe 2018).

In the case of Xinjiang, there have also been long-standing concerns about the government's interference with religious practice. Complaints include claims of intense and expansive surveillance during Muslim holidays, and the oppressive policing of religious festivals. As described earlier, the government has been particularly aggressive in its efforts to crackdown on religious activities that have taken place outside the confines of what is approved by state authorities. Uyghurs claims that people have been sent to internment camps for activities ranging from possession of religious books to wearing a shirt bearing a Muslim crescent image (Buckley 2018). This interference in religious freedoms again demonstrates the limits to the autonomy provided to these communities. This has particular significance to both Tibetans and Uyghurs as it is central to the identity of each group.

A final illustration of the limits to autonomy for ethnic communities in China is in terms of immigration into these regions. China's government has had a long-standing policy of promoting Han immigration into Tibet as a strategy to further integrate the province with the rest of the PRC. Tibetans have experienced a flood of Han migrants into the country's urban areas as a result. According to one estimate, among the 13,000 stores and restaurants within Lhasa, only 300 are owned by Tibetans (Mazumdar 2010). Tibetans have come to perceive this policy of encouraging immigration as a threat to the identity of the TAR as their ethnic homeland and complain that much of the wealth of the region is now being monopolized by members of the majority group.

A similar dynamic is apparent in the case of Xinjiang, with the PRC encouraging migration by the Han into the region. The 2000 census reports that 7.49 million individuals in the province, or 40.6% of all residents, identify as a member of the country's majority group (Clarke 2008, 278). In a further parallel to Tibet, Uyghurs articulate concerns that they might soon be a numerical minority within their own autonomous region and that economic opportunities within the region are being disproportionately directed toward relatively new migrants to the area.

These grievances focused on a lack of opportunities for self-governance, restrictions on religious freedoms, and migration appear to form the basis for the continued opposition and hostility by ethnic communities to the Chinese state. Tibetans and Uyghurs both perceive the autonomy guaranteed to them by the PRC's constitution and laws to have never been realized in practice. Their acts of resistance thus serve as reminders of the hypocrisy of the Chinese state and a demand that the government abide by its commitments.

Alternative Approaches to Ethnic Relations in the PRC

What approaches exist for addressing the continuing sense of grievance among China's ethnic communities? As described earlier, one approach that has been favored by some members of the Han majority is intended to reshape government policy in ways that discourage minorities from maintaining their separate identities. In keeping with the suggestions of Ma Rong, this would include ending the practices associated with the reform era of distributing political and economic benefits on the basis of ethnicity. Through the promotion of policies that favor assimilation, the hope and expectation is that conflict based on ethnic difference would become less salient.

There are obvious reasons to doubt that adopting this approach is a realistic possibility. It would undoubtedly invite further resistance by minority communities that have already engaged in activities indicative of their opposition to a state that they perceive to have limited their opportunities for self-governance. Doing away with affirmative action policies and other accommodations would only do further harm to ethnic relations that have already been badly damaged by years of hostile actions by the state.

An alternative approach has been favored for a number of years by the Dalai Lama. Conceding that the Chinese government is unlikely to ever accept Tibetan independence, the Tibetan leader has shifted to advocating for greater and more meaningful autonomy for Tibet. Early in the 2000s, the Dalai Lama pointed to China's use of a "one country, two systems" approach for integrating the former colonies of Hong Kong and Macau. Both regions have been incorporated into China based on guarantees that they would enjoy substantial opportunities for self-government (He and Sautman 2005/2006, 612–613). The Dalai Lama's suggestion was that China and Tibet might have the potential to develop a similar arrangement.

Perhaps in recognition of the fact that the Chinese government has become increasingly interventionist in the politics of Hong Kong in recent years, the Dalai Lama has more recently pointed to the European Union (EU) as an alternative model. He notes that the EU demonstrates that people of different nationalities and political systems have found a way to cooperate and coordinate over key issues such as foreign policy (Reuters 2018). The suggestion is again that this may serve as a means of structuring the relationship between China and Tibet.

Just as Ma Rong's proposals seem unlikely to be adopted in practice, there are very real reasons to be skeptical that the Chinese government would cede greater autonomy to territories such as Tibet and Xinjiang. As noted previously, these areas have both strategic and economic significance to the PRC; it is thus unlikely that the state would willingly place limit on its control over them. It is also the case that the government would have very real concerns about the possibility that concessions provided to one or more groups and territories would lead to a deluge of demands by other minority communities for similar accommodations.

Conclusion

In the near future, the most likely scenario for the ethno-politics of the PRC is that it will continue down the path that was set at the initiation of the reform era. Limited and incomplete accommodations for minorities in the form of weak territorial autonomy arrangements and affirmative action-style policies will remain the government's favored approach for addressing the issue of diversity. These policies will likely continue to prove insufficient for addressing the grievances and sense of insecurity among ethnic communities. Episodes of protest and violence have the potential to continue as the means by which China's minorities express their continuing discontent.

Cross-References

▶ Ethnicity and Cultural Rights in Tibet
▶ The State and Minority Nationalities (Ethnic Groups) in China

References

Blum SD (2001) Portraits of "primitives": ordering human kinds in the Chinese nation. Rowan & Littlefield, Lanham

Buckley C (2018) China is detaining Muslims in vast numbers. The goal: 'transformation.' New York Times. 8 September. https://www.nytimes.com/2018/09/08/world/asia/china-uighur-muslim-detention-camp.html. Accessed 30 Oct 2018

Clarke M (2008) China's "war on terror" in Xinjiang: human security and the causes of violent Uighur separatism. Terrorism Polit Violence 20:271–301

Dodin T (2008) What policies has the Chinese government adopted in regard to minority nationalities? In: Blondea A, Buffetrille K (eds) Authenticating Tibet: answers to China's 100 questions. University of California Press, Berkeley, pp 191–197

Dreyer JT (2004) China's political system, 4th edn. Pearson, Upper Saddle River

Goldstein MC (1997) The snow lion and the dragon: China, Tibet, and the Dalai Lama. University of California Press, Berkeley

Goldstein MC, Jiao B, Beall CM, Tsering P (2006) Development and change in rural Tibet: problems and adaptations. In: Sautman B, Dreyer JT (eds) Contemporary Tibet: politics, development, and society in a disputed region. M.E. Sharpe, Armonk, pp 193–213

He B (2006) The Dalai Lama's autonomy proposal: a one-sided wish? In: Sautman B, Dreyer JT (eds) Contemporary Tibet: politics, development, and society in a disputed region. M.E. Sharpe, Armonk, pp 67–84

He B, Sautman B (2005/2006) The politics of the Dalai Lama's new initiative for autonomy. Pacific Affairs 78:601–629

Heberer T (1989) China and its national minorities. M.E. Sharpe, Armonk

Hoddie M (2006) Ethnic realignments: a comparative study of government influences on identity. Lexington Books, Lanham

Hoddie M, Lou D (2009) From vice to virtue: changing portrayals of minorities in China's official media. Asian Ethn 10:51–69

Holdstock N (2014) Islam and instability in China's Xinjiang. Norwegian Peacebuilding Resource Centre Report. March. https://www.files.ethz.ch/isn/179639/3ba335a7680451de2612c693a481eb96.pdf. Accessed 30 Oct 2018

Jacobs A (2008) Ambush in China raises concerns as Olympics near. New York Times. 5 August. https://www.nytimes.com/2008/08/05/world/asia/05china.html. Accessed 3 Dec 2018

Jacobs A (2014) Train station rampage further strains ethnic relations in China. New York Times. 3 March. https://www.nytimes.com/2014/03/04/world/asia/han-uighur-relations-china.html. Accessed 30 Oct 2018

Johnson T (2011) Tragedy in crimson: how the Dalai Lama conquered the world but lost the battle with China. Nation Books, New York

Karmel S (1995–1996) Ethnic tension and the struggle for order: China's policies in Tibet. Pac Affairs 68:485–508

Kaup KP (2000) Creating the Zhuang: ethnic politics in China. Lynne Rienner, Boulder

Liu A (1996) Mass politics in the people's republic: state and society in contemporary China. Westview Press, Boulder

Ma R (2007) A new perspective in guiding ethnic relations in the twenty-first century: 'depoliticization of ethnicity in China. Asian Ethn 8:199–217

Mackerras C (1994) China's minorities: integration and modernization in the twentieth century. Oxford University Press, Hong Kong

Mazumdar S (2010) China finally realizes how badly it bungled Tibet. Newsweek. 27 January. https://www.newsweek.com/china-finally-realizes-how-badly-it-bungled-tibet-71141. Accessed 30 Oct 2018

Narabe T (2018) Discussions on Dalai Lama's succession could begin this year. Asahi Shimbun. 16 March. http://www.asahi.com/ajw/articles/AJ201803160023.html. Accessed 6 Dec 2018

Reuters (2018) Tibet can exist with China like 'European Union': Dalai Lama. Reuters World News. 16 March. https://www.reuters.com/article/us-china-tibet/tibet-can-exist-with-china-like-european-union-dalai-lama-idUSKCN1GS0C7. Accessed 6 Dec 2018

Sautman B (1998) Affirmative action, ethnic minorities and China's universities. Pac Rim Law Policy J 7:77–116

Sautman B (1999) Ethnic law and minority rights in China: progress and constraints. Law Soc 21:283–314

Sautman B (2006) "Demographic annihilation" and Tibet. In: Sautman B, Dreyer JT (eds) Contemporary Tibet: politics, development, and society in a disputed region. M.E. Sharpe, Armonk, pp 193–213

Sautman B (2012) Paved with good intentions: proposals to curb minority rights and their consequences for China. Modern China 38:10–39

Self-Immolations by Tibetans (2018) International campaign for Tibet, Washington, DC. http://www.savetibet.org/resources/fact-sheets/self-immolations-by-tibetans/. Accessed 30 Oct 2018

Shakya T (1999) The dragon in the land of snows: a history of modern Tibet since 1947. Columbia University Press, New York

Smith WW (1996) Tibetan nation: a history of Tibetan nationalism and Sino-Tibetan relations. Westview Press, Boulder

Sugimoto T (1993) The political stability of ethnic regions in China. International Institute for Global Peace, Tokyo

Van Schaik S (2011) Tibet: a history. Yale University Press, New Haven

Van Wie Davis E (2008) Uyghur Muslim ethnic separatism in Xinjiang, China. Asian Aff 35:15–29

Wong E (2008) China has sentenced 55 over Tibet riot in March. New York Times. 5 November. http://www.nytimes.com/2008/11/06/world/asia/06tibet.html. Accessed 6 Dec 2018

Wong E (2009) Clashes in China shed light on ethnic divide. New York Times. 7 July. http://www.nytimes.com/2009/07/08/world/asia/08china.html. Accessed 6 Dec 2018

Ethnicity and Cultural Rights in Tibet

17

Jianxia Lin

Contents

Introduction	302
China's Tibet Policies: Rationales and Criticisms	304
Interpretation of Depoliticization in Tibet Context	307
Non-separatism Self-Representation as an Alternative	309
Conclusion	310
Cross-References	311
References	311

Abstract

The debates on the so-called Tibet issue between the exiled Tibetan government and the Chinese central government have caused misunderstandings of Tibetan ethnicity. The manufacturing of an image of passive Tibetans either as victims or recipients of aid under China's economic and cultural policies in Tibet is questionable. The arising discussions on the improvement of China's ethnic policies provide theoretical possibilities of breaking the impasse of Tibetan ethnicity and cultural rights. The proposals of Chinese scholars to depoliticize Tibet-related issues, as well as the idea of non-separatism self-representation, are supposed to allow more space for Tibetans to exercise ethnicity and maintain the prosperity of their culture through their own voice.

Keywords

Tibetan ethnicity · Tibetan cultural rights · Misrepresentation · Depoliticization · Self-representation

J. Lin (✉)
University of Leeds, Leeds, UK
e-mail: ssjli@leeds.ac.uk

Introduction

In 1950, the People's Republic of China (PRC) launched nationality identification to identify ethnic minority groups within the country. This was completed by 1983, confirming the presence of 55 ethnic minorities, named "shaoshu minzu (少数民族)" in Chinese. This is in addition to the Han ethnic group, which comprises the majority of the Chinese population, meaning that there is a total of 56 official identified ethnic groups in China.

The sixth national census showed that while the Han ethnic group makes up over 90% of the population, ethnic Tibetans comprise only 0.47%. The population of Tibetans is distributed in the Tibetan Autonomous Region (the TAR) and other Tibetan-concentrated areas in four provinces that surround the TAR: Qinghai, Gansu, Yunnan, and Sichuan Provinces. It is necessary to clarify the different definitions of "Tibet" claimed by the two parties. The central government officially confirms the TAR as "Tibet," whereas the Tibetan exiled government emphasizes the idea of "cultural Tibet," which includes not only the TAR but also the Tibetan areas in the four near provinces.

It is important to be clear on the different definitions of Tibet's scale because the central government implements different policies toward Tibetan people in the TAR and toward those in the neighbor provinces. The latter experience more relaxed management from the central government. It should be noted that Tibetans are not themselves unified; many of them remain antagonistic toward different groups of Tibetans (Karmel 1995; Frangville 2009). Divided regions consist of several groups and subgroups of Tibetan language and culture (Karmel 1995). As a result, when the exiled government speaks on behalf of Tibetans without distinguishing the different experiences of the two groups of Tibetans, this creates a misrepresentation of Tibetan ethnic groups. If the exiled government cannot answer the question of where the Tibet boundary lies, they are not able to speak effectively in the name of Tibet.

This divergence on the scale of Tibet between the central government and the Tibetan exiled government is a taste of the complicated political disputes between the two parties in relation to the Tibet issue. The Tibet issue is fundamentally about the sovereignty of Tibet. The Tibetan exiled government is led by Dalai Lama and his supporters, known as the Dalai Clique on the one side of the debate and the Chinese central government on the other. Along with countless rounds of debate between these two parties, the attitudes of the exiled Tibetan government tend to be dynamic, while the central government maintains an uncompromising political stance.

The political expectation of the exiled Tibetan government has experienced a shift from the independence of Tibet to autonomy stipulated by China's constitution (Frangville 2009). In a statement made by Dalai Lama in 1961, he appealed to Tibetans who remained in China to strive for independence of Tibet and to Tibetan diaspora to get ready for returning and building a greater Tibet (The Office of the Dalai Lama 1961). Then in a memorandum sent to the central government in 2008, Dalai Clique applied a "middle way" approach to obtain "genuine autonomy" for Tibet in which the autonomy in 11 areas regulated in the PRC Constitution was cited

(Davis 2014: 100; Central Tibetan Administration 2008). This dramatic shift from expectations of absolute independence to the willingness of compliance with the Constitution shows the increasing uncertainty and divergence within the community of Tibetan exiled (Frangville 2009; Davis 2014).

In contrast to the dynamic political stances of Tibetan-in-exile, the central government allows no flexibility on negotiations and accepts no charges from the exiled government. By sustaining this hard position, the central government has experienced great pressure, both internally and externally (Goldstein et al. 2010). Therefore, the central government focuses on developing Tibet's economy, with the intention to domestically connect Tibetans economically with mainland China and to show internationally that the Tibetans live well under the management of the central government (ibid.).

One of the keywords of China's economic strategies in Tibet is "aid." Campaigns launched by the central government to support Tibet include but not limit to the "counterpart aids to Tibet (对口援藏)," which assigns more affluent provinces to sponsor Tibet, "develop the west (西部大开发)," in which huge capital and subsidies were allocated to constructing basic infrastructure in Tibet, and the "comfortable housing project (安居工程)," which offers funds directly to Tibetan households to improve their living environment. It is evident that the development of the Tibetan economy relies heavily on investment from the central government. Nevertheless, Tibetan economy still ranks at the bottom of the country's financial statistics.

Instead of factoring other disadvantages of the region, such as geographic limitations of and the preexisting vulnerabilities of the society's production mode, to the inadequate economic performance of Tibet, the political disputes surrounding Tibetan ethnic group have linked its economic weakness to its ethnicity (Zhu and Blachford 2012). The two parties each have their own views.

The exiled Tibetan government feels that the market-oriented economy has been marginalizing Tibetans and declassing them to "an increasingly disenfranchised minority in their own land" (The Tibet Policy Institute 2017: 2). This view presents Tibetans as victims of either being discriminated by the Han-dominated market or are denied of their cultural rights. Furthermore, the exiled government regards itself as the protector of Tibetan ancient culture and feels that it is required to speak on their behalf.

In contrast, the central government is keen to praise the success in developing the Tibetan economy and improving the living standards of Tibetans. The official propaganda of Tibet always reports the noticeable economic improvement in comparison to the backwardness of old Tibet and suggests that Tibetans are in dire need of aid from the government. The image of Tibetans and Tibet areas as targets of aids has therefore been generated, and the stereotype of material lacking and deficiency gradually becomes a preconceived view of the backwardness of the Tibetan community as a whole (Schwartz 2008).

While the two parties have conveyed their views on various occasions and have drawn attention from the international stage, the voices of Tibetan individuals are unheard. Beyond the two political accounts are the living Tibetan individuals, who practice their ethnicity as a way of life and make adaptations when faced with challenges and find ways to lead a better life by seizing opportunities. The misrepresentation arising from the political disputes has not only ignored the efforts made by the Tibetan people but has also caused misunderstanding of Tibetan ethnicity and resulted in the term "Tibet" becoming a synonym of "political sensitivity." How to break this impasse is therefore a topic worth studying.

Starting from the discussion on the misrepresentation of Tibetan ethnicity that has been created by the two parties of the debate, this chapter will then look into China's economic and cultural policies in Tibet and analyze the narratives behind them. Following that, the recent domestic debates on the issue of "depoliticizing" China's ethnic policy, as well as the proposal of the non-separatism self-representation, will be represented and explained in the context of Tibet. Lastly, a conclusion will be drawn that more attempts must be made to improve Tibet policies in order to allow more space for Tibetans to exercise their ethnicity and cultural rights.

China's Tibet Policies: Rationales and Criticisms

China's economy has experienced tremendous growth since the country's opening-up reform in the late 1970s. In parallel with the rapid improvement of the national economy is the rising inequality of development among different regions: in the west of China, where most of the country's ethnic minority groups live, the economy is less vibrant than in the southeast area. Ranked at the bottom of the country's financial statistics, Tibet is a salient representative of those west and less developed ethnic minority groups (Fischer 2005). The gap between the reality of this inadequate economic performance of Tibet and China's propaganda on the great economic success in Tibet leads to the questions on the efficiency of China's Tibet policy.

The preference and tendency of China's policies in Tibet are most intuitively reflected in the Tibet Work Forums. Tibet Work Forums are conferences that the central committee holds to make plans for Tibet's development and to summarize the achievements and disadvantages of past stages (Yang 2012). They are key conferences that make the most important policy guidelines for the development of Tibet. Since its initiation, the forum has been held six times, in 1980, 1984, 1994, 2001, 2010, and 2015. Each forum has a directive theme, which indicates the preferences of the government in terms of developmental strategies in Tibet.

The Third Tibet Work Forum in 1994 is regarded as an important transition point of the Tibetan economic process (Barnett 2012). At this forum, it was decided to push Tibet toward a market economy by means of large-scale investment and subsidies (ibid.). Based on this decision, the economic development in Tibet sets out on a path of basic infrastructure construction. Most of the subsidies were used for the establishment of hardware such as high-speed roads, airports, and railways. In association of the large flow of investment into Tibet were numerous migrations from the inland China who were attracted by the preferential policies in Tibet and came to Tibet with the intention of seeking economic opportunities (Fischer 2005).

In spite of the decision on the economic development strategies, the Third Tibet Work Forum launched an unprecedented cultural intervention with the decision to openly boycott Dalai Lama against his individual role as a religious leader of Tibetan Buddhism and of diluting the religious atmosphere in Tibet by restricting religious events (Barnett 2016). This policy has remained since then, setting a stage for the prolonged disputes about Tibet's cultural rights (ibid.).

There are two main rationales behind this cultural policy. Firstly, the policy initially aimed to prevent separatism and curb separatist events. The cultural decision made at the Third Forum was based on the assertion that separatism and local nationalism in Tibet comes from Tibetan culture, which is religion-oriented (Karmel 1995).

The central government has attempted to prevent separatism and local nationalism since the Mao Zedong era of 1949–1976. At the time before the Third Forum, the international context of the dissolution of the Soviet Union which the Chinese officials factored to the failure of its cultural policies and the continuous domestic unrests led by the religious figures in Tibetan areas from 1987 to 1989 had both alarmed the Chinese officials of the dangerous role that cultures could play in the separatist events (Karmel 1995). As a result, the belief that Tibetan culture and religion could be the source of separatism and local nationalism had developed and gradually deep rooted in the minds of the decision-makers (ibid.).

The cultural strategies of restraining Tibetans' religious activities achieved its success by sharply reducing the cases of riots in Tibet in the late half of the 1990s (Barnett 2016). However, this decision was considered to be a temporary measure that would be detrimental to the long-term interests of the country (ibid.). The eruption of many ethnic conflicts at the beginning of the twenty-first century was the manifestation of this prophecy. One of the most prominent of such cases was the unrest in Lhasa, which hit the world news headlines in 2008. In response to questioning about the effect of Tibet policy in aggravating the conflicts, the government did not examine the potential flaws of the current policy but again blaming on Tibetan separatists' and religious extremists' sinister motives of splitting up China (Elliott 2015).

Secondly, the cultural policy was a reflection of the recrudescence of Han ethnocentrism (Sautman 2014). It was believed that the value of Tibetan culture is typically dismissed by the decision-makers because they take an ethnocentric attitude toward it (Karmel 1995). As an evidence, most of the official propaganda on Tibetan culture emphasizes its previous backwardness when Tibet was a feudal society full of darkness and barbarity (Karmel 1995). And the central government is presented as playing the role of lifting Tibet away from its darker history. This theme has connected the present and past propaganda on Tibetan culture. The 2008 White Paper on Tibetan culture and the 2015 White Paper on Tibet maintain the same tone as the earlier 1992 White Paper. For example, the 2008 paper describes how old Tibet society "was even darker than the European society of the Middle Ages" with "a system of feudal serfdom under theocratic rule," and the central government brings the "hope to the protection and development of Tibetan culture" (The State Council Information Office of the People's Republic of China 2008: Foreword). The idea of taking material backwardness into social and moral inadequacies is further reflected in many Chinese studies regarding Tibetan traditional cultures. Although Tibetan cultures are portrayed as treasured culture heritage for China and the world, many parts of it are regarded as against modernity and are seen to need improvement (Zhang and Xu 2011; Zhao 1993).

These narratives behind the China's policy in Tibet indicate that the policy is not unassailable, rather its deficiencies exist at the very beginning of the decision-making process. Nevertheless the implementation of these policies still brings benefits, such as improved living standards and more approaches of income making, to Tibetans. However, in the views of Tibetans exiled, the advantages of the policies are not worth mentioning, but the so prominent disadvantages deserve strong criticism as they are ruining the Tibetan community.

The inflows of Han population from inland China to Tibetan areas are deemed by the Tibetan exiled government as great threat to the homogeneity of Tibetan culture. Because the local Tibetans are easily at an unfavorable position in the competition with their Han compatriots (Fischer 2005). The disadvantage is mostly reflected in their decentralized role in their participation in the market sector. Tibetans have fewer opportunities to obtain a good job in the labour market because of disadvantages in language and technological skills. As a result, most Tibetans take jobs which have a lower salary such as building workers and truck drivers (Goldstein et al. 2008; Fischer 2005).

While the economic policies in Tibet are charged as central government's tool of exploiting the resources and facilitating the control in Tibet (Central Tibetan Administration 2015), the cultural policies are also continuously criticized by the Dalai Clique as they exaggerate its deficiencies and accuse the central government of committing cultural genocide in Tibet. In a report generated in 2017, China's policies in Tibet are portrayed by the exiled administration as "the complete annihilation of the Tibetan culture and way of life." The policies had maintained the superficial integrity of Tibetan culture but destroyed the Tibetan ethnic identity in a "fundamental and irremediable manner" (The Tibet Policy Institute 2017: 119).

As stated by Kolas and Thowsen (2005), the reality is never as black and white as both the central government and the Tibetan exiled government have described. In terms of the central government, the desire to shape policy around the Tibetans and to convince them that being close to the "motherland" is in their long-term interests is beyond reproach considering the initial intention of the policy design. However, it can be seen to create a sense of ethnic superiority of the Han majority by attributing all the progress in Tibet to the help from the Han people. The exiled Tibetan government is criticized for ignoring or underestimating the strength and abilities of the Tibetan people. Tibetans who are under the management of the central government still develop their culture, but the exiled Tibetan government holds the belief that Tibetan cultures are fading because there is no leadership from the Dalai Lama.

One same problem of both the accounts is that they have either neglected the positive parts of Tibetan culture or omitted the great efforts made by those Tibetan individuals in the creation and reconstruction of Tibetan culture.

Tibetan religion, which is viewed by the central government as superstition and a source of separatism, is deeply rooted in Tibetan ethnicity. The positive effects of religion on Tibetan market development have long been unvalued. In fact, it "enhances shared norms that promote the incentive compatibility of non-contractual or legally enforceable exchange" (Tu et al. 2011: 62) and helps to build a fair and honest trading atmosphere in the market (Wang 2009). Because the nature of Tibetan Buddhism emphasizes karma and the afterlife, so believers are taught to care about spiritual desire rather than desire for materials and money. Chasing material desires will lead to suffering in the next life (Wang 2009).

Meanwhile, ordinary Tibetans are making efforts to live the culture and to express ethnic identity on their own. As Kolas and Thowsen (2005) summarize, both preservation and creation of culture are vibrant in Tibet. In order to protect their traditions, Tibetans are trying to revive religious activities, and greater attention is being paid to the preservation of Tibetan literacy and written language. In constructing new cultural products, Tibetan stakeholders are manufacturing new cultural commercials in the tourism industry, while young Tibetans are constructing modern Tibetan identity through the combination of traditional symbols and fashion media, such as popular music and video. Furthermore, Tibetans are increasingly expressing their identity and voicing their views through new platforms on social media (Grant 2017; Kehoe 2015).

Interpretation of Depoliticization in Tibet Context

These misrepresentations of Tibetan ethnicity can be attributed to the misleading politicization of the Tibet issue. The depoliticization of Tibetan ethnicity is therefore necessary. And the process of depoliticizing Tibetan ethnicity if it is possible is inevitably linked with the general context of China's ethnic relations management. Because no matter how controversial the Tibetan issue is, the Tibetan people are fully under Chinese jurisdiction, and the Tibetan region is affected by China's ethnic policy.

China has a long history of being a multiethnic country. The PRC has long used politics as a way of dealing with ethnic issues; the country "views ethnic groups mainly as political entities" and "emphasizes integrity, political power, and 'territorial' conservation of ethnic groups"(Ma 2007: 202). The implementation of regional ethnic autonomy (民族区域自治) and preferential policies (优惠政策) in regions inhabited by ethnic minorities are examples of this (Sautman 2014). While this approach has its advantages, it also has negative side effects. Conflicts between ethnic minority groups and the Han majority groups and unrest in regions inhabited by ethnic minorities continue to occur, making ethnic conflicts one of the main concerns for the PRC government and a controversial academic topic (Ma 2014).

Therefore, in recent years, some scholars have brought out and discussed some proposals of the adjustment of China's current ethnic policies. There are advocates on a "second generation" of the ethnic policies. The leading academics are Hu Angang (胡鞍钢) and Hu Lianhe (胡联合). They call for the gradual cancelation of the preferential policies in minority autonomous regions to achieve facto equality among all ethnic groups in China (Hu and Hu 2011). Meanwhile, there is another proposal emphasizing the idea of depoliticization of China's ethnic issues. One of the leading academics is Ma Rong (马戎) (2007, 2014); he suggests breaking the political barriers among the 56 minzu in China so that those minzu will not be distinguished by their "political status in administrative and social systems (Ma 2014: 238)." Rather, they will be recognized with different cultures and traditions (Ma 2014).

Ma Rong labels this "culturalizing," a way of managing ethnic relations in China that "prefers to treat ethnic relations as cultural interactions (Ma 2007: 202)." It treats the problems among minority groups as problems among individuals who belong to different cultural groups, instead of treating them as collective problems of the whole groups (Ma 2007; Sautman 2014). This new direction for ethnic management lacks general support within China's domestic academic circle, whereas its theory of replacing "politicization" with "culturalizing" is suitable for Tibet and can be interpreted into two layers of meaning when applied in Tibetan context.

The first layer supports Ma's view that the central government should change the emphasis of its ethnic policies in Tibet to focus more on Tibetan culture and to protect the Tibetan traditions. The government should recognize the characteristics of Tibetan culture and make flexible policies to enable its diverse development, instead of copying the development mode from the relatively developed coastal cities to Tibet (Ma 2014). The second layer of "depoliticizing" Tibetan ethnicity is to tear up the tag of "a political-sensitive ethnic group" currently placed on the Tibetans. This requires the two parties on the debate of Tibet issue could give more space for the Tibetans themselves to develop, instead of speaking on their behalf. On the one hand, the exiled Tibetan government is expected to consider the real situation of Tibetans rather than hiding political tools behind narratives of so-called historical fact and appealing Tibetans for unrealistic political aims (Frangville 2009).

In terms of the central government, on the other hand, in spite of the fact that new perspectives should be taken regarding the relationship with the Tibetan ethnic group, more freedom is also necessary for Tibetans to seek economic and cultural prosperity in a way that is suitable for their ethnicity. This requires avoidance of excessive support and aid from the government on many economic aspects because the suitable support is needed, but over-intervention is not, particularly when the intervention is under the name of preferential policies (Zhu 2013). It is argued by Ma (2014) and two Hus (2011) that the preferential policies for minorities can be helpful at earlier times but cannot last forever due to the fact that the privileges and protections enjoyed by the ethnic minorities are causing further inequalities between ethnic minority groups and Han majority populations.

Also, the Han dominance position in implementing these preferential policies can limit the space for Tibetans practicing their ethnicity in market sector. The positive influences of Tibetan ethnicity on the trading environment, such as religion, will only become apparent when a spontaneous market is available for local people to participate in positively and play a greater role. It has to be recognized that the assertion that local ethnicity is dragging back the economy is unfair and misleading because the virtues rooted in the traditional community's ethnicity have barely had the opportunity to contribute to the development of the economy due to the government's strict management. To allow them to function better in the way they should, more space and freedom is needed.

Non-separatism Self-Representation as an Alternative

Ma has been questioned whether the ethnic issue can really be "depoliticized" because any issue relate to "ethnicity" cannot avoid a nature of political color. It is reasonable to question the same problem on the depoliticizing of Tibetan ethnicity because neither of the two layers of interpretation of the depoliticization theory in Tibet context could bypass the political debate. Even those requirements of adjustments from the two parties, which aim to depoliticize Tibetan ethnicity, are ideal but unable to be fulfilled in short future. Considering the limitation of the interpretation of depoliticization in Tibet context, further exploration in the design of Tibet policy is needed.

In addition to China's present ethnic policies and the proposals for a new ethnic strategy, Sautman (2014) provides a third option: developing the Tibetans' cultural self-representation with the denial of self-determination or separatism. According to Sautman (2014: 175), the cultural ethnic self-representation enables the members of ethnic group to "articulate their understandings of their ethnic group's history and culture."

There are both similarity and disparity existing on the grounds of Sautman's conception of cultural self-representation and Ma's theory of depoliticization. First of all, they both advocate the important influences of securing self-esteem of minority in maintaining harmonious coexistence of minority groups. Two Hus' proposal of the second-generation ethnic policy emphasizes the importance of restraining ethnic elites' roles as representatives and spokesmen of their ethnic groups in preventing them from becoming leaders of separatist events (Hu and Hu 2011; Ma 2014). Ma Rong objects this suggestion by assuming that only when the dignity of the minority intellectuals is fully respected that they could play positive role in facilitating the cooperation among minority groups (Ma 2014). This emphasis on the dignity and happiness of ethnic minorities echoes with Sautman's argument that the realization of cultural self-representation of ethnic minority relies on the enhanced ethnic dignity (Sautman 2014). This requires internally "empowering minorities to mould perceptions of their groups within a multi-ethnic policy," and meanwhile externally making sure that cultural characteristics of minorities are respected, the contributions made by minorities to the development are recognized, and minorities are not discriminated in a Han-dominated market and society (Sautman 2014: 179).

Meanwhile, the differences between Sautman and Ma are on their assertions of the measurements of separatism prevention. As mentioned previously, the main concern regarding China's Tibet policy is the potential for separatism and local nationalism in Tibet. Therefore, if recommendations are made for changes to the Tibet policy, the decision-maker must be assured that the changes will not cause social instability. Ma's theory applies an outside pressure on minority groups to keep away from political appeal of self-determination and independence, urging them to "move in the direction of cultural and socioeconomic demands (Ma 2014: 241)," whereas Sautman's proposal suggests minorities' actively rejecting self-determination or separatism (Sautman 2014).

In the particular context of Tibet, this active abandon of separatism and self-determination requires a prerequisite that Tibetans realize the claim of self-determination lack legitimacy. Based on his political expectation of self-determination, Dalai Lama tends to cite international regulations as legitimacy of his claim of self-determination. For instance in the report accusing "cultural genocide" from the central government, the exiled government cites the statement of International Covenant on Economic, Social and Cultural Rights that "All peoples have the right of self-determination. By virtue of that right they freely determine their political status and freely pursue their economic, social and cultural development" to back up its argument of Tibetans' self-determination rights (The Tibet Policy Institute 2017: 28).

However, this ethnic-based self-determination claimed by Tibetan exiled government is actually "a *cul-de-sac* under international human rights norms" (Sautman 2014: 180). Because the "external self-determination as a gateway to separation" only suits in the cases of "colonialism and foreign occupation" (Sautman 2014: 180), but Tibet is not a colonial subject. And the internal self-determination sought by Dalai Lama which stresses the choice of the system of government is also out of the rights granted by international law (Sautman 2014; Matsuno 2014).

The self-determination claimed by Dalai Lama is not only unwarranted from international law but also lacks internal supports. Both external and internal self-determination, as concluded by Rob Dickinson (2014), are characterized by violence, while the nature of religion-oriented Tibetan society stresses nonviolence and determines the impossibilities of Tibetans' support for using violence to achieve self-determination (Dickinson 2014).

In comparison to Ma and the two Hus whose new propositions fail to offer a feasible measurement of preventing Tibetans from separatism, Sautman may take advantages of his suggestions of minorities' inside-out denial of self-determination in promoting cultural self-representation in the context of Tibet.

Conclusion

Just as the political debates between the Chinese central government and the Tibetan exiled government have no end in sight, the fundamental adjustment of China's ethnic policies in Tibet is also out of the question. However, the open discussion regarding changes to ethnic policies in China is a good sign that the problems are realized and possible solutions are explored. Although this is not backed up officially, or widely supported in academia, it offers a possibility that is lacking in the current system. In Tibet context particularly, the interpretation of the idea of depoliticizing ethnic issues infuses new blood to the impasse of Tibetan issue.

Regardless of how strong the political stances of the two parties on the Tibet issue are, their manufacturing of Tibetans' experiences and misrepresenting Tibetan ethnicity should be questioned (Frangville 2009). It is vital to look beyond the political narratives produced by the two parties in the Tibet issue debate to see the images of Tibetans in reality. Firstly, they are neither victims nor recipients of aid. They are people who participate in the market while practicing their ethnicity just as other ethnic groups in China, facing both challenges and opportunities, benefiting from the market, and bearing any side effects of the market-oriented economy (Zhu and Blachford 2012). Secondly, they are neither a backward ethnic group who are in dire need of mother state's help with cultural preservation nor "uniquely spiritual, peaceful and enlightened people nestled in a far-off, wild and sacred frontier (Kehoe 2015: 314–315)" who are easily overwhelmed by the numerous changes and cannot make adjustments just because they have no leadership from their religious spiritual leader.

These misunderstandings towards Tibetan may not be sanctioned by the two accounts, but the two parties are responsible for the generation of them. Because the political discourses made in the political debate has squeezed the space and freedom for Tibetans to practice their ethnicity and cultural rights through their own voices. In this case, the idea of cultural self-representation without separatism, which enables Tibetans to represent their culture while at the same time remains this self-representation within the demands of separation preventing, is worth consideration. If self-representation can ever be used by the Chinese government to deal with Tibetan related issues, this may greatly help to ease the conflict between Tibetans and other ethnic groups. In addition, as Sautman (2014: 185) puts it, this action will "go further in China towards mitigating ethnic problems than it has elsewhere."

Cross-References

▶ China: Modernization, Development, and Ethnic Unrest in Xinjiang
▶ Ethno-politics in the People's Republic of China
▶ The State and Minority Nationalities (Ethnic Groups) in China

References

Barnett R (2012) Restrictions and their anomalies: the third forum and the regulation of religion in Tibet. J Curr Chin Aff 41(4):45–107
Barnett R (2016) Imagining the borderlands: managing (to prolong) conflict in Tibet. Nations Nationalism 22(4):706–724. https://doi.org/10.1111/nana.12252
Central Tibetan Administration (2008) Memorandum on genuine autonomy for the Tibetan people. http://tibet.net/important-issues/sino-tibetan-dialogue/memorandum-on-geniune-autonomy-for-the-tibetan-people/. Accessed 22 Sep 2018
Central Tibetan Administration (2015) Tibet was not part of China but middle way remains a viable solution: central Tibetan administration's response to China's white paper on Tibet. http://www.

tibet.net/2015/09/full-text-of-ctas-response-to-chinas-whitepaper-on-tibet/#. Accessed 22 Sep 2018

Davis M (2014) China and the UN declaration on the rights of indigenous people: the case of Tibet. In: Woons M (ed) Restoring indigenous self-determination theoretical an practical approaches. E-International Relations, Bristol, pp 96–104

Dickinson R (2014) Tibetan self-determination: a stark choice for an abandoned people. In: Woons M (ed) Restoring indigenous self-determination theoretical an practical approaches. E-International Relations, Bristol, pp 106–112

Elliott M (2015) The case if the missing indigene: debate over a "second-generation" ethnic policy. China J 73:186–213. https://doi.org/10.1086/679274

Fischer AM (2005) State growth and social exclusion in Tibet: challenges of recent economic growth. NIAS Press, Copenhagen

Frangville V (2009) Tibet in debate: narrative construction and misrepresentations in seven years in Tibet and Red River Valley. Transtext(e)s Transcultures. Available via OPEN EDITION. https://journals.openedition.org/transtexts/289. Accessed 13 Sep 2018

Goldstein MC, Childs G, Wangdui P (2008) "Going for income" in village Tibet: a longitudinal analysis of change and adaption, 1997–2007. Asian Surv 48(3):514–534. https://doi.org/10.1525/as.2008.48.3.514

Goldstein MC, Childs G, Wangdui P (2010) Beijing's "people first" development initiative for the Tibet autonomous Region's rural sector – a case study from the Shigatse area. China J 63:57–75. https://doi.org/10.1086/tcj.63.20749194

Grant A (2017) "Don't discriminate against minority nationalities": practicing Tibetan ethnicity on social media. Asian Ethn 18(3):371–386. https://doi.org/10.1080/14631369.2016.1178062

Hu A, Hu L (2011) 第二代民族政策:促进民族交融一体和繁荣一体 (the second generation of nationality policy: promoting integration and prosperity of nationalities). 新疆师范大学学报 (J Xinjiang Normal Univ) 32(5):1–12

Karmel SM (1995) Ethnic tension and the struggle for order: China's policies in Tibet. Pac Aff 68(4):485–508. https://doi.org/10.2307/2761273

Kehoe T (2015) I am Tibetan? An exploration of online identity constructions among Tibetans in China. Asian Ethn 16(3):314–333. https://doi.org/10.1080/14631369.2015.1015254

Kolas A, Thowsen MP (2005) On the margins of Tibet: cultural survival on the sino-Tibetan frontier. University of Washington Press, London/Seattle

Ma R (2007) A new perspective in guiding ethnic relations in the twenty-first century: "de-politicization" of ethnicity in China. Asian Ethn 8(3):199–217. https://doi.org/10.1080/14631360701594950

Ma R (2014) Reflections on the debate on China's ethnic policy: my reform proposals and their critics. Asian Ethn 15(2):237–246. https://doi.org/10.1080/14631369.2013.868205

Matsuno A (2014) Ethnic groups' right to Independence: self-determination, secession and the post-Cold War international relations. Asia Peacebuilding Initiatives. http://peacebuilding.asia/ethnic-groups-right-to-independence-self-determinationsecession-and-post-cold-war-international-relations/. Accessed 22 Sep 2018

Sautman B (2014) Self-representation and ethnic minority rights in China. Asian Ethn 15(2):174–196. https://doi.org/10.1080/14631369.2014.880588

Schwartz R (2008) Introduction. In: Barnett R, Schwartz R (eds) Tibetan modernities: notes from the field on cultural and social changes. Brill, Leiden, pp 1–34

The Office of the Dalai Lama (1961) Statement of his holiness the Dalai Lama on the second anniversary of the Tibetan National Uprising day. https://www.dalailama.com/messages/tibet/10th-march-archive/1961. Accessed 22 Sep 2018

The State Council Information Office of the People's Republic of China (2008) White paper: protection and development of Tibetan culture. http://www.china-un.org/eng/gyzg/xizang/t521512.htm. Accessed 22 Sep 2018

The Tibet Policy Institute (2017) Cultural genocide in Tibet: a report. https://tibetpolicy.net/wp-content/uploads/2017/10/Tibetocide.pdf. Accessed 22 Sep 2018

Tu Q, Bulte E, Tan S (2011) Religiosity and economic performance: micro-econometric evidence from Tibetan area. China Econ Rev 22(1):55–63. https://doi.org/10.1016/j.chieco.2010.09.008

Wang S (2009) Policy impact on Tibetan market participation. Asian Ethn 10(1):1–18. https://doi.org/10.1080/14631360802628418

Yang M (2012) Local responses to the "comfortable housing policy" in the Tibetan Autonomous Region A case study based on the actor-oriented approach. 中国藏学英文版 (China Tibetology English) 2012(2):76–99

Zhang Q, Xu P (2011) 西藏跨越式发展与民族文化的调试 (Tibet's leapfrog development and its culture adjustment). 中国藏学 (China Tibetology) 2011(2):65–69

Zhao D (1993) 试论西藏的传统文化与现代化 (Discussion on the traditional culture and modernization of Tibet). 西藏大学学报 (J Tibet Univ) (2):1–6

Zhu H (2013) How do farmers and herdsmen participate in the market? In: Wang L, Zhu L (eds) Breaking out of the poverty trap: case studies from the Tibetan Plateau in Yunnan, Qinghai and Gansu. World Century, Hackensack, pp 35–52

Zhu Y, Blachford D (2012) Economic expansion, marketization, and their social impact on China's ethnic minorities in Xinjiang and Tibet. Asian Surv 52(4):714–733. https://doi.org/10.1525/AS.2012.52.4.714

Volga Tatars: Continuing Resilience in the Age of Uncertainty

18

Renat Shaykhutdinov

Contents

Introduction	316
Historical Background: The Origins of People and Name	317
Early Contacts with the Muscovy/Russia	319
Tatars and the Imperial Russia: Suppression, Resilience, and Reform	320
Transition from Communism: New Hopes and Regrets	322
Conclusion	327
Cross-References	328
References	328

Abstract

The purpose of this chapter is to trace social and political processes of Volga, or Kazan, Tatars – the largest ethnic minority in the Russian Federation and one of the largest stateless ethnonational groups of Europe and the world. In doing so, some of the major developments concerning Tatar history, traditions, and their interaction with the Russian state will be surveyed. In addition to some of the key scholarship on Tatars published in English, several Russian- and Tatar-language sources will be employed. Following the introductory remarks, the origins of the people and their name will be examined alongside their early history. Competition with the Russian lands and the consequences of the loss of statehood will then be discussed. These include strategies of resilience, especially efforts at reforming culture, tradition, and the way of thinking. Post-communist struggle for greater self-governance, achievement of the power-sharing treaty with Moscow, and the post-Yeltsin policies will also be investigated. Brief assessment of the prospect of Tatar survival will be offered in the concluding section.

R. Shaykhutdinov (✉)
Florida Atlantic University, Boca Raton, FL, USA
e-mail: rshaykhu@fau.edu

© The Author(s), under exclusive license to Springer Nature Singapore Pte Ltd. 2019
S. Ratuva (ed.), *The Palgrave Handbook of Ethnicity*,
https://doi.org/10.1007/978-981-13-2898-5_148

Keywords

Volga (Kazan) Tatars · Russian Federation · Tatarstan · Idel-Ural · Volga-Urals region

Introduction

Volga, or Kazan, Tatars are a nation autochthonous to the Volga–Urals region located in the eastern part of the East European Plain at the confluence of the Volga (İdel) and Kama (Çulman) rivers "whose current republic of Tatarstan (one of 21 within the Russian Federation), ranks among Russia's most prosperous, highly developed and industrialized regions" (Daulet 2003, 3). Tatars boast rich political tradition; they speak a version of the Kypchak Turkic language and culturally and linguistically are close to the neighboring Bashkirs and Chuvash (Tanrısever 2001, 46). According to the ranking of top 100 most spoken languages in the world compiled by *the Ethnologue* in 1996 and updated in 1999, the Tatar language with its 8 million speakers occupied the 95th position globally; was among top 21 European languages (including Turkish), ahead of several official EU languages; and was the second most commonly spoken minority language of Europe (after Lombard) (Grimes 1996). The demographic attrition of the Tatar-speaking population is now counted in millions in just a handful of years between two Russian censuses. As such, the Tatar language has likely ceded its positions drastically. In fact, by 2009 *the Ethnologue* would exclude Tatar from the global top 100, downgrading the language to a still close 101st position (6.5 mln speakers) (Lewis 2009). Nevertheless, the language, culture, and legacy of Volga Tatars do remain an important phenomenon on a global ethnonational landscape. Tatars are still widely considered to be "Russia's biggest minority" (Massimo 2015). They are currently one of the largest, if not the largest, stateless ethnonational groups in Europe.

Following a rich history of independent statehood, people that came to be known Volga Tatars were the first non-Slavic and non-Christian people to be fused into the Muscovy, paving the way for that (proto-)Russian state to eventually become a continental empire. Alongside the history of conflict with Russia, Tatars were nevertheless instrumental in Moscow's expansion to Central Asia in a later period of czarist rule. Experiencing periodical campaigns, targeting their identity and very existence, and masterminded or condoned by the Russian state, Tatars nevertheless benefitted immensely from brief periods of Russia's liberalization and cooling off of its imperial and "civilizing" zeal. Short-lived political opportunities coupled with growing concerns about their existence within the Russian state led to the formation of a reform movement among Volga Tatars that aimed at reevaluating their values, culture, and thought system and has been widely considered among the most far-reaching reformist endeavors in the Islamic world. Among their major aspiration was greater self-governance, which included a maximal desire for the formation of their own state, during the czarist, communist, and post-communist periods. During much of their history, and perhaps most tellingly, at present, these aspirations have been fueled and undercut by assimilationist policies of the Russian state. These developments will be expanded on in the rest of the chapter.

The title of this chapter draws on two important books, one published at the beginning of Gorbachev's perestroika in 1986 – *The Volga Tatars: A Profile in National Resilience* – by historian Azade-Ayşe Rorlich was the "first Western-language study of the history of the Volga Tatars" (1986, xv) and for a long time perhaps the most authoritative study on that nation. Another is by Alan-G. Gagnon (2014) – a renowned scholar of ethnicity and federalism – who recently published a study that examines minorities at "the age of uncertainty." Resilience and uncertainty inform and set a tone for the rest of this chapter where, from this author's perspective, a brief but comprehensive account of historical and contemporary developments will be provided. Both terms of resilience and uncertainty, however, should be qualified for space and time, in which Volga Tatars find themselves. Resilience provides a positive outlook suggesting that Tatars are able and willing to recover from stresses placed upon them in history and perhaps even more so by contemporary challenges. Whether Tatars' resilience has limits or will help them survive as a distinct collectivity is nevertheless an open question as their resilience is tested hard by the current "age of uncertainty" in which many ethnonational minorities are faced with adverse state policies having little hope for redress and justice. State actors often act in subtle manner, engaging in ethnocide, cultural, and linguistic genocide, but stopping short of outright ethnic cleansing. Such instances, including one in which Volga Tatars find themselves, may even be dubbed as hybrid ethnocide. The age of uncertainty at the level of general dominant discourse spells an uncertain future driven by "objective" forces of history, and is supposed to result in "neutral," "natural," and even favorable outcomes for these groups. However, alternative views suggest that such future is far from uncertain and will bring about unfavorable, if not ominous, consequences to ethnic groups pushed by the actions of their "host" states. This contradiction of the new age is perhaps illustrated well by Valery Tishkov, a former Russian cabinet minister for nationality affairs and ex-head of the Institute of Ethnology and Anthropology in Moscow, in a recent interview: "no peoples [in Russia] have disappeared" in the last 20 years. Yet, "if the 20th century was the century of minorities, the 21st will be the century of majorities." In Russia, "Assimilation is also helping the ethnic Russians [...P]eople who live in Orthodox culture are making a voluntary choice in favor of Russian culture and the Russian language" (Goble 2016a). At one level, this quote gives hope for the survival of Russia's ethnic minorities, but at another points to their hybrid disappearance.

Historical Background: The Origins of People and Name

Volga Tatars have also been called *Kazanis* (*Qazanlılar*), *Bulgars* (*Bolğarilär*), *Mishars* (*Mişärlär*), and *Tatars* (*Tatarlar*). However well into the mid-nineteenth century, they were called and favored to be called as Muslims (Rorlich 1986, 3), perhaps not unlike the Bosniaks. Both the ethnonym (name) and ethnogenesis (origins and subsequent development) of Volga Tatars are subject to scholarly and popular debates which bear major political and even individual psychological implications. As Shafiga Daulet (Şafiğa Däwlät) points out, the ethnonym *Tatar* is associated with massive brutality and all things negative. Consequently, many in Russia and elsewhere think that violence and repression, past and present, directed against the Volga Kazani population is well-justified. Daulet counters this reasoning suggesting that the indigenous people of Volga-Urals have long professed a tradition of peace and nonviolence and suffered immensely from both the Mongol and Russian brutality. She also claims that they have been ashamed and reluctant to own and use *Tatar* as their ethnonym and choses to refer in her work to this population as *Kazani(an)* over *Tatar*. Taking Daulet's qualification of the Tatar national character as peaceful even further, İskändär Ğıylācev (Iskander Gilyazov), the editor of the Kazan Institute of the Tatar Encyclopedia points out that "We are an excessively modest and subservient people...We live according to the principle 'today things are like this but tomorrow we will see.' We aren't capable to defend [...] ou[r] interests" (Goble 2018a). Faller thinks that by tracing their history directly to the (pre-Mongol) Volga Bulgar state allows the present-day Volga Tatars to claim their status as an indigenous nation of the Volga-Ural region (Faller 2011). In deconstructing the myth of the "Tatar Yoke," Bilz-Leonhardt further shows that Western historiography has long been critical of the hegemonic negative view that Tatar rule was detrimental to the Russian principalities and suggests that a similar historical revisionism in Russia was largely made possible only in the post-Soviet period. She further opines that the recently qualified and reinterpreted history allowed the Volga Tatar population to reclaim their national pride and positively influenced Tatarstan's sovereignty project (Bilz-Leonhardt 2008).

Two versions exist regarding how the ethnonym *Tatar* originated – a Turkic and a Mongolic one. The Mongol version traces the roots of *Tatar* to the Chinese *Ta-Tan* (or *Da-Dan*) a derogatory name used by Chinese for Mongols. According to this version, *Tatar* refers to a Mongol tribe subjugated by Genghis Khan and "*Tatar*," which appears on the Orkhon Inscriptions, is believed to signify them. Mongol Tatars lived together with Turkic tribes and witnessed the destruction of the seminomadic Turkic kaganate (6–7 centuries A.D.) before being overtaken by Genghis Khan (1202–1208). Mongol Tatars together with Central Asian and south Siberian Turkic tribes were incorporated in the army of Batu, Genghis Khan's grandson. At the time of the conquest by Batu (and his three sons) of the east European *ulus* (lands), the Mongols came into relation with Turkic Kypchaks who at the height of their power (12–13 centuries) ruled enormous territory between Irtysh and Danube called *Dasht-i Kypchak*. Mongols and Mongol Tatars constituted a minority in Batu Khan's military; their ratio was even smaller in the newly formed "Golden Horde" that appeared after the conquest of the European ulus west of the Urals. As such, they have been assimilated both culturally and biologically by the Turkic peoples alongside whom they resided (Rorlich 1986, 4–5).

The ingathering of all Mongol tribes by Genghis Khan could only be possible by breaking the opposition of the Mongol Tatars. This has been symbolically marked by Genghis Khan's 1206 command to name all conquered people as *Tatar*; Tatar meant a subjugated people. However, as Mongols themselves have been assimilated by the peoples they had previously conquered, they would eventually adopt *Tatar* as their name. Most peoples of the Golden Horde would appear to embrace the name *Tatar*; however, the ancestor of Volga Tatars would resist that name in the sixteenth century (Rorlich 1986, 5).

The Turkic version is accepted by a minority of scholars who think that the Turkic people named *Tatars* existed before the Mongol invasions and it was them whose name passed on to the residents of the Golden Horde. It has also been argued that the ethnonym *Tatar* could have been used independently for two different groups of people – a Mongol tribe called Tatars and a Turkic tribe that resided at the far end of Eastern Europe, west of the Ural Mountains. This view draws heavily on Mahmud al-Kashgari's dictionary of Turkic languages, the *Diwan-i Lugat it-Turk*, which suggests that a Tatar arm of the Turkic languages was spoken in the area west of the Irtysh river (Rorlich 1986, 5).

The ethnogenesis of Volga Tatars is likewise very complex. Despite the disagreement about the origins, there is no division among scholars that by the sixteenth century Kazan Tatars were residing in the territory that included the northern part of the former Volga Bulgar state. This territory was still referred to in the western maps as *Bulgaria Magna*, yet it coincided with the area of the Kazan Khanate. The extensive network of firmly populated urban and rural settlements points to a degree of economic and cultural development and continuity of Kazan Tatars that sets them apart from their (semi) nomadic neighbors. The disagreement on the origins, however, is illustrated by two main theses – Kypchak and Bulgar. The Kypchak school of thought maintains that Volga Tatars descent directly from the Tatars of the Golden Horde, whereas the Bulgar claims that the forefathers of Kazan Tatars were Bulgars – a Turkic group that settled in the Middle Volga and lower Kama after being displaced from their ancestral lands located at the Sea of Azov by Arab raids. Volga Bulgaria was then conquered by Mongol Tatars (1236 and 1237) but their culture survived disappearance of their state and provided base for the rise of present-day Kazan Tatars. The latter thesis is deemed more categorical and less flexible (Rorlich 1986, 6) and even primordial while the former is likely to align with the constructivist scholarship of ethnic origins.

Historical complexity, ideological pressures, control, and periodic suppression of the study of Tatar history led to a situation where most Tatars, despite a rich written tradition, do not exhibit deep knowledge of their national origins. This is captured well in an interview with German journalist and writer Kai Ehlers who thinks that "Tatars do not know who they are, but know what they want":

> It seems to me that many Tatars do not quite understand who they are. [Are you d]escendants of the Huns? The Mongols? You cannot answer this question. At the same time, I have a feeling that you are as if telling others that "We are Tatars, we want to live our own way. We work. We follow our own path. We are strong and very hardworking." I would say that Tatars know what they want. Very practical people. (Etatar.Ru 2011)

Early Contacts with the Muscovy/Russia

The conditions and developments surrounding the tragic loss of independence by Volga Tatars provide some fascinating details that underscore the continuity of peaceful coexistence between Tatars and Russians but also challenge some widespread views concerning brutal treatment of Russians in the hands of Volga Tatars. In fact, Kazan, Moscow, and Crimea were equal heirs to their "host" state, the Golden Horde and cooperated with each other in their rivalry with Sarai (the capital of the Golden Horde). Alliances, counter-alliances, and cooperation and rivalry both within and between those entities marked their relations. Eventually, however the history of the Tatar Kazan and less significant Ästerxan (Astrakhan) Khanates would be characterized by conflict with and "their resistance to Russian counterinvasion" (Grousset 1970, 473). Historically, Tatar fragmentation is exemplified by multiple centers of power at the last stages of the Golden Horde and in its aftermath – Kazan, Crimea, and Astrakhan – which allied with Moscow in their conflict with Sarai. These centers of power, which, in turn, were internally divided by the time of the Russo-Tatar competition. The Muscovy was not necessarily responsible for the emergence of all the divisions within the Tatar elites. The quest for power among the rulers of the Kazan Khanate and the inability to check it by Kazan is an example. However, the Muscovy's provision of a "Czardom"/Khanate to Qasim, the brother of Kazan's ruler Mahmudek, was a crucially important direct move. The Kasimov Khanate was a vassal entity subordinate to the Muscovy; the cooptation of Tatar elites had arguably peaked with its establishment. The Kasimov Khanate has been instrumental in Muscovy's involvement in the competition between the Kazan khans, which would ultimately undercut the influence of Kazan and, after its fall, that of other Tatar khanates.

Specifically, following his decision to end the independence of Kazan, the ruler of the Muscovy Ivan IV (the Terrible) (1533–84) besieged Kazan in June, 1552 with the strong support of the Russian artillery. "On October 2, he took it by assault, massacred a large part of the male population, enslaved the women and children, pulled down the mosques, and annexed the territory of the khanate" (Grousset 1970, 475). The end of the Kazan Khanate precipitated the swift change in the balance of power between the Jenghizides and the Russian state as the Ästerxan Khanate fell almost immediately in 1554, though the Crimean Khanate was to survive for another 200 years.

Tatars and the Imperial Russia: Suppression, Resilience, and Reform

Following the conquest and loss of statehood, Kazan Tatars were subjected to direct pressures from the state. Subsequent repressive policies of the czarist regime led to the destruction of mosques, seizure of property, and building of churches and monasteries (Davis et al. 2000). Imperial Russia's policy of coopting the Tatar aristocracy via religious conversion was unsuccessful as only a small portion of Tatars adopted orthodox Christianity (Tanrısever 2001, 46). Consequently, the locals who refused conversion were forced to relocate 30 kilometers away from Kazan and the riverbanks (Faller 2002). As the Russian peasantry was transferred to the area [and exempt from serfdom, which was in place in the rest of the Muscovy], to colonize the newly conquered lands, Tatars found themselves expelled from their rural areas to arid lands (Faller 2002, 82). Scholars, such as Kopanski (1998), claim that all-Russian orthodox hegemonism has always been in place across political and economic regimes in Russia. It is implied, however, that its salience has been conditioned by state's capacity/weakness. Instability and state-wide crises that led to greater freedoms were in part produced by Tatars (and Bashkirs) themselves during the uprising of Batırşa; by the external forces as at the time of troubles; or the combination of both, when, for example, Tatars and Bashkirs took part in the peasant war of 1773–1775 alongside the Russian serfs. Among other notable factors determining the level of relative freedom is the higher degree of enlightenment of autocratic rulers, with Catherine II and Mikhail Gorbachev being perhaps the most prominent examples. Still, even for rulers widely deemed democratic and enlightened, economic resources are claimed to be a decisive factor in shaping their political reputation. According to Russian commentator for *Deutsche Welle* Igor Eidman, "Yeltsin was just as much a crazy imperialist as have been practically all other Russian rulers over the last several centuries," yet "he simply did not have the economic resources for carrying out an imperial policy at the international level. But judging from his conversations with Clinton, he like his predecessors very much wanted to be master of half of the world" (Goble 2018b).

Even though Kazan came to be a central city for missionary efforts, Slavic colonization, and Russia's assimilationist endeavors accompanied by periodic Tatar revolts against Russification, an understanding between the two groups developed with respect to mutual benefit and cohabitation (Toft 2003, 46). Tatars were increasingly becoming mediators between the Christian imperial core and the Turkic peoples conquered more recently contributing to their coexistence. Their central geographical location within Russia and social role allowed Tatars to enjoy a relative prosperity that led to the establishment of a large Tatar middle class (Toft 2003, 46–47). Tatars exhibited high literacy rates, developed national consciousness, and grew concerned about de-Tatarization and the challenges to the Tatar way of life (Toft 2003, 46).

Historically, perhaps the most important intellectual movement that forged and exhibited national resilience was that of the progressive reformist Muslim Tatar movement of *jadidi*s who sought to reform and energize the Tatar ways of life in an effort to counter what they saw as an impending and almost certain extinction of the nation. An important *jadidi* was a classic of the Tatar literature Ğayaz İsxaqıy (Iskhaki) (1878–1954), who published in 1904 a famous novel titled "Disappearance After 200 Years" ("200 Yıldan Soñ İnqıyraz"). İsxaqıy was widely seen as a talented and passionate spokesman for the radical renewal of Tatar social life as a condition for the preservation and development of the nation (Ämirxanov/Amirkhanov 1997).

Another scholar who is (re)gaining attention in Kazan is Musa Bigiyev, sometimes referred to as Luther of Islam, "a Tatar Muslim theologian of the first half of the 20th century whom many have called Islam's answer to Martin Luther because of his call for a reformation in the ways Muslims approach the Koran and who spent time in both Soviet and British jails." Bigiyev was a major figure in the Muslim renaissance of 1905, having put together records of the All-Russian Muslim Congresses and participating in the early phases of the Tatar national movement. He was noted in

1909 for what others dubbed as "the errors in the Qur'an" that he had identified. In reality, however, he did not talk about the errors in the Qur'an, but instead about errors of people who read it as in the way the Qur'an was currently written there are "more than 60 places" where interpretation of the Arabic has been challenging. The version of the Qur'an that he had corrected received a far-reaching acceptance among the *ulema* (Islamic scholars) in the Muslim world. This was his first major "victory" in what was seen by some as the reformation in Islam. He subsequently produced books where he utilized his revised version for rereading and reinterpreting earlier Islamic scholars (Goble 2018c; Xäyretdinov (Khairutdinov) 2018).

As the system was democratizing, by the end of the czarist rule, Muslim Tatars were able to acquire political representation in the Russian Duma and assert their aspirations for self-government. A leading contemporary scholar of Islam in Russia claims that in contrast to the previous period, by the beginning of the twentieth century, the political side of their relationship with Russia became especially important to Tatars; the Russian revolution brought "hopes and aspirations for democratic liberties; the notion of the 'motherland' gained a new civic substance, which implies the equality of political rights and duties..." (Möxämmätşin (Mukhametshin) 2009, 137). The Tatar intelligentsia clearly understood that the success of Tatars' national aspirations was inexorably tied to "the democratization of the entire political system of Russia," offering a model of Russia's political restructuring based on pluralistic principles long familiar in the West (Möxämmätşin 2009, 139). In the context of Russia such model, first suggested by I. Gasprinski, placed Tatars and Russians in the position of formal equality. As the Muslim fraction in the second State Duma published in its program, "as the most appropriate form of state structure for Russia under the current conditions the fraction recognizes the constitutional parliamentary monarchy, in which the highest state authority belongs to the monarch constrained in her rights by the Constitution, and the people embodied by their representatives who act on the base of the same constitution" (Möxämmätşin 2009, 138).

By the end of the nineteenth century, they agreed that a Tatar homeland should exist in the middle Volga region (Toft 2003). The Idel-Ural state (1917–1918) uniting Tatars, Bashkirs, and the Finno-Ugric people of the area was formed during the World War I, but proved to be short-lived as Bolsheviks took over. Political repression of the 1920s–1930s suppressed the Tatar national movement (D. M. Iskhakov et al. 2005, 11). The entire Tatar intelligentsia was purged in 1930s due to the accusation of bourgeois nationalism (Faller 2002, 82). "By midsummer [of 1937] the entire Government of the Tatar Republic was under arrest," which reflected a likely "general decision to destroy old Parties in the national Republics" (Conquest 1968, 251).

Transition from Communism: New Hopes and Regrets

By the end of the Soviet period, Tatarstan had become one of the most industrially developed areas of the country (Gorenburg 2003, 20). It produced 50% of all Soviet trucks in one of the largest factories in the USSR. By 1970s, the republic was the largest producer of oil in the Soviet Union (Gorenburg 2003) with an industrial potential superseding that of the three Baltic republics. In spite of the industrial developments, the borders of Tatarstan formed by Soviet ethnic engineers were explicitly designed to divide Tatars and weaken the Tatar identity, laying ground for the expression of the ethnically driven demands by the end of the Soviet rule (Toft 2003, 48).

The policies of *perestroika* initiated by Gorbachev in 1985 gave ethnic groups within the communist bloc an opportunity to express their grievances. During the early transition, the Tatar forces are represented by two key players within the republic – Tatar nationalizing intellectual and political elites – who largely defined the political landscape in Tatarstan and Tatarstan's relationship with Moscow (Giuliano 2000; Kondrashov 2000; Toft 2003). Both intellectual and political elites have constantly pressed for the greater autonomy of Tatarstan since the late Soviet period. Both intellectual and political elites in Tatarstan were, to a degree, the products of what Giuliano calls "an overt, publicized strategy of nativization (*korenizatsiia*) and a covert strategy of Russification" of the ex-USSR (Giuliano 2000, 304). Nativization led to the increased social mobility of the minority titular populations, but it also meant that titular nationality groups had to play by the rules of the game, which implied education in Russian and communication in Russian at work. The urban Tatar intelligentsia became quite isolated from the Tatar culture. Hence, it was advocating the need for language revival. Russified Tatar intellectuals were the founders of the first (and most dominant) non-state nationalist organization Tatar Public Center (TOTs) (Giuliano 2000).

Substantive demands of parties, clubs, and social organizations of Tatar intellectual elites ranged from purely cultural and educational, such as *Mäğärif*, to overtly political, such as the *Suverenitet* Committee, *İttifaq*, *Azatlıq* Association, and TOTs. Programmatic statements of the groups avoided references to violence and, as did *Watan*'s program, explicitly "reject[ed] violence and terror" putting emphasis on attaining party goals through peaceful means (D. M. Iskhakov 1992, 23).

Regarding the rights of other nationalities, TOTs stipulates equality of all citizens and congruence of the republic's law with international norms (1992, 14). *İttifaq*'s program suggests that "social rights and freedoms of the people of other [non-Tatar] nationalities should be respected" and "all conditions for satisfaction of national and cultural needs are provided" (1992, 21). *Watan*'s program stipulates equality of all nations, good neighboring relationships between different peoples, recognition of their territorial integrity, as well as respect for the rights of other nationalities in a restored Tatar state. *Watan* also claims to promote social and national equality and different forms of property ownership (1992, 23). Islamic Democratic Party of Tatarstan grants "native peoples of the republic…status of a native nation" while taking "an active role in the defense of ethnic interests of all nationalities residing in the republic, their language, culture, education and religious conscience" (1992, 24). *Suverenitet* Committee "purports to express the interests of all citizens who actively support the politics of reform within the country and the growth of the state sovereignty of Tatarstan regardless of their nationality, social status, religion or partisanship"; it supports human rights of individuals without regard to their ethnic background and calls for restoration of the ideals of humanism (1992, 26).

Smaller groups that split from TOTs – *İttifaq* and *Azatlıq* – voiced more extreme demands, yet as Toft shows, they "never drew large following" and their demands for "Tatarstan for Tatars" calls for a ban on Tatar–Russian marriages, and extension of citizenship rights for any Tatars living outside of Tatarstan were "counterbalanced by equally extreme groups on the other side" (Toft 2003, 51).

The issue of language revival advocated by many Tatar intellectuals did not attract much support from Tatar-speaking Tatars, most of who resided in the countryside and already fluently spoke Tatar. A perceived cleavage in social status between the urban and rural Tatars might have resulted in a more limited support of the nationalist aspirations. Despite their inferior status in the eyes of some urban intellectual elites, the Tatar-speaking Tatars from the countryside came to play the most important role in the political elite of Tatarstan. These elites were formed under the leadership of the Tatar communist party *obkom*'s (republic, oblast' level party branch) first secretary Tabeev in the 1960s–1970s. While in office, he brought to Kazan people from the local and town administrations (Giuliano 2000). By the time Tatarstan entered the period of national revival, the republic was headed by Tabeev's successor Mintimer Shaymiev. Shaymiev and his administration employed conciliatory actions and rhetoric that emphasized nonviolence.

Despite splinter groups, Tatar intellectual elites, Tatar political/presidential elites, and pro-Russian unity groups have been the main forces on the political scene of Tatarstan. Throughout the period, there was a shifting balance of forces among them; however, between 1988 and 1992, the nationalist movement "set the agenda," but from 1992 "[n]egotiation with Moscow over the republic's resources came to be determined by [ruling] elite interests" (Giuliano 2000, 54).

From summer 1989, TOTs advanced a nationalist discourse in the republican media and organized street campaigns. Tatar political elite complemented nationalist protests organized by grassroot organizations. A Tatar MP read a TOTs' petition addressing Gorbachev and Yeltsin at the Russian Congress of People's Deputies in Moscow (McAuley 1997). By the end of August 1991, the Tatar Declaration of Sovereignty was adopted.

Yeltsin quickly reacted to the mounting, yet, peaceful pressures coming from Tatarstan. He traveled to the republic in late summer and held a number of visits with the representatives of economic enterprises, intelligentsia, and members of the Tatar parliament. It was also during this visit when Yeltsin made a legendary announcement inviting Tatarstan and, indeed, other republics to take as much sovereignty as they could swallow (Malik 1994).

Despite Yeltsin's efforts, Shaymiev and the republican political elite cooperated with Gorbachev's Union forces with the purpose of gaining a Union republic status for Tatarstan. Hence, when Yeltsin tried to introduce in Gorbachev's referendum the question on the formation of the Russian presidency, the republic's elite excluded this question from the referendum. After the elections of the Russian president were permitted, the nationalist organizations resisted them and by the end of April 1991, an approximately 10,000-strong rally stipulated the recall of the Tatar deputies from the Russian parliament (Beissinger 2002). A demonstration of some 15,000 participants on May 21 is also noted, which included the members of *İttifaq*, who went as far as to start a hunger strike; newspaper *Novosti* wrote of daily rallies and protest meetings (Toft 2003). These events were critical as they led to the onset of negotiations between the Tatar and Russian political elites and resulted in a power sharing treaty between Kazan and Moscow in February 1994. The treaty solidified interethnic and interreligious concord as an integral part of social and political identity of Tatarstan, and the republic "was presented as an example of tolerant coexistence of the different people and faiths, as center of the Tatar and Muslim cultures" (Nurutdinova 2016, 34).

Since Putin's election as Russian president in 2000, he embarked on the construction of the *power vertical* centralizing regional competencies in Moscow. Among the first policies were the formation of the federal districts in 2000 as an intermediate layer between Moscow and regions; stripping governors and heads of regional parliaments of right to represent their entities in the federal senate; replacing direct gubernatorial elections with effective, though indirect, appointments; and amalgamation of ethnic autonomous district (*okrugs*) with predominantly Russian regions. There were also more direct pressures on Tatarstan. According to a source interviewed by Faller (2011, 11):

> In 2000 – his first year as Russia's president – Vladimir Putin came to Kazan during the annual Sabantuy celebrations in June and held a 24-hour-long closed-door meeting with Tatarstan President Mintimir Shaimiev and Bashkortostan President Murtaza Rahimov. According to a source close to Shaimiev, Putin threatened to 'discover Wahabbists' on the two presidents' territory, which he would use as justification for 'making a Chechnya' out of Tatarstan and Bashkortostan, unless both republics relinquished their adherence to the power-sharing agreements they had concluded with Moscow in 1994...Tatarstan immediately agreed to cede at least 50% of the revenues generated on its territory to Moscow, which, as in Soviet times, were not redistributed back to the republic.

However, the instances of violence remained infrequent, though more salient. The Global Terrorism Database, which tracks information on terrorist incidents around the globe from 1970 to 2014 found evidence for only seven occurrences in Tatarstan, with an isolated event in 1997 and the remaining cases taking place in equal numbers in 2012 and 2013. The dataset misses explosions that took place in December 1999, targeting gas pipelines in the border region of Tatarstan and Russia's Kirov oblast. That incident was blamed upon students at the Yolduz (Yoldız) madrasa and linked to the Arabs teaching at that school and Chechen rebels. That incident resulted in the republic-level anti-terrorism campaign that led to detention of some Yolduz students with suspected affiliations with al-Qaeda (Malashenko and Yarlykapov 2009; cited in Khurmatullin 2010) and the eventual shutdown of that madrasa in 2000 (Khurmatullin 2010). While the incident, referred to at times as the Quqmara [Kukmor] event, was not widely reported by English-language outlets, the twin terrorist attacks that occurred a little over a decade later would bring world-wide attention to a region known for its peaceful and pragmatic approach to religion.

The terrorist acts of July 19, 2012, represent perhaps the most vivid example of a security issue that leaped to the very top of public concern and government attention. The vice mufti of the central Russian republic of Tatarstan, Wäliulla Yaqup (also spelled Yağqup and Yakupov), was assassinated in front of his house, while *mufti* (chief Islamic religious figure) Fäiz's (Fäyez, Fayzov, Faizov) car was subjected to three explosions at a busy intersection of the central streets in the capital city of Kazan. Fäiz suffered a broken leg and was hospitalized. A series of important developments followed the incidents. One was the rapid detention of five suspects, including four Tatarstanis. These were the head of the board of directors of the *İdel-Xac* (*Idel-Hajj*) company Röstäm Ğataullin (Rustem Gataullin), the leader of the Muslim organization *Waqıf* Murat Ğaliev (Galeev), the businessmen Azat Ğäynetdinov (Gainutdinov) (from Tatarstan's Layış district), and Ayrat Şakirov (Airat Shakirov) (from Biektaw district), together with a national of Uzbekistan, Abdunozim Ataboyev. Overall, it is reported that several hundred people were detained by the authorities (up to 700, according to Keenan (2013, 75)). A video would later surface featuring an appeal to the republic's Muslims to fight the Russian regime by a self-proclaimed Tatarstani jihadist leader, later identified as Räis Miñğäliev (Rais Mingaleev), who pledged allegiance to the Caucasus Emirate. By August 16, a manhunt for the prime suspects, Räis Miñğäliev, Robert Wäliev (Valeev), and Albert İsmağıylev (Ismagilov) was declared. Approximately one month after the attacks, on August 20, a car exploded on the Kazan-Yäşel Üzän highway leaving three passengers dead. Authorities attributed the cause to an accidental detonation of a homemade explosive by the suspected members of an underground Islamist group. A violent standoff in a Kazan apartment on October 24 left four dead, including three suspects and one member of the FSB (Russian security service). Ammunition apparently intended to be used in terror attacks was uncovered during the operation. According to Russia's National Anti-terror Committee (NAC), the militants killed were suspects in the attack on mufti Fäiz; the *RIA Novosti* news agency referencing NAC claimed that two of the killed, Qaşapov (Kashapov) and Wäliev, were members of Miñğäliev's group. However, some within the Tatar intellectual elite interpreted the event differently. The Head of the Institute of History of the Academy of Sciences of Tatarstan, Rafail Xäkimov (Rafael Khakimov), maintained that ordinary crime rather than terrorism was behind the tragic events of October 24 in Kazan: "I believe that this is a continuation of the attack on the mufti. This is not an Islam-related affair, it is criminality. I think this is not terror…I wouldn't say that some sort of ideology is at play here. Organizing explosions before the holidays only looks like someone is pulling wool over our eyes" (RFE/RL 2012). Meanwhile, a reclusive Islamic sect led by its own prophet, Fäyzraxman Sattarov, dubbed the "catacomb sect" of Faizrakhmanists (Fäyzraxmançılar) because it operated from the basement of a house, became the target of a special operation by the authorities. The sect, totaling 70 members, did not interact with the outside world, did not let anybody in their residence at the outskirts of Kazan, did not use communication technology, and was not connected to the terror events. However, the group's Tatar language literature was confiscated and sent off for expert examination for extremist content. In November of 2013, a Kazan court ruled that the sect should be evicted from their house. By April 2014, the sect was included in the registry of extremist organizations and 15 members remaining in the house were eventually evicted. Similarly, the Äl-İxlas (Al-Ikhlas) parish/mosque was pronounced extremist and shut down by the government.

On the weekend of November 16 and 17, 2013, another series of events shook Tatarstan. On the 16th, four rockets were fired at a chemical facility within the confines of the petro-industrial city of Tübän Kama (Nizhnekamsk) along with an arson attack on two churches in Yaña Çişmä and Çistay districts. The following night was marked by a deadly crash of the Tatarstan Airlines Boeing 737-500 jet airliner, which took the lives of some 50 people, including the son of Tatarstan's president. These events resonated with the initial twin terror attacks of July 19, 2012, underscoring a sense of popular insecurity. The coverage of the terror events in the Russian and western media focused on apocalyptical scenarios for Tatarstan as far as risks for the subsequent terrorism are concerned; however, most locals downplayed the significance of that threat in online forums (Shaykhutdinov 2018).

Many online commenters saw recent violence in Tatarstan as an assault on the republic and Tatars more broadly. In addition to violence, many were concerned about the catastrophic demographic situation: between 2002 and 2010 the number of active Tatar speakers has reportedly diminished by some 1 million; the 2010 figure for the total number of Tatar speakers in the Russian Federation was 4,280,718 (including 3,647,137 ethnic Tatar speakers of the language). This change can at least partly be attributed to a range of policies intended to centralize Russian federalism through the *power vertical*. The policies targeting ethnic non-Russian population (and Tatars and Tatarstan, specifically) include the prohibition on the use of the Latin alphabet for republics' state languages; refusal to allow students to take the country-wide university entrance examination (EGE) in languages other than Russian; "optimization" (economic cuts) in the education system leading to disproportionate closure of Tatar-language schools (187 in 2011–2016); and diminishing opportunities for higher education in the Tatar language.

Conclusion

What does future hold for Volga Tatars? Unfortunately, recent developments are less than encouraging. Among them are the effective termination of territorial autonomy for Tatarstan in July 2017 and the ban on Tatar language classes in the mandatory curricula of Tatarstan's public schools in November 2017. The federal center refused extending the treaty between governments of Russia and Tatarstan in July 2017, allowing that document to lapse in August 2017. The language ban followed a July statement by President Putin that "Forcing a person to learn a language that is not native to him/her is just as unacceptable as reducing the level of teaching of Russian" in the national republics. Apparently, the expiration of the treaty allowed the Russian government to unilaterally modify the education policy. In November, the republic's prosecutor delivered a speech at the session of the parliament of Tatarstan, in which he threatened that no "statements of extremist nature" concerning the issue of language education will be tolerated. Following the speech, the parliament, holding no discussion, in the best Soviet traditions terminated the mandatory education of Tatar in Tatarstan. Students who gathered in front of the parliament to sing a Tatar folksong in protest were threatened by their university's administration. Tatar intellectuals also expressed worries that the likelihood of dissolution of Tatarstan is high. In the meanwhile, Volga Tatars who are also a recognized minority group in the People's Republic of China are being interned in the reeducation camps in the Xinjiang Autonomous Region alongside Uyghurs, Kazakhs, and others.

Many Tatars concerned about future of their nation are "negative nationalists," who view their position in the world through the prism of survival and interest. To the extent that Tatars' rich historical tradition, peaceful coexistence with others, and resilience influences their transformation into "positive nationalists" – ones "who think they are going to win because they are on the winning side of history" – Volga Tatars may stand a chance at survival. Such survival may take unusual form, consciously or unconsciously feeding on the assimilationist policies currently at work. As such, those policies may backfire in a grand manner. While linguistic Russification and "Irelandization" of the Tatar culture is increasingly the topic of discussion for urban Tatar intellectuals (Säetov/Saetov 2017), some observers warn that "some Russian-speaking non-Russians may have a stronger sense of national identity than their [unassimilated] ancestors" who spoke native languages and consequently are "likely to be the Irish of the 21st century" (Goble 2016b).

Cross-References

▶ Ethno-politics in the People's Republic of China

References

Ämirxanov/Amirkhanov, Raşat/Rashat (1997) Fatíx Ämirxan/Fatikh Amirkhan: 'Vse prezhnee vo mne prevratilos' v pepel (Fatíx Ämirxan/Fatikh Amirkhan: 'Everything that was inside me has turned into ashes'). Ğasırlar Awazı – Ekho Vekov (Voice/Echo of Centuries)
Beissinger MR (2002) Nationalist mobilization and the collapse of the soviet state. Cambridge University Press, Cambridge/New York
Bilz-Leonhardt M (2008) Deconstructing the myth of the Tatar yoke. Centr Asian Surv 27(1):33–43
Conquest R (1968) The great terror: Stalin's purge of the thirties. The Macmillan Company, New York/Toronto
Daulet S (2003) Kazan and Moscow: five centuries of crippling coexistence under Russian imperialism (1552–2002). Kase Press, Hudson/New Hampshire
Davis H, Hammond P, Nizamova L (2000) Media, language policy and cultural change in Tatarstan: historic vs. pragmatic claims to nationhood. Nations and Nationalism 6(2):203–226
Etatar.Ru (2011) Kai Eilers: 'Tatary Znaiut, Chego Khotiat' (Kai Ehlers: 'Tatars know what they want'). Etatar.Ru. http://etatar.ru/top/40214
Faller HM (2002) Repossessing Kazan as a form of nation-building in Tatarstan, Russia. J Muslim Minor Aff 22(1):81–90
Faller HM (2011) Nation, language, Islam: Tatarstan's sovereignty movement. Central European University Press, Budapest

Gagnon A-G (2014) Minority nations in the age of uncertainty: New paths to national emancipation and empowerment. University of Toronto Press, Toronto

Giuliano E (2000) Who determines the self in the politics of self-determination? Identity and preference formation in Tatarstan's nationalist mobilization. Comp Polit 32(3):295–316

Goble PA (2016a) Crimea annexation restored ethnic Russian share of country's population to 1989 level, Tishkov says. Window on Eurasia – New Series. http://windowoneurasia2.blogspot.com/2016/01/crimea-annexation-restored-ethnic.html

Goble PA (2016b) A warning to the Kremlin: Its non-Russians likely to be the Irish of the 21st century. Window on Eurasia – New Series. https://windowoneurasia2.blogspot.com/2016/10/a-warning-to-kremlin-its-non-russians.html

Goble PA (2018a) Tatarstan now under attack and probability it will disappear is 'extremely high,' Gilyazov says. Window on Eurasia – New Series. http://windowoneurasia2.blogspot.com/2018/09/tatarstan-now-under-attack-and.html

Goble PA (2018b) Yeltsin was just as much an imperialist as Putin is but lacked resources to act broadly on his views, Eidman says. Window on Eurasia – New Series. https://windowoneurasia2.blogspot.com/2018/09/yeltsin-was-just-as-much-imperialist-as.html

Goble PA (2018c) 'Muslim Martin Luther' jailed by both Soviets and British recalled in Kazan. Window on Eurasia – New Series. http://windowoneurasia2.blogspot.com/2018/08/muslim-martin-luther-jailed-by-both.html

Gorenburg DP (2003) Minority ethnic mobilization in the Russian Federation. Cambridge University Press, Cambridge

Grimes BF (1996) Ethnologue. *Ethnologue*. https://www.ethnologue.com/13/top100.html

Grousset R (1970) The empire of the steppes: a history of Central Asia. Rutgers University Press, New Brunswick

Iskhakov DM (1992) Neformal'nye ob"edineniia v sovremennom tatarskom obshchestve (Informal associations/organizations in contemporary Tatar society). In: Iskhakov DM (ed) Sovremennye natsional'nye protsessy v Respublike Tatarstan (Contemporary national processes in the Republic of Tatarstan). Rossiiskaia Akademiia Nauk – Kazanskii Nauchnyi Tsentr (The Russian Academy of Sciences – Kazan Science Center), Kazan

Iskhakov DM, Sagitova LV, Izmailov IL (2005) The Tatar national movement of the 1980s–90s. Anthropol Archeol Eurasia 43(3):11–44

Keenan R (2013) Tatarstan: the battle over Islam in Russia's heartland. World Policy J 30:70–79

Khurmatullin A (2010) Tatarstan: Islam entwined with nationalism. In: Dannreuther R, March L (eds) Russia and Islam: state, society and radicalism. Routledge, London/New York, pp 103–121

Kondrashov S (2000) Nationalism and the drive for sovereignty in Tatarstan, 1988–92: origins and development. St. Martin's Press, New York

Kopanski AB (1998) Burden of the Third Rome: the threat of Russian Orthodox fundamentalism and Muslim Eurasia. Islam and Christian–Muslim Relations 9(2):193–216. https://doi.org/10.1080/09596419808721148

Lewis MP (2009) 'Statistial Summaries', ethnologue: languages of the world, 16th edn. SIL International. https://www.ethnologue.com/16/ethno_docs/distribution/size/

Malashenko A, Yarlykapov A (2009) Radicalisation of Russia's Muslim community. MICROCON Policy Working Paper 9. Brighton: MICROCON

Malik H (1994) Tatarstan's treaty with Russia: autonomy or independence. J South Asian Middle East Stud 18:1–36

Massimo C (2015) Do minorities have a place in Putin's Russia? Wilson Q. https://wilsonquarterly.com/stories/do-minorities-have-a-place-in-putins-russia/

McAuley M (1997) Russia's politics of uncertainty. Cambridge University Press, Cambridge, UK/New York

Möxämmätşin (Mukhametshin) RM (2009) Osnovnye etapy vozvrashcheniia islama v obshchestvenno-politicheskuiu zhizn' v volgo-ural'skom regione (Main phases of Islam's return in the socio-political life in the Volga-Urals region). In: Iskhakov DM (ed) Konfessional'nyi faktor v razvitii tatar: kontseptual'nye issledovaniia (Confessional factor in the development of Tatars: conceptual research). Institut istorii im. Sh. Marjani AN RT; Rossiiskii Islamskii Universitet (Sh. Marjani Institute of History of the Academy of Sciences of the Republic of Tatarstan; Russian Islamic University), Kazan

Nurutdinova AN (2016) The newspaper discourse dynamics of religious extremism in the Tatarstan Republic. J Org Cult Commun Confl 20(2):33–38

RFE/RL (2012) Rafail Xäkimov: 'Atışlar artında islam eşläre tügel, ä kriminal' (Rafail Xäkimov/ Rafael Khakimov: 'Criminality is behind the shootings, not Islam-related affairs'). Azatlıq Radiosı—Radio Free Europe/Radio Liberty. http://www.azatliq.org/a/24750710.html

Rorlich A-A (1986) The Volga Tatars: a profile in national resilience. Hoover Institution Press, Stanford

Säetov/Saetov İ/I (2017) Kommentarii. Tataro-mongol'skoe EGE. Kak v Rossii stroiat etnonatsional'noe gosudarstvo (Commentary: The Tatar-Mongolian EGE (Unifed State Exam). How an ethnonational state is being built in Russia). Novaya Gazeta, № 103, September 17. https://www.novayagazeta.ru/articles/2017/09/18/73884-tataro-mongolskoe-ege

Shaykhutdinov R (2018) The terrorist attacks in the Volga region, 2012–13: hegemonic narratives and everyday understandings of (in)security. Centr Asian Surv 37(1):50–67. Routledge

Tanrısever OF (2001) The impact of the 1994 Russian-Tatar power-sharing treaty on the post-soviet Tatar national identity. Slovo 13(1):43–60

Toft MD (2003) The geography of ethnic violence: identity, interests, and the indivisibility of territory. Princeton University Press, Princeton/Oxford

Xäyretdinov (Khairutdinov) A (2018) Musa Bigiyev govorit, chto nuzhno reformirovat' ne islam, a nashe ponimanie islama (Musa Bigiyev says that it is not Islam that needs to be reformed, but our understanding of Islam). BIZNES Online (BUSINESS Online). https://www.business-gazeta.ru/article/392614

Identity and Conflict in Northern Ireland

19

Cathal McManus

Contents

Introduction	332
Background to the Conflict	333
Northern Ireland: A Legacy of Sectarian Division	335
Conflicting Cultures: The Politics of Identity	336
Comfort in Sectarianism?	340
Conclusion	344
Cross-References	344
References	344

Abstract

For almost 30 years, Northern Ireland society was torn apart by a conflict based along competing ethno-religious lines. The signing of the Good Friday (Belfast) Agreement in 1998, however, promised a peace process that would bring an end to the militancy of previous decades and the establishment of new political arrangements that would see the competing groupings of Irish Nationalism and Ulster Unionism share power in a devolved Northern Ireland assembly. Despite much progress in the 20 years since the Agreement, many problems remain, and often bitter sectarian tensions continue to blight Northern Irish society and block progress toward full implementation of both the Good Friday Agreement and the subsequent St Andrews Agreement of 2007. This chapter will examine the nature of these ongoing divisions and highlight the role that competing identities have come to play in maintaining a sectarian divide since 1998. Arguing that Northern Ireland has yet to confront a legacy of "Othering" between the two conflicting communities, it will be stressed that much work remains to be done to fulfil the

---

C. McManus (✉)
School of Social Sciences, Education and Social Work, Queen's University Belfast, Belfast, Northern Ireland
e-mail: c.p.mcmanus@qub.ac.uk

promise and optimism of 1998 and to create a Northern Ireland at peace with its diversity.

Keywords

Northern Ireland · Othering · Peace process · Reconciliation · Identity · Sectarianism

Introduction

In July 1997, the Irish Republican Army (IRA) declared an "unequivocal restoration" of the ceasefire it had previously called in August 1994, bringing about a "complete cessation of military operations." The ceasefire was an important milestone in bringing to an end a conflict that had raged for almost 30 years and had claimed the lives of over 3,500 people. Central to this conflict were the competing national aspirations of Ulster Unionism/Loyalism, who seek to protect Northern Ireland's position within the United Kingdom, and Irish Nationalism/Republicanism who strive to bring about some form of political unification with the Irish Republic.

The decision by the IRA to restore its ceasefire also helped to create a political climate that made negotiations toward a new compromise settlement possible, negotiations that were to culminate 9 months later with the signing of the Good Friday (Belfast) Agreement (the Agreement) in April 1998.

At the heart of the Agreement was a new power-sharing/consociational assembly headed by a governing executive, positions to which were allocated via the d'Hondt system with each party being allocated ministerial posts based on the number of votes gained in elections (HMSO 1998). This helped to ensure that power would largely be shared between the two dominant political blocs with the smaller cross-community alliance party occasionally holding one or two ministerial positions.

In addition to establishing the power-sharing assembly, the Agreement also provided for reform to policing, the release of paramilitary prisoners, and the decommissioning of illegally held weapons by these groups which included not only the IRA but also loyalist organizations such as the Ulster Volunteer Force (UVF) and the Ulster Defence Association (UDA).

Furthermore, and in an important addition to the consociational frameworks proposed by Arend Lijphart (1977), the Agreement also established new North-South ministerial bodies to develop greater cooperation between Northern Ireland and the Republic of Ireland on "matters of mutual interest" and new institutions designed to improve working relations between both parts of Ireland and the United Kingdom (McGarry and O'Leary 2009).

For proponents of this consociational democracy, the Agreement ought to have provided a long-term settlement to the long-running constitutional question having accommodated the competing nationalist yearnings of both Irish nationalists and Ulster Unionists. In protecting the immediate future of Northern Ireland by attaching it to the principle of consent and developing stronger UK ties, the Agreement had much to reassure Unionists. With the establishment of the power-sharing assembly, the creation of new (and potentially further) cross-border ties, the guarantee to the right of Irish citizenship, and a promise to protect and promote Irish cultural identity, there was also much to reassure Irish Nationalists and Republicans.

Yet, implementation of the Agreement has proven to be hugely problematic as Northern Ireland remains bitterly divided along its historic sectarian lines. Indeed, at the time of writing, Northern Ireland has been without a government for 19 months following the collapse of the assembly in January 2017 in part because of issues related to the introduction of an Irish Language Act (Acht na Gaeilge). This dispute is merely the latest in a long line of disagreements that have had cultural issues at their heart, leading some to argue that we are now witnessing the old military conflict being fought out over matters of identity (McManus 2017).

This chapter will examine the causes of these cultural disputes and, in particular, highlight how processes of "Othering" are continuing to shape negative attitudes toward "the Other." It will be argued that although the Agreement was designed to provide a long-term solution to what was once deemed an intractable conflict, it has also helped to feed and sustain the sectarian divisions that have characterized Northern Ireland society throughout much of its history.

Background to the Conflict

Although the conflict in Northern Ireland finds its immediate roots in the crisis generated by the civil rights campaigns of the 1960s, it has a much longer ideological lineage (Bew 2009). At its heart lies the question of the constitutional relationship that should exist between the island of Ireland and its nearest neighbor Great Britain – a question that has been framed by political, economic, religious, and cultural considerations.

This was to become an increasingly important issue following the Act of Union of 1800/01 which brought an end to the historic Irish parliament in Dublin, with representation shifting to Westminster as part of the new United Kingdom of Great Britain and Ireland (Bew 2009). Opposition to this Union grew throughout much of the nineteenth century, mainly within the Catholic population but initially with considerable backing from within the radical elements of Protestantism. The radical nationalist movements of the nineteenth century, which included such groups as the Young Irelanders, were greatly influenced by developments elsewhere in Europe, including the emergence of a cultural nationalism that served to define nationhood around the possession of a distinctive identity (McManus 2016; English 2006). McManus (2016) argues that because Ireland "was seen to possess its own distinctive cultural identity, including its own language," it provided a "greater legitimacy" to nationalist claims for nationhood and, as such, the island "was deserving of political independence" (pp. 46–47).

The emergence of a cultural nationalism during the 1890s, however, merely helped to reinforce wider divisions that had appeared throughout the nineteenth century and which, increasingly, became defined by religion. Many Irish Protestants had hoped that the Union with Britain would lead to a decline in the Catholicism of the majority population of the island – aided by increased support for proselytization furthered by the establishment of a new National Schools system. Leading figures within Irish Protestantism looked down upon Catholicism as little more than an "idolatrous superstition" (McManus 2015, p. 54) but also, crucially, viewed the church as a threat to their "established" status, especially as Catholicism became better organized and structured as the century progressed (Bew 2009). This fear intensified with the emergence of the various Irish nationalist movements, culminating in the Home Rule movement from the 1880s, which commanded a very public support from leading figures in the Catholic clergy (English 2006). Opposition to Home Rule – a limited form of self-governance that would also maintain the UK – came predominantly from within the Irish Protestant population, particularly in North East Ulster, who rallied around the belief that Home Rule would mean Rome Rule and, as such, posed a huge threat to Protestant interests in Ireland (Walker 2004).

A crucial component of the political culture in Ireland during the period of the Union (1801–1922) was the processes of Othering that helped to define attitudes toward the Other (McManus 2017). Two elements are important in this Othering process: possessing a sense of superiority over the Other but also, at the same time, fearing the Other as a threat to "our" way of life.

As can be seen above, for example, Irish Protestants looked down upon the Catholicism of the majority population from a theological perspective, but this was also to be reflected in their attitudes toward the Irish cultural heritage as it was defined by the various cultural nationalist movements (Loughlin 1999). This was particularly true of the Irish language which was seen as a backward language of the peasantry with little practical use in a modern society (Crowley 2008). What is more, this backwardness was seen as one element of the wider threat posed by Irish nationalism to the superior British way of life in Ireland (McManus 2015). In other words, not only were the Catholic Irish a numerical threat; they also represented a cultural threat (Loughlin 1999).

McManus (2017) maintains that Othering, by its nature, is a two-way process and that it is this that helps to feed conflict (see also McManus Forthcoming). As such, over the course of the nineteenth century, many Catholics/Irish nationalists also came to view their religion and cultural heritage as being superior to that of Protestantism and Britishness (Boyce 1995; Hutchinson 1987). Furthermore, for many nationalists, the nature of Protestantism and Unionism in Ireland meant that it posed an existential threat to the Irish way of life – a perception seemingly reinforced by Unionist opposition to Home Rule and their apparent willingness to partition the nation by 1912 (English 2006). As a result, elements of radical Irish nationalism adopted something of an anti-colonial narrative that emphasized the need to protect the nation including its cultural identity (English 2006; Howe 2000).

These divisions meant that the two communities came to feel permanently threatened by their Other. This reinforced a sectarianization of Irish society in which neither community could nor would seek to understand the position of their Other or reach out in an effort to incorporate them into their vision for the Irish nation (McManus 2017). Rather, both political communities focused mainly on their own priorities and continued to ignore the complex realities of diversity on the island. The outcome, of course, was the creation of an ever more sectarianized society and, ultimately, the partition of Ireland (Bew 2009).

Northern Ireland: A Legacy of Sectarian Division

Northern Ireland was established in 1921 amid chaos across the island of Ireland (English 2006). The IRA, predominantly in the southern provinces, were waging a guerrilla campaign against the British establishment, while in Northern Ireland itself, the sectarian violence had escalated so dramatically that civil war effectively raged on the streets of Belfast and other major towns (Bardon 2005).

These violent origins helped to shape the political culture of the new Northern state (McManus Forthcoming). Of particular significance was the impact the violence had on attitudes toward the Catholic minority – representing one-third of the total population – who were immediately labeled as an internal threat being aided by external and hostile forces from the South (McGarry and O'Leary 1995). This sense of threat, McManus argues, helps in part to explain "why the Unionist government failed to use the new opportunity presented to them to build a state capable of representing all its citizens":

> The reality was that the combined sense of hostility towards and fear of their "Other" made any movement towards conciliation unlikely. Although "most Catholics did not actively work against the Northern Ireland state," both the passive hostility of the majority and the active opposition of a minority helped to feed unionist fears and convince them that their negative perceptions of the Other was accurate. (McManus Forthcoming)

The sectarianism of the previous century, therefore, continued to frame the political culture of Northern Ireland (Brewer and Higgins 1998). A sense of anti-Catholicism, alongside a dislike for and fear of anything "Irish," was evident in Unionist government circles from the foundations of the state (Walker 2004; Elliott 2000). This was to manifest itself in various policy approaches that led to discrimination against the Catholic population in terms of housing allocation, employment opportunities, and voting (Elliott 2000) – issues that would come to the fore in the campaign for civil rights during the 1960s and which would eventually push the state toward crisis (English 2006).

It was also evident, however, in the negative attitudes expressed by Unionists toward aspects of Irish culture that Northern Catholics continued to define themselves by. In particular, there was considerable opposition among Unionist politicians toward giving support – financial or educational – to the Irish language which they viewed as backward and useless. In a debate at Stormont over the position of an "organiser of Irish language instruction," in May 1923, one Unionist Member of Parliament (MP), Robert Lynn, queried:

> …whether a circular has been issued…saying that in cases where Irish is taken up history may be dropped. I respectfully suggest to the Ministry of Education that history – that is, real history, not imaginative history of the Irish type – would be of more benefit to the schools

than the teaching of Irish. That is purely a sentimental thing. None of these people who take up Irish ever know anything about it. They can spell their own names badly in Irish, but that is all. I do not think it is worth spending any money on. (Lynn 1923, p. 663)

The language used here emphasizes the negative and sectarian attitude of many Unionists toward the Catholic Irish and, more specifically, the Irish language. This was again highlighted in 1933 when the MP for North Belfast, William Grant, declared in parliament that "the only people interested in this language are the people who are the avowed enemies of Northern Ireland" (Grant 1933, p. 773).

Such remarks, as shocking as they often are, need also to be contextualized. As Richard English (2006) highlights, the views and actions of Unionists in the early decades of the state were, to a large extent, "determined by Irish nationalism":

IRA violence in the founding years of Northern Ireland heightened unionist anxiety, as did the increasing Catholicization and Gaelicization of independent Ireland once de Valera came to power in 1932, and the understandable sense among northern nationalists themselves that the new northern state was neither fair nor legitimate. (p. 342)

Although Unionists unquestionably looked down upon Gaelic Irishness, they also had very genuine fears concerning the threat posed by Irish nationalism. As such, they felt justified in taking the actions, outlined above, that would limit the political influence of Catholics (Patterson and Kaufmann 2007; Elliott 2000).

McManus (Forthcoming) argues that what emerged in Northern Ireland was a political climate fed by a series of "self-fulfilling prophesies." Unionists, for example, in preventing Catholics from fully participating in the state (for what they deemed to be defensive reasons), merely reinforced the negative views held by the Catholic population toward both, the Unionist administration and the state itself. This negativity fed a continuing sense of alienation that would manifest itself in an ongoing support for nationalist and/or republican political movements – thus, in itself, reinforcing unionist fears that Catholics remained disloyal (English 2006). It was these fears that helped, in part at least, to frame Unionist attitudes toward the civil rights movement during the 1960s – while Catholics argued that they all they wanted was "British rights," Unionists feared that this was little more than a new nationalist/republican plot to undermine Northern Ireland by other means (McManus Forthcoming; English 2006). It is within this context that violence was to erupt in the late 1960s. As English has succinctly summed it up, "[c]ulture, economy, symbols, religion and politics all combined to produce...the worst combination in the north: a disaffected minority and an under-confidant majority" (2006, p. 369).

Conflicting Cultures: The Politics of Identity

The crisis surrounding the civil rights movement quickly escalated, and street violence – largely organized along sectarian lines – became a regular feature of Northern Irish society (Hennessey 2005). Moreover, as English argues, an inadequate response from the Unionist government at Stormont only helped to further inflame tensions:

> ...a one-sided curfew in Catholic Belfast in 1970, the introduction of an equally one-sided and clumsy internment in 1971, and the disaster of the Bloody Sunday killings in 1972 all backfired, and helped destroy the chance of a rapprochement between the British state and the Catholic working class. (2006, p. 370)

The use of the British military and the Royal Ulster Constabulary in this response further alienated many Catholics from both, and, as a result, elements within the community turned to the IRA for protection from loyalist attacks (Taylor 1998; McCleery 2015). McManus (Forthcoming) argues that this turning to the IRA had significant implications for the movement who found their ranks swelling with "significant numbers of young men and women angered by events around them" (p. 10) but who lacked a significant grounding in traditional Irish republican ideology.

The outbreak of violence in 1969/1970 had, to some extent, caught the IRA by surprise, and they initially lacked the resources necessary to help defend nationalist areas in an effective manner (Taylor 1998). Although they worked to quickly correct this military weakness, less time was taken to deal with the absence of an ideological background among its members (McManus Forthcoming; Adams 1995). When such efforts did emerge, it was very much reflective of the republican movement of the early twentieth century and had, as a key component of its ideological narrative, an anti-colonial outlook (McManus 2016, pp. 53–54). Central to this was, again, the Irish language which, McManus argues, gained "a more prominent status within what was seen as a wider political struggle against the effects of British colonialism on the island" (2016, p. 53). As political activity grew in importance for republicans, so too did the significance of the Irish language, with considerable efforts made to promote the language in nationalist areas. Throughout the 1980s and 1990s, Irish-medium schools were established in greater numbers, and programs of adult education courses became a common occurrence in community halls (McManus 2016).

The importance of the Irish language to the Nationalist and Republican community(ies) can be seen in the status afforded to it within the Good Friday Agreement. Under the terms of the Agreement, the British government committed "where appropriate and where people so desire it" to:

- Take resolute action to promote the language.
- Facilitate and encourage the use of the language in speech and writing in public and private life where there is appropriate demand.
- Seek to remove, where possible, restrictions which would discourage or work against the maintenance or development of the language.
- Place a statutory duty on the Department of Education to encourage and facilitate Irish-medium education in line with current provision for integrated education (HMSO 1998, pp. 19–20).

In addition to this, the British government, in a further Agreement reached at St Andrews between Sinn Féin and the Democratic Unionist Party (DUP) in 2006, committed to introducing "an Irish Language Act reflecting on the experience of Wales and Ireland and work with the incoming Executive to enhance and protect the development of the Irish language" (NIO 2006, p. 12).

The prominence of the language was part of a concerted effort by the nationalist parties, the Social Democratic and Labour Party (SDLP) and Sinn Féin, to gain a greater recognition for the Irish cultural identity of Northern Catholics and to provide developmental support for a language that they believed had been suppressed by both the British and Unionist governments (Adams 2005, pp. 78–88). For both parties, but increasingly for Sinn Féin as it became the biggest nationalist party in the North, governmental support for developing the Irish language was part of a rights-based and equality agenda. As Gerry Adams (2005), a prominent figure in the Republican movement since the 1970s, has argued:

> The negotiation for the Good Friday Agreement involved rights and safeguards for cultural expression, including the promotion of the Irish language. These rights and safeguards had been absent from the Six Counties since its foundation. (p. 84)

That Sinn Féin were arguing for the protection and development of Irish sat uncomfortably with many Unionists with three key reasons helping to explain this.

In the first instance, many Unionists continue to look down upon the language with many believing that it is not worth protecting. The former aspect was demonstrated by a controversial incident in the Stormont Assembly in November 2014 when a senior DUP politician, Gregory Campbell, mocked the language as he stood to give a statement (BBC 2014). Later in the same month, as the controversy still raged, another prominent Unionist, Jim Allister, was quoted as having described Irish as "a dead language that will never bring jobs to anyone" (Strabane Chronicle 2014).

A second, and more prominent reason, was that Unionists feared the Irish language was being used by Sinn Féin for political reasons – specifically, they believed that it was part of a wider agenda to undermine the Britishness of Northern Ireland. In support of this, they could point to various campaigns and policy statements developed by the party during the years of conflict which emphasized the role of Irish in a "reconquest" of the island (McManus 2016, pp. 53–54). As late as 2005, indeed, Gerry Adams was writing that "it is impossible to separate national liberation from cultural revival" (Adams 2005, p. 84).

Such a viewpoint has been aided by the fact that although the political arrangements provided for in the Agreement were seen to protect the position of Northern Ireland in the UK in the short to medium terms, the Agreement also legitimized Nationalist aspirations for Irish unity and, under certain circumstances, catered for a border poll to be held to determine the North's future constitutional status. McManus (2017) maintains that this has fed unionist fears regarding key elements of the peace process and particularly those aspects designed to protect what are deemed as component parts of an Irish culture:

> Working under the terms of the Agreement, northern Catholics have sought greater recognition and equality for their political and cultural identity…Unionists, however, interpret this as part of a new nationalist strategy designed to undermine the 'Britishness' of the state and advance their cause of Irish unity – an analysis seemingly reinforced by the opposition of Nationalists to Unionist/Protestant culture such as Orange parading. (p. 422)

This leads therefore to the final consideration which centers on the above idea that while Sinn Féin were promoting Irish as part of an "equality" and "rights-based" agenda, they were also seemingly attacking Unionist culture and rights. This perception stemmed from various disputes that emerged during the 1980s and 1990s over the right of the Orange Order, a Unionist and Protestant organization, to parade through predominantly Catholic/Nationalist neighborhoods (McManus 2017; Bryan 2000).

In the mid-1990s, as the peace process was still emerging, disputes about these parades in Derry, Belfast and, most famously, Portadown, led to significant outbreaks of sectarian violence (Bryan 2000). Unionists believed that the emergence of residents' protest groups were part of a deliberate strategy by Republicans to undermine Unionist and Orange culture while at the same time promoting an Irish agenda (McManus 2017). Such were the fears of Unionism in this period the then leader of the Ulster Unionist Party (UUP), David Trimble, predicted that "culture is going to be a political battleground" (quoted in McManus 2017, p. 422).

In many ways, this prediction has come to pass. In the two decades since the signing of the Good Friday Agreement, progress has been stalled at various intervals over disputes related to identity politics that have included not only Orange Order parading but also the flying of Union flags on civic buildings, loyalist commemorative bonfires and, most recently, the implementation of the Irish Language Act seemingly promised in the St Andrews Agreement (Nolan 2014; Nolan et al. 2014). Divisions over the latter, indeed, had a role to play in the collapse of the Northern Ireland Assembly in January 2017 when Sinn Féin's Martin McGuinness resigned his position as deputy First Minister. In his resignation letter to the Speaker of Assembly, McGuinness accused "elements of the DUP" of having "exhibited the most crude and crass bigotry" toward those "who wish to live their lives through the medium of Irish" (McGuinness 2017).

Although the primary reason for Sinn Féin's decision to bring down the Assembly was an alleged financial scandal involving the DUP, the primary issue preventing its return has become the Irish Language Act (Dunlevy and Mainnin 2017). Sinn Féin claim that there will be no return of the Assembly until the St Andrews Agreement is implemented in its entirety which, for them, means the introduction of an Irish Language Act. The DUP, however, have claimed that they never agreed to this in the St Andrews negotiations and that its inclusion was part of a side deal agreed only between Sinn Féin and the then Labour Government in Westminster. Yet, despite this, the party did come close to signing a fresh agreement with Sinn Féin in early 2018 which would, according to a prominent Belfast journalist, have included a self-contained "Irish Language Act" only for that deal to collapse due to a huge swell of opposition within grassroots Unionists (Mallie 2018).

Comfort in Sectarianism?

Opposition toward the Irish Language Act within grassroots unionism provides a useful insight into current political thinking within that community and highlights the extent to which unionist leaders have failed in selling what they deem to be political progress to their support base (Shirlow 2012; McAuley 2010). This failure, indeed, highlights an important consequence of Othering in that it demonstrates the extent to which it is difficult to break free from the sectarian politics it creates, even if doing so has potentially positive outcomes for the in-group. To assess the nature of this in more detail, it is important to understand the nature of Unionism and, more especially, the brand of Unionism represented by the DUP.

As the DUP rose in electoral strength at the turn of the century, it sought to portray itself as the party of strong and confident unionism – a unionism that would stand up to the threat of Irish nationalism and republicanism and which would, as a result, win a fairer peace than that secured by the UUP in 1998 (McAuley 2010). Although there was much initial anger and resentment at the party's decision to share power with Sinn Féin – a party they had previously promised to "smash" – they successfully managed to contain the disquiet and held off the challenges from a rival, anti-Agreement party, the Traditional Unionist Voice (TUV) led by former member Jim Allister (Tonge et al. 2014). By 2012, the then party leader and Northern Ireland's First Minister, Peter Robinson (despite having lost his own Westminster seat in 2010), was keen to portray the success enjoyed by the DUP over the previous 5 years and how they had successfully contained the threat posed by Irish nationalism. He told his party conference in November of that year that the "siege has lifted, the Troubles as we knew them are over, and the constitutional debate has been won" (Robinson 2012). Almost a year later, in October 2013, he proclaimed that the "simple and unchallengeable reality is that the Union has never been stronger...Support for the Union has never been higher" (Robinson 2013).

This confidence, however, has not been reflected across Unionism and, in particular, within its working-class loyalist communities. Indeed, within a couple of months of Robinson's 2012 speech, Belfast was once again subjected to a period of violence and sectarian tension following Belfast City Council's decision to limit the number of days the Union flag would fly at City Hall (Nolan et al. 2014). Although there is evidence that the DUP had sought to exploit anger at the vote to win back Robinson's lost Westminster seat in East Belfast, there is little doubt that the party was also, to some extent, sidelined in the loyalist protests (Nolan et al. 2014). For these protestors, the decision by the Council was yet another attempt by Sinn Féin – now the largest party in Belfast – to undermine the British identity of the City and Northern Ireland more widely, and it was seen to make a mockery of Robinson's more optimistic outlook (Tonge et al. 2014).

For many Unionists, therefore, the flag dispute in Belfast again highlighted what they perceived to be an ongoing cultural war being waged against the Protestant/ Unionist identity (Tonge et al. 2014, pp. 120–122). Sinn Féin's campaign for the Irish Language Act is very much seen within this context, and, as such, there appears to be a strong determination within grassroots unionism to frustrate it.

This was evident during the negotiations between Sinn Féin and the DUP as they sought an agreement that could restore the Stormont Assembly. Even as talks were progressing, it was clear that opposition to an Irish Language Act was strong within grassroots Unionism with an Orange Order lodge at Queen's University Belfast issuing a stark warning to party leaders that Unionists had "no appetite" for further compromise. According to this lodge, an Irish language act would have "far ranging ramifications across civil society" that would not have "a positive impact on the nation." They further claimed that the "promotion of cultural supremacy, under the guise of equality, will only further entrench divisions in Northern Ireland" (Queen's LOL 2018).

Such attitudes reflect the views gathered by Tonge et al. (2014) in their study of the modern DUP. They found among grassroots members that:

> The idea that the DUP are engaged in a 'culture war' has been given further momentum by perceptions that attacks on Orange Order halls are not just sectarian, but also politically inspired. This understanding is also applied to other issues, such as restrictions placed on Orange marches, or the limiting of the flying of the Union Flag on Belfast City Hall to designated days. Such actions are interpreted by the DUP as evidence of a broader campaign of 'anti-British bigotry' waged by Irish republicans. (Tonge et al. 2014, p. 121)

Such views, however, raise an important question for Unionists, particularly within the context of Peter Robinson's 2012–2013 speeches arguing that the Union was safe: if the Union has been secured should they now take moves to better facilitate the Irishness of Northern Catholics in an effort to create greater political stability?

To examine this question, a number of important issues need to be considered.

Firstly, Robinson's claim that the Union "has never been stronger" was based on a growing perception that more and more Catholics were content with the political status quo – that is to say, they were willing to support a form of Union with devolved powers to Northern Ireland. Robinson, indeed, in his 2013 speech was keen to emphasize that:

> Support for the Union has never been higher. When Republicans can't even persuade a majority of their own people of the case for a United Ireland you know their game is up. For the first time in generations Northern Ireland has stable political structures. (Robinson 2013)

These claims have been backed by findings from the Northern Ireland Life and Times Survey (NILT), which has been conducted annually since 1998 by researchers from both Queen's University Belfast and Ulster University. These findings show a consistent support for Northern Ireland remaining within the United Kingdom (with devolved power) with a majority of Catholic respondents supporting that position between 2010 and 2016 (Fig. 1). Notably, in that period, there was a significant degree of political stability and functionality at Stormont despite ongoing tensions on the ground.

This data would suggest that the political aspirations of those labeled "Nationalist" are more complex than is often allowed for and hint at the idea that respect for

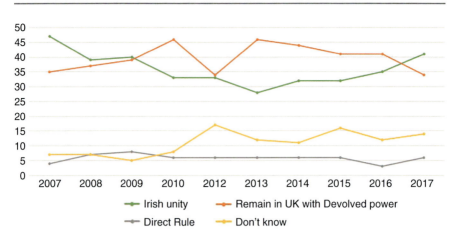

Fig. 1 The long-term policy for Northern Ireland should be? (Catholic respondents only). (Source: NILT)

the Irish identity of Catholics could facilitate a degree of contentment with the state (McManus 2016).

The second consideration, therefore, centers on how Unionism has responded to such findings. While there has been lip-service paid to these changing dynamics – as highlighted by the speeches of Peter Robinson – Unionist leaders have failed to move beyond this rhetoric in any meaningful way. This is evident not only in their failure to engage with the idea of an Irish Language Act but, perhaps more symbolically, in the fact that they continue to refer to the Irish language in such derogatory terms. The high-profile examples of Gregory Campbell and Jim Allister have already been highlighted but perhaps even more crucial was the intervention of Arlene Foster, the current DUP leader and former First Minister. Speaking at a DUP event in February 2017, Foster claimed that the party would "never agree to an Irish language act" and claimed that because there were more Polish speakers in Northern Ireland than Irish speakers, a Polish Language Act should take precedence. Regarding Sinn Féin's demand for an Irish Language Act, she quipped that "if you feed a crocodile it will keep coming back for more" (Foster 2017).

Such views do little to lessen the Catholic population's alienation from the Northern state which has potentially been further reinforced by Britain's 2016 decision to leave the European Union – a decision supported by the DUP but opposed by the vast majority of Nationalists (Murphy 2018). Indeed, polls during the referendum campaign suggested that 85% of Catholics supported Remain – a stark contrast to the 41% of Protestants that did so (Murphy 2018).

Moreover, in the immediate aftermath of the vote, questions started to be asked concerning the compatibility of "Brexit" with the political arrangements established by the Good Friday Agreement – an issue that had been largely neglected in the mainstream debates leading up the referendum (Murphy 2018). In particular, the issue of the Irish border – soon to be the only land border between the UK and the EU – became a significant stumbling block to progress in Brexit negotiations given the possible necessity of new custom checks should any divergence emerge between the UK and Ireland (Hayward 2017). Such a possibility angered Irish nationalists who firmly oppose any return of a visible and/or physical border between the North and the Republic (Murphy 2018).

The issue has been further complicated by the DUP's continued support for Brexit, despite the fact that a majority in Northern Ireland voted in support of Remaining (56% Remain – 44% Leave). What is more, the party continues to espouse an uncompromising Leave position that will tolerate no special treatment for Northern Ireland that might help to prevent the reintroduction of border checkpoints even in the case of a no deal scenario.

All of this has seemingly had an impact on political attitudes in Northern Ireland. According to the 2017 NILT survey, for example, there has been a rise in support for Irish unity within the Catholic population from 35% in 2016 to 41% in 2017.

This analysis suggests that Unionism can be, at times, its own worst enemy. This leads to an obvious follow on question to that posed above: why don't unionist politicians do more to reach out to the Catholic/Nationalist population if they are willing to support the Union under certain circumstances?

One answer to this is that it brings little electoral advantage to the DUP in the short term. Although many Catholics/Nationalists will express a willingness to support some form of Union, they have not yet come to see themselves as Unionist and are not, therefore, likely to vote for the DUP. Moreover, should the DUP reach out on issues such as the Irish language, it is likely they would anger their own political community who may turn against the party in elections.

A second reason is that Unionism continues to fear the normalization of Irishness in Northern Ireland society. Such a normalization would serve, as stated by the Queen's LOL 1845, to undermine what is deemed the British character of the state and to reinforce the idea that it is a place apart. Indeed, this fear of being viewed as different has been evident in relation to the Brexit question and how any customs checks on the island should be managed. While those in favor of Remaining in the EU have argued for Special Status for Northern Ireland, this idea has been rejected by Unionists who see it as a "trap" and a Sinn Féin ploy to "break up the Union" (Murphy 2018, pp. 133–134).

It is important also to contextualize this situation within the framework of Othering. McManus (Forthcoming) has argued that a fear of the Other (as well as a sense of superiority) will lead to an in-group taking measures that often contradict what it claims to stand for. In this case, although Unionists will talk about representing open and tolerant British values and express a desire to see stable political structures operating in Northern Ireland, they often lack the political leadership necessary to implement those measures that might achieve such ends.

Conclusion

Identity has played an important role in helping to frame the sectarian divisions in Northern Ireland that fed conflict for almost 30 years. It has been instrumental in shaping long-term processes of Othering that generate an in-group sense of superiority over the Other but which also, as a consequence, feeds a sense of fear over the threat posed to "our" way of life.

Although the Northern Ireland peace process has provided the basis for a political settlement, the failure to address the processes of Othering has allowed a cultural war to emerge that is perpetuating the divisions caused by the military conflict. Most recently, this has focused on the implementation of an Irish Language Act, but there is also a very real possibility that Brexit could become a further strand of this such are the levels of polarization it is creating. Indeed, with an apparent unwillingness to compromise now evident in both communities, it appears that any resolution to the political deadlock that has taken hold since January 2017 will be far from easy and will require a brave leadership to emerge – something that has been lacking in the recent times.

Cross-References

▶ Cultural Socialization and Ethnic Consciousness
▶ Ethnic Conflicts and Peace-Building
▶ Ethno-cultural Symbolism and Group Identity
▶ Historical Memory and Ethnic Myths

References

Adams G (1995) Free Ireland: towards a lasting peace. Brandon Books, Dingle
Adams G (2005) The New Ireland: a vision for the future. Brandon, Dingle
Bardon J (2005) A history of Ulster: new updated edition. Blackstaff Press, Belfast
BBC (2014) 'Curry my yoghurt': Gregory Campbell, DUP, barred from speaking for day. Retrieved September 18, 2018, from BBC News: Northern Ireland: https://www.bbc.co.uk/news/uk-northern-ireland-29895593
Bew P (2009) Ireland: the politics of enmity, 1789–2006. Oxford University Press, Oxford
Boyce D (1995) Nationalism in Ireland. Routledge, London
Brewer JD, Higgins GI (1998) Anti-Catholicism in Northern Ireland, 1600–1998: the mote and beam. Macmillan Press Ltd., Basingstoke
Bryan D (2000) Orange parades: the politics of ritual, tradition and control. Pluto, London
Crowley T (2008) Wars of words: the politics of language in Ireland, 1737–2004. Oxford University Press, Oxford
Dunlevy DA, Mainnin MO (2017) Debate over Irish language is central to power-sharing talks in Northern Ireland. Retrieved from The Conversation: https://theconversation.com/debate-over-irish-language-is-central-to-power-sharing-talks-in-northern-ireland-79285
Elliott M (2000) The Catholics of Ulster: a history. Allen Lane: The Penguin Press, London

English R (2006) Irish freedom: the history of nationalism in Ireland. Macmillan, London
Foster A (2017) Arlene Foster on Sinn Féin: 'if you feed a crocodile it will keep coming back for more'. Retrieved from The Journal.ie: http://www.thejournal.ie/arlene-foster-gerry-adams-3225834-Feb2017/
Grant W (1933) Stormont Papers, 15 (1932/33). Retrieved from http://stormontpapers.ahds.ac.uk/pageview.html?volumeno=15&pageno=773
Hayward K (2017) Bordering on Brexit: views from local communities in the central border region of Ireland/Northern Ireland. Queen's University Belfast, Belfast
Hennessey T (2005) Northern Ireland: the origins of the troubles. Gill & Macmillan, Dublin
HMSO (1998) The agreement: agreement reached in multi-party negotiations. HMSO, Belfast
Howe S (2000) Ireland and empire: colonial legacies in Irish history and culture. Oxford University Press, Oxford
Hutchinson J (1987) The dynamics of cultural nationalism. Allen & Unwin, London
Lijphart A (1977) Democracy in plural societies: a comparative exploration. Yale University Press, New Haven
Loughlin J (1999) "Imagining Ulster": the north of Ireland and British national identity, 1880–1921. In: Connolly S (ed) Kingdoms united? Great Britain and Ireland since 1500: integration and diversity. Four Courts Press, Dublin
Lynn RJ (1923) Stormont Papers, 3 (1923). Retrieved from http://stormontpapers.ahds.ac.uk/pageview.html?volumeno=3&pageno=663
Mallie E (2018) New light shone on draft agreement. Retrieved from EamonnMallie.com: http://eamonnmallie.com/2018/02/new-light-shone-draft-agreement-eamonn-mallie/
McAuley JW (2010) Ulster's last stand? Reconstructing unionism after the peace process. Irish Academic, Dublin
McCleery M (2015) Operation Demetrius and its aftermath. Manchester University Press, Manchester
McGarry J, O'Leary B (1995) Explaining Northern Ireland: broken images. Blackwell Publishers, Oxford
McGarry J, O'Leary B (2009) Power shared after the deaths of thousands. In: Taylor R (ed) Consociational theory: McGarry and O'Leary and the Northern Ireland conflict. Routledge, London, pp 15–84
McGuinness M (2017) Martin McGuinness resignation letter. Retrieved September 18, 2018, from Sinn Féin: http://www.sinnfein.ie/files/2017/Martin_McGuinnessResignationLetter.pdf
McManus C (2015) "Bound in darkness and idolatry"? Protestant working-class underachievement and unionist hegemony. Ir Stud Rev 23(1):48–67
McManus C (2016) Irish language education and the national ideal: the dynamics of nationalism in Northern Ireland. Nations Nationalism 22(1):42–62
McManus C (2017) Dealing with the legacy of ethnic conflict: confronting 'othering' through transformative adult education – a Northern Ireland case study. Ethnopolitics 16(4):411–429
McManus C (Forthcoming) Conceptualising Islamic "Radicalisation" in Europe through "Othering": lessons from the conflict in Northern Ireland. Terrorism and Political Violence
Murphy MC (2018) Europe and Northern Ireland's future: negotiating Brexit's unique case. Agenda Publishing, Newcastle upon Tyne
NIO (2006) The St Andrew's agreement. Retrieved from Gov.UK: https://assets.publishing.service.gov.uk/government/uploads/system/uploads/attachment_data/file/136651/st_andrews_agreement-2.pdf
Nolan P (2014) Northern Ireland peace monitoring report: number three. Community Relations Council, Belfast
Nolan P, Bryan D, Dwyer C, Hayward K, Radford K, Shirlow P (2014) The flag dispute: anatomy of a protest. Queen's University Belfast, Belfast
Patterson H, Kaufmann E (2007) Unionism and Orangeism in Northern Ireland since 1945: the decline of the loyal family. Manchester University Press, Manchester

Queen's LOL (2018) Not too late to stop Irish language act: Orange lodge. Retrieved from Belfast Newsletter: https://www.newsletter.co.uk/news/not-too-late-to-stop-irish-language-act-orange-lodge-1-8376176

Robinson P (2012) Most Catholics want to stay in UK. Irish Independent. Retrieved from https://www.independent.ie/breaking-news/irish-news/most-catholics-want-to-stay-in-uk-28905862.html

Robinson P (2013) Speech by Peter Robinson (DUP), Castlereagh Borough Council. Retrieved from CAIN: http://cain.ulst.ac.uk/issues/politics/docs/dup/pr_2013-10-18.htm

Shirlow P (2012) The end of Ulster loyalism? Manchester University Press, Manchester

Strabane Chronicle (2014) "Irish language is dead" – Jim Allister. Retrieved 18 Sept 2018, from Strabane Chronicle: http://strabanechronicle.com/2014/11/irish-language-is-dead-jim-allister/

Taylor P (1998) Provos: the IRA and Sinn Féin. Bloomsbury, London

Tonge J, Braniff M, Hennessey T, McAuley JW, Whiting S (2014) The democratic unionist party: from protest to power. Oxford University Press, Oxford

Walker G (2004) A history of the Ulster unionist party. Manchester University Press, Manchester

Immigration Policy and Left-Right Politics in Western Europe

20

Trevor J. Allen and Misty Knight-Finley

Contents

Introduction	348
Situating the Far Right in West European Party Systems	349
The Expert Survey Data and Analyses	352
Immigration, Multiculturalism, and the Traditional Left-Right	352
Theoretical Implications for Immigrants and Immigration Policy	356
Conclusion	358
Cross-References	358
References	359

Abstract

Immigration and migrants have been increasingly politicized across Western Europe in the twenty-first century, corresponding to the rise of the radical right. Focusing events in the early 2000s lent salience to a now-familiar far right brand of ethnocentric, anti-immigrant identity politics, as distinct from emphases on immigration's economic impacts. This research considers the extent to which multiculturalism and ethnocentrism, exploited by the far right, remain disconnected from economic conflict in West European party systems. Specifically, we evaluate the relationship between the traditional left-right economic dimension and a more recent multiculturalism-ethnocentrism dimension structuring party competition in nine Western European nations. We use expert positioning of political parties to describe the evolution on these two dimensions at four time points from 1999 to 2014. While party positions on multiculturalism are mostly

T. J. Allen (✉)
Department of Political Science, Central Connecticut State University, New Britain, CT, USA
e-mail: allentj@ccsu.edu

M. Knight-Finley
Department of Political Science and Economics, Rowan University, Glassboro, NJ, USA
e-mail: knightfinley@rowan.edu

distinct from positions on economics in 1999, positioning on the two dimensions becomes highly correlated by 2009, increasing further in 2014. The shift is driven both by the far right's de facto absorption of rightist economic policies, and the mainstream right's increasing ethnocentrism. It is proposed that the far right is the principal actor behind this realignment, and policy implications are explored.

Keywords
Far right parties · Party systems · Multiculturalism · Western Europe

Introduction

Following focusing events in the early 2000s (e.g., 9/11 and the London and Madrid bombings), immigration in terms of national identity has become increasingly politicized. Muslim immigrants and their descendants, in particular, have increasingly been targeted with value laden rhetoric by Europe's far right (Zúquete 2008). For instance, the 2007 French *Front National* (FN) manifesto regards religious difference as the greatest impediment to Muslim integration in France (Williams 2010, see also Byng 2008). Similarly, the FPÖ's Haider criticized Islam as being at odds with Austrian values towards women (Betz 2003). During the French headscarf affair, feminists and the FN were reasonably similar in their treatment of Muslims as a monolithic anti-modern foil (Scott 2009). More recently, a 2017 AfD election ad featuring a picture of a baby pig standing in lush green grass read: "Islam? It doesn't fit in with our cuisine." Paradigmatically, the flash-pan *Lijst Pim Fortuyn* (LPF) achieved historic success mobilizing against multiculturalism in the Netherlands, by promoting both immigrant assimilation (Joppke 2004) and value pluralism (Akkerman 2005).

Evidence suggests far right parties have been instrumental in casting immigration as a question of national identity rather than (say) labor migration (Schain 2006). However, the impact of this rhetoric on party systems more broadly is less than univocal. Moreover, the extent to which far right parties themselves influence policy is contestable. In this chapter, we consider together research on party families, immigration and integration policies, and public policy processes to examine the critical role of far right parties in immigration politics and policymaking.

We take as our starting point the debate as to whether the "new politics" of far right parties belongs on the left-right continuum historically structuring party competition in Western Europe, or whether far right parties remain orthogonal to this traditional dimension. We hypothesize that the initial ambiguity around far right parties' situation in the competitive party space has crystalized, and use 15 years of expert data to evaluate the evolving relationship between party positions on the left-right continuum and a scale of ethnocentrism and multiculturalism, a proxy for anti-immigrant positions *qua* issues of national identity. Subsequently, we evaluate far right parties' influence over immigration policymaking in light of our results, suggesting that incorporation of immigration into traditional left-right corresponds to the issue's increased salience and its incorporation into national citizenship regimes.

Before proceeding with these empirical analyses, we begin with a discussion of the development of far right parties and an examination of the debates that considered immigration, ethnocentrism, and multiculturalism independently from traditional left-right politics. In so doing, we discuss immigration as an issue of "new politics." After presenting our empirical methods and results, we discuss the implications of this work.

Situating the Far Right in West European Party Systems

The far right mobilizes most successfully on grievances about immigration, especially when cast as a cultural issue of national identity – the battle between ethnocentrism and multiculturalism – rather than as a matter of left-right economics (Betz and Meret 2009; Ivarsflaten 2008; Schain 2006; Hooghe et al. 2002). This brand of anti-immigrant identity politics became especially available to far right actors following twenty-first century terrorist attacks in New York and London, the Danish cartoon affair, and the assassinations of Theo van Gogh and Pim Fortuyn. It is generally agreed that the extreme right made their anti-Islam message increasingly overt as these events unfolded. For instance, Williams (2010) finds after 9/11 "virtually all parties and formations on the radical right made the confrontation with Islam a central political issue." Likewise, Eatwell (2003) characterizes the attacks as a "godsend" to the extreme right. Others qualify that the far right's interest in immigration is informed by ethnopluralism and civic nationalism, rather than racism or issues surrounding labor migration (e.g., Rydgren 2005; Schain 2006), in keeping with arguments to "value pluralism" (Akkerman 2005).

An examination of the development of individual far right parties reveals strategic pivots in party messaging, narrowing focus on populism, nationalism, and radicalism or extremism to expand party ranks (Golder 2016; Lehmann et al. 2017). The evolution of Germany's *Alternative für Deutschland* (AfD) illustrates the point, but is only one of several examples. In 2012, three prominent members of the country's Christian Democratic party (CDU) started a political action group – *Wahlalternative 2013* – advocating for an electoral alternative to the traditional parties in the 2013 election. After proposing a failed party list with the Federation of Independent Voters in the January 2013 state elections, *Wahlalternative*'s leaders founded AfD. The group drafted a short manifesto focusing primarily on economic policy issues, with a few references to education and immigration ahead of the 2013 federal elections (Arzheimer 2015). Ultimately, AfD fell just short of the 5% threshold required to earn seats in parliament but gained more votes than any new party in over 50 years (Arzheimer 2015). Much like the far-right parties gaining popularity throughout Europe, AfD filled a space created by voters disaffected by traditional parties – typically younger, less-educated, male, blue-collar, anti-immigrant, anti-establishment voters (Allen 2017; Arzheimer and Carter 2006; Savelkoul and Scheepers 2017). In an effort to court more dissatisfied voters, the AfD manifesto grew from 80 quasi-sentences to 1,151, and included entire chapters on "Culture, Language, and Identity" and "Immigration,

Integration, and Asylum" by 2017 (Alternative für Deutschland n.d.; Lehmann et al. 2017). This shift in issue attention paid off; as of this writing, AfD is the third-largest party and the primary opposition party in the Bundestag.

The story of AfD's transformation from an unsuccessful single-issue party to a successful far right party is not unique. In their early days, far right parties exhibited considerable cross-national variation. In Austria and Switzerland, far right populists co-opted existing right parties. The French FN consisted of a variety of far right elements at its founding including Poujadists, monarchists, Old Right militants – a "hodgepodge of political cranks" (Art 2011: p. 2). Many of the Scandinavian far right parties began as anti-tax "progress" parties. The Swedish far right has roots in interwar fascism (Ignazi 1992), but has since evolved. UKIP and the AfD were principally Euroskeptic parties at their outset, but developed programmatically in other areas as they matured. In Italy and Belgium, successful far right parties developed from explicitly regional movements. Nascent Dutch and Norwegian far right parties were idiosyncratic vehicles for their charismatic leaders. However, as all of these parties realized a toehold in their party systems, they began to reflect the contours of those systems, operating in space vacated by so-called mainstream parties – that is, Christian and Social Democrats – after the transition to advanced capitalism. The number of countries with competitive far right parties has increased since the early 1980s, as has the far right's share of the total vote (Bale 2003; De Lange 2007; Golder 2016; Koopmans 2010; cf. McGann and Kitschelt 2005). Furthermore, the party family has survived various tenures in government (e.g., Austria, the Netherlands) and party splits (e.g., France, Austria), and its impact on Western Europe's party system is increasingly manifest.

Though the far right represents a durable addition to the party families of Western Europe, there remains a debate as to whether and where these parties belong on the left-right continuum historically structuring party competition in the area. On one hand, the far right's narrow preoccupation with ethnocentric, anti-immigration rhetoric; characteristic populism (Derks 2006; Kaltwasser 2014); and advancement of both right and left economic positions (Ivarsflaten 2005; McGann and Kitschelt 2005) have led some scholars to exclude economic platforms entirely from studies on the extreme right (Mudde 2007). Similarly, given these parties' "ideological promiscuity," other scholars have questioned whether the "right" label is appropriate (Arter 2010, p. 494). A study of UKIP pithily summarizes the difficulty in placing the party family on the continuum, suggesting the party is neither right, nor left, but represents those "left behind" (Ford and Goodwin 2014). On the other hand, far right parties have grown increasingly popular and positions associated with the far right have gained respectability among mainstream voters and parties (Betz and Meret 2009; Williams 2010; Zúquete 2008). At the same time, the far right may have moderated some of its views to posture for coalitions with or in support of mainstream center-right parties (see Bale 2003).

Either of these possibilities, or a combination of the two, could represent absorption of the immigration debate into traditional left-right politics. Some scholars describe the ethnocentrist immigration attitudes of the far right as a "rightist" stake in "new politics" – characterized by noneconomic, quality of life issues (Dalton 2013; Inglehart 1977) – orthogonal to the traditional left-right dimension (Bornschier 2010; Ignazi 2003).

The intervention of new values into the continent's once-ossified party systems is typified by green movements (Dalton 2008; Kitschelt 1989), and there is reason to consider the far right's mobilization against immigration as operating on the same dimension (Bornschier 2010). Where mainstream parties did not integrate new values, new interest groups, and eventually new political parties, formed (Kitschelt 2004; Ford and Goodwin 2014). For the far right, as social democratic parties' economic platforms moved rightward and trade unions disintegrated, the working class – former partisans of the Old Left – became attracted to the far right's sociocultural authoritarianism (Ivarsflaten 2005; Kitschelt 2004; Oesch 2008; Rydgren 2009). At the same time, far right parties have intentionally underemphasized economic programs to unify a voter base consisting of blue-collar workers and the *petit bourgeoisie* on this second dimension of political competition (Kitschelt 2007; Ivarsflaten 2005).

Relatedly, the "conspiracy of silence" hypothesis suggests the mainstream left and right prevented immigration from gaining traction in the competition between mainstream alternatives (Bale 2003). This purportedly allowed the far right to attract the portion of the electorate susceptible to ethnocentric anti-immigration rhetoric (Bale 2003; Givens 2005; cf. Ignazi 2003; Kitschelt and McGann 1995). From these perspectives, anti-immigrant mobilization, while consistent with a broader constellation of preferences anticipated by both economic and sociocultural consequences of post-industrialism, remains disconnected from an economic dimension of party competition.

Conversely, the continued salience of immigration and changes in political opportunity structures consequent for all party families cast doubt on the argument that the immigration debate remains separate from the traditional left-right dimension. First, pressure on the center right to coalesce with extreme right parties has increased since the success of Green parties expanded the coalition possibilities for the center left, seemingly forcing the center right to align itself with far right positions on immigration (Bale 2003). Some mainstream parties' have responded to the message of the extreme right by incorporating restrictive immigration programs in response to the issue's politicization and symbolically addressing sociocultural issues dredged up by the extreme right (Yılmaz 2012; Williams 2010; Bale 2003). This noticeable shift suggests the absorption of far right party platforms into Western European party systems (Williams 2010; Yılmaz 2012; cf. Bale 2003).

Contrary to early accounts, the far right's preoccupation with immigration does not make it a single-issue party, and there is a reasonably durable constellation of sociodemographic characteristics of far right supporters (Arzheimer and Carter 2006; Mudde 1999). As such, some scholars simply place the far right on the extreme end of the single left-right dimension (Abedi 2004; Carter 2005) or suggest the far right is something of a "halfway house" for disenchanted center left voters as they move to the mainstream right (Mudde 2007). Other influential accounts ascribe obvious rightist qualities to far right parties. Kitschelt and McGann's (1995) seminal work includes an opposition to redistributive politics among the constituent characteristics of the new radical right. Moreover, the far right has generally supported conservative economic policies when in or supporting government (Bale 2003). There is also evidence to suggest the far right has moderated somewhat since its inception, perhaps to appear more "coalitionable" (Williams 2006). These latter scholars emphasize the degree to which post-industrial political opportunity structures, in general, and the extreme right, in particular, have impacted and refocused party systems along a single dimension (e.g., Kitschelt and McGann 1995).

Next, we examine these contrasting perceptions. Specifically, we consider whether immigration, especially in terms of multiculturalism and national identity, has come to correlate with an existing left-right dimension since its politicization alongside the rise of the far right, or if positions on immigration are still best characterized as perpendicular to a left-right understanding of party competition.

The Expert Survey Data and Analyses

We measure the relationship between party position on immigration as a question of multiculturalism and national identity, and on the traditional left-right dimension of politics using expert surveys at four time points. Our data come from the European Election Studies' (EES) Euromanifesto Study (Schmitt et al. 2016), where after coding manifestos experts are asked to assess party positions on several issue areas. Although the expert evaluations are not formulaically derived from the manifesto coding, the degree to which manifestos are coded on multiculturalism is largely dependent on how immigrant integration, related to a national way of life, is addressed in the manifesto. We use the four most recent waves of EES data – 1999, 2004, 2009, and 2014. The t_0, 1999, represents the dataset immediately preceding the political impact of 9/11, 7/7, and the other events of importance to far right actors detailed in the previous section. We consider the nine EU-15 countries with far right parties by 2014, which is appropriate given the historical determinants of the traditional left-right dimension. Thus, our cases are Austria, Belgium, Denmark, Finland, France, Germany, Netherlands, Sweden, and the United Kingdom.

To compare party positions on the economic and immigration dimensions, we use two key variables from the data that asked party experts to position parties along 1–10 point scales:

(1) Left versus Right (10)
(1) Multiculturalism versus Ethnocentrism (10)

We expect the left-right scale to display the traditional economic conflict between social democratic and conservative parties. If immigration debate remains distinct from economic conflict (see Bornschier 2010), the multiculturalism dimension should have far right parties at one pole and traditional parties at the other.

Immigration, Multiculturalism, and the Traditional Left-Right

We examine the contrasting perceptions of how immigration as a question of national identity has become politicized in the party systems of Western Europe by mapping the changing correlations between the left-right economic dimension and the dimension measuring multiculturalism versus ethnocentrism between 1999 and 2014. In so doing, we can evaluate the two differing perspectives on whether and where far right parties fall on the left-right continuum. The first perspective emphasizes the conspiracy of silence surrounding immigration, and the far right's participation in a new dimension of politics distinct from the traditional left-right continuum. Here, immigration represents the "rightist" stake in "new politics." If this school of thought is correct, we should see minimal correlation between parties' positions on multiculturalism (or ethnocentrism) and economic issues.

The alternative camp emphasizes the currency of immigration in Western European politics, because of which mainstream parties of both left and right have taken positions on immigration, facilitating its integration into the unidimensional left-right continuum. These latter scholars observe the many mainstream parties now proposing plans not altogether dissimilar from the ones previously proposed by their system's far right party (Williams 2010). Mudde (2013) indicates that social democratic parties have shown a tendency to move rightward on immigration only when there is a successful extreme right party present, though other impressions are mixed (Bale et al. 2010). Center right parties seem to be moving in that direction almost irrespective of extreme right party performance and have thoroughly legitimized the message of their far right competitors, radicalizing discourse and polarizing the party system (e.g., Bale 2003; Ignazi 2003). If this latter school of thought prevails, we should see increased correlation between the two dimensions.

Figure 1 shows the correlation between experts' assessments of parties on the 10-point left-right economic dimension and the 10-point multiculturalism-ethnocentrism dimension at four time points: 1999, 2004, 2009, and 2014. The data points are rounded to the nearest integer, so the data clearly indicate more populated coordinates. The figure provides insight as to how multiculturalism has been absorbed into the left-right dimension. In this sense, "rightist" positions on immigration represent not only more restrictive policies but also more ethnocentric ones. This distinguishes rightist parties who might oppose immigration in cultural terms from other parties that might oppose labor migration for protectionist, economic reasons.

The chart mapping 1999 party placement represents the period before the focusing events discussed above (i.e., 9/11, 7/7, etc.). In this chart, the economic dimension reflects largely predictable patterns, with far left and social democratic parties left of center, and liberal parties to the right of the center. Christian Democratic and conservative parties and far right parties, by contrast, can be found across the left-right dimension. For far right parties, the pattern illustrates efforts to corral economically diverse voters vís a vís non-economic immigration issues – namely, immigration as a matter of national identity (Kitschelt 2007; Ivarsflaten 2005). On the multiculturalism dimension, all of the far right parties are found at the top of the graph – the space representing stronger ethnocentrism. There is minimal correlation (r=0.36) between parties' placements on the economic and multiculturalism dimensions overall. This spatial alignment supports early assessments (Ivarsflaten 2005) of far right parties and the immigration issue as orthogonal to the traditional economic cleavage.

By 2004, multiculturalism positions become significantly more correlated (r=0.72) with expert assessments and remain that way through 2009 (r=0.73) and

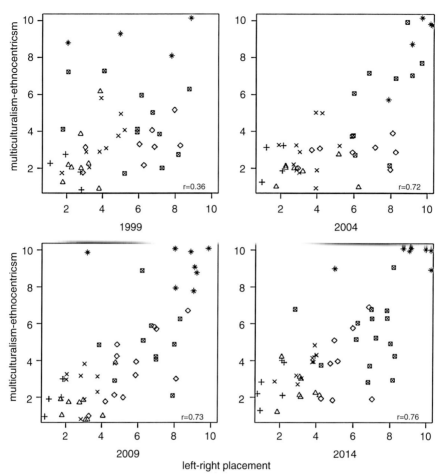

Fig. 1 Party positions on multiculturalism-ethnocentrism and left-right, 1999–2014

2014 (r=0.76). Between 1999 and 2004, Christian Democratic and conservative parties and far right parties assume rightist economic platforms and the moderate right grows increasingly ethnocentric. The lonely point in the upper left corner of the 2009 chart belongs to the radical right Finnish True Finns (PS) (Art 2011), indicating some durable programmatic heterogeneity among the far right as regards economic policy. By 2014, party families clearly cluster together on both the economic and multiculturalism dimensions, though the liberal party family displays the greatest variance, as it includes "social" liberals like the Dutch D66 and United Kingdom's Liberal Democrats, "right" liberals like the Dutch VVD, and Scandinavian Agrarian parties (Ennser 2012).

The clustering of party families suggests the incorporation of immigration as a question of national identity into the traditional left-right dimension of party competition in Western Europe. Possible sources of this realignment include the diminished ideological base for post-communist parties in the aftermath of the cold war (Dalton 2008) and pressure on the center right to respond to or coalesce with extreme right wing parties (Carter 2005; Bale 2003). Contrary to the above, it does not seem to be the case that the far right has appreciably tempered its positions on immigration, rather the center right has moved in a restrictive direction (Fig. 2 below). The salience of immigration corresponds to more restrictive preferences among the electorate and in policy (Howard 2009), so this trend is not terribly surprising. There remains considerably more noise on the left side of the continuum, which is consistent with the comparatively wide variety of strategies identified for Social Democrats in the climate of far right success (Akkerman 2015; Bale et al. 2010).

To better examine this apparent realignment, Fig. 2 tracks the movement of party families over time on a single chart. We use the average value for each party family at two time points to better assess how each party family participates in the realignment of the dimensions examined above. Party families are useful for a more granular analysis in part because specific parties may differ between the two time points. This is especially true of the comparatively nascent far right where several countries have had multiple members of the party family emerge and disappear since 1999. We expect to see center right parties move toward more ethnocentric positions. Some movement by the far right on this dimension is also possible. More likely, however, would be far right movement on the economic dimension toward more traditionally rightist positions. Figure 2 may also shed light on the response of Social Democratic parties.

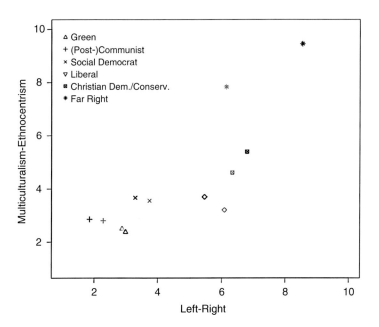

Fig. 2 Multiculturalism-Ethnocentricsm positions over time

The black shapes in Fig. 2 represent party family positions in 2014; the grey shapes represent the 1999 averages. In 1999, there is a relative convergence by most parties on the multiculturalism dimension. By 2014, most party families move as predicted. Already by 1999, it seems the radical (post-communist) left has become integrated into the post-industrial dimension of party competition (Dalton 2008). There is an increase in ethnocentrism in center right (Christian Democratic, conservative, and liberal) party families. Contrary to the prospect of a more moderate far right, the far right moves significantly in an ethnocentric dimension, reflecting the potency of that strategy in Western Europe (Rydgren 2005). The Green parties in the sample move to the bottom left, indicating a dimension of party competition for which Green Parties and far right parties are the anchors (Bornschier 2010; Cole 2005). Lastly, perhaps as a result of their variegated strategies on multiculturalism, there is little movement by the Social Democrats on that dimension (Akkerman 2015; Bale et al. 2010). There also seems to be some polarization in both dimensions, due possibly to the onset of the Eurozone crisis (Cramme et al. 2013), or influence of the far right on electoral politics (Carter 2005; Bale 2003).

Through this analysis it appears as though immigration as a question of national identity became increasingly accessible in terms of the traditional left-right direction over the first decade of the twenty-first century. While a relationship is present in 1999, it is considerably strengthened by 2014. As such, although it may not be accurate to fully endorse the "conspiracy of silence" hypothesis, it is apparently the case that the party systems of the EU-15 integrated immigration and national identity as the issues realized greater salience in the twenty-first century. Likewise, the far right party family does not appear to have moderated into the continent's party systems, but has instead pulled center right actors toward its positions on immigration and multiculturalism.

Theoretical Implications for Immigrants and Immigration Policy

That immigration *qua* a question of national identity has become tethered to traditional left-right political conflict raises questions about the implications for immigrants and immigration policy. Indeed, these results have significant consequences for theoretical and practical debates. First, given that the increased politicization of immigration as a question of identity means increased salience and issue attention, tractable solutions to the influx of forced migrants are fleeting. Second, given the challenges of policymaking in high salience policy spheres (Givens and Luedtke 2005), governments may look to bureaucratic and technical policy changes to subvert criticism from the left while assuaging fears of the center and right. Finally, to the extent that immigration policy can be made at all amidst such heightened awareness, policy outputs are likely to be more restrictive (Givens and Luedtke 2004, 2005) and lay the groundwork for nationalistic, anti-immigrant policy regimes.

Existing work has identified hyper-awareness to immigration issues as a threat to the harmonization and liberalization of immigration policy in the European Union (Givens and Luedtke 2004). Though citizens' attitudes toward immigration liberalized during the 1990s, the 2000s have seen a slight increase in preferences for more restrictive and nationalistic policies (Caughey et al. 2017). Far from insignificant, this shift stands in contrast to the decided liberalization of social policy issue attitudes across Europe (ibid.). With immigration issues in the limelight, political parties and their legislators face increased scrutiny and pressure over actions in this policy sphere. As concern over immigration rises and pressure to implement more restrictive policies builds alongside the refugee crisis, parties must wrestle with the competing interests of voters and the humanitarian needs of the region. This reality complicates and politicizes the refugee crisis, unfortunately leaving few acceptable solutions.

Amidst the challenges of making policy in high salience issues areas, governments may rely on bureaucratic and technical policy solutions in an effort to manage competing constituent concerns. Specifically, as increased issue salience illuminates socially constructed conceptualizations of immigrants and immigration, elevates discussions of deservingness, and promotes calls for congruent policymaking, countries may bifurcate their administration of immigration policy based on individual immigrant utility and status (Schneider and Ingram 1993). That is to say, countries may increasingly adopt divergent rhetoric and strategies for skilled and unskilled labor or for prospective new arrivals and already present immigrants (Givens and Luedtke 2005; Wright 2017). Importantly, these public preferences may justify restrictive regulatory and administrative changes even in the absence of more substantive policy change. For instance, countries across Europe have developed integration requirements for citizenship and settlement, requiring migrants to demonstrate language competency and civic knowledge (Goodman 2012). These sorts of changes to immigration policy are likely to be met with less resistance than more substantive changes, but will still assuage the fears and concerns of attuned anti-immigrant voters. Thus, technical policy changes offer politicians an option for balancing competing constituent interests.

The European Election Voter Study reflects a secular increase in citizens identifying immigration as their countries' most important problem between 1999 and 2014. To the extent that policymakers succeed in making policy in this sort of high salience issue area, their policy outputs are likely to be more restrictive (Givens and Luedtke 2004). Given the growing pressure to reign in immigration and the corresponding stereotyping of immigrants as deviants, restrictive policymaking is congruent policymaking (Schneider and Ingram 1993). Beyond the shorter-term, normative implications of restrictive immigration policy, the development of restrictive policy may lay the groundwork for long-term policy shifts toward nationalistic and anti-immigrant policies. Specifically, research on policy feedback demonstrates that policymaking is iterative and self-reinforcing (Goodman 2012). Thus, the establishment of such policies may provide a foundation for increasingly restrictive immigration policies under the banner of national pride.

Conclusion

The emergence of immigration as a defining issue in European politics reflects, along with the rise of environmental movements, the political opportunity structures in postindustrial societies where quality of life issues are increasingly salient. The incorporation of immigration as a question of national identity into party politics too reflects this change. To the extent that anxiety in the electorate regarding immigration was unrequited by mainstream parties, it opened the door for the far right. As the far right continued to gain popularity, and ultimately seats in parliaments, other parties were predicted to adjust their platforms in response.

The foregoing analysis assessed the relationship between a general left-right dimension of party competition and immigration in terms of multiculturalism. Immigration and multiculturalism have come to correlate with the existing left-right dimension much more strongly during the first decades of the twenty-first century. The right side of the spectrum has become more consistent than the left in their appropriation of restrictive and ethnocentric positions, with Conservative and Right-Liberal parties adopting more ethnocentric programs Indeed, the increased role of immigration and multiculturalism in electoral politics attests to the "absorbency" of the traditional left-right dimension in Western Europe. Even in the relatively brief period examined here, the impact of immigration, multiculturalism, and the far right on EU-15 party systems seems clear, as does the party systems' ability to incorporate these comparatively new issues. While other literature has considered the far right to be moderating, perhaps in an effort to be more "coalitionable" for the center right, we find little evidence of that here. Rather, the far right seems to have had a polarizing effect. This is a finding with important implications for the timbre of electoral politics, especially in the context of potential economic nationalism (cf. Brubaker 2011).

The increased salience of immigration as a question of national identity has implications at all levels of analysis. More restrictive policies toward - immigration and citizenship exist where immigration is salient, and the far right is a principal actor in immigration's politicization. This politicization also has ramifications at the systemic level as suggested by the analysis above. Perhaps most importantly, the expected shifts in policy outputs may produce lasting and meaningful shifts in migrant flow (e.g., Alarian and Goodman 2017). In sum, it appears that most party families have in some way repositioned themselves to correspond with a postindustrial dimension of party competition that features immigration as a question of national identity. The implications of this repositioning and attending increased salience of immigration alongside the myriad crises besetting Europe marks a critical juncture for European integration and for Europe itself.

Cross-References

▶ Multiculturalism and Citizenship in the Netherlands
▶ The Significance of Ethno-politics in Modern States and Society

References

Abedi A (2004) Anti-political establishment parties: a comparative analysis. Routledge, London

Akkerman T (2005) Anti-immigration parties and the defence of liberal values: the exceptional case of the list Pim Fortuyn. J Polit Ideol 10(3):337–354

Akkerman T (2015) Immigration policy and electoral competition in Western Europe: a fine-grained analysis of party positions over the past two decades. Party Polit 21(1):54–67

Alarian HM, Goodman SW (2017) Dual citizenship allowance and migration flow: an origin story. Comp Pol Stud 50(1):133–167

Allen TJ (2017) Exit to the right? Comparing far right voters and abstainers in Western Europe. Elect Stud 50:103–115

Alternative für Deutschland (n.d.) Manifesto for Germany. https://www.afd.de/wp-content/uploads/sites/111/2017/04/2017-04-12_afd-grundsatzprogramm-englisch_web.pdf

Art D (2011) Inside the radical right: the development of anti-immigrant parties in Western Europe. Cambridge University Press, New York

Arter D (2010) The breakthrough of another west European populist radical right party? The case of the true Finns. Gov Oppos 45(4):484–504

Arzheimer K (2015) The afd: finally a successful right-wing populist eurosceptic party for Germany? West Eur Polit 38(3):535–556

Arzheimer K (2017) The alternative for Germany. Programming, development and political positioning

Arzheimer K, Carter E (2006) Political opportunity structures and right-wing extremist party success. Eur J Polit Res 45(3):419–443

Bale T (2003) Cinderella and her ugly sisters: the mainstream and extreme right in Europe's bipolarising party systems. West Eur Polit 26(3):67–90

Bale T, Green-Pedersen C, Krouwel A, Luther KR, Sitter N (2010) If you can't beat them, join them? Explaining social democratic responses to the challenge from the populist radical right in Western Europe. Political studies 58(3):410–426

Betz H-G (2003) The Growing Threat of the Radical Right. In: Merkl, P. H., & Weinberg, L. (eds.) Right-wing Extremism in the Twenty-first Century. Psychology Press. 74–92

Betz HG, Meret S (2009) Revisiting Lepanto: the political mobilization against Islam in contemporary Western Europe. Pattern Prejudice 43(3–4):313–334

Bornschier S (2010) Cleavage politics and the populist right: the new cultural conflict in Western Europe. Temple University Press, Philadelphia

Brubaker R (2011) Economic crisis, nationalism, and politicized ethnicity. In: The deepening crisis: governance challenges after neoliberalism. pp 93–108

Byng MD (2008) Complex inequalities: the case of Muslim Americans after 9/11. Am Behav Sci 51(5):659–674

Carter E (2005) The extreme right in Western Europe: success or failure? Manchester University Press, Manchester

Caughey D, O'Grady T, Warshaw C (2017) Policy ideology in European mass publics, 1981–2014

Cole A (2005) Old right or new right? The ideological positioning of parties of the far right. Eur J Polit Res 44(2):203–230

Cramme O, Diamond P, McTernan M (eds) (2013) Progressive politics after the crash: governing from the left. IB Tauris, London

Dalton RJ (2008) Economics, environmentalism and party alignments: a note on partisan change in advanced industrial democracies. Eur J Polit Res 48(2):161–175

Dalton RJ (2013) Citizen politics: public opinion and political parties in advanced industrial democracies. SAGE, Thousand Oaks

De Lange SL (2007) A new winning formula? The programmatic appeal of the radical right. Party Polit 13(4):411–435

Derks A (2006) Populism and the ambivalence of egalitarianism. How do the underprivileged reconcile a right wing party preference with their socio-economic attitudes? World Polit Sci Rev 2(3):175–200

Eatwell R (2003) Ten theories of the extreme right. In: Merkl PH, Weinberg L (eds) Right-wing extremism in the twenty-first century, 2nd rev. ed, pp 23–46. Frank Cass, London

Ennser L (2012) The homogeneity of west European party families: the radical right in comparative perspective. Party Polit 18(2):151–171

Ford R, Goodwin MJ (2014) Revolt on the right: explaining support for the radical right in Britain. Routledge, Abingdon

Givens TE (2005) Voting radical right in Western Europe. Cambridge University Press, Cambridge, MA

Givens T, Luedtke A (2004) The politics of European Union immigration policy: institutions, salience, and harmonization. Policy Stud J 32(1):145–165

Givens T, Luedtke A (2005) European immigration policies in comparative perspective: issue salience, partisanship and immigrant rights. Comp Eur Polit 3(1):1–22

Golder M (2016) Far right parties in Europe. Annu Rev Polit Sci 19:477–497

Goodman SW (2012) Fortifying citizenship: policy strategies for civic integration in Western Europe. World Polit 64(4):659–698

Hooghe L, Marks G, Wilson CJ (2002) Does left/right structure party positions on European integration? Comp Pol Stud 35(8):965–989

Howard MM (2009) The politics of citizenship in Europe. Cambridge University Press, Cambridge, MA

Ignazi P (1992) The silent counter-revolution hypotheses on the emergence of extreme right-wing parties in Europe. Eur J Polit Res 22(1):3–34

Ignazi P (2003) Extreme right parties in Western Europe. Oxford University Press, Oxford

Inglehart R (1977) The silent revolution: changing values and political styles among Western publics. Princeton University Press, Princeton

Ivarsflaten E (2005) The vulnerable populist right parties: no economic realignment fuelling their electoral success. Eur J Polit Res 44(3):465–492

Ivarsflaten E (2008) What unites right-wing populists in Western Europe? Re-examining grievance mobilization models in seven successful cases. Comp Pol Stud 41(1):3–23

Joppke C (2004) The retreat of multiculturalism in the liberal state: theory and policy. Br J Sociol 55(2):237–257

Kaltwasser CR (2014) The responses of populism to Dahl's democratic dilemmas. Polit Stud 62(3):470–487

Kitschelt H (1989) The logics of party formation: ecological politics in Belgium and West Germany. Cornell University Press, London

Kitschelt H (2004) Diversification and reconfiguration of party systems in postindustrial democracies. Internat Politikanalyse, Friedrich-Ebert-Stiftung, Bonn

Kitschelt H (2007) Growth and persistence of the radical right in postindustrial democracies: advances and challenges in comparative research. West Eur Polit 30(5):1176–1206

Kitschelt H, with McGann AJ (1995) The radical right in Western Europe: a comparative analysis. University of Michigan Press, Ann Arbor

Koopmans R (2010) Trade-offs between equality and difference: immigrant integration, multiculturalism and the welfare state in cross-national perspective. J Ethn Migr Stud 36(1):1–26

Lehmann P, Matthieß T, Merz N, Regel S, Werner A (2017) Manifesto corpus. Version: 2017-2. WZB Berlin Social Science Center, Berlin

McGann AJ, Kitschelt H (2005) The radical right in the Alps: evolution of support for the Swiss SVP and Austrian FPÖ. Party Polit 11(2):147–171

Mudde C (1999) The single-issue party thesis: extreme right parties and the immigration issue. West Eur Polit 22(3):182–197

Mudde C (2007) Populist radical right parties in Europe, vol 22, no 8. Cambridge University Press, Cambridge, MA

Mudde C (2013) Three decades of populist radical right parties in Western Europe: so what? Eur J Polit Res 52:1–19

Oesch D (2008) The changing shape of class voting: an individual-level analysis of party support in Britain, Germany and Switzerland. Eur Soc 10(3):329–355

Rydgren J (2005) Is extreme right-wing populism contagious? Explaining the emergence of a new party family. Eur J Polit Res 44(3):413–437

Rydgren J (2009) Social isolation? Social capital and radical right-wing voting in Western Europe. J Civ Soc 5(2):129–150

Savelkoul M, Scheepers P (2017) Why lower educated people are more likely to cast their vote for radical right parties: Testing alternative explanations in The Netherlands. Acta Politica 52(4):544–573

Schain MA (2006) The extreme-right and immigration policy-making: measuring direct and indirect effects. West Eur Polit 29(2):270–289

Schmitt H, Braun D, Popa SA, Mikhaylov S, Dwinger F (2016) European Parliament election study 2014, Euromanifesto study. GESIS Data Archive, Cologne. ZA5162 data file version 1.0.0. https://doi.org/10.4232/1.5162

Schneider A, Ingram H (1993) Social construction of target populations: implications for politics and policy. Am Polit Sci Rev 87(2):334–347

Scott JW (2009) The politics of the veil. Princeton University Press, Princeton

Williams MH (2006) The impact of radical right-wing parties in west European democracies. Palgrave Macmillan, New York

Williams MH (2010) Can leopards change their spots? Between xenophobia and trans-ethnic populism among west European far right parties. Nationalism Ethn Polit 16(1):111–134

Wright CF (2017) Employer organizations and labour immigration policy in Australia and the United Kingdom: the power of political salience and social institutional legacies. Br J Ind Relat 55(2):347–371

Yılmaz F (2012) Right-wing hegemony and immigration: how the populist far-right achieved hegemony through the immigration debate in Europe. Curr Sociol 60(3):368–381

Zúquete JP (2008) The European extreme-right and Islam: new directions? J Polit Ideol 13(3):321–344

Lost in Europe: Roma and the Search for Political Legitimacy

21

Neil Cruickshank

Contents

Introduction	364
Roma	366
Europe	369
Four Pillars of Political Legitimacy	370
Transnationalism	372
Internationalism	374
Nationalism	375
Cosmopolitanism	377
Conclusion	378
Cross-References	379
References	379

Abstract

In trying to locate/identify avenues for political representation and contestation in Europe, this chapter examines four discrete approaches that in various ways and guises have animated (and continue to animate) Romani mobilization (and the Romani movement) over the past few decades. In no particular order, these are: nationalism, transnationalism, internationalism, and cosmopolitanism. The argument hinges on two assumptions: (1) the European Union, and Europe generally, has the institutional capacity to accommodate a non-territorial, post-Westphalian, form of belonging and representation and (2) Europe's largest contiguous minority, Roma, could realize enhanced political legitimacy and efficacy through one of the suggested models. An important caveat to the discussion at hand is that "institutional capacity" is not the same as institutional willingness or desire,

---

N. Cruickshank (✉)
Political Scientist and Dean of the Faculty of Arts, Science, and Technology, North Island College, Courtenay, BC, Canada

Faculty Associate, Centre for European Studies, Carleton University, Ottawa, ON, Canada
e-mail: neil.cruickshank@nic.bc.ca

© The Author(s), under exclusive license to Springer Nature Singapore Pte Ltd. 2019
S. Ratuva (ed.), *The Palgrave Handbook of Ethnicity*,
https://doi.org/10.1007/978-981-13-2898-5_150

and the gulf between what could work and what lawmakers are prepared to endorse is, at this point, sizable. Various attempts to integrate Roma have failed, and it looks like that without a significant change in how Roma interact with politicians and jurists, at the EU and state level, they will remain peripheral and disenfranchised, and politically lost.

Keywords

Roma · Transnationalism · Europe · European Union · Nationalism and political legitimacy

Introduction

One thing is for certain: For Roma rights to advance, something has to change. The promise of an integrated, open, and more humane Europe that would assist in the delivery of political and social rights has not materialized. Putting things in context, Zeljko Jovanovic, director of the Open Society Roma Initiatives, is quoted as saying: "When we started some of the major initiatives on Roma rights in 2003 and 2004, we saw more political will and less money than we have today available for addressing the situation for Roma" in Europe, he said. "We don't have a scarcity of resources, we have a scarcity of political will" (Surana 2016). This "scarcity of political will," and the dearth of political legitimacy that accompanies it, is the focus of this chapter. The concern is not with discrimination and racist attitudes per se, though they are both a cause and consequence of disenfranchisement, but with the possibility of political empowerment through new and different institutional arrangements. It is important to take a look at what different models offer; institutions and networks that might help Roma achieve political legitimacy and in turn improve group cohesion and identity.

It should be said from the outset that Roma are not "lost" in the literal sense, and the title should not be interpreted or construed in this way. Drawing this distinction is important because the last thing this chapter would want to do is contribute to the mistruths, falsehoods, and racist discourse that paint Roma as itinerant, exotic, and politically inattentive. Having participated in workshops, conferences, and research projects with and about European Roma, most recently in Budapest, I can say with relative certainty that Roma know exactly who they are, where they are, and what their contributions to European society have been since they migrated to Europe nearly seven centuries ago. Despite having lived in Europe since the early medieval period, only now are there opportunities in place, like the Romani Studies Program at Central European University, to study Romani language, politics, art, and culture. Going forward, the European Roma Institute for Arts and Culture (ERIAC), having opened its doors in June 2017, will surely serve as a hub for the study, curation, and preservation of Romani music, literature, and artifacts.

Speaking about representations of Roma in popular culture and ERIAC, Timea Junghaus said: "The stereotypical view of us is as a romanticised, sexualised, criminal people. The effect is false and destructive. Now we're claiming our own right to represent ourselves," she said. "Self-expression will hopefully challenge these long-held assumptions and prejudices" (Connolly 2017). In this way, Roma are not only taking control of their cultural destiny but also working to develop institutions, organizations, and discourses that aid in their quest for political power, legitimacy, and representation. The time is ripe to discuss the sorts of representative models that will aid in this development and enable Roma to work across and through political frontiers. The existing arrangement, which relies upon States to integrate Roma, develop and implement strategies to enhance Roma representation at the State and local levels and work through European institutions to coordinate policies and construct metrics (to evaluate the effectiveness of those policies) has proven ineffectual.

This chapter is concerned first and foremost with political legitimacy and political representation and the ways in which both, or perhaps either of these, could be achieved through the various approaches described below. Therefore in the context of this chapter, "lost" denotes an uncertain position or spot among European states, nations, and institutions, both at the EU and European (i.e., continental) levels, wherein Roma exist uncomfortably (and simultaneously) at the local, national, international, transnational, and supranational levels. Lost also suggests fluidity and flux, constant movement and searching – in the political sense – at all levels and within all available institutions and organizations. There is no titular Roma state, and no homeland that could be used to mobilize the whole Romani community, worldwide. A population that numbers in the tens of millions. And differences remain with respect to the depth (and intensity) of attachment between any particular Romani community and their host state, or between any two Romani communities living in the same state. Like any diverse population, especially one that displays transnational or diasporic qualities, Roma are properly understood as an amalgam of ethno-politically similar, yet distinctive groups, rather than a single, culturally homogenous and ethno-linguistically unified population.

There are a lot of uncertainties, but it is unfair to assume that just because questions persist about the organizational density of the pan-European Romani community, scholars and lawmakers should not examine Roma as a contiguous population, deserving of group rights and representation. They display the sorts of ethno-linguistic, socioeconomic, and political markers that both invites one to examine Roma through a transnational framework and consider orientations that emphasize group belonging and expression. The problem, and why this chapter is reviewing four discernible paths to political legitimacy, is expressed by McGarry (2010): "from an academic point of view, Roma fall through the cracks of conventional theories on minorities which have so far failed to account for this diverse community..." (p. 3).

On that note, after orienting the reader to the history and plight of Roma, this chapter will first discuss Europe and the European Union, the backdrop to the theorizing, before outlining four possible (and potentially emancipatory) avenues to greater political legitimacy: transnationalism, internationalism, nationalism, and cosmopolitanism.

Roma

The question is often asked: Who are the Roma? In his book, *The Romani Gypsies* (2015), Yaron Matras uses this question to animate his opening chapter and then, as a way to give shape to a group that sometimes seems more mythical than real, spends considerable time outlining the many stereotypes and prejudices Roma are subject to. Popular misconceptions of Roma, as vagabonds, fortune tellers, hustlers and worse, criminals, still shape popular discourse to such an extent that it is difficult to know where the fictional Roma ends and the nonfictional begins. Some of these inaccuracies and misrepresentations are so commonplace, like the idea that Roma are nomadic, that Europeans and non-European alike are quick to identify Roma as voluntarily stateless or itinerate. Such a belief excuses all sorts of unsavory policies and practices, permitting non-Roma to ignore and/or rationalize living conditions that are truly deplorable and treatment that is cruel and callous. Jean-Pierre Liégeois argues (2012), "it must be underlined that the majority of Roma are not nomadic, and many would prefer not to be bug are obliged to be so in order to adapt to changing and often threatening living conditions" (p. 26). It is also for this reason that Roma have emigrated from central Europe to Canada, the USA, and to other Western European states (like the UK and Ireland).

It is hard to find a time when Roma were not subject to mistruths, falsehoods, and cruel stereotypes. One of the more outrageous yet enduring claims concerns the idea that "Gypsies" are kidnappers of non-Roma children. The idea being that "nomadic Gypsies" would kidnap children as they travelled from town to town, village to village, with their itinerancy making it nearly impossible for authorities to find and rescue the abducted children. But this sort of mindset, as obviously prejudicial as it is, is far from historical.

In 2013, a young girl with blonde hair and blue eyes named Maria was "rescued" by Greek authorities when she was discovered living with a Roma couple outside Athens. News outlets around the world ran with the story, publishing articles and broadcasting stories that assumed, first, that Maria was most certainly not Roma (because of her complexion and hair color) and, second, was clearly the victim of a "Gypsy" kidnapping. Tabloid newspapers, like the *Daily Mail,* asked rhetorically if Maria could one of the many missing girls reported from the UK or elsewhere. Within days of the Maria story airing in Europe, *Fox News* (in America) published the story "Missing Missouri child could be a match for gypsy girl, attorney says." Hysteria and racist discourse is all too common when Roma are involved, and especially when an event or alleged crime, like the abduction of Maria, fits the narrative of Roma being itinerant, dishonest, predatory, and non-European. The custodial parents of Maria, a Roma couple living in Greece, explained to authorities that they were minding her for a family friend, who lived in Bulgaria, and asked for their help because she could not afford to care for her. This explanation for why Maria was in their custody was met with credulity and ridicule. They were asking, as many were, how could it be that a blond haired, blue-eyed girl with a fair complexion is living, *legitimately,* with a Roma family?

In the end it was discovered, through DNA testing no less, that Maria did in fact belong to a Roma woman living in Bulgaria, and that the explanation given to police and child services by Maria's guardians was, indeed, the truth. Moreover, Maria *is* Roma. So, Maria is not a "mystery girl," a "kidnap victim," and she is certainly not the "missing Baby Lisa." As Zeljko Jovanovic (2013) points out, "when the glare of the media spotlight fades, Maria will go back to a life of exclusion, without basic documentation or rights" (np). Clearly, there is a sinister side to the sort of mythologizing that produced the inaccurate and racist narrative around Maria's apprehension; it permits and excuses all manners of prejudicial and cruel behavior. This is something that Roma are continually dealing with, trying to overcome and having to fight against. And this is why an appreciation (or better yet, an understanding) of how prevailing discourses and imagery complicate any discussion related to Roma activism, Romani political mobilization, and, the issue at hand, political representation and legitimacy.

Peter Vermeersch (2006) a scholar of Romani political mobilization, spends considerable time contemplating the use of the term "Roma" and its implications. He argues "the introduction of the term 'Roma' (...) clearly represents an attempt to break away from the social stigmas and to produce a more positive, more neutral, and less romanticised image" (p. 13). The term, Roma, while being somewhat imprecise because it covers Sinti, Manouche, Travellers, Gypsies, etc., is now used by enough IGOs and organizations, and researchers and journalists, to make it the preferred noun for the whole group heretofore referred to (most often pejoratively) as Gypsies. While this chapter does use the term Roma, it does so in the knowledge that the term is a shorthand for a remarkably diverse community that has lived in Europe, uninterrupted, since before the European state system emerged.

For Vermeersch (2006) "Romani identity is the result of a complex process of labeling, categorization, and self-categorization. To study the Romani movement means to study that process of labeling, categorization, and self-categorization in political action" (p. 3). He goes on to caution, "a serious analysis should not simply focus on specific forms of lifestyle, traditions, descent, language usage, and so forth; it should ask why and in what social and political circumstances such phenomenon become generally accepted as markers of Romani identity" (p. 3). The enduring debate about (what is) Romani identity, (who represents and can speak on) Roma culture, and (who are) Romani people is in some respects the by-product of decades – if not centuries – of unhelpful, and at times racist, discourses.

In Europe, Roma are a contiguous minority numbering approximately 12 million. The majority of Roma live in central and Eastern Europe. This number, however, is just an estimate. The uncertainty stems from poor record keeping, internally displaced Roma lacking proof of citizenship and/or residency, and state bureaucracies unconcerned with obtaining reliable census data. Also, not everyone from a Roma family will self-identify as such. It is a sad truth, but many Roma have traded their ethnic identity for enhanced life chances. Simply put, in Europe non-Roma are more likely to find employment and suitable housing than Roma.

Roma are Europe's largest minority and live in all areas of Europe, and all EU states. It is generally accepted that Roma arrived in Europe approximately seven centuries ago, living and working alongside non-Roma for just as long. Since their arrival, Roma have contributed to European economies and culture. They are as much a part of Europe as any other ethnic group and just as entitled to the fruits of European "civilization" as anybody else. Despite these objective truths, Roma continue to be scapegoated and treated as "outsiders." Aiden McGarry (2017) refers to this condition as Romaphobia. He defines it as:

> Romaphobia is the hatred or fear of those individuals perceived as being Roma, Gypsy or Traveller; it involves the negative ascription of group identity and can result in marginalization, persecution and violence. Romaphobia is a manifestation of racism: it is cut from the same cloth. Romaphobia is no different in form and content to Islamophobia or anti-Semitism, both of which are on the rise in Europe, but its causes can be particularised. There is something *specific* about Romaphobia, even if its racist core is familiar (p. 1).

Subject to segregated schooling, coercive sterilization, pogroms, and physical violence, Roma have never really enjoyed full citizenship rights in Europe. This chapter's preoccupation with legitimacy and representation speaks to this continued marginalization. The models being advanced, presumably, can help with the development of a more robust political identity.

In this context, and how the concept is being applied here, political legitimacy is a term that denotes the level, degree, or efficacy of a subject's involvement in formalized political processes and decision-making. If an actor or organization has "political legitimacy," they are deemed to be a part of political decision-making and, most importantly, are thought to represent a discrete segment of society. With legitimacy, Roma can engage with other stakeholders, as a stakeholder, and not have to worry about communicating through others, be it states, NGOs, or lawmakers, to decision-makers at the European or State level. Frankly, legitimacy is the difference between being ignored and being heard. Moreover, legitimacy begets legitimacy. As Dür (2011) argues, "interest groups' resources mentioned in the literature include money, *legitimacy,* political support, knowledge, expertise and information (…) By dealing with certain political bureaucratic actors (in particular officials that are not directly elected, such as those in the European Commission), interest groups may also be able to convey legitimacy upon them" (p. 112).

The argument here proceeds on two foundational assumptions. First, the European system, which consists of a lattice work of EU institutions and protocols, structures, and, regimes, along with overlapping and cross-cutting bilateral and multilateral agreements, partnerships, and working groups, and an emergent European public space, is ripe for transnationalism, transboundary (or cross-border) activism, and cosmopolitan thinking. Second, Europe's largest contiguous minority population, Roma, are in a position to take advantage of (or derive political legitimacy from) this transnational turn in European politics. However, the argument proceeds cautiously. As the title of this chapter implies, being *in a position* to take advantage of new political opportunities is certainly not the same things as actively taking advantage of them.

There is no panacea at this point, but the proposed models seem appropriate, in different ways, for a European space that utilizes multilevel decision-making and governance. It is important to acknowledge that some EU states are actively challenging this orthodoxy and pushing back against EU institutions and, in particular, principles fundamental to the European project, like freedom of movement. These challenges to some aspects of European integration, however, fall short of undermining its core institutions and the bulk of the treaty law dating back to 1951.

Europe

To say that Europe has undergone a fundamental political-economic transformation since the end of World War II is hardly contentious. The development of the European Union, both horizontally and vertically, and its impact on the pace and character of democratization in central and Eastern Europe has both been remarkable and profound. Even a cursory examination of the transition period beginning 1989 will yield countless examples of how the drive to join the EU (for states like Poland, Czechoslovakia, and later the Czech Republic and Slovakia, Hungary, Romania, and Bulgaria) and the official accession process influenced decision-making around economic planning, public policy, and the structure and function of newly created democratic institutions. Moreover, with emphasis on governance and civil society, a new expanded Europe looked a perfect match for a transnational community searching for new political opportunities and enhanced legitimacy.

It was with central and Eastern Europe in mind that in 1993, the EU developed its accession criteria ("the Copenhagen Criteria"). Among these criteria was "stability of institutions guaranteeing democracy, the rule of law, *human rights and respect for and protection of minorities*" (emphasis added). While abstract, and arguably aspirational, the articulated concern for minority rights and the prominence it was given during the accession period was for many a step in the right direction. It was at this point, as well, that Roma and human rights NGOs were optimistic and hopeful. There was a belief that the new institutions of democracy, coupled with an open, diverse, and reenergized civil society, would advance a kind of participant political culture that would be inclusive to Roma. However, this did not materialize. As Ringold et al. (2005) discovered: "For several interwoven reasons, Roma poverty is rooted in their unfavorable starting point at the outset of the transition from planned to market economies. Low education levels and overrepresentation among low-skilled jobs led to labor market disadvantages..." (p. xiv). In other words, everything perpetrated against Roma during the socialist period, in particular the practice of segregated schooling, conspired to limit any potential gains they could have made during the transition period.

The transition to democracy and accession to the EU occurred by way of a complex and complicated process. The two processes, democratization and Europeanization, are in many ways mutually reinforcing. Some of the changes occurred at the institutional level, involving the *acquis communautaire*, which is the whole body of European law new members are expected to adopt, and others occurred (and are still occurring) at the cultural and discursive levels. Through the process of Europeanization, accession countries (like the Czech Republic, Poland, Slovakia, Hungary, and Romania) learned not only how to practice democracy, but most critically, activists learned how to utilize pan-European networks to advance their claims.

The other important development has been the creation of a human rights regime. The regime, comprising both European and EU institutions, rules and treaties, offers minority groups recourse to universal standards and fundamental human rights. This regime, consisting of the EU Charter of Fundamental Rights, the European Convention on Human Rights ("the Convention"), the European Court of Human Rights (ECtHR), which serves as a final appellate court for anyone residing in a signatory state, and the Court of Justice of the European Union, is remarkable advancement in the practice and application of transnational human rights. In short, this regime constitutes an important institutional and discursive development.

In the first instance, it affords minority ethnic groups, like Roma, additional opportunities to query and challenge discriminatory practices that occur at the state level. In D. H. and Others *v* the Czech Republic, a case heard by the ECtHR in 2007, the majority of jurists ruled that segregated schooling violated several principles of European law, including Article 14 ('Prohibition of Discrimination') of The Convention. Article 14 reads: "The enjoyment of the rights and freedoms set forth in this Convention shall be secured without discrimination on any ground such as sex, race, colour, language, religion, political or other opinion, national or social origin, association with a national minority, property, birth or other status." In the second instance, which is perhaps more difficult to see, the presence European-wide rights discourse not only reinforces the idea that human rights are universal but also routinizes the application of law in matters of discrimination and unequal treatment.

Four Pillars of Political Legitimacy

As a heterogeneous and geographically dispersed population, and a group without the strong national, religious or linguistic bonds that many other ethno-political groups claim to have and rely upon to create social cohesion, it is impossible to speak of a single Roma political movement or ideological orientation. It is equally difficult to speak of a single, encompassing Roma identity, be it ethnical, racial, sociopolitical, socioeconomic, or otherwise. Saying this, it is important to recognize that Roma, regardless of where they live, share a common condition. They are viewed by the majority population in similar terms, through a racialized lens, and very often subject to the same indifference. So, despite differences between and among Roma and Romani groups, Roma are united by a common history and the acute discrimination they experience across Europe and throughout the world. However, they are also united in their pursuit of justice, social and economic rights, political legitimacy, and in their concern for overcoming systematic, institutionalized and often public expressions of anti-gypsyism.

With that, and in the hope of moving the discussion about Roma rights forward, this chapter looks to identify four popular and potentially viable models available to Roma for the enhancement of both political representation and legitimacy. Before proceeding with that discussion, it is important to summarize where we are, in terms of Roma rights and representation, and what the principal concerns are relative political legitimacy and representation. The current situation can be boiled down in this way:

1. Despite attempts to integrate Roma, initiated primarily at the European level, they continue to experience discrimination, harassment, and maltreatment in a variety of ways and forms. Physical violence, forced evictions, and segregated schooling continue to happen across Europe. Programs designed to assist with integration, like the Decade of Roma Inclusion 2005–2015, started with great fanfare but, as with other top-down initiatives, fell far short of delivering any tangible improvements. It goes to reason that either the existing institutions are ill-equipped to deal with ongoing marginalization of Roma, or Roma lack the political power, and by extension legitimacy, needed to bring about change through contentious politics.
2. The European Union, a system that encourages informal decision-making and governance, is home to a constellation of actors and organizations actively working across political frontiers. Power is highly diffuse. Social movements, contentious politics, and collective action occur with little regard for jurisdiction and Westphalian norms. The presence of the European Court of Human Rights, coupled with deepening and widening human rights law, changes the parameters of contention in a very real (and still uncertain) way. Some activists, and some Roma, are still holding out hope for the EU Framework for National Roma Integration Strategies (EU Framework), which began in earnest in 2011. The idea being that each EU member-state should know how to best integrate Roma living within their territory, as each city, town, and village will present differently when it comes to Roma–non-Roma relations. Noting the previous point (no. 1), Roma are beginning to look at models and approaches that move beyond status quo, take advantage of new European institutions, laws and norms, and offer the possibility of emancipation.

So, the models being examined here align with new and emerging possibilities. The post-structural turn in Romani research has ushered in a new sense of optimism, and with this a reimagining of governance, representation and legitimacy.

The four approaches overlap in some ways, though they each tend to emphasize a different element of relational politics and decision-making. In functional terms, each approach is different as well. They demand different things as far as institutions are concerned and draw the eye to different levels or spheres of governance. While they can be applied at the same time, some of the incompatibility that exists between them will make it very difficult to advance more than one or two models simultaneously. But, it is possible to advance from one model to another.

Internationalism, for example, functions according to the principle of sovereign equality and on the basis that each group, being a named community, will assume the personality of a discrete (potentially juridical) actor. Responsibility resides with the representative of each group to communicate concerns to a larger group, and the larger group in-turn takes decisions on behalf of the whole. If this sounds like representative democracy or intergovernmentalism, it should. A model premised on internationalism would adhere to the notions of subsidiarity and collective decision-making, and focus attention on each community.

Transnationalism is first and foremost a process whereby information, ideas, and norms travel across political frontiers, and political actors feel unconstrained by traditional identities and boundaries – be it citizenship, geography, or language. Linking the idea of transnationalism to migration, Portes et al. (2009) contented the concept is suggestive of "a permanent back-and-forth movement in which migrants lived simultaneously in two or more societies and cultures, tying them together into 'deterritorialized' communities" (p. 568). The appeal of this approach is that it can accommodate multiple identities and belongings.

In some ways, nationalism appears incompatible with the new, integrated, and multileveled European Union. After all it was nationalism and the horrors of World War II that motivated Jean Monnet and Robert Schuman, among others, to develop the European Coal and Steel Community in the first instance. However, in trying to build cohesion and a robust identity, it might be appropriate for Roma to advance a doctrine of nationalism. Nationalism, as Ernest Gellner (1983) argues, "is primarily a political principle, which holds that the political and the national unit should be congruent" (p. 1). As it has been advanced so far, Romani nationalism is less concerned with statehood than the development of solidarity between Romani communities. With devolution, subsidiarity, and federalism, not to mention The European Committee of the Regions (CoR) that actively seeks input from sub-national governments, it looks like a form of nationalism can be advanced that does not myopically pursue statehood.

Cosmopolitanism has both an empirical and normative dimension to it. One of its principal opponents, David Held, offers this definition:

> Cosmopolitanism elaborates a concern with the equal moral status of each and every human being and creates a bedrock of interest in what it is that human beings have in common, independently of their particular familial, ethical, national and religious affiliations. It does not deny the historical, sociological, and political significance of these kinds of identity, but argues that they can obscure what it is that all people share – the bundle of needs, desires, anxieties and passions that define us all as members of the same species (Held 2010, p. x).

With its focus on morality, subsidiarity, and universal human rights, it is not hard to see why Roma activist and sociology professor, Nicolae Gheorghe, advanced this approach as a way to reconcile local concerns with pan-European institutions and norms.

The next few pages will delve a little deeper into each of the identified approaches.

Transnationalism

As a community contiguous to Europe, with familial bonds that stretch across political frontiers and with a history that predates the European state system, Roma appear not only well-situated to become a transnational community but, objectively speaking, *are already* a transnational community. With EU expansion in 2004 and 2007 came the institutional framework that would (and could) help facilitate the further transnationalization of European Roma, and more importantly, created among lawmakers, at both the European and State levels, a sense that Roma are a "European" community. The development of a European public space, a European civil society, and a European human rights regime, as mentioned above, all contributed to this new discourse. The United Nations identifies the constitutive elements of a transnational community:

> Trans-national communities are one aspect of trans-nationalism. Trans-national communities are groups whose identity is not primarily based on attachment to a specific territory. The notion of a trans-national community puts the emphasis on human agency: such groups are the result of cross-border activities which link individuals, families and local groups (UNESCO 2013).

Recall, Roma are peripheral actors in all European States, continually being derided for their culture and ethnicity, which many posit is not or non-European. We now know that Roma have lived in Europe for nearly a millennia, but the idea that Roma are from somewhere else persists. This defies logic, but as McGarry points out, Romaphobia involves a denial of fundamental truths and wanton disregard for Romani history and culture. There is no question that Roma migrated to and across Europe at some point during the early medieval period. However, moving back to the here and now, todays Roma are geographically dispersed and heterogeneous, speak different languages, and have a more profound attachment to their own community – not the broader European diaspora. The question is, how do Roma develop political bonds while retaining their regional and/or clan differences?

The answer lies, it would seem, with the kind of transnationalism being described below. It is easy to speak of Roma as a single population, especially with the advent of the term, "Roma." A term that is, admittedly, imprecise. But it is not considered pejorative, like the term Gypsy, and is favored by all European institutions, including the EU. Despite the homogenizing effect the term Roma has had, cleavages within the Romani community exist, are sometimes profound, and often make consensus difficult if not impossible to achieve. Recognizing this, it might be that a transnational model is the only possible way to balance the needs of the whole group with the wants of each Romani community. The quote, below, provides a strong endorsement of this model.

> There is no substitute for having human rights everywhere; this is the logic of seeking to define Roma as a transnational rather than a national minority. It is not so much that the rights of ethnic minorities must be protected, as that ethic majorities must be in themselves deconstructed. The foundation of global human law must shift from the self-contradictory illusion of national self-determination to a new bedrock of individual human self-determination. The unfolding agenda of Gypsy activism may be nothing less than the abolition of the nation-state. The mere existence of such an agenda has profound implications for any sociology of group conflicts (Gheorghe and Acton 2001, p. 69).

A transnational approach would prompt Roma to develop connections across and between political boundaries and look to supranational institutions for the mediation of political disputes. Moreover, it would empower individual Roma to exert their rights, as members of an ethnical group. This could be the compromise needed to push the discussion of rights forward.

Internationalism

In some respects, the international model is subsumed within "transnational" and "national." So, this section really serves as a bridge between the two. However, there are two important things to keep in mind.

First, separate from a transnational identity, Roma have acquired an international personality that in some instances, through the United Nations (UN) system for example, has allowed activists to directly communicate their grievances to world leaders and agencies with global reach. A 2013 position paper authored by the Roma Regional Working Group of the United Nations Development Group (RRDG) outlines the advantage of the UN system:

> As the guardian of the international human rights system, the UN has a unique role in supporting and strengthening national and local authorities and others to ensure effective domestic implementation of human rights. More particularly, UN entities frequently have operational strengths in the field in particular countries, making them well-placed to assist authorities in securing Roma inclusion (RRDG 2013. p. 1).

As it has been documented elsewhere, and despite good intentions, Roma are still very much at the margins of society with little in the way of dynamic political power. However, whereas in the early 1990s Romani issues were thought to be specific to Europe, they are now of international concern. Part of this has to do with the movement of Roma from Europe to North America, primarily, but also South America and Australia.

Second, the establishment of the International Romani Union (IRU) in 1977 effectively reoriented the focus of some Romani activists. The hope was to involve global actors and institutions in the pursuit of political rights and ultimately the amelioration of anti-gypsyism around the world. However, to achieve international personality Roma would first have to develop as a coherent nation. As reported by Acton and Klimová (2001):

> Dr Ščuka continued that gadje saw Roma as a minority group, social group or even a criminal group and was adamant that Roma should not let themselves be defined in that way by outsiders. Roma were, above all, a nation in their own right, and should be seated as a nation in organizations like the UN and UNESCO.

With the president of the IRU, Dr. Ščuka, identifying Roma as a nation, it might be that before any of the models can be pursued, especially internationalism and transnationalism, Roma must first contemplate the efficacy of nationalism.

Nationalism

Unlike the Scottish, Welsh, Catalans, or Basques, all subnational groups that are geographically rooted, Roma are without a single, coherent delimited territory, other than Europe as a whole, and the particular regions/areas they inhabit within existing states. And unlike Indigenous people in Canada that have been recognized at the constitutional level, they lack the juridical right to self-government and a historical claim to territory. There is no process in place to identify Romani lands or areas that might be understood as historically Roma, or populated by Roma. So when discussing the parameters of Romani nationalism, it is a non-territorial (non-irredentist) form of nationalism that is being considered. Calls for cultural, legal, and political rights have been issued, but not territorial rights. Since the early 1970s, some Roma, particularly those associated with the IRU, have been discussing nationalism and presenting a program of non-territorial political rights. In this way, Romani nationalism departs from other forms of European nationalism. Some comparative analysis has been done between European Jews and Roma, the form of nationalism practiced by each and how each group mobilized in the nineteenth and twentieth centuries. While there are some commonalities, the cases are idiosyncratic, and there is no Romani equivalent to Zionism.

Unsurprisingly, researchers have given Roma nationalism some thought (Fosztó 2003; Liebich 2007; McGarry 2011, 2014). This has also involved looking at the utility of the paradigm, used more confidently (and commonly) by people making an irredentist claim, like Québécois or Catalans. It is not a common approach, admittedly, but given the structure and function of the European Union, it makes sense to contemplate how a Romani nation would interaction with European lawmakers. Having presented on the topic of "Roma Nationalism," to audiences in Europe and North America, it became apparent early on that many European Roma, and non-Roma for that matter, equate nationalism with Nazis or Fascists. The interwar period, 1919–1939 was marked by nationalism and nationalist discourse, and the targeted killing of Roma, Jews, and others deemed "inferior." It is not surprising that Roma, today, are skeptical of nationalist.

Thoughts of the former Yugoslavia, once beset by ethnonationalist violence, were also top of mind. Given this association, it makes perfect sense that most Roma would not want to embark on a nationalist program. In *Europe is Ours: A Manifesto,* Ethel Brooks (2018) asserts: "We claim nationhood without aspiring to the hierarchy of the nation-state; nor do we aspire to the tyranny of the border or the imperative to empire that are part of the legacy of Europe, embodied in the current system of nation-states."

Like all good areas of scholarly inquiry there are plethora of approaches, theories, methodologies and concepts available to the earnest researcher. Sometimes it looks like there is more disagreement than agreement when it comes to the study of nations and nationalist movements, and this applies to the utility of the term "nation" itself. Looking back at the Warwick debates (1996), between eminent theorists of nationalism Ernest Gellner and Anthony D. Smith, it is easy to see just how unsettled some of the basic assumptions about nations and nationalism are. The debate, for example, revolved around the questions: The nation: real or imagined? and "Do nations have navels?" There is still fundamental disagreement about how and when nations are created, their scope and character, and the value of looking at groups of human beings through a nationalist lens.

Further complicating matters is the splitting of nation into "ethnic" and "civic." Having reviewed several political science textbooks and books on nationalism, this taxonomical shorthand is becoming all too common and with that accepted. Michael Ignatieff (2006), for example, argues "civic nationalism (...) maintains that the nation should be composed of all those – regardless of race, color, creed, gender, language, or ethnicity – who subscribe to the nation's political creed" (p. 6). He goes on to say in the same paragraph that this type of nationalism is democratic, inclusive and is "a community of equal, rights-bearing citizens, united in patriotic attachment..." (ibid.). According to Ignatieff, "ethnic nationalism claims (...) that an individual's deepest attachments are inherited, not chose. It is the national community that defines the individual, not the individual who define the national community" (p. 8).

Intersectionality assumes people might share ethnic or national markers, like Roma do, but is also supposed that members of the same group belong to other discernable groupings. Smith (1996) definition, below, is a useful starting point:

> Ethnic community (or 'ethnie') as a named human population of alleged common ancestry, shared memories and elements of common culture with a link to a specific territory and a measure of solidarity; a 'nation' as a named human population sharing a historic territory, common myths and historical memories, a mass, public culture, a common economy and common legal rights and duties; and 'nationalism' as an ideological movement for the attainment and maintenance of autonomy, unity and identity on behalf of a population some of whose members deem themselves to constitute an actual or potential 'nation' (p. 446)

Martin Kovats (2003) offers a critique of Roma nationalism, arguing among other things that Roma, as a heterogeneous, diasporic, and loosely aligned community can never really achieve anything akin to a nation-state. His analysis is striking and worth quoting at length.

> Roma nationalism represents the politicisation of the Romantic racial myth of the 'Gypsy people'; this, though intellectually discredited, has been thrown a lifeline due to its political utility. The application of 'Gypsy' identity has traditionally been used to marginalise the status of these communities, and Roma nationalism accords with this tradition by legitimating the ideology of segregation and suppressing democratic political development in order to sustain the marginalisation and isolation of 'Roma' people so they become politically dependent on the nation's elite. The nationalist agenda can only be realised by ripping Roma people from the societies in which they are citizens. It tells Roma people it is pointless trying to use the established mechanisms for democratic political accountability within their home countries; nor should they seek political support from amongst their 'non-Roma' fellow citizens. Indeed, attributing the problems experienced by Roma people to the racism of their neighbours could not be more important to an ideology which deliberately seeks to exacerbate social tensions (ibid.).

There is an implicit assumption that nationalism, and by extension the formation of a nation, is counterproductive and somehow destabilizing and would only work to sow more distrust between Roma and non-Roma, and between Roma themselves. Kovats also asserts that a Roma nation would effectively rip Roma "from the societies in which they are citizens" (ibid.). When one of the biggest problems facing Roma is political representation, or rather lack thereof, it might be time to pursue a nationalist agenda.

Cosmopolitanism

One of the more intriguing developments of the past two decades has been the renewed interest in cosmopolitanism. This model is being applied to Roma, certain aspects of the EU, and more generally to what have been identified as a post-Westphalian world order. As social scientists grapple with new kinds of governance, what appears to be an ever intensifying globalization that links people from disparate regions in awkward and exhilarating ways, and the spread of NGOs, IGOs, and transnational corporations (TNCs), they are looking to novel (and granted, some less novel) theoretical approaches to help explain forces behind contemporary decision-making and political mobilization. As the closest thing to a cosmopolitan order, a confederation of sovereign states working under the direction of supranational institutions, the EU has attracted a lot of attention from empiricists and theoreticians alike. And for good reason, as the EU acquires a genuine public space and civil society, and further establishes its human rights regime, which features a charter of rights and convention (i.e., *Charter of Fundamental Rights of the European Union* and *European Convention on Human Rights*) and an appellate court to adjudicate human rights violations (i.e., the European Court of Human Rights), and continues to rely on pan-European political networks and systems of governance to legitimate its political decision-making, it looks to approximate. Van Hooft (2014) suggests:

> But cosmopolitanism is not just another name for egalitarianism or liberal humanism. What it targets are forms of discrimination that arise from the victim's being of a different nationality, ethnicity, religion, language, race or any other form of identity that is use to classify people into discrete groups (...) It is the division between people that are created primarily by religion, race, nationality and ethnicity that are of central concern to cosmopolitanism (p. 5)

There is a danger when applying cosmopolitanism to Roma and Romani ways of knowing and understanding that one might, rather unintentionally, fall victim to romanticism. This is something that should be guarded against. Roma have been portrayed as itinerant, carefree vagabonds that travel throughout and across Europe (in wagons or caravans) with little concern for civility or societal norms. Many believe Roma are fortune tellers, mystics, and musicians. While cosmopolitanism is worth considering, it is an approach that could further malign Roma and provide lawmakers a reasons to shirk their responsibilities with respect to Roma living in their state.

Conclusion

The discussion here has been about legitimacy and representation. The arithmetic is fairly simple: Roma lack political clout and power, and therefore within the existing institutional framework have been unable to acquire the political legitimacy that would normally translate into meaningful representative authority. In this way, as the title of this chapter suggests, they are lost, perpetually navigating an institutional environment devoid of real political opportunities. Complicating matters, and despite being a contiguous, diasporic ethnic community with a territorial claim to many parts of Europe, they never developed the accoutrement of a Nation. (Although the existence of a Romani flag and anthem are indication of some movement toward that possibility.) Further, their status as a diaspora, of Europe's largest ethnic community, has not translated into increased political power. As this chapter has argued, changes at the structural and discursive levels are the only way to ameliorate this condition of political impotence and marginalization. But critically, and for it to be effectual, this structural change has to occur outside existing channels, either above, below, or in-between European national states. The four perspectives covered, nationalism, internationalism, transnationalism, and cosmopolitanism, even if combined in some way, shape or form, will undoubtedly provide that opportunity.

Moving away from (or pulling out of) existing political institutions to build cohesion and political legitimacy might seem wrongheaded, even regressive, but such a move will help Roma develop connections, between and among themselves, and the social capital required to effect change. True, national states should be prepared, willing, and indeed able to address the maltreatment and disenfranchisement of Roma. After all, Roma are citizens deserving of rights, protections, and ultimately the same life chances accorded non-Roma. However, 30 years after the collapse of state socialism in central and Eastern Europe, Roma are no better off, with little to no improvement in their per capita wealth. Poverty, ill-health, and illiteracy disproportionally impact Roma. So, they are poor, undereducated, and subject to a host of discriminatory policies and practices, including segregated schooling, deportation, and forced relocation. Denial of citizenship, and the internal displacement it produces, is the net result of continuing, endemic forms of institutionalized racism. With many Roma inhabiting a legal gray zone, authorities are able to intimidate, coerce, and simply ignore whole swaths of the Romani population.

Only through an examination of the policies, practices, and prejudices that have prevented Roma from realizing full political participation at the State and regional levels can one begin to fully comprehend the breadth and the depth of the representative deficit. With this in mind, and with an eye to the future, it is important to contemplate models that move beyond *status quo* and in parallel look for ways to build capacity among Roma. This chapter attempted to do this. Admittedly, the discussion here is not altogether novel nor ground-breaking, as the approaches presented above have been examined elsewhere and applied across disciplines. However, by presenting transnationalism, internationalism, nationalism, and cosmopolitanism as alternative frameworks capable of producing political legitimacy, this chapter is contributing to an ongoing discussion about ethnopolitical mobilization, minority group representation, and identity politics.

Political empowerment has not come easily for Roma, and where gains have been made, they have often been modest, incremental, and episodic. Realizing this, this chapter is just the start of longer, more in-depth exploration of different representative models and sources of political legitimacy.

Cross-References

▶ Ethno-cultural Symbolism and Group Identity
▶ Stereotypes of Minorities and Education

References

Acton T, Klimová I (2001) The international Romani union: an east European answer to west European questions? In: Guy W (ed) Between past and future: the Roma of central and Eastern Europe. University of Hertfordshire Press, Hertfordshire

Brooks E Europe is ours: a manifesto. European Roma Rights Centre. http://www.errc.org/news/europe-is-ours-a-manifesto. Last Accessed 8 Oct 2018

Connolly K (2017) A place to call our own: Europe's first Roma cultural centre opens in Berlin. The Guardian. https://www.theguardian.com/world/2017/jun/08/roma-artists-launch-art-cultural-centre-institute-berlin. Last accessed 10 Aug 2018

Dür A (2011) Interest groups in the European Union: how powerful are they? In: Beyers J, Rainer E, Maloney WA (eds) Interest group politics in Europe: lessons from EU studies and comparative politics. Routledge, Oxon

Fosztó L (2003) Diaspora and nationalism: an anthropological approach to the international Romani movement. Regio: Minorities, Politics, Society 1:102–120

Fox News. Missing Missouri child could be a match for gypsy girl, attorney says. Web. https://www.foxnews.com/world/missing-missouri-child-could-be-a-match-for-gypsy-girl-attorney-says. Accessed 10 Jan 2019

Gellner E (1983) Nations and nationalism. Cornell University Press, Ithaca

Gheorghe N, Acton T (2001) Citizens of the world and nowhere. In: Guy W (ed) Between past and future: the Roma of central and Eastern Europe. University of Hertfordshire Press, Hertfordshire

Held D (2010) Cosmopolitanism: ideas and realities. Policy Press, Cambridge

Ignatieff M (2006) Blood and Beloning: journeys into the new nationalism. Penguin Books, Toronto

Jovanovic Z (2013) Maria is Roma – so now she will become invisible once again. The Guardian. Web. https://www.theguardian.com/commentisfree/2013/oct/28/maria-roma-invisible. 28 Oct Accessed 10 Jan 2019

Kovats M (2003) The politics of Roma identity: between nationalism and destitution. openDemocracy. https://www.opendemocracy.net/people-migrationeurope/article_1399.jsp. Last Accessed 8 Nov 2018

Liebich A (2007) Roma nation? Competing narratives of nationhood. Natl Ethnic Polit 13(4):539

Liégeois J-P (2012) The Council of Europe and Roma: 40 years of action. Council of Europe Publishing, Strasbourgh

McGarry A (2010) Who speaks for Roma?: political representation of a transnational minority. Continuum, London

McGarry A (2011) The Roma voice in the European Union: between national belonging and transnational identity. Soc Mov Stud 10(3):283–297

McGarry A (2014) Roma as political identity: exploring representation of Roma in Europe. Ethnicities 14(6):756–774

McGarry A (2017) Romaphobia: the last acceptable form of racism. Zed Books, London

Portes A, Escobar C, Radford AW (2009) Immigrant transnational organizations and development: a comparative study. In: Ben-Rafael E, Sternberg Y (eds) Transnationalism: diasporas and the advent of a new (dis)order. Brill, Boston

Ringold D, Orenstein MA, Wilkens E (2005) Roma in an expanding Europe: breaking the poverty cycle. The World Bank, Washington, DC

Roma Regional Working Group of the United Nations Development Group (2013) The Role of The United Nations in Advancing Roma Inclusion. www.europe.ohchr.org

Smith AD (1996) Culture, community and territory: the politics of ethnicity and nationalism. Int Aff 72(3, (July)):445–458

Surana K (2016) Roma Fleeing the EU's 'Broken Promises' Seek Asylum in the US. Foreign Policy. 22 Sept Web. https://foreignpolicy.com/2016/09/22/roma-romania-migration-united-states/

United Nations Educational, Scientific and Cultural Organization (UNESCO). Learning to Live Together. Web. http://www.unesco.org/new/en/social-and-human-sciences/themes/international-migration/glossary/trans-nationalism/. Last Accessed 20 Oct 2018

Van Hooft S (2014) Cosmopolitanism: a philosophy for global ethics. Routledge, New York

Vermeersch P (2006) The Romani movement: minority politics and ethnic mobilization in contemporary Central Europe. Berghahn Books, New York

Part III
Stereotypes and Prejudices
Part Introduction

This part of the book comprises 14 chapters that describe, dissect, and critically examine the nature of stereotyping, prejudice, and racism; and the consequences of these cognatic and behavioral dimensions of fairly ubiquitous ways of thinking and acting, as well the struggles against racism. The authors draw case studies from various parts of the world.

One of the salient features of modern-day societies is the occurrence of various forms of discrimination based on ethnicity and race among almost all multiethnic member states of the United Nations. The extent of state responses to quell discrimination and promote multiculturalism and antiracism varies considerably. In many countries, the promotion of cultural diversity and equality of opportunity in a situation of institutionalized racism remains a major challenge.

The first chapter by Vijay Naidu provides a conceptual and historical overview of race and racism, and the following chapter by Paul Spoonley provides a sociological assessment of stereotypes and how they are institutionalized and manifested in human relationships. approach them differently in relation to how they are applied in different contexts. The chapters which follow provide a variety of unique case studies from various parts of the world. Alois Mlambo provides a critical analysis of colonialism in Zimbabwe (Southern Rhodesia) and documents the profoundly debilitating effects of discriminatory policies on Indigenous Africans in relation to land, education, labor, residence, and livelihoods. Land appropriation by the colonizers was central to tensions and conflict between Indigenous peoples, the white settlers, and the colonial government.

The history of discrimination based on skin color survives in various forms in contemporary societies. This theme is taken up by a number of authors in this part. They include racialized identity in apartheid South Africa Suryakanthie Chetty and racism against black people in Europe by Stephen Small. Paul Bagguley and Yasmin Hussain discuss how the impact of institutionalized racism and inequality created conditions for riots in the UK in 2001.

Contemporary forms of stereotyping, prejudice, and racism are also taken up by authors whose chapters address the mass media's role in constructing, reinforcing, and sustaining stereotypic images of ethnic minorities and "others." Tara Ross critically examines how negative images of Pacific peoples are framed by mainstream New Zealand media and how these reinforce intergroup perceptions. Karl Cheng Chua discusses the imageries of the Japanese in the Philippines literature and how this has changed over the years. The Japanese have been portrayed as villains with cruel disposition in the postwar era, but their image has become more nuanced as having both "good" and "bad" and the "ugly" among them. The final chapter looks at the dilemma relating to racial justice in education and implications on "white fragility."

Vijay Naidu

Race and Racism: Some Salient Issues

22

Vijay Naidu

Contents

Introduction	384
The Notion of Race	384
Racialization: An Overview	385
The Ideology of Racism	388
Racism in the Contemporary World	390
"Old" and "New" Racism	391
Race Relations and Anti-racist Struggles	392
Conclusion	393
References	394

Abstract

It can be said that virtually all member states of the United Nations are multiethnic, and yet racism and ethnic discrimination remain significant features of many of these countries. This chapter examines the notions of race and ethnicity, the origins of racialization and racism, as well as ethnic discrimination. It alludes to the historical significance of the enslavement of millions of Africans to labor in the plantations and mines of the Americas and Caribbean islands, colonialism in Africa, Asia, and the Pacific, and international labor migration to contemporary forms of racism and interethnic relations. The violent displacement and movement of thousands of refugees and asylum seekers from Iraq, Afghanistan, and Syria to Western countries have given rise to xenophobia, Islamophobia, and racism in the latter states. Interethnic tensions and conflicts remain legacies of an earlier epoch of uneven and unequal development as well as discriminatory practices in most postcolonial states. The struggle against racism and ethnic discrimination is an ongoing process.

V. Naidu (✉)
University of the South Pacific, Suva, Fiji
e-mail: vijaynaidu61@gmail.com; vijay.naidu@usp.ac.fj

© The Author(s), under exclusive license to Springer Nature Singapore Pte Ltd. 2019
S. Ratuva (ed.), *The Palgrave Handbook of Ethnicity*,
https://doi.org/10.1007/978-981-13-2898-5_25

> **Keywords**
> Race · Racism · Ethnicity · Colonialism · Anti-racist struggles

Introduction

In the early twenty-first century, notions of race and racism are widely used and their manifestation can be seen in everyday life at global, national, and local levels. Most recently, the terrorist attack on worshippers that resulted in 50 deaths and 50 injured and hospitalized in Christchurch, New Zealand, show that a relatively remote and apparently peaceful country is not spared the extreme violence of a white supremacist. International main stream media and social media cover matters relating to race, ethnicity, and racism on a routine, if differential basis. Prominent among these are statements and actions of President Donald Trump and the reassertion of white supremacist views and activities by American and European right wing and neo-Nazi groups; the "Black Lives matter movement"; European countries' responses to the immigration of displaced civilian men, women, and children of Iraq, Syria, Afghanistan, and a number of African countries; Islamophobia in Western countries fueled by fundamentalist Muslim terrorists; the ethnic cleansing in Myanmar (Burma) of Rohingyas; the forceful appropriation of white-owned farms in Zimbabwe; ethnic profiling by security forces including at points of entry into countries; the treatment of Palestinians by the Israeli state; rising anti-Semitism; the suppression of Ugihurs and Tibetans by China; and the continuing marginalization of first nation peoples and interethnic conflict in many postcolonial states.

This chapter examines some selected trends in intergroup relations and racism in the contemporary era.

The Notion of Race

The idea of race and especially its use in pseudoscientific disciplines such as eugenics is relatively recent in terms of human history. It denotes the classification of human beings or *Homo sapiens* in terms of patterns of physical appearances beginning with skin color (pigmentation), facial features, hair texture, physical size, and head shape. Patterns of these phenotypical features spread over geographical space and reflect both periodic isolation and intermixing among human populations. Biologists accept that all human beings belong to the one species of *Homo sapiens* and physical differences have arisen out of environmental conditions and over time, reproduction in relatively isolated gene pools. They have also maintained that biologically "race" is a meaningless notion as irrespective of phenotype and genotype human beings can and do interbreed to produce virile offspring. However, "race" is a social construct of dominant groups to identify themselves and other people who vary in physical appearances and may or may not have cultural differences. Over time, there has been a wide acceptance of racial categorization globally, regionally, and nationally. These categorizations include social and cultural attributes, self-identification, political-state based identification, and institutional definitions and practices (Banton 1967; Cohen 1999; Cox 1948; Rex 1983; Sivanandan 1982; Yeboah 1988).

The UNESCO Declaration on Race and Racial Prejudice (1978) has unequivocally declared that "all human beings belong to a single species and are descended from a common stock." However, "Legal and political language use the term *races* in the plural sense in order to cover different ethnicities or geographically characterizable subgroups, such as Caucasians, Africans, Mongoloids. Because of the well-established (but erroneous) custom, political and legal language is still using this term." (Gayle 2018).

There is some overlap between the concept of race and ethnic group. According to Stavenhagen:

> ...ethnic groups are historically given collectivities which have both objective and subjective characteristics, that is, their members acknowledge sharing common traits such as language, culture or religion, as well as a sense of belonging...Ethnic boundaries are socially constructed and may be more or less permeable....Ethnic group identity is the result of internal factors (common lifestyles, share beliefs), but also the outcome of relations the group entertains with other distinct but similarly constituted groups and with the state in any given country (1996, 4).

Historically, at the very beginnings of the categorization of human beings into races, intellectual, behavioral, and normative – therefore cultural – dimensions were included in the definition of race.

In the mid-eighteenth century, Carl Linnaeus, the renowned Swedish zoological taxonomist, classified human beings in the order of primates and belonging to the single species of *Homo sapiens* and several major subspecies. By the time of his writing, the European world had expanded to most parts of the world and knowledge about peoples in these places was shared among European scholars. His fourfold categorization included *Americanus, Asiaticus, Africanus*, and *Europeanus*. He proceeded to imbue these supposed subspecies with traits derived from Eurocentric perceptions. *Europeanus* were white, and supposedly gentle and inventive. *Asiaticus* were melancholic and greedy. *Americanus* were red, ill-tempered, and subjugated. *Africanus* were black, lazy, and impassive. "...Linnaeus correlated skin color with medical temperament—Americans turned out to be 'choleric,' Europeans 'sanguine,' Asians 'melancholic,' and Africans 'phlegmatic'—moral characteristics, preferred clothing, and form of government" (Muller-Willie 2015, 597). The association of human anatomical features with intellect and other nonbiological attributes has been a feature of subsequent classification of varieties of human beings (Fredrickson 2002, 56). Linnaeus and, following him, Blumenbach, accepted that these varieties of human beings belonged to the one species (Ibid., 57).

Racialization: An Overview

This categorization of vastly culturally diverse groups of people both in physical appearance and in terms of their cultures became an integral dimension of both identifying these groups in rather simplified categories, ascribing certain immutable attributes, and discriminating against them. European exploration and colonialism was accompanied by this process of naming and ascribing. In a number of cases, the names have stuck, even when they were blatantly in accurate from the start. Two examples should suffice. The term "Indian" was applied to the huge number of nations and ethnicities in the Americas and the Caribbean region. The Pacific island countries were divided into three regions based on the early explorers designation of them as Melanesian (black islands), Polynesian (many islands but inhabited by lighter skinned people), and Micronesian (very small islands, inhabited by brown skinned people). As pointed out by William Alkire, there is no clear demarcation between these islands, and indeed because of considerable intermixing in the one village, "The range of physical types found in most Oceanic communities is great, and it is fairly simple in Micronesia to find within the same village individuals whom anthropologists of 30 years ago would have labelled 'Mongoloid', Negroid; or Caucasoid'" (Alkire 1977, 9).

The role of dominant groups and states in defining "race" has been significant in the institution of discriminatory racist policies and practices. For examples, in the United States, one drop of black blood meant that the person was black irrespective of what the person looked like. This definition emerged in the southern states of the United States and was adopted at the national level (Davis, ND). Racial classification in Apartheid South Africa by the 1950 Population Registration Act stipulated three races: "white," "native" (black African), or "colored" (neither white nor "native"). Appearance and public perception were the two criteria for designating a person's race. Thompsell describes a simple racial test in South Africa thus:

> Over the years, certain unofficial tests were also set up to determine the race of individuals who either appealed their classification or whose classification was challenged by others. The most infamous of these was the "pencil test", which said that if a pencil placed in one's hair fell out, he or she was white. If it fell out with shaking, 'colored', and if it stayed put, he or she was 'black'. Individuals could also be subjected to humiliating examinations of the color of their genitals, or any other body part that the determining official felt was a clear marker of race (Thompsell 2018).

Racialization has a long history and is associated with contact and interaction between people of different physical and cultural backgrounds. For instance, the expansion of the ancient Egyptian empire brought together Africans, Asians, and Europeans – in short, the inhabitants of two large continents: Africa and Eurasia. In AD 325, Alexander the Great led a military expedition across Asia Minor into the Indus valley conquering and subjugating various groups on the way. He was accompanied by a scholar, Megasthenes "who wrote the Indica, recording strange races of people in India: dog-headed men, men without mouths who got their nourishment from smelling fruits, men with their faces on their chests" (Palat 1998). This type of grossly distorted, exaggerated, and imaginary descriptions of non-European people became common place as European explorers and adventurers journeyed to Africa, Asia, the Americas, and the Pacific. These generally negative imageries and associated attributes were reproduced in caricatures of colored peoples in foreign lands.

Apart from conquest, trading was also a way of connecting groups. For instance, the Silk Road provided traders and travelers from the Far East, the Middle East, the near East, and parts of "civilized" Europe to establish networks and relationships across diverse regions and cultures (Gordon 2008). Presumably, in these relations, there would have been both positive and negative stereotyping that would have informed the trade partnerships that were engendered.

Colonialism also played a central part in the racialization process. Early Portuguese and Spanish intrusion into Africa and the Americas in the sixteenth century, followed by other Europeans, namely, the Dutch, the British, the French, the Germans, Italians, Belgians, over the subsequent 300 years resulted in several negative outcomes for peoples of the non-European world. Colonial conquest, the subjugation and decimation of native peoples, expropriation of the land of first nation peoples, their enslavement, as well as the scramble and partition of Africa, and much of the rest of the world have been held as morally reprehensible by Adam Smith. He stated that European superiority of force "enabled to commit with impunity every sort of injustice in those remote countries" (Smith 1811, 459; see, Ince 2017). Terms such as primitive accumulation (Karl Marx) and booty capitalism (Max Weber) could be applied to this phase of human history. European expansionism for economic and geopolitical reasons was accompanied by ideas of racial superiority over colored and black people. Such ideas emerged even more powerfully from the rationalization of the slavery of non-Christian native peoples and especially Africans, and subsequently by pseudoscientific racism beginning with social Darwinism, and then in the early twentieth century by eugenics. Rudyard Kipling wrote of the "white man's burden" and although Christianity coexisted with the enslavement of indigenous peoples and Africans for the better of 400 years, it lived with the contradiction of human beings made in the image of god and the horrendous treatment of black people and people of color. In fact, a pope accepted African slaves as gift in the sixteenth century endorsing the kidnapping and enslavement of non-Christians of color.

It is noteworthy, that in the post-WWII world following the revelation of the horrors of the Holocaust, the ideology of racial purity and superiority waned (together with Eugenics as a "science"), and the United Nations stood strongly against all forms of racism. However, Howard Zinn, the American historian, has written that:

> Fifteen years ago, when I was teaching at Boston University, I was asked by a Jewish group to give a talk on the Holocaust. I spoke that evening, but not about the Holocaust of World War II, the genocide of six million Jews. It was the mid-eighties, and the U.S. government was supporting death squads in Central America, so I spoke of the deaths of hundreds of thousands of peasants in Guatemala and El Salvador, victims of American policy. My point was that the memory of the Jewish Holocaust should not be circled by barbed wire, morally ghettoized, kept isolated from other atrocities in history. To remember what happened to the six million Jews, I said, served no important purpose unless it aroused indignation, anger, action against all atrocities, anywhere in the world " (Zinn 1999).

Numerous atrocities akin to the Holocaust have been committed against mostly people of color over the last five centuries. The genocide and apparent extinction of the indigenous people of Tasmania, with the death of Truganini in 1876 is one example of the atrocities committed against native peoples by white settlers during early periods of colonization (Alexander 2006).

In 2008, Stanford University researchers estimated that the Americas had 40–80 million native peoples when European explorers arrived in the late fifteenth century. Within a very short period of time, 90% of the native peoples died because of their lack of immunity to European diseases, such as small box, influenza and measles, or were killed by the invaders. The sudden demise of these indigenous inhabitants in such large numbers resulted in rapid reforestation of the Americas and the reduction in the amount of carbon dioxide in the atmosphere. This engendered the "little ice age" that Europe experienced from 1500 to 1750 (Yirka 2011). The British used "germ warfare" against native peoples by deliberating infecting them with small pox (Dixon 2005).

It has been pointed out that in Australia there are numerous statues and war memorials in large and small cities and towns but there is no such commemoration of the war of conquest over Aboriginal peoples. A campaign to exterminate indigenous communities settled in Australia for over 65,000 years took place between 1788 and 1872. It is estimated that over 500 massacres occurred mainly by white settlers of aborigines and 250 massacre sites have been identified by researchers (Wahlquist 2018) and were rarely investigated, and no one was prosecuted for their homicide. The deaths in custody of first nation people continued after the 1991 Royal Commission of Inquiry in Aboriginal Deaths in Custody (Allam et al. 2018).

As noted earlier, slavery and colonialism have been pivotal in the evolution and inculcation of racist attitudes and behaviors. These will be addressed in the following section.

The Ideology of Racism

Although it is now accepted by nearly all scholars of human populations and biology that *Homo sapiens* evolved in sub-Saharan Africa over 250,000 years ago and spread over the rest of the world in the following centuries mixing with other varieties of local human species, there have been the purveyors of multiple origins of the human species. The later have argued that Europeans (Caucasians) evolved separately from black, yellow, and brown people. Another line of argument by other pseudoscientists of race is that white people are at a higher stage of evolution than black and colored people, or that the latter are degenerated races (see discussion on Yeboah 1988, 55 and 64).

Beyond these types of racial thinking, the ideology of racism derived from five sources. The first has its origins in the prejudice and treatment of the European peasantry or serfs by those who lorded over them. Those who labored in the fields and did menial work were deemed to be inferior breeds of humanity whose station in life was to toil and serve those whose station in life placed them in upper echelons of society. They were regarded for many centuries by the aristocracy, clergy, and commercial classes with "contempt, derision and fear" (Davis 1991, 180). They were deemed to be intellectually inferior, of loose morals, and inclined to have great sexual appetite as seen by the relative number of offsprings they had (a la Malthus) (Caldwell 1998) https://ucmp.berkeley.edu/history/malthus.html. In the earliest period of European settlement of the New World, people from this category were taken as slaves and as indentured laborers.

Second, racism emerged in tandem with the kidnapping, transportation, and the sale of Africans into slavery in the Americas and West Indies. The Atlantic triangular trade began in the sixteenth century and reached its apex in the mid to late nineteenth century. Between 10 million and 15 million were sold into slavery. Much of African stagnated as the continent's able bodied and productive young people were abducted and enslaved (Rodney 1972). Some of the negative stereotypes associated with European serfs were extended to black people and new ones added. Africans were deemed to be an inferior species of human beings closer to apes and monkeys. They were intellectually inferior, indolent, driven by emotions, sexually inclined, dishonest, dependent, and lacked creativity. African man had large penises (Yeboah 1988, 64). (Shakespeare's Othelo alludes to some of these negative qualities of the Moor.) There was Biblical justification provided for the inferiority of serfs as there was for black slaves. For the latter, Noah's curse on Ham permeated to all his descendants who were blacks. Without examining empirical evidence of any kind, a number of prominent European philosophers like Voltaire, Rousseau, David Hume, Immanuel Kant, and Hegel emphatically considered Africans to be inferior. Some of these philosophers maintained that Africans had not built a civilization (Henry 2004; Camara 2005).

The so-called "Polynesian labor trade" involved primarily the kidnapping, shipping, and forced labor of Melanesians from the Solomon Islands, Vanuatu, and islands of Papua New Guinea, as well as Micronesians, namely Ikiribati people, to a number of countries in the Pacific. Prominent among these were Australia (Queensland and New South Wales), Fiji, New Caledonia, and Samoa. Peruvian slavers also descended on Tuvalu to abduct whole villages of their inhabitants to work in guano mines of Peru and Chile. The periodic discovery of skeletal remains of these victims of slavery in Queensland and New South Wales evoked anger among Pacific islanders but also showed to them the systematic discrimination practiced by white planters in these countries against them (Armbruster 2017).

Third, anti-Semitism also appears to have its origins in the Bible, both old and new. The distinction between "God's chosen people," the Jews and Gentiles provided a problematic basis for inclusion and exclusion. Moreover, with Christianity, prejudice, discrimination, and pogroms against Jews were rationalized on the basis that they were the killers of Christ. Negative stereotypes included Jews as misers, money lenders, cunning and crafty, and dishonest. As a distinct religious minority, Jews suffered systematic discrimination over the centuries including violent pogroms in and forced exiles from many parts of Europe. Not unusually this was associated with nationalism and the rise of the modern European states. The Holocaust in Nazi Germany saw the horrific genocide of 6 million Jews in gas chambers of holding concentration camps in Germany and in Poland.

Fourth, European imperialism and colonialism meant the conquest, suppression, and subjugation of people of color in the Americas, Africa, Asia, and the Pacific.

Accompanying these historical events were the notions of Darwinian "natural selection" and "survival of the fittest" to which was added "manifest destiny" as thousands and millions of indigenous people perished with European incursion and invasion. The conquest and occupation of the regions of the Global South was taken as evidence of both European racial superiority and the "white man's burden" to civilize and Christianize the rest of the world. Rampant racism accompanied the wars of appropriation against first nation peoples and European settlement of the Americas, parts of Africa, and Australasia (Zinn 1999; Davidson and Scarr 1970). Nuclear colonialism in many ways reflected the little regard for the well-being and lives of Micronesians, Tahitians, and aboriginal Australians by the United States, France, and Britain (Winchester 2015; MacLellan).

The fifth source of racist thinking and ideology derives from language and particularly the English language (and extends to other European languages). Language was (and is) an extremely portent ground for the evolution of racist thinking and practice. Fundamentally, the color black is associated with the devil and evil, and just about everything else that is bad and unpleasant, "black death," black list, black market, black arts, black magic, black Friday, and black attire associated with mourning and death. By contrast, the color "white" is associated with purity and good things, even lies could be made light with the reference to "white lies."

Sixth, racial and ethnic stereotypes and prejudices are to be found in most countries, including postcolonial states where certain groups who may physically appear to be similar have a history of competition and conflict often manufactured by divide and rule policies of the former colonizing power and/or by local dominant groups. These stereotypes, prejudices, and competitive relationship have led to horrific violence with scores of thousands being killed for instance during the partition of British India, in the "Biafran war" in Nigeria, and in the genocide in Rwanda. They also have fueled the long-standing conflict in Northern Ireland, Sri Lanka, and Kashmir. Black and colored people have expressed their racism in recent times towards to immigrants in South Africa and India.

The active recruitment of labor to work in colonial plantations and mines and the encouragement of the immigrant laborers to settle in the colonies together with bringing together diverse nationalities, ethnicities, and "tribes" in colonial states created complex multiethnic societies including the so-called plural societies. In nearly all these states, there have been issues relating to interethnic relations and systemic discrimination against minorities. The discrimination can be based on language, religion, physical appearance, and ethnic identity more generally.

Racism in the Contemporary World

Over the last 300 years, countries of the world have become increasingly diverse, although there have been counter trends as well. For instance, Argentina's African inhabitants have diminished quite markedly over the last century. "The demographic shift has been sharp. In 1800, on the eve of revolution with Spain, blacks made up more than a third of the country, 69,000 of a total population of 187,000, according to George Reid Andrews's 2004 book *Afro-Latin America*. In 2010, 150,000 identified themselves as Afro-Argentine, or a mere 0.365 percent of a population of 41 million people, according to the census, the first in the country's history that counted race" (Luongo 2014). Currently, it could be argued that virtually all the 193 member states of the United Nations are multiethnic. The diversities in nearly all states have been the outcome of population migration as well as the political incorporation of culturally diverse groups by emergent states (Castles 2000; Stavenhagen 1996). The United States is perhaps the most culturally diverse country in the world with nationalities and ethnic groups from numerous parts of the planet. Even the most apparently homogenous countries of the world such as Japan and Samoa have minorities.

Racism based on discriminatory treatment by dominant groups is as widespread as the ubiquity of multiethnic societies. The concept has cognitive and behavioral dimensions. Stereotypes both negative (prejudice) and positive exist in ethnic (and racial groups). These originate in socialization, and experience including through the exposure to mass media with its portrayal of those who are different in appearance and who may have different cultures. Behavioral dimension of racism is usually associated with relative power and the capacity to discriminate against those of different ethnicity or "race." When such discrimination is systemic, the term institutionalized racism is used to distinguish it from inter-personal discrimination. A "culture of racism" exists in Britain and indeed in many countries of the world. As racial discrimination and racist behavior has at its core unequal power relations, such practices are found in wealthy countries that have drawn migrant laborers, and by those who comprise the dominant groups and classes in societies. In the notions of "old" and "new racism," distinction is drawn between the expression of open prejudice and discriminatory treatment of black people by whites of the period before the 1980s to more subtle forms in the last 30–40 years.

"Old" and "New" Racism

Basically, "old" racism denotes open forms of discrimination which in their extreme manifestation were seen in state-sponsored racism of Jim Crow, USA, and Apartheid South Africa. Prejudiced and racist behavior by whites were openly expressed, condoned, and even encouraged by law. With the Civil Rights Movement and the enactment of the Civil Rights Act (1964), open segregation, discrimination in education, employment, housing and in access to public utilities and services were proscribed in the United States. However, it is maintained that more subtle forms of racism continued and these are labelled "new racism." The opposition to affirmative action for Afro-Americans and other disadvantaged groups and the claims of "reverse racism" in a supposed social context of "equal opportunities" for all are perceived as new racism. The empirical evidence from countries where there has been a history of racism show that both institutionalized discrimination and interpersonal expression of prejudice continue to exist, and in some contexts thrive.

In the early twenty-first century nationalism, xenophobia and racism have been on the rise in Europe and the United States. These have been especially manifest in the response to the exodus of refugees and asylum seekers who traveled, including on foot to European country borders during the wars in Syria and Afghanistan, and the campaign for Brexit and its aftermath (Gayle 2018). But all European countries and especially those states that have been former colonial powers have deeply ingrained "cultures of racism" which is manifested at institutional and individual racist practices. This is reinforced by extreme right, neo-Nazi groups, and nationalistic political parties. As noted by other scholars, racism becomes amplified during times of economic crisis and wanes when the economic performance of European states is on the rise. Globalization, demographic changes, and the arrival of refugees and asylum seekers have given rise to a siege mentality among Europeans in a number of countries including Britain, France, Denmark, and Germany.

Institutionalized racism has been evident over and over again by the slowness of police in investigating and prosecuting perpetrators of hate crimes and violence against minority black and colored communities, and by police practice that has disproportionately targeted these communities. Police in Europe and the United States have a proclivity to stop, question, and search a disproportionate number of black persons. Criminal justice systems have been largely used to penalize individuals and groups from minority communities. A combination of institutional and individual racism has undermined minority access to education, employment, health, housing, and welfare. The "race riots" of the 1970s and 1980s, and in 2001 in the cities of United Kingdom, and subsequently in other European cities bought to the fore issues relating to how dominant communities, local governments, and central state institutions had been discriminating against minorities.

Race Relations and Anti-racist Struggles

With the rise of tensions and overt conflicts exemplified by demonstrations, riots, and response to police brutality and white racism in the United Kingdom, policies to dialogue and co-opt black community organizations and leaders become widespread. Although some scholars pointed out that the issue of racism and exclusion of minorities lay with the dominant group, and this is what has given rise to the "race problem," a number of local and national level initiatives led to the growth of race relations bodies. Some of these entities have been well funded and have been involved in promoting dialogue, reconciliation, mediation, and tolerance between whites and blacks. However, both institutionalized and interpersonal racism is deeply entrenched and racism continues in the United Kingdom (Sivanandan 1991).

Opposition to racism has been undertaken by both those who have been its victims as well as those who opposed social injustices committed on racial grounds. The decimation of indigenous peoples the world over was opposed by individual Europeans, some were clergy men. Slave uprisings were common in the Caribbean region and there were white individuals who opposed slavery. In the nineteenth century, the abolition of slavery movement gained traction with the changing demands of capitalist enterprises. Slavery came to an end in the British Empire in the 1830s, and the American Civil War ended slavery in the United States in 1865. The French ended slavery in their colonies in late 1840s and Brazil did so in 1888. Other forms of forced labor were to follow as for example the Indian Indenture Labour System (Tinker 1974).

However, racial equality was severely undermined during the late nineteenth century and well into the 1960s by Jim Grow laws in the southern states of the United States, colonialism in the Global South, the emergence of Apartheid in South Africa, and the color bar against the Windrush generation and their Asian counterparts in Britain. Responding to Enoch Powell's racist anti-immigration campaigns the British government enacted its first immigration legislation beginning in the 1960s which was eventually followed by the Immigration Act of 1971 and the Nationality Act of 1981. These sought both to encouraged black people to return to their countries of origins but also to restrict possibilities of long-term migration to Britain. Australia put in place a white Australia policy following its federation in 1901. Anti-racist struggles have been underway in North America, Europe, and South Africa for much of the twentieth and early twenty-first centuries. The American Civil Rights Movement led by Dr. Martin Luther King helped confront the openly racist system of segregation found in the southern states of the United States. The fight against racism continues in the post-Obama era with the "Black Lives Matter" movement in the United States. Far too many Afro-Americans, and especially young men are being killed by police in the United States.

The African National Congress with Nelson Mandela at its helm and their allies engaged in a peaceful campaign and an armed struggle to end Apartheid in South Africa. The internal struggle within South Africa was accompanied by a powerful international movement that finally led to the collapse of the racist regime. While racism persists in Britain and other European states, people of color and progressive white people have continued their struggle against institutional and interpersonal racism. Increasingly, this struggle has extended to campaigns against Islamophobia, as well as against the reemergence of anti-Semitism.

Conclusion

Racism is a socially constructed discourse and practice that has emerged over time and space. It is historically linked to anti-Semitism, slavery, colonialism, and contemporary national immigration policies of countries of the Global North. In fact, one could argue that the international division of labor itself reflects the long history of racism at the global level. The rise of right wing white neo-Nazi organizations and the apparent willingness of individuals with extremists believes to engage in extreme violence armed with semiautomatic weapons as well as using motor vehicles to run over people are contemporary phenomenon.

Racism is not limited to white people only as negative stereotyping but prejudice and discrimination are also found among people of color. The treatment of Dalits, Muslims, and other minorities in India remains a matter of concern for human rights defenders. The Chinese state has suppressed minorities such as Tibetans and Uighurs. Discrimination and interethnic tensions and conflict are to be found in most postcolonial states in Africa, Asia, South and Central America, the Caribbean, and the Pacific. Anti-Chinese riots have occurred in Tonga and the Solomon Islands, and Fiji has experienced political turmoil and four military coups that have featured indigenous Fijians and Indo-Fijians.

Clearly the wide prevalence and ubiquity of racism and the struggles to counter it means that no single paper or book can provide in-depth coverage of its many features, manifestations, and consequences.

References

Alexander A (2006) Truganini, Centre for Tasmanian Historical Studies. http://www.utas.edu.au/library/companion_to_tasmanian_history/T/Truganini htm
Alkire WH (1977) An introduction to the peoples and customs of Micronesia, 2nd edn. Cummings Publishing, Menlo Park
Allam L Wahlquist C, Banister J, Herbert M (2018) Indigenous Australian Deaths in Custody. https://www.theguardian.com/australia-news/ng-interactive/2018/aug/28/deaths-inside-indigenous-australian-deaths-in-custody
Armbruster S (2017) Islander graves rediscovered on 150th anniversary of 'sugar slave' trade. https://www.sbs.com.au/news/islander-graves-rediscovered-on-150th-anniversary-of-sugar-slave-trade
Banton M (1967) Race relations. Basic Books, New York
Caldwell JC (1998) Malthus and the less developed world: the pivotal role of India. Popul Dev Rev 24(4):675–696. See also https://ucmp.berkeley.edu/history/malthus.html
Camara B (2005) The falsity of Hegel's theses on Africa. J Black Stud 36(1):82–96
Castles S (2000) Ethnicity and globalisation. Sage Books, London
Cohen P (1999) New ethnicities, old racism. Zed Books, London
Cox OC (1948) Class, caste and race. Doubleday, New York
Davidson JW, Scarr D (1970) Pacific Island portraits. In: Canberra: Australian National University press
Davis FJ (1991) Who is black? One nation's definition. https://www.pbs.org/wgbh/pages/frontline/shows/jefferson/mixed/onedrop.html
Dixon D (2005) Never come to peace again: Pontiacs uprising and the fate of the British empire in North America. University of Oklahoma Press, Oklahoma
Fredrickson GM (2002) Racism a short history. Scribe Publications, Melbourne
Gordon S (2008) When Asia was the world. Da Capo Press, Philadephia
Gayle D (2018) UK has seen 'Brexit-related' growth in racism, says UN representative. https://www.theguardian.com/politics/2018/may/11/uk-has-seen-brexit-related-growth-in-racism-says-un-representative
Henry P (2004) Between Hume and Cugoano: race, ethnicity and philosophical entrapment. J Specul Philos, New Series 18(2):129–148. Identity and Ethnicity (2004)
Ince OU (2017) Adam Smith, settler colonialism and cosmopolitan overstretch. Singapore Management University, Singapore. https://ink.library.smu.edu.sg/cgi/viewcontent.cgi?article=1017&context=soss_research_all
Luongo MT (2014) Argentina rediscovers its African roots, New York Times (12 September), http://www.mixedracestudies.org/?tag=afro-argentines
Muller-Willie, S (2014/2015) Race and history: comments from an epistemological point of view. Sci Technol Human Values 39(4):597–606. https://doi.org/10.1177/0162243913517759
Palat RA 1998 'Warne, Waugh and Western Hypocrisy'. New Zealand Herald (16 December)

Rex J (1983) Race relations in sociological theory. Routledge and Kegan Paul, London
Rodney W (1972) How Europe underdeveloped Africa. Bogle-L'Ouverture Publications, London
Sivanandan A (1982, 1991) A different hunger. London: Pluto Press
Smith A (1811) The works of Adam Smith, LL.D., vol 3. London/Edinbugh. https://books.google.com.fj/books?id=DFpZAAAAcAAJ&pg=PA459&lpg=PA459&dq=adam+smith,+enabled+to+commit+every+sort+of+injustice+in+those+remote+countries%E2%80%9D&source=bl&ots=3Fm8R3sEOB&sig=ACfU3U0e9-_6FwYEnmRHapTqU2HMLM59FA&hl=en&sa=X&ved=2ahUKEwiyxpTvqabhAhXRWisKHbIqA04Q6AEwA3oECAcQAQ#v=onepage&q=ad am%20smith%2C%20enabled%20to%20commit%20every%20sort%20of%20injustice%20in%20those%20remote%20countries%E2%80%9D&f=false
Stavenhagen R (1996) Ethnic conflicts and the nation state. Macmillan Press, London
Thompsell A (2018) In the Apartheid state of South Africa (1949–1994), your racial classification was everything. https://www.thoughtco.com/racial-classification-under-apartheid-43430
Tinker H (1974) A New System of Slavery The Export of Indain Labour Overseas, 1830–1920, Hansib Publications, London
Wahlquist C (2018) Evidence of 250 massacres of indigenous Australian mapped. https://www.theguardian.com/australia-news/2018/jul/27/evidence-of-250-massacres-of-indigenous-australians-mapped
Winchester S (2015) Pacific: the ocean of the future. William Collins, London
Yeboah SK (1988) The ideology of racism. Hansib Publishing Limited, London
Yirka B (2011) Research team suggests European Little Ice Age came about due to reforestation in New World. https://phys.org/news/2011-10-team-european-ice-age-due.html
Zinn H (1999) Respecting the Holocaust. Third World Traveler. http://www.thirdworldtraveler.com/Zinn/RespectingHolocaust.html

Media and Stereotypes 23

Tara Ross

Contents

Introduction	398
Mainstream Media Representations of Racial and Ethnic Minorities	400
News Media	400
Popular Media	403
Media Effects	405
Ethnic Media, Representation, and Stereotypes	406
Conclusion	410
Cross-References	411
References	411

Abstract

Mass media have huge reach in society and are a key filter through which people learn about each other, yet countless studies demonstrate that these media continue to reproduce ethnic and racial stereotypes, with often harmful effects. In various mediums – news, drama, and gaming – ethnic minority groups are typically marginalized and overlooked. Very often, when they are represented, they are shown only in narrowly stereotyped roles, such as the model Asian migrant or the exotic Latina, or depicted negatively as the problematic "other," disproportionately represented as violent or criminal, and "less than" dominant groups (i.e., less intelligent, less wealthy, less powerful). Ethnic minority media – that is, media produced by and for ethnic minority groups – generally offer more positive representations and a counter narrative to mainstream stereotypes but can also be prone to narrow typecasting and stereotype. The resulting pervasiveness of stereotyped representations across media formats and type is partly the outcome of complex media production processes, norms and values, commercial

T. Ross (✉)
University of Canterbury, Christchurch, New Zealand
e-mail: tara.ross@canterbury.ac.nz

© The Author(s), under exclusive license to Springer Nature Singapore Pte Ltd. 2019
S. Ratuva (ed.), *The Palgrave Handbook of Ethnicity*,
https://doi.org/10.1007/978-981-13-2898-5_26

drivers, and a lack of ethnic minority media producers. Nonetheless, their impact, though hard to measure, is potentially significant. Mass media play a role in shaping collective identities and intergroup attitudes and, by typecasting certain groups, distort the picture that audiences see of different groups. There is evidence to suggest these skewed media representations can not only promote public hostility toward other ethnic groups but also lower ethnic minority individuals' self-esteem. As a result, research into ways to combat stereotypes and promote more positive representations in the media is critical.

Keywords
Media · Ethnic media · News · Stereotype · Audiences

Introduction

When it comes to the representation of different groups and the reproduction of racial and ethnic stereotypes, the media matter – partly because they are a key filter through which groups learn about each other. It is impossible for us to interact with everyone directly and much of what we know or understand about one another is often mediated by news and popular media. Coupled with the massive reach of mass media that makes these media powerful social agents.

Not surprisingly then, they are also the subject of close study. In terms of ethnicity and the media, a dominant line of research has concentrated on media content and representational problems in relation to the use of racialized stereotypes, systematic under- and misrepresentation of minority ethnic groups, and the marginalization of minority media producers. Media scholars have drawn on theorists such as Michel Foucault (1980), Stuart Hall (1980, 1996), and others to theorize the connections between these mediated constructions of difference and structures of power and/or structural inequalities (Jedlowski and Thomas 2017), essentially arguing that the media are, if not a source of dominant ideas about race and ethnicity, at least highly influential in structuring social ideas about race and ethnicity (van Sterkenburg et al. 2010). That is partly due to the media's role in constructing and reaffirming stereotypes – McLaughlin et al (2018, p.4) note that the more a stereotype is repeated in media content, the more it becomes naturalized and can influence the ways individuals think about different groups. Much of the existing research tends to privilege the analysis of Western representations of "its" others, and research on non-Western societies' representations, particularly of other non-Western societies, is much rarer (Jedlowski and Thomas 2017, p. 64). This chapter attempts to address some of that bias but is limited by the paucity of literature on ethnic groups and the media, particularly in relation to Africa, Latin America, parts of Asia, and the Indian subcontinent (Matsaganis et al. 2011, p. 265).

To understand how and why stereotypical representations are reproduced, it is useful to look not just at theories of communication, but also at the characteristics of media industries, as their occupational routines and structures play a key part in shaping what we see and hear in media content. In terms of news media, for instance, scholars have demonstrated how the use of news values to select and prioritize what is news, along with news routines and professional norms of objectivity, has tended to advance dominant views and values and marginalize ethnic minorities (Cottle 2000). News media play a key role in reaffirming unequal power relations in society by systematically over-accessing people in powerful and privileged institutional positions – officials, experts, politicians – often to the detriment of alternative viewpoints. Budget and resource constraints often mean little attention is devoted to searching for noninstitutional voices or viewpoints (ibid.), and some issues are overlooked. For example, the time constraints of deadline-driven newsrooms make it easier to focus on *what* happened rather than *why*, ruling out the deeper political and economic analysis that is needed to understand longstanding structural inequalities (Abel 2004). Commercial pressures – the drive to attract maximum audiences and thereby advertising revenue – mean stories tend to be centered on the middle ground of dominant (often White) opinion and interests, and the lack of diversity in many newsrooms means they tend to reflect the experiences and assumptions of a largely White, middle-class workforce (ibid.).

Erigha's (2015) overview of research on inequalities in Hollywood film and television production, for example, demonstrates how a lack of representation within the ranks of media producers has led to stereotypes and a lack of diversity in entertainment media content. She cites studies that show Hollywood to be a predominantly White sphere, where racial and ethnic minorities are highly underrepresented in various roles, including acting, writing, and directing: Black filmmakers directed only 7% of all theatrically released Hollywood films between 2000 and 2011; more than half of theatrical films had casts that were 10% or less minority; and writing occupations showed similar patterns of White over-representation and minority under-representation (ibid., p. 81). This matters, because the structural inequalities of media production play out in on-screen representations. Smith and Choueiti's 2011 study of 100 top-grossing Hollywood films in 2008 (cited in Erigha 2015, p. 86) showed that an absence of ethnic minorities behind the scenes corresponded with fewer and less empowered characters on-screen, while greater diversity behind the scenes positively impacted the quality of on-screen images. And it is not just an issue of numerical under-representation. It is also an issue of representational quality, that is, the kinds of roles that people occupy. Typically, ethnic minorities are limited to narrow roles and genres: actors are typically cast in stereotyped and racialized roles, directors and writers are similarly typecast in ethnic genres, and ethnic minorities are less likely to belong to core talent agencies or major studios. (ibid., p. 82). Recent figures suggest the picture may be getting worse, with the Directors Guild of America (2018) annual study of US feature films finding ethnic diversity has dipped to a new low. In 2017, only 10% of the 651 films measured were led by directors of color – down 3% on the previous year, and the lowest figure since the guild began its reporting in 2013.

Given our media-saturated lifestyles – and the potential for media to shape views on diverse groups – it is important, therefore, that we examine closely the media's role in the production and reproduction of racial and ethnic stereotypes and the quality of their content (Mastro 2015, p. 3).

Mainstream Media Representations of Racial and Ethnic Minorities

Whether you look at primetime television, newspapers, TV news, advertising, film, sports, or videogames, Mastro (2015) says media representations have generally been unfavorable toward racial/ethnic minorities. In the United States, numerous scholars have documented problematic media depictions of Native Americans, Arab Americans, Asian Americans, and Hispanic and Latino minorities (Schneeweis and Foss 2017, p. 1147). Elsewhere, scholars have documented problems with media depictions of immigration as a threat and the framing of ethnic relations in terms of problems or within discourses of "us" and "them" that reproduce the power of dominant groups.

Though the media representation of ethnic minorities has tended largely to be negative, representations have differed across different mediums, such as news, drama, and video games. Depending on people's media consumption, Mastro (2015, p. 3) says that can distort the picture people see of different racial/ethnic groups. For example, while the representation of Blacks in US primetime entertainment television has improved over time, print and television news continues to portray them as violent and criminal. Similarly, the portrayal of Latinos in dramas has improved, but their portrayal in sitcoms is still problematic (ibid.). As such, audiences who follow one form and not another will get a more or less distorted view. This is particularly important when it comes to the news format. How mainstream news media portray ethnic minorities deserves particular attention, because audiences' belief in the news media's supposed objective presentation of information means they are even more likely to view them as reliable sources of information about different ethnic groups. Yet media scholarship demonstrates repeated problems with the representation of ethnic minorities in news media.

News Media

International research shows that news reports routinely use criminalizing language when reporting on ethnic minorities and that ethnic and racial minorities are routinely over-represented as criminals or perpetrators compared to dominant racial groups (Dukes and Gaither 2017, p. 790; Ewart and Beard 2017, p. 169). In Australia, researchers have shown how news media have portrayed Lebanese Australians as violent and criminal or as terrorists; Chinese Australians as illegal immigrants; and Sudanese Australians as criminal, deviant and the perpetrators rather than victims of serious violent crimes. The most frequent categorization for stories involving an ethnic minority was crime (Ewart and Barnes 2017). Foster et al. (2011) tracked the ways in which the Australian press wrote about Arabs, Muslims, and Islam and demonstrated a reliance on xenoracist stereotypes and "them"/"us" dichotomies that essentialized and simplified what it meant to be Arab or Muslim. In New Zealand, mainstream news media have tended to depict Muslims as terrorists, Pacific peoples as unmotivated, unhealthy and "criminal others," and indigenous

Māori as under-achievers involved in conflict, violence, or crime (Allen and Bruce 2017, p. 227). These representations can add up to a picture of crime and danger for whole neighborhoods or areas. Allen and Bruce's study of news media coverage of the mostly ethnic Pacific community of South Auckland revealed it was depicted primarily as a place of violence and crime. More than a third of news articles focused on crime, amounting to a higher proportion of crime-related stories than the highest level reported in an international meta-analysis of crime reporting (Allen and Bruce 2017, p. 238).

More significantly, research also shows that these skewed media representations can promote public hostility toward ethnic minority groups. Dukes and Gaither (2017) write that Blacks are less likely to be depicted as victims of crime than Whites, and when they are shown as victims they are often demonized and criminalized. They cite Smiley and Fakunle's 2016 content analysis of media coverage of the deaths of six unarmed Black men by law enforcement (ibid., p. 791). That study found news stories focused on the victims' behavior as criminal, their physical stature and attire, and the location where they were killed or lived as crime-ridden and impoverished, and they included negative, stereotypical elements about the victims' lifestyles (ibid.). In their own 2017 study, they found that the type of information reported about shooting victims significantly shaped not just people's sympathy and empathy for victims but also how people attributed blame and recommended punishment. When negative Black stereotypical information was given about a shooting victim, they found that it significantly colored those victims as being more at fault for their own deaths.

Most often, these representations are not deliberate – most journalists do not go to work aiming to slander an entire ethnic group. Instead, these stereotypes are often the result of unconscious bias and newsroom pressures. Within the demands of live, 24/7 real-time news production, journalists often have little time to review their work, which raises the risk that they might fall back on – and reinforce – widely circulating stereotypes. For example, in 2012 ESPN sacked a journalist (and suspended another) after he used the loaded headline "chink in the armor" in a mobile news story about the under-performance of rising Asian-American basketball star Jeremy Lin. Jason Fry (2012) says the reporter was working in the middle of the night, virtually alone (the mobile team operated without a copy editor and the only other journalist working alongside him was too busy to double-check his work) and at speed. Better practice would be to allow time to step back and deliberate over content, but as-live production allows little room for that. Indeed, various content analyses of live sport media commentary, which is similarly produced at speed and with fewer opportunities for considered reflection, reveal a pattern of crude stereotypes that might be different if content was produced in a less time-pressured way. For instance, one study found live football commentators gave White players more play-related praise and represented them in a more positive light than Black players, and depicted Black athletes as naturally gifted and strong compared with White athletes, who tended to be depicted as intelligent and hard-working (van Sterkenburg et al. 2010, p. 822).

So, there are clearly problems with how news media portray ethnic minorities. There are problems, too, with *how often* they portray them. Ethnic minorities are often overlooked and even rendered invisible in mainstream news media, which limits the resources that members of these groups can draw on to build a secure sense of identity and community. Ewart and Beard's (2017) overview of Australian literature found that the continuing marginalization of ethnic minorities was a significant feature of the Australian mediascape. They cited Phillips' 2011 study of current affairs stories, which found that of 209 stories, 139 had no ethnic minority faces at all, not even incidentally in the background (cited in Ewart and Beard 2017, p. 173). ter Wal et al. (2005) noted similar patterns of erasure in European Union and Dutch domestic news media, where they found that, even in stories *about* ethnic minorities, majority ethnic subjects appeared more often as the main news actors than minorities themselves – and ethnic minorities were underrepresented in reports about politics and government and in the role of politicians and professionals, and overrepresented in crime news.

Overall, news media representations of ethnic minorities have tended to be negative. However, they are also crosscut with other dominant constructions – about class, gender, sexuality, and so on – and as such there are differences in how different groups are portrayed, with some treated more negatively than others. van Doorn's (2015) analysis of racial and ethnic patterns in the US newsweeklies' pictorial coverage of poverty found the poor were disproportionately represented as Black. His study found that the composition of coverage was well out of step with the actual demographics of poverty: Blacks were overrepresented by more than a factor of two (and overrepresented in stories about welfare and stories that were unsympathetic to the poor), while Hispanics were underrepresented, making up less than 10% of newsweekly pictorial content but 21% of US welfare recipients. Elsewhere, Stamps (2017, p. 410) argues that the news media's routine focus on poor African American families (despite the fact they make up less than 26% of welfare recipients in the USA) means many people understand welfare to be an African American issue.

van Doorn's analysis of pictorial coverage (2015) usefully highlights the importance of the visual, as opposed to just textual dimensions of media content. By analyzing a major US daily newspaper's photographs for emotion, Rodgers et al. (2007) were able to pick up subtle differences in the way different ethnic groups have been framed. They found the average African American was visually portrayed as happy, excited, and submissive, while the average Latino and Asian American was seen as sad, calm, and submissive. The authors argued that these images reinforced to readers that this was what ethnic minorities should be like and, by framing them as emotionally calm or submissive, these messages helped readers to understand the operation of power in US society. Elsewhere, Harrison et al. (2016) have shown how the visual representation of Chinese in South Africa has both simplified and exaggerated the stereotypes found in media texts. Interestingly, they also found evidence of the ways in which visual messages could *subvert* stereotypes – by humanizing, rather than labeling, ethnic minority actors.

As with the intersection of ethnicity and class, the intersection of dominant ideologies about race/ethnicity and gender has generated different stereotypes. An analysis of gendered race representations in popular American magazines

(Schug et al. 2017) found that, relative to the proportions of Whites, Asians depicted in the magazines were more likely to be women and Blacks were more likely to be men. In this way, Asians were stereotyped as more feminine and Blacks as masculine, and those who did not fit the prototype – Asian men and Black women – were rendered largely invisible (ibid., p229). The authors argued (ibid., p. 230) that the type of discrimination faced by people who were deemed prototypical and nonprototypical clearly differed, and where previous research suggested that individuals who matched their group prototypes face more discrimination (e.g., Black men), nonprototypical groups, such as those who did not match the gendered race stereotype, might also suffer from discrimination in the form of invisibility.

Popular Media

Many of the stereotypes we see depicted in news media are echoed in other entertainment media, such as popular film and television, comedy, reality television, and video games. Tyree's study (Tyree 2011) of ten reality television shows airing in the USA between 2005 and 2008 found all ten shows had at least one stereotyped African American participant. More than half of the shows' African American participants fit the characteristics of a stereotype, and African American participants were often catalysts in arguments, disagreements, and physical altercations with other Black and White participants. Tyree said that added up to a significant reinforcement of negative stereotypes by a genre that played a major role in shaping pop culture (ibid., p. 409).

Latinos are the largest ethnic minority in the United States (comprising about 16% of the population), yet account for less than 10% of prime-time television portrayals – and those portrayals are often limited to crime dramas and sitcoms, thereby typecasting a group in narrow ways (Martinez and Ramasubramanian 2015, p. 210). On a positive note, Guzman and Valdivia (2010) write that strong demand from US ethnic audiences for more inclusive programming had increased the production of more diverse film and television shows in terms of race, ethnicity, gender, and class (though programming continued to include homogenizing discourses and problematic stereotypes, such as Latina/o tropes of tropicalism (bright colors, rhythmic music, and brown or olive skin) and sexual availability and exoticism).

This kind of narrow typecasting and "othering" remains a problem in popular media, not just in the USA but also internationally. Jedlowski and Thomas' (2017) study of Ethiopian popular films found Chinese characters were depicted often negatively as the "other" and in ways that reinforced closed definitions of what it meant to be African. Donovan (2017) found similar othering of Chinese migrants in Spanish film and media, where they were portrayed as both the racialized "other" and as a threat to the Spanish way of life. Elsewhere, Cabanes' (2014) analysis of entertainment media in Manila found a racially hierarchical view of both Filipino subjects and other ethnic groups: Depictions of local Filipinos who were so-called Mestizo (light- and fair-skinned) were privileged over those who were brown- or dark-skinned, and depictions of the city's Indians and Koreans (which tended to marginalize these groups) similarly valorized lighter-skinned Koreans over darker-skinned Indians.

Racial and ethnic stereotyping is also evident in interactive, participatory media, such as video games, but in these forms media stereotyping is further complicated by the fuzzy line between what we understand to be real and/or virtual. Burgess et al.'s (2011) multipart study of race in video games found overt racial stereotyping was common. In their content analysis of top-selling video game magazines, they found that minority men were generally underrepresented when compared with US Census and gamer demographics but overrepresented as thugs using extreme guns, and also as athletes (compared with White males who were almost exclusively portrayed using technology). Their content analysis of video game covers found that minority men were again underrepresented, and when they were present, they were more likely than White males to be portrayed as athletes or as aggressive, and less likely to be depicted using technology or in military combat. This last point is an interesting one. The study's authors noted that not a single minority was portrayed in a socially sanctioned (i.e., military) setting, and where 51% of aggressive minorities were depicted in fighting scenes, only 37.8% of Whites were, adding up to a picture where Blacks were more likely to be engaged in illicit rather than socially sanctioned aggression (ibid., p.297). The authors concluded (ibid., p. 303) that video games taught a number of stereotypes:

> Blacks are athletes or unprovoked social menaces with extreme weapons; Asians are martial artists; Hispanics are in short supply. White men fight in fantasy realms or defend their country in heroic war settings. Alien characters outnumber minority males. Women of color are invisible.

Given their interactive and participatory nature, video games pose extra questions for researchers interested in questions of representational bias, because the traditional distinctions that have been drawn between the real and virtual are problematic in this space. Cover (2016) argues that the way we think about film or television – where racial and ethnic difference is seen to be either grounded in the "real" and represented on-screen as "virtual" or represented in the media sphere and then enacted in reality – does not fit interactive gaming. Because gaming involves bodies on-screen or as game-players "who are neither disembodied nor radically separated from those on-screen representations," Cover says we need new ways of understanding issues of race and ethnicity that can account for the performativity of gameplay (ibid., p. 5).

Many of these studies focus on overtly negative stereotypes, but some scholars have drawn attention to the "othering" effect of what might seem on the surface to be "positive" stereotypes. In an analysis of Asian American stereotypes in popular film, Kawai (2005) argues that the stereotype of the "model minority" (i.e., the good migrant) should be considered as simply the benign flipside of the negative "yellow peril" stereotype and, thereby, understood as being just as implicated in racial hostilities and violence toward Asian Americans. Schneeweis and Foss' (2017) analysis of the portrayal of Roma communities in 60 years of US fictional and reality television programs found similar parallels between overtly negative, age-old stereotypes (the ethnic "other," the swindler, the fortune teller) and the contemporary, more politically correct construction of the "misunderstood" Gypsy. In all cases, they were characterized as outsiders, "sometimes feared, sometimes pitied, but always separate from mainstream culture" (ibid., p. 1151). Thus, though there might be differences in character and tone, media stereotypes generally still tend to portray ethnic minorities in ways that are othering and one-dimensional.

Media Effects

The picture, then, is not pretty, but so what? Do these distorted and negative representations have any consequence? That is difficult to answer. Put simply, the processes of representation are complex and do not end with publication. To understand the media's role in stereotyping, we need to also understand audiences and what they do with media, and that is not so easy. Audiencing is a messy concept and, when it comes to ethnic minority audiences, there are relatively few studies to draw on. Early traditions of media effects research focused narrowly on what media did to audiences, painting a picture of media as an all-powerful institution that "injected" a message into a passive audience with direct effects. Theoretical approaches to audiences have moved on since then and alternative approaches have adopted a view of audiences as more active and complex in their uses and interpretation of media. Research into the meaning-making practices of audiences (based on Hall's (1980) suggestion that the meanings embedded in media texts are not necessarily taken up by audiences) has shown that audiences are active producers of meaning. We cannot assume that the meaning intended by media producers – or the unintended meaning buried in their content – is the meaning that will be interpreted by their audiences. Furthermore, audience members' everyday practices are messy and cannot be neatly categorized. The mere fact of having a television switched on does not indicate audience-hood; people interact with television in complex and different ways and their degree of attention, type of watching, and empathy with a program varies (Morley 1990 in Toynbee 2006, p. 123). In fact, audiences are not discrete, homogeneous groups that use media in isolation from everything else in their lives. Cordoning people off by their use of a particular medium or genre – or by categories of "racial" or ethnic grouping – is problematic (Bird 2003), as is isolating their media practice from their everyday practice and context. People slot in and out of a range of media, use multiple forms simultaneously, and interpret meaning based on their familiarity with different media and different socio-cultural contexts. Cultural meanings, including stereotypes, are generated from within the complex messiness of people's lived experience, of which media are just one part.

Notwithstanding these caveats, there is evidence to suggest that mass media play some role, at least, in shaping collective identities and intergroup attitudes. Tyree (2011, p. 399) says television audiences tend to believe that what they watch is a true representation of cultures and people, particularly when they have little or no direct experience with those cultures and people. For example, Schneeweis and Foss (2017, p.1148) cite studies that have found Caucasian people who learn about Latinos from television are much more likely to believe negative stereotypes than those who have personal interaction with Latinos; that heavy viewers of television are more likely to believe ethnic stereotypes than those who watch fewer hours of television; and that fans of television news tend to hold more negative attitudes toward African Americans than light news viewers. Interestingly, in a US national survey measuring participants' exposure to Latina TV characters, McLaughlin et al. (2018) found that exposure was related to more favorable feelings toward Latinas (which they ascribed to the positive portrayal of reoccurring Latina characters) and to higher levels of stereotyped views of Latinas as sexualized and melodramatic (because portrayals, though positive, were frequently one-dimensional and relied on old stereotypes of the emotional, hypersexual Latina). The authors argued (ibid., p.1321) that we need to develop theoretical models that can "account for the complicated manner in which media portrayals produce both positive and negative societal effects" – and do so simultaneously.

As well as playing some role in shaping people's attitudes about others, the media also play some role in shaping beliefs about oneself and one's own group – often negatively. Various studies have shown that exposure to mainstream media stereotypes can lead to lower self-esteem and negative self-concepts (Ramasubramanian et al. 2017; Tukachinsky et al. 2017). In a national US study of the effect of prime-time ethnic stereotypes on Latino and Black Americans, Tukachinsky et al. (2017) analyzed two decades of the most viewed television shows and examined their relationship with Latinos and Blacks' feelings about their own ingroup. They found that negative representations reduced Latinos' and Blacks' warm feelings towards their ingroup, while favorable characterizations contributed to feelings of warmth (ibid., p551). The study's authors concluded that negative media representations might pose a tangible identity threat to ethnic minorities – and they highlighted the critical importance of promoting positive media representations and limiting negative media depictions (ibid.). Other authors have suggested that the media can also shape support for social policy. Sue Abel (2017) says that news media representations of indigenous Māori, which have tended to focus on violence, crime and Māori as a threat to "the nation," have contributed negatively to policy-making in New Zealand. She argues that governments need the goodwill of the majority non-Māori population to put in place policies that might redress the historic wrongs of colonization, but negative attitudes toward Māori, fostered in part by mainstream media, have impeded such legislation.

Ethnic Media, Representation, and Stereotypes

Much of the literature on ethnicity and stereotypes has been focused on ethnic minorities' under- and misrepresentation in mainstream media, but there is a smaller literature on ethnic minority media (i.e., media produced by and for ethnic minorities) that reveals different insights into the relationship between media and stereotypes. There are gaps in that literature – studies of ethnic minority audiences, in particular, are relatively rare, and very few studies have much to say about how people use ethnic media – but various works attempting to pin down the role of ethnic minority media suggest they serve several functions, including combating negative stereotypes and providing a counter-narrative to mainstream media reporting, as well as providing self-representation, that is, "telling one's own story and celebrating one's own culture in one's own way" (Browne 2005, p. 31).

Ethnic media have largely been equated with providing an alternative or counter-narrative to mainstream news. Matsaganis et al. (2011) describe various examples of the ways in which ethnic media have emerged from a community's frustration with its representation in mainstream media and/or served as platforms for an ethnic community's campaigns for voice, social equality and other social and political demands (e.g., South Africa's "homeland" radio stations in the late 1970s and early 1980s, Black and Native American newspapers in the United States, German-Turkish media in Berlin, Aboriginal newspapers in Australia, and Greek media in London). In her work on New Zealand's indigenous TV channel, Māori Television, Smith (2016) says the station's programming has enhanced individual and collective wellbeing by routinely broadcasting strength-based representations of Māori people and things Māori.

Ramasubramanian et al. (2017, p. 1890) write that where the representation of minority members in mainstream media is largely negative, ethnic media have provided minority members with an alternative and relatively more positive source of information about their ethnic identity, "which subsequently make minority members feel more positive and secure about their ethnic identity by increasing their ethnic pride and ethnic performance." However, they note that ethnic media, as with mainstream media, have also marginalized certain groups, for example, lighter-skinned compared with darker skinned members of a group or indigenous voices. Just as in mainstream media, the impact of intersecting identities can lead to the privileging of some identities over others in ethnic minority media.

Some scholars have suggested that ethnic media can also tend to freeze communities in relation to each other and to majority ethnic groups, by enacting representations of ethnicity that are too narrow. A study of New Zealand's Pacific media representations (Ross 2014, 2017) demonstrates the risks of over-simplifying identity in this way. By celebrating and foregrounding certain identities within a group (usually traditional, "authentic" prototypes), ethnic media can reify some identities and marginalize others. A thematic analysis of Pacific ethnic media content revealed that New Zealand's Pacific media tended to privilege migrant identities over hyphenated or New Zealand-born identities, so that what counted as authentically "Pacific" was tightly tied to traditional island "homelands" and villages, and not the urban landscape of New Zealand-born Pacific youth. Many Pacific media producers are aware of this risk and some have taken steps to respond (Ross 2017): A television show was attempting to include Pacific identities that were less rigidly rooted in notions of "home" or tradition; a magazine had embraced a Polynesian identity that was more inclusive of Pacific peoples who also identified as Māori; and a Tongan news website had adopted English language as well as Tongan content to address a diverse audience – and included a dedicated section dubbed "Diasporic Pacific Islanders" for news about Tongans in New Zealand, the United States, Australia, and Tonga, to speak to an emergent, younger Pacific transnational identity.

Notwithstanding these efforts, Pacific media were not free of weaknesses. Key media tended to represent Pacific peoples as athletes (often within the dominant racialized discourse of physical flair versus leadership or strategic ability), performing artists, and church-goers, but not business owners, scientists, or IT professionals (Ross 2014). Interviews with Pacific media producers (Ross 2017) revealed producers aimed to tell "brown" stories in "brown" ways to differentiate from and fill the gaps in mainstream media coverage, but that often set limits on how "Pacificness" could be legitimately performed. So, for instance, a belief in Pacific identity's roots in an ancestral homeland ruled in scripts and representations of grass skirts, sand, and palm trees and ruled out those of the urban Pacific Rim. Indeed, by emphasizing ethnic minority identity in certain ways, the study suggested that ethnic media risked falling back on well-established versions of identity, including racialized versions, thereby paradoxically reproducing the dominant stereotypes found in mainstream media.

Several scholars have raised questions about the extent to which ethnic minority media actually offer an alternative voice to mainstream media by demonstrating that they can be, in fact, a copy of such media. Daniels' (2006) case study of Native American media revealed that, far from producing their own "ethnic" content, some ethnic media republished mainstream content in large quantities – up to 95% of their product. Browne (2005) and Riggins (1992) have similarly noted heavy use of mainstream media content, production values, and styles by ethnic media. Moran's (2006) content analysis of mainstream and Spanish-language television news channels revealed Spanish media followed the conventions of mainstream media, just in a different language. They had similar story types, corporate structures, news values, presentation, focus on profits and even their journalists shared largely the same training. In their book on ethnic media, Matsaganis et al. (2011) noted that mainstream media had even acquired key ethnic media, leading some to suggest that, by losing control over their production practices, those ethnic media would become no different from the mainstream (p. 244).

What this demonstrates is that it is too simplistic to assume that ethnic media producers will produce only progressive representations of their in-group. As already outlined, media content is shaped by many complex factors and the ethnicity of the media producer is only one factor. Perhaps controversially, bell hooks (1996) argues that because they must appeal to mass (White) audiences and/or they have internalized white aesthetics, Black filmmakers' representation of blackness often replicates dominant stereotypes.

> Until both colonizer and colonized decolonize their minds, audiences in white supremacist cultures will have difficulty 'seeing' and understanding the images of blackness that do not conform to the stereotype. (1996, p. 72)

Interestingly, her critique suggests that ethnic audiences also play a part in shaping stereotypical representations. By pushing for more positive images of their group, audiences create a straitjacket for producers' work. hooks contends that in all areas of cultural production in the USA, the work of Black artists, especially filmmakers, has been subject to heavy policing by consumers around whether or not the work is authentic or positive and so on – and that has actually restricted producers' ability to subvert dominant stereotypes.

The role of the audience in co-creating stereotypes is woefully under-studied and an area for further research. In the contemporary Web 2.0 and social media landscape, audiences not only consume media but also create and interact with it, leading some to ask where the boundary can be drawn between audience member and media producer. Strong and Ossei-Owusu (2014) traverse some of these questions in their examination of the YouTube videos (and comment threads) of the Naija Boyz, two Nigerian-born, US-based brothers who became a YouTube hit for their "African Remix" genre of hip hop video parodies. Strong and Ossei-Owusu (ibid., p.194) argue that, on one hand, the Naija Boyz' success demonstrates how the proliferation of new media channels, especially user-generated media like YouTube, has given ethnic minority artists and audiences "unprecedented levels of agency in their production, consumption, and social interaction." However, on the other hand, they suggest that the independence of that media production, which sits outside the traditional institutions of mainstream and ethnic media, has not guaranteed the absence of stereotype. In fact, the brothers' videos and comment threads contain xenophobic discourses and problematic tropes of Africa and black America (e.g., the "true African" vs. the Black American "swagger jacker" or charlatan) that are viewed by some as caricatures (ibid., p. 197). Clearly, neither the ethnicity of media producers nor their independence from traditional media institutions is guarantee against stereotypical representation.

Matsaganis et al. (2011) suggest some ethnic minority media have adopted too narrow a view of their audience – and thereby limited the identities they portray – particularly in relation to language (Smith [2006] offers a similar warning in relation to Māori Television's 'staging' of cultural identity in a way that privileges language fluency). Publishing or broadcasting in an ethnic minority language is seen by many scholars as an important function of cultural maintenance and revival, but it can also act as a threshold – and stereotype – of authenticity that rules in those who "really" belong and those who do not. The authors give the example of the Japanese-American community in the USA, which has low rates of language proficiency, particularly among second- and third-generation Japanese Americans, yet most Japanese-American newspapers are still written primarily in Japanese rather than English, and their circulations have declined as a result.

Johnson (2010) and Mora and Kang (2016) draw on social identity and self-categorization theories to argue that ethnic media play an important role in generating and reinforcing socio-cultural categories. They hypothesize that individuals form and adopt collective or social identities based on processes that accentuate in-group prototypes. In their study of social identity and English-language Latino programs, Mora and Kang (2016, p. 32) found a positive association between the programs' hyphenated and pan-ethnic social identities and the self-worth and ethnic solidarity of their respondents, who were mostly second-plus generation Latina or Latino. Conversely, respondents' self-worth declined when program characters' Latino social identity was identified through an arguably too-narrow, specific ethnic label such as Mexican, Cuban, or Puerto Rican.

These various studies suggest that the range of representations available in ethnic media – and their fit with different ethnic communities' everyday realities – is important. A broad and inclusive range of identities is crucial to how well media representations resonate with ethnic audiences and effectively combat stereotypes. Ramasubramanian et al. (2017, p. 1892) found that ethnic media exposure could mitigate the negative effects of mainstream media stereotypes for ethnic minorities. As such, they argued that as well as addressing negative portrayals of ethnic groups in mainstream media, it was important to nurture alternative spaces where ethnic communities could create, consume, and share their own media: "These alternative mediated spaces can help improve group vitality, boost collective ethnic pride, and increase willingness to engage in ethnic performance for minority groups" (ibid.).

Conclusion

In summary, the media scholarship demonstrates both the vexing pervasiveness of ethnic and racial stereotyping in the media *and* the critical importance of promoting positive media representations and combating negative representations (Tukachinsky et al. 2017). What it is less clear about is how to challenge and change such stereotypical representations. Some have argued that new digital media might provide an effective challenge by enabling spaces for alternative, grass-roots storytelling and a democratization of content from a more diverse range of producers. For example, Guins (2008, cited in Erigha 2015, p. 87) found that artistic practices online offered more racial and gender diversity than traditional media studios, while Erigha (2015) describes evidence that suggests millennials, regardless of race, are more likely than members of previous generations to watch and seek out media by or about people from racial/ethnic groups different from their own. These tendencies may strengthen, she says, as more people drift to the Internet and alternate channels for media content (YouTube, social media, etc.) – and, potentially, compel decision-makers in traditional and dominant media to include more diverse cultural creators and content to compete for audience attention (ibid., p. 88).

Scharrer and Ramasubramanian (2015) argue that the media can either promote or call into question racial and ethnic stereotypes, and there is potential for media to use their influence positively to mitigate the effect of social stereotypes. They cite research that shows exposure to counter-stereotyping exemplars in the media can increase positive attitudes and have a positive effect on intergroup relations. The pair suggest that media literacy efforts, especially with young people, could help to address prejudice and racial bias, promote appreciation for diversity, and foster more nuanced understandings of identity and social groups. Clearly, more research into ways to combat stereotypes and promote more positive representations in the media is critical.

Cross-References

▶ Japanese Representation in Philippine Media
▶ Rewriting the World: Pacific People, Media, and Cultural Resistance

References

Abel S (2004) All the news you need to know? In: Goode L, Zuberi N (eds) Media studies in Aotearoa/New Zealand. Pearson Education, Auckland, pp 183–196
Abel S (2017) Māori, media and politics. In: Bahador B, Kemp G, McMillan K, Rudd C (eds) Politics and the media. Pearson, Auckland, pp 257–271
Allen J, Bruce T (2017) Constructing the other news media representations of a predominantly 'brown' community in New Zealand. Pac Journal Rev 23(1):225–224
Bird S (2003) The audience in everyday life: living in a media world. Routledge, New York
Browne D (2005) Ethnic minorities, electronic media and the public sphere: a comparative approach. Hampton Press, Cresskill
Burgess M, Dill K, Stermer S, Burgess S, Brown B (2011) Playing with prejudice: the prevalence and consequences of racial stereotypes in video games. Media Psychol 14(3):289–311. https://doi.org/10.1080/15213269.2011.596467
Cabanes J (2014) Multicultural mediations, developing world realities: Indians, Koreans and Manila's entertainment media. Media Cult Soc 36(5):628–643
Cottle S (ed) (2000) Ethnic minorities and the media: changing cultural boundaries. Open University Press, Buckingham
Cover R (2016) Digital difference: theorizing frameworks of bodies, representation and stereotypes in digital games. Asia Pac Media Educ 26(1):4–16. https://doi.org/10.1177/1326365X16640322
Daniels G (2006) The role of native American print and online media in the era of big stories: a comparative case study of native American outlets' coverage of the Red Lake shootings. Journalism 7(3):321–342
Directors Guild of America (2018) Available via https://www.dga.org/News/PressReleases/2018/180621-Feature-Film-Director-Diversity-Remained-Low-in-2017.aspx. Accessed 24 June 2018
Donovan M (2017) "Se ríen de la crisis": Chinese immigration as economic invasion in Spanish film and media. Revista de Estudios Hispánicos 51(2):369–393
Dukes K, Gaither S (2017) Black racial stereotypes and victim blaming: implications for media coverage and criminal proceedings in cases of police violence against racial and ethnic minorities. J Soc Issues 73(4):789–807
Ewart J, Beard J (2017) Poor relations: Australian news media representations of ethnic minorities, implications and responses. In: Budarick J, Han G (eds) Minorities and media: producers, industries, audiences. Palgrave Macmillan, London
Erigha M (2015) Race, gender, Hollywood: representation in cultural production and digital media's potential for change. Sociol Compass 9(1):78–89. https://doi.org/10.1111/soc4.12237
Foster N, Cook K, Barter-Godfrey S, Furneaux S (2011) Fractured multiculturalism: conflicting representations of Arab and Muslim Australians in Australian print media. Media Cult Soc 33(4):619–629. https://doi.org/10.1177/0163443711399034
Foucault M (1980) Power/knowledge. Harvester, Brighton

Fry J (2012) How ESPN published "Chink in the Armor" Jeremy Lin headline & what's happened since. Available via Poynter. https://www.poynter.org/news/how-espn-published-chink-armor-jeremy-lin-headline-whats-happened. Accessed 24 June 2018

Guzman I, Valdivia A (2010) Brain, brow, and booty: Latina iconicity in U.S. popular culture. Commun Rev 7(2):205–221. https://doi.org/10.1080/10714420490448723

Hall S (1980) Encoding/decoding. In: Hall S, Hobson D, Lowe A, Willis P (eds) Culture, media, language. Hutchinson, London, pp 128–138

Hall S (1996, c. 1989) New ethnicities. In: Hall S, Morley S, Chen K (eds), Stuart Hall: critical dialogues in cultural studies. Routledge, London, pp 441–449

Harrison P, Yang Y, Moyo K (2016) Visual representations in South Africa of China and the Chinese people. J Afr Cult Stud 29(1):25–45. https://doi.org/10.1080/13696815.2016.1253460

Hooks B (1996) Reel to real: race, sex, and class at the movies. Routledge, New York

Jedlowski A, Thomas M (2017) Representing 'otherness' in African popular media: Chinese characters in Ethiopian video-films. J Afr Cult Stud 29(1):63–80. https://doi.org/10.1080/13696815.2016.1241704

Johnson M (2010) Incorporating self-categorization concepts into ethnic media research. Commun Theory 20(1):106–125

Kawai Y (2005) Stereotyping Asian Americans: the dialectic of the model minority and the yellow peril. Howard J Commun 16(2):109–130. https://doi.org/10.1080/10646170590948974

Martinez A, Ramasubramanian S (2015) Latino audiences, racial/ethnic identification, and responses to stereotypical comedy. Mass Commun Soc 18:209–229. https://doi.org/10.1080/15205436.2014.907427

Mastro D (2015) Why the media's role in issues of race and ethnicity should be in the spotlight. J Soc Issues 71(1):1–16. https://doi.org/10.1111/josi.12093

Matsaganis M, Katz V, Ball-Rokeach S (2011) Understanding ethnic media: producers, consumers, and societies. Sage, Thousand Oaks

McLaughlin B, Rodriguez N, Dunn J, Martinez J (2018) Stereotyped identification: how identifying with fictional Latina characters increases acceptance and stereotyping. Mass Commun Soc 21(5):585–605. https://doi.org/10.1080/15205436.2018.1457699

Mora A, Kang S (2016) English-language Latino themed programming and social identity: the relationship between viewing and self-esteem among Latina/os. Howard J Commun 27(1):16–37

Moran K (2006) Is changing the language enough?: The Spanish language 'alternative' in the USA. Journalism 7(3):389–405

Ramasubramanian S, Doshi M, Saleem M (2017) Mainstream versus ethnic media: how they shape ethnic pride and self-esteem among ethnic minority audiences. Int J Commun 11:1879–1899

Riggins S (1992) Ethnic minority media: an international perspective. Sage, Newbury Park

Rodgers S, Kenix L, Thorson E (2007) Stereotypical portrayals of emotionality in news photos. Mass Commun Soc 10(1):119–138. https://doi.org/10.1080/15205430709337007

Ross T (2014) 'Telling the brown stories': an examination of identity in the ethnic media of multi-generational immigrant communities. J Ethn Migr Stud 40(8):1314–1329. https://doi.org/10.1080/1369183X.2013.831547

Ross T (2017) Locating ourselves: an analysis and theoretical account of strategic practices of identity and connection in Aotearoa/New Zealand's Pacific news media. Unpublished PhD thesis. University of Canterbury, Christchurch

Scharrer E, Ramasubramanian S (2015) Intervening in the media's influence on stereotypes of race and ethnicity: the role of media literacy education. J Soc Issues 71(1):171–185

Schneeweis A, Foss K (2017) "Gypsies, Tramps & Thieves": examining representations of Roma culture in 70 years of American television. J Mass Commun Q 94(4):1146–1117

Schug J, Alt N, Lu P, Gosin M, Fay J (2017) Gendered race in mass media: invisibility of Asian men and black women in popular magazines. Psychol Pop Media Cult 6(3):222–236

Smith J (2006) Parallel quotidian flows: Maori Television on air. New Zealand Journal of Media Studies 9(2):27–35

Smith J (2016) Māori Television: the first ten years. Auckland University Press, Auckland

Strong K, Ossei-Owusu S (2014) Naija boy remix: Afroexploitation and the new media creative economies of cosmopolitan African youth. J Afr Cult Stud 26(2):189–205. https://doi.org/10.1080/13696815.2013.861343

Stamps D (2017) The social construction of the African American family on broadcast television: a comparative analysis of The Cosby Show and Blackish. Howard J Commun 28(4):405–420. https://doi.org/10.1080/10646175.2017.1315688

ter Wal J, d'Haenens L, Koeman J (2005) (Re)presentation of ethnicity in EU and Dutch domestic news: a quantitative analysis. Media Cult Soc 27(6):937–950. https://doi.org/10.1177/0163443705057681

Toynbee A (2006) The media's view of the audience. In: Hesmondhalgh D (ed) Media production. Open University Press, Maidenhead, pp 91–132

Tukachinsky R, Mastro D, Yarchi M (2017) The effect of prime time television ethnic/racial stereotypes on Latino and Black Americans: a longitudinal national level study. J Broadcast Electron Media 61(3):538–556

Tyree T (2011) African American stereotypes in reality television. Howard J Commun 22(4):394–413. https://doi.org/10.1080/10646175.2011.617217

van Doorn B (2015) Pre- and post-welfare reform media portrayals of poverty in the United States: the continuing importance of race and ethnicity. Policy Polit 43(1):142–162

van Sterkenburg J, Knoppers A, De Leeuw S (2010) Race, ethnicity, and content analysis of the sports media: a critical reflection. Media Cult Soc 32(5):819–839. https://doi.org/10.1177/0163443710373955

Japanese Representation in Philippine Media

24

Karl Ian Uy Cheng Chua

Contents

Introduction	416
Representing the Japanese	418
Children's Literature	418
Postwar Postscript	423
My Father (?)	424
Concluding Remarks	425
Cross-References	426
References	426

Abstract

The Japanese are often depicted in as one of the countries worst villains in Filipino history textbooks despite the fact that they were in the Philippines for only 3 years, while Spanish colonial rule lasted almost 400 years, and the Americans, 40 years.

However, when we look beyond formal education, at images of the occupation period in movies, memoirs, television shows, and other forms of popular media, different views of the Japanese often emerge. Instead of demonizing them, a number of accounts seek to distinguish "good" and "kind" Japanese from their "brutal" or "evil" compatriots. Popular Filipino accounts of the war thus convey complex and often contradictory images of Japan.

This chapter aims to present how the Japanese were represented in the Philippine children's literature in the present, when relations with Japan have

K. I. U. Cheng Chua (✉)
History Department, Ateneo de Manila University, Quezon City, Philippines
e-mail: kchengchua@gmail.com

© The Author(s), under exclusive license to Springer Nature Singapore Pte Ltd. 2019
S. Ratuva (ed.), *The Palgrave Handbook of Ethnicity*,
https://doi.org/10.1007/978-981-13-2898-5_27

gradually softened. The findings of this investigation illustrate the evolution of Filipino images of the Japanese and the factors affecting these representations.

Keywords

Children's literature · Representation · Historical memory · Japan · Philippines

Introduction

The recent years marked significant commemorations between the Philippines and Japan, with 2015 memorializing the 70th Anniversary of the end of World War II, and the following year, 2016 honored the 60th year since the "normalization of diplomatic affairs" between the Philippines and Japan. This created much solemn fanfare with two nations whose relationship was marred by invasion and occupation of the Philippines by Japan. The highlight would be a state visit by the last Japanese Emperor and Empress of the Heisei year, which marked their second visit to the Philippines, who are personally committed to remembering his country's past by making statements such as "renewed sense of sorrow" and "feeling of deep remorse of the last war" (Tatsumi 2016).

Amidst the somber celebrations, Filipino impressions on Japan's wartime actions are predominantly negative. In the same state visit, aging women from Lila Pilipina, an organization comprised primarily of comfort women and supporters of their plight, addressed then Philippine President Benigno Aquino, III that "the abuses against us must be addressed. We have yet to receive real justice. We were so young, but a lot was already taken from us. We lost our dignity. We weren't able to go to school. We suffered under the Japanese soldiers" (Kyodo News 2016). This is just one of several negative impressions of Filipinos concerning the Japanese, as written accounts of the period focused on themes such as the atrocities committed by Japanese soldiers. Setsuho mentions that "the victimization of the Philippines during this time in its history, however, extends far beyond the battlefield" (Ikehata and Jose 1999, 1–2).

The writing of Philippine history and its legitimacy has been a point of argument from historians of the Philippines who cite the oft repeated from Jose Rizal "*He who does not know how to look back at where he came from will never get to his destination.*" which emphasized the importance of history towards nation building. The task proves to be more challenging after a country emerges from a difficult event, as the country struggles to understand what had just happened. To gain legitimacy, formal education in history took a nationalist turn to appeal to the people for support in the postindependence period. Historians wrote grand narratives which spoke of a Philippines "discovered"; and "civilized" by the Spanish, "developed" by the Americans, and "destroyed" by the Japanese. While such an emplotment seemed apropos for the immediate postwar period, the problem of the grand narrative is that it has not changed much from its inception. That is why aside from establishing political and economic structures, participation of the education and media sectors were also integral towards the successful support these government-led projects.

However, generations of postwar Filipinos are slowly distancing themselves from the memory and experience of the war. A number of individuals who lived through the occupation period are reassessing their relationship with the former colonial master. This was reflected in a closed survey conducted by Japanese government in 2016 regarding Japan-ASEAN relations which resulted in 90% of Filipino respondents perceived Japan as a friend of the country, an important and reliable partner. Furthermore, looking beyond school texts, different media have presented varied images of the Japanese. Instead of demonizing the Japanese, popular Filipino accounts of the war convey the complex and often contradictory images of Japan and the Japanese.

In a previous study (Cheng Chua 2013), I charted the changing of visual representation of Japanese in Philippine *komiks* published in a popular magazine, *Liwayway,* which began in 1922 and has a wide semi-intellectual readership. The extent of readership expanded to major vernaculars with translated versions in Bisaya, Hiligaynon, Bikolano, and Ilokano. The study highlighted the shifting representation of Japanese addressing issues that Filipinos were coming to terms with from the immediate postwar up to the present.

Children's literature offers an interesting perspective as paired with the formal education of the classroom and the nonformal education of the home, the informal education offered through children's media was a means by which young Filipinos were socialized and prepared for adult subjecthood. Through their consumption of the various works, their identities become unconsciously formed. The contents begin to shape their world view as well as how they see themselves, through the information they have learned and the illustrations they enjoyably consume.

There are various forms of popular media available for society to consume. Media geared towards children seem to be the most influential as Children's Literature scholars would claim. Kutzer in her work, *Empire's Children: Empire & Imperialism in Clasic British Children's Books* (Kutzer 2000), would identify children as future adults and will comprise future society, and it is through the education of these children, whether formally (in the form of schooling) or informally (through the reading of books), that the form of the future society is built. Furthermore, Griffiths would add that children's media is the best way to understand the values of adults of the period, as well as the often yawing gap between what they say and do, by looking at the process by which they transmit knowledge of all types to children (Griffiths 2007). Thus as a medium of influence, children's literature should not be ignored by scholars.

With all this in mind, this researcher chose to look at how the Japanese were represented in the Philippines' children's literature of the present, when Japanese popular culture and other vehicles for "soft power" have permeated Filipino society. The findings of this investigation illustrate the consistent evolution of Filipino images of the Japanese.

Representing the Japanese

The study of the representation of Japanese in the Philippines is not new. Yu-Rivera has published two books entitled, *Patterns of Continuity and Change: Imaging the Japanese in Philippine Editorial Cartoons, 1930–1941 and 1946–1956* (Yu-Rivera 2005) and *A Satire of Two Nations: Exploring Images of the Japanese in Philippine Political Cartoons* (2009). (Yu-Rivera 2009) and points out that editorial cartoons were immune from censorship, thus making them more powerful than the written text. The effectiveness of editorial cartoons partly relies on the fact that they are published in widely circulated tabloids and newspapers. Thus presenting impressions of public intellectuals concerning issues revolving around Japanese, and how they were able to influence general thought during the period.

Terami-Wada has written two articles on the topic: "Japanese Images of Prewar Filipinos" (Terami-Wada 1991) and "Postwar Japanese Images in Liwayway Short Stories and Serialized Novels, 1946 1988" (Terami-Wada 1992) survey representations of the Japanese in the magazine's short stories and serialized novels, identifying three main categories: (1) Japanese as main characters, (2) Japanese as supporting characters, and (3) Japanese mentioned in passing or as a people (i.e., a collective group).

By contrast, a study I conducted on *komik* serials (rather than novels or short stories), published in *Liwayway* from the 1940s to the 1970s, aim in demonstrating the complex and often inconsistent ways in which these represented the Japanese. It sheds further light on how popular images of Japan and the Japanese changed, and on the ways in which they were influenced by shifts in Filipino society and politics. The main focus is on the portrayal of "enemies" or "villains" in the *komiks*. As O'Barr (2009) notes, studying representations of the other can tell us, first of all, how a particular external group is imagined within a particular society. Secondly, it can elucidate the nature of social relationships, or popular perceptions of these, in this case through describing how "heroes" and "villains" interact with each other. By the same token, it also shows us how inequality and the distribution of power within Filipino society are popularly perceived. Thus, by looking at the representations of the "enemy" or "villain" in a medium such as children's literature, we can gain a clearer picture of how Filipino identity was conceptualized in the popular imagination.

Children's Literature

Lin Acacio-Flores is a prominent children's literature who has presently written 16 books since 1996. *The Secret* published in 1997 is a 107-page lavishly illustrated fictional work which is supposed to reference the author's own war experience. This novel for children tells the story of Rica and her experience of the war in the convent where she, and others like her, sought refuge from the conflict. The work includes actual headlines from various newspapers of the period, presenting the Japanese aggression which elicits fear and power (Acacio-Flores 1997).

On December 7, 1941, Japanese planes attacked Pearl Harbor, crippling half of the United States Navy.

Blazing Headlines of the *Japan Times* and *Advertiser* declared:
U.S. PACIFIC FLEET WIPED OUT!

Emperor Hirohito issued a formal declaration of war:
We, by the grace of Heaven, Emperor of Japan, seated on the throne of a line unbroken for ages eternal, enjoin upon you, our loyal and brave subjects: We heareby declare war on the United States of America and the British Empire.

Headlines from *The Tribune,* Manila, Philippines, Tuesday, December 9, 1941:
U.S. DECLARES WAR ON JAPAN
NICHOLS FIELD RAIDED
ATTACK 7 P.I. (Philippine Island) Points
IN FIRST DAY OF WAR
DAVAO bombed twice,
Baguio, 2 Cagayan Towns Once

By Associated Press:
The Japanese used fleet units and their air power to hit along a front extending from Thailand and British Malaya to Hawaii with the Philippines in the very center of the conflagration.

The story features a "good Japanese" – a Captain Nokumura who befriends the nuns and the children. Nokumura asks for permission to read the books in the convent's library and is described as "an unusual Japanese, courteous, bowing to Sister Angela whenever he came. He spoke perfect English, and he said he had studied in London" (Acacio Flores 2002, 70). Despite Captain Nokumura's redeeming qualities, the narrative also highlights the brutality of many Japanese soldiers by featuring an episode in which one of them is trying to find gold hidden inside the convent. Threateningly addressing one of the nuns, this soldier says "you hiding gold of yourrr churrrch, now properrrty of Japanese Imperial Arrrmy and Emperrror of Japan!" (Acacio-Flores 1997), and then draws his saber and puts the blade against Rica's throat. The nun retorts by invoking Captain Nokumura, upon which the soldier beats a hasty retreat. While the dichotomy of "good" and "evil" Japanese nuanced the period, the juxtaposition of an educated Japanese who spoke perfect English against that of what seems like an "uneducated" Japanese due to the speech pattern represented by the author through imperfect English represented the pro-American sentiment that was prevalent in postwar Philippines due to the success of American colonial policies which included the promotion of an English-language education by the Thomasites and led to an English-speaking population during the Japanese occupation period (Okada 2009).

Another fictional work is Lin Acacio-Flores' *Adventures of a Child of War* (Acacio-Flores 2002), a novel about Eduardo, a young boy whose life is turned upside-down by the war. Unlike the previous work which used original illustrations, this work used as supplementary material, stock photographs of the period, and scans of Japanese propaganda material, as well as instructional pamphlets such as how to build air raid shelters. While the book also included "posed" photographs related with the story, interspersed in the pages created a believable effect on the young readers who could further imagine life during the Japanese occupation period of the Philippines. Similar to her previous work, she also features a benevolent Japanese character, in the form of Captain Abe. Abe takes a liking to Eduardo because "he rike my *musuko*, my boy. In Japan" (Acacio-Flores 2002). She further presented the generous side of Captain Abe, who gives supplies and a horse named *Nakama* (friend) to Eduardo's family, and later reveals that he is educated, like Eduardo's father: "Me, engineer, arrso" (Acacio-Flores 2002). Towards the end of the war, when the fleeing Japanese were killing innocent men, women, and children, Eduardo made to remark: "But I was sure that Captain Abe wouldn't have done anything like that" (Acacio-Flores 2002) The representation may confuse the readers, as the author veers away from her previous trope of contrasting "good" and "evil" through their English-language skills. However, this humanizes the Japanese as more than just an "enemy" through information that Captain Abe has a family as well. She goes back to her trope by emphasizing the fact that good Japanese had to be "educated" as they are not capable to the violence.

Barbara-Ann Gamboa Lewis wrote her semi-autobiographical piece entitled *Barefoot in Fire: A World War II Childhood* (Gamboa-Lewis 2005), narrating her family's life during the Japanese Occupation period. It was initially published in 2000 in the United States under the title of *Pocket Stones: A Child's Story of World War II in the Philippines* and was republished under the current title in 2005 for local distribution. Unlike many other works that deal only with the Japanese Occupation of the Philippines, the story covers the prewar, wartime, and immediate postwar periods, highlighting the flux that occurred. The author blatantly identifies her family as being "leftist," and thus having a perspective that is quite different from most Filipinos, who hid their political inclinations during the period. This ideological slant is evident from the way in which the author and her family criticize fellow Filipinos, whom they accused of making the war even worse through their passive or active collaboration. Such perspective slowly gained ground in the Philippine psyche in the 1960s, almost two decades after the war, which slowly distanced the survivors from nationalist narratives, and the beginning of the normalization of Philippine-Japan relations in 1956. This initially began with the act of executive clemency by then President Elpidio Quirino in 1953 to 105 Japanese war criminals, some with death sentences (Philippine News Agency 2018). This continued with the negotiations for reparations and arguments for further clemencies until the 1970s. Another unique feature of this work is the introduction of new "villains with reason" never mentioned in the *komiks*: Koreans. Lewis writes, "The Japanese Army that invaded the Philippines included Korean soldiers. This was because Japan had conquered Korea in 1910, taking it over for themselves with the approval of the United States and major powers in Europe. The Koreans were considered inferior by the Japanese and were used as menial laborers; they were often mistreated. This was probably why, in many instances, the Korean soldiers were more cruel to the Filipinos than were the Japanese soldiers" (Gamboa-Lewis 2005, 76–77). This was a common rumor that began to propagate in line with the success of the normalization of Philippine-Japan relations, and the need to identify a "new villain" in the realms of nationalist histories. However, this was disproven by Yu-Jose who stated that while Koreans were in the Philippines as colonial subjects, their numbers were few and far in-between from the Japanese. Nonetheless, this rumor continues to spread since the roles of Koreans are not properly discussed in official narratives (Yu-Jose 2012). Finally, the author uses a similar trope by Acacio-Flores, by redeeming the former "enemy" via the introduction of an unnamed Japanese officer showing his humanity by crying at the sound of the protagonist's violin, commenting on how this made him think of his son, also a violin player.

A more nuanced narrative emerged with a picture book written by Corazon O. Calica entitled *Good Night, Lala* in 2013. (Calica 2013) Her biography mentioned that she was born in Pampanga in 1936, which presumes that she had lived through the war as a child. This is her first and only book on the topic. The introduction by her daughter and editor, Maya O. Calica highlight that the story was about her mother's life growing up during the Japanese Occupation period of the Philippines, as her legacy to her *apos* (grandchildren). Mara states that "despite the terrors of World War II, Mommy (Corazon) saw fun in the bleakest moments (Calica 2013). The overall narrative presented a state of "normalcy" which nationalist narratives would often refer to as Japanese propaganda but turned out to be real in certain parts of the Philippines (Cheng Chua 2005). The pro-American narrative was also present via the character of the grandmother, Ima who "said something about General MacArthur leaving the country and how the barrio folk awaited his return" (Calica 2013). Thus reflecting a popular sentiment of American colonial success, echoing the statement of General Douglas MacArthur in statement with Australian journalists on his arrival, "I came out of Bataan and I shall return." This piece was one of a few children's literature works which also dealt with the controversial topic of comfort women. The story talks about "many stories of the abuse of young women (by the Japanese)" and continued with her parents worried about their sister, Victoria or *Acheng Toring*. *Acheng Toring*'s beauty worried the parents 1 day brought her out late at night, and returned with a "young boy with short, cropped hair." They disguised *Acheng Toring* as a boy and finally said "She is safer as a boy for now." This was a common practice by Filipinos in protecting their daughters and wives from being take as comfort women. But the skill of dealing with a complex topic can only be done within the realms of children's literature, which according to Kutzer (2000), allowed the "unpalatable to be palatable" due to the consumption habits of children who would reject media they do not like. Finally, another interesting actor introduced by piece were the *Huks* which was an acronym for *Hukbo Laban sa Mga Hapon* (People's Army against Japan) whom were rebels which the locals believed to keep them safe from the Japanese. Lala's family planned to escape the provincial capital of San Fernando, to a small town 10 km away claiming that "the rebel Huks were in the barrios and outskirts of Pampanga (province where they were) and gave villagers a sense of safety because they (Huks) were around" (Calica 2013). The curiosity of the introduction of the Huks was that despite being labeled as heroes during wartime, the group would be discredited during the postwar when the Americans mistrusted them due to their Communist inclinations and the emergence of the Cold War.

On 2001, a children's book publisher, Adarna launched their *Batang Hitoryador* (Child Historian) series which had five books set at different periods of Philippine history: *Si Pitong, Noong Panahon ng mga Hapon* (Pitong During the Japanese Occupation) (Rivera 2001). Not only was there reference to Japanese raping women which began the theme of "comfort women" prior to *Good Night Lala* but also went a peculiar step further by introducing a scene where in evacuating their home in Tarlac, had to paint his face with soot to "disguise" himself. This was peculiar as this was an act to prevent the rape of girls to make them look like tramps. The author's confusion can also be seen when he referred to Japanese soldiers as *kempeitai* even though *kempeitai* only referred to the military police of the Imperial Japanese Army. Nonetheless, memory of *kempeitai* lasted with Filipinos through their oral accounts as they were identified as the Japanese would slap them if they did not salute the soldiers, as what was done to Pitong in the story.

Finally, narratives of the Japanese occupation period could be found in the picture book biography of Socorro Ramos. *Nanay Coring* (Socorro Ramos) is the founder of National Book Store, the largest bookstore chain in the Philippines. Yet while the biography of *Nanay Coring: The Story of National Book Store's Socorro Ramos* by Yvette Fernandez (2012) may seem to not have anything to do with the Japanese Occupation period, *Nanay Coring* lived through the war and began her business during the period. The story mentions a policy by the occupation forces which affected her business, the banning of books which were written by the enemy, in her case stories about America. Thus, to survive, she began to sell products which catered to the needs of her customers, pencils, pens, paper, candy, and soap, things you may not find in a typical bookstore. Rather than treat the Japanese as "enemies," the story presented that *Nanay Coring* treated them as customers. "I [also] found out that the Japanese soldiers liked rubber slippers called *tsinelas*. At night, they liked wearing slippers after walking around in boots all day long. So I went to Divisoria, a market, where I bought slippers at a cheap price, and sold them at our store at a higher price. That's how we made money. We sold hundreds and hundreds of pairs of slippers" (Fernandez 2012). She also developed good relations with her Japanese customers, which further humanized them. When *Nanay Coring* gave birth to her twin sons, she remembered a Japanese soldier giving her children matching red flannel blankets to keep them warm, to which she gave the soldier coconut candy called *bokayo*. There seemed to be no ill feelings between her and her Japanese customers. Rather, the tragedy she narrates is that when the Americans returned to liberated the Philippines. "Then the American soldiers arrived, bombing the city of Manila to send the Japanese away. The bombs killed many people and destroyed many homes and buildings. Our little store burned down and we lost all our soap, slippers, pencils, pens and paper. We lost everything" (Fernandez 2012). This last section veers away from standard tropes of Filipinos which was eager for the Americans to return, as in the story by Calica. Rather, through *Nanay Coring*, the author presented a new "enemy," the Americans through their air raids which is commemorated as the Battle of Manila. In the commemoration of 70th year of the end of the war, Filipinos have now nuanced their war memory as Morales wrote "it was mainly the United States' casualty-avoidance policy that resulted in unrestrained and indiscriminate application of overwhelming firepower by forces under MacArthur, which caused the utter devastation of Manila and the loss of 100,000 Filipino lives in 1945" (Morales 2015).

Postwar Postscript

The beginning of restoration of Philippine-Japan relations was marked by the unpopular decision by then President Elpidio Quirino in granting executive clemency on 4 July 1953 to 114 Japanese nationals who were accused as wartime criminals. In response to public uproar on his decision, Quirino replied stating that "I should be the last one to pardon them as the Japanese killed my wife and three children, and five other members of my family. I am doing this because I do not want my children and my people to inherit from me the hate for people who might yet be our friends for the permanent interest of our country" (Ocampo 2016). Thus beginning the attempt to separate the memory and hatred of postwar Filipinos to the Japanese.

In the signing of the "Treaty of Peace with Japan" and "Reparations Agreement Between Japan and the Republic of the Philippines" on July 1956, diplomatic amicable relations was expected. Nonetheless, the relationship remained precarious, with suspicions by Filipinos of the Japanese. Aside from diplomatic relations, business and economic interests normalized with the establishment of the Philippine-Japan Society on 17 January 1972, and the Japanese Chamber of Commerce and Industry of the Philippines on November 1973. This coincided with Japan's economic miracle.

With a booming Japanese economy vis-à-vis a struggling one in the Philippines, then President Ferdinand Marcos promoted international tourism with the establishment of the Philippine Tourism Authority in 1973 which became the policy implementing arm of the Department of Tourism. Unfortunately, with haphazard projects, the surge of tourist, the boom also included the advent of sex tourism in the 1970s. The Department of Tourism saw an increase of tourist arrivals who would stay in the Philippines for an average of 12.6 days (National Statistics Office 2011). Even as late as the 1980s with attempts by both governments to prevent the entry of sex tourists, official figures have stated around 134,261 inbound tourists from Japan

Table 1 Changes in the number of new arrivals of Philippine nationals by selected status of residence (MOJ 2009). (Changes in new arrivals refer to **flow** of migrants to Japan as they go through immigration control at various ports of entries – e.g., airports and seaports. Changes in number of alien registration meanwhile refer to the **stock** of migrants once they register to their various localities under the alien registration system (*Gaikokujin Touroku*))

Status of residence	2004	2005	2006	2007	2008
Entertainer	82,741	47,765	8,608	5,533	3,185
Spouse or child of Japanese national	5,038	5,530	8,257	6,687	5,133
Long-term resident	2,893	3,109	3,410	4,068	3,811
Trainee	3,635	4,311	4,941	5,843	5,678
Specialist in humanities/international services	66	88	138	127	98
Temporary visitor	51,617	69,285	63,171	58,931	54,678
Total	147,817	132,745	91,474	84,198	75,651

via 1,448 tourist agency members of the Japan Association of Travel Agents who were offering packaged tours, including sex tours by male groups (Yu-Rivera 2006). This caused a resurgence of negative imagery of Japanese from the male soldier to the predatory sex tourist.

Media would engage in this space with the representation of the Japanese sex tourist, predominantly men, who would be compared to the negative archetype of the soldiers of the yesteryear (Yu-Rivera 2009). With the crackdown on sex tourism by both governments, a surge of Filipino migrant workers, including Filipino entertainers entered Japan with around 9075 workers and 5,299 dependents registered in the records of the Immigration Bureau of Japan in 1986 (Yu-Jose 2007). Thus beginning the three waves of gendered migration into Japan. With the "entertainer ban of 2005" of the Japanese government, the advent spouses and rural brides became imminent. This can be seen in the number of entertainers gradually decreasing (Table 1).

The last wave of this migration came with the signing of the Japanese-Philippine Economic Partnership Agreement in 2006 which allowed for the entry of care workers into Japan.

The result of such was the rise of cross-cultural partnerships and the birth of multicultural children. Their identities would shift from the *Japino* which has acquired a negative nuance as children who are "abandoned," "illegitimate," "poor," and "offspring of a sex worker." They have shifted to a more neutral term, referring to themselves as Japanese-Filipino Children (JFC). (Asis and Liao 2017) It is through the stories of the JFC that representation of the Japanese in children's literature reappear.

My Father (?)

While the literature would focus primarily on the JFC, the subject of the Japanese would be referenced through the distant or absent father. Hanna's story focused on the food rituals of her family, particularly on difference between the food prepared by her mother, who cooks Filipino food, her grandmother, who cooks provincial Filipino food, and her father, who "occasionally cooks" Japanese food. Distance is felt when Hanna says: "I've never asked why my father ate upstairs in his room in front of the TV watch NHK, CNN, or whatever anime has taken his fancy." (Asis and Liao 2017) She also mentions that her father didn't live with them, as he was managing their family's business.

There is also the theme of real absence through the story of Arisa who spells out her situation. "There was once an overseas Filipina worker and a Japanese contractual agent who met in an entertainment club in Takamatsu, Kagawa-ken in 1992. Their relationship blossomed, and in 1993, she found out that she was pregnant with her first child....Upon his return to Japan, the mother kept calling him, but the number seemed to be out of coverage...She came to the realization that she and her child vanished in his life" (Asis and Liao 2017). The rest of the story continues with the theme of the absent father.

The same themes are reflected in a manga compilation of JFC entitled *Yoghi Manga* (Neri 2009) which stands for Youth Organization Gives Hope and Inspiration. The three stories tell of the issues of the JFC children who are bullied for their multicultural background, due to the World War II experiences of Filipinos. Yuki Nakamura tells his friend that he is used to the bullying since "our people suffered a lot from the Japanese Occupation" with the backdrop of Filipinos suffering and Japanese soldiers. Naomi was also harshly treated by her grandmother because she was abused by Japanese soldiers. Furthermore, her father is absent as well during the entire story.

The absence of the Japanese in these stories creates a solution to the dilemma of the previous narratives. As nuanced representations of Japanese are gradually presenting itself in children's media, the introduction of another villain archetype would complicate the modern day relations of Filipinos and Japanese who are moving forward towards creating families with each other, perfect and imperfect. Thus supplementing the representations of the Japanese by simply relegating the nuanced villain as part of a past.

Concluding Remarks

While commemorations of the 70th year of the end of the war came to a close, negative stereotypes of the brutality caused by the Japanese still persists in the children's literature, since this image corresponds not only with the lived experience of so many older Filipinos but also the dominance of static nationalistic historical narratives. However, the same children's literature have nuanced their narratives to include the figure of the "good Japanese," and at times also present "new enemies" such as the Koreans or the "once-favored" Americans. Regardless, the trope of the "evil Japanese" persisted with the qualification that "good Japanese" not only by his moral qualities but his superior level of education and occasional fluency in English. While the group that emerges best out of these accounts should be the

Americans – ironically, would also be subject to a more critical gaze by postwar generations as well.

As the Philippines emerged from the ravages of war, a desire to boost the collective national ego was evident in postwar works, which juxtaposed the heroics of Filipino guerillas – and the country's eventual American saviors – with the almost uniformly evil Japanese. However, this depiction would disappear in the twenty-first century as the Philippines not only has to come into terms with its colonial past but with its postcolonial present.

With the gradual thawing of Filipino-Japanese relations, Filipinos can now ask a once taboo question: "Perhaps the Japanese were not all so bad after all?" This, at least, is the sort of shifting national mindset that these children's literature appear to reflect and which they perhaps helped to pass on to the next generation's historical memory.

Cross-References

▶ Cultural Identity and Textbooks in Japan: Japanese Ethnic and Cultural Nationalism in Middle-School History Textbooks
▶ Ethno-cultural Symbolism and Group Identity
▶ Foreign Military Occupations and Ethnicity
▶ Historical Memory and Ethnic Myths
▶ Media and Stereotypes
▶ Museums and Identity: Celebrating Diversity in an Ethnically Diverse World
▶ Racism and Stereotypes
▶ Rewriting the World: Pacific People, Media, and Cultural Resistance

References

Acacio-Flores L (1997) The secret. Cacho Publishing House, Mandaluyong
Acacio-Flores L (2002) Adventures of a child of war. Cacho Publishing House, Mandaluyong
Asis MBM, Liao ASK (2017) Moving portraits: life stories of children of migrant and multicultural families in Asia. Scalabrini Migration Center, Quezon City
Calica OC (2013) Good night, Lala. Adarna House, Quezon City
Cheng Chua IUK (2005) The stories they tell: Komiks during the Japanese occupation, 1942–1944. Philipp Stud 53:59–95
Cheng Chua Ian Uy Karl (2013) Friend or foe: representations of Japan in print media in the Philippines, 1940s to the present. In: Morris Paul, Vickers Edward, Shimazu Naoko (eds) 著: Imaging Japan in postwar East Asia: identity politics, schooling and popular culture, 脚本. Routledge, New York, pp 85–105
Fernandez Y (2012) Nanay Coring: the story of National Book Store's Socorro Ramos. Dream Big Books, Metro Manila
Gamboa-Lewis B-A (2005) Barefoot in fire: a World War II childhood. Tahanan Books, Makati
Griffiths O (2007) Militarizing Japan: patriotism, profit, and children's print media, 1894–1925. Asia-Pacific J 5(9), September 3. https://apjjf.org/-Owen-Griffiths/2528/article.html
Ikehata S, Jose RT (1999) The Philippines under Japan: occupation policy and reaction. University of Hawaii Press, Honolulu

Kutzer MD (2000) Empire's children: empire & imperialism in classic British children's books. Garland Publishing, Inc., New York

Kyodo News (2016) Filipino 'comfort women' want plight raised with Japanese Emperor. ABS CBN News, January月23日

Ministry of Japan (2009) 2009 Immigration Control, Japan: Immigration Bureau

Morales CR (2015) The Americans destroyed Manila in 1945. Rappler, February月4日

National Statistics Office (2011) Tourism industry in the Philippines. J Philipp Stat 62(3):1–14

Neri VB (2009) Yoghi Manga. Batis Center for Women, Quezon City

O'Barr WM (2009) Culture and the Ad: exploring otherness in the world of advertising. Westview Press, Colorado

Ocampo AR (2016) Elpidio Quirino's act of faith in humanity. The Philippine Daily Inquirer, June月22日

Okada T (2009) Colonies and the English language awareness of English in the American colony of the Philippines from the perspectives of theory of imperialism of the languages. Gengo Shakai 3:263–278

Philippine News Agency (2018) A tale of two Presidents: normalization of relations with Japan. May月22日. http://www.pna.gov.ph/articles/1036022

Rivera A (2001) Si Pitong, Noong Panahon ng mga Hapon (Pitong during the Japanese occupation). Adarna Publishing House, Quezon City

Tatsumi Y (2016) Japan's emperor visits the Philippines: major takeaways. The Diplomat

Terami-Wada M (1991) Japanese images of Prewar Filipinos. Solidarity 130:26–32

Terami-Wada M (1992) Postwar Japanese images in liwayway short stories and serialized novels, 1946–1988. In: Barte G (ed) 著: Panahon ng Hapon: Sining sa Digmaan, Digmaan sa Sining (Japanese Occupation Period: Art in War, War in Art), 脚本. Museo ng Kalinangang Pilipino, Adarna House, Quezon City, Philippines, pp 83–91

Yu-Jose L (2007) Why are most Filipino workers? Perspectives from history and law. Kasarinlan: Philipp J Third World Stud 22:61–84

Yu-Jose L (2012) The Koreans in Second World War Philippines: rumours and history. J Southeast Asian Stud 43:324–339

Yu-Rivera H (2005) Patterns of continuity and change: imaging the Japanese in Philippine editorial cartoons, 1930–1941 and 1946–1956. Ateneo de Manila University Press, Quezon City

Yu-Rivera H (2006) The Wakaoji abduction and the Ropponggi property sale: perspectives from the Philippine press. Philipp Stud 54:82–110

Yu-Rivera H (2009) A satire of two nations: exploring images of the Japanese in Philippine political cartoons. University of the Philippines Press, Quezon City

Racism in Colonial Zimbabwe

25

Alois S. Mlambo

Contents

Introduction	430
Defining Racism	430
Scientific Racism and the White Man's Burden Idea	431
Racism and the Black Peril Phenomenon	433
White Racism and the Alienation and Racialization of Land	436
A Racialized Labor Regime	439
Some Are "More White" than Others (Mlambo 2000)	441
The Invisible Minorities	442
Political Marginalization and Other Forms of Discrimination	443
Conclusion	444
References	444

Abstract

Colonial Zimbabwe (known as Southern Rhodesia until 1965, and Rhodesia thereafter until independence in 1980) was established in 1890 under the sponsorship of Cecil John Rhodes and his British South Africa Company (BSAC). Rhodes was a firm believer in the White-Man's Burden idea of the duty of the Anglo-Saxon race to help "civilize" the "darker" corners of the world and regarded British imperialism as a positive force for this purpose. The settlers who occupied colonial Zimbabwe shared this view of the world and treated the indigenous African population as children who needed their guidance, protection, and civilization. The policies which the settler state adopted and implemented, therefore, whether in politics, constitution making and governance, education, economy, land and labor policies, social relations, or residential policy, were based on this sense of racial superiority and the determination to promote white interests at the expense of the nonwhite population. Racial segregation permeated the entire colonial project at every level,

---

A. S. Mlambo (✉)
University of Pretoria, Pretoria, South Africa
e-mail: alois.mlambo@up.ac.za

whether it was in sports, hotel facilities, or the use of public conveniences and amenities. White racism in colonial Zimbabwe was also informed by a sense of fear, given the fact that whites were grossly outnumbered in the country throughout the colonial period and were always afraid of being overwhelmed by the African majority. This contributed to their determination to control the Africans and keep them in their place. Attempts at promoting racial partnership in the 1950s achieved little. State sponsored white racism ended with Zimbabwe's independence in 1980.

Keywords

Racism · Imperialism · Colonization · Black peril · Land · Education · Labor · Rhodes · Rhodesia · Settler

Introduction

Late nineteenth-century European imperialism and colonization in Africa were motivated by a range of factors, including a predominant European racist view of the world which regarded the Anglo-Saxon race as the most civilized of all the races and, therefore, duty-bound to spread the benefits of their civilization to the "lower" races of the world. Called the White Man's Burden or "civilizing mission" and "mission civilisatrice" in the English and French world, respectively, this idea was celebrated by Rudyard Kipling in his 1902 poem entitled "The White Man's Burden," which was, partly, in celebration the United States victory over Spain in the Cuban-American- Spanish War and, mainly, an assertion of the Anglo-Saxon race's right to rule other races. As will be shown, the founder of Rhodesia, Cecil John Rhodes, was a strong believer in the civilizing mission idea and had no doubt whatsoever that his race was the best in the world. He firmly believed that bringing the land between the Limpopo and the Zambezi under British rule was for the unquestionable benefit of the indigenous people of that territory. Rhodesian white settlers shared Rhodes' world view. Not surprisingly, therefore, racism remained the foundation and the pervasive ethos of white colonial rule from the establishment of the British colony in 1890 until the collapse of white rule in 1979, mainly because of the African liberation movements' determination to dismantle the racist colonial system by any means necessary, including taking up arms.

Defining Racism

For purposes of this study, racism means "any action or attitude, conscious or unconscious, that subordinates an individual or group based on skin colour or race ... [whether] enacted individually or institutionally." Institutional racism manifests itself in discriminatory policies based on race in schools, businesses, employment, religion, and media, among others, which are designed to "perpetuate and maintain the power, influence and wellbeing of one group over another." Such discriminatory policies often manifest in the denial of benefits, facilities, services, and opportunities to a person or a group of people on the basis of their racial origins. In addition, racism also exists when "ideas and assumptions about racial categories are used to justify and reproduce a racial hierarchy and racially structured society that unjustly limits access to resources, rights and privileges on the basis of race" (Tatum 2003).

Scientific Racism and the White Man's Burden Idea

While racism and racial prejudice have a long history, as evident in the racial justifications of the transatlantic slave trade as beneficial to the enslaved because it took them away from their savagery in Africa and exposed them to Western civilization and the dignity of manual labor, it is the specific manifestation of this phenomenon in late nineteenth century Western Europe which has a direct bearing on the partition of Africa in general and the colonization of Zimbabwe in particular. Based on the intellectual arguments advanced by American and European Social Darwinists, such as Spencer and Alfred Mahan, which regarded the Anglos-Saxon race and its civilization as the most evolved and best, this version of racism, particularly in Late Victorian Britain, postulated that it was the Anglo-Saxon race's duty to spread Anglo-Saxon civilization to the "darker" corners of the world through colonial domination for the benefit of the colonized peoples (Hofstadter 1944; Rogers 1972). There was no doubt, for instance, in British arch-imperialist Cecil John Rhodes' view that British imperial domination was the best thing that could happen to the world at large. He wrote:

> I contend that we [the English] are the finest race in the world and that the more of the world we inhabit the better it is for the human race. Just fancy those parts that are at present inhabited by the most despicable specimens of human beings what an alteration there would be if they were brought under Anglo-Saxon influence, look again at the extra employment a new country added to our dominions gives. (Rhodes 1877)

With respect to Africa, specifically, Rhodes stated:

> Africa is still lying ready for us. It is our duty to take it. It is our duty to seize every opportunity of acquiring more territory and we should keep this one idea steadily before our eyes that more territory simply means more of the Anglo-Saxon race more of the best the most human, most honourable race the world possesses. (Rhodes 1877)

The White settlers who entered the territory of what was to become Southern Rhodesia (Zimbabwe) in 1890 as part of an invading group of adventurers known as the Pioneer Column which Rhodes sponsored were imbued by this sense of mission and superiority which made them regard the indigenous African majority as a lesser breed to be controlled and guided toward Western civilization. Following their victory in the 1893 Anglo-Ndebele War and the subsequent successful suppression of the *Chimurenga/Umvukela* armed uprisings of 1896, colonial settlers not only claimed the right to rule by conquest, but also consolidated their white supremacist ideology and the conviction that the African majority was a subject race, not only in need of moral guidance and civilization, but also of strict and close control. The determination to control the majority of Africans as closely as possible stemmed from the fear of them inspired by the 1896 uprisings and the ever-present fear of the largely outnumbered white settler population of being swamped by the Africans. Not surprisingly, little effort was made to understand the Africans and their worldview, while a determined resolve prevailed to "civilize" the so-called natives. (This innocuous term normally used to denote indigenous peoples of original inhabitants of a place took on a rather derogatory meaning in colonial Zimbabwe where it increasingly implied inferiority and lack of civilisation. Hence, it will be used in this chapter only in quotation marks.) Thus, the gulf between the races was entrenched in Rhodesian society from the very onset of European colonialism.

According to Anthony Chennells, the white Rhodesian self-image which developed in the early years of colonialism "was based on the idea that they were civilisers of the wilderness, taming its violence. They saw themselves as peace-bringers and profoundly moral beings, in contrast to the less-than-human blacks that embodied brute nature" (Sicilia 1999). Not surprisingly, therefore, whites generally regarded Africans as perpetual children to be firmly and strictly controlled by the civilized settlers. Africans were, thus, perpetually infantilized and were routinely referred to as "boys" or "girls" regardless of their age, as in the then common references to "houseboys" and "house girls" for grown-up African men and women.

Increasingly, therefore, whiteness became a mark of superiority and civilization and, therefore, power and privilege to be promoted guarded and defended at all times, and remained so throughout Zimbabwe's colonial history. This was very evident in the way the successive generations of white political leaders asserted this superiority and white entitlement and repeatedly affirmed the white people's civilizing mission in the colony. For instance, Godfrey Huggins, Rhodesian Prime Minister from the 1930s onwards, declared that "the greatest civilising influence in Southern Rhodesia is the White settler, as long as he is really white inside," while dismissing Africans as incompetent and incapable of holding political or administrative office. When discussions were under way to set up the Federation of Rhodesia and Nyasaland or the Central African Federation, Huggins was adamant that Africans should not be given any administrative positions in its governance structures. He made it abundantly clear that his vision of the proposed Central African Federation had no place for blacks at all in its structures because, "they are quite incapable of playing a full part ... They may have a university degree, but their background is all wrong." In response to a seeming insistence by politicians in the United Kingdom to make the Federation more inclusive, Huggins asserted: "It is time for the people in England to realise that the white man in Africa is not prepared and never will be prepared to accept the African as an equal, either socially or politically" because there was "something in their [Africans] chromosomes which makes them more backward and different from peoples living in the East and West" (Turnbull 1962: 90). Given this racist attitude toward the Africans, it came as no surprise that Huggins spearheaded the policy of separate development which he labelled the two-pyramid system when he became the colony's Prime Minister in the mid-1930s. As the name suggests, the policy had much in common with the later policy of separate or parallel racial development which was the foundation of the South African apartheid system when the Nationalists came to power in that country in 1948.

Similarly, Ian Smith, the Prime Minister of Rhodesia, in the Unilateral Declaration of Independence (UDI) government from 1965 to 1979 justified UDI by saying that by preventing black majority rule in the country, they had "struck a blow for the preservation of justice, civilisation and Christianity."

Racism and the Black Peril Phenomenon

A clear manifestation of pervasive White settler racism and the fear of the African majority which accompanied and underpinned it was the black peril phenomenon of the early twentieth century which saw White settler society experiencing collective hysteria over the alleged sexual threat of African males to white womanhood. The fear, it seems, stemmed from the 1896 uprisings which had resulted in the killings of almost 10% of the total white population and the resulting and ever-present specter of racial swamping, especially given the ratio of Africans to whites of 45:1 in 1901 and 22:1 in 1931 (Mhike 2016). Constantly aware that Africans resented their domination, White settlers were apprehensive about their future in the country and of the likelihood of Africans seeking revenge at some point, including through possible sexual abuse of white women by the, generally, depraved black males driven by irresistible primitive animal sexual instincts. Commenting on this pervasive and ever-present fear of the Africans stemming from the 1896 uprisings, Katherine Gombay stated:

> The 'Rebellion' confirmed the settlers' preconceptions about the brutishness of the Africans, while also awakening in them a sense of their own vulnerability which diminished little over the next two or three decades. It was this legacy of fear and hate which found expression in phenomena such as the black peril. (Gombay 1991)

Imagining Africans as less than human and naturally depraved and brutish was not difficult for the settlers, given that they regarded Africans as little more than children who were ruled by emotions and, therefore, capable of the most violent outbursts of anger and dark acts of sexual passion. Such attitudes were fed by the "scholarship" of the day which was steeped in the racist principles of Social Darwinism, which "formed such a crucial ideological underpinning to colonial conquest" (Pape 1990) and claimed that Africans were subhuman. An example was Professor Henry Drummond's book entitled *Tropical* Africa, published in 1890, in which he characterized Africans as "tribes with no name, speaking tongues which no man can interpret" and who were "half animal half children, wholly savage and wholly heathen" (Drummond 1890). According to such "scholarship," Africans were still at a lower level of evolution and were not yet capable of controlling their sexual urges. This is what was reflected in the statement by one member of the

Legislative Assembly in 1916 that "the male native more or less has a tendency to commit rape" (*Rhodesia Herald* 14 July 1916). Similarly, describing African girls, N. H. Wilson stressed that African morality was low and that African girls passions "are stronger, they have much more of the animal in them in sex matters and they have not the restraint and control that white women have" (Mushonga 2013). This toxic combination of fear and racial hatred of the Africans inevitably led to the determination to impose strict legal controls on Africans in order to monitor and govern their every activity.

Because Africans were believed to be little more than infants, it was presumed that they could not handle European liquor, hence the passage of the 1898 Sale of Liquor to Natives and Indians Regulations. Also, to keep Africans out of white residential areas, the government passed the Native Locations Ordinance in the same year. In 1901 came the Master and Servants Ordinance designed to enforce African workers' obedience and subservience to their white employers, as well as to limit their work and economic options. Most significantly, in order to address the settler community's fear of the abuse of white womanhood by African males, colonial authorities passed the Immorality Suppression Ordinance of 1903, followed by the Immorality and Indecency (Suppression) Ordinance of 1916. Thus African actions and behaviors were systematically criminalized.

The 1903 Ordinance, specifically, outlawed sexual relations between white women and black men and made such transgressions punishable by a maximum sentence of 2 years in prison for white women and 5 years for black men. In addition, black men could be condemned to death for any act legally defined as "attempted rape." Significantly, there was no law preventing white men from having sexual relations with black women or pronouncing on attempted rape of black women by white men. Indeed, the growing number of children of mixed race, known in Southern Rhodesia as Coloureds, is testimony to the prevalence of white male and black female sexual relations over time. Indeed, while white males who married or cohabited with black women were ostracized or criticized by fellow whites, evidence abounds that such sexual arrangements were quite common in the early decades of the twentieth century (Mushonga 2013; Schmidt 1992). Attempts to pass laws criminalizing white men's sexual interaction with black women were continually unsuccessful until the 1950s.

Indeed, as Pape pointed out, while the black peril legislation was the result of white male anxiety and sense of insecurity arising out of the fear of the African majority, it may also have been a diversionary tactic designed to divert attention from their sexual shenanigans with black women. Thus,

> By encouraging white rage against black sexual offenders, settler men were able to hide their own far more widespread and often violent sexual relations with black women. This was the real sexual 'peril' in colonial society, but it can only be discovered by reading between the lines of the tirades against [Africans accused of such crimes]. (Pape 1990)

Moreover, white settler society seems to have downplayed the role that some white women may have played in encouraging or initiating sexual relations with their black servants for purposes of self-gratification or out of curiosity. Mushonga reports that there were 46 cases of white women who used their authority as employers of black men to "persuade" them to have sexual relations with them between 1899 and 1914 (Mushonga 2013). Vambe argued that consensual sexual relations between white women and black men were not that uncommon and that it was only when a white woman involved with a black man was exposed that she would cry rape. Power relations were such, he argues, that even if the black man was reluctant to have sexual relations with a white woman, if the white woman ordered the servant to sleep with her, he had little choice, lest he be falsely reported as having attempted to rape the mistress (Vambe 1976).

According to McCulloch, as a result of the immorality and indecency in legislation, no less than 20 African men were "charged and executed for sexual assault of white women," while, approximately, "two hundred others were either imprisoned or flogged between 1902 and 1935" (West 2003). The sentences meted out to alleged offenders by white-only male kangaroo-type courts, which were "quick to convict African men for any behaviour which could be construed or misconstrued as being threatening to white women" (Vambe 1976), were, most likely, unfair and unjustified and spoke more to the ingrained racial prejudices of white settler males and the hysterical public rhetoric of the threat to white womanhood at the time than to evidence of actual sexual assaults. West observes that:

> The brief kangaroo proceedings that passed for trials went hand in hand with the public expression of white outrage, as exemplified in rallies, fulminations in the press, and demands for still tougher action by the colonial legislature and the administration. (West 2003)

The settlers' hostility to interracial sexual relations persisted for most of the colonial period, as evidenced by the fact that when an African, John Matimba, who had married Adriana von Hoom, a white woman of Dutch descent while studying in England, returned to the country in the mid-1950s, he and his wife found it impossible to settle in the country because of the hostility of the local white society. Not only could they not find anywhere to stay because of the 1930 Land Apportionment Act (LAA) which divided the country into white and black areas and did not provide for mixed marriage accommodation, but they also came under hostile attack in the press, while their marriage was the subject of such acrimonious public debates that they decided to go into exile in 1959 (Mushonga 2008).

Meanwhile, as late as the 1950s, new white female immigrants into the then Federation of Rhodesia and Nyasaland were still warned "never to allow their female children to exhibit any degree of nakedness and for themselves to make their own beds, wash their own underwear and avoid appearing in a state of casual undress ... [as this would put them] at risk at the hands of male servants" (Mlambo 2014).

Doris Lessing's *The Grass is Singing* captures the persistent white fear of the back peril and disapproval of interracial sexual relations between white women and black males very well in her portrayal of the murder of Mary Turner, the main white female character, by her African male servant under circumstances which smacked of an intimate relation gone wrong. Lessing's representation of the settler community's reaction to this tragic event suggests that, for many, this merely confirmed what was expected of such an unnatural and undesirable interracial liaison. Pointedly, the novel's opening words are:

> Mary Turner, wife of Richard Turner, a farmer at Ngesi, was found murdered on the front of their homestead yesterday morning. The houseboy, who has been arrested, has confessed to the crime. No motive has been discovered. It is thought he was in search of valuables. The newspaper did not say much. People all over the country must have glanced at the paragraph with its sensational heading and felt a little spurt of anger mingled with what was almost satisfaction, as if some belief had been confirmed, as if something had happened which could only have been expected. (Lessing 1950)

As shown, racism, which was informed by Social Darwinism at the turn of the twentieth century, underpinned the European colonization project in Africa and gave the incoming settlers a sense of superiority which translated into negative attitudes toward the African majority and discriminatory policies against them.

Indeed, as time went on, the settlers' sense of Africans as infantile and in need of "civilization" deepened, with adult men continuing to be referred to as "boys" who were expected to behave respectfully toward their elders (whites of whatever age) and whose "insolent" behavior, which might include speaking in a loud voice, appearing angry toward any authority figure, and "laughing outright and grinning when being interrogated by the police," was prosecutable behavior (Shutt 2007). In tandem also developed white ideas of "native stupidity" and "inferiority," particularly among the semiskilled whites.

White Racism and the Alienation and Racialization of Land

White racism in colonial Zimbabwe was most pronounced in the manner in which the incoming white settlers arrogated themselves the right to land without any consultation with the local inhabitants whom they found already in the country and then proceeded to decide what parts of the country Africans could legally occupy based on their race. The expropriation of land by the whites commenced with the arrival of the Pioneer Column in 1890. Through his British South Africa Company (BSAC), Rhodes funded a group of adventurers called the Pioneer Column to occupy the land north of the Limpopo River and promised them 3000 acres of land claims each for participating in the occupation. No negotiations with local African authorities had been conducted prior to this decision being taken and then implemented; the assumption being that, either the land belonged to no one or the incoming whites had the right to allocate the land as they wished. This right, it was assumed, was bestowed on the settlers by the Royal Charter given to the BSAC by the British Government, authorizing it to govern the territory it was, yet, to establish. It was assumed, therefore, that the company could dispose of the colony's land on behalf of the British Crown.

It can be argued that the settlers' decision to arbitrarily expropriate and allocate land was, initially, based on a misconception that any uninhabited land at the time of occupation belonged to no one and was, therefore, available for the taking, whereas, the situation was very different. In African society, land did not belong to either individuals or chiefs and kings, but to the community as a whole, together with the yet to be born and those who had passed on. Individuals only had usufruct rights on the land which was allocated to them and which was administered by the traditional leaders. The fact that there were stretches of land which were not occupied at the time of the British occupation did not necessarily mean that the land belonged to nobody, as local populations and their rulers knew exactly which group owned which stretch of land, without boundary pegs or picket fence demarcations.

In the early years of occupation, Whites used very little of the land allocated to them as they concentrated mainly on prospecting for gold. After all, most early settlers had entered the colony in the hope that they would make their fortunes from the fabled gold deposits that, reportedly, were as rich as those at the Rand in South Africa. With time, however, disappointed at not finding the reported rich gold deposits, many of the pioneers either abandoned their land and drifted back to South Africa or sold the land to a number of speculative land companies that were emerging in the colony. Some settlers turned to agriculture, but for a long time, this was little more than subsistence farming. Meanwhile, the small, but growing white settler population depended on the agricultural produce of the African peasant farmers who had responded favorably to the market opportunities offered by this incoming population and increased their output for sale in the mines and other emerging white settlements. Eventually, more Whites took up farming for a living and sought government support for their industry. In the process of developing white agriculture, the colonial government, under pressure to promote and defend the white agricultural sector, proceeded to destroy African agriculture and to promote white agriculture, instead.

The destruction of African agriculture was effected, mainly, through land alienation and confining Africans to designated areas of the country known as African reserves. The first three African reserves, namely Gwaai, Tsholotsho, and Nkai, were established in 1893 in Matebeleland, following the recommendations of the Commission of Enquiry on future land policy set up by the Company Government in that year. What all three areas had in common were poor soils and little rainfall. They were also far away from the emerging urban centers which provided viable markets for agricultural produce. This pattern was to characterize most of the African reserves established by successive governments throughout the colonial period. By 1905, 60 reserves had already been established. More reserves were established following the recommendations of the 1913 Reserves Commission, most of them also located in areas "with little rainfall and far away from major transportation lines and market towns" in order to eliminate competition from African farmers in the agricultural market (Mlambo 2014; Phimister 1988). By 1914, Whites, whose population amounted to only 28,000 people or 3% of the total population, controlled 75% of the land, while Africans, numbering 836, 000 people and accounting for 97% of the population, were confined to only 23% of the land in the agriculturally marginal areas of the country (Mushunje 2005).

The most defining law of Southern Rhodesian's racially based land segregation was Land Apportionment Act (LAA) of 1930 which became the pillar and key symbol of racial segregation in colonial Zimbabwe. Dividing the colony's land surface into white, African, and crown lands, the Act decreed where the two racial groups could legally own land or reside, with a minority population of whites amounting to 50,000 people receiving 52% of the land, while the 1 million African majority were allocated a mere 29.8%, designated as Tribal Trust Lands (TTLs). In order to create a buffer class between whites and Africans, the Act also provided for the so-called Native Purchase Areas (NPAs), where Africans could purchase land. The Crown lands were owned by the state in reserve for future allocation, as well as for public parks and state forests. The 1930 LAA was a close copy of the South African 1913 Native Land Act, which also sought to cripple African agricultural self-sufficiency in order to generate cheap African labor, among other objectives.

When, as expected, the growing African population began to exert pressure on the allocated land resources through soil erosion and other forms of environmental degradation, the colonial governments placed the blame on poor African agricultural practices and imposed cattle destocking measures as well as a number of very unpopular soil conservation policies which alienated a growing number of Africans. These measures were accompanied by the 1951 by the Native Land Husbandry Act (LHA), Native Land Husbandry Act (NLHA), which was designed to reform the African land tenure system from communal to individual ownership, ostensibly, in order to improve efficiency in African agriculture. A not-so-obviously stated objective was to promote stable labor in the emerging industries in the colony's emerging towns and cities by creating a class of Africans permanently divorced from the land and, therefore, obliged to provide labor in the emerging industries. The last major piece of land legislation during the colonial period was the Land Tenure Act of 1969 passed by the Rhodesian Front government of the day, which replaced the LAA and still unfairly allocated an equal amount of land to Africans and whites, even though whites comprised only 5% of the colony's population. Thus, approximately 5 million Africans were to share 44.9 million acres at the ratio of 67.9 persons per square mile, while less than a quarter of a million whites shared 44.95 million acres at 3.2 persons per acre (Austin 1975). As was presaged by the first three African reserves created in 1893, most of the land allocated to the Africans in subsequent legislation was in dry areas with marginal and unproductive soils, thus contributing greatly to the economic marginalization and underdevelopment of the African majority. In the words of Reg. Austin,

> Apart from tenure and scale, Africans suffer other disadvantages: The main roads and railway lines were planned only in relation to white areas. Urban centres and, hence, industry and associated activities are concentrated in white areas. In relation to soil fertility and rainfall, the better agricultural land is predominantly in white areas. By and large, whites have almost as much 'good' land as 'bad' land, while the African land is three-quarters 'bad' and only a quarter 'good'. (Austin 1975)

A Racialized Labor Regime

A dilemma facing early white settlers was how to maintain spatial racial segregation while ensuring the constant supply of cheap African labor. The solution was found in the creation of African reserves where Africans could permanently reside but be allowed to provide labor in the white areas as transient laborers. For this reason, there was great resistance to the provision of urban housing and social amenities to Africans, especially since there was also a widely held belief that Africans were "unhygienic" and most likely to engender disease outbreaks which would impact negatively on the white population. According to Ginsburg,

> Under the policy of segregation, Africans were categorised as temporary lodgers in white cities to fulfil the most menial of tasks. It was believed that physical proximity meant more chance of social mixing, miscegenation and the spread of disease ... Africans were seen to carry infectious diseases over to the white population and this provided a powerful justification and motivation for urban segregation. (Ginsburg 2017)

Consequently, the state passed the Native Urban Locations Ordinance (1906) and the Private Locations Ordinance (1908) restricting Africans to designated native areas or native locations which were very basic, since they were regarded as only temporary homes for the transient laborers who had their permanent homes in the Reserves.

In order to control African labor, the state passed the 1901 Masters and Servants Ordinance and the 1902 Natives Pass Ordinance, both designed to enforce labor contracts and to regulate African labor mobility. The first regulated relations between white masters and African servants in ways which gave the former unchallenged control over the latter, while the second was meant to control the movement of male laborers in the colonial economy and to reduce desertions, among other goals. Indeed, the lives of African males above the age of 14 years became closely governed by a variety of passes, namely registration certificates, work-seeking passes, visiting passes, contract service passes upon gaining employment, and passes to get out of the employers' premises at night. Meanwhile, mine owners adopted the compound system which housed laborers, mostly migrant workers from the surrounding countries of Northern Rhodesia, Nyasaland and Mozambique, in prison-like institutions where they were closely monitored and could be easily disciplined. To get the labor out, the state introduced a range of taxes, including the Native tax, dog tax, dip tax, and a tax for every second and subsequent wives; all payable in money and, therefore, necessitating Africans to seek for employment in the white economic sector in order to raise the required amounts.

Meanwhile, white workers, like white farmers, remained strongly hostile to African competition, as evidenced in the open hostility by white artisans to the training of African artisans at Missions in the early 1920s, resulting in the commitment by the country's Chamber of Mines under pressure from the white trade unions that "coloured employees should not be employed on certain skilled work" (Steele 1972). Opposition to possible African competition in the work place was pushed vigorously by the Rhodesian Labor Party in the 1920s, which, reminiscent of white workers on the Rand in South Africa at the time, insisted on guaranteeing the white workers' future through an industrial color bar that would ensure that African artisans would be permitted to work only in their own areas. It maintained that Africans should be employed in white areas only as unskilled workers. Significantly also at its foundation in 1929, the White Rhodesia Association, whose first chairman was the future Prime Minister, Godfrey Huggins, proposed to stem African competition in the labor market through increased white immigration which would result in the country having more whites than Africans and, thus make African labor redundant. It was partly under this pressure that Prime Minister Huggins promulgated his two-pyramid policy in which whites and Africans were to develop separately from each other.

This was followed by the state passing the Industrial Conciliation Act of 1934, which was enacted partly "in response to a strike by European workers within the building industry who felt threatened by being replaced by African workers" (Ginsburg 2017). The Act effectively introduced a labor color bar by providing for the establishment of trade unions and industrial councils for employers as part of an industrial conciliation system, but pointedly excluding Africans from the definition of employees and, thus, making it unlawful for them to be part of trade unions. Meanwhile, apprenticeships were restricted to whites under the Act. This was in addition to the fact that the Public Services Act of 1921 had already excluded Africans from employment in the civil services, meaning that Africans could not work as "foremen, telegraphists, postal sorter, salesmen, typists, printers, dispensers, or even mechanics employed by Government or industry." Despite such restrictions, an African middle class developed, nevertheless, over time, much to the consternation of some white workers (Ginsburg 2017).

Justifying his policies, Huggins stated:

> The Europeans in this country can be likened to an island of white in a sea of black, with the artisan and tradesmen forming the shores and professional classes the highlands in the centre. Is the native to be allowed to erode away the shores and gradually attack the highland? To permit this would mean that the leaven of civilisation would be removed from the country, and the black man would inevitably revert to a barbarian worse than before. (*Bulawayo Chronicle*, 31 March, 1938)

Under the Huggins administration, African workers faced other restrictive discriminatory legislation, including the 1936 Native Registration Act, which regulated the movement of African males into the urban centers by requiring that, in addition to the registration certificate introduced earlier in the century, one had to have either a "pass authorising him to seek work in town, a certificate to prove that he was employed in the town, a certificate signed by a native commissioner" testifying that he was "earning a living in the town by lawful means" or a visiting pass from his employer if employed outside town (Phimister 1988). With time, however, Huggins realized that separate development was not practical in the Rhodesian context and moved more toward a discriminatory but more integrated development model.

Discrimination between white and black workers persisted into the Unilateral Declaration of Independence (UDI) years from 1965 until the country's independence in 1980, during which period many white workers supported the Rhodesian Front Party's policies to maintain "segregation, land apportionment, the colour bar" and "to protect the white settler state" and its claims to fighting to maintain "standards" and against communism. While the official rhetoric was that of defending Christian civilization, white workers, in fact, sought to maintain so-called standards, "through upholding racist labour practices" and "conflated their own fate with the idea of 'white civilisation'" (Ginsburg 2017).

Some Are "More White" than Others (Mlambo 2000)

Racism in Southern Rhodesia manifested itself, not only along the white and black racial divide, but also among whites themselves, with settlers of English stock regarding themselves as superior to whites from other countries or regions of the world. While Cecil John Rhodes had dreamt of developing Southern Rhodesia as a white man's country, this was not to be because Rhodesian governments were very particular about who they let into "their" country, preferring to accept only the "right type" of immigrant, by which they meant British immigrants. In fact, despite the semblance of unity, the white Rhodesian community was deeply divided by, among other factors, racism and racial chauvinism which emanated, largely, from settlers of British stock and which evoked equally strong animosities from other white groups, particularly the Afrikaners. By the 1920s, Afrikaners were generally regarded as illiterate, indigent, and undesirable and a group which was once described as "neither black not white but really worse than animals; and … mentally deficient" (Townsend 1964). British settlers also dismissed Afrikaners as people with "no code of honour such as is understood by the Britishers," "low class," and "persons of a poor and shiftless type, physical degenerates, sick and diseased" as well as people who were "low in mentality and mode of existence … little removed from the native" (Mlambo 2003). Also looked down upon were Poles, Greeks, Italian, Spaniards, and people of the Jewish religion (Mlambo 2003).

Writing in the 1920s, E. Tawse Jollie, the only female member of the Southern Rhodesian Legislative Council, noted that the "average-born Rhodesian feels that this is essentially a British country, pioneered, bought and developed by British people, and he wants to keep it so" (Jollie 1921). Similarly, in 1939, C. Harding of the Department of Internal Affairs gave the official Southern Rhodesian government position on immigrations as follows:

> The policy of the government in regard to immigrants is to maintain a preponderance of British subjects in about the same proportions as last year when the total number of immigrants was 3 500 of whom 3 000 were British subjects and 500 aliens i.e. 6 to 1. (Mlambo 2003)

Ginsburg reported that the 1933 Immigration Bill listed "Levantines, Europeans from Eastern Europe, Europeans from South Eastern Europe, Low class Greeks, low class Italians, 'Jews of low type and mixed origin and other persons of mixed origin and continental birth'" as undesirable immigrants (Ginsburg 2017).

As Gann and Gelfand correctly observed, in the post-Second World War years as well as in earlier years, "After dinner speakers would extol 'white Rhodesia' but agreed that white aliens should not be allowed to overrun the country but must only be assimilated in penny packets"(Gann and Gelfand 1964).

The Invisible Minorities

In addition to the racial categories of European and "native," there was also another category, that of Asians and Coloureds, who Muzondidya calls the "invisible subject minorities ... who held an intermediate status in the Rhodesian racial hierarchy, distinct from the white and African populations." (The category of "natives" comprised two distinct groups, namely the so-called colonial natives, who included all the Africans in the country and who originated from outside the country, and indigenous natives, i.e., those descending from tribes indigenous to Rhodesia.) Included in this category were local and foreign descendants of mixed race, including "Griquas, Malays and Cape Coloureds from South Africa" and Indian immigrants (Muzondidya 2007). The settler state strongly discouraged Indian immigration into the country, resulting in the Indian population in the country remaining small for much of the colonial period. The immigration of Indians into Rhodesia was regarded with both fear and hostility. The fear was of economic competition as Indians were accused of undercutting European merchants which threatened the very existence of whites in the country (Douglas n.d.). In 1908, the state passed the Asiatic Immigration Ordinance of 1908 designed to discourage Indian immigration except at the discretion of the Company Administrator. The ordinance was rescinded following protests from the British India Association and the Indian Government (Mlambo 2003).

Despite being regarded as inferior to whites, the invisible minorities were considered superior to the "natives" and were, accordingly, granted some privileges which were denied the indigenous population. For instance, they did not have to carry passes and had easier access to the urban areas. They also were free to live in the urban areas and were not confided to the Locations, until the passage of the 1930 LAA after which they were required to reside in segregated areas. Asians and Coloureds also had access to white hospitals, schools, and other social amenities and had some voting powers, at least until the Rhodesian Front removed this right in its 1969 Constitution. These privileges notwithstanding, the subject races were still discriminated against in the types of employment they could take up and "remained on the margins of colonial society where they faced exploitation, discrimination and denial of full citizenship because of their race and origin" (Muzondidya 2007).

Political Marginalization and Other Forms of Discrimination

Throughout the colonial period, Africans remained politically marginalized even though, technically, the vote was open to everyone who met the various stipulated qualifications. The main problem was that these qualifications were set so high that very few Africans could meet them, so the majority of the African population could not vote. A good example is the 1923 Constitution which granted the vote to all men (White women had been allowed to vote in 1919) who were British subjects over 21 years of age and literate enough to fill the particulars of the application form but set the conditions that to be eligible, applicants for enrolment must have an income of £100 per annum, occupy buildings worth £150, or own a mining claim. Given the fact that the average wage of an African was £3 a month, only whites were eligible to vote under this constitution (Mutiti 1974). Subsequent constitutions raised the property qualification bar to levels that excluded the African majority as well as demanding specified educational levels that were unattainable to most Africans in an educational system which favored white children over blacks in several ways.

The state discriminated against African children in education by showing no interest in African education and leaving it in the hands of the missionaries until well into the 1940s and encouraging mostly industrial education in those schools through a grant system which it provided the mission schools with (Dierdorp 2015). The state had no interest in providing a well-rounded education for African children, for as one member of the Southern Rhodesian Legislative Assembly emphasized in 1927:

> We do not intend to hand over this country to the native population or to admit them to the same society or political position as we occupy ourselves ... We should make no pretence of educating them in exactly the same way as we do the Europeans.

Following that logic, African education was consistently underfunded throughout the colonial period. In addition, while education was made compulsory for all white children from 1930, over 50% of African children were not attending school as late as 1979, while the government established the first secondary school in the country only in 1946 (Mlambo 2014). It is no wonder most Africans could not meet the educational requirements for voting.

Apart from the political marginalization, as in South Africa, Africans in Rhodesia were also governed by petty discrimination legislation barring them from using Whites-only toilets, park benches, and other public facilities, and, until the late 1920s, from walking on the pavements in the towns. Until the 1960s, the major hotels in Salisbury, the Miekles and the Ambassador, enforced a color bar and did not serve Africans in their bars and restaurants. The third, the Jameson, was multiracial but deliberately exclusive of the African majority by insisting on certain standards of "culture," "civilization," and dress code. Lastly, until 1959, "it was illegal to accommodate Africans in hotels that were located in European areas (and vice versa)" without special permission from the Secretary of Native Affairs (Craggs 2012).

There was also rampant discrimination in sports (Novak 2012, Dierdorp) and in other social spaces. Such discrimination belied the official policy as a member of the Central African Federation (1953–1963) which was, officially, one of promoting partnership between the races, although it later turned out that the partnership which was envisaged was that between a rider and a horse, rather than one based on genuine equality. White liberal organizations, such as the Interracial Association (IRA) and the Capricorn Africa Society (CAS), mushroomed in this period and maintained the fiction of racial partnership, succeeding in attracting the attention of a few African nationalists for a while until the Africans realized that partnership was a sham (Mlambo 2014; Townsend 1964; Craggs 2012). It was the cumulative result of the many years of political, economic, social, educational, and other types of marginalization on the basis of race which eventually led to the rise and intensification of African nationalism which culminated in the armed struggle as African nationalists fought to end white settler colonialism in the country.

Conclusion

Colonial Zimbabwe was born out of a racist ethos espoused by its patron, Cecil Rhodes, and rooted in the late nineteenth century scientific racism, social Darwinism, and the white-man's-burden philosophy which extolled the virtues of whiteness and Western civilization and denigrated everything African. Not surprisingly, the African population was treated as second-class citizens and marginalized in every walk of life throughout the colonial period, resulting in African nationalists taking up arms in a bitter struggle to overthrow the racist colonial dispensation. The result was Zimbabwe's independence in 1980.

References

Austin R (1975) Racism and apartheid in Southern Africa: Rhodesia: a book of data. UNESCO Press, Paris
Bulawayo Chronicle (8 February, 1895; 20 September 1895; 31 March 1938)
Craggs R (2012) Towards a political geography of hotels: Southern Rhodesia 1958–1962. Polit Geogr 31(4):215–224
Dierdorp L (2015) Segregated education in South Africa and Southern Rhodesia. MA thesis, Utrecht University
Douglas RGS (n.d.) The development of the Department of Immigration to 1953. Cyclostyled paper in the National Archives of Zimbabwe
Drummond H (1890) Tropical Africa B. Alden, New York
Gann LH, Gelfand M (1964) Huggins of Rhodesia: the man and his country. George Allen and Unwin, London
Ginsburg N (2017) White workers and the production of race in Southern Rhodesia, 1910–1980. PhD thesis, University of Leeds
Gombay K (1991) The black peril and miscegenation: the regulation of inter-racial sexual relations in Southern Rhodesia, 1890–1933. MA thesis, McGill University
Hofstadter R (1944) Social Darwinism in American thought. Beacon press, Boston
Jollie ET (1921) Southern Rhodesia. S Afr Q III:10–12

Lessing D (1950) The grass is singing. Heinemann, London
Little Brown (1916) Rhodesia Herald, 14 July 1916
Mhike I (2016) Deviance and colonial power: a history of juvenile delinquency in colonial Zimbabwe, 1890–c1960. PhD thesis, University of the Free State
Mlambo A (2000) Some are more white than others: racial chauvinism as a factor in Rhodesian migration policy, 1890 to 1963. Zambezia 17(2):139–160
Mlambo A (2003) White immigration into Rhodesia: from occupation to federation. University of Zimbabwe Publications, Harare
Mlambo AS (2014) History of Zimbabwe. Cambridge University Press, Cambridge
Mushonga M (2008-9) The criminalisation of sex between 'black' and 'white' and miscegenation Hullabaloo in Rhodesia: an analysis of the marriage of Patrick Matimba and Adriana von Hoom, 1955 to 1959. Lesotho Law J: J Law Dev 18(2):435–456
Mushonga M (2013) White power, white desire: miscegenation in Southern Rhodesia. Zimbabwe Afr J Hist Cult 5(1):1–12
Mushunje A (2005) Farm efficiency and land reform in Zimbabwe. PhD, University of Fort Hare, Alice
Mutiti AB (1974) Rhodesia and her four discriminatory constitutions. Presence Afr 90:261–275
Muzondidya J (2007) Jambanja: ideological ambiguities in the politics of land and resource ownership in Zimbabwe. J South Afr Stud 23(2):325–341
Novak A (2012) Sport and racial discrimination in colonial Zimbabwe: a reanalysis. Int J Hist Sport 29(6)1–17
Pape J (1990) Black and white: the 'perils of sex' in colonial Zimbabwe. J South Afr Stud 16 (4):699–720
Patel H (1974) Indians in Uganda and Rhodesia: some comparative perspectives on a minority in Africa. University of Denver Press, Denver
Phimister I (1988) An economic and social history of Zimbabwe, 1890–1948: capital accummulation and class struggle. Longman, London
Rhodes C (1877) Confession of faith. In: John E. Flint, Cecil Rhodes (Boston: Little Brown, 1974), pp. 248–52
Rogers JA (1972) Darwinism and social Darwinism. J Hist Ideas 33(2):265–280
Schmidt E (1992) Peasants, traders and wives. Baobab, Harare
Shutt A (2007) The native are getting out of hand: legislating manners, insolence and contemptuous behaviour in Southern Rhodesia, c. 1910–1963. J South Afr Stud 33(3):633–672
Sicilia O (1999) There is no such thing as a spirit in the stone! Misrepresentations of Zimbabwean stone sculpture: an anthropological approach. Dissertation Com, Florida, Boca Raton
Steele MC (1972) The foundations of a native policy in Southern Rhodesia, 1923–1933. PhD thesis, Simon Fraser University
Tatum B (2003) Why are all the black kids sitting together in the cafeteria?: a psychologist explains the development of racial identity. Basic Books, New York
Townsend HG (1964) Colour bar or community: reflections on Rhodesia. New Blackfriars 45 (531):367–375
Turnbull CM (1962) The lonely African. Simon & Schuster, New York
Vambe L (1976) From Rhodesia to Zimbabwe. University of Pittsburgh Press, Pennsylvania
West MO (2003) Review of black peril, white virtue: sexual crime in Southern Rhodesia, 1902–1935 by Jock McCulloch. J Soc Hist 36(3):815–819

Ethnic Riots in United Kingdom in 2001

26

Paul Bagguley and Yasmin Hussain

Contents

Introduction	448
What Happened in 2001?	449
The Burnley Disturbances	451
Bradford 2001	452
The Power of Surveillance Policing	454
Community Cohesion	457
Conclusion	460
Cross-References	461
References	461

Abstract

This chapter analyzes the context causes and consequences for ethnic relations of the 2001 riots in the North of England. Between May and July 2001, a series of riots occurred in the Northern former textile towns of Oldham, Burnley, and Bradford. The social context and key features of the riots in each of the towns are examined. This is followed by a discussion of the policing and subsequent prosecution of the rioters, especially in Bradford where the most serious disturbances occurred. Finally the chapter analyzes the emergence of community cohesion policy as one of the longer-term consequences of the riots.

Keywords

Ethnic relations · South Asian · 2001 riots · Bradford · Oldham · Burnley

P. Bagguley (✉) · Y. Hussain
School of Sociology and Social Policy, University of Leeds, Leeds, UK
e-mail: P.Bagguley@leeds.ac.uk

© The Author(s), under exclusive license to Springer Nature Singapore Pte Ltd. 2019
S. Ratuva (ed.), *The Palgrave Handbook of Ethnicity*,
https://doi.org/10.1007/978-981-13-2898-5_30

Introduction

The year 2001 is better remembered for the 9/11 attacks and the beginning of the long "war on terror" (Sayyid 2013). However, from May to July 2001, there were a series of riots in Oldham, Burnley, and Bradford in the North of England. The three towns shared the characteristics of being former centers of the textile industry and had lost most of this employment since the 1980s and also had substantial British South Asian populations. This wave of riots began in Oldham over 26–29 May involving around 500 people, injuring two police officers and three members of the public. The resulting damage to property was estimated at £1.4 million. A month later in Burnley, similar disturbances involving around 400 people occurred on 24–26 June. In this case 83 police officers were injured along with 28 members of the public. The most serious riot that summer occurred in Bradford over 7–9 July involving 500 people. Those injured during the Bradford disturbances included 326 police officers and 14 members of the public (Bagguley and Hussain 2008).

Rude (1981: 10–11) suggested that it is necessary to ask what happened in a riot and why and with what consequences and what were the response of the forces of law and order and the longer-term consequences of the event. This chapter provides such an overview of the riots of 2001 in the UK. It begins with a consideration of what kinds of places were Oldham, Burnley, and Bradford in 2001 and what is known about who was involved and who or what they were attacking. This is then followed by a section on the response of the police and the criminal justice system to the riots with a special focus on the political responses to the riots. The final section of the chapter looks at the longer-term consequences of the riots in terms of the changes that resulted in the state's management of "ethnic relations" in the UK in terms of the emergence of the discourse and practice of community cohesion.

It is important to locate the events of 2001 in the longer-term history of racialized riots in the UK (Bagguley and Hussain 2008; Joshua and Wallace 1983; Keith 1993). The conventional view is to see the character of these riots changing over time from white crowds attacking ethnic minority men in the riots up to the 1950, often with police standing aside, with the 1980s onward as a period of "black resistance" (Joshua and Wallace 1983). However, in this chapter it is suggested that the 2001 riots do not quite fit this historical generalization as shall be seen from the discussion of the riots below. If anything the riots of 2001 have several similarities with the riots of the first half of the twentieth century, especially given the role of neofascist groups and white crowds instigating some of the violence.

Prior to the riots, there had been heightened media and political concerns around young South Asian men giving rise to a populist image of "the Asian gang" Alexander's (2004). These populist discourses suggested that while young Bangladeshi and Pakistani women apparently need defending from forced marriages and male violence, the rest of "us" need defending from the young men from the same backgrounds. South Asian men are no longer stereotyped in media and political discourses as passive feminized victims as they were prior to the 1990s, but since then they have been increasingly seen as the new aggressors (Alexander 2004). All of this marks a reworking of the meaning of ethnicity as it is imposed upon South

Asian communities by others. While previously the concern was to define ethnicity in this context in terms of supposedly traditional, fixed, and internally homogenous collectivities based upon the national origins of the initial migrants, this has now shifted to focus upon religion as the defining characteristic. In particular Muslims are now seen as the most problematic group and the ones who are reluctant to assimilate, the most deprived, and the most dangerous. The 2001 riots in the UK and the wider responses to them were a key turning point in how Muslims were perceived in the UK.

What Happened in 2001?

This section examines the social contexts of Oldham, Burnley, and Bradford in 2001 and who was involved in the riots. Despite the popular impression of Oldham, Burnley, and Bradford as centers of settlement of the South Asian, and especially Pakistani, diaspora in Britain, all three locations at the time had predominantly White British populations. According to the 2001 Census, 4.9% of the Burnley population, 6.3% of the Oldham population, and 14.5% of the Bradford population reported their ethnic origin as British-Pakistani (Bagguley and Hussain 2008: 40). Furthermore, these were still predominantly working class places compared to the rest of the country. Over 50% of the population in each of these towns reported their employment as being in blue-collar or working class occupations to the 2001 Census, compared to England and Wales as a whole where most people reported that they were in white-collar or middle class occupations. The riots occurred against local backgrounds of high unemployment. The unemployment rates for men from the two principal British South-Asian ethnic groups in the three localities were twice as high as the White British male population (Bagguley and Hussain 2008: 41).

Oldham was the first place which experienced unrest in 2001 and had experienced deteriorating relationships between the local police and the local communities prior to this (Ray and Smith 2004). This saw the emergence of a "moral panic" about racially motivated crimes by South Asians on local white people (Ray and Smith 2004: 687). The release of these statistics to the media and how they were interpreted heightened the sense of conflict between the white and South Asian communities in Oldham. The police claimed that during the 1990s gangs of young South Asian men had been trying to create "no-go" areas for whites in certain areas of Oldham (Kalra 2002). In January 2001 the police figures purported to show that over 60% of the racial incidents were by South Asians on whites. Consequently the local press reported the rise in racist offending against whites in typically lurid terms (Ray and Smith 2004: 691). This undermined the confidence of ethnic minority communities in the local police. In such a context, underreporting of racist incidents against ethnic minority communities tends to follow, further distorting the picture represented in official statistics (Ray and Smith 2004).

The media interest in these issues led the neofascist British National Party (BNP) to see the town as a potential area for recruitment and possible electoral contests, and the central theme of this mobilization was the defense of white rights and the vilification of Muslims (Allen 2003: 26). Following a rally in the town on 3 March, the Party staged a protest outside the local police station against South Asian violence toward whites. This was followed up by the National Front planning a march in Oldham at the end of the month. The march was banned by the Home Office, but this was followed by national media interest in the form of BBC's Radio 4 reporting on the creation of no-go areas for whites in the town.

Unfortunately these events were followed by an attack by a group of South Asian youths on a 76-year-old white war veteran. Although this did not take place in one of the putative "no-go areas," the attack did attract further attention to the issue. National newspapers claimed that the attack was racially motivated with headlines such as "Whites beware" and "Beaten for being white," despite the victim's family arguing that it was not a racially motivated crime. Over the following weeks during the general election campaign groups of members of neofascist organizations such as the BNP, the National Front and Combat 18 met regularly in Oldham pubs, and one of these meetings played a key role in the riots that followed (Asian News, 1 December 2001).

On the evening of 26 May 2001, two South Asian boys aged 11 and 14 were walking along a street on the boundary of the mainly South Asian Glodwick neighborhood. A 16-year-old white youth threw a brick at them which struck one of them on the leg. He ran into a nearby house pursued by the victim and his 19-year-old brother. As they kicked the front door of the house, a 36-year-old white woman who lived there became alarmed and was racially abusive toward them and attempted to slap one of them as she followed them down the street. Other South Asian youngsters became embroiled in the argument, and the woman phoned her 25-year-old brother telling him: "Some Pakis have kicked the door in." He had spent the day in Oldham pubs with up to 12 friends variously described as members of the neofascist group Combat 18 as well as the Fine Young Casuals firm of football hooligans singing songs such as "Keep me English," "No surrender to the IRA," and "If you all hate Pakis clap your hands" (Bagguley and Hussain 2008: 47).

The group arrived at the house shortly after 8:00 pm and proceeded to attack nearby South Asian people and their property with iron bars and piece of wood. Up to 200 White people were reportedly in the area retreating into local pubs after their attacks. Windows were smashed, and a South Asian woman 34 weeks pregnant had to receive hospital treatment for shock after her house was attacked (Kundnani 2003). As a result South Asian men responded in the midst of rumors that the police were not responding to the attacks. The police arrested some of the South Asian men who arrived on the scene while protecting white people they had arrested, and at 8:45 pm the police withdrew from the area. Later that evening and into the early morning, around 500 South Asian men built barricades and threw petrol bombs and other missiles at police. In addition the offices of the *Oldham Evening Chronicle*, a local newspaper widely seen as anti-Asian, 4 public houses and 32 police vehicles were damaged.

It was over 2 years later that the 12 white defendants were tried and sentenced for their role in the riots. Despite the court accepting that they had played a key role in instigating the violence, nine men and one woman were sentenced to 9 months each for affray, and a 16-year-old boy received a 12-month supervision order and a 17-year-old girl a conditional discharge. In comparison 22 South Asian men had been sentenced for an average of 3.5 years in prison and ranging up to 7 years for riot for their actions during the Oldham disturbances. The 12 white defendants had originally been charged with riot by the police, but the judge ruled that there was insufficient evidence so they were tried for the lesser offences of affray and common assault (Kundnani 2003).

The Burnley Disturbances

The events in Burnley on 23–25 June 2001 followed after those in Oldham. There is an official account from the police of the disturbances in Burnley that, although it was accepted by the Burnley local authority's Task Force as an accurate account of events (Clarke 2001: 36), has been critically discussed by others (King and Waddington 2007). Prior to the disturbances, it has been noted how politics in the town had moved to the right. The local council was accused of giving preferential treatment to areas of South Asian residence in its investment, and there had been calls for the Equal Opportunities coordinator and translation unit to be closed. Furthermore, the BNP had recently won 21% of the vote in a local authority by-election, and the party achieved its second highest vote in the area in the 2001 general election. In addition the local South Asian community had reportedly lost its trust in the police in the light of a number of incidents immediately prior to the riots (King and Waddington 2007).

The focus of the disturbances in Burnley was in the north of the town in the Stoneyholme, Danehouse, and Duke Bar districts. These areas are the main concentrations of ethnic minority residence in the town with Danehouse, for example, being the heart of the local Pakistani community and Stoneyholme that of the Bangladeshi community. Prior to the disturbances, a number of incidents have been identified as playing a role in their development including a dispute between white and South Asian neighbors and attack on a South Asian taxi driver and a series of violent incidents in the Danehouse and Colne Road areas that the police account described as being related to conflicts over drug dealing (King and Waddington 2007: 125).

That evening on Saturday 23 June, a group of white men gathered outside the ground of Burnley football club before attacking several South Asian-owned takeaways. After warnings were given to the South Asian family who lived there, an off-license in the Burnley Wood district was looted and destroyed in an arson attack. Similarly Shafi's store in Oxford Road was looted and set on fire by white rioters. Subsequently at around 11:00 pm, around 70 South Asian men attacked the Duke of York public house in the Duke Bar district, smashing its windows and knocking two customers unconscious and wrecking the pub with a fire bomb attack. The police interpretation of this was that it was an act of revenge in retaliation for the attack on the South Asian taxi driver (Clarke 2002; King and Waddington 2007).

The Duke of York pub had been previously largely cleared of its customers on police advice amidst rumors of an attack on the premises. Many moved to a nearby pub, the Baltic House, which had a reputation as a gathering place for neofascist sympathizers (King and Waddington 2007: 126). In addition a member of the Commission for Racial Equality, the son of the Deputy Mayor of Burnley and at that time the only ethnic minority member of the National Executive of the Labour Party, Shahid Malik was hit on the head by up to four police officers and required hospital treatment on the evening of 25 June. He was trying to persuade a crowd of South Asian men who were facing a line of police in full riot gear to disperse. The police subsequently arrested him on suspicion of inciting violent disorder, but the charges were dropped (Bagguley and Hussain 2008: 49).

One of the distinctive features of the Burnley disturbances compared to those in Oldham and especially Bradford was that most of those arrested for their role in them were white. At the time of their submission to the Burnley Task Force inquiry, the police had arrested 101 out of 157 of those sought for offences during the disturbances. Of these 101 around two thirds were white and the remainder were South Asian. The largest single group of offenders were white men aged over 30 (Clarke 2002, appendix 10 k). White middle-aged man hardly fits the stereotype of the rioting South Asian youth that has dominated most debate since the riots.

Bradford 2001

The Bradford disturbances in early July 2001 followed those in Oldham and Burnley. As will become clear, there are a number of distinctive elements to the development of the violence in Bradford. According to Allen (2003) early in 2001 the neofascist British National Party leafleted extensively in North Bradford with leaflets carrying the slogans: "Islam out of Britain" and "I.S.L.A.M. – Intolerance, Slaughter, Looting, Arson and Molestation of women." These leaflets claimed that these actions were encouraged by the teaching of the Koran and that the issue is not a matter of race as Hindu and Sikh activists had published warnings against the dangers of Islam. In the May 2001 elections, the BNP's candidate won 1,600 votes in Bradford North. The day before the riots, a meeting in the Ravenscliffe area of Bradford for BNP activists and sympathizers was addressed by the BNP leader Nick Griffin (Bagguley and Hussain 2008: 55).

Around noon on Saturday 7 July 2001, several hundred people of a variety of ethnic backgrounds gathered in the center of Bradford to attend a demonstration organized by the Anti-Nazi League and their allies against a threatened march in the city by the National Front. The police had successfully requested the Home Office to ban the march and a countermarch planned by the Anti-Nazi League. In addition this had been communicated widely to the local community by the police and local politicians; there was sufficient skepticism for there to be a reported 600 present. This skepticism had been fuelled by the last minute cancellation of the "World in a City" music festival scheduled to take place in Centenary Square in the center of Bradford. After taking advice from the police, Bradford City Council cancelled the event a matter of days before it was due to happen. This was because of the fear that a few members of another small neofascist group – the National Front (NF) - visiting

Bradford and provoking violence that could have been a wider threat to public safety. This decision was criticized by some local politicians as giving in to the NF and for it continuing to fuel the rumors that they were coming to Bradford despite the ban on their march (Bagguley and Hussain 2008; Bujra and Pearce 2011).

By 3:00 pm the Anti-Nazi League rally was winding down, although some of those attending were still present in Centenary Square and the police were requesting them to disperse having been herded into a corner of the square. Some of the politicians who had attended at least were leaving, and the event had reportedly ended quietly at 2:30 pm. At this point it may be inferred that some of the crowd were dispersing as well. Around 2:45 pm the police turned back five NF supporters who had arrived at Bradford Interchange railway station, and it was reported that they had complied with the police and left Bradford. However, at around 4:00 pm news of the racist attack on an Asian man in Ivegate outside Addison's bar reached some in the crowd in Centenary Square a matter of yards away (Bagguley and Hussain 2008; Bujra and Pearce 2011; Waddington 2010).

The principal damage to property during this time was an arson attack Lister's BMW garage on Oak Lane, a similar arson attack on the Labour Club on Whetley Hill, from which 30 people narrowly escaped, the Upper Globe pub on Whetley Hill and Arthur's bar on Heaton road. In addition, the Lower Globe pub on Heaton road suffered fire damage as did a butcher's shop on Oak Lane, while in the city center, various shops had broken windows. The police had to draw in a further 425 officers from 9 other police forces to reinforce the 500 already present. Of these 326 were injured. The police eventually recorded 452 crimes including criminal damage, arson, assaults on police officers, robbery, and serious assault. The overall property damage was estimated at £7.5 m (Bagguley and Hussain 2008; Bujra and Pearce 2011; Waddington 2010).

In the press conferences immediately afterward, senior police officers admitted that they had lost control over the situation. Furthermore, despite stopping a small group of NF supporters at the railway station and ordering them to leave the city, they also admitted that "between 12 and 30" had successfully travelled to Bradford in spite of the ban on their march. Various attempts by so-called community leaders to negotiate between the rioters and the police mostly failed. However, the main phase of violence ended at around 1:00 am when some South Asian community members persuaded those involved in the violence to given up. However, those involved in this successful initiative were not the elected local politicians or publicly recognized "community leaders" (Bagguley and Hussain 2008).

The immediate response of politicians and senior police officers was to criminalize the rioters (Allen 2003). Although several of the newspaper headlines and comment used the language of "race riots" to describe the events in Bradford, senior police officers and politicians were quick to dismiss that label. They were equally quick to dismiss any role for factors such as economic and social conditions in the inner city. The predominant explanation as reported in the media that came from the police and politicians was simply to label the events as simply criminal. Several local politicians emphasized the need to "root out" the criminals (Bagguley and Hussain 2008: 61–2). These statements are a straightforward expression of the "law and order" discourse that emerged in the 1970s and 1980s (Keith 1993). Given that these are Labour Party MPs, this just illustrates how this discourse of the Conservative right has now become dominant.

Others highlighted issues that were to become central theme of the predominant community cohesion discourse that featured so strongly in the subsequent reports on the disturbances in Oldham and Burnley. These issues were on the one hand the perceived spatial and social segregation of different ethnic communities and on the other hand the question of speaking English and the more general undesirable transnational marriages of some in the South Asian community. These express the underlying culturally racist notion that the causes of the riots were ultimately to be found in the culture of south Asian Muslim communities themselves (Bagguley and Hussain 2008).

The Power of Surveillance Policing

One of the most striking features of the state's response to the 2001 riots was the long sentences that the rioters received. Most of the youth prison sentences for riot were for up to 18 months, whereas most of the adults were sentenced for 4 or 5 years for riot, with some sentences ranging up to 9 years (Carling et al. 2004). These were longer than comparable sentences given to those involved in the riots in Burley and Oldham that summer. This was part of a centrally sanctioned exercise in the strategic repression of those involved in the riots and their communities.

Toward the end of July 2001, the police began to release photographs of those wanted in relation to the riots. Through posters displayed in police stations, mosques, and schools as well as the police website and through the local press, 212 photographs were released. Three years later 305 people ranging in age from 13 to 47 had been arrested in connect with offences committed during the disorders, and 259 were charged with offences of which 183 were charged with the most serious public order offence of riot. At least 188 received custodial sentences of some kind in relation to offences committed in connection with the disturbances. The longest sentences were 12 years for arson and 8.5 years for throwing petrol bombs. Of those arrested 88% were South Asian, 10% were White, and 2% were African Caribbean. Furthermore 86% came from Bradford, 7% from nearby Keighley, and 5% from elsewhere in West Yorkshire, leaving only 3% from outside the county (Bagguley and Hussain 2008).

The most important prerequisite for the success of the state in punishing those involved in the Bradford violence was the changes in the law relating to riot as a result of events in the 1980s. Under the older public order legislation, very few people were ever charged or successfully prosecuted for the crime of riot in the second half of the twentieth century (Joshua and Wallace 1983). These failures to successfully pursue charges of riot against those involved in more serious disturbances in 1981 was one of the reasons for the reform of public order legislation, although concerns with public order going back to the 1970s played the most significant role. The 1986 Public Order Act introduced a much more promiscuous legal definition of riot. One that would make prosecutions much more feasible in case such as the riots experienced in England during the 1980s. The 1986 Public Order Act specifies a sentence of up to 10 years. More important for the process of prosecuting rioters, however, was the redefinition of riot as follows:

> (1) Where twelve or more persons who are present together use or threaten unlawful violence for a common purpose and the conduct them (taken together) is such as would cause a person of reasonable firmness present at the scene to fear for his personal safety, each of the persons using unlawful violence for the common purpose is guilty of Riot. (2) It is immaterial whether or not the twelve or more persons use or threaten unlawful violence simultaneously. (3) The common purpose may be inferred from conduct. (4) No person of reasonable firmness need actually be, or be likely to be, present at the scene. (5) Riot may be committed in private as well as in public places. (Carling et al. 2004: 11)

Critical in this redefinition was, firstly, that violence need not be threatened nor used simultaneously by those involved and, secondly, that common purpose could now be inferred from the conduct of those charged. These removed the possibility of much of the detailed legal debate about the definition of riot and how it could be proven. Furthermore, it facilitated the use of video and photographic evidence. In particular as common purpose can now be inferred from conduct, if the police have video of someone being there in the crowd that has been defined as a rioting crowd, guilt pretty much automatically follows.

It is rare for the police to prefer the charge of riot in preference to less serious charges under the 1986 Public Order Act. The police are required to gain the consent of the Director of Public Prosecutions for each time someone is charged with riot, and as Allen (2003: 34) suggests, this raises the possibility that the whole approach to the charges, trials, and sentences in Bradford had at least the tacit approval, if not the active support of the Prime Minister and the Home Secretary. Reflecting back on his comments in his autobiography, Blunkett remained unrepentant and proud of his approach:

> Thugs are thugs, from whatever community, ethnic or faith background. The problems that they articulate need to be addressed, but their methods need to be crushed. That was the message that I promoted... The reaction from the police was remarkable. The fact that I had stood up for law and order and for tough – though fair – action in dealing with the self-destruction of home and community was widely welcomed. In other words, I had established a very clear message, that we were not prepared to tolerate mindless violence and the counterproductive undermining of all our efforts, and that we would take any action necessary to stop it. (Blunkett 2006: 280)

Carling et al. (2004) completed a detailed analysis of the sentencing of those convicted for offences committed during the riots. Over 69% of those involved were charged with riot under the 1986 Public Order Act. Of the remainder 17% were charged with violent disorder and the rest with other offences (Carling et al. 2004: 15). They also found that the average age of those charged with riot or violent disorder was significantly lower than that of those charged with other offences. Over 90% were convicted of their offences (Carling et al. 2004: 23), a seemingly historically high rate of conviction for offences committed in these types of disturbance. In 2001 the authorities had at their disposal the changes in the law and the criminal justice system, principally the provisions of the 1986 Public Order Act. The police used video evidence both to identify perpetrators and to use in evidence in court. For the most serious offence of riot, 96% of the adults were given prison sentences, compared to 21% of those aged under 18, with most of them being given Detention and Training Orders. Over 70% of the adults convicted of violent disorder also received prison sentences (Carling et al. 2004: 23–6).

In Bradford the police did not initially make it clear what the specific charges were that the offenders would be charged with, nor was it or could it be made clear what the sentences would be when they appealed for people to hand themselves in or for information from the public. Consequently many individuals voluntarily handed themselves into the police or were identified to police by friends and family in response to the release of photographs of those wanted by the police in connection with the riots. These photographs appeared in the local press, on the police website, and in police stations as well as mosques and local schools. At the time it was the country's largest criminal investigation. What followed was an act of collective goodwill by a majority of those sought by the police, their families, and the wider South Asian community as a step toward reconstructing good community relations. As Allen (2003: 34) argued: "the vast majority of these were not only community or self volunteered, but were also first-time offences without any history of criminal activity."

In response to the initial sentences, the Fair Justice for All Campaign was launched by some of the female relatives of some those who had been arrested and convicted. This sought to provide a support network for those who had been sent to prison and their families, as well as challenge legally the sentencing. Of the 145 convicted for riot offences considered by Allen, many did not receive any reduction in their sentence for not having previous convictions (Allen 2003: 38).

Also important in the Bradford sentencing was the high public profile of the principal judge in the cases Judge Stephen Gullick. For his efforts he was appointed to the newly created position of Honorary Recorder by the City Council. He repeatedly defended the lengthy sentences that he gave out against the growing criticism, and a length statement was published after the initial sentences were handed down toward the end of 2001 (Bagguley and Hussain 2008: 131). The strategic intent of deterrence was quite transparent here, and the consequence was a kind of collective punishment and criminalization of a whole ethnic community.

One important feature of the trials after the Bradford riot was the use in the courts of video evidence gathered by the police. During the trials themselves, two videos were often shown. The first was an edited series of scenes from the disturbances, and the second was evidence of the actions of the particular individuals who were being tried. These videos were shown despite the fact that many of the defendants had handed themselves into the police and had pleaded guilty to the offence of riot quite early on in the process. This use of video evidence helps to account for the very large numbers convicted of riot offences.

The Pakistani community in Bradford generally felt that the sentencing of the rioters was unfair and excessive in most cases. There was the sense that people with and without previous records received the same sentences and that this was unfair. In addition some felt that the personal and family circumstances of the rioters should have been taken more account of in the sentencing. Finally, there was a strong sense of racial injustice emerging, with the Pakistani Bradford rioters being treated much more harshly than the white rioters. One consequence of this was a further loss of confidence in the police (Bagguley and Hussain 2008: 135–41).

The local Pakistani community saw the issuing of "wanted posters" by the police as shaming and criminalizing the whole community. It was felt that this was a form of punishment being meted out to the local community by the police with the collusion of the media. The idea to use what became popularly known as the "wanted posters" arose from the police, and it was first put to the police liaison committee which includes many representatives of the local community who would have been aware of the impact of the shame on the families of those concerned. One aspect often noted that the shame led parents to hand in their sons to the police. However, the result was often harsh treatment in terms of sentencing and long-term disenchantment with the police and the criminal justice system generally. The overall result of the use of the wanted posters and the harsh sentencing was an increase in mistrust in the police and the judicial system. People felt that they had trusted the police and the criminal justice system by cooperating with the search for those wanted in connection with the riots. However, with the lengthy sentences imposed, this trust had quickly turned to hatred and accusations of racially motivated collective punishment of the Pakistani community in Bradford (Bagguley and Hussain 2008: 137–8).

The British state has a long tradition of severe punishment of those involved in rioting, and the effectivity of the forces of law and order is one of the central questions that Rude (1981: 11) urges us to pose when analyzing collective violence. The tradition of generations of punitive punishment of those involved in riots and the forces of law and order were ruthlessly efficient this time. Whereas in the 1980s the state often found the existing traditional laws of riot difficult to enforce (Joshua and Wallace 1983), the state resorted to the simple expedient of changing the law in the form of the 1986 Public Order Act to make it easier next time. From the perspective of those in favor of this kind of response, the events in Bradford in 2001 were the most significant test so far.

Community Cohesion

One of the most enduring legacies of the 2001 riots has been the emergence and of the official discourse and policy of "community cohesion," sometimes referred to as social cohesion. The 2001 riots triggered a major shift in government public discourse around race, ethnicity, religion, national identity, and citizenship. Implicated in this debate has been a wholesale rejection of the discourse of multiculturalism. This section considers the emergence of this discourse.

Despite the emphasis given to "institutional racism" during the 1990s, it is strikingly absent from the official reports into the 2001 riots. These reports like other instances of contemporary governance have mobilized the discourses of community in support of government goals. While the principal policy responses to the riots of the 1980s were dominated by a "law and order" discourse (Solomos and Rackett 1991), the response to the riots of 2001 rejected this interpretation (Denham 2002: 9). Central to the reports have been themes of "community cohesion" and "ethnic segregation" (Burnett 2004; Kalra 2002; McGhee 2005; Rhodes 2009; Robinson 2005).

The discourse of community cohesion is best thought of as having a variety of origins. The theme of segregation that became central to populist, political, and policy debates emerged from the debates about the causes of the riots. Some of this emerged through the media and in particular the consideration of the situation in Oldham and the discussions about "no-go" areas and similar myths. As the Oldham disturbances took place when parliament was in recess due to the general election, there was no formal debate about them. However, the issue of segregation was introduced into parliamentary debate about the Burnley disorders by David Lidington the Conservative MP for Aylesbury and the then opposition spokesperson on Home Office matters. His question was received favorably by John Denham who suggested that these issues should be addressed at the local level (Hansard 2001: Column 388).

However, the significance of segregation and how to address it was by no means clearly established in the parliamentary debates at the time of the riots. While there was a broad political consensus about the negative features of segregation, there was a striking lack of clarity and reluctance to be specific about policy proposals at this stage.

There was an affinity between populist media reports about ethnic segregation in housing being the "cause" of the riots, some intellectual trends around the importance of community cohesion and social capital for the quality of life in urban neighborhoods, certain themes in the Ouseley Report (2001) into ethnic relations in Bradford, and a striking cross-party consensus on the issue of segregation. The product of this was the emergence of the community cohesion agenda. The Cantle Report in particular highlighted ideas on community cohesion from Canada (Cantle 2001: 69), while the idea about their expression locally in connection with social capital was based upon a discussion by Forrest and Kearns (2001). As Robinson (2005) noted all of this resonated nicely with the New Labour preoccupations with communitarianism.

Consequently, since the 2001 "riots," there has been a shift away from multiculturalism and ethnic diversity in political debates. This has been replaced by an assimilationism that demands integration reminiscent of the policies of the 1950s and 1960s. Immediately after the Bradford "riot," a report on "race relations" in Bradford by Ouseley (2001) was published. Although the work and writing on this report was completed before the "riots," certain themes within it contributed to the agenda of the "riot" reports. In particular the report identified residential segregation as a particular issue facing Bradford. In this sense the report helped to set the agenda and focus for the subsequent reports that we are principally concerned with here are those by Denham (2002) Building Cohesive Communities, which arose from a Ministerial Group on Public Order, coordinated by the Home Office. Closely associated with this was the report by Cantle (2001) Community Cohesion, which was produced by an "independent" Community Cohesion Review Team. A tension runs through this report between assertions of "common values" and "valuing difference," between a static traditionalist conception of "common values" and the dynamic nature of cultural identities, and especially between first- and second-generation South Asians. Cantle avoids analyzing why the riots occurred; it avoids "political" questions and focuses on the "management" of cohesion – achieving cohesion through managerial techniques. The Denham and Cantle reports are thus part of the same administrative process and were concerned with defining the policy agenda in response to the riots from within the specific remit of the Home Office. A common feature of the reports was that they constructed issues in terms that can be "managed." The "riots" themselves are depoliticized and reduced to criminal justice questions, a feature that they share with policy response to the British inner city "riots" of the 1980s (Keith 1993).

The issue of residential ethnic or racial segregation became central to the reports, media representations, and popular understandings of the causes of the riots (Burnett 2004; Kalra 2002). This binary opposition between "community cohesion" and "segregation" has become the dominant frame through which the riots are now popularly understood with segregation seen as exemplifying a "dysfunctional South Asian Muslim community." Much of what was and is claimed about ethnic residential segregation in Bradford, Burnley, and Oldham contradicted recent academic research both at the time and subsequently (Phillips et al. 2007; Simpson 2003).

In relation to Bradford, research concluded that "Increasing residential segregation of South Asian communities is a myth" (Simpson 2003: 668). While more neighborhoods (census enumeration districts of between 100 and 200 households) have South Asian majorities, others have become more mixed, and fewer are overwhelmingly White. Overall Simpson found that there were fewer "mono-racial" areas in 2001 than in 1991, while the favored index of segregation was 0.74 in 1991 and 0.75 in 2001 (Simpson 2003: 671). In national terms then Bradford has a relatively high but stable level of overall segregation, but it is not a polarizing city with "ghettoes."

In summary the reports into the riots of 2001 constructed segregation as pathological, as evidence of a "dysfunctional community" in contrast to the "integrated community" characterized by community cohesion. They present no evidence regarding segregation other than hearsay and do not examine its causes and consequences in any detail. The theme of segregation directs attention away from economic inequalities (McGhee 2005), lets the authorities and especially the police off the hook (Kalra 2002: 22), and effectively shifts the blame for the "riots" and the futile search for ultimate causes onto South Asian communities themselves. It has been an effective exercise in the mobilization of "community cohesion" at the level of discourse for the purpose of depoliticization.

The discourse of segregation and social cohesion has narrated the segregated communities as "the problem." Whenever the reports discuss South Asian communities, apart from rather generalized and stereotyped discussion of culture and food, they are pathologized, especially in arguing that South Asian communities are in a state of "crisis." They are repeatedly represented as disintegrating from within, lacking leadership (Clarke 2002: 49) and riven by intergenerational conflict. Cantle, Clarke, Ouseley, and Ritchie all draw attention to the extent which young people's voices have been largely ignored by decision-makers in the areas where there were disturbances. Some young people complained that the older community and religious leaders who claimed to represent them failed to articulate the experiences of the young (Denham 2002: 14). These themes have become central to official public discourse around the South Asian family in relation to issues such as forced marriages and honor crimes prior to the reports, with their colonialist references to ancient practices.

Conclusion

The 2001 riots occurred largely in response to threats of neofascist mobilization. The towns of Bradford, Burnley, and Oldham had superficially similar characteristics: former textile towns still overwhelmingly working class and with substantial South Asian Muslim communities. However, the rioters in each case were rather different. In Oldham both Whites and South Asians were involved in attacks on each other. In Burnley most of the participants were white, while in Bradford they were overwhelmingly of British-Pakistani origin. The patterns of economic and social inequality were contextual factors rather than playing a causal role. In contrast it is more useful to see the riots as the outcome of political process involving multiple collective actors including national politicians, national and local media, the police, and neofascist social movements.

The response of the police and the criminal justice system was also significant especially in relation to the Bradford rioters. The application of the relatively new public order legislation was on an unprecedented scale before and since. Also notable was the use of police video evidence to secure the majority of the convictions and the lengthy sentences typically of 3- to 4-year imprisonment of 300 local men. This chapter has also examined how the discourse of community and related ideas of segregation, community cohesion, and social capital have been deployed in the official reports produced in response to the riots in 2001. In the reports produced in close association with the Home Office, in particular social cohesion was counterposed to the segregated, crisis-ridden South Asian communities. In doing so they created a particular public "official memory" of the 2001 "riots," one structured by the discourse of community cohesion. This is critically important since as Keith argued in relation to the 1980s: "It is how uprisings or riots are remembered rather than how they actually occurred that dictates policy reaction and future popular mobilisation" (1993: 198).

Cross-References

▶ Contemporary Ethnic Politics and Violence
▶ Negotiating Ethnic Conflict in Deeply Divided Societies: Political Bargaining and Power Sharing as Institutional Strategies
▶ Religion and Political Mobilization

References

Alexander C (2004) Imagining the Asian gang: ethnicity, masculinity and youth after the 'riots'. Crit Soc Policy 24(4):526–549
Allen C (2003) Fair Justice: the bradford disturbances, the sentencing and the impact. Downloadable at: http://www.fairuk.org/policy10.htm
Bagguley P, Hussain Y (2008) Riotous citizens: ethnic conflict in multicultural Britain. Ashgate, Aldershot
Blunkett D (2006) The Blunkett Tapes: my life in the bear pit. Bloomsbury, London
Bujra J, Pearce J (2011) Saturday night and sunday morning: the 2001 Bradford riot and beyond. Vertical Editions, Skipton
Burnett J (2004) Community, cohesion and the state. Race Class 45(3):1–18
Cantle T (2001) Community cohesion: a report of the independent review team. The Home Office, London
Carling A et al (2004) Fair justice for all? The response of the criminal justice system to the Bradford disturbances of July 2001. University of Bradford, Bradford
Clarke T (2002) Report of the Burnley Task Force. Burnley Task Force, Burnley
Denham J (2002) Building cohesive communities: a report of the ministerial group on public order and community cohesion. The Home Office, London
Hansard (2001) https://hansard.parliament.uk/
Joshua H, Wallace T (1983) To ride the storm: the 1980 Bristol riot and the state. Heinemann, London
Kalra V (2002) Riots, race and reports: Denham, Cantle, Oldham and Burnley inquiries. Sage Race Relat Abstr 27(4):20–30
Keith M (1993) Race, riots and policing. UCL Press, London
King M, Waddington D (2007) Coping with disorder? The changing relationship between police public order strategy and practice-a critical analysis of the Burnley riot. Polic Soc 14(2):118–137, 2004
Kundnani A (2003) From Oldham to Bradford. Race Class 43(2):105–131
McGhee D (2005) Intolerant Britain? Hate, citizenship and difference. Open University Press, Maidenhead
Ouseley H (2001) Community pride not prejudice. Bradford Vision, Bradford
Phillips D et al (2007) British Asian narratives of urban space. Trans Inst Br Geogr 32:217–234
Ray L, Smith D (2004) Racist offending, policing and community conflict. Sociology 38(4):681–699
Rhodes J (2009) Revisiting the 2001 riots: new labour and the rise of colour blind racism. Sociol Res Online 14(5)
Robinson D (2005) The search for community cohesion: key themes and dominant concepts of the public policy agenda. Urban Stud 42(8):1411–1427
Rude G (1981) The crowd in history 1730–1848. Lawrence and Wishart, London
Sayyid S (2013) The dynamics of a postcolonial war. Def Stud 13:277–292
Simpson L (2003) Statistics of racial segregation: measures, evidence and policy. Urban Stud 41(3):661–681

Solomos J, Rackett T (1991) Policing and urban unrest. In: Cashmore E, McLaughlin E (eds) Out of order: policing black people. Routledge, London
Waddington D (2004) Contemporary issues in public disorder. Routledge, London
Waddington D (2010) Applying the flashpoints model of public disorder to the 2001 Bradford riot. Br J Criminol 50:342–359

Racialized Identity Under Apartheid in South Africa

27

Suryakanthie Chetty

Contents

Introduction	464
The Colonial Era	464
Mining and the Criminalization of Race	467
Intellectual Underpinnings	468
Afrikaner Identity	470
African Identity	474
Colored Identity	475
Indian Identity	476
Fighting the Good War	477
"Non-racialism" Under Apartheid	478
Conclusion	480
References	481

Abstract

The apartheid state emphasized the distinct racial identities that were the hallmark of South Africa's defining population. Racial distinctiveness and, with it, hierarchy had, however, its origins in South Africa's colonial past and can be traced throughout much of the country's turbulent history prior to 1948. Even within broad racial categories, there existed further distinctions based on class and affiliation. The line between race and class was itself blurred, and inequalities may be contextualized by ideological as well as socioeconomic and political concerns, a pattern that may be traced long before the rise of the apartheid state. However, there also existed a competing form of identity based on multiracialism. This emphasized unity and was particularly evident in political activism that

---

S. Chetty (✉)
University of South Africa, Pretoria, South Africa
e-mail: chetts@unisa.ac.za

agitated for full political equality. The history of racial identity in South Africa has therefore been linked to the tension between the opposing strands of unity and divisiveness.

Keywords

Apartheid · Colonialism · Nationalism · Bantustan · Black consciousness · Segregation

Introduction

The ascendance of the National Party under D.F. Malan in the election of 1948 marked the onset of apartheid in South Africa that was to last until 1994. Not simply perceived as a simple dichotomy of white and black, the policies of the apartheid state and the reactions they provoked marked a complex negotiation of race, ethnicity, and national identity. Yet the origins of this lie far earlier than 1948, beginning with the colonial encounter in the seventeenth century.

There are, therefore, certain key periods in South African history that influenced racial identity and ideas of race that would culminate in the fixed notions of race and exclusion that were the hallmarks of the apartheid state. The ideological origins of this state may be located broadly in three features of the South African past – slavery at the Cape under the Dutch East India Company, the requirements of mining capitalism in the late nineteenth century, and the segregation era in the early twentieth century. Simultaneously, notions of race and identity were made and remade for much of the country's turbulent history and not isolated from international trends. This chapter therefore traces the history of racial identity in South Africa as ultimately expressed under the apartheid state by focusing on the colonial era, the economic impact of mining, the formulation of scientific thought on racial distinction, the segregation era, and, ultimately, the apartheid state.

The Colonial Era

The region that was to become South Africa was subject to two successive waves of colonialism – first by the Dutch under the aegis of the Dutch East India Company (VOC) in the mid-seventeenth century and subsequently by the British in the early nineteenth century. It was under the VOC that slaves were imported to the Cape largely from Dutch possessions in Southeast Asia as well as other parts of Africa. Their labor was imperative for a burgeoning settlement that found it difficult to attract waged labor to such a remote outpost, and slaves were used both by the VOC and by the increasing numbers of farmers that stood at the forefront of territorial expansion further inland. Both labor requirements and the status of slaves as property meant that manumission was relatively rare. Those slaves that were freed, however, went on to form a "free black" community who were largely of Asian origin and tended to embrace Islam rather than Christianity. Also included in the population of the Cape were the peninsula's indigenous inhabitants, the Khoi who – as their pastoralist lifestyle was increasingly curtailed by settler incursion and conflict – were compelled to serve as a laboring underclass (Keegan 1996: 15–20).

Early settlement was characterized by an imbalanced sex ratio which contributed to a fluidity between the various groups with European men fathering children with slave and Khoi women. This was compounded by the Cape's status as a key stopping point on the voyage between Europe and the East that led to periodic influxes of sailors and soldiers. While many of these encounters were temporary, formal marriages did take place. All of this contributed to the growth of a mixed or "Bastaard" group. This racial mixing, however, often took place at the lower levels of society, presenting little challenge to class and racial dominance. With the growth of a middle class and the notion of respectability associated with it in the mid-eighteenth century, already existing racial distinctions became increasingly entrenched. During the final years of Dutch control at the Cape, to be considered a free burgher or citizen with all the associated rights and responsibilities, one had to be of European descent whose immediate ancestry was not tainted by slavery. Due to the patriarchal nature of the society where power was held by men, those most affected tended to be male offspring (Keegan 1996: 20–21, 23–24).

When the British assumed control at the Cape, racial hierarchies – and associated discrimination – became, if anything, more entrenched. Both slaves and black residents at the Cape were subject to restrictions on movement, and there was no amelioration in these restrictions for Christian slaves. Under British rule, the various and varied groups that comprised Cape society were organized in a clearly delineated hierarchy that positioned middle-class, white men at the apex. Simultaneously, discrimination also took on a class dimension with the white working class perceived to be an underclass akin to that of "free blacks." This was partly a product of racial prejudice that associated labor with race – since the initiation of slavery at the Cape, labor had become a marker of racial distinction from which respectable whites were exempt (Keegan 1996: 24). Under British rule, slavery also highlighted the contradiction between the infringement on the natural right to liberty and that of private property. British rule was based on an espousal of capitalism, and the preservation of private property was therefore integral to this. Even British liberals argued for gradual emancipation that would allow both for compensation for slave-owners and the inculcation of the roles and responsibilities associated with freedom in slaves (Keegan 1996: 112). The last, in particular, would continue over the next century in relation to extending political equality to black South Africans. Yet, even as "free" labor, the Khoi in particular were subject to legal and administrative controls over their movements. The ostensibly greater liberalism associated with British rule proved little different from their predecessors. The Khoi were subject to labor contracts that tied them to particular employers and places of residence. Movement was governed by the issuing of permits or passes, and those without passes or contracts could be held without trial, subject to corporal punishment, and forcibly contracted to employers. Although their treatment was regulated by the legal system, this system was overwhelming biased in favor of the colonists due to the assumption that, as the Khoi were lower in the racial hierarchy, their "natural rights" were necessarily circumscribed (Keegan 1996: 54–55).

Even as liberals sought a qualified amelioration of entrenched inequality, racial distinction was hardened by the periodic conflict that arose as a result of white expansion. From the period of Dutch settlement, interactions between the colonists and the indigenous Khoi and San were marked by both cooperation and conflict with an emphasis on the latter over time. The military superiority of the Dutch – often operating outside government control – allowed them to suppress Khoi uprisings based on territorial encroachment, confiscate Khoi cattle, and appropriate Khoi labor. For the hunter-gatherer San, there was implacable hostility to means of subsistence that were irreconcilable. Violence, theft, and forced labor were the precursors to policies that bordered on extermination, and the effect was the confinement of these hunter-gatherer groups to marginalized environments unsuited for agriculture and stock farming (Keegan 1996: 30–33). As European expansion continued unabated, they were to come into conflict with a more formidable foe – the Xhosa. Unlike the nomadic San and seminomadic Khoi, the Xhosa formed settled, stable chiefdoms with strong leadership and were thus able to marshal resources for organized military conflict. While trade occurred between the two groups, conflict was also apparent, and the solution was a process of negotiation rather than the violent dispossession that characterized relations with the San and the Khoi. Yet, inevitably, agreements regarding boundaries were not adhered to, and both groups engaged in periodic and violent warfare (Keegan 1996: 34–35).

Initial British policy at the Cape was built on the exclusion of Africans, both legally and through the use of force if required. This contextualized the promotion of British settlement as exemplified by the arrival of settlers in 1820. Serving as a means of making more British the character of the settlement, advocating the virtues of capitalism and assuming the societal position of a white working class, these settlers were the most visible part of a British policy of both creating and maintaining a white British identity at the settlement as well as racial exclusion. White settlement also served an important strategic and military purpose. The Napoleonic Wars had had an adverse effect on military resources, particularly in the colony, and settlement had the potential to provide a buffer against the depredations of the Xhosa on the eastern frontier. The results of settlement, however, were unexpected. The opportunities at the Cape, both for trade and the acquisition of land, meant that the new settlers were hardly content with the role of a laboring class. Ironically, it was their very advocacy of capitalism that made them less inclined to fulfill the expectations of the colonial administration. A decade later, the ambition of the settlers led to them becoming the key agents of colonial expansion and, associated with it, the seizure by force of African land, thus entrenching racial conflict (Keegan 1996: 61–62, 67–68).

As the nineteenth century progressed, it was again the forces of capitalism that would consolidate racial inequality, and this would reach its zenith with the discovery of valuable mineral resources that would permanently alter the economic, political, and social landscape of Southern Africa.

Mining and the Criminalization of Race

It was the need to control black labor – first on the diamond mines of Kimberley and then on the Witwatersrand gold mines – that set in motion much of the legislation upon which the apartheid state would later draw. The early years of diamond mining drew in large numbers of black migrant workers from all over southern Africa. The demand for labor and subsequent competition between diggers gave workers an edge, allowing them to engage in short-term contracts and driving up wages. Yet, over time, as rural societies were drawn into a monetized economy, waged labor became less a choice and more a necessity in order to meet increasing demands for lobola (bride price) as well as manufactured goods (Worger 1987: 87–89). In the 1880s, the consolidation of smaller claims and the growth of mining monopolies gave mining interests greater economic and political control which was used to promulgate legislation that served their interests; chief of these was the control of black workers (Worger 1987: 131–132). A key concern was the theft and illicit trade in diamonds, and, while there were limits to the preventative measures that could be taken against white workers, the same did not apply to black labor with legislation controlling the movement of black workers through arbitrary searches, the institution of a pass system, corporal punishment, and a closed compound system. Black workers were subject to raids, arrests, and imprisonment, all of which contributed to the notion of a criminalized black working class and increased the distance between black and white labor (Worger 1987: 134–135).

The nature of the extensive gold deposits on the Witwatersrand – in particular the great depths at which the seams lay and the equipment required to both mine and process the ore – promoted the amalgamation of the gold mining industry as well. It was also the Kimberley mining magnates that had the capital available to exert their dominance on the gold mines as well (Davenport 2013: 181–182). Key to the profitability of gold mining was black labor. Due to the practice of job reservation, skilled categories of work were reserved for white workers, and mines had to offer competitive salaries in order to attract the requisite skilled labor (Davenport 2013: 234). Black workers, however, were confined to unskilled work and thus had little bargaining power. It was, therefore, only through controlling black labor in the form of long-term contracts, the housing of workers in compounds (as in Kimberley), and low rates of remuneration for black workers that the gold mining industry could maintain its profit margin. Workers were thus housed in compounds based on ethnic distinctions and were subject to strict control by their employers (Davenport 2013: 290). Ethnically segregated compounds and job reservation were real obstacles to working-class unity across racial and ethnic lines and emphasized the divisions that would be reinforced through subsequent decades.

For much of its history, then, race and class have been closely intertwined, and it was the convergence of the two that underlay the inequalities that permeated South African society. Yet, even as class served as a marker of racial distinction, races were not homologous entities and were rent with internal distinctions that shaped the way in which racial identity was constructed. It is also important to note that, although there are broad trends that can be traced in the development of identity over time, identities are a relational category and cannot be easily isolated.

Intellectual Underpinnings

Despite its geographical isolation on the southern tip of the African continent, South Africa was part of the networks of empire in the nineteenth and early twentieth centuries and, as such, was not unaffected by the intellectual milieu that revolved around ideas of race. This was compounded by the presence of hunter-gatherer groups which piqued the interest of anthropologists as well as the numerous discoveries of hominid fossils in East and Southern Africa that added complexity and controversy to debates about human origins.

With the rise of the Enlightenment in eighteenth century Europe and the use of reason and the scientific method, there was greater focus on taxonomy and the classification of the natural world. More than mere classification, however, it was an attempt to create a hierarchy that inevitably included race. This incorporated ostensibly scientific and mathematical methods to support pseudoscientific thinking that emphasized difference and racial typology such as phrenology in the nineteenth century (Dubow 2005: 25–29). This was accompanied by growing ethnographic focus on groups such as the "Bushmen" or "Hottentots" that took on an urgent impetus as the transition to a modern state spelled the ultimate demise for "traditional" ways of life (Dubow 2005: 32–35). With the end of the First World War and into the 1920s, the discovery of fossilized remains of hominids culminating in Raymond Dart's discovery of the Taung child – classified as *Australopithecus africanus* – provided compelling evidence for the antiquity of humankind in Africa and the significance of the continent in the history of human evolution (Dubow 2005: 39–44). In line with these paleoanthropological discoveries, Dart suggested that the hunter-gatherer people of South Africa were themselves remnants of prehistoric human societies, living fossils (Dubow 2005: 46).

Paleoanthropological and anthropological studies in South Africa were thus supportive of Social Darwinian notions of natural selection and, with it, eugenics in the 1920s. Associated with right-wing extremism in the wake of Nazi policies of racial extermination during the Second World War, understandings of eugenics were more complex during the period of segregation in South Africa. There were two contrasting strands of eugenics – the first was based on the notion of "survival of the fittest" and the identification of those considered inferior who were subject to discrimination ranging from isolation to forced sterilization. The second was associated with reform – by improving societal conditions and intervening in areas such as health care, education, and housing, populations could be improved (Dubow 2005: 124). In South Africa this coincided with the increasing urbanization of Africans as a result of the growth of secondary industry and the unsustainability of "native reserves." The association of black with white in the cities also raised the specter of racial degeneration which was compounded by concerns over the "poor white" population – the weak link in the ideology of racial superiority. This, along with an ostensible desire to prevent the urban "corruption" of Africans, underpinned racial segregation (Dubow 2005: 168–170). In Natal African urbanization led to the implementation of the "Durban system." Increasing African urbanization in Durban compounded by the widespread use of "togt" or casual labor led to growing concerns over the control of black labor. This was expressed in the passing of the Native Beer Act in 1908 that sought to control the use of liquor among urban Africans and, with it, the concomitant effects of drunkenness on public order, discipline, and morality. With the Beer Act, the municipality attained a monopoly over the brewing and selling of African beer, creating municipal beerhalls in which the alcohol was consumed. The resulting revenue was then used to fund the administration of Africans in urban areas and led to the creation of a Municipal Native Affairs Department to police Africans in the city. This thus had the effect of making Africans unwittingly complicit in their own subjugation and was a system of administration that would be adapted by the apartheid state (La Hausse 1982: 63–67).

While segregation and racial distinction had been a hallmark of southern Africa since the earliest days of colonization, it was in the wake of the South African War when the foundation was being laid for the new state that segregation came into its own. The Lagden Commission was tasked by Sir Alfred Milner to resolve the "native question," and its resolution was racial segregation with separate political representation and living spaces demarcated for the races. The Lagden Commission served as a blueprint for subsequent segregation legislation and ideology that progressively removed Africans from equal political participation and relegated them to separate representative structures (Davenport 1978: 332–333). This contextualized the landmark 1913 Land Act that sought to prevent Africans from squatting on white-owned farms and restrict them from purchasing land. Under the terms of the legislation, Africans were permitted to purchase and occupy land only on the demarcated African reserves. The land allocated to the reserves was subject to betterment policies in order to promote agriculture but remained woefully inadequate, even when the original allocation was increased. It served to restrict the aspirations of an African middle class and fostered the system of migrant labor – which served both the interests of mining and a growing secondary industry (Davenport 1978: 334–337). These reserves would later form the core of the homeland or Bantustan system implemented by the apartheid state.

Of just as great concern was the influx of Africans into urban areas. Drawing upon both liberal ideas of social welfare and concerns over racial degeneration and miscegenation, attempts were made to regulate the slum areas that had inevitably arisen in the towns and cities. Underlying this was the belief that the African presence in urban areas was a necessary evil to be tolerated but not condoned. It was a temporary situation designed only to fulfill the needs of labor. The Native (Urban Areas) Act of 1923 allocated racially distinct spaces within urban areas leading to the creation of townships such as Soweto and the forced relocation of racially mixed areas by the apartheid state such as Sophiatown and District Six. Associated with urban segregation was the use of a pass system to regulate African movement in urban areas with concomitant policing that led to arrests for pass violations (Davenport 1978: 339–342).

Yet, even as segregationist fears would later be incorporated into apartheid-era legislation, the Second World War saw dissent over understandings of race that offered the potential for a brief interlude from the racist ideology that would take root in 1948.

Afrikaner Identity

While apartheid has simplistically been viewed as white oppression, white society was itself divided by ethnicity and language evident in those of English and Dutch origins, and, even within Afrikaner society, tensions and divisions existed. It was this complex interplay that was ultimately responsible for the ousting of Smuts at the conclusion of the Second World War and the rise of the National Party and, with it, the promulgation of apartheid in 1948.

The transition from Dutch to British rule in the early nineteenth century saw the arrival of successive waves of British settlers who were faced with established Afrikaners. While British settlers were of largely working class origin, they were nonetheless the representatives of Empire and the cultural superiority associated with it. They found themselves confronted with Afrikaners – largely rural and uneducated farmers, distant from the European metropole and with convoluted relationships with indigenous groups that were marked by both cooperation and conflict. The British arrival also posed a quandary for these Afrikaners who, like the new settlers, were colonialists furthering expansion and, at its most positive, adopting a paternalistic attitude to indigenous people. Simultaneously, they sought to identify themselves as a group distinct from the British. An incipient nationalism saw the start of the civilizing mission, not with the onset of British control but with the arrival of VOC official Jan van Riebeeck in 1652 – a date that would acquire an almost mythic status. It is within this context that Afrikaners defined themselves as a separate group rooted firmly in southern Africa, and the term "Afrikaner" highlighted their status as a people of Africa rather than Europe. Yet, even as this nascent identity was being formed, it was placed under threat by British policies that prioritized "Anglicization" in the organs of church, state, and business (Giliomee 2003: 195–197).

The process of Anglicization had a dual effect. The first was the creation of an urbane class of Afrikaners, the "Cape Dutch" or "Anglomen" who were the products of Anglicization and embraced the English virtue of "progress" and, with it, British culture. Other Afrikaners sought to assert their unique cultural identity and history in the face of English hegemony (Giliomee 2003: 198–199). Held in particular disdain by English settlers were rural Afrikaners, viewed as the very antithesis of progress and the Victorian idealization of "improvement." Increasingly the split between Afrikaners took on a class aspect with the upper echelons favoring an Anglicized identity that would allow them access to the colonial structures of power and lead to their dominance in Afrikaner society as well (Giliomee 2003: 202–203).

The perceived liberal attitude of the British toward the Khoi and the Xhosa precipitated what would become a seminal moment in the construction of an Afrikaner national identity – the Great Trek (Giliomee 2003: 152). Viewed as an assertion of Afrikaner independence, the Great Trek was the migration of Afrikaner groups into the interior. Their braving of the unknown and encounters with hostile groups assumed an almost Biblical status, akin to the Israelites wandering the desert until they reached the Promised Land. The Promised Land would be the independent Boer Republics created in the interior, the bastion of Afrikaner identity – the Zuid Afrikaanse Republiek (ZAR) and the Orange Free State. Due to a migration that was in part a protest against racial equality (albeit a qualified equality), the constitutions of both Boer Republics were unequivocal in their limited notion of citizenship – burghers or citizens were white adult men (Giliomee 2003: 176). Yet, as evident throughout South African history, racial inequality did not translate into exclusion, and Boers or farmers developed a reliance on black labor either through coercion or negotiation. The dominance of the former coupled with Boer expansion contributed to hostility from which the better armed Boers ultimately emerged triumphant (Giliomee 2003: 181–183).

The geographic distance of the independent Boer republics from the Cape Afrikaners was symbolic of a deeper ideological divide with the latter believing that it was only by assimilation with Britain that the future of the Afrikaner would be assured. The distinctions between the two groups, however, would be tested by the discovery of gold on the Witwatersrand and the subsequent conflict this provoked with the British (Giliomee 2003: 239). The two poles of Afrikanerdom were embodied in the figure of Jan Smuts – born at the Cape, studied law at Cambridge University, and eventually gave up his British citizenship to become state attorney of the ZAR on the eve of the Anglo-Boer War (Giliomee 2003: 243). The outbreak of conflict and subsequent British actions in setting up concentration camps and the destruction of farms provoked anti-British sentiment among the Cape Afrikaners, uniting them with their northern kinsmen (Giliomee 2003: 256). The years of bitter conflict that culminated in a hard-won British victory did much to further Afrikaner identity – it would become yet another episode in the mythology of Afrikaner nationalism (Giliomee 2003: 263).

In the aftermath of the war, Alfred Milner, British High Commissioner, pursued a vigorous policy of Anglicization which, in turn, provoked an equally virulent emphasis on Afrikaner identity, culture, and language, particularly evident in the church and schools (Giliomee 2003: 268–269). Smuts provided something of a middle ground – a future South Africa would require the union of the two former British colonies and the two Boer republics and, with it, the reconciliation between English and Afrikaans-speaking white South Africans. For this to be achieved, the nascent country had to maintain her ties with Britain, ideally as a dominion within a commonwealth of nations that would simultaneously allow the country to retain its independence (Giliomee 2003: 277). Smuts' willingness – and desire – to continue to maintain ties with Britain did not go unopposed and was manifest in the rebellion led by prominent Afrikaner generals during the First World War and the opposition in the South African parliament to South Africa's entry into the war in support of the Allies in September 1939.

Internal divisions within Afrikaner society once again became linked to class. The process of modernization and, with it, the transition to commercial agriculture spelt the death knell for many Boer farmers who were ultimately forced into the cities – there to be become a laboring underclass but one which was in competition with black workers (Giliomee 2003: 321). In this context, Smuts with his ties to the British symbolized capitalism and, with it, imperial domination. His opposite was J.B.M Hertzog, founder of the National Party, who had distanced himself from Smuts' (and first Prime Minister, Louis Botha's) South African Party due to its "capitalist policies." The "poor white" problem also aroused the attention and empathy of Daniel Francois Malan who was dedicating to elevating the Afrikaner socially and economically while upholding their unique cultural heritage. And, linked to the upliftment of the Afrikaners was the maintenance of racial – and class – divisions with an aspirant black middle class which posed a threat to white economic and political supremacy (Giliomee 2003: 327–328). As Prime Minister, Smuts' government further alienated white workers when a strike by white workers on the Witwatersrand was crushed by government troops using military weaponry and air strikes (Giliomee 2003: 334–335).

Economic struggles went hand-in-hand with cultural assertion. Language was the first step in asserting Afrikaner identity. As editor of *De Burger*, D.F. Malan did much to dispel the stereotype of the anti-intellectual Afrikaner in his advocacy for Afrikaner independence and the resolution of the "poor white" problem while, simultaneously, condemning imperialism and its supporters. In 1922 – the year of the strike – the newspaper changed its name from the Dutch *De Burger* to the Afrikaans *Die Burger*, symbolic of an Afrikaner identity rooted in South Africa (Giliomee 2003: 374). Afrikaner struggles were given a sense of purpose with the formation of the Afrikaner Broederbond in 1918 dedicated to preserving Afrikaner cultural identity. A decade later, at a meeting of the Broederbond, the Federasie van Afrikaanse Kultuurvereniginge (Federation of Afrikaans Cultural Associations) was formed which comprised all Afrikaner cultural organizations across the country with the aim of promoting the language (Giliomee 2003: 400–401). The formation of Afrikaner identity reached its zenith in 1938 with a reenactment of the Great Trek that mythologized settler expansion and struggle. The event whipped up a frenzy of nationalism as Afrikaners donned the clothing of their Voortrekker ancestors and adopted an anthem, "Die Stem van Suid-Afrika" (The Call of South Africa). While theoretically nonpartisan and holding events at which both Smuts and Hertzog were present, it was Malan who emerged as the voice of Afrikaners (Giliomee 2003: 432–433). The seeds were sown for the division that would come during the Second World War.

The outbreak of war in September 1930 saw a division in the South African parliament with Prime Minister calling for South African neutrality. In this he was opposed by Jan Smuts who advocated South African active involvement in the war as an ally of Britain. The ensuing vote led to victory for Smuts who became the new Prime Minister. The dissent in parliament, however, was symbolic of a division within Afrikaners. The far right had already developed Nazi sympathies with the formation of the South African Christian National Socialist Movement – popularly known as the Greyshirts – in 1933. After the outbreak of war, one of Hertzog's former ministers, Oswald Pirow, formed Nuwe Orde (New Order). The right-wing organization that had the greatest support, however, was the Ossewabrandwag (OB), which took its inspiration from the celebrations commemorating the centenary of the Great Trek. OB storm troopers or *stormjaers* carried out sabotage within the union for the duration, presenting a perpetual security problem for the state. War measures such as internment of anti-war figures as well as the implementation of rations and military defeats such as that at Tobruk only inflamed right-wing Afrikaner resentment. The anti-war sentiment was conceded to in the form of an oath taken by South African troops to fight beyond the borders of the country. This was symbolized by an orange tab worn on the shoulders of their uniforms. For war supporters, this signified their loyalty, whereas it was considered an imperialist act of treason by the right (Giliomee 2003: 440–443). The ultimate legacy of South African participation in the Second World War, however, was the shift in support for the far right that would ultimately culminate in Smuts's electoral defeat and the accession to power of the National Party under the leadership of D.F. Malan in 1948 (Giliomee 2003: 446).

With the growing agitation for independence in Africa and Asia that followed the Allied victory in 1945 and the insecurity of a white minority population, the National Party advocated the policy of apartheid or the separation between races as a means of maintaining white political and economic supremacy (Giliomee 2003: 496–497). The apartheid state was defined by a system of legislation – the Population Registration Act of 1950 that legally categorized people according to race, the Immorality Act that forbade sexual relations between different race groups, and the Group Areas Act which segregated racial groups in urban areas. The culmination came in the 1960s with the creation of the homeland system where separate geographical areas, considered "independent" Bantustans were established for the various African ethnic groups who would be excluded from any form of citizenship within white South Africa.

The apartheid state was militant and oppressive, privileging white Afrikaner dominance and racial subordination. Yet it did not go unopposed. Liberal protest, black activism, and international condemnation compounded by economic sanctions exerted pressure on the National Party and challenged its stranglehold on power. Initially economically successful due to the utilization of cheap black labor, the middle of the 1970s saw a dramatic drop in economic growth that was precipitated in part by an international oil crisis. Job reservation had an adverse effect on the required skills necessary with a corresponding shortage of black skilled workers and insufficient numbers of white workers to compensate (Giliomee 2003: 597–599). The implementation of economic sanctions exacerbated the situation as did the growing unrest such as the Soweto Uprising of 1976 in reaction to the implementation of Afrikaans as the medium of instruction in black schools. Just as economics had been a significant catalyst in the creation of a particular Afrikaner identity, it now challenged the notion of a unified Afrikaner identity. The 1980s saw the beginning of concessions made to halt the inevitable with Afrikaners' split between the *verkramptes* who resisted change and the more liberal-minded *verligtes*. The ideological difference mirrored an economic one – a hallmark of the historical divisions in Afrikaner identity: the *verligtes* tended to be more economically affluent and educated than their counterparts, and political change was therefore a pragmatic decision (Giliomee 2003: 549). It was this that would ultimately allow for political change, leading to unbanning of the ANC and the first democratic elections held in 1994.

African Identity

Prior to the formation of the Union of South Africa, African political activism was centered on their full political and social inclusion within existing societal structures. The disparate voices found a focus with the formation of the South African Native Congress in 1902. This organization emphasized the loyalty of indigenous Africans to the British Empire and advocated the more inclusive nonracial Cape liberalism as the basis for a new South African state in contrast to the racial policies of the northern provinces and Natal that prioritized white settler concerns over land and labor. In contrast, the Cape system allowed for the theoretical equality and assimilation of other race groups. The South African Native Congress was led by an African intellectual elite that clearly differentiated itself from the greater part of the indigenous population, seeking to both represent and lead this group until full assimilation was achieved (Greenstein 1994: 4–5).

A more ambivalent response to imperial hegemony was evident in the formation of the African Ethiopian churches in the late nineteenth century. Despite clear Christian influences, these religious movements sought emancipation from colonial rule and drew a membership across tribal and ethnic division, a forerunner to the creation of a unified African identity. The formation of a Christian identity distinct from that of the colonizer and settler was also an assertion of indigenous identity, albeit one shaped by Christianity (Greenstein 1994: 5–6).

The creation of the Union of South Africa in 1910 led to a shift in black political activism. The Union had dashed the hopes of the national extension of Cape liberalism and the maintenance of racial political inequality led to a united response on the part of Indians, coloreds, and Africans who appealed unsuccessfully to the British government. Realizing the inefficacy of using white liberals to address their plight, the South African Native Congress (later to be renamed the African National Congress) was formed in 1912. From the outset its membership was envisaged as a national one, drawing members from the four provinces that comprised the union as well as the British protectorates. Its first constitution emphasized the unity of indigenous people, but, as yet, it did not incorporate other race groups (Greenstein 1994: 7–8).

A major obstacle to unity, however, was the presence of "traditional" structures of leadership that colluded with the state as a holdover from the British policy of indirect rule. Traditional leaders or chiefs found themselves caught between functioning as part of the apparatus of state rule on the "native reserves" – symbols of ethnic and racial segregation – and resistance. A further distinction was evident in the urban-rural divide. While the ANC largely represented an urban population, resistance occurred sporadically in rural areas due to land dispossession and the incorporation of Africans into waged labor in the form of the migrant labor system. Rural movements incorporated indigenous elements as they engaged with the repression of the modern state. Again, this was symbolized by the Ethiopian churches where a group calling themselves the Israelites (based on the Old Testament) resisted the payment of taxes and illegally occupied land in Bulhoek. An attempt to remove them led to increasing tension that culminated in open conflict between the Israelites and the police, leading to the deaths of more than 200 Israelites (Greenstein 1994: 8–9).

The ANC emphasized the unity of Africans across ethnic lines, particularly evident under the presidency of Pixley Seme who drew upon figures significant to the Zulu and Xhosa, for instance. This would mark the pattern for the ANC from then on (Greenstein 1994: 11). During this period, African political interests were represented by the Native Representative Council comprising both whites and Africans who were elected by Africans indirectly through councils, committees, and chiefs. While not a lawmaking body, the NRC could theoretically represent African interests in parliament and was seen as a forerunner of direct parliamentary representation. It was, however, a toothless entity creating a sense of disillusionment and leading to African opposition to it a decade later (Greenstein 1994: 12–13). With the failure of the NRC, however, African political activism became more inclusive, transcending local, ethnic, or traditional identities to espouse a more unified African and, ultimately, South African identity (Greenstein 1994: 14). This would lie at the heart of the radicalization of black nationalist politics evident across the various political organizations in the 1940s.

Colored Identity

South Africans termed "colored" were a heterogeneous mix of indigenous Africans, slaves, and white settlers that had come to develop a unique identity, embracing either Christianity or Islam and, like their white counterparts, largely speaking Afrikaans. They occupied an unenviable position in the racial hierarchy, caught in the middle ground between black African and white, and this was reflected in their political activism over the course of the twentieth century. Coloreds – the largest numbers of which were found at the Cape – had had a long and ambivalent history with white South Africans. In many cases their common ancestry and the ability of some individuals to "pass" as white in appearance had blurred the boundaries of race and predisposed some to highlight their distinctiveness from black Africans. This served as a significant obstacle to racial and political solidarity in the wake of the formation of the Union of South Africa in 1910. Even the increasingly discriminatory racial legislation that characterized the new country failed to drum up sufficient support for the political unity advocated by colored political leader Dr. Abdullah Abdurahman, founder of the African Political Organization. Despite their common cause, both African and colored segments of the population would, in the early years of the country, consider themselves distinct based on differences in language, culture, and the preferential treatment accorded to coloreds in the racial hierarchy, due to the greater ease with which the latter could potentially be assimilated (Simons and Simons 1983: 120–121).

As with the other race groups, the years prior to the outbreak of the Second World War saw a growing radicalization in colored politics led by Cissie Gool – daughter of Abdurahman – who served as president of the newly formed National Liberation League formed at the end of 1935. Agitating for equal political rights, the League looked beyond the colored population to forge ties with other "non-Europeans" in a quest for "national liberation" that cut across racial and ethnic lines (Simons and Simons 1983: 486–488). This stemmed from a realization that the common oppression experienced by the black races of South Africa necessitated a united opposition. The earlier isolated engagement between each racial group (and its political representatives) with the state had proved fruitless. Simultaneously, the heterogeneous mix that comprised the colored population also served as a concrete reminder of the artificiality and constructed nature of racial categories that would later be enforced by notorious pieces of legislation such as the Population Registration Act. On the eve of the Second World War in 1938, as right-wing Afrikaner nationalists were becoming increasingly vociferous, the National Liberation League formed part of a conference comprised of groups with allied interests and proposed the formation of a "Non-European United Front of Africans, Colored and Indians" in common resistance against racial discrimination (Simons and Simons 1983: 489).

Indian Identity

From the outset there was a clear class and ethnic distinction within the Indian diaspora in South Africa that would shape the way in which South African Indian identity was articulated. The bulk of the Indian population that arrived in Natal in the mid-nineteenth century was composed of indentured laborers drawn largely from South India. They were soon followed by the Gujarati merchants from the north with a sizeable Muslim population. Indentured labor was the solution to the labor problem in Natal – in particular, the cultivation of sugar. The Zulu kingdom had, at this point, retained its independence, and the Zulu were thus not easily drawn into waged labor. Indentured labor, with its 5-year contracts, also allowed for a greater control of labor, making easier the transition from slavery to waged labor. Moreover, British imperial domination over both India and Natal allowed for the easy movement and control of Indians (Reader's Digest Illustrated History of South Africa: The Real Story 1995: 222–225).

The difficult conditions and general isolation of indentured laborers led to an alienation from their subcontinental origins. This was in contrast to the merchant Indian class who maintained financial, social, and cultural ties with their ancestral villages. For the indentured laborers then, there was a growing tendency to construct a particularly South Africanized Indian identity. This was evident in the eventual creation of stable family units, the use of organized religion as evident in the construction of temples, and the absence of the caste distinctions that were a hallmark of Indian society, even as distinctions based on religion, language, and ethnicity were maintained (Freund 1995: 8–9).

A growing Indian population compounded by the economic competition represented by the merchants or traders provoked white settler hostility and discrimination. This was the context of the arrival of M.K. Gandhi in 1893. A year later Gandhi had formed the Natal Indian Congress, a political organization designed to advocate for political equality for the largely merchant class through passive resistance. While the Congress eventually included issues that affected the working class of indentured origin such as opposition to the imposition of a £3 tax, it was the Colonial-Born and Settlers' Indian Association – formed in 1933 – that briefly came to represent the interests of the descendants of indentured laborers who identified strongly with their South African origins (Kuper 1960: 45–47). In the early decades of the twentieth century, however, as Indians found themselves the subject of discriminatory legislation designed to limit them economically and politically, it was the Natal Indian Congress that came to represent their interests. Indian political activists from Natal and the Transvaal would come together to form the South African Indian Congress which would become increasingly radical in the 1940s (Reader's Digest Illustrated History of South Africa: The Real Story 1995: 537).

Fighting the Good War

The period leading up to the Second World War was marked by a growing militancy in black nationalist politics. This was evident in the emergence of radical factions within existing political groups – the Nationalist Bloc within the Natal Indian Congress and Transvaal Indian Congress, the ANC Youth League, and the National Liberation League of South Africa that represented colored activists who agitated for "complete social, political and economic equality for non-Europeans with Europeans" (Lewis 1987: 179). Dissatisfied with the way in which the existing black political leadership had campaigned for social, political, and economic reform, the new generation of radicals would find the Second World War the perfect means of highlighting the incongruity of Allied ideals with domestic suppression and agitate for equality based on equal participation in the conflict.

The traditional African leadership such as Mshiyeni ka Dinizulu, Paramount Chief of the Zulu, and Chief Jeremiah Moshesh of the Basotho threw their weight behind the war effort urging their followers to enlist due to the greater threat presented by the Germans to freedom and, on a more pragmatic level, the remuneration of military service. Also evident was the desire to prove their loyalty through war service – that could ultimately culminate in the reward of equal citizenship. Of particular note was the relegation of black men to support or auxiliary services with their concomitant exclusion from combat. It was this that took on a special significance as it precluded them from equal participation in the war, mirroring their secondary status in South African society (Chetty 2012: 53–79).

The Communist Party of South Africa, on the other hand, condemned black support for the war – and for a state that oppressed them. Their stance was to change with the German invasion of the Soviet Union in 1941, but, nevertheless, the CPSA emphasized equal participation in the war and the use of black soldiers in combat roles. This placed the Union Government – already dealing with the hostility of right-wing Afrikaners – in an untenable position (Chetty 2012: 53–79).

Yet, the setbacks of the war such as the defeat at Tobruk suggested the possibility of reform at home. "Segregation has fallen on evil days" was the oft-quoted phrase from Jan Smuts in 1942. The high number of casualties led to the creation of a dilution policy where black noncombatants were placed in previously all-white units, freeing white men to take up combatant roles. Here, the inequalities became more pronounced as did the resentment of black soldiers. Yet, as the tide of war turned in favor of the Allies, equality receded ever further. Segregation would continue unabated with the formation of Colored Affairs Department to administer coloreds as a separate group as well as the Trading and Occupation of Land (Transvaal and Natal) Restriction Bill in 1943 designed to restrict Indian access to land and alleviate white fears of Indian "penetration" into white areas in Natal (Chetty 2012: 53–79). Thus, while representing a moment of real change, opportunities for racial equality had ultimately been significantly decreased by the end of the war. The war had itself provoked a resurgence of right-wing Afrikaner nationalism that would culminate in Smuts's electoral defeat and the creation of the apartheid state in 1948.

"Non-racialism" Under Apartheid

When Archbishop Desmond Tutu described South Africa as a "rainbow nation" in the wake of the first democratic elections held in South Africa in 1994, he was echoing the sentiment of the Freedom Charter almost 50 years earlier, "...South Africa belongs to all who live in it, black and white." Drawn up in 1955, the Freedom Charter was the expression of the ideology of the South African Congress Alliance composed of the ANC, the South African Indian Congress, the Colored People's Congress, and the leftist, anti-apartheid, and largely white South African Congress of Democrats. It was an articulation of a multiracial and inclusive identity that would be a hallmark of mainstream black protest politics. The Freedom Charter was the culmination of the expression of a multiracial identity that had begun with the Defiance Campaign in 1952, the large-scale coordinated passive resistance protest against the apartheid state. Through the use of strikes and boycotts, activists courted arrest, demonstrating the militancy that had been in evidence since the 1940s (Reader's Digest Illustrated History of South Africa: The Real Story 1995: 383–388).

In contrast to the Freedom Charter and the inclusive identity espoused by the Congress Movement, the Pan-Africanist Congress or PAC adopted a more radical approach under the leadership of Robert Sobukwe. Initially a member of the more moderate ANC, Sobukwe was disillusioned with the multiracial nature of the organization and subsequently broke away to form the Pan-Africanist Congress in 1959. Inspired by the ideals of Pan-Africanism – a movement begun by the African diaspora and strengthened with anti-colonial struggles and the creation of new

African states in the wake of decolonization – the PAC promoted African unity across the continent and a disavowal of racial categories with an emphasis on socialism. The defining moment for the PAC came in March 1960 during a protest against the carrying of passes in Sharpeville. The protestors came under police fire resulting in the deaths of 69 people in what infamously became known as the Sharpeville Massacre. Sobukwe was subsequently imprisoned on Robben Island. The unwelcome media attention of the Sharpeville incident caused no small amount of embarrassment to the South African government which took immediate action by issuing a state of emergency and, a month later, banning both the ANC and PAC (the Communist Party of South Africa had already been banned a decade earlier). With the banning, imprisonment, and exile of key black political figures, protest politics entered a period of quiescence that was eventually broken by a new generation of activists (Reader's Digest Illustrated History of South Africa: The Real Story 1995: 398–407).

This decade highlighted the power of the state which began to refine apartheid policy. This led to a privileging of distinct ethnic identities in contrast to the sense of unity that had permeated black nationalism in the preceding decade. It was epitomized by the independent homeland system. Hendrik Verwoerd, the "architect of apartheid," served as Prime Minister and initiated the Bantustan or independent homeland system envisaged as the means by which Africans (segregated according to their "tribal" or ethnic affiliation) would exercise their political rights. Taking earlier policies of segregation to their extreme, the homeland system meant that Africans could never be considered citizens of white South Africa, and their presence in urban areas and as laborers would be temporary. In all, ten homelands were created for the different ethnic groups, and four of them ultimately attained their independence. The system, however, was an exercise in the theoretical over the practical. The homelands were not economically self-sustaining and served mainly as labor reserves for the dispossessed who were compelled to work in "white" South Africa (Reader's Digest Illustrated History of South Africa: The Real Story 1995: 378–380). Their emphasis, however, on ethnic identity and, with it, division and distinction left a legacy with KwaZulu, for instance. Its leader, Chief Mangosutho Buthelezi, formed the Inkatha Freedom Party that focused on Zulu cultural identity and ultimately challenged the power of the ANC in the region. Buthelezi clearly preferred a federal system of government in 1994, allowing for greater regional autonomy and the maintenance of IFP power. This system was ultimately rejected. The tension between the two groups was manifest in violent conflict between ANC and IFP supporters prior to the first fully democratic elections in 1994 (Reader's Digest Illustrated History of South Africa: The Real Story 1995: 509, 526–527).

The late 1960s and 1970s saw the growth of Black Consciousness which occurred within the milieu of decolonization in Africa, radicalized student politics in America and Europe, and a similar radicalization of student politics in South Africa exemplified by the National Union of South African Students (NUSAS) and the South African Students Organization (SASO), with its largely black membership. Also influential were the remnants of earlier radicalism in the form of the Ethiopian churches as well as the ANC Youth League (Rich 1989: 6). Influenced by the work of Frantz Fanon, Black Consciousness emphasized a common black identity that sought equality on their own terms without having to concede to white liberals and identifying a sense of black pride. The movement was epitomized by the figure of Steve Biko, founding member of SASO – who would be subsequently killed while held in police custody in Pretoria in 1977. Black Consciousness embraced the adjective "black" as a marker of identity rather than the negatively defined "non-white" favored by state bureaucracy. By utilizing a common identity, the movement hoped to unite the various races in common cause against oppression (Hook 2014: 22–23). For Biko, the aim of Black Consciousness was not merely "integration" into South African society with its hegemonic espousal of European values but the assertion and validation of indigenous belief systems (Hook 2014: 242–243).

The catalyst for the new generation of student radicals was the Bantu Education Act passed in 1953 which was designed to maintain Africans at an education level suitable only for menial labor. Despite a growing realization of the need for skilled African labor, education disparities between race groups remained a source of discontent and resistance to the implementation of Afrikaans as a medium of instruction which broke out in Soweto in 1976, spreading throughout the country. Affiliated to both SASO and the Black Consciousness Movement, violent clashes occurred between students and police. Many of these protestors would go into exile, joining groups such as the ANC and PAC and returning in secret to South Africa to conduct subversive attacks against the apartheid regime. This would mark a growing radicalization and increasing confrontation with the state that characterized the opposition to apartheid in the ensuing decade (Reader's Digest Illustrated History of South Africa: The Real Story 1995: 446–451).

Even as Africans continued to be marginalized from political participation in white South Africa, the 1980s saw some attempt at cursory reform on the part of the state. This was the Tricameral Parliament which allowed for the establishment of limited representation for coloreds and Indians. Perceived correctly to be window dressing in an attempt to avoid real political change, the system was given little credibility and was opposed by the United Democratic Front (UDF). The UDF continued in the multiracial pattern of protest established with the Congress movement in the 1950s. Also influential – and an acknowledgment of the convergence of race and class – was the involvement of trade unions. With the dawn of a new decade and the unbanning of the ANC, SACP, and PAC in 1990, the UDF's role became superfluous (Reader's Digest Illustrated History of South Africa: The Real Story 1995: 474, 477–478, 538).

Conclusion

On the eve of the end of apartheid and the first democratic election in 1994, there remained – and continues to remain – the tension that had existed in the formation of racial identity in South Africa from its colonial beginnings. Along with the identification as members of a larger group sharing common aims and aspirations – whether it was the preservation of white minority power, black nationalist protest politics, or the creation of a unified multiracial nation – there existed a tendency toward fragmentation. This was evident in the assertion of certain racial or ethnic identities that served the needs of special interest groups in the struggle for social, economic, and political power that characterized the history of the country.

References

Chetty S (2012) Subjects or citizens? Black south Africans and the dilemma of the second world war. J Natal Zulu Hist 30:53–79

Davenport TRH (1978) South Africa: a modern history, 2nd edn. Macmillan Publishers, Johannesburg

Davenport J (2013) Digging deep: a history of mining in South Africa, 1852–2002. Jonathan Ball Publishers, Johannesburg

Dubow S (2005) Scientific racism in modern South Africa. Cambridge University Press, Cambridge, UK

Freund B (1995) Insiders and outsiders: the Indian working class of Durban, 1910–1990. Heineman, James Currey, Portsmouth and University of Natal Press, Pietermaritzburg

Giliomee H (2003) The Afrikaners: biography of a people. Tafelberg Publishers Ltd, Cape Town

Greenstein R (1994) Identity, democracy and political rights: South Africa in a comparative perspective in University of the Witwatersrand History Workshop, 13–15 July 1994 Democracy: Popular Precedents, Practice, Culture

Hook D (2014) Steve Biko: voices of liberation. HSRC Press, Cape Town

Keegan T (1996) Colonial South Africa and the origins of the racial order. David Philip, Cape Town

Kuper H (1960) Indian people in Natal. Natal University Press, Natal

La Hausse P (1982) Drinking in a cage: the Durban system and the 1929 beer hall riots. Afr Perspect 20:63–75

Lewis G (1987) Between the wire and the wall – a history of South African 'Coloured' politics. David Philip Publisher, Claremont

Reader's Digest Illustrated History of South Africa: The Real Story (1995) The Reader's digest Association of South Africa. University of Cape Town Press, Cape Town

Rich P (1989) Liberals, radicals and the politics of black consciousness, 1969–76. Unpublished Seminar Paper, 24 July 1989, African Studies Institute, University of the Witwatersrand

Simons J, Simons R (1983) Class and colour in South Africa, 1850–1950. International Defence and Aid Fund for South Africa, London

Worger WH (1987) South Africa's City of diamonds: mine workers and monopoly capitalism in Kimberley, 1867–1895. AD Donker, Craighall

Racism and Stereotypes

28

Paul Spoonley

Contents

Introduction	484
Race as Science	485
Racism: Reviewing and Rescinding Race	486
Stereotypes	489
Stereotypes and Education	491
Stereotypes and the Media	493
Stereotypes and Humor/Satire	495
Conclusion	496
References	497

Abstract

One of the major shifts in scholarship in the twentieth century was to move away from a reliance on the science and popular understanding of "race" to a more critical and nuanced approach that included a focus on ethnic identity and a vocabulary that included racism. These shifts prompted the race-inspired genocide of the Holocaust combined with the growing decolonization politics of the colonized, both those that were colonized as part of a process of occupation and settlement or those that were excluded and marginalized as a result of the racism of hegemonic communities or institutions of those states. The decolonization politics of the mid-twentieth century included those residents in metropolitan economies and societies as a result of what was often a process of forced migration. The struggle for recognition and equity also included those that had existed as preexisting nations within colonies but were now subjugated peoples.

P. Spoonley (✉)
College of Humanities and Social Sciences, Massey University, Auckland, New Zealand
e-mail: P.Spoonley@massey.ac.nz

© The Author(s), under exclusive license to Springer Nature Singapore Pte Ltd. 2019
S. Ratuva (ed.), *The Palgrave Handbook of Ethnicity*,
https://doi.org/10.1007/978-981-13-2898-5_36

One of the most important components to these politics of colonization and ongoing marginalization were the presence of stereotypes, the attribution of certain characteristics, typically negative in tone or content, to a whole group of people. As racism has changed in the late twentieth century and through the first decades of the twenty-first century, some stereotypes have remained constant while others have changed or new ones emerged. These stereotypes are invoked and reproduced in a range of settings, including institutions such as the media (new as well as traditional or education, or as an aspect of social commentary and exchange, such as comedy and humor) and as part of humor.

Keywords
Race · Racism · Stereotypes

Introduction

An explanation of phenotypical, cultural, and intellectual differences was embodied in the notion of "race" that was part of a (long) period of European expansion and colonization. Popular understanding of what constituted race was underpinned by the "science" of race, including as a justification for exploitation and colonization. These world views were contested by a growing opposition to slavery from the late 1700s, but it was the deployment of arguments about race and the use of these to justify genocide in Europe during World War II that prompted a significant shift: to critique arguments about race and to acknowledge cultural identity (ethnicity) as an alternative.

This period, dating from the late 1940s, paralleled a period in which decolonization politics were more forcefully articulated as subjugated peoples and nations fought for recognition and to contest cultural and economic marginalization. The civil rights movement added another dimension to these politics of resistance. A more critical science of difference and inequality emerged, and common to both, the movements of resistance and social science was a concern with the presence and impacts of racism. There was an interest in the process by which particular categories/groups of people became racialized (defined and problematized as a "race").

One of the key elements in the product and reproduction of racism is the presence and utilization of stereotypes. Essentially, these are the attribution of characteristics, in a simplistic way, to a group that has been racialized. This attribution or categorization of others is typically couched in negative or hostile terms, and these stereotypes sustain derogatory views of others – and to justify, discrimination and various forms of exclusion. This chapter explores the nature of these stereotypes and uses two institutional settings – the media and education – to explore the nature and impacts of stereotypes and ends with a discussion of comedy and humor. Stereotypes are widely used in such settings and what is – or is not –acceptable is an interesting test of public sentiment and analyses of racism.

Stereotypes remain an important part of the vocabulary and practice of racism. In one sense, they can be relatively innocuous and simply part of the way in which humans understand and explain their social world in a banal and mildly problematic way. But this characterization tends to undermine their ongoing contribution to popular and political racism, to ignore the impact on those being stereotyped and to resist the perniciousness of contemporary racism.

Race as Science

While the idea of "race" is now seen as problematic, at least in academic circles, during a period of European expansion and underpinned by scientists and science of the period, race was a key concept in both explaining phenotypical difference and in justifying the attitudes and actions towards others, essentially the non-European "other" (including Jews). The explorations and expansionism of Europeans from the 1600s onwards brought those explorers and then subsequently colonizers/settlers into contact with people who were physically and culturally different. Race became a core concept in explaining these differences and the "superiority" of the European colonizers and the "inferiority" of those encountered (and therefore their rights to subjugate and enslave). The developing biological sciences helped in this process by providing a scientific justification for these beliefs. The mid-nineteenth century development of eugenics is one of many examples of racial classification and the development of the science of measuring racial difference, and ultimately, resulting in the differential treatment of races. A second element was the appearance of social and economic systems such as slavery which required the absolute subjugation of certain peoples. As the opposition grew to systems such as slavery from the late 1700s, justifications were sought to preserve an economic and social system that depended on the subjugation and exploitation of others. The science of race and the beliefs of elites and hegemonic communities reinforced the key elements in race: that groups could be classified in terms of their phenotypical differences; and that these phenotypical differences reflected innate characteristics between races; that races could be ordered into hierarchies based on how differences in terms of intellect or competence were differentially allocated amongst races according to those doing the allocation (Banton 1978; Miles 1989). Underpinning these beliefs, both scientific and popular, were stereotypes (which will be explained in more detail below) about the perceived nature and key characteristics of groups who were being racialized.

A key moment in relation to the science of racism and the use of race to categorize and justify exclusion and subjugation came in the mid-twentieth century as the full realization of the Holocaust was made clear. The fact that a "modern, advanced" state, in this case Germany, could utilize beliefs about the "superiority" of Aryans and "inferiority" of many others, but especially the Untermenschen – Jews and Romany in particular – in order to justify genocide invited many to revisit beliefs in race. After the end of World War II, international agencies lead a debate about the nature and consequences of beliefs in race. Probably the most significant came from UNESCO who sponsored a series of expert panel meetings in the 1950s and 1960s. A statement noted that race is essentially an arbitrary social classification that then gained a dubious science to underpin these social beliefs. The preexisting science of race and the Holocaust were based on a "scientifically untenable premise" (Miles 1989: 46). The issue of deciding who is or is not a member of a particular race is problematic and relies on social conventions and beliefs – and characterizations of phenotypical difference. There is now a substantial literature which discounts race as a scientific concept (UNESCO 1975; Banton 1978) and which points to the ideological and political content of the term – and the very destructive consequences of these beliefs.

Racism: Reviewing and Rescinding Race

While there had been concerns expressed about both the scientific validity of race and the way in which it was used to denigrate and exploit since the late 1700s and through the 1800s (see Quaker campaigns against slavery), and some of those who were on the receiving end of racism resisted subjugation and denigration in various ways, international understanding and skepticism was muted. For example, the allied countries and their leaders did not accept the stories about Jewish and Romany genocide until the evidence of the death and concentration camps at the end of the war forced a re-evaluation. Through the late 1940s through to the 1970s, scientific communities began to unpack and critique the science of race and populist beliefs about race. This was accompanied by the decolonizing politics of the colonized (cf Fanon 1967; Freire 1968) and the civil rights movement.

Racism, as an increasingly widely used term, was used to signal the presence of ideological beliefs that people can be classified into races and that these racial differences explain physical/intellectual differences and the outcomes of social variation (Miles 1989). In this sense, racism refers to the beliefs about racial difference and typically that these differences signal innate characteristics which translate into hierarchies of superiority and inferiority. It includes a "mix of prejudice, power, ideology, stereotypes, domination, disparities and/or unequal treatment" (Berman and Paradies 2010: 228). In the latter half of the twentieth century, as part of a varied set of decolonizing politics, the connection of racism with colonization and power differentials became an important part of academic and public discourse – and of resistance. Commentators such as Fanon (1967) and Freire (1968) provided a powerful critique of colonialism and what was required to decolonize. Civil rights and Black activists in the United States added to this element, notably in the introduction of concepts such as institutional racism in the late 1960s. This notion, institutional racism, supplemented the existing focus on personal prejudice and the impacts of racism on those targeted and began to stress the structural components and outcomes of racism. Institutional racism "refers to the ways in which groups are differentially treated by institutions as a result of a set of organizational policies and procedures" (Spoonley 1995: 21) whereby certain discriminatory practices are normalized and routinized within the organization (cf Downing and Husband 2005). The institutions referred to typically those that are at the core of states and the allocation of goods, status, and services – education, justice, welfare, housing, employment – and the assumption is that the behaviors of individuals who occupy positions in those institutions are less significant than the way in which the institution operates to disadvantage particular racial groups. This might involve differential access, or limited access, to resources and services and the emphasis on the norms and expectations of hegemonic ethnic groups to the detriment of indigenous or minority ethnic groups, with the result that life chances and outcomes vary considerably depending on the ethnic group in question. One of the interesting arguments in relation to institutional racism is that those in the institutions might not be racist themselves but that the key factor was that the institution in question contributed to inequity by operating in a racially advantageous or disadvantageous way.

Through the 1970s, the emphasis on racism being a combination of prejudice plus power, and an increasing focus on the structural impacts of racism, guided understanding of racism. And these politics and emphasis began to be seen more widely in academic understanding. For example, Rex and Moore (1967) wrote about housing classes in the UK, to signal the way in which the housing market was determined by racial exclusion. But perhaps the more important shift came in the 1980s when writers like Robert Miles and Stephen Castles linked migration and racism to neo-Marxist arguments about structural disadvantage. A classical Marxism, they argued, was inadequate because of its exclusion of ethnic dynamics in contemporary (or historic) capitalism and the reductionism of economic inequity to class. Miles (1982) argued for the political economy of labor migration which argued that the underlying driver of capitalism was capital accumulation and the need to find more profitable ways of producing and exchanging goods. In post-war capitalist economies, one strategy was to recruit workers from the periphery, often former colonies of the urban-industrial centers of capitalist production. But as Miles went on to point out, not only were these workers a source of waged labor, they brought a different culture and were defined as races that were often problematized. Political and ideological relations were altered as contact and exchange took place in the metropolitan centers of capitalism. In Miles' (1982) terms, relationships between these different groups were "racialized." The migrants are defined as physically and culturally different, that is as "races" that drew upon preexisting notions of inferiority and superiority of these socially constructed races. Moreover, these racialized migrants and their presence were seen as problematic in terms of issues such as contributing to the decline of urban areas, law and order and as a cultural threat. And the class structures and advantage/disadvantage of capitalism was now significantly structured by these racialized relationships, so that the groups racialized were excluded or marginalized in significant ways. Castles et al. (1984) added to this approach, and it was underscored by contributions such as Paul Gilroy's (1987) *There Ain't No Black in the Union Jack* and the attention paid to forms of resistance by those colonized or racialized.

Miles (1982), influenced by Fanon (1967), referred to racialization, or the way in which "relations between people have been structured by the signification of human biological characteristics in such a way as to define and construct differentiated social collectivities" (Miles 1982: 75; see also Murji and Solomos 2005). This, in Fleras's (2014: 73) terms, reflected an important conceptual shift with a focus on the "process of defining, categorizing, and evaluating people and their activities along racial lines" with the emphasis on the ideological underpinnings (including the deployment of stereotypes) and category construction. In this way, defined groups are constructed by a process of attributing racial significance and problematized in various ways. The significance of this shift is to underline the process of social construction using (largely) negative perceptions and characterizations, and thereby rejecting any suggestion that racism is a "natural outcome of intergroup contact" (Fleras 2014: 74). The social construction of these world views rely on categories and stereotypes, what Goldberg (1993) refers to as "preconceptual primitive terms" that simplify and explain as part of the logic of racism.

These evolving approaches to racism were reflected – and influenced by – activists and writers from those colonized. For example, in New Zealand, these ideas (from Fanon through to more contemporary neo-Marxist approaches) were influential in contributions from the indigenous and subjugated Māori and can be seen in statements such as Donna Awatere's (1984) *Māori Sovereignty* which provided an interesting analysis of racism and the idea that the sovereignty of the modern state, in this case in New Zealand, could be renegotiated to ensure that indigenous peoples, Māori, could exercise their own (albeit partial) sovereignty. An indigenous scholar, Ranginui Walker (1990), provided a powerful critique in his book, *Ka Whawhai Tonu Matou. Struggle Without End*, in which he linked colonial dispossession and racism with contemporary (highly negative) outcomes for Māori, and argued that both personal and structural racism needed to be confronted. Such approaches continue to remain influential in relation to contemporary understandings of racism in Aotearoa/New Zealand (see, for example, Moewaka Barnes et al. 2013) so that structural racism (in Moewaka Barnes et al. 2013) is seen as being central to both societal and institutional racism with impacts for individuals and groups (notably Māori) in terms of detrimental health outcomes.

The use of the term racism, the process of racializing particular groups, and the critique of institutional racism were central to academic and popular understanding by the second half of the twentieth century. This was accompanied by the recognition that racism could and did take a variety of forms. For example, Fleras and Elliot (1996: 71-83) describe the variety of forms that racism takes, from the everyday and polite versions to more structural and institutionalized forms, and that the targets of racism and the perpetuators of it may equally take a variety of forms. They go on to argue that at its essence, racism is a powerful form of social control whatever its ideological underpinnings, content, or the way in which it is expressed and practiced.

> ...racism has played and continues to play a formidable role in establishing and maintaining patterns of inequality and control. (Fleras and Elliot 1996: 87)

If racism is now seen in a more nuanced way, it is also true that the extensive scholarship and interest provides some challenges. The term itself, racism, has a variety of definitions and is "seldom defined with any precision or consistency" and it is important to recognize that the term refers to a range of attitudes and behaviors (cf Fleras 2014) to a wide spectrum of contexts (Miles 1989 argued that the nature of racism was a product of particular contexts and historical trajectories). It is one of the enduring areas of scholarship and of political activism, and as the politics of the USA, or Hungary, or the UK in recent decades remind us, there is still significant currency in negative beliefs and actions directed at a visible or despised other. Despite an extensive literature, ample evidence, and resistance from those who are targeted by racism, beliefs about racial difference and threat can still be mobilized by nationalist and populist leaders. Despite the political and moral power of a description that some person or action is racist, beliefs about race and behavior based on those beliefs remain a potent and deployed explanation for certain constituencies (see Hochschild 2016).

Integral to racism are certain categorizations and beliefs – and central to these are the presence of stereotypes. What follows is a discussion on the nature of stereotypes and how they operate in certain institutional settings.

Stereotypes

Hurwitz et al. (1997: 31) define stereotypes as "cognitive structures that contain the perceiver's knowledge, beliefs, and expectations about human groups." But this is missing the evaluative or judgmental component in relation to racial categorizations and beliefs. The attribution of characteristics normally embodies a normative component and the attributed characteristics are either negative or positive depending on the group in question (cf Jewell 1993). It might be that stereotypes are neutral or even reflect positive views of others (see Downing and Husband's 2005: 33 discussions of "white stereotypes of Whiteness"). But stereotypes, especially as an underlying component of racism, embody simplistic, negative categorizations of a racialized other. They are categorizations that are "commonly infused with attitudes of hostility and hatred towards the group in question" (Giddens 1993: 256), thereby underpinning the racism with which such stereotypes are associated. As Fleras and Elliot (1996: 68) note, "stereotyping reflects a universal tendency to reduce a complex phenomena to simple (istic) explanations that are generalized to a wider category without acknowledging individual differences." As they go on to argue, these uni-dimensional images can be employed to justify "daily violence or structural oppression" and are an extension of social control" (Fleras and Elliot 1996: 69).

There are different disciplinary approaches to an understanding of stereotypes. For psychologists, there is an interest in cognition and the way in which racism is constructed and practised at the individual and/or contextual level (Fiske 2000). In responding to the question, "how have social psychologists approached this patchwork quilt of categorical thoughts, feelings, and behaviour?" (Fiske 2000: 299) in reference to stereotypes and prejudice, she notes that there are three major approaches to prejudice in relation to intra-individual dynamics that derive from earlier studies by contributors such as Adorno et al. (1950):

(1) Modern or symbolic racism...focuses on policy beliefs that all happen to disadvantage minorities...
(2) ...ambivalent racism ... notes the tension between 'pro'-black attitudes (paternalistic pity for the disadvantaged) and 'anti'-black attitudes (hostility towards the oppositional deviant)...
(3)...aversive racism focusses on the tension between not wanting to be racist and simultaneous, unconscious cognitions that reflect racism. (Fiske 2000: 301)

All involve stereotyping in some form. The alternative approach, according to Fiske, derives from contextual analyses originating with writers such as Tajfel and Turner (see Tajfel and Turner 1986; Turner 1987). This is normally categorized as social identity theory (SIT) and centers on the argument that "people identify with and value their ingroup, thereby derogating the outgroup...[with] both cognitive (categorization) and motivational (self-esteem) foundations" (Fiske 2000: 303), so that there is a tendency to "accentuate differences between categories and minimize differences within categories" (Fiske 2000: 304). It is this tendency towards homogenizing categorized groups that underpins and reinforces stereotypes and "category-confirming information" is privileged (Fiske 2000: 304). Therefore:

People using strong stereotypes neglect ambiguous or neutral information...and assimilate others to the stereotype...[and] people seem to prefer stereotype-matching information...and may ask stereotype-matching questions...[and people privilege stereotype information. (Fiske 2000: 307)

Sociologists and others have often taken their lead from psychologists, notably in the connection between attitudes (prejudice) and negative categorizations (stereotypes). For examples, Macionis and Plummer (1998: 329) define stereotype as a "prejudicial, exaggerated description of some category of people." Here the connection to attitudes and prejudice is explicit. Other sociologists, such as Fleras and Elliot (1996: 68–69) stress the connection between stereotypes and ethnocentrism are "context and consequence" dependent. The interest here is on the presence of stereotypes in institutional practices, such as the media or popular culture (such as ethnic jokes). And the emphasis is on the role that stereotypes play in social control (Fleras 1998: 69). There is still an interest in the role that stereotypes place in prejudicial attitudes but also a strong connection to behavior whether in relation to discriminatory acts or institutional racism. There is some interesting analysis of the role of stereotypes in the practices of employers (McDowell 2008: 59), the visibility/invisibility/hypervisibility of individuals and groups as central to stereotypes (Nagel and Staeheli 2008: 85–87), or victimization stereotypes of Asian women (male controlled, subject to arranged marriages; see Anthias and Yuval-Davis 1992: 125).

One way to test the relationship between stereotypes and the way in which race is refracted by communities is to look at how major public events or disputes are seen through a race lens. Those who take the Implicit Association Test (Nesbit 2016) in the USA show that almost 90% of white Americans display an inherent racialized (positive) bias towards whites. They reflexively and subconsciously associate images of African-Americans with negative (stereotypical) labels and whites with positive descriptors. This is supported by research from the National Opinion

Research Center at the University of Chicago that shows that "many Americans...harbour beliefs about racial and ethnic minorities that are based on racial stereotypes" (Nesbit 2016). It is daunting to realize that more than half of the respondents in the survey rated African-Americans as "less intelligent" than whites, and that this included 30% of the African-Americans answering the survey. In contrast, there are stereotypes about Asian educational performance in the USA. In some research, Asian-Americans were seen in a similar light to Jewish students, specifically in relation to excelling in education while remaining apart from the mainstream as a result of both agency and structural factors (Dhingra 2007: 92), a version of a model-minority stereotype. The latter is an interesting stereotype (how much of it is based on real world educational outcomes as opposed to a simplistic and inaccurate categorization) and it combines negative connotations ("Asian geek" stereotypes) with a begrudging respect.

Stereotypes underpin and contribute to racist categorizations and racialization in a range of ways as the above brief survey indicates. There are also a range of disciplinary emphases, from the role that stereotypes play in social identity theory to the visibility/invisibility of color in different settings. To illustrate the above, a discussion of stereotypes in selected institutional settings is offered.

Stereotypes and Education

Educational systems are critical in socializing younger members of society and providing a sense of self, of norms, and roles and acceptability. The transfer of knowledge, both formal and informal, is critical but so is an understanding of how individuals or groups are to be characterized and understood. So a central research and policy/political question is whether stereotypes exist and operate in educational institutions, what form they take, and what impact they might have, especially on those targeted.

To explore these dynamics, American research has looked at the presence of stereotypes in young students and the role that these stereotypes play in identity formation. A study of seventh and eighth-grade African Americans tested the degree to which they endorsed race stereotypes or whether self-perceptions would be moderated by what the researchers called "racial centrality" (Racial centrality is the "extent to which race is a central aspect of an individual's determination, and the research question concerns the degree to which an individual identifies with a racial group and the relationship between an individual's self-perceptions and stereotype endorsement). Hence, "for these youth, identity development entails forging an understanding of how race – including the centrality of race for the individual, as well as the meaning ascribed to race by others in the society – is intertwined with personal identity" (Okeke et al. 2009: 2). This draws on earlier research that argued that an awareness of negative stereotypes can negatively impact on the performance of group members, giving rise to stereotype consciousness (McKown and Weinstein 2003). These researchers and others found that both African-American and white middle schoolers were more likely to be aware of race stereotypes, in this case relating to academic performance (whites are smarter than African-Americans) than fourth graders. In the case of the Okeke et al. (2009) research, they found that a range of influences and factors were relevant (personality, school characteristics, experiences) and that while causality between stereotypes and self-perception is difficult to establish with cross-sectional data, there remains a concern that some youth are more vulnerable to racial stereotypes.

There is evidence to indicate that stereotypes contribute to educational opportunity outcomes, the education opportunity gap, or educational life chances, from the expectations of key educational players or influential others, and the internalization of these stereotypes for those who are characterized in various and often negative ways. By the time students reach higher education, the education opportunity gap is obvious in advanced economies; although this is played out in different ways depending on which group is the focus. A number of American universities began to operate policies to limit the proportion of Asians in certain programs or institutions – because of what were seen as "educational over-achievement." In this case, stereotypes centered on success (although at times that success was portrayed in negative stereotypes: the Asian "nerd" or "geek" whose only success was educational). Others have focused on the achievement gap that disadvantages African-American and sometimes other groups.

Johnson-Ahorlu (2012), rather than describing the educational outcomes gap between African-American and white Americans as an achievement gap, describes it as an "opportunity gap" to highlight the broad nature of educational inequity and to draw attention to the impacts of racism and stereotypes. She examines the "relationship between racism, stereotypes and the ways in which they hinder academic opportunity" (Johnson-Ahorlu 2012: 635), and she does this by moving away from psychological influences and dynamics and uses Critical Race Theory (CRT). This focusses attention on broader societal influences, dominant discourses (in this case, the role of stereotypes), and accepts that the testimonies of African-Americans (here described as "People of Color") are valid in their own right as a source of data and as providing details of the lived realities of the victims of racism and stereotypes. This approach to understanding the role of racism and stereotypes in educational outcomes offers a more critical and politically nuanced approach. This can be seen in her definition of stereotypes, with its focus on structural elements:

> Stereotypes can be defined as gross generalizations applied to a group of people with some shared characteristics. In terms of African Americans and other People of Color, stereotypes are often used to justify racism and can provide a rationale for racial oppression and marginalization. (Johnson-Ahorlu 2012: 637)

The effect, Johnson-Ahorlu (2012) argues is that low expectations, especially from university staff, limit career options and majors with the result that African-American students experience stereotype threat so that racism was underpinned by stereotypes about educational ability which in turn further contributed to inequitable educational outcomes and opportunities.

The available research indicates that stereotypes are present in educational settings, although they typically do not originate in these settings but rather the presence and use of stereotypes in an educational institution tends to reflect broader societal influences and origins. The above research provides evidence that stereotypes:

- Play a role in contributing to inter-group educational outcome gaps (or opportunity gaps);
- That they negatively impact on identity and performance and contribute to stereotype consciousness;
- That race stereotypes might be accepted/endorsed by both the hegemonic group and those targeted in stereotypes.

Stereotypes and the Media

The media have been critical in the perpetuation of stereotypes and sometimes in their creation (see Mastro 2009 for a review). At times, immigrant and ethnic minorities are invisible in the media (which may sustain some stereotypes by omission) but typically, the media have often played a crucial role in using and reinforcing stereotypes. As Fleras and Elliot (1996: 168) argue, "minorities tend to be associated with 'race or gender *stereotyping*'" and while there have been improvements in media coverage in recent decades, there is still the tendency to "situate minorities in [the] context of conflict or tragedy," as "problems" in some sense (from being an economic liability to contributing to law and order issues) or as an "adornment," as a form of entertainment in stereotypical roles. This is particularly true when it comes to reporting crime, for example, where public perceptions are often influenced by stereotypes that are reproduced by the media (Giddens 1993: 135). Stereotypes about the association of certain racialized groups and crime has an enduring effect (Hjorth 2017). In this sense, the media can be seen as a "racialized institution in that they reflect (embody) and reinforce a dominant culture's perspective" and that the media (can) "deny or denigrate racialized minorities" (Fleras 2014: 147). The media play a critical role in setting the public and popular agendas.

The recent centrality of debates about immigration provides evidence of the association between often long-standing stereotypes and anti-immigrant views and politics.

The association of restrictionist immigration views ("build the wall!") towards immigrants from Latin America can be directly corelated with negative media coverage of Mexican immigration (Jimenez 2010: 199). Views about the ways in which Mexican immigrants were believed to contribute to the degradation of local communities, the level of cleanliness, or their behavior in public contributed to stereotypes that then characterized the whole Mexican immigrant community negatively. Existing stereotypes were endorsed and expanded by media coverage that in turn encouraged media attention and the further use of negative stereotypes to characterize a community, in this case Mexican immigrants. (Jimenez 2010: 200, does point out that there were sympathy among others towards immigrants).

Many of the stereotypes that appear in the media remain, in part or in full, from previous periods. In US popular culture, these historical racial stereotypes in relation to African-Americans include the persona or image of Sambo, Jim Crow, Mammy, Aunt Jemimah, Sapphire, and Jezebell (Green n.d.). Sambo, for example, is a "simple-minded, docile, black man" which dates from a "defense of slavery" that was widely used in the media and which reinforced popular culture (Green n.d.: 3).

Adams-Bass et al. (2014: 368) argue that:

> Besides the minstrel-inspired "coons" and "mammies," additional stereotypical characterizations became staple images of Black females ("tragic mulatto"; "sapphire"; "jezebel") and males ("Buck"; "Uncle Tom"...). In spite of social advances, there remains within the TV and film industry a practice of presenting negative stereotype images of Black people scripted from early characters predicated on the racial inferiority of Blacks

They go on to examine how these stereotypes inform and influence adolescent views in the USA towards African-Americans looking at the message transfer between the media and youth. Based on their research, they concluded that there were significant age and gender differences in relation to whether the youth respondents identified the media messages as positive or negative. For example, "males were less likely to identify negative media stereotypes but more likely to endorse the negative messages than females," while younger youth identified more positive media images than older youth (Adams-Bass et al. 2014: 384). Weaver (2011) in discussing Afro-Caribbean comedians in the UK and USA (such as Lenny Henry or Chris Rock) who still employ long-standing racist stereotypes to develop what he calls a reverse semantic effect, or a form of resistance to racist stereotypes. This becomes complicated when a character such as Ali G (Sacha Baron Cohen) is considered, as Weaver (2010) goes on to do. Here there is an inversion of stereotypes, or as Weaver notes, the pretense of a young working class British person from Staines who pretends to a homophobic, sexist, person from an inner-city ghetto in the USA, in this case played by a British Jew who graduated from Cambridge University. It is not unlike other characters such as Alf Garnett in "Til Death Us Do Part" (on British television in the 1960s and 1970s) or Archie Bunker in the American television show "All in the Family" (1970s). Both played racially bigoted individuals and employed a range of stereotypes, both self-directed and at others. There is also the question of how much those targeted by these stereotypes either accept or resist them. One research project (Tukachinsky et al. 2017) examined the effects of television depictions of African-Americans and Latinos on members of the groups. Although the number of African-Americans on US prime time television reached parity with the size (proportion) in the US population, and many of the roles and images had improved, there were still negative portrayals alongside positive ones (Tukachinsky et al. 2017). In comparison, Latinos "are only seen infrequently on television – a pattern that has persisted for decades" (Tukachinsky et al. 2017: 3). Their study concluded that "negative media representations ... pose a tangible identity threat to ethnic minorities" and that these "micro-level psychological processes [identity threat] may be occurring on a societal level as well" (Tukachinsky et al. 2017: 19) with concerns that negative stereotyping has implications for well-being and health.

These negative images and stereotypes have not gone uncontested. Ethnic minorities, indigenous nations, and immigrants have resisted the negative imaging of them by the media (Fleras 2014). In destination countries such as Canada, Australia, and New Zealand, the immigrant and ethnic minority communities build social capital and ethnic identities (hyphenated and third space identities), and from this base, will seek to confront, challenge and provide alternative readings in the media. Or they might be confronted by particular incidents which help mobilize activism to context negative media commentaries and images (such as the beating of Rodney King in Los Angeles). Immigrant and ethnic organizations and activists seek to develop a "more positive image of their collective membership to confront negative stereotyping in the media" (Simmons 2010: 171).

The role of the media, in all its manifestations (old and new), continues to play a role in perpetuating stereotypes, either by commission or omission. The media landscape in countries like the USA or the UK has changed in recent decades, and there is a greater awareness of the need for sensitivity and self-reflexivity when it comes to issues of diversity, in this case ethnic. There have been some powerful public commentaries and the media commons (see Eddo-Lodge 2017). But equally, the proliferation of media options and the development of media echo chambers have provided new opportunities for racist commentaries and opinions to be shared on a one-to-many basis – and often without disclosing a source or authorship.

Stereotypes and Humor/Satire

One of the problem areas in terms of the articulation and reproduction of stereotypes is the area of humor: what is permissible and what is not? For example, is it acceptable for someone to use stereotypes when telling jokes when the teller is from the particular group that is being characterized in a stereotypical way? Are there stereotypes that are acceptable (and to whom?). These are problematic issues in relation to the use of stereotypes. It may be that there is recognition that a stereotype is part of a joke but that does not mean that the recipient is in agreement (Hay 2001: 72). As Piskorska (2016: 34) notes, joke stereotypes need to be mutually known to individuals but that might not mean that they are endorsed. So what is mutually known and endorsed (accepted) in contrast to what is not accepted, and indeed, might be regarded as deeply offensive?

There is an interesting literature on the role and acceptability of stereotypes in humor. And it is an area that often draws quite differing responses (this or that ethnic group has no sense of humor – it is only a joke!). As Aronson (quoted in Piskorska (2016: 7) notes, a stereotype is most often a set of assumptions about social roles and traits, and Piskorska goes on to explore the stereotypes of Scots as the basis for humor, particularly stereotypes about the perceived meanness (or thriftiness) of Scots. She concludes that such stereotypes rely on being combined with everyday scenarios to give rise to incongruity; they can be augmented to become visibly absurd and given that meanness is an object of ridicule, it supports a sense of superiority (Piskorska 2016: 31). In support of this, Weaver (2011) argues that racist humor acts as racist rhetoric (that is, it can be convincing) which can also impact on nonhumorous discourse (racist truth or truth claims). An embodied racism (that is racism which relies on an earlier biological racism) can reinforce notions of hierarchy and a sense of order (orderbuilding) as part of humor and the reliance on stereotypes.

There are ways of expressing humor and what constitutes acceptable humor. One of the significant moments in these debates occurred with the publication of the Prophet Muhammad cartoons in Denmark in 2015. As Weaver (2011: Chap. 8) argues, the intent and impact of these cartoons are complex, and he suggests that there are four different readings, including as a criticism of Islamic fundamentalism, as blasphemous, as Islamophobic and racist, or as satire which is a defense required in terms of the freedom of speech. He uses the notion of liquid racism to characterize the complexity of the issues in this case. Similarly, comedians such as Ricky Gervais, Jimmy Carr, Frankie Boyle, Dapper Laughs, Daniel Tosh, and Sarah Silverman (Weaver and Morgan 2017) tell jokes that can be seen as a way of challenging prejudice, while others see them as unacceptable and racist/sexist (objectification, devaluation, and violence).

> Offensive humour is political and highlights a connection between our identities, politics and the pleasure of laughter. When people engage in joking about rape or sexual assault...there are intended and unintended consequences for society. In contributing to a blurred distinction between a culture of sexual abuse and humour, rape jokes may contribute to the normalisation of such abuse and make it more difficult that it is already for victims of sexual abuse to speak out. (Weaver and Morgan 2017)

Humor often relies on stereotypes – and humorous stereotypes continue to play an important role in popular culture and thinking. But the use of stereotypes as part of comedy or satire, or as part of informal humor in social situations, is highly problematic. Are there stereotypes that are both understood and acceptable? In what circumstances? And does it matter who articulates the stereotypes – and who the audience is. Is it ever acceptable to joke about the Holocaust? Is a joke that relies on a disrespectful stereotype acceptable if the person telling the joke is from the stereotyped community? As Weaver (2011) notes above, even an important example such as the Prophet Muhammad cartoons is open to a range of readings. Often the issue of the use of stereotypes as part of humor is a complex, multidimensional issue.

Conclusion

Stereotypes play a key role in racial categorization and the racialization of "other" groups. There are arguments that suggest that stereotypes are part of how humans understand a complex social world, a way of simplifying and making that world understandable. However, stereotypes – as defined here – also involve attributing negative characteristics and behaviors to members of racialized groups, and this contributes to racist world views and discriminatory behavior. Stereotypes contribute to the social control of others and to denigration and/or exclusion. There are real world consequences to the use of stereotypes as part of the presence of racism.

Since the late 1940s, there has been a shift in the acceptability of race as a conceptual underpinning for understanding people and cultures, and the development of both academic and popular understandings that are critical of the presence of racism. This has impacted on some policy and political agendas. However, the recent turn to an exclusive nationalism in countries ranging from the USA to Hungary to Germany has reinvigorated debates about the racism directed towards an "other," and has reintroduced questions about the underpinnings of racism, including the reproduction of often long-standing stereotypes.

References

Adams-Bass VN, Stevenson HC, Kotzin DS (2014) Measuring the meaning of Black media stereotypes and their relationship to the racial identity, Black history knowledge, and racial socialization of African American youth. J Black Stud 45(5):367–395

Adorno TW, Frenkel-Brunswik E, Levinson DJ, Sanford RN (1950) The authoritarian personality. Harper, New York

Anthias F, Yuval-Davis N (1992) Racialized boundaries. Race, nation, gender, colour and class and the anti-racist struggle. Routledge, London

Awatere D (1984) Māori sovereignty. Broadsheet Publications, Auckland

Banton M (1978) The idea of race. Westview Press, Boulder

Berman G, Paradies Y (2010) Racism disadvantage and multiculturalism: toward effective anti-racist praxis. Ethn Racial Stud 13(2):214–232

Castles S, Booth H, Wallace T (1984) Here for good. Western Europe's new ethnic minorities. Plunto Press, London

Dhingra P (2007) Managing multicultural lives. Asian American professionals and the challenge of multiple identities. Stanford University Press, Stanford

Downing J, Husband C (2005) Representing 'race'. Racisms, ethnicities and media. Sage, London

Eddo-Lodge R (2017) Why I'm no longer talking to white people about race. Bloomsbury Circus, London

Fanon F (1967) The wretched of the earth. Penguin, Harmondsworth

Fiske ST (2000) Stereotyping, prejudice, and discrimination at the seam between the centuries: evolution, culture, mind, and brain. Eur J Soc Psychol 30:299–322

Fleras A (1998) Working through differences. The politics of "isms" in Aotearoa. New Zealand Sociology 13(1):62–96

Fleras A (2014) Racism in bicultural Canada. Paradoxes, politics and resistance. Wilfred Laurier University Press, Waterloo

Fleras A, Elliot J (1996) Unequal relations. An introduction to race, ethnic and aboriginal dynamics in Canada (second edition). Prentice Hall, Scarborough

Freire P (1968) Pedagogy of the oppressed. Seabury Press, New York

Giddens A (1993) Sociology. Polity Press, Oxford

Gilroy P (1987) There ain't no black in the Union Jack. The cultural politics of race and nation. Chicago University Press, Chicago

Goldberg DT (1993) Racist culture. Philosophy and the politics of meaning. Blackwell, Oxford

Green L (n.d.) Stereotypes: negative racial stereotypes and their effect on attitudes towards African-Americans. https://ferris.edu/HTMLS/news/jimcrow/links/essays/vcu.htm. Accessed 17 Sept 2018

Hay J (2001) The pragmatics of humor support. Humor 14(1):55–82

Hjorth F (2017) The influence of local ethnic diversity on group-centric crime attitudes. Br J Polit Sci. https://doi.org/10.1017/S0007123417000424
Hochschild B (2016) Strangers in their own land. The New Press, New York
Hurwitz J, Peffley M, Sniderman P (1997) Racial stereotypes and whites political views of blacks in the context of welfare and crime. Am J Polit Sci 41:30–60
Jewell SK (1993) From mammy to miss America and beyond: cultural images and the shaping of US policy. Routledge, New York
Jimenez TR (2010) Replenished ethnicity. Mexican Americans, immigration and identity. University of California Press, Berkeley
Johnson-Ahorlu RN (2012) The academic opportunity gaps: how racism and stereotypes disrupt the education of African-American undergraduates. Race Ethn Educ 15(5):633–652
Macionis JJ, Plummer K (1998) Sociology. A global introduction. Prentice Hall, New York
Mastro D (2009) Effects of racial and ethnic stereotyping. In: Bryant J, Oliver MB (eds) Media effects. Advances in theory and research. Lawrence Erlbaum, Hillsdale, pp 325–341
McDowell L (2008) On the significance of being white: European migrant workers in the British economy in the 1940s and 2000s. In: Dwyer C, Bressey C (eds) New geographies of race and racism. Ashgate, Aldershot, pp 51–64
McKown C, Weinstein RS (2003) The development and consequences of stereotype consciousness in middle childhood. Child Dev 74:498–515
Miles R (1982) Racism and migrant labour. Routledge and Kegen Paul, London
Miles R (1989) Racism. Routledge, London
Moewaka Barnes A, Taiapa K, Borell B, McCreanor T (2013) Māori experiences and responses to racism in Aotearoa New Zealand. Mai J 2(2):63–77
Murji K, Solomos J (eds) (2005) Racialization. Studies in theory and practice. Oxford University Press, Oxford
Nagel C, Staeheli LA (2008) Integration and the politics of visibility and invisibility in Britain: the case of British Arab activists. In: Dwyer C, Bressey C (eds) New geographies of race and racism. Ashgate, Aldershot, pp 83–94
Nesbit J (2016) America has a big race problem. https://www.usnews.com/news/articles/2016-03-28/america-has-a-big-race-problem. Accessed 17 Sept 2018
Okeke NZ, Howard LC, Kurtz-Costes B (2009) Academic race stereotypes, academic self-concept, and racial centrality in African American youth. J Black Psychol 35(3):366–387
Piskorska A (2016) Humour and popular stereotypes of Scots In: Korzeniowska A, Szymańska I (eds) Scottish culture: dialogue and self-expression. Semper, pp 369–379. https://www.researchgate.net/publication/303719570_Humour_and_the_Popular_Stereotypes_of_Scots. Accessed 21 Sept
Rex J, Moore R (1967) Race, community and conflict. A study of Spankbrook. Oxford University Press, New York
Simmons AB (2010) Immigration and Canada. Global and transnational perspectives. Global and transnational perspectives. Canadian Scholars Press, Toronto
Spoonley P (1995) Racism and ethnicity. Oxford University Press, Auckland
Tajfel H, Turner JC (1986) The social identity theory of intergroup behaviour. In: Worchel S, Austin WG (eds) Psychology of intergroup relations. Nelson-Hall, Chicago, pp 7–24
Tukachinsky R, Mastro D, Yarchi M (2017) The effect of prime time television. Ethnic/racial stereotypes on Latino and Black Americans: a longitudinal national level study. J Broadcast Electron Media. https://doi.org/10.1080/08838151.2017.1344669. Accessed 2 Oct 2018
Turner H (1987) Rediscovering the social group: a self-categorization theory. Basil Blackwell, London
UNESCO (1975) Race, science and society. Allen and Unwin, London
Walker R (1990) Ka whawahi tonu matou. Struggle without end. Penguin, Auckland
Weaver S (2010) The 'other' laughs back: humour and resistance in anti-racist comedy. Sociology 44(1):31–48
Weaver S (2011) The rhetoric of racist humour. US, UK and global race joking. Ashgate, Farnham
Weaver S (2013) The rhetoric of racist humour. Routledge, London
Weaver S, Morgan K (2017) What is the point of offensive humour. The Conversation, 10 May. http://theconversation.com/what-is-the-point-of-offensive-humour-76889

Discussing Contemporary Racial Justice in Academic Spaces: Minimizing Epistemic Exploitation While Neutralizing White Fragility

29

Adele Norris

Contents

Introduction	500
Emotional Discomfort and Discussions of Racism	501
Impediments to Beneficial Racial Dialogue	502
Situating my Social Location and Teaching Introduction to Sociology	503
White Fragility and White Guilt	503
Logic of Diversity in an Increasingly Multiracial Society	506
Colorblindness and the Possibility for Social Change	507
Epistemic Exploitation	509
Conclusion	509
References	510

Abstract

In light of contemporary racial justice issues in the United States, the academic classroom can be a precarious environment to engage in intellectually humble dialogue on racial injustice. This chapter expands upon the concept of *epistemic exploitation* raised in Nora Berenstain's 2016 article, which explains the exploitative and emotionally taxing burden marginalized persons feel when compelled to educate privileged persons about their unearned privilege and the nature of marginalized person's oppression. I argue that epistemic exploitation is more likely to occur in academic classrooms if white guilt and fragility are not acknowledged and neutralized. My assertion is based on the premise that as racial justice conversations increasingly occur, the need to satisfy white fragility exceeds the need to engage in healthy discussions on racism and white supremacy. Race is, therefore, deemphasized and other social status markers (e.g., gender, class, age, sexuality orientation) are overly emphasized or are used as proxies

---

A. Norris (✉)
School of Social Sciences, Sociology and Sociology Program, The University of Waikato, Hamilton, New Zealand
e-mail: adele.norris@waikato.ac.nz

for race. In such cases, colonizing narratives of groups racialized as non-white are perpetuated via colorblind explanations about social problems.

Keywords

Epistemic exploitation · Racial justice · Diversity ideology · Colorblind ideology · White fragility/guilt

Introduction

In 1963, a racially contentious time in the United States, James Baldwin published the essay *A Talk to Teachers*. During this time, racism, social inequalities, and stratification were severe and profound (Smith 2017). Given the 2017 neo-Nazi march across the University of Virginia campus and the ongoing gross police brutality against blacks—which spurred a national movement—we are, again, living in a contentious time. The message Baldwin (1963) delivered to educators in his essay is just as relevant today when he says that educators should not make peace with the conspiracies designed to destroy us but rather assume the obligation to teach students to examine society critically and truthfully. In Clint Smith's (2017) reflection on Baldwin's essay, Smith implores educators not to fall victim to wanting to create an apolitical space in the classroom. "The very decision to not discuss certain things in your classroom" he says, "is in and of itself, a political decision," especially when students' lives are impacted by political decisions every single day (Smith 2017, 3).

It is well documented that explicit and implicit social status markers (race/ethnicity, gender, social class, ability status, and sexual orientation) contribute to barriers that prevent people from engaging in open-minded, intellectually humble dialogue that stimulates a critical consciousness and engagement with the world (Berenstain 2016; Collins 2013; Lorde 1995; Nadan and Stark 2016; Smith 2017). My view, which serves as a pivotal aspect of this discussion, is that social status markers are more important in determining whether one accepts a particular position than is the content of the position itself. I posit that social cues, specifically related to race/ethnicity, trigger implicit biases and are more likely to drive academic discussions of injustices experienced by members of structurally disadvantaged racial groups than the need to unlearn colonizing narratives that are regurgitated within the classroom. For example, Katie Reilly's (2016) *Time* article, *How Guns on Campus Could Change What Texas Teaches*, draws attention to how gun laws influenced the removal of controversial content from university classrooms. In the wake of the campus-carry law, which allows Texans with concealed handguns license to carry guns on public university campuses, university professors were urged to consider changing their curricula to avoid controversial subjects (Reilly 2016).

Scholars have noted a new trend among racially conscious white individuals, on the one hand, ostensibly advocating for racial inclusion and challenge colorblind ideology, while, on the other hand, maintain white supremacy (Bell and Hartmann

2007; Smith and Mayorga-Gallo 2017). With an increasingly multiracial society that seemingly celebrates efforts of diversity and inclusion, groups racialized as non-white often bear the burden to still prove their oppression (Berenstain 2016) while whiteness remains unquestioned (Smith and Mayorga-Gallo 2017). Berenstain (2016) refers to this process as epistemic exploitation. In an increasingly race-conscious society, expanding our understanding of epistemic exploitation is an important step if we are to advance academic discussions of racism and racial justice. This chapter argues, however, that as a part of deconstructing epistemic exploitation, careful and sustained attention must be used to identify the ways in which "white fragility" and "white guilt" are mobilized to establish a moral equivalence between all racial groups. Effectively a form of "White protectionism," as Charles Mills (1998) calls it, white people's claims of emotional injury and victimhood, fueled by the discourses of diversity and colorblind ideology, amplifies the epistemic exploitation of oppressed groups who are called upon to protect the white ego from reflective engagement with unearned privilege.

Emotional Discomfort and Discussions of Racism

I begin this discussion by first defining epistemic exploitation set forth by Nora Berenstain (2016). Epistemic exploitation occurs when individuals from racially/ethnically subjugated groups are called upon to educate individuals from racially privileged groups on their oppression and to prove that the systems of power that work to oppress them exist (Berenstain 2016). I argue that in order to avoid or limit epistemic exploitation, white guilt and fragility must be accounted for and neutralized. This will be challenging. My claim is grounded in the reality that contemporary racism arises in complex forms where diversity claims are in fact promoted by white individuals. However, many people hold subconscious or unarticulated racist beliefs, often without having considered that these beliefs are racist (such as, for example, the claim that the problem is solely social class based, rather than the possibility of racism). These forms call for innovative pedagogical strategies that examine the underlying beliefs that operate to reject or constrain one's understanding of institutional and structural racist practices. Essential to this complexity is the widespread belief that society has achieved racial equality. Those who are consistently told that racism is a problem of the past, will have some reason to cease to look for it as an explanation of behaviors and practices in the present. It is not surprising that students would grapple with examining features of modern-day racism, especially when many of them have grown up in a world where words such as *diversity* and *multicultural* are freely embraced and dominate mainstream discourses (Alexander 2012; Collin 2013; Davis 1996; Mohanty 2004; Norris 2017; Pitcher 2011; Smith and Mayorga-Gallo 2017; St. Clair and Kishimoto 2010). The problem arises when this discomfort is ignored and goes unexamined. Failing to examine the causes of our modern discomfort, both to talk and to hear about race and racism, stops us from understanding the extent to which it influences and impedes discussions of racism and racial justice.

There is a growing scholarship on the emotional discomfort stimulated by discussing the nature of racism and racist stereotypes (Boler 1999; Burke 2017; Collins 2013; Ladner 1971; Nadan and Stark 2016; Zajicek 2002). Developing pedagogical strategies that equip students to reflect upon their personal biases is far from new and crosses disciplinary boundaries (Collins 2013; Cooper 2008; Boler 1999; Murphy-Erby et al. 2009; Nadan and Stark 2016). It is imperative students are equipped to engage in healthy discussions of racism, especially as social inequalities deepen and, through corporate media penetration, we are aware that the world is culturally diverse (Nadan and Stark 2016). Taking the stark reality that social inequality is both ubiquitous and is becoming worse as my point of departure, I now move to explicate its implications for the politics of embodied knowledge and emotional labor involved in respecting race-talk in the classroom.

The remainder of the chapter is organized into two parts. First, I situate this discussion in the philosophical context of epistemic exploitation. The extent that academic classrooms can effectively challenge racial hierarchies rather than replicate them rests upon the extent that such spaces can minimize epistemic exploitation while neutralizing white guilt and fragility. In doing so, the theoretical insights presented are supported by my personal experiences as a transnational educator who has taught Introduction to Sociology in two predominately white countries. Thus, this work poses theoretical arguments. Second and relatedly, I review three overlapping themes identified in the literature that often dominate formal classroom settings: (1) white guilt and white fragility, (2) diversity ideology, and (3) colorblind ideology. Each of these are core features inherent to the ubiquity of whiteness that dominate formal settings, which in turn influences the type of scholarly material utilized in classes, how it is delivered, and possibilities for how it is understood.

Impediments to Beneficial Racial Dialogue

Trayvon Martin, Michael Brown, Eric Garner, Sandra Bland, Walter Scott, Philando Castile, Alton Sterling, Terence Crutcher, and Jordan Edwards are only a few names embedded in the United States discourse on racism and police brutality. The untimely deaths of these African Americans coupled with the mass incarceration of black and brown people launched the widely known social justice movement, Black Lives Matter. Such dismal events are evidence of a growing twenty-first century racial justice problem with centuries old roots. Yet, contemporary understandings of the enormity of racial injustices lag considerably behind the urgency to achieve racial justice. The fight for racial equity has spurred a plethora of discussions; however, these discussions are too often tempered by the need to assuage white discomfort. That is, while communities, activists, and public figures alike are now willing to strongly criticize particular instances of violence against African Americans, fewer are as yet willing to analyze the structural and social features of institutions such as the police. Presumably this "hierarchy of credibility" is determined by the overdetermined ideological conception that police are "protectors" and neutral arbiters of conflict resolution.

Situating my Social Location and Teaching Introduction to Sociology

As a heterosexual Black woman from rural Mississippi who has taught Introduction to Sociology and other sociology and women studies courses in two predominately white countries, speaking about racism comes fairly naturally. This ease comes in part because of my daily experiences, and I rely heavily on my experiences growing up in the Deep South during the 1980s. I inform my class of my earliest memories of having to learn about racism. Only a minority of students can relate to experiences of racism coupled with having to understand it at the age of five or six, especially during a time many students perceive as post-Civil Rights and therefore post-racial. But most of my comfort comes from having had to engage in hostile environments towards blacks and having hostile teachers most of my life. Such experiences bring with it an understanding and/or expectancy of white hostility and discomfort with discussions of race/racism. However, despite my comfort with delivering material on race/racism, most of my students do not share the same level of comfort hearing or learning about racism.

As with any topic, I am aware of students' engagement and receptiveness. While comfort levels for different topics vary across classrooms and geographic regions, I have recognized that with discussions of race/racism/white supremacy, there is a consistent hostility and discomfort that are more pronounced, which often manifest visibly (e.g., defensive body language, awkwardness) and verbally (e.g., types of questions posed, defensive comments and tone of voice). Albeit unknowingly, these responses work in tandem to gain control of the space and to direct the discussion to more palatable takes on racism or to complete dismissal. These types of responses are powerful and are also evidence that there is an acute lack of understanding of racial injustice and white supremacy despite the plethora of diversity and multicultural initiatives. I use this discomfort as evidence a problem exist, and then pose the question: *How can we dismantle a system that we cannot discuss?* While I do not gain everyone's attention, I do get enough students involved to counter classroom discomfort and get the class to a place for those who want to learn will gain some insights and confidence to challenge their peers.

White Fragility and White Guilt

Discomfort arises somewhere between acknowledgement of the problem and criticism of those enacting racism. In discussions of race in formal settings, like academic classrooms, emotional discomfort is often elevated to higher levels of importance than difficult and complicated substantive discussions of racism that are beneficial and productive. The concept of "safe space" is mobilized by whiteness to protect the biases and insecurities of white students, teaching assistants and even professors. Robin DiAngelo's (2011), ground breaking work on white fragility, regards theses dynamics as a function of whiteness. Consider the lengths public figures feel they must go to separate their criticism of particular police officers from any perceived criticism of the police as an institution, when speaking out against atrocities. This is the "bad apple" versus the "bad barrel" polemic, as if the two cannot exist simultaneously. The idea that police forces are institutionally racist cannot be broached without causing public discussion to veer away from the issues at hand, to a discussion about what criticisms can and should be uttered publicly. In this way "political correctness" is a slur projected at those seeking to legitimate alternative and oppositional narratives, whereas it is in reality discursive strategies that seek to constrain radical analysis that are politically correct.

Robin DiAngelo (2011) defines whiteness as including three fundamentals: (1) a location of structural advantage and race privilege; (2) a standpoint for which white people look at themselves, at others, and at society; and (3) a set of cultural practices that are usually tied to "othering" of non-white people. Goodman (2011) argues that the limited examination of whiteness is a societal cost connected to the predominant way history is told. Since history is told from the perspective of the dominant group that emphasizes and embellishes the accomplishments of this group, readers receive a partial and distorted view of the past (Baldwin 1963; Collins 2013; Goodman 2011). Poor exposure to an inclusive history, also a function of white supremacy (Baldwin 1963; Woodson 1933), limits and skews the views of different lifestyles, perspectives, and people (Goodman 2011). Consequently, a "whiteness conditioning" develops and impedes the critical interrogation of whiteness and privilege, especially by white students (Goodman 2011; Loewen 2007). Loewen (2007) identifies this issue as the primary reason white students, in particular, leave high school with weak to nonexisting foundations upon which to encounter knowledge about race and social inequalities. If the material is all/primarily told from a particular perspective, discussions will fail to make students leave the classroom thinking critically, which also speaks to the structural inequalities rooted in "diversity" initiatives. Meaning, the structural inequalities in society are maintained by the standard choices of educators regarding subject matter, such that even in classrooms with a diverse range of students from diverse backgrounds, the students do not develop critical approaches to knowledge.

Luft (2009) argues that it is important to first consider the logic of the system for which one plans to impart information or facilitate discussion. This process requires understanding varying levels of power in the classroom setting (Collins 2013). For example, DiAngelo (2011) argues that college courses designed to meet multicultural educational requirements rarely challenge the racial understanding of white students much less address white privilege and white supremacy. Instead the norm is to deliver information using racially coded language such as "urban," "inner city," or "disadvantaged" but rarely "white," "over-advantaged," or "privileged" (DiAngelo 2011, 55). Content designed to teach cultural competency that does not directly address racism inherently caters to the comfort of white students via the use of palatable language. Researchers note that in educational programs/courses that comprehensively tackle racism and the privileging of whites, a common response among white students is anger, withdrawal, emotional incapacitation, argumentation, and guilt (DiAngelo 2011; Smith and Mayorga-Gallo 2017; Spanierman et al. 2005). DiAngelo locates these reactions within the broader frame of white fragility.

Advanced by Robin DiAngelo (2011), white fragility describes the condition when white people regard racial stress, even minimal, as intolerable. Widespread protection received by white people in social environments in North America insulates them to the point that their expectations for racial comfort are taken-for-granted as a right. Thus, white fragility evokes defensive reactions which include outward demonstrations of emotions (anger, fear, and guilt) and conduct (argumentation, silence, and leaving the stress-inducing situation), which all function to reinstate white racial equilibrium (DiAngelo 2011). In the broadest terms, white fragility, originates from the failure to understand and interrogate whiteness (DiAngelo 2011).

Critical race scholars focusing on whiteness pedagogy explain this discomfort as part of the complexity of white identity wherein *guilt* and *fragility* are often present but rarely confronted (DiAngelo 2011; Yeung et al. 2013). White guilt, as a domain of white identity (Lydacker et al. 2014) is a cognitive reaction of collective and individual awareness of unearned privileges and racism (Iyer et al. 2003; Swim and Miller 1999). Refusal to support ameliorative racial equity policies, cast in the context of white protectionism as unearned and unfair, amplifies white guilt, manifested as fragility, which in turn articulates itself through white projection onto the other. Conceptually, white guilt is a culturally and context-bound expression of guilt more generally: an emotion that combines self-deprecation and shame. Because white guilt is a consequence of systemic oppression and racism, its distinction lies in the process of reflecting on negative events and attributing blame about racial injustice to individuals and not a system of policies, institutions, and cultural norms (Lydacker et al. 2014).

Studies of white guilt are diverse, ranging from understanding the emotional influence on eating disorders, attitudes towards affirmative action, and pedagogical strategies (see, e.g., Iyer et al. 2003; Swim and Miller 1999; Goodman 2011). These studies highlight the value of understanding the benefits and limitations of group-based guilt (white guilt). Largely due to the unmarked but ever present nature of whiteness, white guilt receives little attention in racial and social justice discourses (DiAngelo 2011; Gans 2007; Goodman 2011; Todd and Abrams 2011; Zajicek 2002). Even when white guilt emerges in discussions of racism, some scholars question its effectiveness to bring about social change (Kirabo 2015; Younge 2015).

For example, in the debates surrounding the culture of racism in the United States after the 2015 Charleston church shooting, some have spoken of white guilt as an impediment to social change. Kirabo (2015) argues that an emotional response such as white guilt does not translate to an authentic understanding of contemporary racism and its structural formation. Thus, it is not an effective tool to combat social inequality and address prevalent racial injustices (Kirabo 2015; Younge 2015). The problem with white guilt, according to Kirabo (2015), is that it attempts to diminish the focus aimed at issues integral to marginalized groups and redirect attention to a wasteful plan of apologetics and ineffective assessments.

Since white guilt and fragility are unavoidable, it is important to discuss these modus operandi as integral components with the power to influence and obstruct valuable discussions on racial justice issues. Thus, a thoughtful understanding of white guilt and white fragility is required. Given the intensity and power of the emotional responses attached to discussions of racism, I argue that having a firm grasp of white fragility/guilt is as important as the content delivered. Individuals who do not learn to process these emotions in a healthy manner are less equipped to properly engage in and process discussions of racism. Moreover, engaging in discussions that facilitate deeper insights into structural processes that engender racial inequalities, is thwarted by the power of white discomfort, which potentially shifts the learning environment into a space where racially marginalized students' experiences would have to be defended or they are called upon to prove how racism is different from any other type of oppression or suffering. This is particularly problematic given that students must learn to thoughtfully navigate the contemporary highly racially charged sociopolitical climate and rhetoric that coexists with the widespread belief in a diverse and a colorblind society.

Logic of Diversity in an Increasingly Multiracial Society

As stated earlier, it is important to understand contemporary features of racism wherein words such as diversity and inclusion are commonplace and embraced by broader society. Yet, as Smith and Mayorga-Gallo (2017) maintain, diversity ideology is embedded within neoliberal logic. Meaning that neoliberalism is a "governing agenda that included the increased privatisation of government programs and institutions like public schools or even prisons," and it "also involves an intensifying rhetoric that is grounded in the belief that markets, in and of themselves, are better able than governments to produce, in particular, economic outcomes that are fair, sensible, and good for all" (Cohen 2010, as cited in Smith and Mayorga-Gallo 2017, 897). Smith and Mayorga-Gallo (2017) define diversity ideology as a way whites maintain dominance even in multiracial spaces. It is similar to colorblind racism but differs in that it centers an appreciation and lauding of racial differences. It essentially highlights race to "achieve" colorblindness.

Smith and Mayorga-Gallo's 2017 study analyses the responses of 43 face-to-face interviews with white Millennials in an attempt to understand how whites continue to maintain power, economic apartheid, in a society that is becoming increasingly multiracial. The authors found that educated white Millennials, in fact, adhere to and use diversity ideology to navigate contemporary racial issues. The study found that diversity ideology helped whites move between valuing diversity and maintaining a lack of support for policies that would bring those values to fruition. In such cases, "otherness," as it pertains to non-white people, became commodified. In this case, diversity was viewed or used as a good to be consumed by whites to fulfill an individual desire or to market themselves as more attractive in the marketplace (Smith and Mayorga-Gallo 2017). The authors found that diversity for most of their white respondents was defined as symbolic representation that may or may not have included racial diversity, with no thought of the ongoing structural impact of various individuals' life chances.

Smith and Mayorga-Gallo (2017) findings provide insight into the gap between diversity ideology and having solid understanding of existing power relations and racial hierarchies. Within the context of diversity ideology, St. Clair and Kishimoto (2010) argue that diversity initiatives can prevent fruitful implementation of college and university course content covering race and ethnic groups/studies in ways that thwarts understanding the white supremacist system that continues to produce racial hierarchies. The integration of race into college settings in the 1960s and 1970s brought about specific challenges to teaching about race (St. Clair and Kishimoto 2010) and to decolonizing school curricula (Cooper 2012; Smith 2012). With the emergence of diversity and multiculturalism in the 1980s, these challenges became more arduous in response to the demand to accommodate multiculturalism in an increasingly privatized and corporatized society (Mohanty 2004; Smith and Mayorga-Gallo 2017; St. Clair and Kishimoto 2010). Ethnicity/race-related courses or topics runs the risk of being compartmentalized in college curricula and are often co-opted and transformed as diversity and multiculturalism requisites that in turn dodge challenging issues including White privilege, institutional racism, social position and oppression (Deckert 2014; Kitossa 2012; St. Clair and Kishimoto 2010).

Colorblindness and the Possibility for Social Change

An extensive scholarship exists that expounds upon the workings and the negative implications of colorblindness as well as the recent call to move beyond its early articulation (see, e.g., Alexander 2012; Burke 2017; Bonillia-Silva 2006; Burke 2017; Collins 2006, 2013; Robertson 2015; Smith and Mayorga-Gallo 2017; Vargas 2014). Colorblind discourse hides white privilege behind the mask of meritocracy which renders institutional arrangements that perpetuate racial inequality invisible (Alexander 2012; Bonillia-Silva 2006; Burke 2014/2017; Vargas 2014). Eduardo Bonilla-Silva's (2006), now, classic work examines how colorblind ideology preserves white supremacy. He argues that while not all whites adhere to white supremacy, a majority do in a casual, uncritical fashion, which works to sustain the prevailing racial order. For example, Vargas (2014), in his study of the relationship between racial contestation and colorblind adherence, found that contested whites, individuals who identify racially as white but are perceived by others as non-white, express similar or amplified notions of colorblindness as their non-contested white counterparts. His study suggests that because contested whites find themselves at the margins of whiteness they often seek to legitimate their group membership as white by adhering to colorblindness. Since race and racisms are believed to be inconsequential in a supposedly post-racial society, adherents to colorblindness believe the best way to get past racism is to simply stop talking about race. Those who embrace colorblindness believe that talking about race perpetuates the belief that there is a race problem (Bonilla-Silva 2006; Burke 2017; Collins 2013; Vargas 2014). Of course, we should believe there is a race problem. As evidenced by the gross racism and social inequalities in the United States, which clearly indicates that the country is not a post-racial paradise.

For example, Sarah Maddison (2011) examination of the challenges between black and white relations in Australia revealed that discussions of race/racism are avoided in efforts to circumvent or deny guilt. Yet, such attempts do not erase the existence of racism or guilt. Therefore, Maddison (2011) argues that considerable attention should be devoted to understanding collective guilt and its potential to facilitate meaningful social change (Maddison 2011). For example, investigations of the dimensions of white guilt revealed that it is important to distinguish healthy white guilt from unhealthy white guilt, stating that the former leads to change and transformation while the latter leads to paralysis and inaction (DiAngelo 2011; Maddison 2011; Spanierman et al. 2005). When the focus or concern is on how one *feels* (as a white person) about the issue of race and racism (inward focused), the guilt is deemed unhealthy thereby inhibiting progressive actions towards social justice. Even if one is motivated by white guilt to take a particular action, unhealthy guilt leads to white saviorism wherein white superiority stance/belief remains unquestioned and intact (Finnegan 2013). For example, Amy C. Finnegan (2013) examined young white-middle class North American female attraction to the Kony 2012 political movement, which sought the capture of the leader, Joseph Kony, of the Lord's Resistance Army in Eastern and Central Africa. In her article, *The White Girl's Burden*, she interviewed young white evangelical women participating in the Invisible Children organization. Her study found that many of the young girls/women, ages 14–24, had very little to no knowledge of the history of the African countries affected and the social forces creating the harsh realities, especially the United States' role in constructing the structural violence in that part of the world. Participation in the movement was described as sexy and a mark of individuality. Most of the participants expressed that belonging to something bigger than themselves evoked feelings of specialness. Finnegan (2013, 33) called attention to the remoteness of the conflict as an important source of attraction.

> The remoteness of the conflict facilitates an easy, noncontentious form of activism that does not threaten the students' futures. By inspiring them to think beyond themselves, to set bold goals, and to be creative in their efforts to raise awareness and funds for children in eastern and central Africa, the organization offers opportunities for young Americans to feel that their contributions are truly unique and noteworthy. Ultimately, however, Invisible Children also promotes policies that are highly controversial; its state-centric orientation seeks to eliminate the LRA through U.S.-supported military intervention carried out by the Ugandan army.

Finnegan's (2013) study found that the actions taken contributed very little to mitigating the structural violence in the affected areas in central Africa but, instead, perpetuated the exoticization of the *other* and reinforced a white superiority position. Actions (e.g., fundraising, rallies, and visits) were taken with very little examination of whiteness/privilege.

I found the enthusiasm to come to the aid of the *exotic other* is pervasive among many sociology students. However, students' enthusiasm tends to wane when asked to identify the social forces in their own communities, states, and countries that have contributed to unequal experiences of citizenship today. Thus, unhealthy guilt does not seek to understand whiteness and examine contemporary ways white supremacy is exercised and benefits white individuals. Whereas healthier responses to guilt use guilty feelings to *understand* the sources and outcomes of the injustices in a racist system (outward focused) (Maddison 2011). Actions are then directed to oppose racism and racist/discriminatory policies/practices rather than adopting an "apolitical" stance or becoming ambivalent. Maddison (2011) argues that the personal nature of guilt, when collective, can be a powerful political tool, specifically as a driver of transformative change, if guilt is recognized and processed in ways that are healthy.

Epistemic Exploitation

Like white guilt, epistemic exploitation is also physically and emotionally draining, but it lacks the comforts of privilege for which to retreat. Black feminist scholars across different genres have spoken for years about this type of exploitation as an extension of oppression (see, e.g., Cooper 2015; Dotson 2011, 2014; Morrison 1975). Characterized by unrecognized, uncompensated, emotionally taxing, coerced epistemic labor, epistemic exploitation maintains structures of oppression by making the needs and desires of dominant groups central to the interactions all people have in society (Berenstain 2016; Dotson 2014). Formal settings, such as the classroom, can be prime locations where emotional and cognitive labor is exploited. Instead of being an intellectual space used to tackle racism and equip students to reflect and become active participants in creating a just society, formal spaces can be disempowering for individuals from structurally disadvantaged groups. This occurs because individuals within these structurally disadvantaged groups are tacitly (or even explicitly) expected to be the ones who take on the burden of explaining how and why disadvantage has accrued, and the burden of arguing for changes that will ameliorate this burden both for currently existing persons and for future persons (Berenstain 2016). Meanwhile, those who benefit from the status quo are not expected to shoulder this burden.

Conclusion

This chapter argues that white guilt and fragility are almost always present, albeit in diverse forms depending on the country in question. It argues that colorblind and diversity ideologies are intricately linked to white fragility/guilt as some type of colorblind stance is likely a strategy deployed to minimize charges of racism. Burke (2017) argues for the need to more deeply examine the mechanisms of contemporary colorblind racism. Because racial dynamics evolve and shift over time and space, so too will the ideologies and discourses that surround them (Burke 2017). Enhancing our understanding of how white fragility and guilt influence discussions of race/racism is paramount if we are to engage in fruitful discussion of racial justice.

From this basis, I argue that diversity ideology caters to white fragility and guilt in specific ways. The massive appeal to be a part of something that is supposedly inclusive and celebrates differences, but never interrogates whiteness and white supremacy, has worked to strengthen white supremacy, which undergirds unequal life chances and experiences of citizenship. Academic classrooms should be the space where critical thinking about race/racism occurs. If white fragility/guilt is not accounted for and neutralized, academic spaces cannot equip students with the correct knowledge to bring about racial justices. Moreover, even those spaces created to discuss and implement diversity needs becomes another space to placate white guilt and therefore reproduce the same outcomes in the absence of a so-called diversity program. Diversity, in this neo-liberal era, inadvertently caters to the demands of white comfort and individuals racialized as non-white are again called upon to justify their claims and explain what makes racial oppression different from other social ailings experienced by racially advantaged groups such as disability, sexuality, or social class. If change is to occur, white fragility and guilt must be recognized as a prevailing feature preventing critical discussions of racial injustice.

References

Alexander M (2012) The new jim Crow: Mass incarceration in the age of colorblindness, revised edn. New Press, New York

Baldwin J (1963) A talk to teacher. The Saturday Review, December 21

Bell JM, Hartmann D (2007) Diversity in everyday discourse: the cultural ambiguities and consequences of happy talk. Am Sociol Rev 72(6):895–914

Berenstain N (2016) Epistemic exploitation. Ergo 3(22):569–590

Boler M (1999) Feeling power: emotions and education. Routledge, New York, NY

Bonilla-Silva E (2006) Racism without racists: Color-blind racism and the persistence of racial inequality in the United States (2nd ed.). Oxford, England: Rowman & Littlefield

Burke MA (2014) Colorblindness vs. race-consciousness – an american ambivalence. In: Hartmann D, Uggen C (eds) Color lines and racial angles. W.W. Norton, New York, pp 165–176

Burke MA (2017) Colorblind racism: identities, ideologies, and shifting subjectivities. Sociol Perspect 60(5):857–865

Collins PH (2006) From Black power to hip hop: racism, nationalism, and feminism. Temple University Press, Philadelphia

Collins PH (2013) On intellectual activism. Temple University Press, Philadelphia, PA

Cooper G (2008) Tawhaki and Māui: critical literacy in indigenous epistemologies. Crit Lit Theor Pract 2(1):37–42

Cooper G (2012) Kaupapa Māori research: epistemic wilderness as freedom? N Z J Educ Stud 47(2):64–73

Cooper B (2015) Black America's hidden tax: why this feminist of color is going on strike. Salon. Retrieved 10 Oct 2017 from https://www.salon.com/2015/02/25/black_americas_hidden_tax_why_this_feminist_of_color_is_going_on_strike/

Davis A (1996) Gender, class, and multiculturalism: rethinking 'race' politics. In: Gordon AF, Newfield C (eds) Mapping multiculturalism. University of Minnesota, Minneapolis, pp 40–48

Deckert A (2014) Neo-colonial criminology: quantifying the silence. Afr J Crim Justice Stud 8:39–60
DiAngelo R (2011) White fragility. Int J Crit Pedagog 3(3):54–70
Dotson K (2011) Tracking epistemic violence, tracking practices of silencing. Hypatia 26(2):236–257
Dotson K (2014) Conceptualizing epistemic oppression. Soc Epistemol 28(2):115–138
Finnegan AC (2013) The white girl's burden. Context 12(1):30–35
Gans E (2007) White guilt, past and future. Anthropoetics 12(2):1–8
Goodman DJ (2011) Promoting diversity and social justice: educating people from privileged groups. Routledge, New York
Iyer A, Leach CW, Crosby FJ (2003) White guilt and racial compensation: the benefits and limits of self-focus. Personal Soc Psychol Bull 29(1):117–129
Kirabo S (2015) Want to help end systemic racism? First step: drop the white guilt. Retrieved 31 Aug 2015 at http://thehumanist.com/commentary/want-to-help-end-systemic-racism-first-step-drop-the-white-guilt
Kitossa T (2012) Criminology and colonialism: counter colonial criminology and the Canadian context. J Pan Afr Stud 4:204–226
Ladner JA (1971) Tommorrow's tommrrow. Doubleday and Company, Garden City
Loewen JW (2007) Lies my teacher told me. Touchstone, New York
Lorde A (1995) Age, race, class, and sex: women redefining difference. In: Beverly Guy-Sheftall (ed) Words of Fire: An anthology of African-American feminist thought. The New Press, New York, pp 284–292
Luft R E (2009) Intersectionality and the risk of flattening difference: gender and race logics, and the strategic use of antiracist singularity. In: Berger M T, Guidroz K (eds) The Intersectional Approach: Transforming the Academy Through Race, Class, & Gender The University of North Carolina Press, Chapel Hill, NC, pp. 100–117
Lydacker JA, Hubbard RR, Tully CB, Utsey SO, Mezzeo SE (2014) White public regard: associations among eating disorder symptomatology, guilt, and white guilt in young adult women. Eat Behav 15:76–82
Maddison S (2011) Beyond white guilt: the real challenge for black-white relations in Australia. Allen and Unwin, Australia
Mills C (1998) blackness visible: essays on philosophy and race. In: Ithaca. Cornell University Press, London
Mohanty CT (2004) Feminism without borders: decolonizing theory, practicing solidarity. Duke University Press, Durham
Morrison T (1975) A humanistic view. In: Public dialogue on the American Dream Them, Part 2. Panel conducted by the Portland State Black Studies Center, Neville.
Murphy-Erby Y, Hunt V, Zajicek AM, Norris AN, Hamilton L (2009) Incorporating intersectionality in social work research, education, policy, and practice. National Association of Social Workers Press, Washington, DC
Nadan Y, Stark M (2016) The pedagogy of discomfort: enhancing reflectivity on stereotypes and bias. Br J Soc Work 47(3):683–700
Norris AN (2017) Are we really colour-blind? The normalization of mass female incarceration. Race Justice 1–25. https://doi.org/10.1177/2153368717718028
Pitcher B (2011) Radical subjects after hegemony. Subjectivity 4(1):87–102
Reilly K (2016) How guns on campus could change what texas teaches. Time, February 26.
Robertson DL (2015) Invisibility in the color-blind era: examining legitimized racism against indigenous peoples. Am Indian Q 39:113–153
Smith L (2012) Decolonizing methodologies: research and indigenous peoples, 2nd edn. University of Otago Press, Dunedin
Smith C (2017) Why James Baldwin's 'A talk to teacher' Remains relevant 54 years later. Wbur. Retrieved 9 Oct 2017 from http://www.wbur.org/hereandnow/2017/10/03/james-baldwin-talk-to-teachers

Smith CW, Mayorga-Gallo S (2017) The new principle-policy gap: how diversity ideology subverts diversity initiatives. Sociol Perspect 60(5):889–911

Spanierman LB, Todd NR, Anderson CJ (2005) Psychosocial costs of racism to whites: understanding patterns among university students. J Couns Psychol 56(2):239–252

St. Clair D, Kishimoto K (2010) Decolonizing teaching: a cross-curricular and collaborative model for teaching about race in the university. Multicult Educ 18(1):18–24

Swim JK, Miller DL (1999) White guilt: its antecedents and consequences for attitudes toward affirmative action. Personal Soc Psychol Bull 25(4):500–514

Todd NR, Abrams EM (2011) White dialectics: a new framework for theory, research, and practice with white students. Couns Psychol 39(3):353–395

Vargas N (2014) Off white: colour-blind ideology at the margins of whiteness. Ethn Racial Stud 37(13):2281–2302

Woodson CG (1933) Mis-education of the Negro. Khalif Khalifah, Drewryville

Yeung JG, Spanierman LB, Landrum-Brown J (2013) Being white in a multicultural society: critical whiteness pedagogy in a dialogue course. Journal of Diversity in Higher Education 6(1):17–32

Younge G (2015) White guilt won't fix America's race problem. Only justice and equality will. The Guardian, August 31

Zajicek AM (2002) Race discourses and antiracist practices in local women's movement. Gend Soc 16(2):151–170

Ethnicity, Race, and Black People in Europe 30

Stephen Small

Contents

Introduction 514
Racial Discrimination in 1968 and Ethnic Murder in 2016 516
Distinct Ethnic Differences in Black Populations Nationally Across Europe 517
Striking Racial Similarities in Black Populations Europe-Wide 522
Historical Background to Black Presence in Europe 524
Discussion 528
Conclusion 532
References 533

Abstract

This chapter provides a definition and examples of the concepts of ethnicity and race, by describing and explaining the presence and experiences of black people in Western Europe at the present time. And it provides examples of the range of ethnic differences in the white population of Europe at a time of increasing national and populist movements. There are currently just over 7 million black people in the 46 nations of Europe, the majority of whom are born and raised in Europe. The black population reveals a wide range of ethnic differences in terms of religion, language, national origins, family format, gender, as well as in music, film, literature, and food. At the same time, regardless of their ethnic origins, all black people in Europe share three common experiences that result from racial stereotypes and discrimination. These are ambiguous hyper-visibility, entrenched vulnerability, and irrepressible resistance and resilience. It is argued that race, ethnicity, and other variables such as economics and gender are intricately entangled with one another in both populations in ways that make it difficult to predict outcomes for different populations.

S. Small (✉)
Department of African American Studies, University of California, Berkeley, Berkeley, CA, USA
e-mail: small@berkeley.edu

© The Author(s), under exclusive license to Springer Nature Singapore Pte Ltd. 2019
S. Ratuva (ed.), *The Palgrave Handbook of Ethnicity*,
https://doi.org/10.1007/978-981-13-2898-5_169

Keywords

Race · Ethnicity · Ambiguous hyper-visibility · Entrenched vulnerability · Irrepressible resistance and resilience

Introduction

Europe is currently experiencing a series of intense and enduring problems with increasing demands on its politicians and increasing anxiety and reactions among the general population. At the forefront of these issues is the rising threat to the existence of the Europe Union precipitated by extensive financial and economic worries, anti-globalization movements, the ascendancy of right-wing political parties, the Brexit vote, and the increasing divergence of goals and priorities between Europe and the USA, including a trade war. Donald Trump's unexpected rise to the US Presidency in 2016 – and his erratic, contradictory policies and statements while president – has increased tensions. Politicians and the public are worried about high levels of unemployment and low economic growth, exacerbated by the political precariousness of the Eurozone. Economic austerity has been embraced by several governments with widespread adverse effects, especially for the unemployed and those in poverty. Migration across the Mediterranean is a major issue, too.

Many political groups and individuals are motivated by xenophobia and racism for the pursuit of political advantage or electoral gain. Right-wing and populist movements have dramatically increased their share of the vote in many Europeans nations, and a number of right-wing groups from France, Germany, and the Netherlands met in Koblenz, Germany, in January 2017 to savor the Brexit vote and Donald Trump's victory and to proclaim the year 2017 as the year of far-right reawakening. Since then, they have increased in strength, with the governments of Austria, Italy, and Hungary the most visible. Hostility to Muslims in Europe – and to Islam in the Middle East – is widespread, deeply entangled with other political and economic issues that are worrying non-Muslim populations. Violent atrocities in Paris in November 2015, the horrific attack in Nice in July 2016, and in Germany have raised anxieties tremendously.

In this context, ethnic, cultural, and national differences among whites in Europe have become far more salient, as more and more Europeans at the national level talk about protecting "our own people." In England, British people don't like white immigrants (like Poles and Romanians) and talk about Britain for "white British." In Sweden there is antagonism toward Finns, in Germany and Spain toward Romanians, and in Greece toward Albanians and Bulgarians. Nationalist and populist groups assert their wish to keep Austria, Austrian; Denmark, Danish; Britain, British; and Italy, Italian.

One group typically absent from these debates and headlines – with a few exceptions – is black people of African descent. There is very little talk about black people, especially black citizens, even though the vast majority of black people in Europe are citizens and legal residents. Yes, black Europeans appear in the news in highly stereotypical ways, for example, as illegal immigrants dying in the Mediterranean, black women victims of sex trafficking or drugs, and black men as criminals or thugs. Typically called sub-Saharan Africans, the majority of the black population in Europe traces its origins directly to West, East, and Southern Africa. Most of the rest are from the Caribbean, and South America, themselves the descendants of Africans kidnapped, transported, and enslaved during the several hundred years of the European transatlantic slave trade. Significant numbers of black people have been in Europe only since the 1990s and many others from the 1950s; and small yet symbolically significant black populations – and communities – go back several centuries, for example, in the port city of Liverpool, England. While they are not at the forefront of discussion, a description and assessment of black people in Europe highlights a wide variety of issues of ethnicity and race.

Ethnicity and race are often used popularly as interchangeable terms. Many social scientists – myself included – argue that although they are frequently intertwined in practice, analytically we get greater insights by keeping them separate from one another. But what are race and ethnicity? While there is no clear-cut and universally accepted distinction between the two, the idea of race tends to highlight physical and mental issues, often regarded as permanent and unchanging and always organized hierarchically in terms of superiority and inferiority. Historically, this is how Europeans, who defined themselves as white (and Christian), defined and treated Africans and their descendants (whom they defined as black and barbarian). Racist ideologies that originated and were disseminated in Europe attributed and imposed such beliefs on Africans and established political institutions and labor systems (via slavery, colonialism, and imperialism) to do so. In contrast, ethnicity typically highlights social and cultural issues, usually regarded as variable (you can change your religion, language, music, and food tastes), not always regarded in a hierarchy, and often embraced by different groups. Such ethnic differences – in terms of language, religion, family structures, and political values – have been at the heart of Europe even before Europeans came into contact with Africans (or other peoples across the world). Complicating things further, ethnicity and race almost always operate in ways that intersect with, and are often greatly affected by, other variables, including economics and class, religion, nationality, and especially gender. Issues of ethnicity and race are complex; they are not mutually exclusive and are best regarded as situational, contextual, and contingent. We need to pay attention to these complexities.

In this chapter I describe and assess black people's presence and experiences in Europe today in order to discuss the relationship between ethnic and cultural differences on the one hand and racial differences on the other. In Europe today, we can find fascinating examples of these complexities. Comparison of different types of ethnic, racial, and national differences – including discrimination – raises important questions about the nature of ethnicity, ethnic difference, and ethnic conflict and about the nature of race, racism, and racial conflict. What is the relationship between ethnicity and race? How does cultural difference and nationalism intersect with ethnicity and race? We also see some of the ways in which attention to gender complicates matters even further.

Racial Discrimination in 1968 and Ethnic Murder in 2016

In England in the late 1960s, a large-scale empirical study took place on racial and ethnic discrimination. The results were published in the book, *Racial Discrimination in England* (Daniel 1968). The study tested the attitudes and behavior of British-born white people toward black immigrants from the Caribbean, Indian immigrants from India, and several white immigrants from Europe. The goal was to assess the extent to which discrimination was based on race, culture, or nation. The study found that while there was some discrimination against European immigrants to England, the most serious discrimination that occurred was racial with most discrimination happening against black and Asian immigrants. This discrimination varied "from the massive to the substantial." Furthermore, later studies found that the children of white immigrants – who were born, raised, and socialized in England and spoke with English accents – faced no discrimination. They were racially indistinguishable from white British people, while the children of black Caribbean immigrants and Indian immigrants continued to faced discrimination like their parents, in education, in jobs, and often in the form of violence (Small 1983). An interesting issue here is that the black Caribbean immigrants to England were culturally very similar to English people – they spoke English as a first language, were mainly Christians, followed football and cricket, and ate similar food. They were racially different but culturally similar (though not identical). Whereas the white immigrants from Europe were racially similar but culturally different (spoke English only as a second language, were often Catholics, ate different food, etc.).

Compare this to the situation in June 2016, when Britain voted by 52–48% (though by a much higher margin in England) to quit the European Union. Leading up to the election, there was a great deal of publically expressed hostility to immigrants – black, Indian, and Middle Eastern. There was also significant hostility toward white immigrants from Europe. Sometimes the hostility to white immigrants met and surpassed the hostility to immigrants of color. For example, not long after the vote, Polish, Bosnian, and Romania immigrants to England discussed the extensive hostility they faced. And shortly after the vote, an ethnically Polish person was murdered outside a Polish cultural center. Complicating the matter further, a small but significant number of British-born black people of Caribbean origin and British-born people with origins in India or Pakistan also expressed hostility to white immigrants and voted in favor of Brexit. By this time the phrase "white British" had emerged, to distinguish white immigrants from white British, while in the 1960s, white invariably meant British and developed in opposition to black and Asian immigrants. So, in the 1960s there was hostility to racially different but culturally similar people (black Caribbeans); and by 2016 it was joined by hostility to racially similar but culturally different people (white immigrants). Racial discrimination against black people in England at this time, in 2016, had not disappeared. Black citizens and immigrants in 2016 still faced widespread discrimination (Small 2018). This was evident in employment, housing, and education (Small 2018). So, things are not so simple.

This entanglement of race and ethnicity, of national and cultural differences, is not just the case in the UK. There are examples in France where there is hostility toward Spanish and Romanians and in Spain, where there is discrimination against Roma and Romanians. In Germany, where there is discrimination against other immigrants from around Europe, such as Poles and Lithuanians. In Sweden, where there is discrimination against Finns. And in Spain and Greece, where there is discrimination against Albanians and Bulgarians. Hostility, discrimination, and violence have also increased toward Jews in several nations, especially in France.

Distinct Ethnic Differences in Black Populations Nationally Across Europe

The black population of Europe is highly stratified by ethnicity, including language, religion, and family structure, as well as ancestry and national origins. It is also stratified by citizenship and gender. Further cultural differences can be found in music, food, film, literature, art, dance, and performance. How many black people are in Europe, and where are they located? Well, it all depends on how we define Europe – which is not as easy as one might suspect. But let's begin with what is Europe. In 2018 Europe currently has 46 states – with an estimated population of at least 770 million. Several sources, including the United Nations, define Europe as having 51 independent states, including Kazakhstan, Armenia, Azerbaijan, Georgia, and Turkey, but I exclude these five nations because I suspect that they are not considered European by most commentators, including politicians and public. The European Union (EU) currently has 28 nations with more than 505 million people; the UK is in the process of exiting the EU, but that won't happen formally before at least 2019. The Euro zone has 19 nations, all of whom are in the EU. There are currently 26 Schengen nations, which includes 22 nations in the EU and 4 nations outside it (Iceland, Liechtenstein, Norway, and Switzerland). Schengen nations allow passport-free travel across nations, at least on paper.

It also depends on how we define black people and on what kind of data we have on black people. The truth is that we just don't know for sure how many black people there are in Europe. The refusal of most nations in Europe to collect data by race (except the UK and the Republic of Ireland) means that we have no direct nationally collected data. Where numbers exist, they are typically based on "country of origin" of immigrants, with an estimate of the number of native-born children of such immigrants. Hardly an infallible technique. Besides, we know that many black people that settled or lived in Italy, Spain, and Portugal have moved on permanently to England, Germany, or the Netherlands, mainly for economic reasons.

Exactly who is black, is identified as black, and/or chooses to identify as black is unclear. For example, the majority of Africans in France (overwhelmingly from Algeria and Morocco) are not regarded as black and do not identify themselves as black. My definition focuses mainly on black people of African descent and includes those that identify themselves (or are identified by others) as black, African, African-Caribbean, Afro-European, African Americans, or some other national variation and who trace their origins to Africa and the Americas. Some call themselves "Afropean" or "Afro-European." I also include people of mixed black and non-black origins, if they define themselves as black (though across Europe, the evidence suggests that the majority of people, with at least one black parent, do not define themselves as black, but as "mixed").

Bearing these problems in mind, I estimate that there are more than 7 million black people in these 46 nations out of a total population of 770 million people. And I estimate that over 93% of black people in Europe (6,717,000) can be found in just 12 nations (which have a total estimated population of more than 380 million people). These nations are the UK, France, the Netherlands, Belgium, and Portugal; Spain, Italy, and Germany; and Denmark, Norway, Sweden, and the Republic of Ireland. There are almost certainly black people in every other nation in Europe, but we just don't know how many. In my recent study, I estimated that there were no more than 500,000 (Small 2018). The general numbers of black people in each of these 12 nations are as follows: the UK (2 million), France (2 million), the Netherlands (323,000), Portugal (150,000), Belgium (250,000), Spain (500,000), Italy (325,000), Germany (800,000), Denmark (46,000), Norway (78,000), Sweden (180,000), and Republic of Ireland (65,000). For a total black population in the 12 nations of 6,717,000. If the numbers are correct, then the UK and France have more than 55% of all black people in these 12 nations. But these numbers are misleading; that's because as many as 700,000 black people in France actually live in the Caribbean – in Martinique and Guadeloupe. These two "*départements*" (administrative districts) are legally and officially France.

It's highly probable that the majority of black people in these nations are women, as is the case with the gender balance in most nations in Europe, and across the world. And the black population has a higher proportion of young people. However, the relative proportion of men and women in each nation is variable, again as might be expected.

Within these 12 nations, black people are concentrated in a limited number of urban areas – mainly because that is where the jobs were to be found when black people were recruited in significant numbers from the early 1900s or where they were directed as refugees since the 1990s. For example, in England more than 60% of black people live in the Greater London area, with smaller groups in Birmingham and Manchester. In mainland France, the majority of black people live in Paris, with smaller numbers in Lyons and Marseilles and much smaller populations in Bordeaux and Toulouse. In the Netherlands, more than 50% of black people live in four cities – Amsterdam, Rotterdam, The Hague, and Utrecht. In Portugal, they are mainly in Lisbon and in Belgium mainly in Brussels; in Germany, black people are mainly in Berlin, Hamburg, and Frankfurt; in Spain, they are in Barcelona and Madrid. In Italy, most black people can be found in Rome and Milan, in Denmark in Copenhagen, in Norway in Oslo, in Sweden in Stockholm, and in the Irish Republic in Dublin.

What are some of the ethnic, national, and religious backgrounds of black people across Europe? The majority of black people in the UK, France, and the Netherlands have backgrounds from across West Africa and the Caribbean and those in Belgium and Portugal, from other parts of Africa. It seems clear that the vast majority of people with a Caribbean background live in the UK, France, and the Netherlands. The numbers of people from the Caribbean elsewhere in Europe are tiny. In Spain, there are few people from the Spanish Caribbean, for obvious reasons (including Spain's historically poor economy, fascism, and preference by Spanish-speaking Caribbeans for migration to the USA). In the Irish Republic, most black people are West African, from both English- and French-speaking nations. There are also black people in Europe from many nations in Southern Africa, East Africa, and the Horn of Africa. In Denmark, Norway, and Sweden, the majority of black people are from the Horn of Africa, most arrived as refugees and have been resident in significant numbers for no more than three decades (McIntosh 2014). In Italy, most black people were from the Horn of Africa, until the early twenty-first century, when the number of West Africans rose rapidly and is now a majority. In general, then, the majority of black people across Europe are from Africa or the children or grandchildren of Africans. After that, it is the children and grandchildren of (English-speaking or French-speaking) Caribbeans. There are no nations in which southern Africans are dominant, though they can be found in small numbers in several nations.

All 12 nations have large numbers of native-born black people and significant numbers of black people who are citizens or permanent residents. The exact number in each category is unclear. In the UK, France, Netherlands, Belgium, and Portugal, it seems clear that the majority of black people are native-born and/or citizens. In Germany, native-born black people are probably a majority, but in Spain and Italy, probably not. In Denmark, Norway, Sweden and the Irish Republic, a minority of black people are probably native-born. What is clear is that millions of black people – and probably a very large majority – are citizens or legal residents.

The languages spoken by black people in Europe certainly number in the hundreds. Not surprising given that most black people come from Africa, which itself has more than a thousand languages. European-origin languages are the most common spoken, not only because so many black people were born, raised, and schooled in Europe but also because of the colonial legacy across Africa and the Caribbean. English and French became the national languages in more than 40 nations across Africa, as did Spanish in most of the nations across South America, Portuguese in Brazil, and Dutch in Suriname. English, French, Spanish, and Dutch are spoken widely across the Caribbean. In addition to the legacy of colonial languages, there is also creole and patois. Sometimes called dialects or slang. They are a mixture of European languages and diverse African languages, as some indigenous languages. In Jamaica, they are called "Patois"; in Martinique and Guadeloupe, they are called "creole"; in Curacao and Aruba and Bonaire, it is Papiamento. These languages have been put to great creative – and political – use in the novels, poems, and other writings of a wide range of black Europeans. They remind us that languages are highly diverse, creative, and flexible. To quote one famous Jamaican poet, folklorist, writer, and educator – Louise Simone Bennett-Coverly – known professionally as "Miss Lou" who ridiculed the British for saying Patios is a dialect and English is a language, when English itself is made up of so many different languages and dialects.

There are significant differences in religion and faith communities in the black population across Europe. Much of this has to do with legacies of colonialism and imperialism, especially with regard to the fact that the vast majority of black people in Europe – as with black people in Africa and across the Americas – are members of several denominations of two mainstream religious communities, that is, Christianity and Islam. The evidence suggests that the majority of black people in Europe are Christians of various denominations. They come from nations in Africa and the Caribbean that were once colonies of European nations and where Christianity was imposed onto the colonial populations. Many are Protestant, and many others Catholic. There are also variations – like Pentecostalism and Evangelicals. These nations include Nigeria, Ivory Coast, Angola, and South Africa; they include Kenya and Uganda. And they include Suriname, Jamaica, Trinidad and Tobago, and Barbados. The majority of black people in England, the Netherlands, Germany, France, Spain, and Portugal are Christian. And the evidence suggests that many are in black led congregations, because of discrimination in the mainstream congregations.

There are large numbers of black people in Europe that are Muslims. They come from nations like Senegal in West Africa, Somalia and Eritrea in the Horn of Africa, and Angola in Southern Africa. The majority of Africans in Sweden, Norway, Denmark, and Italy are Muslims.

The relationship between the continent of Africa with its diverse racial populations and the racial and religious identities of black people in Europe raises an interesting issue. If you read most of the political debates in Europe about Muslims, they invariably treat Muslims as if they are not black (Scandinavia is the exception). But there are at least several hundred thousand Muslims, who trace their backgrounds to black Africa. The evidence indicates that they face significant discrimination. But are they racially "black"? And do they face racial discrimination because they are black? Or ethnic discrimination because they are Muslim? The answer is not clear. But I suspect that few black people are targeted for violent harassment or discrimination simply because they are Christian. However, we know that Muslims are targeted for attack simply because they are Muslim, which means that many black people are also targeted for discrimination primarily because they are Muslim. And black women that are Muslim occupy a unique intersection that may involve the contempt of white men and the condescension (or pity) of white women. It might be reflected in their names, or in how they dress, or in their interactions with their Mosque. In other words, for those who are black and Muslim, identifiably Muslim to the European gaze, then problems of race and religion – more accurately racism and religious persecution – are likely to befall them.

There are other faith communities in which we find significant numbers of black people. These are what would typically be defined as syncretic religions, that is, that combine elements of Christian and non-Christian faiths and rituals (drawing on religious beliefs that can be traced to many areas in Africa and to Native American beliefs in the Americas). These groups are primarily of Caribbean or South American origins, and they developed as a result of the establishment and growth of state-sanctioned slavery across the Americas by Europeans and their descendants.

Most of the non-Christian elements are associated with African religious, ritual, or cultural practices. This includes Rastafarians and followers of Santeria, Candomblé, and Vodou. Candomblé in Europe traces its origins to northeastern Brazil, Santeria to Cuba, and Vodou to Haiti and Louisiana. The practitioners of each no doubt highlight the differences in belief, faith, and ritual, among them, but as compared to the so-called mainstream Christian communities, these three share more in common with one another, than they do differences.

It is likely that the majority of black people in Europe that are Christians are in multiracial congregations. However, because black people faced discrimination in these multiracial churches – they were denied positions of leadership even when they had equal of superior qualifications to white people – there now exist hundreds of black-led congregations. This is the case in England, Germany, and elsewhere.

It's clear then that there are a wide variety of ethnic differences among black people in Europe in terms of national origins and citizenship. The same is true for family format – in terms of the relative roles of men and women in the family and various forms of single-parent, nuclear, and extended families. There are many differences across cultures in the roles allocated to women and men inside the home and outside in the public sphere and workplace. Adding further complexity is the clear existence – and increasing public visibility of black people that are gay or transgender. They have always been present and active in the black population – fighting for equality and justice for all (El Tayeb 2011). Their visibility was restrained, and their voices mostly silenced, but not any longer. They are increasingly present and active in a range of black social movements and protests, including in Germany, the Netherlands, the UK, and elsewhere (Small 2018).

Space does not allow me to detail the many and fascinating cultural differences among black populations in Europe in the fields of music, food, film, literature, art, dance, and performance. Suffice it to say that there are vast differences. In popular music, there is Hip-Hop, Jazz and Gospel, Reggae, Reggaeton, Calypso and Zouk, Latin Jazz and Samba, or Highlife and Afrobeat. The Montreux Jazz Festival in Switzerland, running for more than 50 years, may be the oldest. No carnival is bigger than the Notting Hill Caribbean Carnival that began in London in 1966. Black music clearly mixes with non-black music forms in creative transformations. There are examples in France and Portugal and in Sweden and Switzerland. In England, black people and non-blacks have been mixing Reggae and Indian music (especially Bhangra) for decades. In France, they have been mixing African and Caribbean music with various influence from Islamic music for decades too. Similar and extensive variations can be found in film, literature, art, dance, and performance. And food. A black European that traces his or her origins to Nigeria may recognize few things about the culture of Tanzania or Kenya or Zimbabwe. Just as a Jamaican may not know the ins and outs of Samba or Merengue. But I suspect that all blacks in Europe are familiar with African American music and reggae music. These two musical forms, for various reasons, are global.

The variety and vitality of black culture is endless – drumming from Ghana; political theater from South Africa; and Ethiopian painting and artwork contrasts markedly with art work from the Democratic Republic of the Congo, Angola, and

Benin. Just go into any major museum in Europe to find a staggering variety of black cultural products. The so-called Benin Bronzes are scattered across museums in the UK (London, Liverpool, and Oxford), Germany (Hamburg, Leiden, Leipzig, and Cologne), Denmark, and elsewhere. Other items are in the *Koninklijk Museum voor Midden-Afrika* (Royal Museum for Central Africa) in Belgium. The largest collection of Egyptology in Europe is found in the *Museo Egizio* (Egyptian Museum) in Turin, Italy. Other museums across the continent possess collections acquired during colonial and imperial rule, including the *Tropenmuseum* (Tropical Museum) and the *Rijksmuseum* (Dutch National Museum) in Amsterdam and the *Museo Antropologica* (Anthropology Museum) in Madrid. See also Copenhagen's Glyptotek and Sweden's ethnology museum.

Finally, there are tens of thousands of community groups, cultural organizations, and centers that are black-led or mainly black. Examples abound in London and Paris, Oslo and Copenhagen, and across Germany, Spain, and Italy (Emejulu and Bassel 2017; Small 2018). And there are political and community organizations and conferences that combat racial discrimination. The work of groups like these can be traced back decades and, in some nations like England, centuries (Adi 2013). It is because of the active work, dedication and commitment of these groups that racism is not far worse in Europe.

Not only is black culture from across Africa and the Americas generated within Europe by black people living in Europe, but each year tens of thousands of performers, writers, filmmakers, and musicians from Africa and the Americans visit to perform and give talks across Europe. Ethnic differences and black culture are highly diverse and hardly surprising given that the continent of Africa has well over a billion people and African-origin people across the Americas numbering perhaps more than 200 million. The African diaspora shares culture with blacks in Europe in a dynamic mix, vibrant, and far-reaching mix (Hine et al. 2009; Clarke and Thomas 2006).

Striking Racial Similarities in Black Populations Europe-Wide

The previous section has demonstrated that there are important ethnic and cultural differences within the black population of Europe. They are major and consequential. They can be summarized in the following way. In the UK, France, and the Netherlands, black people are long-time residents, arrived speaking the national language, were primarily Christians, and arrived as citizens. In contrast, in Sweden, Norway, Denmark, and Italy, black people are recent residents (most since 1990s) and did not speak the national language when they arrived, the vast majority are Muslims, and they arrived primarily as refugees. Black people in other nations – like Germany, Belgium, and the Republic of Ireland – reveal contrasting configurations of demographic, national, ethnic, and religious configurations (White 2012; Mazzocchetti 2014).

Despite the wide range of ethnic and cultural differences in the black population of Europe, there are at least three striking similarities in their experiences across these nations. These similarities are racialized, because they impact all people perceived as black (or African) without regard to the major ethnic differences already listed or the nation in which they live. The first similarity is ambiguous hyper-visibility, which means that in all the major media – press, television, film, social media – there is a high visibility of gendered negative images of black people in highly stereotypical arenas. They overwhelmingly appear as subservient, poor, and needy. For example, black men are stereotyped as irresponsible, dangerous, violent, and criminal and black women as irresponsible, or angry, as sex workers and "drug-mules," or the victims of sex trafficking. Both men and women appear in low-level jobs, among the unemployed, on welfare, in poverty, as criminals, in prison and illegal immigrants. There are very few images of successful or highly achieving black people, which means few or no images of black women chief executives, medical doctors, professors, or lawyers. These images are ambiguous, because it is possible to find what some people call "positive images" of black people. But the success is also in highly stereotypical arenas like music and entertainment business and in sport such as soccer and athletics. Many of these images are of Americans, for example, Oprah Winfrey, Beyonce, Nicki Minaj, and Serena and Venus Williams. They also include people like Usain Bolt and Bob Marley. Many are of European-based black people, like Olympic champions and athletes such as Nafissatou Thiam (Belgium), Kaddi Sagnia (Sweden), Patricia Mamona (Portugal), and Jessica Ennis-Hill (UK). The impression given is that black people are a success, which is highly misleading because except for soccer, only a minuscule number of black people are successful in any of these arenas. Apart from a tiny handful, most black people in these industries occupy subordinate roles (such as backup singers and performers and support staff). At the same time, black people are also subject to hyper-invisibility in the upper echelons of all these arenas of wealth, status, and power (with the exceptions just mentioned).

The second similarity is entrenched vulnerability. Which means that across Europe, black people are over-concentrated in the lower ranks of every major political, economic, and social hierarchy; from political representation, in business, educational and medical occupations; and in the nonprofit sector. And from agriculture and construction to public transport. They are over-concentrated in the ranks of the unemployed, the homeless, and the confines of prisons. They receive wages rather than salaries, do work that requires little or no educational qualifications or specialized training, and in part-time and insecure jobs. Black women (native-born or immigrant) are overrepresented in the so-called caring sector – domestic and public service jobs and in sex work. Black women in nursing are an exception. In general, the economies of southern Europe are poorer than those of Northern Europe. Black people are even worse off there. This is true for black citizens and legal residents as it is for immigrants and refugees. Several authors have argued that black women citizens in the UK, despite having been born and raised in the UK, and despite having the same or superior qualifications to non-blacks, are still at a disadvantage compared to non-blacks. The issue is racism not immigration, they argue.

In politics, for example, at present there are almost 4200 nationally elected politicians in the 12 nations that are the focus of this chapter (there are of course far more at the city and local level). I identify no more than 23 nationally elected black politicians in this block of 12 nations (around half of 1% (0.50%) of the total). Eighteen of these politicians are in England alone, leaving just 4 black politicians in the remaining 11 nations. This is staggering inequality.

A third similarity can be found in the mobilization of black people around racial identity and in the formation and importance of black and black-led organizations and in multiracial organizations. Protests, demonstrations, boycotts, as well as longer-term activities exist in all nations. The same is true for writers, artists, and film directors. Black women are certainly a majority in many these activities as well as in black women's organizations (Emejulu and Bassel 2017; McEachrane 2014; Virdee 2014; McIntosh 2014; Mazzocchetti 2014). This includes groups like Operation Black Vote and Abasindi black women's organization in England; Afro-femme and Brigade Anti-Negrophobia in France; Plataforma Gueto in Portugal; and Foja Organisacion in Spain. It includes the Black Europe Summer School, New Urban Collective, and Amrit Publishers in the Netherlands, as well as work by Jeanette Ehlers in Denmark, and Fred Kuwornu and Medhin Paolos in Italy.

Also, given how few black people there are in European universities, many black organizations and individuals focus their mobilization and activities around knowledge production outside the academy, both present and past. Central here is the challenge to the largely whitewashed and self-aggrandizing histories of slavery, colonialism, and imperialism produced in schools and universities across the continent. This includes collaborations with some progressive European academics. Knowledge production and collaborations are abundantly clear for the topic of reparations for slavery, a topic almost completely absent from scholarly analysis and completely rejected as a valid topic for consideration by politicians and in the public sphere (Hira 2014; Beckles 2013). At the forefront of these groups and individuals and working across national boundaries is the work of Professor Emejulu Akwugu, one of the co-founders of the annual conference on Black Womanism, Feminism and the Politics of Women of Colour. This conference brings together women and transindividuals – who are professors, writers, poets, and activists – to address the irrepressible intersections of race, gender, religion, and class.

I don't want to suggest that non-blacks do not recognize or act on the many ethnic or cultural differences among black people in Europe. But my main point is that anti-black and anti-African racism is consistently experienced by these populations, regardless of the very real ethnic differences between them and that while variations occur, they do so largely as a result of intersections with other criteria, such as gender, religion, and nationality.

Historical Background to Black Presence in Europe

Before we go any further, I suspect that there many readers outside Europe who did not know anything significant about the black population in Europe. They are probably surprised by these facts. And it is not only people outside Europe; many non-black people in Europe often ask "why are there so many Black people in

Europe?" But we could equally ask "why are there so few black people in Europe?" Whether there are many or few depends the criteria of evaluation being deployed. Analytically, I suggest it is far more insightful to ask why are there so few black people in Europe. Why? It is a fact that Europe invaded and colonized Africa; invented, articulated, and disseminated various forms of racism (from biological racism to scientific racism and, later on, from Social Darwinism and eugenics to cultural racism); and did this before all of the current nation-states in the Americas even came into existence. And yet the black population in Europe is currently much less than 1% of the total population of Europe. The numbers in the past have never been greater than a tiny fraction of 1%, as I explain shortly.

There are two narratives about why black people are in Europe. The first and dominant narrative occurs in political and public discourse, and in schools and universities, and highlights how Europe has helped black people. In this narrative Europe is advanced, civilized, Christian, decent, tolerant (and white), and doing the right thing for the poor and needy of the world. It highlights the European empires as being mainly mutually beneficial to those colonizers and colonized, good for everyone in the metropolis and colonies. In this way, it highlights a shared history shared culture, common languages, citizenship, and opportunities in Europe for education, work, residence. This is especially that case in the UK, France, the Netherlands, Portugal, Spain and Belgium, and to some extent Italy and Germany. These were the most intrusive and enduring European colonizers in Africa and the Americas, and it is because of them that there are more Catholics in Latin America than anywhere else on the planet, that Spanish and Portuguese are the dominant languages, and that English is the official language in North America and in more than 25 nations in Africa, just as French is the official language in more than 15 nations in Africa. Relatedly, Sweden, Norway, and Denmark, who historically had limited opportunities to compete with the larger imperial nations, deny any involvement in colonialism (which is not true) and highlight how they have helped refugees, asylum seekers, and victims of sex trafficking to escape war, famine, poverty, and persecution in the underdeveloped nations of Africa and achieve a more prosperous life in Europe (McEachrane 2014). Many other nations in Europe deny any involvement in colonialism at all, though the evidence reveals that they benefitted directly and indirectly in very real economic, cultural, and political ways.

The second narrative occurs in black community organizations, among progressive organizations and some independent writers. It is slowly moving into public discourse, but its advocates have far less resources and traction, for all the obvious reasons, than the dominant discourse. This counter narrative is reflected in the slogan "we are here because you were there" popularized during a labor strike involving many black and Asian women in the UK in the 1970s. The phrase is now common among black people and other immigrants in nations across Europe. In this narrative Europe colonized Africa, creating nations, political, economic, and social systems for their own political and economic benefit, systems that were entirely based on race; kidnapped, transported, and enslaved black people in colonies across the Americas; denied any real opportunity for equality to black people after slavery was legally abolished; maintained white supremacy in the colonies after slavery and when independence was reluctantly granted in Africa – frequently as a result of sustained anti-colonial struggles – left the colonies with surplus labor; and left African nations with dependency. This narrative is captured in the book by Walter Rodney *How Europe Underdeveloped Africa* and in the article *Discourse on Colonialism* by Aimé Cesaire.

Each narrative has elements that appeal to different sections of the European population. The main point that needs to be made here is that for centuries, as Europe plundered Africa, and transported and exploited black labor in the Americas, Africans and other black people allowed into Europe were kept to tiny numbers until the twentieth century. We were prevented from entering Europe in all but the tiniest numbers; denied the opportunity for any significant formal political participation; almost totally excluded from political office and representation; directed into the narrowest, the lowliest, and the most undesirable of jobs; and with miniscule exceptions, prevented from acquiring any formal education. Any positions that involved authority or power over white people were strictly forbidden. The overwhelming majority of black men and women brought to Europe – or born there – occupied subordinate and subservient roles.

There is evidence of black people in Europe in Ancient Greece and Rome and in the Roman armies in England. Black men worked as servants, tradesmen, and soldiers in the military and black women as maids, concubines, and prostitutes. Both men and women performed music and dance. We have evidence of tiny numbers, mainly in southern Europe, through the year 1400. Far more black people were forced into Europe after the 1400s, as Europe intruded further and further into Africa and as it colonized more and more of the Americas. They seem to have reached a peak in Spain and Portugal in the 1400s, when a significant proportion of the population of Lisbon was black. Black men were unskilled laborers, and black women were domestics. In Spain, several thousand Africans lived in Andalucía and Valencia. Most of the black people in Spain and Portugal were enslaved. The same is true for the estimated 15,000 black people in England in the 1770s. Tiny numbers of enslaved Africans and African Americans found their way to European nations during slavery. Many involuntarily as the property of their white master-enslaver owners; others voluntarily having escaped slavery or served in European forces against American independence. There were also Africans, mainly men, who went – or were brought – to Europe to study religion or law. Although no census data are available during these periods, it is clear the numbers were a miniscule fraction of 1% of the total European population.

From the early twentieth century, tens of thousands of black people – overwhelmingly men – were actively recruited to fight or work in the military in two world wars. England and France brought the most. Small but significant numbers remained in Europe after the wars. Then with massive war deaths of European men, black people were recruited in hundreds of thousands after the Second World War – to work in Europe. This is the case in the UK, France, the Netherlands, and Portugal. The UK recruited men to work in British Rail and London Transport and women to work in the National Health Service. They were overwhelmingly in low-level jobs that local white people did not want to do or were available in insufficient in numbers. France also recruited thousands of black men, after World War II, especially in the 1960s when they were needed for work in hospitals and post offices. The Netherlands received thousands of black people (and others) leading up to and after the independence of Suriname in the 1970s. Portugal also recruited thousands of black people, mainly from Cape Verde. Thousands more black people arrived during and after the decolonization in Africa, with small but significant numbers going to Portugal, Belgium, and elsewhere. They were joined by students and others. In Germany, there were several thousand Africans resident before German colonies in African were confiscated by the allies after World War I (Zimmerman 2010; Rosenhaft and Aitken 2013). And several thousand black children with African American fathers and white German mothers remained in Germany after World War II.

Finally, from the mid-twentieth century, several thousand black students were recruited to Russia and other socialist or communist nations, including Poland, Hungary, East Germany, and Bulgaria, as part of the Cold War efforts to counter the US cultural influence. Many of them studied medicine. The majority of them left after their studies finished, but tiny numbers remained, and their descendants are still resident today.

During these twentieth century arrivals, there were far more men than women, and most women came as dependents, with husbands or fathers. But among those that arrived in England, prior to the 1980s, especially from the Caribbean, large numbers of women arrived independently, seeking work and social mobility there. Many sent remittances back to children and families in the Caribbean, and some eventually brought their children to Britain. There were also significant numbers of women from Cape Verde who arrived independently in Portugal and Italy. At the turn of the twenty-first century, tens of thousands of black people have arrived as refugees; many of whom have experienced horrific journeys, and many of whom have died.

So, let's come back to the question – why so few black people in Europe? If black people were first in Europe in the tens of thousands in the 1400s, 1500s, and 1700s and if European empires – and their descendants in what became the USA – by the early 1900s already controlled territories with hundreds of millions of black people (in the Americas and across Africa), why are the numbers in Europe so small? The short answer is white racism and discrimination. European states systematically kept black people out of Europe. It did not suit the needs or interests of European governments to bring significant numbers of black people to Europe or to allow them to come of their own accord. Even after slavery legally ended, any attempts by black people to move to Europe were systematically obstructed in a range of direct and indirect ways. Those who came did so mainly at the whims of whites – for curiosity and spectacle, or for subordinate economic roles, and always for financial or cultural exploitation. The exception to this pattern are the black people that came to Euorpe to fight racism, colonialism and imperialism.

Discussion

It is obvious that the black population across Europe is highly diversified ethnically and culturally. This is evident in language and religion, in national origins and citizenship, and in a wide array of cultural practices involving family, music, film, literature, art, and performance. At the same time, they are a highly racialized population, frequently treated stereotypically, that shares similar experiences of hypervisibility, entrenched vulnerability, and irrepressible social mobilization for equality and justice. The ethnic differences and the racial similarities highly intersect with, and are affected by, other variables, including economics and class, religion, and gender. In this regard, there is a combination of intricate and entangled variables that shape black people's lives, opportunities, and outcomes.

It is self-evident, yet it also needs to be said that ethnic variables are equally complicated in the white population – perhaps more so than in the black population – given the far larger numbers of white people in Europe. There are also many ethnic differences in other populations, that is, the wide array of European residents that trace their origins in the last 100 years to India, Algeria, Turkey, Indonesia, and multiple nations in the Middle East. Clearly there are millions of Europeans (typically self-defined as white) that live in nations other than the ones in which they were born. Migration across nations in Europe has been happening for centuries. There was a dramatic increase in migration across nations within Europe with the formation of what has become the European Union. At present there are around three million EU residents living in the UK. This includes whites from Germany, France, Portugal, and Spain, as well as Poland, Romania, and Hungary. In France, there are many whites from Italy, Spain, and Portugal. A further increase in migration occurred as nations from across what used to be Eastern Europe migrated westwards, after the fall of the Berlin Wall in 1989. There are also significant numbers of other people, many born in Europe, with origins outside Europe. For example, in England there are at least four million people of Asian origin (India, Pakistan, Bangladesh, Malaysia); several million of Turkish origin in Germany; and many more of Turkish origin in the Netherlands, Belgium, and France. Several millions of North African origins (Algeria, Morocco, Tunisia) are in France. They are overwhelmingly concentrated in cities. This is what one well-known analyst has called "super-diversity" (Vertovec 2007). In this context, how are we to approach the issues of ethnicity and race?

While nonspecialists frequently use the terms race and ethnicity interchangeably, most social analysts agree that they should be distinguished for analytical purposes. And it should be recognized that they overlap with many other factors. Historically, in Europe and elsewhere, the idea of race typically indicated a belief in the existence of naturally occurring groups, each exhibiting real and/or imagined biological and mental attributes regarded as fixed and hierarchical. In Europe historically, so-called scientists, philosophers, prominent writers, and politicians developed and articulated theories of race to defend these views. Such as David Hume, Robert Knox, Rudyard Kipling, Thomas Carlyle, and Herbert Spencer; Geoffrey St Hilaire, Georges Buffon, Georges Cuvier, and the Comte de Gobineau; Hegel, Blumenbach and

Ernst Haeckel; Cesare Lombroso and, laying a foundation for all of them, Carl Linnaeus (Hondius 2014). This involved biological racism, social Darwinism, and eugenics.

Such explicit and rigid views of racial difference are no longer commonly expressed by major politicians, but there are concrete examples of right-wing political groups in several nations that are outright racist; the legacy of racist ideas remains pervasive in Europe, and there are still many forms of cultural racism and widely held stereotypes against black people that draw of stereotypes and caricatures (Araújo and Maeso 2015; Wekker 2016). Several nations provide evidence of direct, subtle, and camouflaged racism. The exaggerated and offensive character known as Zwarte Piet (black Piet) in the Netherlands is one such example. In this case, tens of thousands of white Dutch people paint their faces black and their lips bright red, every November, and parade in the streets (Essed and Hoving 2014). Historically, the racial category of "black" and "negro" was forced onto Africans from diverse ethnic groups (Nigeria, Cameroun, and Angola) who were kidnapped, transported, and enslaved in the Americas, though they had little in common with one another. At the present time, racial identities are frequently embraced by black people – in the form of organizations and political groups as a form of survival and resistance (Small 2018; Sivanandan 1990). And they are intertwined with ethnic identities.

Ethnicity, in contrast to race, usually highlights a wide range of social and cultural issues; it is typically viewed as something that is highly variable and not necessarily organized in a hierarchy. Many groups, families, and individuals steadfastly embraced these cultural practices. And as mentioned above, ethnic differences – in terms of language, religion, family structures, and political values – have been at the heart of Europe even before Europeans came into contact with Africans (or other peoples across the world). These ethnic differences are ubiquitous across all racial populations in Europe.

It is clear that race and ethnicity are complex phenomena, intertwined and entangled with one another and with many other variables too. They are highly situational, contingent, and contextual. And while I have demonstrated this with regard to the black population, many similar variations, entanglements, and consequences apply to other populations across Europe. Complicating things further, ethnicity and race almost always operate in ways that intersect with, and are often greatly affected by, other variables, including economics and class, religion, nationality, and especially gender. One lesson from this is that it's difficult to analyze ethnicity independent of its relationship to these other variables. Ethnicity and cultural differences are not factors that unfold or are always played out independently of other variables, like race (and gender). So we need to pay attention to how ethnicity unfolds via other variables. Just as I have done in this chapter.

The cases and incidents mentioned in this chapter provide some examples of how the complex ethnic and national differences with the black population – and the complex ethnic and national differences within the white population – can become deeply entangled in strange and unusual ways. Black people in Europe are highly diversified ethnically but are still frequently treated racially in terms of discrimination and hostility. The majority of politicians in Europe deny that there is racism or racial discrimination – despite the evidence – because they use an old-fashioned definition of racism, associated with slavery in the Americas, apartheid in South Africa, and with legal racial segregation in the USA. They assume racism only exists when it is explicit, legal, and deliberate. Nothing could be further from the truth. Racism still exists where it is operationalized through indirect and subtle measures, stereotypes, and caricatures.

In ethnic, cultural, and national terms historically, European nations competed with one another as separately as the fingers of a hand. The largest and most intrusive European empires fought with one another over land in Africa, the Caribbean, and North America (and in other parts of the world). They also fought over control of labor populations, trade routes, and access to minerals, raw materials, and spices. They had been in competition with one another well before they ever set foot in Africa or the Americas. So this competition was not new. But in racial terms, during colonialism and imperialism, these nations also worked together like a clenched fist in colonial and imperial goals and operations. They downplayed ethnic differences of language, religious denomination, and others elements, for the common goals of colonialization for political and economic reasons. They signed treaties and made agreements over colonies (Haiti independence); over territories in Africa (e.g., the Berlin Conference 1884); over territories in the Americas (Dutch, French, and British Guiana); and over the confiscation of colonies (the allies after World War I) and decolonial treaties. They agreed with one another that Europeans (whites) were superior in politics, economics, and culture, especially Christianity, and that they should remain superior in any competition with non-Europeans. Because, to paraphrase George Orwell, all European nations are equal, but some nations are more equal than others. For example, Scandinavian nations provided wood to the Netherlands to build slave ships, as well as other materials, as well as cattle for food (Moore 2010). The Netherlands kidnapped and transported hundreds of thousands of Africans to become enslaved in Spanish colonies (Nimako and Willemsen 2011). That is why the British, French, Germans, and Belgians were able to capture and colonize more land in Africa, than other nations, just as the Spanish and Portuguese were able to capture and colonize more land in what became the Americas. There is substantial evidence that Sweden, Denmark, and Norway also sought to capture and colonize territories in these continents, but they could not outcompete the larger European nations (McEachrane 2014).

But that was the past and times have changed. What is the situation today? We see a highly complicated interplay of racial and ethnic factors. We see common patterns of racial discrimination against black people despite ethnic differences. And we see common ethnic discrimination among whites, despite racial similarities. For whites, ethnic differences face competing trends of salience and diminishment. The formation and expansion of the EU was meant to highlight what Europeans share in common and to build and consolidate institutions to achieve these goals. But it has not worked fully.

Why did it not work fully? And why has ethnic discrimination against whites – which was relatively low in Europe in the 1960s – become so much more salient? The answer can be found by relating ethnic variables to other variables. In the 1960s, when Spanish, Portuguese, and Italians migrated to live and work in the UK, the Netherlands, Belgium, and Germany, the economics of these nations were stronger and they needed labor. Also, importantly the migrants assimilated – learning language and cultural practices – and after 1–2 generations were largely invisible to locals. Even in the 1980s as the EU was further consolidated, assimilation was the major force. This was before globalization had taken off. But since the 1990s, two major things have happened. First, the economics, standard of living, and cost of living are relatively weaker than it was in the past. In some nations there is significant austerity, unemployment, and poverty. And second, globalization allows for the retention of ethnic difference because immigrants use social media, internet, and telephone communications, and cheap airlines have enabled far more back and forth travel by migrants.

So this means that while black people that migrated to live in England since the 1950s, in France since the 1960s, in the Netherlands since the 1970s, and in Portugal and Belgium over similar periods were ethnically similar to local white residents of these nations, they were racially different. And they faced significant discrimination. And while whites that migrated to these nations, in all these periods were ethnically different, they were racially similar. And so they faced far less discrimination. The patterns have become far more complex, and these intricate entanglements continue to unfold.

Black people in Europe face discrimination that can be ethnic or racial, and it is almost always interconnected with other variables like class, gender, or religion. It is not always clear what the basis of discrimination actually is, so we have to pay attention to the context, the situation, and the instance at hand. White immigrants to nations across Europe increasingly face discrimination that is typically called ethnic discrimination or nation-based discrimination. Some people have called such discrimination racial discrimination – because it often is based on what seems to be deep-seated prejudice and hostility; and it results in denying white immigrants access to jobs, housing, and education. It can also lead to violence and murder. But I suggest it is not useful to describe the two types as similarly racist. Prejudice, racism, hostility, and discrimination toward black people – whether from Africa or the Caribbean and Latin America – are based on ideologies, political, economic, and social structures (like slavery, colonial and imperial labor systems, laws, statues, and official practice) that have existed for centuries. It is based on belief systems that were first invented, developed, and implemented with the support (and resources) of kings and queens, presidents and prime ministers, and religious leaders of most Christian and related denominations, along with powerful men and women in educational and other arenas. And racial stereotypes, caricatures, and discrimination that confront black people in Europe today draw directly and heavily on a legacy of these practices from the past. There are few counterparts with such depth, historical longevity, and vehement impact in what is happening to white immigrants to Germany, Austria, and Italy at the present time.

Conclusion

In this chapter I have described and evaluated black people's presence and experiences in Europe today in order to explore the intricate and multifaceted relationship between ethnic and cultural differences on the one hand and racial differences on the other. I have provided examples from across Europe today that provide fascinating insights into many of these complexities. I have provided some examples of key dimensions of ethnicity and examples of key elements associated with race and racism. And I have provided examples of some of the other variables that interact with ethnicity and race – including religion and gender.

In Europe today race and ethnicity – and their relationship with other variables – have become increasingly intertwined and complex, given the precarious and dire economic circumstances facing the resident populations of most European nations, especially those populations that believe themselves to be the "true (white) residents" of each nation; and given the increasing levels of international migration, it is important to be aware of the complex nature of race and ethnicity. And it is increasingly important to recognize how they interact with other variables such as class, religion, and gender. There is no common pattern for how these variables interact with one another and no easy way to predict such outcomes. Sometimes ethnic difference will be the most salient factor; at other times, it is (perceived) racial difference that is decisive. Sometimes economic factors will play a salient role; at other times it may be religion or gender. Each situation has to be examined closely in order to identify which set of factors is more important than the other in people's day-to-day lives. During European systems of slavery and colonialism, in many instances, Europeans downplayed ethnic differences among themselves, and among Africans, highlighted racial differences between Europeans and Africans, and asserted and highlighted racial similarities among Africans and their descendants. This perspective served the common economic and political interests of different European nations during that long period.

Across Europe today, politicians and often the general (white) public in individual nations are increasingly highlighting ethnic and cultural differences between themselves and white people from other European nations. At present, it is perceived by many politicians and members of the public that highlighting such differences is in their national interest. At the same time, key institutions of the European Union challenge such distinctions and highlight what Europeans share in common. But while emphasizing common origins and ancestry, Christianity, and values such as a belief in civilization, freedom, and democracy, it has been difficult for such advocates to specify how such values are different from those of non-Europeans. And it has been difficult for them to deny that such emphasis has racial – and racist – connotations. In Europe today, whether racial or ethnic differences among black Europeans (and black immigrants) are highlighted or downplayed depends on context and situations. And whether ethnic differences among white Europeans are highlighted or downplayed also depends on context and situation. These complexities – and uncertainly about their outcomes – are highly likely to remain for the foreseeable future.

References

Adi H (2013) Pan-Africanism and communism. The Communist International, Africa and the diaspora, 1919–1939. Africa WorldPress, Trenton

Araújo M, Maeso SR (2015) Eurocentrism, racism and knowledge. Debates history and power in Europe and the Americas. Palgrave Macmillan, Basingstoke/New York

Beckles H (2013) Britain's Black Debt. Reparations for Caribbean slavery and native genocide. University of the West Indies, Kingston

Clarke KM, Thomas D (2006) Globalization and race. Transformations in the cultural production of blackness. Duke University Press, Durham/London

Daniel W (1968) Racial discrimination in England. Penguin Books, Harmondsworth

El Tayeb F (2011) European others. Queering ethnicity in postnational Europe. University of Minnesota Press, Minneapolis/London

Emejulu A, Bassel L (2017) Minority women and austerity: survival and resistance in France and Britain. Polity Press, Bristol

Essed P, Hoving I (2014) Dutch racism. Thymaris, New York

Hine DC, Keaton TD, Small S (2009) Black Europe and the African diaspora. University of Illinois Press, Urbana/Chicago

Hira S (2014) 20 Questions and answers on reparations for colonialism. Amrit Publishers, The Hague

Hondius D (2014) Blackness in Western Europe. Racial patterns of paternalism and exclusion. Transaction Publishers, New Brunswick/London

Mazzocchetti J (2014) Migrations Susaharienne, et Condition Noires En Belgique. Academia, L'Harmattan, Brussels

McEachrane M (2014) Afro-Nordic landscapes. Equality and race in Northern Europe. Routledge, New York/London

McIntosh L (2014) Impossible presence. Race, nation and the cultural politics of 'being Norwegian'. Ethn Racial Stud 38(2):309–325

Moore JW (2010) 'Amsterdam is standing on Norway' Part II: the global North Atlantic in the ecological revolution of the long seventeenth century. J Agrar Chang 10(2):188–227

Nimako K, Willemsen G (2011) The Dutch Atlantic. Slavery, abolition and emancipation. Pluto Press, London

Rosenhaft E, Aitken R (2013) Africa in Europe. Studies in transnational practice in the long twentieth century. Liverpool University Press, Liverpool

Sivanandan A (1990) Communities of resistance. Writings on Black struggles for socialism. Verso, London/New York

Small (1983) Police and people in London. II A group of young Black people. Policy Studies Institute report no. 619. Policy Studies Institute, London

Small S (2018) 20 Questions and answers on Black Europe. Amrit Publishers, The Hague

Vertovec S (2007) Super-diversity and its implications. Ethnic Racial Stud 30(6):1024–1054

Virdee S (2014) Racism, class and the racialized outsider. Basingstoke, UK, Palgrave

Wekker G (2016) White innocence. Paradoxes of colonialism and race. Duke University Press, Durham

White EJ (2012) Modernity, freedom and the African diaspora: Dublin, New Orleans, Paris. Indiana University Press, Bloomington

Zimmerman A (2010) Alabama in Africa. Booker T Washington, The German Empire & the globalization of the New South. Princeton University Press, Princeton